Governance and Generalized Exchange

 Y0-BVN-129

Public Policy and Social Welfare

 E u r o p e a n   C e n t r e
for Social Welfare Policy and Research

Volume 5

Bernd Marin (Ed.)

Governance and Generalized Exchange

Self-Organizing Policy Networks in Action

•A15043 898328

JC
11
.G687x
1990
West

Campus Verlag · Frankfurt am Main
Westview Press · Boulder, Colorado

Published in 1990 in the United States by Westview Press.
Frederick A. Praeger, Publisher
5500 Central Avenue
Boulder, Colorado 80301

Library of Congress Cataloging-in-Publication Data

CIP data available upon request   90-050983
ISBN 0-8133-8292-0   CIP

CIP-Titelaufnahme der Deutschen Bibliothek

Governance and generalized exchange: self-organizing policy networks in action / Bernd
Marin (Ed.). – Frankfurt am Main: Campus Verlag; Boulder, Colerado: Westview Press, 1990
    (Public policy and social welfare; Vol. 5)
    ISBN 3-593-34398-3 (Campus Verlag)
    ISBN 0-8133-8292-0 (Westview Press)
NE: Marin, Bernd [Hrsg.]: GT

© 1990 by European Centre for Social Welfare Policy and Research, 1090 Vienna, Berggasse 17.
Composition: Beatrijs G. de Hartogh. Printed by Druck Partner Rübelmann, Germany.

For Dalia

CONTENTS

IV Territorial Politics and Intergovernmental Relations

V Generalized Political Exchange and EEC-Policy Synchronisation

VI Beyond Joint Regulation and Cooperative Industrial Governance?

CONTENTS IN DETAIL

Interpretation of the Chemicals Control Policy Based on Political Exchange Theory

Political Exchange on a Perfect Market?
An Alternative Model and an Empirical Test
Peter Kappelhoff / Franz Urban Pappi
1. The Perfect Market Model and its Modifications 2. A First Application of the Restricted Access Model to Hypothetical Data 3. A Second Application of Models to the Empirical System of a Community Elite a: The Operationalization of the Exchange Network; b: The Structure of the Exchange Network; c: Changes in the Power Structure Due to Restricted Access and Price Making Behavior 4. Further Considerations

IV. TERRITORIAL POLITICS, PUBLIC ADMINISTRATION, AND INTERGOVERNMENTAL RELATIONS

Territorial Politics and Political Exchange:
American Federalism and French Unitarianism Reconsidered
Leonardo Parri
1. Introduction: A Theoretical Framework. Exchange Processes in Contemporary Politics; The Development of the Relations Between the Central and the Peripheral Politico-Administrative Structures; Intergovernmental Relations and Political Sociology: The Concept of Territorial Politics; The Notion of Centralization: A Critique and a Reconceptualization; Functional, Territorial and Generalized Political Exchanges 2. Territorial Politics in the United States. Narrow, Fragmented TPEs and Categorical Grant-Based Territorial Politics; The Reaction of the Chief Executives; Block and General Grants as an Instrument of Widening the Scope of and the Control upon TPEs; The Federal State Power Balance in U.S. "Cooperative Federalism" 3. Territorial Politics in France. The Jacobin Leviathan and Territorial Representation; TPEs and the "Locus minoris resistentiae" of the Jacobin Leviathan; Changing the Central-Local Power Balance: The Impact of the Defferre Reforms 4. Comparative Conclusions. List of Abbreviations Used in the Text

Preface

This collection of theoretical essays and empirical studies in two volumes had a most joyful procreation, an easy and happy birth — and a most difficult growing-up into a full-blown, mature publication. As the delay is almost exclusively the editor's responsibility, a word of explanation is owed to all the authors who sent in their contributions in time and to scholarly colleagues who followed the project with sympathy and curiosity. This explanation will also enable the readers to set the two books in their proper time frame.

The project originated in Florence in the mid eighties, where it took its basic shape, before it moved with me to Vienna, where it was finalized and updated. The first ideas have been discussed in my seminars on "Theories of Political Exchange" and on "Network Analysis" at the European University Institute (EUI) since 1984. The paper on "Generalized Political Exchange: Preliminary Considerations" was presented at the XIIIth World Congress of the International Political Science Association (IPSA) in Paris in July, 1985 and then published as a EUI Working Paper (85/190). Its unexpected resonance with a great number of greatly appreciated scholars made me organize, jointly with Sandro Pizzorno (whose meanwhile "classical" 1978 piece on political exchange had initially set me on the track), a conference on "Political Exchange: Between Governance and Ideology" in December 1986, which was generally perceived as having been particularly stimulating, and where most of the contributions published in volumes 4 and 5 of the series have already been presented and discussed for the first time. Later, additional contributions were invited in order to round up the aspects not fully covered by the conference participants and to compensate for the gaps that occured because of my mismanagement by first setting all-too-strict deadlines and later extending them for-all-too long. Thus, active conference participants such as Claus Offe and Sandro Pizzorno and even paper givers such as Tom Burns, Renate Mayntz and Toni Pelinka are not in the books and scholars such as Paolo Ceri, Karen Cook, Mark Elchardus, Ian Macneil, Antonio Mutti, Victor Pestoff, Franz Traxler, Arthur Wassenberg, and Paul Windolf joined in as authors, after having presented their contributions at the EUI. Most of this has been completed when I moved back to Vienna in 1988 after having been nominated the new Executive Director of the European Centre, and this personal reason is the main explanation, but no excuse, for the delay in publication.

Apart from the new challenges and the heavy workload coming with the new task, it did not make sense to publish the volumes in the EUI series (which had been abolished) or to have them published as isolated single books by other commercial publishers while I was negotiating the establishment of a new European Centre book series with Campus and Westview Press. That is why I turned down interesting and specific publications offers by two British publishing companies and integrated the books into the new European Centre series "Public Policy and Social Welfare", once it became clear that '(generalized) political exchange', 'antagonistic cooperation', 'policy networks', 'joint inter-organizational policy-making' and 'cooperative governance' would become central concerns and key notions of the European Centre's research program as the 'welfare-mix' (Evers / Wintersberger eds, 2nd ed. 1990) had already been a focal concept before. Of the projects reflecting this focus

I would like to mention the conference on policy networks jointly organized with the Max-Planck-Institut für Gesellschaftsforschung in late 1989 and to be published soon (Marin/Mayntz eds 1991) as just one example of continous interest in cooperative governance and welfare provision through inter-organizational policy networks.

Apart from the conference participants and authors mentioned so far, I have learned from the papers and discussions with David Baldwin, Jim Coleman, Colin Crouch, Erhard Friedberg, Klaus Gretschmann, Patrick Kenis, Franz Urban Pappi, Leonardo Parri, Fritz Scharpf, Volker Schneider, Michael Wagner and Helmut Willke; as well as from critical comments by Ian Budge, Michel Crozier, Jon Elster, Tony Giddens, Luigi Graziano, Gerhard Lehmbruch, Nino Majone, Dalia Marin, Birgitta Nedelmann, Adriano Pappalardo, Philippe Schmitter, Mike Taylor, and Gunther Teubner — without being able to either take their views adequately into account or to reciprocate my intellectual debts to any of them. This would have implied a far reaching revision of my original article, to which all the invited contributions had meanwhile referred; and while I would now write quite different a paper on GPE, it is reproduced as it was published as a EUI Working Paper for reasons of authenticity and fairness to the other authors' referencing. But I trust that even this first and incomplete attempt might help the emergence of a more general social science discourse on policy networks, generalized political cooperation and inter-organizational governance, which would be interesting to wider debates on the welfare mix — for quite different reasons with each participant.

But if the initial efforts finally developed into something final, this is due not only to colleagial scholarly responses but also due to the caring qualities of many persons assisting the editor in many ways: here, my thanks go to Maureen Lechleitner and James Newell in Florence, as well as to Michael Eigner, Klarissa Guzei, Ellen Kraus, Suzanna Stephens and, above all, to Beatrijs de Hartogh in Vienna, who have helped to bring what has turned from a beautiful and promising, maybe all-too-spoiled child to a somehow neglected youngster back into an adult, civilized and mature book publication.

I dedicate these two books to Dalia, companion, friend and wife for almost two decades. With her I have shared the most in my life and the best, and also some of its darker moments. To her I owe so much more than the books I have written or edited, though I might not have made several of them without her stimulation and support. Significantly, even the interest in generalized media results from our exchange of views about her work as an economist in monetary theory; this had opened theoretical horizons remote and incongruent but exciting and cross-fertilizing for a social scientist working on governance and concerned with welfare production, social integration and *buongoverno*. Still, our intellectual exchange, intensifying over the years, could never live up to the passioning and *beglückende* experience of a generalized exchange medium called love. As a token of our love, a great love, I dedicate these two books to Dalia.

Vienna, 29 September 1990   Bernd Marin

Introduction

Bernd Marin

Generalized political exchange (GPE) is based on a number of simple ideas, developed into a rather complex concept or set of concepts. When I first coined the notion, it was — on the one hand — in order to criticize and even break with traditional exchange theories; and on the other, in order to link policy studies and theorizing on governance and interest intermediation to network thinking and network analysis.

First, it set out to overcome those prevalent economic and rational choice theories which redefine everything from interpersonal relations to international warfare as "exchanges" or reinterpret all kinds of social and political interactions by the economic model of perfect market competition — as if political exchange were simply a market relation between political actors and as if real markets worked according to the textbook scheme. The oversupply of such overly general and misfit "exchange" concepts, I held, inflates their intellectual exchange value and undermines their explanatory power. Instead, a genuine and interdisciplinary social science conceptualization was proposed, restricted to analyse a specific class of phenomena only — but more thoroughly.

Generalized political exchange was meant to become a building block of a middle-range and grounded theory to better understand governance in advanced, industrialized, capitalist market societies. This mode of governance, in particular in the core areas of macroeconomic management and interest intermediation, operates through policy networks or integrated policy circuits, all which are based on self-organization and antagonistic cooperation of constituent collective actors.

As a concept, generalized political exchange should help to uncover exactly what the still prevalent market models of exchange define out of possible understanding: the logic of risky, mutually contingent macro-political transactions between organized actors with functionally interdependent, yet competing or even antagonistic interests, not to be regulated sufficiently by law and contract; the functioning of transaction-chains, where a variety of valuables exchanged flow predominantly in one direction through the policy network, which is kept in order to insure all participants against the threatening uncertainties of complex strategic interactions with indeterminate exchange rates; the joint and value-adding production of public goods by collective actors, organized into a political division of labor in the cooperative governance of a multiplicity of interlinked and asymmetric markets and political arenas.

The GPE concept was also meant to shed light on puzzling phenomena related to governance such as the role of generalized media of exchange within politics, such as political money and political credits; the functioning of social contracts without legal contracts; the role of trust in transactional risks, balancing reciprocity and absorbing political exchange rate fluctuations; the interplay and contradictions between institutions and extra-institutional factors; the logic of public policy-making as a series of interrelated and self-modifying games by corporate actors; etc. And it was meant to provide answers to queries such as the following: are "equal" exchanges between collective actors representing organized interests even conceivable? If not, can unequal exchanges nevertheless be "fair" or otherwise "productive"? What mechanisms are there to (re)balance asymmetric exchanges and how can (generalized) political exchange as such rebalance inequities? Why does the central state need to be decentered as the primary focal point of policy field analysis? Why is the so-called political market no market, neither bazaar nor supermarket? What other schemes could provide a more adequate conceptualization of inter-organizational policy-making?

Looking for responses to these basic queries led to the second underlying theme of the GPE attempt: namely, linking policy field studies and theoretical reasoning on modes of governance and interest intermediation to network thinking and network analysis. Again, the premises were simple: to the extent that governance in a centerless society cannot be achieved by hierarchical control and without complex configurations of horizontal coordination and synchronisation, inter-organizational policy networks become the focus of attention; and in analysing policy networks, exchange network concepts and network analytical methods offer themselves as the most adequate tools at hand. In developing the idea of governance through policy networks and generalized political exchange, a wide variety of intellectual traditions was used, some what ecclectically and arbitrarily, or critically confronted: from Claude Lévi-Strauss' concept of generalized exchange (developed to understand matrilateral cross-cousin marriage and transferred to policy field studies) to Emerson's framework fusing power dependence and social exchange theory to Cook's exchange network theory; from inter-organizational theory (Benson, Evan, Hanf / Scharpf, Aldrich / Whetten, Galaskiewicz) to network analysis (Burt, Marsden, Knoke, Laumann, Pappi); from the political study of industrial labor relations (Crouch) and political exchange (Pizzorno, Baglioni, Ceri, Mutti, Rusconi) to the theory of neo-corporatism (Schmitter / Streeck, Lehmbruch, Katzenstein); from contract theory in law and economics (Macneil, Macaulay, Daintith) to reasoning on social contracts (Bobbio, Macneil); from power theory (Baldwin, Crozier / Friedberg) over the debate on generalized media of exchange in politics (Parsons, Luhmann) to concepts of political money (Coleman); from collective action theory (Olson, Hardin) over cooperation and game theory (Axelrod) to regime theory (Keohane); from neo-institutionalism (March, Olsen) to autopoietic systems and legal theory (Luhmann, Teubner); from economic and cultural anthropology (Einzig, Polanyi, Sahlins) to transaction cost economics (Williamson) and its critiques in organizational theory (Perrow).

If one asks what binds together a perspective that tries to integrate such a variety of partly complementary but largely competing approaches, the *theoretical and methodological orientation* of the editor's initial paper and also the mix of the contributions invited from other authors for criticism and elaboration can be characterised as follows.

First, the theoretical orientation is *inter-disciplinary* and *social science*, not just for the start-up contribution, but also for the collection invited. Social science inter-disciplinarity is evident in the authors' reasoning as well as in their educational and training backgrounds, positions and outlooks: while sociologists provide the greatest number of social scientists presented in these volumes, political science and government, economics (including social economics and political economy), public administration, business administration, management and planning, law, organizational research, education and social psychology are among the more than ten social science background disciplines represented by the various authors.

Secondly, the focus is predominantly on *middle-range theory*, apart from occasional temptations at "grand theorizing" which are discussed as they arise.

Thirdly, politics is analysed from a *meso- and macroscopic* perspective, not from a micro-analytical point of view: its driving forces are organized, collective, corporate actors — not individuals, groups or elites; it deals with inter-organizational relations in public policy-making (outside the arenas of party competition and parliamentarism); it refers to collective action either on the level of societal reproduction and self-regulation, governance and development of the economy, macropolitical guidance and other issues related to the production and distribution of public goods; on the meso-level it refers to specific policy fields (domains, sectors) such as industrial labor relations and labor policy, industrial policy, taxation, chemicals control etc.

Fourthly, it aims at *empirically grounded theory.* This implies that most theoretical reasoning has an empirical underpinning — even in cases where empirical findings are not directly referred to, as is true especially in the first volume on Generalized Political Exchange; and that empirical research has a strong theoretical orientation, as can be seen in particular in the volume on Governance and Generalized Exchange. It furthermore implies a pluralist conception with respect to methodology and techniques used. The books confront various analytical models and methods (from mathematical and game theoretical models to network analytical techniques) with a diversity of empirical evidence, ranging from historical documents and case study material to cross-national comparative statistical data.

Fifthly, many contributions to the two volumes at least try to overcome, *dialectically* if you please, well-established but quite sterile theoretical dichotomies in social and political theory such as power vs. exchange theories, market vs. hierarchy or organisation concepts, structure or system vs. action theories, institutionalist vs. non-institutionalist perspectives, etc. Instead, practically all of the authors hold that neither power nor exchange can simply be reduced to one or the other but must always be thought of as intertwined. Markets are analysed as a specific form and not as an alternative to organization (Friedberg); they are seen not as symetrically linked but as politically ordered into "market hierarchies"

(Wagner). Exchange networks are conceptualized as linking structure to action (Cook), as are the tangled hierachies of self-modifying games presented in the introductory paper. Institutionalism is redefined as comprising non-institutional levels of analysis such as socio-economic conditions and policy games, political goals and strategic choices (Scharpf), etc. Differentiated views of this kind make the labelling of the approaches used more difficult but reading and thinking much more exciting.

Both volumes deal with the basic puzzle: how is societal self-regulation and governance through complex policy networks possible at all? Whereas *Generalized Political Exchange* develops the base by presenting competing as well as converging theoretical perspectives, *Governance and Generalized Exchange* confronts the analytical models with empirical data. The two volumes complement each other and consequently should be read jointly in order to make sense. Though not numbered as volumes I and II, the sequential order suggested is to start with the theoretical volume on *Generalized Political Exchange* before one moves on to the policy network studies assembled in the volume on *Governance and Generalized Exchange.* Because of the large overlaps in the references and bibliographies of the single contributions, each volume contains a single joint bibliography of references made throughout the book — as well as an author index of references and cross-references.

Generalized Political Exchange

The volume on generalized political exchange starts with my original paper from 1985, unchanged for reasons of authenticity, in order to formulate the theoretical stakes and key concepts.

A second section reviews theories of cooperation as well as of political and social exchange in the social sciences. *Paolo Ceri*, sociologist in Trento, one of the leading figures within the rich Italian debate on political exchange, summarizes in his contribution the essence of his previous own reasoning on the specifics of political as opposed to economic exchange, understood as a special kind of social relation within politics and not primarily as an institutional system. His is above all an exercise in taxonomy, working towards a highly complex and sophisticated typology, using the analytical tools of geometry as a heuristic device to unfold and illustrate an elaborated scheme of a great variety of exchange modes. None of those can be simply reduced to power if one avoids the more common opposite trap of reducing power to exchange; power, control and exchange are (apart from extreme exceptions) always intertwined. Given the Italian societal and intellectual context, major efforts go into the distinction of political exchange from newly emerging forms of institutionalized collective corruption such as "mass or categorial clientelism", gradually replacing more conventional modes of clientelistic exchange or patronage. Both mass clientelism and political exchange are seen as complex as opposed to simple exchange systems like markets, conflicts or representation. Ceri's elaborate typology comes close, but stops short of generalized political exchange. The prevalence of selective clientelism or *corporativismo* (which is just the opposite and not at all another variant of neo-corporatism) and the absence of GPE patterns in Italian societal reality prevents him from conceptualizing a largely unknown phenomenon with similar precision.

Whereas Paolo Ceri deals with political exchange leaving out networks of generalized exchange altogether, *David A. Baldwin* has been invited to contribute because of his reputation as a profound sceptic of generalized political exchange. Baldwin, a political scientist, has specialized in power theory and international relations and is the Director of the Institute of War and Peace Studies at Columbia University, New York. He has, among other things, long ago published what may still be the most brilliant, incisive and harshest critique of all attempts at finding media of generalized exchange equivalent to money in the political realm — that is, conceptualizing power accordingly as "political money" (Baldwin 1971a, 1978); be it from a systems-functionalist (Parsons, Luhmann) or from a methodological individualist, actor-centered approach (Coleman).

In this volume, he reconfirms the basic premise that while differences between political and social exchange are hardly significant, the crucial difference "is that between monetized market exchange and everything else". Consequently, political exchange is characterized by "the absence of a generally recognized standard of value that also serves as a highly liquid medium of exchange. There is no political counterpart to money. The error of assuming the existence of political money has probably done more damage in political science than any other error." Baldwin takes the exact counterposition to Lévi-Strauss (1969), who claims that "it is precisely from the economic point of view that exchange should not be envisaged", when he asserts that social science should try to transfer, adjust and build on economic conceptions which have laid the basic groundwork for exchange theory, instead of aiming at genuinely new models (including GPE which he considers "a potentially useful, but also potentially misleading concept for the study of politics"). According to his conviction that social science has well understood similarities but underestimated crucial differences between economic and other forms of exchange, Baldwin sets out to explore the implications of the absence of political money, for instance in the new literature on reciprocity and cooperation which has illuminated opportunities for cooperation but obscured the obstacles to reciprocity, all linked to the lack of a standardized measure of political value.

This is not the place to criticize Baldwin or to juxtapose the editor's own position. Suffice it to say that clear-cut analytical dichotomies might wither away in view of complex realities: the uncertainties of no risky, complex, economic transaction beyond simple spot-like exchanges (from long-term, relational or labor contracts to major investment projects) can be mitigated by money alone or even predominantly. They are as strategic and "political" as any political exchange, generalized or not, with money as just *one* yardstick to determine equivalent values or exchange rates among others, the indeterminacy about other criteria for judgment of equities, and the open search for equivalent mechanisms to price signals to synchronize expectations: trust, history sedimented in structure and operational procedures, status, reputation and legitimacy, reciprocity norms and generalized compliance, rights and guarantees, etc., might all serve to reduce complexity and uncertainty and generalize expectations where money and political money or power are not sufficient.

The next section III, dealing with divergent views on political money, rights, contracting, and power, takes the reader exactly where Baldwin has left him/her at last, i.e., at the search for generalized media of exchange or functional equivalents to money in politics. *James S. Coleman,* sociologist at the University of Chicago and one of the world's most renowned and productive scholars in social science theory and research, continues what he has started with his pathbreaking article on "political money" (Coleman 1970). Now, he postulates that the fundamental tangibles exchanged in all forms of exchange are rights, the crucial difference in their use, partitioning and transfer being their (in)divisibility and externality. While money solves the problem of double coincidence and splits transactions, allowing for the partitioning of divisible goods, rights regarding goods which are difficult to divide or cannot be divided at all, or of several potential uses are most problematic. Coleman dedicates a substantial part of his contribution to an elaboration of the various modes of the partitioning of rights, including the discussion of vouchers (as domain-restricted money, constituting entitlements to public services in health, welfare, housing, education, etc.), complicated variations in voting rights and disjointed authority structures. He also debates the fungibility of rights, i.e. under what conditions they can be exchanged at all and if so legally or legitimately, and what rights are non-transferable by their holders (such as, for instance, voting rights).

His contribution demonstrates to sceptics like Baldwin, how far one can get in taking the quest for a generalized medium of exchange analogous to money serious, *without* falling into the Parsonian trap of systems functionalism. But Coleman's interest is no less ambitious than Parsons', i.e. grand theory, no less than the foundations of a *general* social theory. This ambitious endeavour makes for difficult, but exciting reading. It also made Coleman bypass the interests of many of the other participants in the conference and contributors to the two collective volumes, which were more modest and more specific in wanting to better understand public policy-making through (generalized) exchange networks. Otherwise, he would have concentrated on what he calls fiat money or the equivalent to central clearing house mechanisms for identifying mutual obligations within a policy community. Fortunately, almost all of the remaining authors within this volume have carried on and taken over by specifying one aspect or the other left undetermined or untouched by Coleman's general theory.

As a legal scholar, *Ian R. Macneil* deals with the specific forms exchange relations take under law, that is contracts. While I have defined generalized political exchange by, among other things, a conspicuous absence of legal-contractual devices, Macneil (Professor of Law at Northwestern University School of Law in Chicago and one of the leading scholars in the new field of law and economics in general and of contract theory in particular) has turned the argument around in trying to subsume political exchange, including its generalized version, as a form of what he coined as *relational contract*. Whereas Coleman's archimedic point in analyzing exchange are rights, Macneil's anchor are contractual relations; consequently, relational contract theory is stipulated as a general and comprehensive theory of exchange encompassing, among other forms, political exchange. By analyzing GPE in terms of relational contract theory, he uses Great Britain in the transition to Thatcherism — his view of the "winter of discontent" 1978/79 — as a historical case in point. The reader will see what can be gained from translating a conceptual framework such as generalized political exchange, having itself gained a lot from the insights of (social) contract theory (Macneil 1974a, 1980, 1981, 1985), into exactly that theory considered to be most appropriate for more formalized and enforceable interaction domains. In another article (Marin 1987, in Teubner 1990) I have tried to further clarify this phenomenon of "contracting without contracts" as against commitments, compliance and exchange relations which are binding only to the extent that they are based on law and contract.

Some of these considerations are taken care of in the next section IV, which analyzes the logic of macroeconomic management as cooperation within market hierarchies. The contribution by *Michael Wagner* is crucial to the understanding of generalized political exchange, both from an analytical point of view as well as with respect to the issues at stake. (Wagner is an economist with social science orientation, and Director of the Institute for Economic and Social Research in Vienna).The conceptualization of GPE itself would have been significantly different without joint reasoning and exchange of ideas over many years. I had borrowed the empirical case in point for modelling the simple transaction-chain blowing up the barter scheme of traditional political exchange and adopted some core concepts such as "market hierarchies" in developing the notion of extended and generalized exchange networks a bit further.

Macroeconomic management, the degree of control over economic development indicators, Wagner holds, is a parameter of political effectiveness, despite the paradoxical constellation of limited governmental capacities to influence and the impossibility *not* to influence the economy in a modern, democratic society. Following Keynes, macroeconomic instabilities are seen as inherent to market societies, the "economy" of which is perceived as a network of markets. Economic disequilibria do not spread randomly or symmetrically over all markets, but rather in a structured chain of transmission with unequal adjustment capacities and, correspondingly, dominant directions of adjustment flows (usually from capital over commodity to labor markets, the latter having to absorb the spillovers from markets upstream the flow of adjustments). In contrast to Oliver Williamson's transaction-cost approach (Williamson 1975, 1985) which does not leave the general equilibrium assumptions and the symmetry view on market linkage of standard economics, Wagner follows Clower's (1969) framework of non-symmetric adjustment of markets in postulating a hierarchy of markets — not as a stable structure, but as a variable pattern which can be changed and is determined politically. Such a re-ordering of market hierarchies is done through strategic capacities of collective actors resulting from institutional resources outside the exchange nexus (such as, e.g., property rights, voluntary associations, legal market regulations, political exchange rate interventions). Market hierarchies "are designed to generate favorable outcomes of macroeconomic adjustments to disequilibria". Thus, Wagner allows for "economy failure" and its partial absorption by inter-organizational policy networks like GPE in the same way as Williamson allows for a partial absorption of "market failures" by single organizational hierarchies. His theoretical scheme of institutional economics is based on the idea that a "restructuring of the price-quantity-nexus" (Luhmann 1971) implies an exchange of commitment power for legitimacy derived from macroeconomic performance between the polity and the economy. A correspondence between market hierarchies and the power-relations between collective actors in a policy community makes for equilibrated exchange; if the "correspondence principle" is violated, market hierarchies will change, power will be reallocated and a deflationary spiral will set in; market hierarchies are as fragile or stable as the coalitions underlying the macroeconomic policy network.

The nature and dynamics of such policy networks or integrated policy circuits is the focus of the next section V. *Erhard Friedberg*'s contribution deals with generalized political exchange and its relationship to public policy from an organizational and inter-organizational point of view. (Friedberg is organizational researcher, political sociologist and policy analyst and Research Director at the *Centre de Sociologie des Organisations,* C.N.R.S., Paris). In the tradition of his famous *L'acteur et le Système* with Michel Crozier, Friedberg analyzes public policies as the product of concrete action systems before he deciphers such action systems as resulting from generalized political exchange, considered as one case of inter-organizational policy-making. While the first aspect is too well known to need further mentioning, its application to GPE offers several new insights not to be preempted in the introduction. Instead, I would like to draw the reader's attention to the second, core part of his contribution, where power (and collusion) relations are investigated as the nucleus of games in policy-making. Power is seen as an unbalanced exchange of possibilities for action between interdependent actors; by implication, it is relational, always also involves cooperation as well as asymmetric capacities of influence and appropriation of benefits. It is based on the control of uncertainties relevant to others and on the freedom of action or leeway, i.e. unpredictability. Friedberg dismisses the argument (also voiced during the conference) that unpredictability might be the source not only of power, but also of exclusion from relevant power circles which want to protect themselves against unreliable actors. In his (and Crozier's) model, the unrestricted, pure logic of exchange (in all kinds of interorganizational action-fields) is the *logic of monopoly* (and not that of competitive markets !); and political exchange — as against economic exchange of resources — is characterized by the players' attempt to manipulate and change in one's own favor the rules of the bargaining and exchange game.

Friedberg is radically unorthodox: not free, open, competitive markets but monopolistic tendencies (never to be pushed too far) are natural and predominant games under the prevalent conditions of limited rationality and opportunistic behavior; perfectly competitive markets are fascinating, but they are purely theoretical models and highly "artificial" social constructions as well, most difficult to establish and most difficult to sustain in reality. There is a constant danger of precarious market relations slipping into uncontrolled constellations of bilateral monopoly; and conflictual exchanges will transform themselves into collusive relationships, generated by a common interest from interdependence, both in permanence and in stability. An autonomization of transaction and bargaining processes around more or less implicit rules of the game occurs. "Actual policy-fields will always be in between these two extremes of the continuum", and Friedberg constructs an evolutionary typology of thresholds from tacit collusion to planned cooperation. Renate Mayntz (1986) has underlined that Friedberg's genetic perspective focuses on the emergence of inter-organizational policy networks, whereas Marin concentrates on the system itself.

There is a second, radically unorthodox facet in Friedberg's reasoning: his comprehensive concept of "organization". Organization, according to Friedberg, is not just *one* possibility in solving the problem of "negotiated order" besides markets and solidarity / community, as Willke holds, "it is not the equivalent to Williamson's hierarchy. It is a construct superordinate to these alternatives, a level of reality which structures and conditions markets as well as solidarity and hierarchy. It is that which gives life and existence to cooperative arrangements, whatever form they may take". Thus, Friedberg's is an attempt at nothing less than a general theory of collective action, of antagonistic cooperation and of the integration of inter-organizational policy-making through exchange networks.

The second contribution in this section, written by *Antonio Mutti*, deals with the role of trust in political exchange. (Antonio Mutti is a sociologist and social economist at the University of Pavia and a well-established figure in the Italian discourse on political exchange and in the debate on neo-corporatism, to which he has contributed a number of theoretical pieces as well as some empirical studies).Mutti starts with the puzzle of how it is possible to achieve long-term and generalized political exchanges without the existence of as perfect a generalized medium of exchange as money. How can stable, enduring GPE emerge without being able to quantify the stakes, in particular with respect to hardly divisible regulatory and redistributive policies ? His answer, in accordance with the GPE concept and most other authors, is rules of interaction and communication, the irreducible ambiguity and uncertainty which can only be overcome by trust. This is not the place to reveal his discussions of trust in this context, spanning a wide range of theoretical traditions from Goffman to Luhmann, from Parsons to Garfinkel, from Blau to M. Deutsch and from Ouchi to, above all, Georg Simmel. Simmel's analysis of the trusting expectation, the "almost compulsory power" trust constitutes over those receiving it, its reflexivity (trust in the trust conceded/received) etc., helps to understand why processes of GPE (with stakes difficult to measure and compare, uncertain criteria to calculate cost/benefits, etc.) cannot work without trust and political credit to control opportunistic behavior, save transaction costs for information and surveillance, extend time horizons and strengthen social ties, bringing about a virtuous circle of productive exchange. Mutti shows that trust is superior to legal-contractual formalization and rule specification and that the flexibility and dynamism of GPE is directly related to the amount of trust available. He finally analyzes a series of painful but fundamental organizational dilemmas arising for collective actors through their participation in GPE networks of stabilized trust. Still, the consolidation of trust and acceptable games cannot be sufficiently explained by their strategic choices, but needs a consideration of structural contexts.

Karen S. Cook tries to provide exactly what Antonio Mutti in his very last sentences (for Blau and many other theorists of social exchange) considers to be unresolved and unresolvable for the time being: to bridge action theory and structural analysis, the micro and the macro-level of social exchange theory which he thinks of as "the main logical difficulty of a theory of generalized political exchange". Karen S. Cook, sociologist at the University of Washington and Director of the Social Psychology Laboratory, is more optimistic in this respect, and she certainly has all credentials to be so; many scholars see her as the single most important proponent of exchange network theory today (and, I might add, the concept of generalized political exchange owes more to her meanwhile "classical" articles (Cook 1977, Cook/Emerson 1978) and Emerson's theoretical framework (Emerson 1962, 1972a, b, 1976) than to any other approach). Because of its prominence as well as its degree of complexity and sophistication, not even its basic premises shall be referred to. Instead, I simply point to two implications of her recent contribution: first , those of us who are working on policy networks composed of corporate actors could certainly learn from her new experimental research on generalized exchange systems on the micro-level, in particular as this reasoning is related to macro-processes and actually focuses on the interplay between these two levels; and, secondly, to the conceptual contributions of her theory to a better understanding of GPE.

Empirical research on exchange networks have considerably complexified our conceptual notions regarding linkages between structure and action: network positions such as, for instance, structural centrality determine resource dependencies and power relations between participating actors not in a direct and expected homologous way — centrality might in some exchange network structures imply weakness and not strength in resource control (Cook et al.1983, Yamagishi, Gillmore and Cook 1988). This indeterminacy between network properties and power-dependency relations between actors is further increased if one takes different meaningful conceptions and operationalizations into account: point centrality might be measured by degree-based, betweenness and closeness-based measures and these three measures hardly converge in assessing structures of networks neither very small nor very simple, and none of them corresponds to power distributions in negatively connected networks. Quite obviously, such empirical findings have theoretically far reaching, but ambiguous consequences, as do network-"vulnerability" measures, findings on "power-balancing" mechanisms such as coalition formation, on the determinants of commitment formation in social exchange networks (Cook, Emerson et al.1983) etc.

The second important lesson scholars of GPE policy circuits can learn from exchange network analysts concerns conceptual elaboration. I have borrowed, for instance, Emerson's idea of "productive exchange" involving "value-adding" processes (Emerson 1972a, b, 1976) as a defining element of GPE conceptualization. From Karen S. Cook's contribution in this volume, future work on GPE will have to refine, for instance, its notions of linkages: they are, in Cook's terms, chain-generalized and not group-focused, mainly univocal and only occasionally bilateral; the question who the principals are and who the agents in highly complex inter-organizational exchange networks of collective actors is far from obvious and probably as indeterminate as network-wide power measures; the high vulnerability of GPE networks stemming from the non-substitutability and non-interchangeability of strongly interdependent interests and from the predominant unilaterality of flows has not yet been fully explored; etc. In Cook's words, "These two research traditions need to be integrated, since GPE represents one form of generalized exchange about which there has been too little empirical work within the social exchange tradition. Both Marin's developing exchange framework and social exchange theory more generally stand to gain from such a synthesis". It will be an interplay between a general theory of exchange networks and a middle-range conceptual framework on inter-organizational and integrated policy circuits.

A last contribution elaborates the temporalities of exchange: the case of self-organization for societal governance, by *Mark Elchardus*. (Elchardus is sociologist at the Free University of Brussels and a leading specialist in social theory and social research on time). How are exchanges generalized? How can actors and exchanges constitute each other? How do such interpenetrated actors produce the conditions of exchange? From a temporalist perspective, the structuration of action systems is based on relative invariance and sequential order; time-negating or, in short, atemporal as against temporal models of exchange discount the past, e.g., by ignoring history and structures including costs incurred (sunk costs) at the expense of probabilistic assumptions about the future. Elchardus discusses time-discounting institutions such as transactional, discrete contracts and the ways time intrudes the atemporal strategy; he reflects on the boundaries non-market institutions such as formal organizations or families impose on the generalization of exchange; he understands GPE as a particular temporal mode of exchange, in need of generating its own conditions, and asks for its macro-sociological prerequisites etc. Here, the subtleties of Elchardus' theoretical interpretation of social time in political exchange networks cannot be accounted for. He aims at a theoretical foundation of a phenomenon like GPE, the temporal aspects of which were crucial from its very beginning: they have history and they take their time to evolve — and it takes time to change them; time is one of their most important self-generated and collective power resources; they operate in open, infinite time horizons; they upgrade capacities through frequency of interactions and tightening of coupling procedures; they use timing as a strategic power medium; they synchronize different "times" (temporalities, rhythms, calendars etc.) at work; and it takes time to fully understand them.

Governance and Generalized Exchange

Both volumes deal with the puzzle of how is societal self-regulation and governance through complex policy networks possible at all. Whereas *Generalized Political Exchange* develops the base by presenting competing as well as converging theoretical perspectives, *Governance and Generalized Exchange* confronts various analytical models with a diversity of empirical evidence, from historical documents, case-study material to cross-national, comparative statistical data. At the core of governance in modern, industrialized, market societies lies, of course, the political responsibility for economic reproduction and development and the corresponding social integration. Therefore, the studies collected in the second volume center around queries like: What explains success or failure of joint macroeconomic management in areas such as employment, industrial, technological development, monetary or fiscal policy ? What makes associational interest intermediation in labor relations, what, e.g., makes environmental protection through chemicals control policy viable or ineffective ?

The first section, unfolding genetic-evolutionary and comparative-historical perspectives, bridges the purely theoretical orientation of the first volume with the theoretically oriented empirical study outlook of the second. This section develops the elements of a general theory of the genesis of industrial relations and corporatism (*Franz Traxler*) and traces this developmental pattern towards forms of interest governance by generalized political exchange throughout Western Europe during the Twentieth Century *(Colin Crouch)*. Franz Traxler (who is sociologist at the University of Economics in Vienna and Head of the Department of Sociology at the Federal Academy of Public Administration, also in Vienna, an established scholar of corporatism and industrial labor relations, with books on trade unions and business associations) addresses as his main puzzle the emergence of institutionalized macroeconomic regulation and of inter-class cooperation in industrial labor relations, the second great circuit of any modern polity besides the system of parliamentarism and political parties. He starts by observing the lack of a genetic theory of collective action capable of explaining this historical phenomenon and the conditions of its cross-national variability. In the tradition of the supposed "two logics of collective action"(Offe/Wiesenthal 1980), he links institutional reasoning to the socio-structural, class-specific position of the collective actors participating in governance. By implication, collective bargaining, political exchange and corporatism re-balance power relations in favor of labor, structurally weaker in market economies. He analyses the material, institutional and intentional framework of political exchange in trying to reconstruct the self-interested rationality (as a system property, not individual preferences) inducing both capital and labor to enter and institutionalize joint regulation systems as part of their respective collective action strategies.

Whereas the main problem of labor is recruiting (and eventually also mobilizing) members, capital is faced with the problem of obtaining the members' compliance or loyalty; labor's main collective action problem is associability, capital's problem internal governability. Both have to rely also on selective external incentives in order to come to terms with their own collective action problems. Reciprocal assistance as, for instance, the exchange of union security (automatic fee collection, "closed shop"-policy) for union help to maintain business association member's loyalty is just one example. Traxler reminds us of seemingly perverse phenomena such as trade unions as the most effective lobbyists for business interests in order to advance interests of their own, or the ironical historical fact that it has been unions — and not business associations — which have prevented capitalists from price-cutting against other capitalists by early institutionalizing collective bargaining in fragmented branches with skilled labor, thereby creating a functional equivalent to cartels and syndicates endogenously formed by business in more concentrated sectors and regulating competition between capitalists in this indirect way. In short: effective intra-class collective action requires inter-class collaboration.

The most avanced stage of such cooperation is the transition from collective bargaining to joint macroeconomic concertation and interest intermediation through GPE or what Traxler calls corporatism. But establishing and maintaining macro-corporatist cooperation faces the same dilemmas of collective action the participating associations have to confront at the organizational level (e.g. disciplining "free riders"). Therefore, the costs of cooperation must be compensated for by political exchange, whether in elementary or more refined, generalized forms (e.g. by a "producers' alliance" at the expense of third parties such as consumers or the environment). In order to become workable such precarious arrangements of meta-games need state support to overcome inter-organizational competition, centralized associations with comprehensive domains and a balance of power or class forces; then and only then can political exchange create social order.

This is also the subject of *Colin Crouch* (Colin Crouch, sociologist at Trinity College in Oxford, is author of many well-known books, including the two-volume collection of essays edited jointly with Alessandro Pizzorno which started the recent debate on political exchange). Colin Crouch links the basic theoretical and practical concerns of this debate to historical and empirical realities by providing a genetic or evolutionary theory of GPE systems covering an impressive range of historical evidence between about 1910 and 1975 on 10 to 13 (Western, Nordic, Central, Southern) European countries in a comparative manner. He focuses on the place of labor within the politics of industrial relations and related macroeconomic policy-making at the national level. While he sees collective bargaining as the characteristic mode of exchange in industrial relations pluralism, GPE is considered to be the characteristic mode of neo-corporatism; the latter being defined by more frequent and enduring interactions and negotiations across a wide and constantly expanding range of issues, mixing the exchange of demands and offers with the joint regulation and administration of areas of common interest, relaxing contractual elements for agreed-upon technocratic criteria. Collective bargaining and GPE mark the poles of a continuum with many intermediate cases. Crouch bases his comparative historical review and testing of hypotheses on a simplified model with three independent variables (the power of organised labor, the centralisation of labor movement organisations, and the capacity of employers associations to operate at a centralised level) and one dependent variable (the character of the industrial relations system along a complex of dimensions related to GPE features). Each of these factors is operationalized in a sophisticated way by multiple empirical indicators which cannot be discussed here, before the model is applied in order to interpret the historical changes in European industrial relations systems during this century. Crouch works with a series of "snapshots" at crucial moments of the 20th century: "the eve of the Great War; the mid-1920s after the upheavals of the immediate post-war years had settled into some kind of coherence; the eve of the Second World War; the early 1950s, again after the subsidence of post-war upheaval; and the mid-1970s as the most recent period for which it is already possible to secure some kind of perspective". (Crouch, 1990)

In resuming his broad comparative historical review across countries and periods, Crouch concludes on the "demonstrated usefulness of the idea of GPE" as a heuristic tool of analysis and on the prerequisites of that model. "It has also shown how extensive GPE has been as a tendency towards which many systems move, but at the same time it has both shown the absence of either inevitability or irreversibility in that process". He confirms and refutes a number of propositions of established theories of industrial relations, discusses unexpected and paradoxical findings as well as puzzling historical discrepancies in a comparative view, and locates the heyday of GPE in Europe in this century between 1935/ 45 and 1975. His is a bottom-up built, grounded theory in the best sense of the term, well illustrating the limits to where one could go with pure theory and *a priori* reasoning without empirical evidence. At the same time, his comparative and theoretical account of the rich variety of structural and historical patterns to be observed has important implications for evolutionary theory: it immunizes against simplistic assumptions about unilinear directions towards GPE configurations, about supposedly inevitable trends to higher complexity and organizational development or about an irreversible nature of advanced stages of inter-organizational policy-making through generalized political exchange.

The next section II analyses macroeconomic management and corresponding types of policy regimes from an unorthodox institutionalist point of view. *Fritz W. Scharpf* (political scientist with background in law and research in political economy, government and administration, is Co-Director jointly with Renate Mayntz of the newly-founded Max-Planck-Institut für Gesellschaftsforschung in Cologne after having been founding Director of the International Institute of Management of the Science Center in Berlin for more than a decade) is both an early predecessor of network thinking in policy analysis (Hanf / Scharpf 1978) as well as a most sophisticated empirically working theorist of what he has coined as interorganizational policy-making in the area of macroeconomic management. His core puzzle is nothing less than the core puzzle of economic governance of modern polities around the third quarter of this century: what explains the remarkable and growing divergence of economic performance between advanced industrialized nation states with regard to unemployment and price stability and what is the variation in governance capacities or political management of highly developed market economies ? This core puzzle is not just of most obvious great practical and political but also of major theoretical interest, given that neither conventional theories in economics nor previous political science approaches have generated valid explanations of this phenomenon for all the decades since the sixties.

Scharpf develops his own theoretical framework in order to test it through a comparative analysis of four selected countries, so that both the choice of the period investigated as well as the countries covered can claim systematic and theoretical significance. The world economic crisis after 1973 is seen as a kind of laboratory for "natural experiments" providing ample opportunities for theory-building and theory-testing: for instance, to disentangle institutional factors, economic environmental conditions, political goals and the repertoire of public policy responses and strategic choices. His version of institutionalism is not one-dimensional but operating on several levels (policy games / institutions / economic structures and outcomes, like the generalized political exchange concept, but far more elaborated) and on their interplay. Thus, he combines solid, grounded theory in political economy with the analytical instruments of game theory, convincingly demonstrating to orthodox institutionalists that institutional conditions do not determine public policy and hence can never fully explain economic policy outcomes. But this model of model-building and empirical testing of hypotheses must be read in its complexity and sophistication, as it does not lend itself to easy summaries. What holds for the rich analytical apparatus also applies to the results: they cannot be resumed. But it would be interesting to catalogue empirical findings of Scharpf's contextual analysis, which would falsify or at least significantly modify previous hypotheses: an only marginal role of business associations as *political* actors in explaining macroeconomic outcomes in the seventies (as against Schmitter / Streeck 1981); the crucial strategic importance of unions and their wage moderation for *all* kinds of macroeconomic coordination games (as against Streeck 1984 or Marin 1985); systematic counter-evidence to the competing "class-politics" (Korpi 1983, Esping-Andersen 1985) and "political business cycle" (Nordhaus 1975, Peel 1982) theories; a revision of simple, barter-like conceptions of political exchange, prevalent since Pizzorno 1978, in Lehmbruch, Regini etc., strongly converging with the editor's conceptualization of generalized political exchange: Scharpf works with ideas of network-vulnerability as a generalized resource or rationality assumptions conceiving political calculations as guided by strict but enlightened self-interest, taking into account forms of roundabout payoffs and benefits beyond simple and direct compensations by the parties interacting. Despite theoretical efforts, Scharpf does never forget to link institutional analysis to historical contingencies; that is, to the limits of general theorizing. If he postulates, for instance, an asymmetry between Keynesian and monetarist economic policy regimes, he understands the relevance of neo-corporatist institutions as a prerequisite for Keynesian macroeconomic policy games only; and he sees that to the extent that policy regimes change historically, the explanatory power of institutional factors for economic variance and governance will change as well.

The second contribution to the macroeconomic management section II deals with a most complex, structurally permanent and conflictual domain of generalized political exchange, the taxation game, by *Klaus Gretschmann* and *Patrick Kenis*. (Gretschmann is an economist with social science orientation, coordinating the EC Policy Unit at the European Institute of Public Administration in Maastricht, Patrick Kenis is sociologist and Research Fellow at the European Centre in Vienna). Starting from Knoke and Laumann's (1982) definition of policy domain, Gretschmann and Kenis develop a theoretical framework of their own which goes beyond the conceptualizations of political exchange since Pizzorno, and critically reconsiders the editor's GPE concept as being somewhat overgeneralized and lacking an actor-theoretical foundation. They see the *differentia specifica* of generalized political exchange in what they call its "relational repeatability" ensuring the option of future exchanges despite changing actor configurations within the domain. Political exchange involves elements of threat and counter-threat as well as significant externalities; the lack of political money and, therefore, also the absence of market and shadow prices and exchange rates; correspondingly, gains and losses cannot be calculated easily their distribution will result from strategic action and make political exchange vulnerable to "false trading". Thus, it is not only conflict-settling, but conflict-generating at the same time, making trust and faithful cooperation integral components of political exchanges.

Having elaborated their model and formalized the logic of political exchange involved, Gretschmann and Kenis test its usefulness by analysing the German tax reform package 1986 - 1990 as a case in point of a most complex political exchange transaction pattern. As against economic tax analyses which conceive all kinds of (individual or corporate) tax payers as passive adjusters to legislation only, their political and social science study of taxation looks at how organized corporate actors influence both tax legislation and implementation. The enormous heterogeneity and differentiation of tax payer's interests make the "tax caleidoscope" constituting the "fiscal game" a vastly more complex policy domain than traditional corporatist set-ups. Gretschmann and Kenis provide a most interesting case study of the (West) German three-step tax reform in the second half of the 1980s. They map the process of interest intermediation and political exchange by a great tableau identifying on the one hand relevant collective actors, their affectedness by intended changes, their objectives, crucial resources in political exchange, their positions and attitudes towards the reform package, as well as the concessions offered in the course of the exchange processes; and by identifying, on the other hand, a set of seven most important organized actors in the tax reform, from federal government, business associations, trade unions, jurisdictions i.e., regional authorities and organizations of municipalities, as well as tax payers and tax consultants associations. Despite the high number of potential interest configurations, only three sets of coalitions (an "equity coalition", an "efficiency coalition" and a "revenue coalition") are found empirically; and despite highly divergent gains and losses involved, *all* actors can and do hope for *some* benefits from the tax reform as a whole and formed positive expectations about its advantages apart from positional gains through political exchanges. This way, the analysis of taxation – considered to be the area of what Schumpeter called "the naked interplay of vested interests" – illustrates well the productive, value-adding quality of generalized political exchange; it is capable of transforming the supposedly pure zero-sum fiscal game into a positive-sum game. But Gretschmann and Kenis have other and additional theoretical lessons to draw from their empirical findings: the most remarkable frequency of tax reforms (46 revisions of the income tax code within the last decade alone) constitute a "permanency" of tax changes; this permanency of tax reforms itself is to be explained by the fundamental uncertainty about benefits and costs of tax changes, so that political exchanges simultaneously make for a solution *and* the creation of new problems of adjustments. It is this basic ambiguity or "indeterminacy", creating stability *and* instability, reliability *and* ever-new uncertainty, which the authors see as "the very essence of political and generalized political exchange".

Analysing the policy process and control as its potential generalized exchange medium, is the focus of the next contribution by *Volker Schneider*, opening section III which moves from network thinking and qualitative or formal analysis to empirical network analysis proper. (Volker Schneider, social scientist with studies in economics and political science, is Research Fellow at the Max-Planck-Institut für Gesellschaftsforschung in Cologne). Schneider "applies J.S.Coleman's concept of political exchange as an 'exchange of control' to a policy process. It is argued that the intrusion of the exchange logic to politics changes the character of the policy game from pressure or coercion to cooperation. Applied to chemicals control, this means that government and administration, being dependent on scientific information and cooperative behavior of industry and other groups in policy formation and implementation, allow these groups to participate in some of its own originally exclusive rights to legislation in exchange for the provision of information and self-binding behavior. This in turn facilitates a more effective and efficient control of chemicals by government". Thus, policy outcomes are explained by interaction processes, where corporate actors exchange resources such as money, rights, information etc. according to institutionalized rule systems or regimes in order to solve policy problems.

Unlike the editor or authors such as Friedberg, Schneider conceives political exchange as following the same logic as economic transactions; and he feels reassured in this assumption by Marsden's (1983) and Pappi's elaboration of the Coleman model overcoming the premise of perfect market competition. The case in point investigated by Schneider through network analytical instruments is taken from a detailed and lengthy study worked out as a PhD thesis at the European University Institute in Florence and later published as a book (Schneider, V. 1988), providing a wealth of information and interesting insights into the policy process of chemicals control of the world's most important producers of chemicals. His analysis also induces one to differentiate and to use the GPE concept rather for understanding the implementation phase and less the formation stage of the policy process: legislation is a single, discrete act and not a recurrent event such as implementation; it involves many more actors than law enforcement; enduring relationships can evolve between a few actors with recurrent tasks only as in implementation; the more open dynamic of parliamentarism and the political market does not generate a stable political status order necessary for exercising collective discipline; and the generalized expectation of what Macneil coined as "ordinary troubles" is conceivable with routine implementation problems only. This way, Schneider contributes implicitly to a further development of the GPE concept as much as he does through explicit criticism and modifications.

A second study in section III using network analytical techniques stems from *Peter Kappelhoff* and *Franz Urban Pappi*, one of the pioneers of network methodology in German- speaking countries. (Kappelhoff is sociologist at the University of Kiel, Pappi is political scientist at Mannheim University after having moved from the University of Kiel). The authors build on Marsden's (1983) modification of the Coleman model of political exchange (Coleman 1973, 1986) which no longer assumes the logic of perfect market competition. Using simulated data first, they point out some of the implications of the modified model before they apply it to empirical data on a community elite system, which they had already studied previously in terms of the original Coleman model of collective action (Pappi/Kappelhoff 1984); finally, the authors investigate the different consequences different model assumptions have for the derived power structure of the exchange network due to restricted access and price making behavior. Here, there is not the time and space to discuss either the operationalization measures proposed or the findings of the model application. But it should be pointed out to the reader that the contribution was invited because of the advanced network analytical methodology used, despite the fact that it does not refer to the puzzles addressed by the other authors and despite its fundamental divergence from, if not outright contrast to, the GPE concept: it is explicitly based on individualistic premises contrasted to what are labelled as collectivistic exchange theories from Durkheim to Lévi-Strauss; it is a market model allowing for imperfections applied to social and political situations, not analysing the production of policy outcomes and the political division of labor involved; its networks are composed of individual elite members or single persons, later aggregated into institutional sectors and power structure groups, not of corporate actors or organized collective interests; structural power constellations outside the influence in the decision-making process of the community elite such as market hierarchies are not taken into account; it focuses on power and control in distributional conflicts over valued resources and that is on appropriation without reference to the joint supply of public goods; governance it not at stake at all, etc. Kappelhoff/Pappi, therefore, actually present an alternative model and an empirical test not only to Coleman's original model of social exchange on a perfect market, but even more so to the volume's common focal point of generalized political exchange.

Section IV of the book opens a new area of applying political exchange concepts to issues of governance: *Leonardo Parri* focuses on what is called territorial politics and inter-governmental relations, i.e. relations between the central and the peripheral politico-administrative structures. (Leonardo Parri is social scientist and Researcher at the European University Institute in Florence where he is completing his PhD and has published a number of articles on the subject). His focus diverges from the bulk of neo-corporatist literature which has concentrated on functional interest organization and taken into account territorial aspects to the extent only that they added to the complexity of functional or sectoral differentiation; Parri, in contrast, analyses the second crucial circuit of any modern polity with conceptual instruments such as political exchange originally developed in the context of the other subsystem of industrial labor relations and macroeconomic concertation; and that is what makes his attempt original and interesting. The cases to which he applies his framework are territorial politics in the decentralized United States ("American federalism") and in centralized France ("French unitarianism") in the crucial domain of policy-linked conditional grant/subsidy allocation by central governments. The substance of his findings and interpretations cannot be adequately discussed in short without doing harm to his thick description and stimulating comparative insights but should simply be recommended to scholars of the American and the French political system as well as to those of public administration.

Instead, I would like to pause for a moment at the conceptual instrument developed in order to investigate the dynamic interplay between center and periphery and the remarkable vitality of the latter in asserting its autonomy under different inter-governmental regimes, what Parri calls "territorial political exchange" (TPE). In his approach to policy analysis inspired by inter-organizational theory (Benson 1975, Cook 1977, Crozier / Friedberg 1977 and Friedberg in this volume, Scharpf 1978, Aldrich and Whetten 1981, Galaskiewicz 1982), Parri distinguishes between functional, territorial and generalized political exchanges in the formulation and implementation of public policies. Territorial political exchange (TPE) could be summarized, in my own view, as against generalized political exchange (GPE) in the following schematic way: it is simpler, less complex; less precarious because of stable institutionalization; of overall loose coupling as against GPE which I would like to characterize by a specific mixture of tight functional and often also tight temporal coupling (due to simultaneous synchronization requirements) with a loose social coupling; it is defined by a "bargaining" style of negotiation and not by a prevalence of "problem-solving" orientations such as GPE; it allows for side-payments and log-rolling such as traditional barter, in contrast to the more functionalized transaction patterns emerging in GPE; it is, in the language of March and Olsen used by Renate Mayntz (1986), an aggregative institution and not an integrative project such as generalized political exchange; it rather combines a logic of selective, clientelistic protectionism on territorial grounds with the GPE logic of global, collective discipline through voluntary cooperation; accordingly, territorial political exchange reaches an equilibrium by balancing central guidelines and enforcements with local demands and anarchies. According to Parri, the crucial dimension underlying the continuum – of which GPE and TPE are seen as extremes – is exchange complexity; but it makes him not ignore the striking similarities which also exist.

Section V addresses generalized political exchange and its application to policy-making in the context of the European Economic Community. The first contribution by *Helmut Willke* on 'Political Intervention – Operational Preconditions for Generalized Political Exchange' could as well have been placed in the first, theoretical volume, as it provides sophisticated theoretical reasoning on the prerequisites of GPE and political intervention under conditions of high societal complexity. (Helmut Willke is sociologist at the University of Bielefeld after having been Professor of Planning and Decision Theory). A leading German scholar in systems and state theory, Willke defines the problem of governance – or of "guidance" in his language – in system functionalist terms: because of their growing differentiation, societal subsystems generate a dependency of the state on their capacity for detailed and specialized knowledge, for decentralized implementation and for providing consensus and compliance with decisions taken. The state will try to convert potential competition by organized interests into mutually beneficial collaboration, inducing an exchange of some autonomy for participation in previously inaccessible domains. In order to cope with high complexity, variation and uncertainty, bureaucratic hierarchies are being replaced by emerging modes of societal steering such as GPE. Thereby, the guidance capacity of the polity is increased and policy networks take the place of the central state which has come to limits of governance through "the simple means of law and money". Inter-systemic exchange relations remain improbable despite their ubiquity due to the simultaneous growth of interdependence *and* independence between subsystems; whereas GPE stresses the former, the problems resulting from the latter are considered to be more important because subsystem autonomy is conceptualized as self-referential, "inner-directed", reproduced through autopoietic closure (for autopoietic theory, see also Teubner 1990). Autonomy makes subsystems unsusceptible and relatively indifferent to their environments, so that political interventions cannot but induce self-guidance of resourceful organized actors; political design establishes the exchange logic or "grammar of transformation rules" and "fitting" transaction-chains between operationally closed systems be it through "incrementalism" / "evolution", "planning", or "guidance". Guidance, as the most complex mode of organizing the interrelation between different autonomous actors, consists both of "a reflexive, decentralized framing of contexts which may serve as common 'world views'...and self-guidance of all subsystems within the limits of their autonomy". But no single collective actor can any longer generate this common orientation and generalize it as binding for all others. Thus, societal guidance at best can work indirectly with contextual interventions, "conditionalize contextual conditions", whereas changes can only be self-implemented into the standard operating procedures of any one subsystem. What results from this highly selective and loose coupling is a co-evolution of distinct and autonomous systems, the exchange of which is understood not as a transportation of fixed entities but rather as a concertation of internal orientations.

From this level of abstraction, Willke moves directly to very specific cases, such as public policies promoting international technological competitiveness in the course of Japan's decision to start the Fifth Generation Computer Project. He goes well beyond all other authors of both volumes: while he provides an interesting kind of translation of social exchange theory and the generalized political exchange concept into the framework of an autopoietic version of systems theory, his reasoning always focuses on *inter-system relations* and *not* on *inter-organizational policy-making* within the polity as a subsystem and across its boundaries, thereby operating a level of abstraction higher than the GPE conceptualization and all other contributions.

Whereas Willke argues on an abstract level of systems theory with occasional empirical illustrations top-down, the next author *Arthur F.P. Wassenberg* (Scholar of management at the Rotterdam School of Management and Erasmus University Rotterdam) provides narratives on European Economic Community industrial policy-making (the battle over the Belgian Société Générale and ESPRIT, the European Strategic Programme for Research in Information Technology) which he later reconstructs and interprets as games of antagonistic cooperation among firms and between companies, governments and administrative agencies. His, in contrast to Willke, is an action- or interaction-oriented bargaining framework , looking for political implications of organizational strategies and inter-organizational networking. While he uses some of the taxonomy from the GPE concept such as "antagonistic cooperation", his usage of it as well as the puzzles addressed are rather remote from what were the original queries and attempts at answering them. Still, the remaining intellectual overlap, as well as Wassenberg's own divergent perspective might shed an interesting light on other author's efforts. Wassenberg, for instance, opposes his triadic perspective on the dynamics of inter-organizational cooperation to the more traditional dyadic approaches on policy-making, discounting the network perspective on generalized exchange circuits; still, its implications are interesting for further elaboration of the GPE concept. The same applies to other concepts used: "captive alliances" with decreasing room for strategic choice but increasing degrees of predictability of the emerging order, strongly converge with Friedberg's analysis (in this volume), as does the understanding of power as maintaining one's own flexibility ("deniability") while keeping opponent's predictability ("reliability" of firms, "repeatability" of bureaucracies); the dilemmas resulting from the trade-off between flexibility and stability; the different rationalities applying to different (national, regional , communitarian, and global) levels of strategic behavior in transnational policy games such as modern industrial policies; or the replacement of comprehensive strategies by tactical moves under conditions of rapid technological change and great uncertainty regarding negotiation agenda, arenas and time horizons, so that any analysis of association and dissociation in policy-making will have to focus on the "limits of intentionality" of the corporate actors involved and on ever-changing network structures.

The final section VI leads back to the core issues at stake in generalized political exchange: i.e., joint regulation and cooperative industrial governance, to labor relations and macro-ecoconomic management. Both contributions implicitly share the sceptical historical view taken by both Colin Crouch and Fritz W. Scharpf that the heydays of a negotiated economy might well be beyond and not before us any longer. This is, in particular, the thrust of *Paul Windolf's* analysis on the future of trade unions, where the emergence of so-called productivity coalitions between organized labor and capital on company level is seen as an important symptom of disintegration of mass unionism and, by implication, also of generalized political exchange which cannot operate without highly organized collective actors. (Paul Windolf is sociologist at the University of Heidelberg). Productivity coalitions are defined by a devolution shifting the centre of collective bargaining from the national or branch level to that of the enterprise; by more cooperative bargaining styles between management and unions; and by a replacement of contractual relations by internal bureaucratic regulations and individualized or categorical agreements between management and (groups of) workers. While they might obviously undermine trade union control shares over the labor process, Windolf does not ignore the ambiguous functions of decentralized exchange relations between labor, capital and public authorities. He develops an evolutionary model in order to answer the basic query whether productivity coalitions are a transitory phenomenon due to the economic depression of the 1980s or rather indicators of structural change in industrial labor relations, away from "neo-corporatist" centralized bargaining and generalized exchange between employers associations, trade unions and the state. But if the second development is more probable, would interest intermediation move back to liberal pluralism and fragmentation – and if not there, where else? Could controlled autonomy imply an exchange of higher productivity and collaboration for participation apart from union involvement and corporatist institutions ?

Windolf analyses experiments with such a participation in Italy and Great Britain, as well as experiences with collective agreements on flexibility (in working time regimes) in France and the Federal Republic of Germany. He concludes from his comparative case studies that the decentralization tendencies were closely related to shifts from wage-centered demands to qualitative demands regarding control of new technology, work organization, upgrading skills and qualifications and improvement of working conditions. Decentralization itself has to be seen more differentiated: more leeway for local, plant-level interests does not replace but rather complements broad guidelines still negotiated by central interlocutors. As the trend towards decentralized bargaining reflects structural transformations of world markets, new forms of work organization and technical changes, a cyclical view of the phenomenon is less plausible than an evolutionary one. Politically, this tendency towards decentralization is completely underdetermined: it did and will strengthen more radical or more moderate factions of the union movement, depending on the different forms of internal organization of European labor unions. And whether generalized exchange modes will be part of such a future of European trade unionism, will critically depend on whether productivity coalitions will be integrated into or cut off from comprehensive policy networks. In principle, GPE could be seen as a generalized device for a controlled, bargained flexibility as against a wildcat or unilateral one; it would allow to generate variety, the widest possible range of negotiable options and extended time horizons, while simultaneously reducing the corresponding complexity and conflictuality. Whether or not it will be used in this way will depend not least on the balance of forces determining the choice of policy regimes and their outcomes.

The contribution on joint regulation, meso-games and political exchange in Swedish industrial relations chosen to be the final one is from *Victor A. Pestoff*. (Pestoff, a specialist on co-operatives, consumer policy, voluntary and business organizations, is Research Associate at the Department of Business Administration at the University of Stockholm, Adjunct Professor at the Department of Political Science, University of Helsinki and Consultant of the European Centre, Vienna). Pestoff's analysis deals both with the core issues addressed by the concept of generalized political exchange and uses its perspective: it reconstructs the policy regime prevailing in Swedish industrial labor relations, often considered to be a paradigmatic case of neo-corporatism and GPE modes of governance – from collective bargaining, work environment regulation, co-determination, labor-market insurance, wage-earner funds, lay representation on the governing bodies of central administrative agencies to institutions of conflict resolution; and it looks at this complex configuration of generalized political exchange through the conceptual lenses of generalized political exchange. The case study provides a thick description of the "Swedish model" of a "negotiated economy", complementing the welfare state by a voluntary regime of joint macroeconomic regulation and industrial governance by organized capital and labor unions; and it provides new insights and specifications of the theoretical framework used.

Let me point out, somewhat arbitrarily, a few remarkable findings out of the wealth of empirical information and theoretical implications: in stressing the bi-partite rather than traditional tri-partite structure of socio-economic governance, reducing the state to a "junior partner" of joint self-regulation by organized interests, Pestoff radicalizes the view of the state as just one collective actor among others or what Renate Mayntz (1986) has called the search for the *contrat social* in a centerless society. While Pestoff underlines, in accordance with GPE, the comprehensiveness and all encompassing character of socio-economic bargaining, he also demonstrates that policy fields or meso-games are not only interrelated but also relatively independent from each other, allowing simultaneously for different coping patterns –from joint regulation and compromise in work-environment and labor-market insurance over transitions from compromise to conflict regarding centralized collective bargaining and lay representation to outright conflictual modes with respect to co-determination and, above all, the struggle over wage-earner funds. The latter are highly controversial despite the fact that they involve only a tiny fraction of the resources at stake in the consensual insurance funds, because they imply power questions; that is, attempts at changing established rules of the game. Employers associations, challenged by a union offensive in the seventies, now not only try to regain territories lost and to restore the original power imbalance in their favor, persisting at plant level, also at the meso and macro levels; they start to fundamentally question the "corporativist" regime implemented to rebalance power imbalances in general, demonstrating to what an extent the Swedish "exceptionalism" (similar to the Austrian one) rested above all not so much on union density as on the strong sanctioning powers and commitment of business associations to enforce collective discipline over firms and the business class in the overriding interest of macroeconomic management and performance. More recent developments have shown that even in Sweden alternatives to such an historic compromise are not completely ruled out any longer, though disintegrative tendencies have not yet fully undermined the overall consensus on cooperative governance. Both future continuity and erosion of this show case of organized democracy and joint regulation will provide comparative research with ample evidence on the strengths, weaknesses and overall competitiveness of cooperative industrial governance through generalized political exchange.

Political Exchange, Collective Action and Interest Governance
Towards a Theory of the Genesis of Industrial Relations and Corporatism

Franz Traxler

1. The Lack of a Genetic Theory of Collective Action

The aim of this study is to develop a theoretical framework explaining the institutionalization of corporative forms of interest governance, understood as associational collective bargaining, up to and including its voluntary incorporation into corporatist macroeconomic concertation. Given the antagonistic relationship between capital and labour, these processes are by no means self-evident. Labour's interest organizations traditionally started, from a historical point of view, as a counterforce to capitalism. The antagonism between capital and labour persists up to now and industrial conflicts have not withered away, contrary to the prophecy of Ross/Hartmann (1960), but these conflicts have lost their threat to the established social order. Most labour organizations have given up any anticapitalist claims and have confined their activities to routinized interest representation within the framework of capitalism. Moreover, trade unions have entered into corporatist arrangements in some countries, thus contributing to adjusting their members' interests to the imperatives of capital accumulation.

Although a lot of social science literature draws attention to the dialectic of conflict and integration affecting labour organizations, there is no discussion of a parallel with respect to capital. This may reside in the fact that capital and its interest organizations are not opposed to the principles of a capitalist society. Through this, their integration into society does not create problems in *general*. However, such an absence of a fundamental opposition does not imply that this necessarily leads to their integration into a system of corporative governance in *particular*. Unlike the former integration, the latter is not in line with the basic interests of capital. This can be traced from its class-specific position. Insofar as capital controls the means of production and, thus, disposes of the most powerful economic resources which can be mobilized in order to advance interests, a relationship of individual exchange with labour is the very best choice from its perspective. The asymmetry of power relations between capital and labour is weakened when labour can succeed in establishing a collective form of bargaining which can be considered the main constituent element of contemporary industrial relations in advanced capitalist societies. Consequently, capitalists and their organizations seek to maintain individual exchange as long as it is possible. For analogous reasons, they will resist entering into corporatist arrangements since not only does this bring about a loss of control over the determination of wages and working conditions (as it is in the case of collective bargaining), but also creates a potential threat to other management prerogatives being more relevant for capital (Schmitter 1982: 277).

Taking into account these class-specific interests of capital, it can be argued that its integration into corporative governance is not less doubtful than it is in the case of labour. For this reason, investigating the genesis of these integration processes requires a theoretical framework which is directed to labour as well as to capital. What explanatory capabilities are, at present, available for dealing with this question? In this context, it is reasonable to differentiate between the three "grand" theoretical approaches of social sciences from which theorems dealing with matters of industrial relations have been derived (Schienstock 1981): Marxism, systems theory and actor-centered concepts.

Due to the premise that the reproduction of capitalism ultimately works in the interest of capital and to the disadvantage of labour, Marxist investigations only focus on the problem of labour's integration. In principle, Marxist analyses have elaborated two different explanations for labour's integration: a theorem of mystification and a theorem of manipulation (Traxler 1982b). The former theorem states that the willingness of labour organizations to abandon anticapitalist goals is backed by the false consciousness of the working class and its representatives, which is generated by the mystifying effects of the sphere of circulation in capitalist societies. In entering into exchange relationships, the owners of commodities have to recognize each other as free and equal exchange agents being authorized to dispose of their commodities autonomously (Marx 1969). Concerning the labour market, this shows only the immediate appearances of the relationship between capital and labour while it disguises the asymmetrical distribution of power rooted in the underlying relations of production. Since workers tend to orient themselves towards the immediate appearances of society, this mystification is, according to this theorem, the decisive factor paving the way for being willing to accept capitalism (Redaktionskollektiv: Gewerkschaften 1972). However, this approach lacks the possibility of an empirically based investigation. If the mystification effect is at work in *all* capitalist societies, then differences in the degree of labour's integration and its change (as pointed out by comparative and historical studies) remain unexplained.

While labour's integration is interpreted by the mystification theorem as an unintended outcome of capitalist reproduction, the manipulation theorem places emphasis on strategies deliberately aimed at stimulating the integration. Specifically, it is assumed that the state and (monopoly) capital diffuse integrating values within the working class (Deppe 1979, Hyman/Brough 1975). The main objection that can be raised against this argument is the question of why the dynamics of economic crises do not generate an effect of discrediting harmonizing values and, thus, do not lead to a destabilization of workers' integration.

Regardless of their different reasoning in detail, both theorems have in common two shortcomings: first, they ignore the problem of capital's integration into corporative governance. Second, in contrast to the claim of Marxist theory, they fail to link the material conditions of the capitalist social formation and collective class action in a way that might be regarded as a sufficient explanation of labour's integration. Both theorems reduce integration to a problem of ideology, namely to false consciousness of the working class and, thus, ignore another important factor conditioning individual and collective action: the institutional framework of society (Traxler 1982b). Generally speaking, institutions work like a mechanism mediating between material conditions, and the individuals' consciousness and actions. Insofar as this mediation contributes to the relative autonomy of consciousness and actions from the material conditions of society, it may provide for the maintenance of labour's integration even in economic crises. In disregarding this, Marxist explanations of the integration process oscillate between a "positivistic" concept, the basic assumption of which is the mere determination of consciousness by material conditions, and an "idealistic" one implying a general state of oversocialization which renders individuals responsive to manipulation strategies (Lockwood 1981).

It is precisely in connection with the intermediary function of institutional patterns that systems theory becomes relevant for the integration problem. With respect to industrial relations, systems theory is mainly concerned with the rules governing the cooperation as well as the conflict of capital and labour (Dunlop 1958). Unfortunately, this institutionalist point of reference is not valuable for any analysis of the *genesis* of corporative governance. This follows from Dunlop's assumption that any governance of industrial relations rests on a system of values shared by all actors. At best, this perspective shifts the problem of explaining integration from rules to values. At worst, it ignores the problem by taking for granted the existence of this value system as it is in the case of Dunlop's conceptualization. The latter is the normal case of institutionalist approaches rather than an exception. It is also the reference of that sociological theory which has been of particular significance for the development of institutionalist thinking: the theory of Parsons who, for instance, regards the goals of organizations as necessarily derived from the overall value system (Parsons 1966). Ironically, even the theory of Dahrendorf who explicitly directed his work against the focus on stability and consensus in Parsons' theory contains a covert kind of functionalism. Its investigations of class relations do not center on the causes conditioning the formation of interest organizations and the institutionalization of class conflict, but on their stabilizing effects on society (Dahrendorf 1959). Neither overt nor covert variants of functionalism offer an explanatory framework for analysing the genesis of corporative governance since the stabilizing functions of rules and underlying values cannot be considered a sufficient cause for their existence (Hempel 1965). Even if it may be reasonable to accept Dunlop's (1958) premise that the actors involved have a common interest in corporative governance, this cannot explain its genesis. Following Dunlop's argument implies viewing rules governing industrial relations as a *collective good*. Contributing to this collective good is not necessarily rational for the actors because, from a viewpoint of individual rationality, each individual actor interested in it can benefit from it whether he contributes or not (Olson 1965).

This lack of coincidence between individual and collective rationality draws attention to the subjective interest perception and strategies of individual actors as well as, seen from a more theoretical perspective, to an action-centered mode of analysis. In strong accordance with systems theory, the premise of a common interest of all actors in corporative governance is central to all the different action-centered approaches related to the issue of industrial relations insofar as it is supposed that the actors regard the governance's function of resolving conflicts as a precondition for their mutual survival (Schienstock 1981: 174). Paradoxically, even investigations into industrial relations derived from rational-choice-theory, which basically takes for granted neither a set of values jointly upheld by all actors nor an identity of individual and collective interests, also often presuppose that which is to be explained by a genetic theory of industrial relations: they proceed to analyse interclass relations between capital and labour from the assumption of an already existing system of collective bargaining.[1] There is a substantial and a formal reason for this. Substantially, it has to do with another shortcoming from which, like other forms of action theory, rational-choice-theory is suffering. By concentrating on the investigation of behaviour, important contextual constituents of the actors' behaviour are eliminated from the analytical frame of reference (Berger/Offe 1982). From a formal point of view, a genetic analysis of corporative governance would require a non-cooperative model of bargaining which has not been fully worked out (Elster 1989).

In all, none of the prominent approaches discussed here can simply be adopted and used for analysing the genesis of capital's and labour's integration into corporative governance. However, this does not imply their irrelevance for this problem. It rather seems that each approach can provide a special link for the chain of arguments that a process analysis must include. In this connection, three "links" can be distinguished: *material conditions, institutional conditions* and *intentional actions*. They can be characterized as follows:

Material conditions are generated by the "silent forces" of economic relations. They mainly result from the market mechanisms through which the actors are subordinated to the imperative of competing among one another. Although material and institutional conditions both constrain intentional action, this happens in a basically different form. In contrast to institutional conditions, material conditions cannot be a matter of negotiations. Consider, for instance, the consequences of a violation of institutionalized norms and of economic imperatives. In the case of norms, the consequence might be a sanction which must be deliberately mobilized by a special actor. Due to this, there is the possibility of interpreting the norm and of bargaining about the conditions of sanctioning. This does not apply to the case of economic imperatives. Here, the consequence of violation is economic failure, which takes place automatically and autonomously from any sanctioning actor. In this sense, the genesis of material conditions cannot be described as a process of developing intersubjective meanings (Berger 1978) and, thus, must be analytically differentiated from institutional and intentional determinants of behaviour. Obviously, *Marxism* is mainly related to the analysis of material constraints.

Institutional conditions should not only be differentiated from material constraints, but also from the actors' intentions. What makes the crucial difference in their theoretical status is that the functions of societal institutions transcend the individuals' subjective meanings (Habermas 1970). Most strikingly, this can be demonstrated with reference to the fact that institutions may perform not only manifest, but also latent functions. Within the social sciences, this type of condition is strongly affiliated with *systems theory*.

Considering *intentional action* an explanatory factor in its own right implies the assumption that actors are not completely restricted by material and institutional constraints. Reflections on the question of autonomy in human behaviour have a long tradition in philosophical and sociological theory. Instead of taking up this debate, reference to empirical findings which are of special significance for the issue of interest governance may be helpful to justify the assumption of an existing scope of choice: following recent cross-national research on economic development, political strategies adopted by Western governments to master the present economic problems not only vary from country to country, but also account for differences in achieving macroeconomic goals (Schmidt 1982; 1985, 1986; Scharpf 1985). Focussing on a scope of choice refers to the domain of *action theory*, which is particularly relevant for a process-oriented analysis. For instance, in order to investigate corporatism in a dynamic way, Nedelmann/Maier (1979:108) suggest treating corporatism as an interaction configuration, the changes of which result from "(1) the dominant way in which the actors *define an issue* (or conflict object) on which their interaction is concentrated, and (2) the dominant way in which the actors *define the situation* in which the interaction takes place." Such an actor-and process-related frame of reference can only serve to describe but not to explain the actors' definitions and their behaviour if the basic principles of subjective selectivity which structure the process and outcome of definitions are not specified. In other words, what is needed is not only an actor-centered point of reference, but a theory of action. This raises the question of which action-centered approach may be most appropriate to an investigation of the genesis of interest governance. In this respect, the concept of rational choice based on the premise of individuals acting in a rational and self-interested way seems to be the most promising alternative for methodological as well as for substantive reasons.

Rational choice is particularly fitting in a genetic theory of integration since it opens up an especially useful path of analysing the general question underlying the problem of interest governance: the explanation of the emergence of social order under the conditions of structurally divergent interests of competing actors. Beginning from the treatise of Hobbes, social science has answered this question in different theoretical ways, the antipoles of which focus on norms on the one hand and on interests on the other. From a methodological point of view, it is convenient to focus on the premise of self-interested rationality because this offers an instrument which can be applied easily to empirical research. It can be regarded, so to speak, as the null hypothesis of an action-centered analysis. Following the proposal of Weber (1968), this means that individual rationality is interpreted as the idealtype of social behaviour, serving as the focal point of reference to analyse individual intentions. Seen from a substantive perspective, the question is whether and to what degree self-interested rationality empirically prevails over alternative orientations. For certain, there are differences in its relevance which not only result from different preferences of individuals, but also from different social contexts. It may be correct that consciously weighed and strategic choices are not the rule in the context of day-to-day social activity (Giddens 1982: 535ff).

Concerning matters of corporative governance, as they are in question here, it is reasonable to assume that a high degree of rationality is typical of the actors involved. In the course of achieving their economic goals, workers and capitalists whose activities are to be organized and coordinated in a system of interest governance are exposed to the competitive imperatives of market forces. These conditions do not, in the strict sense, enforce self-interested rational orientations. At any rate, they create a strong tendency towards this orientation since each deviation from the rational path of effective competition results in a threat to economic survival. Thus, market relations are characterized by some kind of built-in mechanism of rendering rational behaviour more likely than other forms of activity. Against this background, self-interested rationality is rather the property of a (competitively organized) *social system* than the property of *individual preferences*. For the purpose of a detailed inquiry into the issue of rationality, this is an important reference to the way in which attention must be paid to the micro- and macro-level of analysis. Primarily, it implies that it is not sufficient to adopt an action-centered perspective for analysing this issue.

2. Political Exchange and its Material, Institutional and Intentional Framework

Material constraints, institutional conditions and rational intentions are the basic "links" of an analytical framework insofar as they are irreducible to one another and contain all dimensions which are relevant for a genetic approach to interest governance. Having these "links" at hand does not automatically provide the knowledge for assembling them in a way that moulds an explanatory "chain". Since these "links" are being deduced from disparate social theories this assembly would require recourse to a "super-theory" systematically integrating all levels of social-scientific analysis (beginning from the individual up to the system-reproduction of society) into a comprehensive frame of reference. Such a super-theory does not exist and there is good reason to suppose that it will never be developed because structural properties of society cannot be completely expressed in terms of intentional behaviour of individual actors (Adorno 1972, Berger 1978). A more pragmatic way to deal with this assembling problem might be to identify a notion which is of analytical relevance for the genesis of interest governance as well as appropriate to serve as a bridge between the divergent traditions of Marxism, systems theory and action theory. The notion of exchange promises to meet these demands.

In lieu of elaborating exhaustively its respective meaning within the framework of each theoretical tradition, it seems to be more useful to point out the basic elements of an exchange-related approach to the genesis of interest governance. This, primarily, requires (i) specification of the properties of exchange relations within the context of interest governance and (ii) an outline of the way in which the main "links" of analysis referring to material, institutional and intentional conditions of action can be assembled along the lines of an exchange concept.

(i) The kind of good which is being traded can be regarded as the decisive criterion for classification. In this respect, exchange concerning interest governance must be differentiated from *commercial* as well as from *social* types of exchange since its objects are neither commodities put on the market by their owners nor social gratifications (like sympathy and reputation) mutually provided by individuals in the process of interaction. Interest governance is linked with a *political* form of exchange. As pointed out by Pizzorno (1978) with regard to industrial relations, by Lehmbruch (1977) with respect to corporatism and by Marin (1985) with reference to social order built on this in general, the issues of political exchange are mutual obligations of collective actors.

Concerning the relationship between capital and labour, the underlying political exchange is related to the question of whether and on what conditions rules of collective interest promotion should be institutionalized. Exchange of this type is political in respect to its *input* as well as to its *process* and *output*.

Since the agents engaged in this kind of bargaining are collective entities (trade unions, business associations and the state) the interests covered by them consist of a variety of at least partly conflicting interests of the individual actors affiliated to them. As a consequence of this, the collective actors are forced to transform the heterogeneity of individual interests into common interests. Thus, *internal* compromise is the necessary *input* to start political exchange. Similarly, compromising is the focal problem of the *process* of bargaining about the rules of promoting collective interests. In contrast to the input aspect, it is a matter of *external* compromise seen from the perspective of collective actors. Finally, effects of political relevance can also be attributed to the *output* of internal and external compromising. In finding a compromise on the conditions for the collective pursuit of interests the actors constitute a system of rules, the specific form of which is of central importance for the efficiency of the economy and the stability of society as comparative research shows (Olson 1982, Schmitter 1981). Besides, these rules define specific conditions for the *organizational* survival of the collective actors involved which are not identical with the conditions for the *economic* survival of their individual members.

(ii) Although compromising on the mode of interest governance can be considered political, it is by no means completely autonomous from material, namely economic conditions. This kind of exchange is induced ultimately by interests, needs, deprivations and the like which are partly located beyond the sphere of constituting intersubjective meanings. Among these material conditions of action the relations of production bring about the most general and fundamental basis of political exchange.

Within the capitalist mode of production, capital and labour are constituted in terms of antagonistic as well as of (asymmetrically) interdependent relations to one another. In order to ensure its competitive viability, capital is forced to accumulate. This implies an increase in the possibilities of capital reproduction at the expense of living conditions and current consumption of the working class. Nevertheless, an element of coincidence of interests is embedded in the relations of production. Since workers surrender control not only over their labour-power, but also over their person, the consequence is that workers are also interested in capital's prosperity. What renders this interdependence asymmetrical is the societal *primacy* of capital accumulation at the level of system integration and the economic *predominance* of capital over labour at the level of social integration. Primacy of capital accumulation means that the interests of capital in general are structurally preferred to all other interests in capitalist societies. Insofar as all countries are exposed to the pressures of competition in the world market, their economic development and political stability strongly depend on gaining and maintaining advantage in the world economic system, the decisive implication of which is profitable capital accumulation. This is also the central point of reference for the activities of the state apparatus because its ability to raise the resources necessary for its own reproduction (e.g. tax receipts) is contingent upon capital's profitability (Offe 1975, Offe/Ronge 1976).[2] Economic predominance of capital ensues from an asymmetrical distribution of strategic options. Compared to labour, capital can reduce its dependence upon labour by substituting machinery for labour-power while labour lacks corresponding economic means of autonomization from capital.

There are two main consequences which follow from this for the pursuit of interests of capital and labour. First, their interests must be pursued in conflict and opposition to one another as a result of their antagonistic relationship. Second, as a result of the functional interdependence of capital's and labour's interests, the possibility of establishing and maintaining corporative governance is also inherent in the relationship between capital and labour. However, as outlined above, both classes are not equally interested in such a system. Due to this asymmetry, such a system does not simply arise out of a common preference of both classes, but requires for its emergence a political exchange suited to trade off the advantages and disadvantages which corporative governance creates for each side. In this sense, the asymmetrical interdependence between capital and labour defines the general "terms of trade" for their political exchange.

Within this material framework of political exchange, the form of interest governance varies over time as well as from country to country. Whether it is corporatist rather than pluralist and whether it furthers the tendency for cooperation rather than for conflict cannot be deduced from material constraints, but requires paying additional attention to the institutional and intentional conditions of action.

There are two points of view from which institutions must be considered relevant for a concept of exchange. On the one hand institutions can function as a framework of exchange constituting the "rules of the game" that each exchange agent is obliged to accept. On the other hand, institutions can be the output of exchange relationships insofar as negotiations may result in a contract containing a code of conduct. From the former perspective, institutions are interpreted as the conditions for exchange, from the latter they are regarded as its result. This twofold relationship between exchange and institutions refers to the most controversial and crucial question in the social-scientific debate on the Hobbesian problem of social order: whether exchange, namely market relations, can generate endogenously through themselves all relevant institutions of society or, conversely, whether exchange and market necessarily require institutional prerequisites for their functioning and, consequently, cannot exist without conditions *external* to them.

Focussing on the formation of corporative governance does not require dealing with the problem of social order in such a fundamental way since relations between capital and labour always take place within an institutional framework provided by the state. The specific mode of industrial relations whether it be "liberal" or "corporatist" is decisively influenced by the state (Crouch 1979). Though it is paradoxical at first glance, even state-free industrial relations are under the rule of the state. Generally speaking, this results from the fact that state regulation is not reducible to direct intervention. A state-free sphere within which capital and labour autonomously arrange their relations between themselves cannot arise unless the state has (at least implicitly) devolved this possibility of autonomous behaviour to them.[3] From this point of view, non-intervention is as well as intervention a mode of state regulation (Offe 1975). This raises the question of what kind of state regulation is required to give rise to a voluntary formation of corporative governance in general and of a corporatism in particular. In this respect, the minimal variant of state regulation can serve as a point of reference for analysis: this is the (non-interventionist) type of guaranteeing freedom of contract and freedom of association. Along with the state, the interest associations of capital and labour are another important institutional determinant of corporative governance. In order to represent interests vis-à-vis their interlocutors, interest associations have to interpret, aggregate and unify the individual interests of their (potential) members. This transformation is not left to chance, but is subject to specific rules of intra-associational policy-formation which are embodied in the associations' organizational structure. By analogy with the institutional framework established by the state, organizational structures substantially affect the process of goal promotion, favouring and suppressing, emphasizing and excluding certain kinds of interests.

Turning now to the intentional dimension of political exchange requires reference to the relationship between individual preferences and collective interests. Given self-interest as the guiding principle of individual actions, it is uncertain whether a collective strategy of interest promotion can be adopted at all. The formation of collective action is burdened with a difficulty which can be described as a prisoner's dilemma, or, in other terms, as a free-rider problem.[4] Collective action always requires some sacrifice of individual payoffs and the benefits of collective action accrue to all individual actors that are interested in them regardless of whether they have shared in its costs, so it is not self-evident for a rational individual actor to participate in collective action. Consequently, a genetic explanation for interest governance voluntarily upheld by capital and labour must be related to two dimensions of collectively promoting interests:

- the formation of collective action on the side of labour as well as of capital. This refers to the *problem of organizing* interests.
- The formation of a durable system of collective exchange relations between capital and

labour. This refers to the *problem of institutionalizing* corporative governance.

These problems are interrelated. On the one hand, the institutionalization of collective exchange depends on the ability to act in a collective way and, conversely, organizing and unifying interests can be supported by a corporative governance system. As a consequence of this mutual conditionality, a step toward the solution of the organization problem can facilitate the institutionalization of common rules and vice versa.[5] As will be demonstrated in detail below, the genesis of corporative governance decisively rests on solving both problems simultaneously. The logic underlying this solution can be conceived of as a form of political exchange.

3. Class-specific Problems of Collective Action as the Starting Point of Political Exchange

Interdependence among the problems of organization and of institutionalization raises the question of what problem should be taken as the starting point of analysis. To begin with the organization problem seems reasonable because, logically, collective bargaining pre-supposes collective action, but a collective mode of interest promotion undertaken by capital and labour does not necessarily lead to an institutionalized form of collective bargaining. Analysing the formation of collective action requires proceeding from two points outlined above: first, the interests to be collectively advanced are rooted in material conditions generated by the modes of production and are influenced by institutional conditions provided by the state. Second, the pursuit of interests is burdened with a conflicting relationship between individual and collective rationality. Although these two points apply to the situation of capital as well as of labour, they affect them in different ways. Before dealing with these differences in more detail, one must distinguish the levels of interest aggregation to which collective rationality may refer in the course of associational action. At the *macro* level, collective rationality is associated with those interests capitalists and workers have in common as *classes*. At the *meso* level, collective action takes place on behalf of *particularistic* interests which pertain to certain subgroups within each class. These subgroups' collective identities may be constituted by properties like branch, region and firm size.

Beginning with class interests of labour, the starting position of forming an association can be characterized as follows: class interests of labour suffer from ambiguity since they are partly in coincidence with the imperatives of capitalist system reproduction and partly in contradiction to them. As a consequence of the primacy of capital accumulation and the predominance of capital, the associations of labour must offensively represent their interests vis-à-vis capital as well as the state. From this it follows that the formation of collective action requires a type of mediation between individual and collective rationality in the course of which the latter is substituted for the former. Associations fulfil a *substitu-tive* function for labour because, from a formal point of view, collective action must replace individual action as a result of labour's class-specific inferiority and, from a substantive point of view, the ambiguity of class interests must be transformed into common political goals.

Compared to labour, the conditions of advancing class interests on the side of capital exhibit the following properties: class interests are unequivocal insofar as they coincide with the imperative of accumulation. Corresponding to this coincidence, capital can confine its collective activities to a strategy of defending its economic predominance and the primacy of accumulation. Given these conditions, associations play only a *subsidiary* role in mediating between individual and collective rationality.

This subsidiary function can be specified as follows: associations of capital are only of subsidiary relevance in the sense that individual rationality is structurally superior to collective rationality. Private control of the means of production offers capitalists the most appropriate way to pursue individual interests. This basically conflicts with the principles of associational action. The subsidiary status of business associations results from the fact that collective action is neither the exclusive nor the most important medium to realize class interests since market competition as well as the state are in their service. Competition does not undermine the interests of capital in general, but rather contributes to their realization. For instance, capitalists may lower their labour costs through a devaluation of skills. The manifest function of this measure is to get the upper hand over competing capitalists. In addition, there is also a latent function at work since the devaluation of skills weakens the power position of workers vis-à-vis capital. Such side effects of a competitive mode of capital accumulation affect not only workers, but also the state. As already mentioned above, it is in the interest of the state to further the interests of capital in general. Thus, the most important mechanism of advancing class interests of capital works like an invisible hand: competition among the individual capitals aimed at attaining their self-interested goals automatically amounts to the realization of their class interests through its economic side-effects affecting labour and the state. Moreover, collective action of capital is subsidiary in terms of the level of interest aggregation at which it mainly takes place. Due to the priority of individual over collective rationality, collective action as a measure to realize capital's interests is of subsidiary relevance at the *micro* level (of promoting *individual* interests). At the *macro* level (of advancing class interests) its subsidiary role follows from the societal primacy of competitive capital accumulation.

Comparatively greater importance for capital accrues to collective action at the *meso* level (of pursuing *particularistic* interests). It is more important for capitalists to pursue particularistic than class interests since market competition and the state serve as a mechanism for advancing the interests of capital in general. Hence, collective action of capital is, at least partly, relieved of representing this kind of interest and is more able to concentrate on and specialize in advancing particularistic interests. Furthermore, there is a special need for a collective mode of pursuing particularistic goals, seen from the perspective of those groups interested in them, since particularistic interests are often in conflict with class interests. Under these circumstances, particularistic interests must be advanced offensively and in opposition to the principles of market competition and/or the basic political priorities of the state.[6] Consequently, meso-collective action must perform

Figure 1:   Classes, Collective Interests and the Relevance of Collective Action

Level of Interest Aggregation	Type of Collective Interest	Relevance of Collective Action for the Pursuit of Interests	
		Capital	Labour
Macro	Class Interests	Subsidiary	Substitutive
Meso	Particularistic Interests	Substitutive	Substitutive

a *substitutive* function for advancing the particularistic interests of capital. Since particularistic interests within capital and labour diverge along the same lines (e.g. according to branch), the pursuit of the interests of both classes does not fundamentally differ at the meso level. Nevertheless, there are remarkable *class-specific* differences in the relevance meso-collective action has in the overall process of advancing collective interests.

Insofar as capitalists can confine their associational efforts to subsidiary activities at the macro level, meso-collective action gains *structural* priority over macro-collective action. This does not hold for labour: since collective action plays a substitutive role at the meso as well as at the macro level, priority among particularistic and class interests is set by *decisions*, the outcome of which will vary with circumstances. Another reason for making meso-collective action especially relevant for capitalists is that they are more competitive with each other (Schmitter/Streeck 1981). While durable interaction in the labour process systematically stimulates working-class cooperation, capitalists lack an equivalent mechanism that might mitigate their competitive relationship. This makes bonds more difficult to form within capital than within labour. Consequently, if capitalists form an association, they will not only tend to pursue particularistic interests rather than class interests which are less affiliated to their immediate economic situation, but also direct more of their activities against groups within their own class than workers do.

Collective action of capitalists is at least as relevant for representing interests vis-à-vis (other) business groups as for representing interests vis-à-vis labour. Capitalists' particularistic collective action opposed to other business groups mainly takes aim at rent seeking (Olson 1982), at ensuring economic survival (Bowman 1982) or, more aggressively, at forcing other competitors out of the market.

Considering these class-specific opportunities and constraints of mediating between individual and collective rationality, it is useful to take into account a central theorem of organizational theory. It states that the willingness of an individual actor to join an organization voluntarily does not necessarily imply his willingness to contribute actively to the realization of the organization's goals (March/Simon 1967). From the organization's point of view, this means that the problem of recruiting members must be differentiated from the problem of obtaining the members' conformity. Labour and capital differ remarkably in their difficulties in meeting these two organizational requirements. These class-specific differences are not convergent in the sense that *both* requirements are more difficult to meet for *one and the same class*. On the contrary, the relationship between difficulties and class-position is *complementary*: while the main problem of labour is "*associability*" (recruiting members), that of capital is "*internal governability*" (obtaining the members' conformity) (Traxler 1989).

On the side of labour, the main problem of collective action appears to be the recruitment of members. From the perspective of workers, the advantages of forming an association are not self-evident because of the ambiguity of interests. Therefore, the individual worker may hesitate to *join* an association. Additionally, member recruitment is complicated by the economic predominance of capital. Due to this, the opportunity to form trade unions is not only dependent on workers but also on capitalists who dispose of effective sanctions to prevent their employees from joining a union. Basically, it is rational for capitalists to make use of these sanctions since an individual form of exchange between capital and labour corresponds more to their interests than a collective mode. Furthermore, the opportunity to form labour organizations largely depends on the relations between workers and the state. These relations are conflict-provoking insofar as labour organizations may become a threat to the primacy of capital accumulation upon which the reproduction of the state depends. Thus, capitalists as well as the state may hesitate to *tolerate* the formation of workers organizations. Historically, the beginning of the labour movement was confronted with "unmitigated persecution and continuous repression" (Webb/Webb 1973: 64). Even after the laws against associations had been abolished, the existence of trade unions remained precarious as a result of continued opposition of capitalists to unionization, covert repressive policies of the authorities and the ambiguity of workers' interests. Their destabilizing effects were intensified under the circumstances of economic crises which additionally weakened the solidarity among members. Such an unfavourable combination of events often led to the total eclipse of trade unions, especially in the early period after their legalization. Although recognition may have replaced repression in the meantime, the class-specific conditions complicating the recruitment of workers are still at work. This is indicated by the fact that union membership is highly sensitive and vulnerable to the business cycle (Visser 1986).

Compared to workers, capitalists are burdened with minor problems of associability. The

Figure 2:   Class Position and the Requirements of Collective Action

Class	Requirements of Collective Action	
	Membership	Members' Conformity
Labour	+	-
Capital	-	+

+ Requirements creating major problems for collective action
- Requirements creating minor problems for collective action

development of their associations was not thwarted by repression in a way comparable to workers'. Even when the law forbade associations of workers as well as of capitalists in the early periods of industrialization, as was the case in Britain, this did not really impede the formation of business associations since the authorities only punished workers for combination (Webb/Webb 1973: 72f). Moreover, in many countries suffering from a delayed economic development, the authorities fostered the formation of business associations. Late industrialization imposed the requirement of actively promoting capital accumulation upon the state. In this respect, business associations promised to be an assistance since they could provide the authorities with information and political support indispensable in designing and implementing the state's industrial policy.[7] The primacy and economic predominance of capital made it possible for capitalists to establish associations a long time before the working class. Connected herewith is the fact that these early business associations are primarily specialized in representing interests vis-à-vis the state. As far as industrial relations are concerned, employers' associations dealing with representing interests vis-à-vis the workers emerged after workers had already succeeded in organizational efforts. This historical sequence also facilitated the formation of employers' associations since workers' collective "attack" made the necessity of forming associations more than evident for capitalists.

In addition, there are two other factors which make it easier for capitalists to associate. As worked out above, they can concentrate on collectively promoting particularistic interests. Thus, business associations are more specialized in their potential members and their tasks. Consequently, the number of business associations usually exceeds the number of trade unions by far.[8] This can be interpreted as a result as well as a condition of the major associability of capital. On the one hand, the larger number and the higher degree of specialization indicate a greater willingness of capitalists to associate. On the other hand, specialization supports the recruitment of members. It goes without saying that a particularistic type of association is more attractive to potential members than an encompassing one which is burdened with more difficulties of internal compromising. Another factor affecting the associability of capital and labour is the difference in the unit of membership. Essentially, business associations represent not individuals but firms. Since a firm itself is a collective entity, business associations have to recruit fewer members than trade unions in order to cover the same number of employees. This also facilitates the formation of business associations compared to unions since the smaller the membership necessary for effective collective action, the more the ability to associate increases (Olson 1965).

Compared to the recruitment of members, obtaining the members' conformity generates, by far, more difficulties for business associations.[9] Furthermore, their difficulties with the conformity dimension exceed those of trade unions. Both can be traced to the central role capital plays in the reproduction of capitalist societies: the private control of the means of production underlying this central role is not only relevant for the interclass relationship between capital and labour, but also for the intraclass relations between capitalists and their associations insofar as it results in a predominance of capitalists over workers as well as over their own interest organizations. This creates serious problems of maintaining the members' conformity for business associations in three respects (Traxler 1987b):

*   Since the systematic gathering of information which is essential to the course of business is routinized in each firm, capitalists are more aware of their individual interests than workers. This difference affects the associations' internal process of unification of interests. The more the members are aware of their individual interests the more difficult the internal decision-making becomes given the fact that the individual interests of members are not identical. Consequently, the high degree of capitalists' awareness of self-interest constitutes peculiar problems in making all members comply with the associations' goals.

*   A second factor which complicates obtaining the members' conformity for business associations is that the costs of compliance with the associations' goals are likely to become considerably higher than the costs of membership. Paying the dues charged by the association is the main cost factor of membership. Conforming to the associations' goals will result in forgoing individual advantages if a goal is not in line with the self-interest of a member. For capitalists, the costs of joining an association are rather irrelevant (Traxler 1986) since membership dues are low, relative to their financial resources, and are often tax deductible whereas compliance with an association's goal that clashes with their individual interest implies sacrifices which weigh more than comparable sacrifices of workers who are less competitive with each other. If capitalists' associational action requires suspension, at least partly, of competitive behaviour in the market (as in the case of representing interests vis-à-vis other business groups or vis-à-vis employees) a special incentive to defect is constituted. A non-cooperative behaviour (e.g. undercutting a collectively fixed price) makes it possible to realize extra profits and/ or extra sales at costs to those competitors complying with the association's expectations.

*   Those parameters of politics which business associations can mobilize as a measure of *collective* interest promotion are, as a rule, at the individual disposal of capitalists, too. For instance, wage policy or public relations which are important parameters of interest politics are not an exclusive domain of business associations, but also measures which each firm can privately take, in order to pursue its individual goals. Hence, there is an asymmetrical power relationship between business associations and capitalists. On the one hand, capitalists exclusively command the means of production, which is the most effective parameter of advancing capital's interests. On the other hand, nearly all parameters of interest promotion which can be brought into associational action are also accessible to individual actions of capitalists. The decisive power resources remain outside business associations (Offe/Wiesenthal 1980) and, furthermore, the internal capacity of business associations to impose binding decisions on their members is remarkably weak. Capitalists can easily thwart the associational realization of collective goals through making individual use of their private power resources.

4. The Genesis of Collective Bargaining and Corporatism

The dilemma of collective action primarily results in a problem of *associability* for labour, while it leads, above all, to a problem of *internal governability* on the side of capital. These differente problems are of relevance for an analysis of collective action because they may require differentiated modes of solution. Basically, an endogenous and an external mode of overcoming the dilemma of collective action can be distinguished if the relationship between the actors interested in collective action and their environment is taken as the criterion for differentiation.

In the case of an endogenous solution, an interest group is able to organize collective action without the assistance of its environment. Following Olson (1965), it can be argued that this may occur under two conditions. Collective action will probably be organized if the size of group is small and the interest in the common goal is highly unequal among group members. Otherwise, group members have to mobilize selective incentives suited to reward participants and/or to punish non-participants. From the perspective of a genetic analysis of collective action, referring to an endogenous mobilization of selective incentives is a fictitious rather than a real explanation since it just transfers the dilemma of collective action from the level of pursuing collective goals to the level of mobilizing incentives. If an autonomous and voluntary formation of collective action is unlikely because the group's size and their internal distribution of interests are not favourable, then it is also unlikely that any member of the group will be willing to bear the costs of mobilizing selective incentives while all other group members will benefit from this without any contribution.[10]

Consequently, the genesis of collective action can only be stimulated through selective incentives provided by actors *outside* the interest group if favourable conditions are absent. Since the existence of favourable conditions can be conceived of as an exceptional case rather than the rule, *external* selective incentives are particularly relevant for the development of continued, institutionalized collective action. An outside actor will help an interest group in overcoming its problem of collective action if he can expect some attractive compensation for this. Thus, external assistance is normally embedded in an exchange relationship between the outside actor and the (members of the) focal interest group. In looking for possible actors outside it is of importance that the collective action problem is posed to capital and labour in a *complementary* form: since the main problem of labour is associability and that of capital is internal governability, this enables workers and capitalists to enter into an exchange relationship serving to overcome their specific problem of collective action in a process of mutual assistance.

Hence, labour receives union security in this exchange. To the extent that capitalists lend assistance in solving the recruitment problem of labour, trade unions gain autonomy from the pressures of economic crises that threaten their organizational stability through undermining the workers' solidarity. Conversely, what a business association can expect to obtain in exchange for its assistance is the unions' support in ensuring members' conformity to those of its goals which are not directed against unions and their members. Since business associations, as a rule, are often concerned with interests which are not to be represented vis-à-vis workers but vis-à-vis other groups such help from trade unions is by no means irrelevant.

Obviously, this kind of relationship is nothing else but a political exchange, since it deals with mutual obligations of collective actors. Following the classification of Marin (1985b), there are three main elements of generalization inherent in this kind of political exchange. First, reference to the other partner is not confined to increasing one's own control capacity. Moreover, it is, as a consequence of the peculiar complementarity of capital's and labour's problem of collective action, necessarily aimed at increasing the control capacity of both partners. Thus, the issue is not only the appropriation but also the *production* of a collective good insofar as the increase of associational power can only be created through coopera- tion. Second, producing control capacity as a collective good is a problem that cannot be solved once and for all in a single act, but is a matter of enduring efforts. For this reason, it is necessary for capital and labour to enter into an open-ended political exchange. All to- gether, these properties of exchange imply certain requirements for behaviour. Above all, they constitute an ordered and durable form of collective relationship. Consequently, the generalization of political exchange in terms of *function* (producing compliance as a collective good) and in terms of *time* (producing compliance enduringly) additionally results in a (third) generalization in *social* terms (institutionalization of collective relations).

With regard to the subject in question here, the most crucial point is the generalization in the social dimension. From it follows that the emergence of political exchange is a process through which capital's and labour's (intraclass) problem of organizing collective action and the (interclass) problem of institutionalizing collective relations between capital and labour can be simultaneously solved. To the extent that capital and labour are incapable of solving their problem of collective action in an endogenous way, they are forced to seek to overcome their problem through reciprocal assistance. They have to recognize each other as interlocutors and have to approve rules governing their relationship. In this sense, political exchange is the decisive mechanism for capital and labour to establish themselves as continuous collective actors capable of integrating and controlling their (potential) members through a mutual transfer of resources, the side-effect of which is the institution- alization of corporative governance.

Most strikingly, empirical evidence of this is afforded by the historical development of collective bargaining. Within the economy, collective bargaining first spread through the skilled trades (like the building trades and the printing trade) which were fragmented into a multiplicity of small and medium firms.[11] Why were employers of such branches more willing to accept common rules on working conditions? The answer lies in the interdepend- ence of the preconditions for interclass and intraclass collective action. The employers' willingness to establish collective interclass relations is linked to a particularly crucial problem of intraclass collective action among capitalists: the tendency towards suppress- ing competition among each other.

As A. Smith (1979: 145) remarked, "people of the same trade seldom meet together, even for merriment and diversion, but the conversation ends... in some contrivance to raise prices". Although this may be a general desire in all trades, there are remarkable differences in the opportunities of satisfying it. The greater the number of single actors is, the more difficult it is to overcome the dilemma of collective action. Given a highly concentrated sector, it is a sufficient condition for an effective sector-wide coordination that a small number of powerful firms agrees on governing their market in terms of price, sales or quality. Therefore, it is very likely that sectors of that type are able to overcome *endogenously* the dilemma of collective action. Contrary to this, regulating competition is contingent on external assistance in the case of a great number of firms. In this respect, collective bargaining offers such an assistance, since it can be used as a mechanism for regulating competition among capitalists in an indirect way based on the help of trade unions. This particularly applies to skilled trades because their course of manufacture is very labour-intensive. Due to the above-average importance of labour costs for fixing the selling-price in these branches, standardization of wages and of working time through collective bargaining can bring about an indirect regulation of price competition.

Seen from this perspective, the earlier institutionalization of collective bargaining in skilled and fragmented branches can be traced to the fact that, for capitalists of these branches, collective bargaining served as a functional equivalent to cartels and syndicates endogenously formed by capitalists of more concentrated sectors. An *external* form of making capitalists conform to this corporative governance was accompanied by this *indirect* mode of regulating competition. Ultimately, responsibility for preventing capitalists from price cutting was not assumed by business associations but by trade unions. Unions could do so because of the strong position of skilled workers in the pre-Fordist and pre-Taylorist labour process. Employers' associations often explicitly incited the unions to use all their influence to compel non-cooperative firms to conform to the collective agreement concluded. For instance, in several industries of Britain, Webb/Webb (1965: 210) found "the trade union acting in alliance with the employers' association, putting its own forms of pressure on dissentient employers, who refuse ... to conform to the arrangements agreed to by the industry as a whole." In this context, the most effective power resource skilled workers could collectively mobilize was their refusal to accept work in a firm ignoring the collective agreements.

In exchange for sponsoring their internal governability, employers and their organizations contributed to union associability in various respects. One advantage to unions was the fact that collective bargaining at the firm level through which unions might be bypassed as workers' representatives was not useful for capitalists if an indirect regulation of competitive practices was intended. Under these circumstances, collective agreements at the sectoral level were required in order to cover as many competitors as possible. For this reason, capitalists and their organizations were forced to negotiate not with particular workmen in a single establishment, but with a broad-based union. One element habitually settled in collective agreements was the employers' obligation to recognize the trade unions' workplace representatives. Since the workplace was (and still is) a particularly relevant area for unions to contact their potential members, the recognition of workplace representatives considerably facilitated the unions' efforts in recruiting members and collecting dues. The external sponsorship of union security took a more direct form when employers themselves assumed the function of recruiting members and raising financial resources on behalf of the union. As Webb/Webb (1965: 210f) also reported, in some industries the employers automatically deducted a certain share from their workers' earnings as the contribution to the union. Another compulsory form of securing the unions' associability was that employers engaged exclusively those workers who joined the union.

Sometimes the logic of trade-off underlying this kind of collective agreement appears curious to the outside observer at least at a first glance. Consider, for instance, an arrangement settled by the employers' association of the Bohemian building trades and its corresponding trade union in 1913. The main components this arrangement contained were the standardization of wages and of working time, the recognition of the union's workplace representatives and, paradoxically, the claim that workers should accept work in firms not affiliated to the employers' association only if their earnings *exceeded* the standard rate of payment settled for firms being members of the employers' association (Traxler 1982a: 49). Seen against the background of capital's and labour's dilemma of collective action, this claim, nevertheless, does make sense. From the perspective of the members of the employers' association, it was a measure to suppress price competition. The employers' association could also take advantage of this claim since the differentiation of payment between members and non-members functioned as an incentive to join the association. Last but not least, this arrangement contributed to union security, too. To the extent that employers joined their association, the union's importance as the interlocutor of the employers' association grew and the process of recruiting members became easier as a consequence of the growing recognition of its workplace representatives.

This example shows very clearly how, in reality, economic and political issues are interwoven in the collective exchange between capital and labour. Nevertheless, it is important to distinguish both dimensions for systematic reasons. On the one hand, collective agreements deal with the *economic* interests of the associations' members in wages, working time and the like. On the other hand, collective agreements concern the *political* interests of the associations in maintaining their organizational stability. While the exchange relationship is based on the commodity form of labour power in the former dimension, the common denominator is compliance in the latter. What makes the crucial difference between these dimensions is the fact that economic interests of members and political interests of associations do not necessarily coincide, at least in the short run. To secure the association's stability and to increase its power it may be necessary to sacrifice short-run interests of the members (Pizzorno, 1978: 283f).

Although these modes and issues of political exchange that brought about the institutionalization of collective bargaining reflect the specific circumstances of the historical period of the early labour movement, they are still important for contemporary industrial relations. This holds good even for the most advanced systems of corporatism as is the case in Austria. In 1957, the parity commission for wage and price policies was founded. Its main function is income policy. In this system, all wages and ca. 25% of all retail prices are subject to corporative governance carried out by the four big associations of capital and labour (Marin 1982). An important reason for capitalists' willingness to accept such a political control of prices is that this system effects a latent cartelization analogous to those collective arrangements described above.

All these examples of political exchange have in common that support in obtaining compliance is afforded in order to overcome competitive behaviour in the market. Certainly, this is only one field in which the dilemma of collective action may arise. A second important field is representing interests vis-à-vis the state. Though collective action in the market is more precarious since it is subject to the forces of competition, the efforts of an association to represent interests vis-à-vis the state may also need political support provided by the opposite association. Especially under the circumstances of a democratic regime, the particularistic interests of a subgroup of capitalists will have a greater opportunity of being noted by the state apparatus if this group acts in alliance with the corresponding union. At present, a wide-spread form of this kind of assistance is branch-related lobbying. In this case, the union lobbies on behalf of business interests in order to advance interests of its own. An example may demonstrate the trade off underlying this type of political exchange in more detail: a union representing workers in a declining sector calls for state subsidies designed for reconstructing the sector. If the union succeeds, then primarily the particular capital to which the subsidies are transferred gains advantage from this lobbying. Additionally, to the extent that state subsidies preserve jobs, this decreases the crisis-induced risk of workers' desolidarization that threatens the union's stability. If the authorities channel the subsidies through the sectoral associations of capital and labour, this results in a mesocorporatist system. By analogy with collective bargaining, the associations integrated into such a system can extract resources ensuring their organizational stability from their cooperation with one another and, particularly, with the state. That explains why, according to a comparative study (Visser 1986), the density ratio of unions integrated into corporatist arrangements is less vulnerable to the present economic crisis than is the case in pluralist countries.

Just as in the case of collective bargaining, political exchange underlying branch-specific lobbying and corporatism serves, from the perspective of the trade unions involved, as a means of making their associability more autonomous from economic pressures. Hence, the conditions and goals of collectively representing interests vis-à-vis the state are closely related to the problem of overcoming competitive behaviour in the market. These two fields of collective action are interrelated. On the one hand, successful lobbying vis-à-vis the state may provide associations with external guarantees of organizational survival and, thus, defuse the dilemma of organizing competitive actors. On the other hand, competition in the market impedes the formation of collective action aimed at representing interests vis-à-vis the state. Since capitalists are more competitive among one another and more able to follow their self-interested goals than workers are, business associations are also confronted with more problems of reaching internal compromises on matters to be represented vis-à-vis the state. In extreme cases, the part the union has to play in a political exchange is to substitute lobbying of its own on behalf of the industry in order to make up for lacking lobbying of business associations. In the Austrian construction industry, for instance, the sectoral trade unions got used to lobbying more actively for an extension of the state's purchases of goods from the sector than the corresponding business associations do (Marin 1987). The reason for this is that lobbying for an increase in public demand is controversial within the sector because the opportunity of receiving an order of the state is not equally distributed among all firms. As a rule, orders of the state can only be taken by large firms. Consequently, small and medium firms are hardly interested in lobbying for an increase in sector-specific public demand. Insofar as this differentiation of interest relates to firm size, it holds true for capitalists as well as for workers. Regardless of that, it is more difficult for business associations to reach a compromise on this matter than for unions on the grounds elaborated above. Additionally, the backbone of unionization is the sector's large firms in which the density ratio is remarkably higher than in small and medium firms. This makes the interests of workers employed in large firms particularly relevant for the unions' politics (Traxler 1987a). Hence, unions are an important ally of large firms for advancing their collective business interests.

However political exchange relations may differ in terms of issues, modes and goals which are all contingent on the specific circumstances of time, sectors and national economies, the basic pattern underlying them is the same: that stabilizing intraclass collective action decisively presupposes interclass collaboration. What remains to be clarified at this point is the question of how institutional forms of political exchange may develop from collective bargaining into corporatism and what role the state plays in this process. First of all, an approach to this question requires clarifying the notion of corporatism. Of the manifold conceptualizations proposed, there are three that can be regarded as representing the main aspects of the phenomenon to which the current debate refers: (i) corporatism as macroeconomic concertation in which interest associations become integrated into the process of governmental policy formation and implementation (Lehmbruch 1977). (ii) corporatism as interest intermediation characterized by a distinctive mode of organizing functional interests by associations (Schmitter 1974). (iii) corporatism as a strategy aimed at a direct and organized mediation between the economy and the state apparatus within capitalist societies (Kastendiek 1981).

It is not difficult to connect each of these aspects with the main dimensions of the genesis of institutionalized collective relations between capital and labour. Obviously, concertation defined as tripartite cooperation between employers' associations, unions and the state at the macroeconomic level refers to the most highly developed form of corporative governance. Corporatist intermediation is nothing but a specific form of associational collective action. Hence, each of these conceptualizations corresponds to one of the two interrelated problems on which political exchange focusses: the interclass dilemma of institutionalizing collaboration between capital and labour and the intraclass dilemma of organizing collective action. The third conceptualization can be linked up with the societal effects of industrial relations on social order. In a society in which the competitive pursuit of interests is the precondition for economic survival, the function of preventing society from disintegration must be devolved upon the state as a special institution autonomous from market competition. However, the autonomy of the state is only relative insofar as the state's reproduction is structurally subject to the imperatives of accumulation and its policies are susceptible to interest politics. As far as industrial relations are concerned, this means that state policy is mainly influenced by the power relations between labour and capital. Given the structural primacy of capital accumulation, the state will presumably follow a strategy of repressing the labour movement as long as capital is not interested in collective exchange. In this respect, the genesis of collective bargaining can be interpreted as the result of a shift in power relations that improved the position of labour.

It would be misleading to interpret this shift as a linear pattern of development that systematically increased the power of labour and the capitalists' willingness to cooperate. Rather, it has been a dialectic and conflict-provoking process since interclass and intraclass power relations habitually vary from firm to firm, across sectors and over time. In the highly concentrated sectors like heavy industry, there did not exist any need for externally sponsored cartelization. Consequently, these sectors were largely unwilling to accept collective bargaining before World War I. For instance, in Imperial Germany, heavy industry put pressure on the employers of fragmented sectors in order to induce them to give up their systems of collective bargaining already established (Ullmann 1977). Furthermore, to accept such a system was also controversial within the working class. In some cases, trade unions were confronted with workers' aversion to institutionalized industrial relations since the common rules usually claimed "industrial discipline" from workers and, thus, confined their autonomy in advancing interests vis-à-vis employers.

However complicated by divergent tendencies this shift in power relations was, to the extent that labour's increase in power resulted in an interest of capitalists and workers in entering institutionalized interclass collaboration, it also became rational for the state to recognize the freedom of association and of collective bargaining. Under the circumstances of an increased tendency of both classes to associate, the institutionalization of collective bargaining contributes to social order because it tends to isolate economic from political issues of class struggle (Dahrendorf 1959). As long as the state apparatus suppresses the labour movement, any collective action of workers, even when it is explicitly limited to economic issues like wages, automatically causes a conflict with the authorities and, thus, leads to a challenge to the political order of society. Conversely, the structural selectivity inherent in the logic of collective bargaining impedes collective action aimed at overcoming capitalism. According to this logic, only interests which are confined to matters of industrial relations are admitted to articulation. Interest articulation is passed through an elaborated system of negotiation and arbitration that reduces the realization of interests to those compatible with capitalist order. This selectivity of interest formation also takes place *within* the unions incorporated in the system since their organizational interests are strongly linked with the emergence and maintenance of collective bargaining. In short, free collective bargaining relieves the state of the responsibility for interfering in industrial relations and furthers the integration of labour into society.

The institutionalization of a system of state-free industrial relations has become more precarious with regard to its effects on the stability of capitalist societies the more state regulation has been transformed from a liberal to an interventionist mode. To the extent that state regulation aimed at attaining macroeconomic goals like economic growth, monetary stability, full employment and the balance of trade has increased, the interest politics of business associations and trade unions have gained in importance for economic policy-making. The reason for this is that the associations of capital and labour autonomously negotiate over economic issues which decisively affect the realization of macroeconomic goals. Hence, the consequences of the rise of the interventionist state are not confined to a quantitative alteration in the degree of regulating the economy. Moreover, a qualitative change in the conditions of maintaining stability of capitalist societies and in the role of associations in performing stabilizing functions has taken place: in Parson's terminology (1959), industrial relations and their collective actors are required to contribute not only to expressive but also to instrumental functions.

These changed preconditions of social order have created the need for a corresponding mode of restructuring the relations between the economy and the state. In this context, the problem is that this results in a contradiction of functional requirements. On the one hand, state-licensed autonomy of associations in governing industrial relations is the most appropriate way of integrating them into the social order of capitalist societies. To the extent that the state's politics of industrial relations consistently follow this principle of non-interference, it grows difficult to keep associations in line with the imperatives of macroeconomic management. On the other hand, the more the associations' autonomy is restricted by directives referring to these imperatives, the more political and economic issues of class struggle tend to coincide and the higher the risks of delegitimation and disintegration are. Beyond a strictly state-free, autonomous industrial relations system and its state-directed, authoritarian counterpart, both threatening the stability of societies at least in the long run, the liberal mode of macro-corporatism offers a possibility of restructuring the relations between the economy and the state in order to optimize the conflicting requirements of social order. Contrary to neo-liberal strategies which try to keep associations conform to macroeconomic goals of the state through exposing them to the compulsion of market relations, liberal corporatism is a direct and organized form of mediation between the economy and the state based on the voluntary cooperation between the associations of capital and labour and the state. There is empirical evidence from comparative studies[12] that corporatism has performed better in terms of economic efficiency and political stability relative to its alternatives. Nevertheless, corporatist macroeconomic management is waning rather than expanding. In many countries, attempts to establish such a system have failed or systems already established have broken down in the meanwhile.

In overall terms, these serious problems of establishing and maintaining a macro-corporatist system result from the fact that this is burdened with a dilemma of collective action quite analogous to that associations are confronted with: realizing macro-economic goals means providing a collective good (Olson 1982). Thus, in the course of macro-corporatist governance, the problem of mediating between self-interested and collective rationality is reproduced at a more aggregated level of interest unification. From the perspective of self-interested rationality, it is reasonable for associations to take a free ride. Under these circumstances, bearing the costs of optimizing macroeconomic development is left to the "others" while the free-riding association is able to concentrate on advancing the special interests of its members. Contrary to this, following the corporatist strategy of collective rationality remarkably complicates intra-associational compromising since it becomes necessary to make members conform not only to their *collective* interests, but also to *public* goals. What, then, can make associations willing to enter into such an arrangement? One explanation might be that cooperation is recognized as the guiding value jointly upheld by them. However, such a value-oriented basis of cooperation is unlikely since corporatism is hardly legitimated by political culture in advanced capitalist societies (Anderson 1979, Offe 1981). Interest politics of associations are, usually, not guided by internalized values but by a rational calculation of gains and losses. When concertation arrangements do not coincide with their interests, then associations will tend to defect. Hence, the formation and persistence of concertation depend on the existence of a payoff structure underlying the relationship between capital and labour that makes cooperation more attractive than conflict through opening a broad scope of options to political exchange the benefits of which exceed its costs.

The specific properties that all together constitute such a payoff structure can be categorized as material, institutional and intentional.

- The material dimension: of these factors, interclass distribution of power relations is the most important determinant. In order to form a corporatist governance system, capital as well as labour must be capable of burdening a conflict-oriented strategy of its opponent with costs that outweigh the costs of cooperation (Marin 1985, Schmitter 1985). This does not necessarily presuppose a "balance of class forces" in the strict sense, but implies that each class has enough power to veto strategies which violate important interests of its own. In this respect, a complicating factor is that the scope of this power configuration must correspond to the scope of interests corporatist arrangements aim to govern. If the reciprocal power to veto is confined to a limited number of sectors, then this does not substantially affect the payoff structure of overall interclass relations. For the emergence of macroeconomic concertation it is necessary that the classes' power to veto prevails in the society as a whole. Such a power configuration is found in small rather than in large countries. This mainly results from a specific form of vulnerability to which small countries are subject: as a rule, their economy is more integrated into the world market system due to the small size of domestic markets. Under these circumstances, maintaining export viability is a particularly important precondition for prosperity, which is in the interest of capital and labour. Realizing this common interest is increasingly jeopardized the more antagonistic class interests are pursued in a conflict-oriented mode. Thus, an above-average exposure to the pressures of the world market increases the costs of conflict and the benefits of cooperation.

- The institutional dimension: business associations and trade unions must be capable of sacrificing the particularistic interests of members for the sake of the common interest in economic prosperity. Capability, in this sense, primarily refers to the institutional pre-conditions of cooperation, namely, to the associations' organizational properties determining the decisive framework for internal compromising. The organizational structure of associations generates a structural selectivity which systematically favours either a more particularistic or a more universal mode of interest representation. Two elements of the associations' organizational structure are of particular relevance for this: the associational domain in terms of tasks and membership and the internal procedures of decision-making. The more tasks and member groups an associational domain encompasses the more conflicting the interests internalized and the more difficult the processes of internal compromising become (Schmitter/Streeck 1981). Encompassing associations can reduce these problems through decentralization making each member group autonomous in representing its interests. Decentralization works in the same way as a narrow domain, giving rise to a particularistic mode of interest representation. If encompassing associations claim to articulate unequivocal demands on behalf of all member groups, they are forced to unify the interests internalized in the course of a centralized decision-making process. In this context, the dilemma is that the internal unification of interests must be achieved *without* regard for their high degree of diversity and, simultaneously, *with* regard for the principle of minimizing internal conflicts which may endanger the association's stability. How can encompassing and centralized associations manage to meet these requirements? For certain, they cannot change the divergent *substance* of their members' interests. However, this interest diversity can be overcome in the *time dimension* through an interest policy which is aimed at improving the situation of all members in the long run. The more encompassing the associational domain is, the more this common denominator of internal compromising corresponds to the requirements of optimizing macroeconomic development. Consequently, encompassing and centralized associations tend to set up universal political priorities which coincide with the requirements of *inter*class concertation merely to find *internal* compromises.

- The intentional dimension: these linkages between organizational forms and political priorities draw attention to the preconditions for the genesis of organizational forms corresponding to macro-corporatism. If associations are forced to compete for members, the emergence of particularistic associational structures is much more likely than the development of universal structures. This follows from the members' tendency to prefer the realization of their short-term, particularistic interests over the attainment of long-term goals. If a potential member can choose, then it is rational for him to join a specialized and decentralized association which is capable of representing his interest in a more authentic way. Due to this, encompassing and centralized associations cannot arise from autonomous collective action, but require external assistance.

Since the conditions of inter-associational competition apply *equally* to the organizations of capital and labour, the problem of forming encompassing and centralized associations is posed to capital and labour not in a *complementary* but in an *identical* way. Thus, there is no basis for overcoming this problem through political exchange carried out only by organized capital and labour. A third party participating in political exchange is needed to sponsor encompassing and centralized organizations of capital and labour. This role is assigned to the state since (re)ordering the associational system of interest intermediation according to the requirements of macroeconomic concertation is in its very interest. Moreover, it is the state, if anybody, that controls those power resources indispensable in performing this function (Streeck/Schmitter 1985). What the state can do is to reduce inter-associational competition and intra-associational pressures of the rank and file towards a particularistic policy-line by attributing a privileged, public status to a limited number of interest organizations. In more detail, the privileges with which interest associations can be equipped mainly refer to associability (e.g. compulsory membership and payment of dues), domain representation (e.g. representational monopoly), internal decision-making (e.g. support in strengthening centralization and sanctioning potentials) and integration into the process of policy formation and implementation (e.g. guarantees of consultation, devolution of public functions to associational self-governance) (Schmitter 1974, Offe 1981). Political exchange, thus including the state as a third party, decisively depends on elaborated linkages between the associations and the party system, government and parliament which serve as an "infra-structure" of coordinating activities and of resource transference from one actor to another (Lehmbruch 1985).

Summing up, the state's role in the development of concertation is quite different from its role in the rise of collective industrial relations. Usually, industrial relations systems were initiated by capital and labour whereas the state adjusted the law to this development with some delay. Throughout the early stages of collective bargaining, jurisdiction embedded in an individualistic system of legal order found it difficult to classify the validity of norms binding collective entities. The state could confine itself to a policy based on the principles of non-interference and of freedom of association since an interclass power configuration rendering political exchange attractive to (subgroups of) capital and labour was a sufficient condition for the genesis of collective bargaining. Characteristically, the state started to change its policy under the circumstances of an increased need for an interventionist regulation of the economy. In many countries during World War I, political exchange was initiated as well as sponsored by the state through providing the associations of capital and labour with guarantees of governance capacity and of organizational security (Crouch 1986). Obviously, all these activities were nothing but first attempts to form a system of macroeconomic management.

Against this background, the conclusion can be drawn that the difference in the state's role in the development of collective bargaining and of concertation is due to the fact that they are not equally important for organized capital and labour. Concluding collective agreements on wages and working conditions is directly linked with the associations' organizational interests insofar as this serves to realize members' interests and to legitimate the existence of the associations involved. Furthermore, it offers the possibility of political exchange contributing to the associations' stability. A comparable linkage between concertation and organizational interests does not exist. Moreover, they contradict one another since optimizing macroeconomic development is a public good. Its provision can create remarkable threats to the organizational stability of participating associations. Hence, political exchange bringing about concertation must be stimulated by the state. In overall terms, this means that the state has to reorganize the associations' payoff structure in a way that renders "responsible" cooperation clearly more attractive to them than conflict.[13] Evidently, collective bargaining also contributes to social stability due to its effect of integrating the working class into society. In this sense its institutionalization may be regarded as a public good, too. What makes the difference between collective bargaining and concertation is that this public good is being created as a side-effect in the case of the former while providing a public good is the main goal of the latter. In this respect, the status of meso-corporatism is ambiguous since the provision of public goods may be its manifest as well as its latent function. To put it in general terms: if, in the course of interclass relations, the provision of public goods shifts from a latent to a manifest function accruing to social order, this is precisely the point where state guarantees become necessary (Figure 3).

Although the state plays the key role in initiating concertation, its development cannot be reduced to a matter of state regulation. The state is able to further the development of corporatism only within certain given confines. Often, institutional and associational structures are deeply entrenched and can be hardly reorganized by the state if they do not fit the requirements of macroeconomic management. Above all, reorganization by the state is limited by material constraints. An important limitation is that the most effective power resources of capital remain outside its associations and, consequently, outside any form of concertation. Due to this, crucial parameters of macroeconomic development (like invest-

Figure 3: Basic Differences in Development and Function of Collective Bargaining and Concertation

Institution	Political Exchange Underlying the Institution	Initiative Actors	Functions Performed by Institutions	
			Manifest	Latent
Collective Bargaining	Bipartite	Interest Associations	Group-Specific Goods	Public Goods
Concertation	Tripartite	State	Public Goods	Group-Specific Goods

ment decisions) cannot be effectively influenced by corporatist arrangements. Conversely, by mobilizing its power resources outside concertation, capital can escape from macroeconomic responsibility without being forced to counteract it explicitly at the level of associational action. Another kind of material constraint is related to interclass power relations. As outlined above, stable concertation is linked to a situation of reciprocal power to veto strategies of the opposite class. Interclass power relations are primarily determined by the accumulation cycle in general and by labour market development in particular. Given the primacy and predominance of capital, only full employment can place labour in a position of possessing veto power. Thus, the existence of corporatism is contingent upon forces, the dynamics of which the state can only soften at best, but not really control. Furthermore, the state's interest in corporatism varies in a way corresponding to economic fluctuations and shifts in power configurations accompanied by them. The more the power of labour wanes with an increasing unemployment rate, the less macroeconomic management requires the integration of trade unions into a system of concertation. So far, the overall picture is that state policy is not free enough from interest pressures and from economic forces as would be necessary to serve as a sufficient precondition for establishing corporatism. Two main conclusions can be drawn from this. First, the development of corporatism cannot be generated by a deliberate political design of the state, though state assistance is essential. Second, as a consequence of this, the non-institutional preconditions of corporatism are of so much more importance. Since the development of interest governance follows the main fluctuations and changes in the material conditions of interclass power relations, a linear trend from collective bargaining to corporatism does not exist.

5. Political Exchange and Social Order

In the contemporary social science debate, the concept of political exchange is primarily related to corporatism. The previous sections of this article should already have made clear that this is an unjustifiably narrow perspective. One reason for this perspective may be that the corporatist mode of political exchange is usually an *overt* process to which the *manifest* function of governing the economy is assigned. This does not hold true for all cases of political exchange. Political exchange underpinning the genesis of collective bargaining is rather a *covert* form of interclass collusion fulfilling *latent* functions of cartelization and of integrating the working class into society. Hence, it is difficult to disentangle the political and economic dimensions of this type of collective arrangements.

However political exchange may differ in goals, appearances and effects, it decisively determines the rise of institutionalized relations between capital and labour. The general logic of political exchange underlying all its different manifestations is that collective actors are being confronted with the problem of making their (potential) members comply with their expectations. To describe this problem more precisely, they have to obtain compliance under the conditions of a prisoner's dilemma situation. Ultimately, this dilemma results from the compulsion of market competition to which the collective actors' members are subject. Corresponding to the respective positions which the collective actors and their members have in society, this dilemma arises in a specific form:

 • In the case of trade unions, it appears as a problem of associability. The workers' membership is the most problematic requirement of collective action.

 • For business associations, the dilemma mainly consists of a problem of capitalists' conformity: it is most difficult for them to keep their members' behaviour in line with their goals.

 • As far as the state is concerned, the dilemma with which it is burdened is, in overall terms, the Hobbesian problem of social order. Among the functions to be fulfilled in this respect, the regulation of interclass relations becomes a main concern of the state given the threat to economic performance as well as to the stability of capitalist societies as a whole generated by class conflict.

The less their (potential) members are capable of voluntarily cooperating, the more useful it is to collective actors to seek an exogenous solution to their prisoner's dilemma instead of an endogenous one: this results in political exchange when two or more collective actors tend to establish a cooperative network among themselves in order to solve their internal cooperation problem in a process of mutual transfers of resources. This means nothing else but establishing a "reflexive" game in the sense that two or more prisoner's dilemmas become interrelated and then solved in a coordinated and simultaneous process of inter-game cooperation.

Above all, the formation of such a collective actors' "reflexive" game is based on three prerequisites which can be categorized as substantive, social and temporal:

• The substantive prerequisite is a complementarity of dilemma problems which offers the opportunity of establishing a symbiotic relationship between the collective actors. In the case of bipartite political exchange, complementarity rests on the fact that the unions' prisoner's dilemma is related to associability and that of business associations to internal governability. Similarly, a complementarity underlies tripartite political exchange inso- far as an increase in regime governability is contingent on state assistance for increasing associability and internal governability of capital's and labour's associations. Relieving the state of public regulatory functions by associations' assistance requires, conversely, relieving the associations of risks of defection by state support.

• The social prerequisite refers to a problem of reducing complexity. Cooperation becomes less difficult the smaller the number of actors is. What renders the cooperation problem of a "reflexive" game easier to overcome than each single prisoner's dilemma is that the number of actors whose cooperation is required is smaller in the "reflexive" game than in each single game. This can be traced to the fact that establishing a "reflexive" game generates or strengthens a tendency toward hierarchization within each game. This can be demonstrated most strikingly by the example of corporatism. The real target groups whose behaviour the state seeks to influence are not associations, but workers and capitalists. However, it is more convenient to the state to cooperate with associations which are then asked to keep their members in line with the goals of corporatist governance.

- In the time dimension, it is of importance that the prisoner's dilemmas with which the actors are burdened are enduring problems. Under these circumstances, the problem of cooperation at the "reflexive" game level is not to reach a single solution restricted in scope and in time, but rather to find a stable framework for permanent compromising. Basically, this long-term perspective facilitates the institutionalization of cooperation.

Whether these prerequisites are in existence, depends on the specific configuration of material and institutional conditions. In the end, they constitute the actors' scope of feasible options, thus defining their possibilities for cooperation. Against this background, some general conclusions can be drawn concerning the applicability of the concept of political exchange to social science issues. Political exchange, understood as a process of interrelating prisoner's dilemma games, cannot be used only for analysing industrial relations and corporatism. Moreover, it is of relevance for analysing the genesis of institutions in all fields of society. Specifically, it can contribute to a general theory of collective action and cooperation through broadening the focus of analysis. In this respect, one finding of this study is that the analysis of a certain group's collective action problems must not be confined to the focal group, but must be extended to its environment. Such a shift in perspective also implies a "sociologization" of analysis. To the extent that the environment in general and outside actors (as possible partners for interrelating cooperation problems) in particular are relevant for the focal group to organize collective action, it becomes necessary to analyse the focal group's relationship to its environment, for instance, in terms of status and class position. There are good reasons to suppose that the activities of groups, of subsystems within the society and even of the society as a whole must be increasingly synchronized with the activities of outside collective actors in order to solve their internal problems of synchronization. This ensues from the growing interdependencies and mutual externalities caused by increasing functional differentiation and specialization at all levels of social aggregation. In many cases, these synchronization problems take the form of a prisoner's dilemma. Thus, analogously with its *analytical* relevance for serving as a bridge between different social scientific theories, political exchange gains in *practical* importance for maintaining social order as a consequence of the growing demand for mediation between interdependent collective entities.

Acknowledgement

I would like to express my thanks for discussion of an earlier version of this paper to K. Hinrichs, R. Pirker and members of the European University Institute, at which this version was presented. I am especially grateful to B. Marin and Ph.C. Schmitter for their comments and criticism.

Notes

1 Elster (1982:472ff) and Lange (1985) can be taken as examples of this assumption. In cases where this assumption is not made, investigations into interclass relations based on rational-choice-theory (e.g. Przeworski/Wallerstein 1982, Schott 1984) center on the conditions of bilateral interclass compromising leaving aside the conditions of intraclass cooperation. Since they do not refer to individual action, they cannot be regarded as action-centered approaches in a genuine

sense.

2 To put primacy of private accumulation into more general terms: accumulation takes place for the sake of profits under capitalism and any improvement of economic conditions depends on accumulation.

3 Whether autonomy in the pursuit of interests is initiated by the state itself or by interest groups struggling for this is contingent on the specific context. In any case, autonomy is granted by the state, by decision or non-decision, since the state has a monopoly over legal power.

4 As Hardin (1982) demonstrated, the free-rider problem of collective action as described by Olson (1965) is logically equivalent to an n-person prisoners' dilemma.

5 At this point, it should be noted that the explanandum of this study is the institutionalization of corporative governance. Organizing collective action is only considered insofar as it is relevant for this question. Hence, a clarification of the *initial* impulses leading to capital's and labour's collective action will not be presented here. However, by reference to its focal problem, this study also contributes to explaining the conditions of *stabilizing* organized collective action.

6 For instance, capitalists of a structurally depressed sector will tend to block entry into their market and will lobby for special government policies that favour them at the cost of promising sectors. Since this reduces macroeconomic efficiency, distorts the conditions of competition and, ultimately, threatens the international competitiveness of the economy, this particularistic interest clashes with the interests of capital in general.

7 The more associations are able to overcome particularistic interest perceptions and to orient themselves according to the imperatives of accumulation, the more they gain importance for this kind of assistance. As outlined above, representing this type of general interest is not the main concern of business associations. Consequently, the authorities had to sponsor associations suited to this function by attributing a public status to them (e.g. compulsory membership, representational monopoly). Chambers of business and commerce, which are the most prominent manifestation of this institutional design of the state, still exist in some European countries.

8 For empirical evidence see the examples of the USA (Schmitter/Brand 1979) and of Austria, West Germany and Switzerland (Traxler 1985). For a statististical analysis of data on 9 countries see Traxler (1989).

9 For empirical evidence see Traxler (1986).

10 An endogenous solution of this second-order free-rider problem is possible if mobilizing selective incentives is remarkably cheaper than realizing the original common goal. In the case of capitalists and workers, this is not likely to happen. Since selective incentives must provide such high rewards that competitive behaviour becomes unattractive (and, on the side of labour that a possibly existing repression is neutralized), their mobilization usually is rather expensive.

11 On this branch-specific spread of collective bargaining see Traxler (1982a: 44ff) for Austria's history of industrial relations; Webb/Webb (1965: 173ff), Sisson (1979) for Britain; Erd/Müller-Jentsch (1979), Hinrichs (1988), Müller-Jentsch (1983), Volkmann (1979) for Germany and Gruner (1963) for Switzerland, Sisson (1979) for France, Italy and Sweden.

12 On this issue see, for instance, the research done by Cameron (1985), Scharpf (1985), Schmitter (1981), Schmidt (1982, 1985, 1986).

13 For this purpose, the state must play an initiative, but not necessarily interventionist role under favourable conditions. In Sweden, for instance, the long survival of the guild system has fostered the development of associational structures conducive to corporatism. Consequently, the mere *threat* of state intervention was sufficient to induce organized capital and labour to establish a cooperative arrangement in 1938 (Pestoff this volume).

Generalized Political Exchange in Industrial Relations in Europe during the Twentieth Century

Colin Crouch

A continuing source of resistance to the use of exchange models in sociological theory is that they seem to reduce all forms of social relationship to market models of contract, when clearly the specific and calculated character of market exchanges marks them out as rather distinctive. At the same time exchange in a more general sense is a very useful tool in social analysis: in any relationship (from love to hate) something is given and something taken. We can make progress by defining the field of exchange generally and by then locating different types of exchanges more precisely within that field.

Figure 1 expresses such a definition diagrammatically. Social relationships between two actors are here considered in terms of two variables. First is the degree of separateness between the actors, rated on a scale ranging from alienation to identity. The limiting case at the former end will be total strangers. We then move through sporadic, hostile contact, through regular but rather formal contact, more friendly relations, until we meet the limiting case where the identity of the actors is so close that they are experienced as the same self, and there is no longer a relationship. The second variable is the extent to which the exchange possesses the specific, calculated qualities of contract, ranging from total absence of calculation to pure contract, that is to complete formal specification of the terms of the relationship.

Combining the two dimensions enables us to map social relationships, and as the illustrative indications on Figure I show, all parts of the space can be occupied. Love and hate, as emotional states, occupy similar positions of low degree of contract, but of course strongly contrasted positions on alienation/identity. Markets, often seen as the archetypical forms of exchange, can be seen as occupying a rather limited space on the total exchange map. They are extremely high on the contract scale, but come rather midway on an alienation/identity ranking.

We can turn the model from a map to a source of theory by hypothesising that, as the sheer number of exchanges between two actors increases, they will move from alienation towards identity, and that as they do so the degree of contract will first rise and then again decline. The former point embodies the hypothesis that alienation is overcome by frequency of

Figure 1   Forms of Variation in Social Exchange

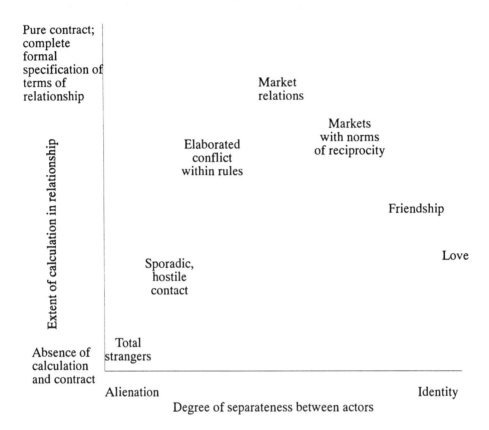

contact. The latter claims that relations between strangers are first made easier by elaborating forms of contract, which gradually become unnecessary as relations of trust are established. However, trust is not a simple function of frequency of contact. Experience may indeed teach that a particular partner is not to be trusted, and there will be a limit to any movement towards the identity end of the alienation-identity axis. There can also be movement in the reverse direction if an intimate relationship moves back gradually into alienation, with a period of elaborate contract facilitating the move. This is most commonly seen in divorce. It is also possible for movement between extreme states to be so rapid that there is no intermediate contract stage.

As in Parsonian theory, this model can be applied to different levels of aggregation of social actors. For sociology, the lowest level is the single human individual. From there we proceed up through groups of increasing scale and complexity until ultimately we reach humanity in general as the highest level, though this is not an actor that normally engages in social relationships with others. Identification of the intermediate levels at which most social interaction takes place will be determined empirically by the substantive area being considered. The actors at successively higher levels are of course comprised of units that might themselves be actors in social relationships at lower levels. One major source of complexity in social relations is that actors may stand in different relationships with each other on the alienation and contract dimensions at different levels. To take an example from our present field of study, industrial relations: individual workers may be in a fairly high-trust near-identity relationship with their individual managers, but both may be part of unions and employers' organisations which are engaged in low-trust bargaining at every step — or, of course, vice versa. A related problem is that the relevant level of action might change as groups and organisations form and fragment.

Such a model can be applied to many areas of human interaction, but I want here to limit it to the place of labour within the politics of industrial relations. These relations are capable of occupying a wide range of spaces on our map of exchanges: from states of alienation so extreme as to include the physical liquidation of opponents to degrees of identity so close that one can hardly talk of industrial relations at all. The levels covered range from individual workers, managers and employers to national-level labour movements and employers organisations. There is also an international level of interaction. In practice this last is of growing importance, but for reasons of length and complexity it has unfortunately had to be omitted from the present paper.

My starting point is the problem central to relations between employees and employers under capitalism (or any other system that separates those who perform work from those who control its performance): on the one hand the employer needs pure contract in its relations with labour, so that effort and its reward can be bound closely together; but it also wants the worker to co-operate like a willing partner. For their part, workers do not want to give any more than they are being paid for, but also want to be treated like reasonable human beings. The issue has received remarkably illuminating treatment in a number of texts (e.g. Bendix, 1956; Baldamus, 1961; Offe, 1970; Fox, 1974; Hirsch, 1977).

As a question of individual relations, this is an important theme in industrial sociology. Somewhat different issues are raised when we consider relations between organisations of employees and employers (the latter including large firms). Interpersonal relations may still be important, as in the many recorded cases of employers and trade union leaders seeking a personal rapprochement to help resolve their organisational conflicts. Our concern here is however with the superpersonal and organisational. What is the range of possible relationships between such entities? In particular, are there circumstances under which they move clockwise through the arc in Figure 1, towards zones normally limited to relations between individuals?

The only collective relations usually seen as embodying a high level of identity and a relative absence of calculated exchange are those described as community, but it is only by an abuse of that term that it can be applied to relations between industrial relations bureaucracies. Streeck and Schmitter (1985) have recently proposed treating 'association' as a form of social order differing from both market and community (and also from the state,

which raises slightly different questions). The difference between the relationships produced by community and those by association is that between mechanical and organic
solidarity identified so long ago by Durkheim (1893). Community rests on similarity and
shared experience. Associations can approximate the solidarity of 'community' only
through close interdependence, by entering into so many exchanges with each other that
they cease to calculate each one and begin to trade demands and concessions across a
lengthy time horizon. This then considerably reduces their incentive ever to leave the
relationship. The organisations become engaged in a rapidly multiplying relationship, in
which they keep seeking out new areas for transactions, so that they might increase further
their scope for trading concessions. They acquire a commitment to the relationship; the
relationship becomes part of their identity, and some movement is made from alienation to
identity, not so much towards the counterpart itself as towards the relationship or some other
reality for which it comes to stand. 'Identity' takes the form, not of identifying with *alter*,
but with the institutional context within which *ego* and *alter* are both defined.

The model does not cease to be one of exchanges, nor is the question of alienation
transcended. The partners remain aware of separate interests; they are trying to maximise
those of their 'side', and they may engage in open conflict from time to time. It is essential
not to mistake this model of action for the claim that 'everyone is on the same side really',
or what Fox (1966) called a 'unitary' model of industrial relations. It does however also
differ sharply from bargaining in a purely contractual sense.

1. Generalized Political Exchange in Industrial Relations

One might investigate the existence of such relationships at various points within industrial
relations, but the level to which we are directed by Marin's (1985) concept of generalised
political exchange (GPE) is that of the nation state, where the range of issues extends beyond
those of industrial relations as such to embrace those of national policy. Marin's model is
an example of what we have been discussing: a dense web of interactions binding together
a small number of actors. This paper is therefore concerned with the possibilities of GPE
developing in relations between organisations of employees and employers.

If collective bargaining is the characteristic mode of exchange in industrial relations
pluralism, and repeated strikes the characteristic mode of contestation, then GPE is the
characteristic mode of neo-corporatism. It describes how the partners in a neo-corporatist
structure deal with each other, and serves a useful incidental purpose in avoiding naive
accounts of corporatist relations as based on 'consensus' and a willingness to forget conflict.

We identify collective bargaining and therefore pluralism when the parties come together
at separate, discrete moments to resolve a conflict of interest through an exchange of
demand, offer, threat and counter threat; the parties can comprise anything from a group of
workers and a manager to a large union and employers' association. Under GPE, the parties
come together on a very frequent basis and across a wide and constantly expanding range
of issues. They mix the exchange of demands and offers with the joint regulation and
administration of certain areas of common interest, and introduce technocratic criteria into

their dealings. The actors are typically the leaders of centralised national-level unions and employers' associations, or indeed confederations of these. This concentration provides the maximum scope for dealing with a wide range of issues. Collective bargaining enables opposed interests to resolve their conflicts by maximising the contractual character of their relationship. GPE makes possible a relaxation of contract. These two types are of course poles of a continuum, and in practice there are many intermediate cases.

The simplest theory of collective bargaining treats it as a function of the strength of labour's organisation. Weak labour can be ignored by employers; but as it grows in strength employers must either break its organisations or come to terms with them by agreeing to the replacement of open conflict by bargaining institutions. And the stronger labour becomes, the more elaborate such institutions have to be. A similarly simple theory of GPE treats it as a function of (1) particularly high levels of union strength, so that the elaboration of institutions goes beyond those typical of collective bargaining; and (2) the existence of a centralised capacity on the part of both capital and labour, so that the process of continual extension of the range of interactions can proceed.

To test this hypothesis we need to assess three independent variables (the power of organised labour, the centralisation of its organisations and the capacity of employers too to operate at a centralised level) and one dependent variable: the character of the industrial relations system defined in a way that would enable us to detect the emergence of GPE.

Labour's organised power, its capacity to make exchanges, will be regarded as being primarily a function of the extent of union membership. Not only is membership a reasonable indicator of a movement's ability to wield sanctions, but it may also be a good guide to the union's perceived usefulness by workers. (In the case of a closed shop, the capacity of a union to secure such a device may also be regarded as an indicator of power.) Since our main concern is with the development of the national importance of organised labour, we shall measure membership primarily as a percentage of the total labour force, including independent and family workers. These are not usually included in measures of union density that are concerned with a union's capacity to organise its target population, but clearly the overall national importance of unionised labour will be affected if there is, say, a large peasant population reducing the significance of normal employed labour. Consideration will also be given to union density within the dependent work force only, as an indication of the significance of unionised labour to employers in general.

Attention must also be paid to labour's political power or potential power, which may be relevant, not only to the state, but also to employers. We assume that, the stronger labour's political presence, the less likely employers will be to try to eliminate labour's organisations. This component can be measured in terms of the share of the poll and/or seats in parliament gained by labour-movement parties in elections, with account then taken of whether the parties are participating in government. There are however major ambiguities in the case of parties that incorporate labour wings which are relatively unimportant to the party's base in general. The base might even include groups hostile to organised labour, as is the case within Christian Democratic parties. Within the language of our earlier model, the presence of workers within these parties raises interesting issues of identity. Such parties clearly contribute to labour's strength, but they also divide and compromise it. We therefore need to take separate account of parties for whom organised labour represents the primary constituency (usually social democratic and communist parties), and those for whom organised labour is a minor constituent.

Reliance will mainly be placed on these direct and quantifiable indicators, but some account also has to be taken of other factors that might significantly affect labour's power, viz: the level of unemployment, as conventionally assessed; major mobilisations in which labour has demonstrated organisational power irrespective of membership, and including consideration of those cases where mobilisations have ended in major and unambiguous defeat; and finally any reasons, other than those deriving directly from labour's industrial and political strength, that render organised labour important to the unity of the society and therefore make it less likely that attempts will be made to obliterate it.

Centralisation, labour's capacity to act strategically in making exchanges, is a question of the concentration of power in labour movements within confederations, and in the leaderships of dominant unions. The following indicators will be used:

i) the percentage of total national union membership covered by unions in the country's main confederation. This cannot be used as the sole consideration, as a confederation may be either a weak assembly or a tightly knit organisation. We must therefore also consider:

ii) whether or not there are rivals to the main confederation. It is assumed that confederal rivalry will weaken the dominance of the central confederation more than will the existence of a number of unco-ordinated individual unions. Separate account then has to be given to cases where there is confederal pluralism but evidence of co-operation between confederations.

iii)does the confederation hold the main strike funds and or monopolise the ability to call strikes?

iv)does the confederation carry out or effectively co-ordinate the bargaining of its affiliates?

v) how many unions are there within the main confederation? It is assumed that the smaller the number the more centralised and concentrated the movement is: first, because it is an indicator of confederal strength to have reduced the number of unions; and second, because the fewer the number of unions, the more effectively co-ordinated can action be.

vi)are industrial unions the basic units of the movement? It is assumed that the construction of a 'tidy' system of industry unions is evidence of confederal strength, and also contributes to internal union centralisation.There are important questions concerning the identity of industrial 'branches' here. An 'industry' is a rather arbitrary construct. For example, sometimes we speak of the metal industry, sometimes of the motor industry, sometimes of the truck-making industry within that. There is a tendency for unions that organise on a branch rather than a craft basis to do so roughly according to Group II of the International Standard Industrial Classification of the United Nations Organisation, which constitutes a broad aggregation of labour, product and raw material markets.

Arbitrary though all this sometimes is, the important point is that such unions are committing themselves wholly to an individual discrete area (or limited number of areas) of the economy, and are committing themselves to more or less the whole of that area and not just a minority of its members as with a craft union. This places the union in the position of potentially accepting some kind of responsibility for that area. At a lower level, similar points apply in a different way to company unions, but they are not the focus of the present paper.

vii) irrespective of what happens at the confederal level, do the leaderships of individual unions effectively dominate their unions' bargaining activity, or are the main initiatives taken by lower-level groups?

Employers' organisations are not the central focus of the paper; we are concerned with their availability as partners for labour. We shall therefore limit attention to a small number of factors: are employers strongly organised? Are their organisations in general centralised? Have they developed relations with government, enabling them to act at the national political level? What kinds of relationship have they sought with unions: centralised or not? What is their practice in relations with unions?

Finally, the character of interactions between capital and labour have to be considered. Relations vary in both extent and intensity. The former is largely a matter of specifying the basic levels of industrial relations action as follows: (1) plant or company level; (2) local or regional level; (3) industry or branch level; (4) national level: (5) state level. There are distinctions within (1) and (2) that we shall have to discuss when we encounter them; and (3) raises the same questions as under centralisation (vi) above. National and state are distinguished in that the former means a coming together of organisations existing at the level of the nation state, but without the state's active participation. State-level action occurs when the government initiates the contact and remains a major actor. The boundary between the two is however indistinct.

Intensity is more difficult because more ad hoc and empirical. We must specify the particular decision-making fields involved, and also state whether the action takes the forms of (a) consultation; (b) bargaining; (c) participation in mediation and conciliation activities; (d) participation in the administration of services.

2. A Comparative Historical Review

We shall now examine how such a model can help us make sense of the changes in European industrial relations systems during the present century. I include all countries that have had a long enough record of action by autonomous labour movements to make discussion worth while; where a movement has obviously been controlled by the state or employers it is not considered. I have also excluded the very small states. There is clearly not space to trace continuous historical development; instead we shall take a limited number of 'snapshots' at important moments of the 20th century: the eve of the Great War; the mid-1920s after the upheavals of the immediate post-war years had settled into some kind of coherence; the eve of the Second World War; the early 1950s, again after the subsidence of post-war upheaval; and the mid-1970s as the most recent period for which it is already possible to secure some kind of perspective.

Before 1914

Tables Ia-d summarise the situation on the eve of the First World War. Countries are ranked in what can be only a rough way. In all countries union power was low by the standards of later in the century. Membership was small, labour-associated parties weak. Unemployment was generally high, but at this stage available statistics are neither comparable nor sufficiently reliable to make use of them worth while. In spite of their weakness, most movements had managed some major mobilisations, though often these had ended in major defeats. Working primarily from membership strength, we might make a rough division into five categories.

In three countries (Denmark, the German *Reich* and the United Kingdom of Britain and Ireland) the unions show incipient strength, with an above average membership and a prominent political presence, though Denmark is the sole clear-cut case. Germany looks similar, but the *Reichstag* in which it had representation was unable to control the executive. British labour, though by far the most powerful industrially, was dependent for most of its political influence on the Labour Party's alliance with the Liberal Party, which was also linked to non-labour interests; but the Liberals formed the government, so British labour was the only movement at this period with major government influence.

The Norwegian and Swedish movements, and in more complex ways the Austrian, Belgian, Dutch and Swiss, lagged behind these, but were showing signs of strength. The membership weakness of Austrian unions was largely a function of the large peasant economy; within the modern sector they were more important. And in a curious way, although it had continuing difficulties with the Hapsburg regime, its commitment to the identity of the existing Austrian state gave social democracy a place of some significance in an empire for whom nationalist struggles often loomed larger than class ones. The Belgian and Dutch movements (like the Austrian, German, Swiss, French and Italian ones) are made complicated by a division between socialist and Catholic unionism, in these two countries the Catholic minority being particularly large.

Finland (still at that time a Russian Grand Duchy) is an odd case. Extreme industrial weakness is partly explained by the exceptionally peasant character of the economy, but the Social Democratic Party was the strongest in Europe and had as early as 1906 become the first European socialist party to hold government office. It stands at the opposite extreme from the British labour movement, having a strong party and a weak unionism. Two countries (France and Italy) are easily classified as weak. France is notable for having no real political component to its labour movement. The unions mistrusted the socialists and were devoted to anarcho-syndicalism.

Degrees of centralisation are shown in Table Ib. In Norway and Denmark there is clear evidence of some centralisation, within both unions and confederations. The Austrian,

Table Ia: Power of Organised Labour, c. 1914, 12 European Nations

Group	Country	1	2	3	4	5	6
A	UK (7)	22.59	26.89	M	6.4 (44.2)	0.25	-
	Denmark	13.02	19.72	M	29.6	-	-
	German Reich (8)	11.38	17.24	M	34.8 (16.4)	-	-
B	Norway	8.53	13.75	H	26.3	-	-
	Sweden	7.14	12.51	X	30.1	-	-
	Netherlands	12.19	16.24	M	18.5 (46.5)	0.25	-
	Belgium	7.45	11.23	H	9.3 (51.1)	0.25	-
	Switzerland	5.68	9.47	M	10.1 (21.2)	0.25	-
	Austrian Reich (9)	4.75	10.25	M	15.89	0.5	0.5
C	Finland (10) (Grand Duchy)	3.35	11.76	X	43.1	-	1
D	Italy	3.97	6.30	X	17.6	-	-
	France	1.93	3.45	X	-	-	-

Notes

1. Total known union membership as percentage of labour force, c.1910-1914.
2. Total known union membership as percentage of dependent labour force, c.1910-1914.
3. Mobilisation: M = important incidents of high labour conflict some time during preceding decade; H = incidents of exceptionally high labour conflict some time during preceding decade; X = important incidents of high labour conflict some time during preceding decade, during the course of which labour suffered major defeats.
4. Share of popular vote in most recent general election secured by: Austrian Reich (allocation of Kuria seats): Social Democratic Party; Belgium: Workers Party (Catholic Party in parentheses); Denmark: Social Democratic Party; Finland: Social Democratic Party; France: no party recognisably allied to unions; German Reich: Social Democratic Party (Catholic Centre Party in parentheses); Italy: Socialist Party; Netherlands: Social Democratic Workers Party (Anti-Revolutionary Party (21.5%), Catholic Party (14.5), Christian Historical Party (10.5%) in parentheses); Norway: Labour Party; Sweden: Social Democratic Labour Party; Switzerland: Social Democratic Party (Catholic Conservative Party in parentheses); UK: Labour Party (Liberal Party in parentheses).
5. Government participation: 0.25 = party(ies) not primarily labour movement parties but with a labour wing represented in government.
6. Evidence of state dependence on organised labour as an element of social order (0.5 = a weaker dependence). In the case of Austria this refers to loyalty of German-speaking organised labour to

concept of the Reich at a time when the main social conflicts were nationalist; in the case of Finland it refers to role of Social Democrats in leading initial drive for autonomy from Russia.

7. UK figures include Ireland.

8. Reich boundaries as at 1914.

9. not including Hungary or Bosnia-Herzgovina.

10. Grand Duchy of Finland, including Karelia; semi-autonomous part of Russian Empire. NB for Finland data for dependent labour are not available; figures in column 2 refer to union membership as a proportion of non-agricultural labour.

Sources: Labour force and electoral data drawn from Flora et al, 1983 and 1987; union membership data from Visser, 1987 (supplemented by national sources for Belgium and Finland and in order to take account of non-confederated unions in France and Scandinavia). Other sources include: Austrian Reich: Traxler, 1982, esp. pp. 63, 71; Belgium: Chlepner, 1956, esp. pp. 116-9; Delsinne, 1936, esp. p. 202; Denmark: Dybdahl, 1982; Hansen & Henriksen, 1980a, esp. p. 92; Galenson, 1952a, esp. p. 29; Finland: Knoellinger, 1960, ch. 3; France: Lefranc, 1967, esp. p. 220; Reynaud, 1975, ch. III; German Reich: Weitbrecht & Berger, 1985, esp. p. 485; Italy: Barbadoro, 1973b, esp. p. 304; Netherlands: Windmuller, 1969; Norway: Galenson, 1949; Sweden: Hadenius, 1976; Korpi, 1978; Switzerland: Höpflinger, 1976, esp. p. 92; UK: Clegg, 1972, ch. 2; 1979, ch. 5; Fox, 1985, chs. 5, 6.

German, Dutch and Swedish movements were also fairly centralised but lacked monopoly. The opposite pattern was found in Finland, France and the UK, with confederations that were weak but which were unrivalled — though in France many unions remained outside the confederation. The other three countries had unambiguously decentralised movements, though the Italian CGdL organised the fourth highest percentage of unionised workers of our group of countries.

Among employers' organisations (Table Ic) we can identify two different forms of centralisation. In both forms employers were grouped in strong, centralised associations that had become (or were associated with trade associations that had become) considerably involved in dealings with government. But in one sub-group — the Scandinavians — these associations insisted that the unions try to bargain with them at a national, cross-branch level, while in the other — the two German *Reich* and the Netherlands — they either kept bargaining at local levels or tried to stop any dealings with unions at all. It should not be assumed from this distinction that the Scandinavian employers were particularly friendly towards labour. They engaged in very tough struggles, calling nation-wide lockouts to enforce their demand for centralisation (especially in Denmark and Sweden; as we have seen, Norwegian labour was already more clearly centralised). But they seemed to take the existence of labour's organisations for granted and were confident they could cope best with highly centralised relations.

Swiss employers differed from those in the above countries in that, while strongly organised and having close dealings with government, they were not at all centralised. This of course reflects the uniquely decentralised nature of the Swiss polity, so Switzerland is treated here as a sub-group of the 'essentially organised' category, sharing the approach to unions of the 'German', not the Scandinavian, group. Finnish employers were also organised, but as a mirror image of the Swiss. They had developed, in imitation of the Swedes, centralised power, but had few dealings with a government that was mainly concerned with

Table Ib: Centralisation of Labour Movements, c. 1914, 12 European Nations

Group	Country	1	2	3	4	5	6	7
A	Norway (LO)	78.0	1	1	-	32	-	1
	Denmark (DsF)	77.9	1	1	-	c50	-	1
B	Austria (GK)	58.5	-	1	-	19	0.5	1
	Germany (GK)	65.0	-	0.5	-	49	0.5	1
	Netherlands (NVV)	30.24	-	1	-	20	-	1
	Sweden (LO)	63.6	-	-	-	27	-	1
C	Finland (FL)	75.0	1	-	-	30	-	-
	UK (TUC)	64.7	1	-	-	207	-	0.5
	France (CGT)	51.5	1	-	-	*	-	-
D	Italy (CGdL)	76.9	-	-	-	*	-	-
	Switzerland (SGB)	64.36	-	-	-		-	-
	Belgium (CS)	48.8	-	-	-	c50	-	-

Notes:

(country boundaries as in Table Ia)
1. Percentage of total union membership within main confederation.
2. Single confederation (1) or more than one (-).
3. Confederation monopolises (1), has important share in (0.5) or has no part in (-) control of strike funds and/or strike calls.
4. Confederation exercises major control (1) or no control (-) over formulation of wage, etc demands.
5. Number of unions within confederation (* signifies that in France and Italy there was a complex pattern of local branches of the confederations alongside individual unions, giving a very large number of units, many of which were however parts of the confederation itself).
6. Industrial-branch union structure dominant (0.5) or not (-) within confederation.
7. Individual unions strongly (1), intermittently (0.5) or not (-) centralised internally.
   CGdL= Confederazione Generale del Lavoro; CGT= Confédération Générale du Travail; CS= Commission Syndicale; DsF= Den samvirkende Fagforbund; FL= Federation of Labour; GK= Generalkommission; LO= Landesorganisasjon i Norge (Norway), Landsorganisationen i Sverige (Sweden); NVV= Nederlands Verbond van Vakverenigingen; SGB= Schweizerischer Gewerkschaftsbund; TUC= Trades Union Congress.

Sources: Union membership data from Visser, 1987 (supplemented by national sources for Belgium and Finland and in order to take account of non-confederated unions in France and Scandinavia). Other sources include: Austrian Reich: Traxler, 1982, esp. pp. 63, 72, 90; Belgium: Chlepner, 1956, esp. p. 120; Delsinne, 1936, esp. p. 222-54; Denmark: Galenson, 1952a, esp. p. 24; Finland: Knoellinger, 1960, esp. p. 51; France: Lefranc, 1967; Shorter & Tilly, 1974, esp. pp. 164-8; German Reich: Müller-Jentsch, 1985, esp. p. 375-7; Italy: Barbadoro, 1973b; Netherlands: Windmuller, 1969, esp. p. 29; Norway: Galenson, 1949, esp. p. 15; Sweden: Hadenius, 1976, esp. pp. 23-30 and Appendix; Switzerland: Höpflinger, 1976; UK: Clegg, 1972, ch. 2; Fox, 1985: chs. 5,6.

Table Ic: Employers' Organisations, c. 1914, 12 European Countries

Group	Country	1	2	3	4
Aa	Denmark	H	1	1	Z
	Norway	H	1	1	Z
	Sweden	H	1	1	Z
Ab	Germany	H	0.5	1	X/W
	Netherlands	H	1	1	X/W
	Austria	H	1	1	X
B	Switzerland	H	-	1	X/W
C	Finland	H	1	-	X
D	UK	M	-	-	X/W
	Italy (north)	M	-	-	X
E	Belgium	L	-	-	X
	France	L	-	-	X
	Italy (south)	L	-	-	X

Notes:

1. High (H), moderate (M) or low (L) level of organisation.
2. Strongly developed peak organisation (1) or not (-) (0.5= strength concentrated in centralised industrial-branch organisations).
3. Regularly involved as organisations with government in economic policy-making (1) or not (-).
4. Dominant strategy in relations with unions: W=accepts collective bargaining at various levels; X=rejects dealings with organised labour; Z= insists on centralised pattern; X/W= mixed pattern.

Sources: Austrian Reich: Traxler, 1982, esp. pp. 101; Belgium: Chlepner, 1956, esp. p. 121; Delsinne, 1936; Denmark: Dybdahl, 1982, esp. pp. 247-50; Galenson, 1952a, ch. V; Vigen, 1950; Finland: Knoellinger, 1960, esp. p. 45; France: Lefranc, 1976, Pt I; Reynaud, 1975, esp. p. 33; German Reich: Leckebusch, 1966, esp. pp. 58-60 and 125-46; Weitbrecht & Berger, 1985, esp. p. 487; Italy: Barbadoro, 1973a, esp. pp. 161-6; and 1973b, esp. p. 180; Netherlands: Windmuller, 1969, esp. p. 46; Norway: Galenson, 1949, esp. p. 80; Lafferty, 1971, esp. p. 189; Sweden: Hadenius, 1976, esp. pp. 21; Samuelssonn, 1968, p. 209; Switzerland: Höpflinger, 1976; Prigge, 1985, esp. p. 404; UK: Clegg, 1972, ch. 4; 1979, ch 3.

issues of national independence and agrarian policy.

In the remaining countries employers' organisations were relatively unimportant, though in Britain and northern Italy these were much stronger than elsewhere.

Putting together the information in Tables Ia and b we can identify very broad groupings of trade union movements: (1) having a potential centralised national role are the movements in Denmark, Germany, Norway; then, much less centralised, Sweden; and at lower levels of power Austria and the Netherlands: (2) powerful but decentralised is the UK and,

Table Id: **Institutional Development of Industrial Relations, c. 1914,**
               12 European Countries

Group	Country	\ Plant	\ Locality	Levels \ Branch	\ Nation	\ State
A	Denmark	(q)	q	q(s)	r	(p)
B	Germany	p	q	(s)		(p)
	Austria	p	(q)	(s)		(p)
	UK		q	(q)		p
	Switzerland	(q)	(q)			(p) (s)
C	Sweden			q	r	
	Norway		q	q		
D	Netherlands		(q)	(q)		
	Belgium		(q)	(q)		
	Finland		(q)	(q)		
E	France		(q)			
	Italy		(q)			

Notes

p = consultative arrangements q = collective bargaining r = formal union involvement in mediation, etc schemes s = formal union involvement in administration of policies (in this period all cases concern administration of unemployment insurance) ( ) indicates weak or patchy development.

Sources: Austria: Lang, 1978, esp. pp. 26-7; Talos, 1981, ch. 2; Traxler, 1982, esp. pp. 48-56; Belgium: Chlepner, 1956, esp. pp. 114-27; Delsinne, 1936, esp. p. 306; Denmark: Galenson, 1952a, esp. pp. 97-107, 226-47; Hansen & Henrikson, 1980a, esp. p. 85; Finland: Knoellinger, 1960, esp. pp 45ff; France: Lefranc, 1967, esp. pp. 81-2, 186; Shorter & Tilly, 1974, esp. p. 27; Germany: Heidenheimer, 1980, pp. 7-11; Ullman, 1977; Weitbrecht & Berger, 1985, esp. pp. 486-8; Italy: Barbadoro, 1973b: esp. pp. 151-9; Netherlands: Windmuller, 1969, esp. p. 45; Norway: Galenson, 1949, ch. VII; Lafferty, 1971, pp. 188-218; Sweden: Korpi, 1978; Switzerland: Parri, 1987; UK: Clegg, 1972, ch. 6; Fox, 1985, chs. 5,6.

considerably weaker, Belgium; among the weakest cases, (3) Finland and Switzerland have some points of strength; (4) but clearly decentralised and weak are France and Italy.

Adding to this our knowledge of employers' organisations, the 'essentially and centrally organised' employers are all found alongside the potentially powerful and centralised union movements, though there is no reflection of the sub-groups within each category. It is less easy to see patterns among the remaining six countries. Mutual lack of centralisation seems to link employers and unions within individual countries, without reference to degrees of potential union strength. This helps account for Belgium and Britain, but leaves the Finnish and Swiss cases unaccounted for. Finnish employers (centrally organised but without political weight) seem the very opposite of their weak, decentralised but political powerful labour counterparts in this agrarian corner of the pre-revolutionary Russian empire. The uniqueness of the Swiss situation is accountable in terms of the country's political system.

Table Id shows the state of the main institutional developments in each country. In the majority of cases the most we find is incipient collective bargaining at the local and branch levels. French and Italian institutions are particularly weak, but three other countries (Belgium, Finland, the Netherlands) differ from them only in having some minor industry-level bargaining. Sweden and Norway present more elaborate, higher-level developments of bargaining, though in rather different ways. Denmark is by far the most elaborate, having developed a centralised system of institutionalised industrial relations in the final year of the 19th century. Labour had developed a rapid mobilising power in this very small economy with few major social divisions, and employers responded by insisting on the establishment of a centralised system.

The remaining four countries all had elaborate systems that, though clearly less complete than the Danish and more developed than the rest, are difficult to compare with each other. Germany and Austria, like Denmark, had unions participating in unemployment insurance schemes and some plant-level workers councils, but the UK, which lacked these features, had more strongly developed collective bargaining and more extensive if less formal consultative relations between unions and government. Swiss unions had, through the particular structure of organisational involvement in public affairs characteristic of that country, achieved a certain level of national participation.

Comparison of this Table with the preceding discussion shows a distinct if partial relationship between independent and dependent variables as expected by traditional institutionalisation theory. On the basis of Tables Ia-c one would expect Denmark to be the most extensively developed, and for German and other Scandinavian nations to have far more developed institutions than Belgium, the Netherlands, Finland, France and Italy. The UK and Switzerland present more of a problem. But in none of our countries can we discern anything resembling GPE at this period. The range is mainly between complete alienation and limited collective bargaining, but with a few incipient developments going beyond the latter; Switzerland is rather separate. It is notable that in the three German-speaking countries (Austria, Germany, Switzerland) institutions have developed at state level without much prior development within industrial relations. This throws into doubt any theory one might construct about gradual upward accretions of institutions from the industrial relations base.

The Mid-1920s

Immediately after this 'snapshot' of 1914, most of these countries were engulfed in a world war, either as participants or as affected neutrals. National integration became an overwhelming issue. States faced a major need to develop identity and transcend alienation at the level of the nation, and the manner in which total war defines people in terms of their national location facilitated this. There were differences within and between nations; indeed one might predict from the foregoing discussion the way in which the majority of the German labour movement moved more readily than the French to accept a patriotic role.

In general, labour movements became important to governments and were incorporated in a manner that dramatically changed the picture presented of their relations with the state in Table Id. In the immediate aftermath of war the momentum of this incorporation continued into grandiose plans for a new tripartite capitalism, the most tangible interna-tional manifestation of which was the formation of the International Labour Office under cross-national tripartite control in Geneva. However, the impact of all this did not reach far down into sub-national or sub-political levels. War-time measures were an emergency, temporary imposition on existing institutions and often contrasted strongly with them. The details of these and their post-war fate are highly interesting, but for present purposes there is not space to analyse them. Instead we take our second snapshot at the century's quarter mark, after events had clarified.

As early as 1920 the first post-war recession had affected most European economies. From being scarce and crucial to the war effort, human labour was now in surplus. The contrast was swift and stark, and enabled employers rapidly to reverse the rise of labour and concomitant institutionalisation of industrial relations that had occurred. The shallow, bolt-on nature of the war-time changes and war-related character of the state's earlier accessi-bility made matters that much easier for them. Unions usually wanted to keep their war-time positions, but their declining strength could often no longer sustain them.

The change was most abrupt in Italy, with the accession of a fascist regime encouraged by industrial unrest and rural employers fearful of labour's militancy in the immediate post-war years. By 1925 Italy lacked an autonomous labour movement of the kind we are studying here, so that country temporarily leaves our analysis. Democracy survived, but the labour movement suffered rapid reverses in France and the Netherlands, where the indus-trial working class remained fairly small and poorly organised. In Britain the very large class remained a pressing political fact even though there were major defeats for the unions within industrial relations. In Belgium socialists took part in a post-war government of reconstruc-tion, but a return to 'normalcy' rapidly followed its fall in 1923.

The story is rather different in the two defeated German-speaking *Reich*, where the discrediting of established elites propelled labour movements to a leading position in the polity. Here, while labour was in rapid retreat in the victor countries, labour-led coalitions set about both advancing labour's rights and entrenching the labour movement as an important representative of the national interest. This made for a rapid advance in both institutionalisation and political access within the context of the awesome task of national reconstruction. But after a few years this proved to be an enlarged, nightmare version of the 'premature' promotion of labour elsewhere during the war. There remained a discontinuity between labour's sudden political importance and growing centralisation on the one hand and its labour-market position and therefore organisational strength on the other, the latter being weakened by both the general recession and the particular dislocation of the defeated economies. The labour movement became a paper tiger. This was by no means the only source of instability that beset those two ill-fated republics, but it was certainly among them. Labour was politically prominent and exposed while being vulnerable to its enemies should it seek to use any of its apparent political strength.

Border changes have affected the identity of some of our cases between 1914 and 1925: Austria has lost its Slav lands and is pressed back into the German-speaking territories around Vienna and the Alps, the loss of both rural and Slav populations greatly enhancing the relative weight and internal unity of labour within the infant republic. Germany loses Alsace-Lorraine to France and also parts of Poland. The UK loses the major part of Ireland, predominantly a peasant economy. The last change gives us a new case to consider: the new Irish Free State, later the Republic of Ireland. And Finland finally secures independence from now revolutionary Russia. At the time of our 'snapshot', 1925, Ireland and Finland were still in the midst of internal conflict surrounding their constitutional status.

Table IIa summarises the state of union strength around 1925. Since 1914 there has been a considerable increase in membership in most countries, and a smaller increase in political strength. Some account should now be taken of unemployment, though this is still rendered difficult by different national counting systems and by low levels of registration of unemployment in countries with large rural sectors. All we can say is that unemployment in Scandinavia and Austria was higher than that in the UK and the Netherlands, which was in turn higher than in Switzerland. Clearly high unemployment did not hamper union recruitment in the high-unemployment countries, but it must have reduced the incentive for employers to bother to come to terms with otherwise impressive labour movements.

Over half our cases now have labour movements with reasonable incipient strength. These are listed as Group A. Denmark and Sweden had labour parties dominating government coalitions at this time, which puts them in a different position from those with higher memberships but less direct political influence. It is difficult to calculate the significance of this, especially when it is compared with the ambiguous 'dependence' of Austria and Germany on their labour movements or the similarly ambiguous factor of Christian labour movements in Austria, Belgium, the Netherlands and elsewhere.

As of 1925, and ignoring what was to follow, the Austrian movement emerges as very strong, especially if we take account of dependent labour only and forget the large remaining peasant population. The movement had suffered some reverses since its immediate post-war dominance, the material situation in the country was appalling, and politically the only state representation of labour was through the highly ambiguous Christian Social Party; but there was simultaneously a curious dependence of the state of Restösterreich on the labour movement. It constituted the only element in the society genuinely prepared to commit itself to the new republic — an advantage that could rapidly become the opposite when other elements finally became disillusioned with that entity. How do we distinguish between this brittle strength and that of Danish labour, with a poorer mobilisation base, but a more secure place in a far more stable polity? Another strong case, one year before a disastrous general strike, was the UK, with a higher overall membership than Denmark (though not if

Table IIa: Power of Organised Labour, c. 1925, 12 European Nations

Group	Country	1	2	3	4	5	6	7
Aa	Denmark	22.80	35.96	H	H	36.6	0.75	-
	Sweden	19.98	31.03	H	X	41.1	0.75	-
Ab	Austria (8)	31.06	48.07	H	X	39.6 (44.0)	0.25	0.5
	UK (9)	28.46	31.83	M	H	33.3	-	-
	Belgium (10)	21.84	30.76	?	H	39.4 (36.1)	0.25	-
	Germany (11)	19.13	28.39	?	X	34.9 (13.6)	0.25	0.5
	Netherlands	18.40	22.99	M	H	22.9 (50.7)	0.25	-
B	Switzerland	12.32	18.95	L	-	25.8 (20.9)	0.25	-
	Norway	13.33	20.13	H	X	33.3	-	-
C	Ireland	8.45	19.00	?	H	10.9 (27.4)	-	-
	Finland (12)	4.09	13.87	?	X	39.4	-	-
	France	4.58	7.60	?	X	9.8	-	-

Notes:

1. Total known union membership as percentage of labour force, c.1925.
2. Total known union membership as percentage of dependent labour force, c.1925.
3. Unemployment: H= registered unemployment clearly in excess of 10% of dependent labour force; M= registered unemployment about 10% of dependent labour force; registered unemployment less than 5% of dependent labour force; ?= official unemployment figures are low, but there are reasons for doubting whether they give a full picture.
4. Mobilisation: M = important incidents of high labour conflict some time during preceding decade; H = incidents of exceptionally high labour conflict some time during preceding decade; X = important incidents of high labour conflict some time during preceding decade, during the course of which labour suffered major defeats.
5. Share of popular vote in most recent general election secured by: Austria: Social Democratic Party (Christian Social Party in parentheses); Belgium: Workers Party (Catholic Party in parentheses); Denmark: Social Democratic Party; Finland: Social Democratic Party (29%) and Socialist Workers Party (10.45%); France: Communist Party; Germany: Social Democratic Party (26%), Communist Party (8.9%) (Centre Party in parentheses); Ireland: Labour Party (Republican Party in parentheses); Netherlands: Labour Party (Catholic Party (28.6%), Anti-Revolutionary Party (12.2%), Christian Historical Party (9.9%) in parentheses); Norway: Labour Party (18.4%), Social Democratic Workers Party (8.8%) Communist Party (6.1%); Sweden: Social Democratic Labour Party; Switzerland: Social Democratic Party (Catholic Conservative Party in parentheses); UK: Labour Party.

6. Government participation: main labour-movement party dominating government coalition (0.75), or having minor role in coalition (0.5); other parties with labour-movement component in government (0.25).
7. Evidence of state dependence on organised element as an element of social order. In this period this occurs only through the dependence of the Viennese and Weimar republics on the Social Democratic labour movement for stability.
8. Republic's boundaries as at 1918; no reliable labour-force data available for Austria until 1934; figure given is an estimate.
9. Not including Republic of Ireland.
10. Workers Party joined government in June 1925, giving a weight of 0.5 plus 0.25 in column 6.
11. Republic's boundaries as at 1918.
12. NB for Finland data for dependent labour force are not available; figures in column 2 refer to union membership as a proportion of non-agricultural labour.

Sources: Labour force and electoral data drawn from Flora et al, 1983 and 1987; union membership data from Visser, 1987 (supplemented by national sources for Belgium, Finland and Ireland and in order to take account of non-confederated unions in France and Scandinavia). Other sources include: Austria: Traxler, 1982, esp. pp. 116-31; Belgium: Chlepner, 1956, esp. pp. 316-8; Spitaels, 1967, esp. p. 31; Denmark: Hansen & Henriksen, 1980a, esp. p. 178-82; Finland: Knoellinger, 1960, esp. p. 4; France: Lefranc, 1967, esp. p. 223-36, 280, 315; Prost, 1964; Germany: Weitbrecht & Berger, 1985; Ireland, McCarthy, 1977, esp. pp. 67-73; Netherlands: Windmuller, 1969; Norway: Galenson, 1949, esp. pp. 25-30; Sweden: Hadenius, 1976; Switzerland: Höpflinger, 1976; UK: Clegg, 1972, ch. 2; Fox, 1985, ch. 7.

dependent labour only is taken into account). Belgian labour's strength has risen sharply since 1914, as has its political presence.

Among the remaining cases there is no real political argument for changing the order indicated by simple membership strength. One might note that German labour shared the dangerous privilege of its Austrian sister of being the only element fully committed to a new republic that some powerful forces repudiated. This emerges strongly from accounts of the French occupation of the Ruhr at this time; while the Social Democrats and unions were suffering the privations of a strike to resist the invaders, German businessmen were secretly negotiating with the French the possible detachment of the Rhineland from the Weimar Republic (Maier, 1975: 390-405).

Norway and Switzerland, though hardly similar to each other, both had membership levels clearly below the first group but well in excess of the weakest cases: Finland, France and Ireland. French labour continued to find it difficult to establish a membership base, and a large part of the movement remained in syndicalist organisations, rejecting political involvement. Acting within a very rural economy and having no distinctive position on the issues raised by the civil war that followed the struggle against the British, the Irish unions had to stand aside from the process of nation- and party-building that accompanied independence. They never capitalised on their 'heroic' leadership role in the period before 1918, and were unable to make the state very accessible to them. There was however no repression or even exclusion of the Finnish kind. In Finland a disastrous Civil War in 1918-21 wiped out labour's earlier political dominance as mobilisers of a successful drive for national independence. This resulted from the impact of the Russian revolution, which led to great ambiguities and divisions within labour's ranks and created great opportunities for nationalist anti-labour forces. Socialism and socialists suffered greatly during the civil war itself, leading to a period of exclusion and repressive industrial relations from which there was only gradual subsequent recovery. On the other hand, Finnish labour retained its precocious parliamentary strength.

Developments in centralisation are shown in Table IIb. There has been a general shift to a concentration of numbers and powers within national unions and confederations. Austria and Norway appear as the most centralised, the former having gained since 1914 from the reduction in heterogeneity in the shift from Austria-Hungary to Restösterreich. The Belgian, Danish, German, Swedish and Swiss movements had also acquired some central powers within their dominant confederations, or in the Swiss case within industrial unions, even if the movements in some of these were religiously divided. The Netherlands and Switzerland are those where religious divisions most weakened the leading confederation, centralised though it was.

The remaining countries all have far stronger monopolies than the Netherlands, but these confederations had little power. They are therefore best ranked against each other by their degree of representativeness, though it should be noted that the British TUC had somewhat more power than the Finnish federation. French labour stands alone as clearly the least centralised.

Combining these data we see, as in 1914, a weak but positive association between labour's power and its centralisation: the only relatively weak but strongly centralised movement is Norway, then in the grip of its Comintern phase. The other Scandinavian and the German-speaking cases remain the leading examples of relatively centralised union power with some advance in Sweden. Belgium has begun to join this group. The Dutch remain a midway case because of the divisions in the labour movement. Finland, France and Ireland are examples of weak, decentralised movements. The UK provides an unusual combination of decentralised power.

The main changes — or apparent changes — to affect employers organisations (Table IIc) were in the defeated powers, where a position of resistance to working with unions was changed into one of being required to do so by the political settlement in the first years of the post-war republics — a settlement which was by 1925 beginning to seem increasingly unnecessary to employers as labour's political strength waned and rising unemployment destroyed its base in the labour market. Otherwise we note a general growth in government involvement, an increasing willingness to deal with unions in the UK, Belgium and Ireland, little change in France, and in Finland a decline in centralisation after the crushing of the unions rendered it less necessary. Only Belgium sees employers accelerating in organisation less rapidly than labour, while Norway is temporarily the most clearly opposite case.

The state of institutional development in the mid 1920s is shown in Table IId. There has been the gradual 'thickening up' of institutions as would be expected by simple evolutionary theories: considerable development of bargaining and mediation arrangements, increasingly at branch rather than local level, and a considerable extension of government consultation of unions. In Austria and Germany there is apparently the kind of institutional

Table IIb: Centralisation of Labour Movements, c. 1925, 12 European Nations

Group	Country	1	2	3	4	5	6	7
A	Austria (GK)	86.67	-	1	-	52	0.5	1
	Norway (LO)	85.00	1	1	-	32	0.5	-
	Denmark (DsF)	77.15	1	-	-	51	-	1
	Belgium (CS)	65.43	-	-	-	31	1	1
	Switzerland (SGB)	65.05	-	1	-	21	0.5	1
	Germany (GK)	65.0	-	0.5	-	49	0.5	1
	Sweden (LO)	73.45	-	-	-	34	0.5	1
B	Netherlands (NVV)	38.62	-	1	-	29	0.5	1
C	Ireland (ITUC)	85.00	1	-	-	50	-	0.5
	Finland (FL)	83.00	1	-	-	20	-	-
	UK (TUC)	60.6	1	-	-	205	-	0.5
D	France (CGT)	51.01	-	-	-	36*	-	-

Notes:

(country boundaries as in Table IIa)
1. Percentage of total union membership within main confederation.
2. Single confederation (1) or more than one (-).
3. Confederation monopolises (1), has important share in (0.5) or has no part in (-) control of strike funds and/or strike calls.
4. Confederation exercises major control (1) or no control (-) over formulation of wage, etc demands.
5. Number of unions within confederation (* signifies that in France there was a complex pattern of local branches of the confederations alongside individual unions, giving a very large number of units, many of which were however parts of the confederation itself).
6. Industrial-branch union structure dominant (0.5) or not (-) within confederation.
7. Individual unions strongly (1), intermittently (0.5) or not (-) centralised internally.
CGdL= Confederazione Generale del Lavoro; CGT= Confédération Générale du Travail; CS= Commission Syndicale; DsF= Den samvirkende Fagforbund; FL= Federation of Labour; GK= Generalkommission; ITUC= Irish Trades Union Congress; LO= Landsorganisasjon i Norge (Norway); Landsorganisationen i Sverige (Sweden); NVV= Nederlands Verbond van Vakvereni-gingen; SGB= Schweizerischer Gewerkschaftsbund; TUC= Trades Union Congress.
Sources: Union membership data from Visser, 1987 (supplemented by national sources for Belgium, Finland and Ireland and in order to take account of non-confederated unions in France and Scandinavia). Other sources include: Austria: Traxler, 1982, esp. pp. 147-60; Belgium: Chlepner, 1956, esp. p. 258-66; Delsinne, 1936, esp. p. 222; Spitaels, 1967, esp. pp. 15-20; Denmark: Hansen and Henriksen, 1980a, esp. pp. 178-82; Jørgensen, 1975; Finland: Knoellinger, 1960; France: Lefranc, 1967, pp. 240-60, 276-8, 315; Germany: Müller-Jentsch, 1985, esp. pp. 376-7; Rauscher, 1985, esp. p. 386; Ireland: McCarthy, 1977; Netherlands: Windmuller, 1969, esp. p. 53; Norway: Galenson, 1949; Lafferty, 1971, esp. pp. 184-6; Sweden: Hadenius, 1976, esp. pp. 35-8; Switzerland: Höpflinger, 1976; UK: Clegg, 1972, ch. 2; Fox, 1985, ch. 7

Table IIc: Employers' Organisations, c. 1925, 12 European Countries

Group	Country	1	2	3	4
A	Denmark	H	1	1	Z
	Norway	H	1	1	Z
	Sweden	H	1	1	Z
B	Austria	H	1	1	Y
	Germany	H	1	1	Y
C	Netherlands	H	1	1	X/W
D	Switzerland	H	-	1	X/W
E	UK	M	-	0.5	W/X
	Ireland	M	-	0.5	W/X
	Belgium	M	-	0.5	X/W
F	Finland	H	-	0.5	X
	France	L	-	0.5	X

Notes:

1. High (H), moderate (M) or low (L) level of organisation.
2. Strongly developed peak organisation (1) or not (-)
3. Regularly involved as organisations with government in economic policy-making (1) or not (-). 0.5 indicates more intermittent involvement.
4. Dominant strategy in relations with unions: W=accepts collective bargaining at various levels; X=rejects dealings with organised labour; Y= required by government to come to terms with organised labour; Z= insists on centralised pattern; W/X, X/W= mixed pattern.

Sources: Austria: Traxler, 1982; Belgium: Chlepner, 1956, esp. pp. 255-6; Denmark: Galenson, 1952a, esp. p. 102; Hansen and Henriksen, 1980a, esp. pp. 178-82; Vigen, 1950; Finland: Knoellinger, 1960, esp. pp. 71-80; France: Lefranc, 1976, esp. pp. 75-95; Germany: Leckebusch, 1966, pp. 70-5 and 110-26; Ireland: McCarthy, 1977; Netherlands: Windmuller, 1969, esp. pp. 45-50; Norway: Galenson, 1949; Sweden: Hadenius, 1976, esp. p. 38; Switzerland: Prigge, 1985; UK: Clegg, 1972: ch 4.

integration that, when combined with the organisational characteristics studied above, might be considered to have encouraged GPE. That had of course been the language talked by industrial spokesmen in the wake of 1918; but by 1925 many sections of industry were resisting this legally imposed system, were not working within the institutions and were returning to their earlier preference for repressing labour instead. The options available in these countries therefore seem to have been either a shift into GPE or a complete dismantling of institutions.

**Table IId: Institutional Development of Industrial Relations, c. 1925,
12 European Countries**

Group	Country	Plant	Locality	Branch	Nation	State
A	Austria	p(s)	(q)	pq(s)	p	p s
	Germany	p(s)	q	(q)(s)		p s
B	Denmark	(q)	q	q(s)	r	p
C	UK		q	q		p
	Sweden		q	q	r	p
	Switzerland	(q)	(q)	(s)		(p) (s)
	Belgium		q	(q)(s)		p
D	Netherlands		r(q)	r(q)(s)		
	Norway		rq	rq		
E	France		(q)	(s)		(p)
	Finland		(q)			(p)
	Ireland		q	q		

Notes:

p = consultative arrangements q = collective bargaining r = formal union involvement in mediation, etc schemes s = formal union involvement in administration of policies ( ) indicates weak or patchy development.

Sources: Austria: Talos, 1981, p. 130 and ch. 4; Traxler, 1982, esp. pp. 111-30; Belgium: Chlepner, 1956, esp. pp. 318ff; Delsinne, 1936, esp. p. 306-8 and ch XXXIII; Denmark: Andersen, 1976; Galenson, 1952a; Finland: Knoellinger, 1960, esp. pp 68-80; France: Lefranc 271-303; Reynaud, 1975, esp. p. 82; Germany: Leckebusch, 1900, esp. pp. 70-5; Weitbrecht & Berger, 1985, esp. pp. 490-6; Ireland: McCarthy, 1977; Netherlands: Windmuller, 1969, esp. p. 43 and 63-5; Norway: Galenson, 1949, pp. 25-30; Sweden: Korpi, 1978; Switzerland: Parri, 1987; UK: Clegg, 1972, ch. 6; Middlemas, 1978, pp. 68-174.

Labour was also being incorporated at a wide range of levels in Denmark, but building up from an industrial rather than political base: less dramatic but also far less exposed. Then comes a group of countries with fairly substantial but diverse developments which it is difficult to rank: Sweden, Belgium, the UK and Switzerland. But with the partial exception of the last this was mainly a combination of orthodox collective bargaining, some involvement in mediation and consultation with government. In Belgium this kind of development was being furthered, as in Austria and Germany, by state initiative, but in the gradual form of *commissions paritaires*. These were bipartite institutions established by the state, at this stage in only a few industries, and charged with the task of both collective bargaining and representing the interests of the branch to government. The Netherlands and Norway differ from this group through the relative absence of national-level institutions.

Finland, France and Ireland confirm our expectations that a low level of organisational growth will be associated with low institutional development.

There remain no cases that can defined primarily in terms of GPE, but beyond that the range of system types in the mid-1920s extends from the elimination of organised labour (Italy) to extended collective bargaining. In general countries occupy the positions anticipated by our thesis, centralised union power and employers' organisational capacity being associated with extensive institutional development. There remains however an unpredictable and purely 'political' element in the extent to which unions are involved in either consultative or shared administrative capacities. The British and Norwegian cases suggest, in their opposite ways, that the greater relevance for institutional development of centralisation rather than union power observable in 1914 did not generally obtain in the 1920s.

The Eve of World War II

Between 1933 and 1938 there were major changes in the industrial relations systems of all but five of our countries. Germany (1933) and Austria (1934 and 1938) came under fascist/ Nazi control and autonomous trade unionism was destroyed. Belgium and France (1936) saw major crises in the politics of industrial relations. Denmark (1935), Norway (1936) and Sweden (1938) witnessed the establishment of major central agreements between labour and capital associated with the accession of labour-movement parties to office. In Switzerland (1937) there was a similar agreement, but initially limited to the dominant metal and watch industries and without immediate overt political development. Beyond our range of countries, these were also the years of the New Deal in the USA. These changes took varied forms and occurred under different circumstances. The only common thread was the need to cope in some way with increasing industrial conflict and economic difficulty. Conflict was initially associated with workers' defensive struggles in the Depression, but in some cases it lasted into the period of recovery, when labour's strength revived while its awareness of accumulated grievances was strong.

The death of autonomous labour movements in Austria and Germany removes two countries from consideration. For the rest, Tables IIIa-d depict the situation in 1938, the last full year of peace before World War II. Table IIIa shows consolidated union strength in most countries. The three Scandinavian nations finally converge from their diverse backgrounds unambiguously to occupy the leading places, each with governing Labour or Social Democratic parties. Belgium can easily be ranked after them. It is difficult to decide whether the industrially strong but politically greatly weakened British unions should rank next or the politically unusually organised Dutch, but both are clearly stronger examples than the rest.

It is reasonable to rank the remaining four countries in order of their membership

Table IIIa: Power of Organised Labour, c. 1938, 10 European Nations

Group	Country	1	2	3	4	5	6	7
A	Sweden	36.01	55.06	D	H	45.9	0.75	1
	Norway	34.29	57.25	D	H	42.5	0.75	1
	Denmark	27.29	38.05	D	H	46.1	0.75	1
B	Belgium	25.33	36.98	D	H	38.2 (27.7)	0.5 0.25	0.5
	UK	28.72	36.86	D	M	38.1	-	-
	Netherlands	24.49	31.16	H	M	21.9 (52.7)	0.25	0.5
C	Switzerland	19.95	28.62	M	M	28.0 (20.3)	0.25	0.5
	France (8)	18.82	33.66	?	H	35.0	0.5	-
	Ireland	15.03	32.60	?	M	10.0 (51.9)	0.25	0.5
	Finland (9)	4.96	11.64	?	X	38.6	0.5	-

Notes:

1. Total known union membership as percentage of labour force, c.1938.
2. Total known union membership as percentage of dependent labour force, c.1938.
3. Unemployment: D= declining from a high peak; H= remaining high, only slight decline from peak; M= moderately high, some decline from peak; ?= doubts about reliability of the figures, largely owing to large size of rural sector.
4. Mobilisation: M = important incidents of high labour conflict some time during preceding decade; H = incidents of exceptionally high labour conflict some time during preceding decade; X = important incidents of high labour conflict some time during preceding decade, during the course of which labour suffered major defeats.
5. Share of popular vote in most recent general election secured by: Belgium: Workers Party (32.1%) Communist Party (6.1%) (Catholic Party in parentheses); Denmark: Social Democratic Party; Finland: Social Democratic Party; France: Socialist Party (19.9%) Communist Party (15.3); Ireland: Labour Party (Fianna Fail in parentheses); Netherlands: Labour Party (Catholic Party (28.8%), Anti-Revolutionary Party (16.4%), Christian Historical Party (7.5%) in parentheses); Norway: Labour Party; Sweden: Social Democratic Labour Party; Switzerland: Social Democratic Party (Catholic Conservative Party in parentheses); UK: Labour Party
6. Main labour-movement party dominating government coalition (0.75), or having minor role in coalition (0.5); other parties with labour-movement component in government (0.25).
7. Evidence of state dependence on organised labour as an element of social order. In the Scandinavian cases labour-movement parties were associated with the new policies that saved the economies during the 1930s. In the three countries given a 0.5 rating, labour-movement parties were integral parts of national alignments in the face of potential aggression by Nazi Germany.
8. Popular Front government fell in April, reducing score on 6. to nothing.
9. NB for Finland data for dependent labour force are not available; figures in column 2 refer to union membership as a proportion of non-agricultural labour.

Sources: Labour force and electoral data drawn from Flora et al, 1983 and 1987; union membership data from Visser, 1987 (supplemented by national sources for Belgium, Finland and Ireland and in order to take account of non-confederated unions in France and Scandinavia). Other sources include: Belgium: Chlepner, 1956, esp. pp. 240-1; Ebertzheim, 1959; Denmark: Hansen & Henriksen, 1980a; Jørgensen, 1975; Finland: Knoellinger, 1960; France: Lefranc, 1967, ch VII; Prost, 1964; Ireland, McCarthy, 1977, pp. 125-33, 144-9 and ch. IV; Netherlands: Windmuller, 1969; Norway: Galenson, 1949; Sweden: Korpi, 1978; Switzerland: Höpflinger, 1976; UK: Clegg, 1972, ch. 2.

Table IIIb: Centralisation of Labour Movements, c. 1938, 10 European Nations

Group	Country	1	2	3	4	5	6	7
A	Norway (LO)	85.00	1	1	1	c63	0.5	1
	Sweden (LO)	84.73	1	1	1	42	0.5	1
	Denmark (DsF)	92.20	1	-	1	c72	-	1
B	Belgium (CGTB)	61.05	-	1	-	24	1	1
	Switzerland (SGB)	58.18	-	-	-	21	1	1
C	Netherlands (NVV)	39.69	-	-	-	29	0.5	1
D	France (CGT)	90.95	-	-	-	38*	0.5	-
	UK (TUC)	77.1	1	-	-	216	-	0.5
	Ireland (ITUC)	71.00	1	-	-	49	-	0.5
	Finland (SAK)	70.00	-	-	-	c20	0.5	-

Notes:

(country boundaries as in Table IIa)
1. Percentage of total union membership within main confederation.
2. Single confederation (1) or more than one (-).
3. Confederation monopolises (1), has important share in (0.5) or has no part in (-) control of strike funds and/or strike calls.
4. Confederation exercises major control (1) or no control (-) over formulation of wage, etc demands.
5. Number of unions within confederation (* signifies that in France there was a complex pattern of local branches of the confederations alongside individual unions, giving a very large number of units, many of which were however parts of the confederation itself).
6. Industrial-branch union structure dominant (0.5) or not (-) within confederation.
7. Individual unions strongly (1), intermittently (0.5) or not (-) centralised internally.
CGT= Confédération Générale du Travail; CGTB= Confédération Générale du Travail Belge; DsF= Den samvirkende Fagforbund; ITUC= Irish Trades Union Congress; LO= Landsorganisasjon i Norge (Norway); Landsorganisationen i Sverige (Sweden); NVV= Nederlands Verbond van Vakverenigingen; SGB= Schweizerischer Gewerkschaftsbund; SAK= Suomen Ammattijarjestojen Keskusjarjesto; TUC= Trades Union Congress.

Sources: Union membership data from Visser, 1987 (supplemented by national sources for Belgium, Finland and Ireland and in order to take account of non-confederated unions in France and Scandinavia). Other sources include: Belgium: Chlepner, 1956, esp. p.265-6; Ebertzheim, 1959;

Denmark: Hansen and Henriksen, 1980a, esp. pp. 178-82; Galenson, 1952a, chs. III, IV; Jørgensen, 1975; Finland: Knoellinger, 1960, ch. 5; France: Lefranc, 1967, ch. VI; Prost, 1964; Ireland: McCarthy, 1977; pp. 108-60; Netherlands: Windmuller, 1969, esp. p. 84-5; Norway: Galenson, 1949; Sweden: Hadenius, 1976, esp. pp. 45-8; Lewin, 1980, esp. pp. 31-8; Stephens, 1979, ch. 5; Switzerland: Höpflinger, 1976; UK: Clegg, 1972, ch. 2; Fox, 1985, ch. 7.

strength, though they all present some problems of analysis. Irish labour is politically much weaker than its industrial strength would suggest, but certain factors render the situation more complicated. The country's main party, Fianna Fail, continued to be 'labour-friendly', though in no sense a labour party, and was during the 1930s finally discovering a national use for the labour movement, or at least part of it. In the drive to render the republic fully independent of the UK, the Fianna Fail government was anxious to try to separate Irish unions from the Irish branches of British unions which still represented about 20% of Irish union membership. This led ministers to take an interest in the unions. However, the government remained committed to an essentially rural concept of Ireland and was not interested in either building an industrial working class or in economic development. Swiss labour, like the Belgian and Dutch, and possibly more implicitly the Irish, continued to gain ambiguously from having a Catholic wing with some political strength.

Labour in Finland had been drastically weakened by attacks from the fascist Lapua movement, but social democracy retained an unusually strong political position. It becomes difficult to measure both industrial and political strength in France at this time. During the peak of the Popular Front period in 1936 union membership had shot up to about 5 million, but it then deteriorated sharply over the following two years, becoming meanwhile an unreliable indicator of any real 'strength'. The political situation is also unclear in that the Socialist Party appears as much more of a labour movement party than previously (or subsequently); but by April of the year in question the Popular Front had fallen.

These were of course years in which labour movements everywhere had been weakened by high unemployment, but it is interesting to note that unions were at their strongest in membership terms where unemployment had begun to decline.

The most significant development between 1925 and 1938 in levels of centralisation is the convergence of the Scandinavians on a high level. The similarity of these three countries makes possible a finer comparison than usual, and it is clear that Denmark, lacking an industrial-union pattern, is now less centralised than the other two. Belgium is less centralised than these cases only because of its socialist/Christian division. Switzerland now also appears moderately centralised, but because of centralisation within individual industry-branch unions, not confederations. The Netherlands has to be treated as a case on its own because, while its unions resemble Belgium and Switzerland in internal structure, their membership was so fragmented among three confederations. Individual unions in Britain and Ireland had become somewhat more centralised as high unemployment weakened the usually strong decentralising forces. In the wake of the temporary unity of the Popular Front, the French CGT appears remarkably centralised. French labour is in fact caught here at a moment of abrupt transition. In 1936 and 1937 it had gained rapidly in power

Table IIIc: Employers' Organisations, c. 1938, 10 European Countries

Group	Country	1	2	3	4
A	Denmark	H	1	1	Z
	Norway	H	1	1	Z
	Sweden	H	1	1	Z
B	Netherlands	H	1	1	W/X
	Belgium	H	-	1	(Y)
	Switzerland	H	-	1	W
C	UK	M	-	0.5	W/X
	Ireland	M	-	0.5	W/X
D	Finland	H	-	0.5	X
	France	L	-	0.5	X

Notes:

1. High (H), moderate (M) or low (L) level of organisation.
2. Strongly developed peak organisation (1) or not (-)
3. Regularly involved as organisations with government in economic policy-making (1) or not (-). 0.5 indicates more intermittent involvement.
4. Dominant strategy in relations with unions: W=accepts collective bargaining at various levels; X=rejects dealings with organised labour; Y= required by government to come to terms with organised labour; Z= insists on centralised pattern; W/X, X/W= mixed patterns.

Sources: Belgium: Chlepner, 1956, esp. pp. 239-40; Denmark: Galenson, 1952a, ch. V; Vigen, 1950; Finland: Knoellinger, 1960, esp. pp. 71-6; France: Brizay, 1956; Lefranc, 1967, ch. VII; 1976, Pt. II, ch. I; Ehrmann, 1957, pp. 24ff; Ireland: McCarthy, 1977; Netherlands: Windmuller, 1969, esp. pp. 84-5; Norway: Olsen, 1983, esp. p. 172; Sweden: Korpi, 1978; Jackson & Sisson, 1976; Switzerland: Parri, 1987; UK: Clegg, 1972, ch. 4.

and unity. By 1938 membership levels had embarked on an equally rapid decline, though the unity persisted.

Overall there are therefore fewer incongruities among these variables than in 1925 or 1914, and this corresponds with the situation among employers (IIIc). Scandinavian employers seem to have acquired the centralised bargaining partners they had consistently sought — though this achievement was interestingly associated with political developments unfavourable to employers, rather than the reverse. Belgian employers and unions both begin to move to a high level of centralised organisation, mainly as a result of state prompting through the new *commissions paritaires*, which had been extended to a wider range of industries. French employers had largely repudiated the involvement of their leaders in the tripartite negotiations of the Popular Front, and consequent changes in the *Patronat* reinforced rather than challenged traditional French patterns. Elsewhere there were few changes.

The state of institutional development (Table IIId) also demonstrates the distinctive position of the Scandinavian countries, who now have systems of bargaining, consultation, mediation and administration binding the main levels of action, in particular filling out the national (as opposed to state) level, where confederations of unions and employers are the principal actors. In each case the installation of a new system was almost formally registered, which is by no means always the case with change in industrial relations systems, and followed a major demonstration of labour's enduring strength at a time of increasing international tension. The not dissimilar Swiss development at the same time (1937), had characteristically involved an agreement at the level of an industry, not a confederation. The union in question was however the dominant metal and watch-making industry, and the influence of the deal spread rapidly to other sectors. At the same time, in the context of events in the bordering nations of Germany, Austria and Italy, the Swiss government had been re-admitting organised labour to participation in the boards representative of organised interests that administer much of Swiss public life in the absence of an elaborate state structure.

Switzerland, the Netherlands and Belgium all saw major steps in institutional elaboration, though in the Low Countries these remained largely state, as opposed to social partner, initiatives. The *commissions paritaires* imposed by the Belgian government to encourage both branch-level collective bargaining and a system of interest-group consultation by government nevertheless provided an important structure for the development of a web of relations at various levels. In 1936, after major industrial conflict, this structure was crowned by the *Conseil National du Travail*, which played an important formal role in the preparation of labour legislation. But beneath all this, many employers remained reluctant to engage in relations with unions. Similarly, though at that stage less formally, the Dutch government had been busy admitting labour to a range of national participation, but again with less response from capital. In some ways these innovations resembled Austrian and German developments in 1918: the political imposition on capital of arrangements for co-operating with labour. However, the degree of engagement offered to labour was far weaker, and Belgian and Dutch labour posed nothing like the threat to capital of post-1918 Austria and Germany.

A strong growth of collective bargaining, but little else, distinguishes Ireland and the UK at this period. Irish developments may, in the light of what was said above, seem somewhat different, but this is illusory. The government was not really interested in industrial development and did not need trade unions for that purpose. If it took an interest in union affairs it was usually to encourage the Republic's unions to separate themselves from the Britain-based unions that still represented many Irish workers, in the interests of national identity. But this mainly took the form of encouraging splits within an already small movement.

On the face of it the French events of 1936 resemble those in Scandinavia, Switzerland and Belgium at the same time, but, as we have noted, employers remained far less willing than even the Belgian to co-operate, the changes introduced were limited, superficial and

Table IIId: **Institutional Development of Industrial Relations, c. 1938, 10 European Countries**

Group	Country	Plant	Locality	Branch	Nation	State
			Levels			
A	Denmark	(q)		Q(s)	Qrs	Ps
	Norway		r(q)	Qr	Qr	Ps
	Sweden		r	Qr	Qr	Ps
B	Switzerland	q	q	Qr(s)		p(s)
	Belgium	q	q	q(s)		P
	Netherlands	(p)	(q)r(s)	pr(q)(s)	p	
C	UK		q	q		p
	Ireland		q	q		(p)
D	France		(q)	(s)	(q)	p
E	Finland		(q)			(p)

Notes:

p = consultative arrangements q = collective bargaining r = formal union involvement in mediation, etc schemes s = formal union involvement in administration of policies ( ) indicates weak or patchy development capital letters indicate particularly strong development.

Sources: Belgium: Chlepner, 1956, esp. pp. 319-21; Spitaels, 1967, esp. p. 76; Fafchamps, 1961; Denmark: Galenson, 1952, pp. 103ff; Hansen & Henrikson, 1980a, pp. 300-10; Vigen, 1950; Finland: Knoellinger, 1960, ch. 5; France: Lefranc, 1967, ch. VII; 1976, Pt. II ch. I; Reynaud, 1975, esp. p. 96-7; Ireland: McCarthy, 1977, esp. pp. 182-3; Netherlands: Windmuller, 1969, esp. p. 72-8; Norway: Galenson, 1949, pp. 175-82; Kvavik, 1976, esp. pp. 133-43; Olsen, 1983, esp. p. 172; Sweden: Korpi, 1978; Jackson & Sisson, 1976; Switzerland: Höpflinger, 1976, esp. pp. 96ff; Parri, 1987; UK: Clegg, 1972, ch. 6; Middlemas, 1979, pp. 174-214.

easily reversed once labour's strength had waned. This change finally took place during 1938 itself. Immediately after 1936 France would have been classified with Belgium and the Netherlands as a case of government imposition on a reluctant capitalism. However, perhaps because it was both politically more powerful but organisationally less well established than capital in Scandinavia, French capital was not prepared to tolerate such changes. The events of 1936 were indeed enough to encourage among some employers political moves similar to those that had taken place in Austria and Germany. However, enough is left of Popular Front institutions by 1938 to set France apart from Finland, where little change had taken place in the country's limited structures.

Comparison of Table IIId with Tables IIIa-c reveals a close relationship clearly developing between our independent and dependent variables. Scandinavia alone shows distinct potential for GPE systems. Belgium, the Netherlands and Switzerland cannot be classified that way, but they are not straightforward collective bargaining either; that term has to be reserved for Britain and Ireland. Finland and France are still best described as contestative.

After the War: 1950

The rapid pace of change that characterised European industrial relations during the 1930s quickened during the Second World War. Further increases in repression came from German occupation and thus exogenously, but in countries not under Nazi or fascist control (Ireland, Sweden, Switzerland, the UK), and in the unique case of Finland (which fought its private war against the USSR in the midst of it all), tendencies similar to those of 1914-18, but far stronger, were evident. Labour was taken deep into national participation. And in several of the occupied countries, political elites, leading employers and unionists often retained clandestine or exiled contact, expressing a shared general national interest against the invaders and often planning together for the future. As in 1914, the war emergency had strengthened identity. People either forged institutions to give expression to that, or planned for an opportunity to do so once Nazi or fascist rule was ended.

As countries were liberated in 1944 or 1945 this latter became a reality; urgent tasks of reconstruction were planned. This extended also to Germany, Italy and Austria as the dictatorships were removed. For a period there seemed complete convergence on a model of tight tripartite co-operation, with centralised organisations of capital and labour establishing elaborate industrial relations institutions and sharing political influence. Only Ireland stood somewhat aside. The country had been less affected than others and had experienced only marginal mobilisation for industrial reconstruction. But temporary domination of a Catholic-oriented confederation extended to Ireland the general characteristics of the period of an assertion of national unity and shared identities.

However, the trend did not long remain universal. After 1947 and in association with the inception of the Cold War, a sharp divergence set in and became entrenched. We shall therefore, as after 1918, re-examine our countries after the immediate post-war period had settled down, and after identities forged in war-time had relapsed into the patterns of everyday capitalist life. We shall focus on 1950.

The most powerful labour movements remain the Scandinavians — particularly the Swedes — but now joined by the Austrians, Belgians and British. The Danes have lost their pre-eminence of earlier in the century; industrial employment remained relatively low, and in October 1950 the Social Democrats lost office, which must for a while place the Danish movement below the Belgian. The strength of the Austrian movement was increased by the fact that its associated party was vital to the stability of the new and still occupied country on the East/West border. In addition, elaborate forms of co-operation had been devised to maintain good relations between Socialist trade unionists and their Catholic (People's Party) colleagues. Austrian and Danish trade unionists, and probably Belgians as well, had to cope with higher unemployment than their counterparts in other countries with strong unions.

Table IVa: Power of Organised Labour, c. 1950, 13 European Nations

Group	Country	1	2	3	4	5	6	7
A	Sweden	51.98	67.68	L	H	52.4	1	0.5
	Norway	40.34	56.74	-	L	51.5	1	0.5
	UK	41.08	45.44	L	M	46.1	1	0.5
	Austria	41.78	64.57	M	L	43.6	0.5	1
						(44.0)	0.25	
	Denmark(8)	38.05	53.47	M	H	44.2	1	0.5
	Belgium	42.21	58.95	-	H	39.2	0.25	-
						(47.7)		
B	Netherlands	30.01	42.33	L	L	33.3	0.5	0.5
						(53.4)	0.25	
	Switzerland	26.27	35.07	L	L	31.3	0.5	0.5
						(21.2)	0.25	
	Ireland	25.11	44.83	M	M	8.7	0.25	0.5
						(41.9)		
	West Germany	24.81	35.04	H	M	34.9	0.25	1
						(31.0)		
	Finland	20.16	34.70	-	H	46.3	-	1
	Italy	26.57	47.45	-	H	31.0	0.25	1
						(55.6)		
C	France	17.93	31.35	-	H	28.6	0.25	
						(26.3)		

Notes:

Post-war boundary changes largely affect West Germany, which is the new federal republic based on western German territories; and Finland, which has ceded Karelia to the USSR.

1. Total known union membership as percentage of labour force, c.1950.
2. Total known union membership as percentage of dependent labour force, c.1950.
3. Unemployment: H= more than 10%; M= 5-10%; L= less than 5%; -=reliable figures not available on broadly comparable basis.
4. Mobilisation: M = important incidents of high labour conflict some time during preceding decade; H = incidents of exceptionally high labour conflict some time during preceding decade.
5. Share of popular vote in most recent general election secured by: Austria: Socialist Party (38.7%) Communist Party (5.1%); (People's Party in parentheses); Belgium: Socialist Party (34.5%) Communist Party (4.7%) (Christian Social Party in parentheses); Denmark: Social Democratic Party (39.6%) Communist Party (4.6%); Finland: Social Democratic Party (26.3%); Finnish Peoples Democratic Union (Communist) (20.0%); France: Communist Party (MRP in parentheses); West Germany: Social Democratic Party (29.2%) Communist Party (5.7%); Ireland: Labour Party (Fianna Fail in parentheses); Italy combined united Communist and Socialist Parties (Christian Democratic (48.5%) and Social Democratic (7.1%) Parties in parentheses); Netherlands: Labour Party (25.6%) Communist Party (7.7%) (Catholic Party (31.0%), Anti-Revolutionary Party

(13.2%), Christian Historical Party (9.2%) in parentheses); Norway: Labour Party (45.7%) Communist Party (5.8%); Sweden: Social Democratic Labour Party (46.1%) Communist Party (6.3%); Switzerland: Social Democratic Party (26.2%) Communist Party (5.1%); (Catholic Conservative Party in parentheses); UK: Labour Party.

6. Main labour-movement party sole governing party (1) dominating government coalition (0.75), or having minor role in coalition (0.5); other parties with labour-movement component in government (0.25).

7. Evidence of state dependence on organised element as an element of social order, stemming from war-time and post-war role of labour movements in reconstruction and/or anti-Communism.

8. Social Democrats lost office in October.

Sources: Labour force and electoral data drawn from Flora et al, 1983 and 1987; union membership data from Visser, 1987 (supplemented by national sources for Belgium, Finland and Ireland and in order to take account of non-confederated unions in France and Scandinavia). Other sources include: Austria: Lang, 1978, ch. 5; Belgium: Chlepner, 1956, esp. pp. 258-91; Ebertzheim, 1959; Spitaels, 1967, esp. pp. 23-31; Denmark: Hansen & Henriksen, 1980b; Finland: Knoellinger, 1960, esp. pp. 100-39; France: Reynaud, 1975; West Germany: Armingeon, 1987; Ireland, McCarthy, 1977; Italy: Turone, 1981; Netherlands: Windmuller, 1969; Norway: Galenson, 1952b; Sweden: Galenson, 1952b; Korpi, 1978; Switzerland: Höpflinger, 1976; UK: Clegg, 1972, ch. 2; 1979, ch. 5; Fox, 1985, ch. 8.

It is difficult to rank Finland, Ireland, Italy, Germany, the Netherlands and Switzerland. All had similar levels of union membership and various degrees of government involvement by unions or dependence on labour for helping to shore up national unity, in some cases because of the position of the country on the new Cold War boundary. Consociational government participation probably ranks the Netherlands and Switzerland above the others. Also, unemployment was very high in Germany, and the Italian movement had been weakened by deep and bitter divisions and by the expulsion of the majority Communist wing of the movement from national respectability. The French movement is once more clearly the weakest.

As Table IVb shows, the Austrian movement is really in a class of its own for centralisation, but the Norwegian and then the Swedish come close behind, followed at some remove by Denmark. Rankings then become more difficult to discern. Post-war reconstruction involved a considerable increase in the centralisation of the Dutch movement. In terms of the proportion of total union membership represented, the NVV was the weakest confederation in western Europe, but this defect in central control was mitigated by the fact that, partly voluntarily, partly under legal constraint, the Catholic and Protestant confederations co-operated rather than competed with it in wage bargaining and incomes policy. *De facto* therefore, Dutch unions were as centralised as those mentioned above, and probably more so than the Danes. The latter had declined considerably in relative centralisation during the previous half century, following their continuing refusal to develop an industrial union structure.

The German and Swiss cases stand rather apart. In some respects they are highly centralised, but it is really concentration, not centralisation, being rooted in a small number of internally centralised industrial unions rather than confederal power as such. When German labour reconstructed itself after its re-emergence from Nazism it did not re-erect

Table IVb: Centralisation of Labour Movements, c. 1950, 13 European Nations

Group	Country	1	2	3	4	5	6	7
A	Austria (ÖGB)	100.00	1	1	1	16	1	1
	Norway (LO)	c90.00	1	1	1	43	1	1
	Sweden (LO)	79.20	0	1	1	44	1	1
	Denmark (DsF)	84.50	1	0.5	1	69	-	1
B	Netherlands (NVV)	32.90	0.5	1	1	21	1	1
C	West Germany (DGB)	93.70	1	-	-	16	1	1
	Switzerland (SGB)	66.46	0.5	-	-	15	1	1
D	Finland (SAK)	76.50	-	1	-	38	1	-
	UK (TUC)	84.30	1	-	0.5	186	-	1
	Belgium (FGTB)	45.74	-	-	-	24	1	1
	Ireland (CIU)	53.38	-	-	0.5	23	-	1
E	France (CGT)	74.75	-	-	0.5	40*	1	-
	Italy (CGIL)	65.30	-	-	0.5	c90*	0.5	-

Notes:

(for border changes, see Note under Table IVa)
1. Percentage of total union membership within main confederation.
2. Single confederation (1) or more than one (-). 0.5 indicates that minor confederations are very small.
3. Confederation monopolises (1), has important share in (0.5) or has no part in (-) control of strike funds and/or strike calls.
4. Confederation exercises major control (1), limited control (0.5) or no control (-) over formulation of wage, etc demands.
5. Number of unions within confederation (* signifies that in France and Italy there was a complex pattern of local branches of the confederations alongside individual unions, giving a very large number of units, many of which were however parts of the confederation itself).
6. Industrial-branch union structure the sole (1), dominant (0.5) or unimportant mode (-) within confederation.
7. Individual unions strongly (1), intermittently (0.5) or not (-) centralised internally.

CGIL= Confederazione Generale Italiana del Lavoro; CGT= Confédération Générale du Travail; DGB= Deutscher Gewerkschaftsbund; DsF= Den samvirkende Fagforbund; FGTB= Fédération Générale du Travail de Belgique; CIU= Congress of Irish Unions; LO= Landsorganisasjon i Norge (Norway); Landsorganisationen i Sverige (Sweden); NVV= Nederlands Verbond van Vakverenigingen; ÖGB= Österreichischer Gewerkschaftsbund; SAK= Suomen Ammattijärjestöjen Keskusjärjestö; SGB= Schweizerischer Gewerkschaftsbund; TUC= Trades Union Congress.

Sources: Union membership data from Visser, 1987 (supplemented by national sources for Belgium, Finland and Ireland and in order to take account of non-confederated unions in France and Scandinavia). Other sources include: Austria: Traxler, 1982, esp. pp. 179-83; Belgium: Chlepner, 1956, esp. p. 268-72; Ebertzheim, 1959; Spitaels, 1967, esp. p. 78; Denmark: Hansen and Henriksen, 1980b; Finland: Knoellinger, 1960, esp. pp. 106-39; France: Reynaud, 1975, esp. pp. 100, 133-7; West Germany: Rauscher, 1985, pp. 387ff; Armingeon, 1987; Bergmann, 1985; Ireland: McCarthy, 1977, ch. IX, pp. 267-78, 536-8; Italy: Contini, 1985, esp. p. 197; Turone, 1981, esp. pp. 180-2; Netherlands: Windmuller, 1969, esp. pp. 105-67; Norway: Galenson, 1952b, esp. pp. 131-3; Sweden: Hadenius, 1976, esp. pp. 56-81, 123ff; Switzerland: Höpflinger, 1976; Parri, 1987; UK: Clegg, 1972, ch. 2; 1979, ch. 5.

the centralised institutions of Weimar; but it did use its potential centralised power to construct a highly concentrated, homogeneous set of industry unions, rather as already existed in Switzerland and was being constructed in Austria. This exceptionally neat and orderly structure, that can result only from considerable acceptance of central direction by individual unions, became and has remained a distinctive feature of the three German-speaking countries. Such a structure might seem relatively easy to achieve in a small country, but West Germany has the largest work force among the countries under study.

The Finnish SAK had acquired some central powers and monopoly position, but in other respects it remained internally fragmented as a result of tension between Social Democratic and Communist groups. The British TUC, with a very high proportion of members affiliated, was relatively centralised at this time and clearly ranks above the similarly structured but in those years divided Irish movement. On the other hand, there was a potentially growing co-ordination of wage policies among Irish unions in the newly emerging pattern of national wage rounds. The Belgians rank below the UK. Although both socialist and Catholic confederations were internally centralised and concentrated — a remarkable change over a quarter of a century — they had not really established the kind of co-operation now to be seen in the Netherlands.

The newly reconstructed and even more recently divided Italian movement ranks below the again not dissimilarly structured but more monopolistic French movement.

Among all the above, the only real exceptions to a reasonable correlation between union power and centralisation are the British and the Belgians.

War-time developments induced some changes in employer practices (Table IVc). The Scandinavians are joined in their commitment to centralised bargaining alongside close relations with government by the Austrians and Dutch. As we have seen, in neither country does this constitute a radical break in terms of centralised structure, but the willingness to deal systematically with unions at that level was new. The return of Austria to its earlier pattern of organisation is remarkable. Also, governments in both countries were now committed to a systematic policy of economic modernisation in a manner that had not been the case in the past. This intensified their interest in dealing with organised capital (as well as labour). Neat, orderly, centralised structures with extensive government involvement are also found in Germany and Switzerland, though here the centre of gravity in industrial relations is, as we would now expect, more in individual industry associations rather than peak bodies. This sets these two apart from the former group.

Table IVc: Employers' Organisations, c. 1950, 13 European Countries

Group	Country	1	2	3	4
A	Austria	H	1	1	Z
	Denmark	H	1	1	Z
	Netherlands	H	1	1	Z
	Norway	H	1	1	Z
	Sweden	H	1	1	Z
B	West Germany	H	0.5	1	W
	Switzerland	H	0.5	1	W
C	Belgium	H	-	1	W/Y
	Finland	H	-	1	W
	UK	M	-	1	W/X
D	Italy (north)	H	1	0.5	W/X
	Ireland	M	-	0.5	W/X
	France	M	-	0.5	X/W
	Italy (south)	L	-	0.5	X

Notes:

(borders as in Table IVa)
1. High (H), moderate (M) or low (L) level of organisation.
2. Strongly developed peak organisation (1) or not (-). 0.5 indicates strongly developed and centralised branch-level organisations.
3. Regularly involved as organisations with government in economic policy-making (1) or not (-). 0.5 indicates more intermittent involvement.
4. Dominant strategy in relations with unions: W=accepts collective bargaining at various levels; X=rejects dealings with organised labour; Y= required by government to come to terms with organised labour; Z= insists on centralised pattern; W/X, X/W, W/Y= mixed patterns.

Sources: Austria: Lang, 1978, esp. p. 31; Talos, 1981, esp. p. 311; Belgium: Chlepner, 1956, esp. pp. 256; Spitaels, 1967, esp. pp. 75-8; Denmark: Galenson, 1952a, ch. V; Finland: Knoellinger, 1960, esp. pp. 96-7; France: Lefranc, 1976, esp. pp. 130-1; Ehrmann, 1957, pp. 125-57; West Germany: Bergmann, 1985; Prigge, 1985, esp. pp. 400-2; Ireland: McCarthy, 1977, esp. pp. 536-8; Italy: Turone, 1981, esp. pp. 184-6; Netherlands: Windmuller, 1969, esp. pp. 232, 258; Norway: Olsen, 1983; Sweden: Korpi. 1978; Switzerland: Parri, 1987; UK: Clegg, 1972: ch. 4; 1979, ch. 3.

In a further three countries (Belgium, Finland, the UK) there were, though in varied ways, important steps towards greater central involvement by employers associations than in the past, but of an unsystematic nature. Northern Italy would also conform to this model, but the country overall appears as less integrated. Employers' organisations in France and Ireland remained weak.

Table IVd: Institutional Development of Industrial Relations, c. 1950, 13 European Countries

Group	Country	Levels				
		Plant	Locality	Branch	Nation	State
A	Austria	Ps		PQRS	pQRS	PS
	Denmark	pQ		Qrs	pQrs	ps
	Norway	pq		Qr	pQrs	PS
	Sweden	pq		Qrs	pQrs	PS
B	Netherlands	p		rs	Qrs	Ps
	Belgium	p(s)		Qs	ps	Ps
C	W. Germany	Ps	Q*	Qrs		Ps
	Switzerland	q	Q*	Q		Ps
D	UK	(p)q		Q	P	P
E	Finland		(q)	qr	r	Ps
	Ireland		q	Q	(q)r	p
F	Italy	p(q)	(q)	(q)	(q)	(p)
	France	p	(q)	(q)		(p)

Notes:

(borders as in Table IVa)

p = consultative arrangements q = collective bargaining r = formal union involvement in mediation, etc schemes s = formal union involvement in administration of policies ( ) indicates weak or patchy development capital letters indicate particularly strong development.

* indicates regional rather than local level.

Sources: Austria: Lang, 1978, esp. p. 31; Talos, 1981, ch. 7; Traxler, 1982, pp. 191-253; Belgium: Chlepner, 1956, esp. pp. 243-54, 315-20; Fafchamps, 1961; Spitaels, 1967, esp. pp. 76-8; Denmark: Galenson, 1952a, ch. VII; Hansen & Henrikson, 1980b, esp. p. 72; Finland: Knoellinger, 1960, esp. pp. 94-7; France: Reynaud, 1975, esp. pp. 265-9; West Germany: Armingeon, 1987; Bergmann, 1985; Drewes, 1958; Ireland: McCarthy, 1977, esp. pp. 536-43; Italy: Contini, 1985, esp. p. 191; Turone, 1981, 140-68; Netherlands: Windmuller, 1969, esp. p. 105-76, 338-400, 435ff, chs. 7, 11; Norway: Kvavik, 1976, ch. 3; Olsen, 1983, esp. pp. 202-3; Sweden: Korpi, 1978; Galenson, 1952b; Switzerland: Höpflinger, 1976; Parri, 1987; UK: Clegg, 1972, ch. 6; Middlemas, 1978, Part II.

Table IVd shows the state of institutional development. Ostensibly it portrays little change since 1938 in Scandinavia, but in practice there had been several developments there, with a growth of institutions tightening the web that bound government, employers and unions together in a diverse mass of relations, reaching out from the central field of wage development to involve matters of economic planning. For the first time we can see the GPE pattern emerging as the thesis predicts, and doing so precisely where Tables IVa-c would lead us to expect it. Also predictable in terms of our thesis and Tables IVa-c, but far from being anticipated by the experiences of the 1930s, are clear signs that Austria is about to embark on a similar path.

Germany and Switzerland maintain the 'split-level' pattern anticipated by our discussion of union structure. At governmental level, confederations and other central bodies are integrated in a manner similar to GPE, though across a narrower range of areas; within industry a more localised pattern prevails.

The only other cases to approximate to an emerging GPE pattern are Belgium and the Netherlands, where government was much more of an active partner in forcing the social partners into forms of co-operation.

Britain is an interesting case in that it shares with the foregoing countries a close involvement of interest associations in economic policy activities, but virtually always in a consultative, advisory capacity, rarely in administrative, decision-making organs (a point made in a comparison between organisational participation in the three Scandinavian countries and in the UK and USA by Olsen (1983: 166-71)). If persons associated with interest associations were involved in administrative bodies, they were carefully placed in non-representative roles. For example, the governing boards of nationalised industries would always include trade unionists. But they would be appointed as individuals, not as representatives; they would always come from an industry different from that involved; and they would often be retired people.

The period around 1950 represents a peak in activity of the kind we are here studying. Every country with the exception of France and Italy is busy binding its interest group representatives into some kind of system of interaction going beyond bargaining. But it is really only in Scandinavia and Austria that the conditions for GPE can be said to exist and be supported by an appropriate organisational structure, though Belgium and the Netherlands were, with state help, in the process of constructing such a system. The German and Swiss approaches share certain attributes, but with a distinct sectoral emphasis that is not the same as pure GPE.

The Mid-1970s

During the following two decades there was further divergence in national systems. The Austrians, Scandinavians, to a lesser extent the Dutch, and in their rather different ways the Germans and Swiss, continued to multiply and deepen the network of relations binding industrial relations actors, in the first four cases at least, in the manner that the theory of GPE expects.

The three countries that appeared in a provisional stage in 1950 diverged. Belgium maintained a strong degree of government-induced central co-operation, but instead of the essentially corporatist, centralised system of the neighbouring Netherlands, the country entered a period of regional and linguistic conflict which could not be resolved through consociational means and which spilled over into industrial relations. In Finland a similar government-induced model was relaxed in 1956, but instead of the planned transition to a centralised Scandinavian model, the system shifted to one of intensive and conflictual bargaining. Political conflict divided the labour movement in ways that were not conducive to central co-ordination until the late 1960s. Meanwhile Britain reverted to a collective bargaining mould as Conservative governments lost interest in economic co-ordination, to the tacit relief of the unions, until the 1960s when there was an increasingly frantic search to re-establish institutions of the kind that had deteriorated during the 1950s. But by that time the trade union movement was becoming increasingly decentralised. Irish governments began to commit themselves to modernisation in the late 1950s and therefore began to interest themselves, employers and unions in relationships going beyond collective bargaining. There was thus some convergence between the UK and Ireland.

France and Italy remained more or less at the low level of institutionalisation that had long characterised them, though with some growth of collective bargaining, especially in state industries.

In the late 1960s there were signs of new major changes. With the exception of the two Alpine nations, all our countries saw a resurgence of industrial conflict and institutional instability some time between 1968 and 1970; after 1973 the first 'oil shock' produced a wave of inflation and decline in purchasing power throughout western countries that wreaked havoc with expectations and institutions. Virtually everywhere the response of governments to this crisis was, at least until the late 1970s, to appeal to central organisations of capital and labour to help restore stability. There was something of the atmosphere of appeals to national identity typical of (and more powerful during) war-time. In some cases these appeals were abrupt, new interventions — attempts at political exchange in the simple sense. In others they were rooted in existing generalised political exchange models.

However, a further new phenomenon which has to be taken into account was a shift in the locus of workers' collective action: disaggregated, localised shop-floor strength of a tenacious kind, differing considerably from either the conservative defensiveness of traditional skilled craft workers or the transient irruptions of anger and unsettled grievance that every system had known from the early days of industrial relations. The new form of action was a product of unprecedented full employment, and it began appropriately enough in the UK, a society that had experienced both sustained full employment and a labour movement already less centralised than most.

Taking a new 'snapshot' in 1975 enables us to consider institutional development when countries were in the midst of this process. The measurement of union power is fairly straightforward in this period. There had been no major social upheavals other than industrial relations crises themselves, and there was a broad tendency for labour movements' electoral strength to be translated into government participation. Some complications arise from different unemployment levels and from a continuing tendency in some East/West border states for the integration of unions in public life to be seen as important to social stability. Overall, union movements can be placed in a rank order of strength rather than grouped (Table Va). Queries have been entered against those countries that could arguably be ranked lower. Thus Denmark and *a fortiori* Belgium might be ranked below Austria and possibly the UK, as unemployment was higher and labour participation in government less secure in the former two countries. Italy might well be ranked below Switzerland on the grounds of the greater political integration of the main wing of the labour movement in the latter. But, generalising broadly, Scandinavia, Austria, Belgium and the UK continue to dominate. The most dramatic change is the extraordinary growth in Finnish union strength, in the wake of that country's recent industrialisation. It now becomes possible to generalise about Nordic rather than Scandinavian union strength.

The stagnation of union power in Switzerland and to an extent in Austria is notable. Ireland, Italy, the Netherlands and Switzerland are difficult to rank as, though their membership levels are similar, other characteristics show considerable heterogeneity. They all rank below Germany because of the role in government of the SPD at that time; and they all stand above France, which was the only labour movement bereft of all government representation as well as the weakest in membership.

Centralisation (Table Vb) becomes more difficult to assess among the high rankers, for a reason having far more than methodological importance. The manual labour confederations of Scandinavia were losing their hegemonic role following the rise of independent white-collar groupings. Even where, as very temporarily in Sweden in 1975, these co-operated with the manual union movement, their confederations were themselves only weakly centralised.

Austrian centralisation remains virtually unscathed; the Norwegian LO keeps, temporarily, its monopoly status as a confederation and retains a bigger share of organised labour than its Swedish counterpart. Both remain very centralised. They are the only two countries to retain both high centralisation and a virtual monopoly of confederal labour representation, with Sweden ranking below them.

Belgium and the Netherlands form a separate group as centralised but not at all monopolistic. Belgium appears more centralised than in the 1950s, largely because the more centralised Catholic CSC has overtaken the social democratic FGTB as the majority confederation. The state-supported Dutch corporatist structure began to collapse in the late 1960s as secularisation eroded the relevance of the *verzuiling* system in which it was rooted. Co-operation among confederations could no longer be assumed; but a high level of centralisation remained within confederations.

The two 'branch-level-co-ordinated' cases, Germany and Switzerland, remain stable in their own terms though with, especially in the Swiss case, some loss of monopoly. It becomes increasingly difficult to decide whether Germany should rank above Belgium and the Netherlands for overall central co-ordinating capacity.

A fourth group comprises those with reasonable monopolies but only moderate levels of centralisation: Finland, Ireland, the UK and Denmark. There have been far-reaching changes in Finland, though internal conflicts within the unions still lead it to be ranked below the countries discussed so far. Ireland and the UK, which have after all the two most impressively monopolistic confederations after the ÖGB, were engaged in major efforts at

Table Va: Power of Organised Labour, c. 1975, 13 European Nations

Group	Country	1	2	3	4	5	6	7
	Sweden	86.08	93.97	VL	M	48.9	1	
	Finland	67.57	85.64	VL	H	43.8	0.5	0.5
	Norway	61.70	74.07	VL	M	35.3	0.75	
	Denmark	61.21	75.47	M	H	34.1	0.75	
	Belgium	61.32	75.24	M	M	26.7	0.25	
						(32.3)		
	Austria	51.24	65.03	VL	-	50.4	1	0.5
						(42.9)		
	UK	48.08	56.37	L	H	39.3	1	
	West Germany	32.55	38.75	L	-	45.8	0.75	
						(44.9)		
	Ireland	35.73	54.30	H	H	13.7	0.5	
						(46.2)		
	Netherlands	32.98	38.71	L	-	31.8	0.5	
						(31.3)	0.25	
	Italy	32.50	46.43	L	H	27.2	0.25	
						(53.5)		
	Switzerland	29.04	34.20	VL	-	24.9	0.5	
						(21.1)	0.25	
	France	19.15	24.27	L	H	21.3		
						(18.9)		

Notes:

(Country borders as in Table IVa)
1. Total known union membership as percentage of labour force, 1975.
2. Total known union membership as percentage of dependent labour force, 1975.
3. Unemployment: H= more than 10% registered unemployment; M= between 5% and 10% registered unemployment; L= between 2.5% and 5% registered unemployment; VL= less than 2.5% registered unemployment.
4. Mobilisation: M = important incidents of high labour conflict some time during preceding decade; H = incidents of exceptionally high labour conflict some time during preceding decade.
5. Share of popular vote in most recent general election secured by: Austria: Socialist Party (People's Party in parentheses); Belgium: Socialist Party; (Christian Social Party in parentheses); Denmark: Social Democratic Party (29.9%) Socialist People's Party (5.0%) Communist Party (4.2%); Finland: Social Democratic Party (24.9%) Finnish People's Democratic Union (Communist Party, also in government) (18.9%); France: Communist Party (Socialist Party in parentheses); West Germany: Social Democratic Party (Christian Democratic Union/Christian Social Union in parentheses); Ireland: Labour Party (Fianna Fail in parentheses); Italy: Communist Party; (Christian Democratic (38.8%), Socialist (9.6%) and Social Democratic (5.1%) Parties in parentheses; Netherlands: Labour Party (27.3%) Communist Party (4.5%) (Catholic Party (17.7%), Anti-Revolutionary Party (8.8%) and Christian Historical Party (4.8%) in parentheses); Norway: Labour Party; Sweden: Social Democratic Labour Party (43.6%) Communist Party

(5.3%); Switzerland: Social Democratic Party (Catholic Conservative Party in parentheses); UK: Labour Party.
6. Main labour-movement party sole governing party (1) dominating government coalition (0.75), or having minor role in coalition (0.5); other parties with labour-movement component in government (0.25).
7. National dependence on organised labour. In only Austria and Finland can it be contended that political elites saw incorporation of organised labour a vital to social order in this period.

Sources: Labour force and electoral data drawn from Flora et al, 1983 and 1987; union membership data from Visser, 1987 (supplemented by national sources for Belgium, Finland and Ireland and in order to take account of non-confederated unions in France and Scandinavia). Other sources include: Austria: Lang, 1978; Traxler, 1982; Belgium: Desolre, 1981; Molitor, 1978; Denmark: Hansen & Henriksen, 1980b; Finland: Koskimies, 1981; Lilja, 1983, esp. p. 225; France: Dubois et al, 1978; Reynaud, 1975, ch. V; West Germany: Armingeon, 1987; Bergmann, 1985; Brandt et al, 1982; Müller-Jentsch and Sperling, 1978; Müller-Jentsch, 1985; Ireland, Hardiman, 1986; Hillery, 1981; Italy: Regalia et al, 1978; Turone, 1981, ch. IV; Netherlands: Akkermans & Grootings, 1978; Visser, 1987; Norway; Kvavik, 1976; Olsen, 1983; Sweden: Korpi, 1978; Switzerland: Parri, 1987; UK: Clegg, 1979, ch. 5; Crouch, 1978; Fox, 1985, ch. 8.

co-ordination with employer and government groups. But their structures remained essential decentral. Denmark seems to be leaving the scope of the 'Scandinavian model', internal decentralisation combining with loss of monopoly.

Italy and France remain structurally similar, though the political pressures on the movements at that time were very different. A few years later the Italian unions were to attempt an alliance similar to that achieved by the different parts of the Dutch movement in the post-war years.

Two changes since 1950 concerned employers organisations (Table Vc). On the one hand even the countries that were weakly developed in 1950 had now experienced some organisational strengthening. On the other hand however employers' organisations have been affected by two developments also relevant to unions: the growth of the tertiary sector and of public employment. The former has been a major question for the Scandinavian employers, whose tight organisational unity had previously been possible partly because they were, like their partner LOs, concentrated in manufacturing and mining. The scope of their organisations now occupies a much smaller part of the economy than in 1950. This is less of an issue for the looser organisations of, say, Britain and Germany, where tertiary firms have long been members of central confederations. The rise of public employment is a problem for all employers' organisations except the Austrian *Kammer* system.

Within these general developments the strengthened position of Finnish employers calls for special note. The salience for the Finnish economy of the major government-negotiated trade relationship with the Soviet Union has rendered Finnish industrial employers dependent on organisation and dialogue with the state. This has then been relevant to organisation for the labour market too.

Since 1950, there has been a strong thickening of the texture of institutional relations. The scheme used in Tables Id to IVd no longer suffices to give an adequate representation. Instead we show, in Table Vd, six broad groups defined in terms of a broad characterisation

Table Vb: **Centralisation of Labour Movements, 1975, 13 European Nations**

Group	Country	1	2	3	4	5	6	7
A	Austria (ÖGB)	100.00	1	1	1	16	1	1
	Norway (LO)	72.60	1	1	0.5	35	0.5	1
	Sweden (LO)(8)	62.80	0.5	1	0.5	25	1	1
B	Belgium (CSC)	51.06	0.5	1	0.5	19	1	1
	Netherlands (NVV)	40.00	0.5	1	-	16	1	1
C	West Germany (DGB)	83.40	1	-	-	17	1	1
	Switzerland (SGB)	50.86	0.5	-	-	15	1	1
D	Finland (SAK)	64.32	1	-	1	28	1	-
	Ireland (ICTU)	97.54	1	0.5	1	89	-	-
	UK (TUC)	91.80	1	-	0.5	109	-	-
	Denmark (LO)	71.60	-	-	1	44	-	0.5
E	Italy (CGIL)	49.10	0.5	-	-	c38*	0.5	-
	France (CGT)	40.80	-	-	0.5	c42*	1	-

Notes:

(Country borders as in Table IVa)
1. Percentage of total union membership within main confederation.
2. Single confederation (1) or more than one (-). 0.5 indicates that minor confederations are very small.
3. Confederation monopolises (1), has important share in (0.5) or has no part in (-) control of strike funds and/or strike calls.
4. Confederation exercises major control (1), limited control (0.5) or no control (-) over formulation of wage, etc demands.
5. Number of unions within confederation (* signifies that in France and Italy there was a complex pattern of local branches of the confederations alongside individual unions, giving a very large number of units, many of which were however parts of the confederation itself).
6. Industrial-branch union structure the sole (1), dominant (0.5) or unimportant mode (-) within confederation.
7. Individual unions strongly (1), intermittently (0.5) or not (-) centralised internally.

CGIL= Confederazione Generale Italiana del Lavoro; CGT= Confédération Générale du Travail; CSC= Confederation des Syndicats Chretiens; DGB= Deutscher Gewerkschaftsbund; ICTU= Irish Congress of Trade Unions; LO= Landsorganisasjon i Norge (Norway); Landsorganisationen i Danmark (Denmark); i Sverige (Sweden); NVV= Nederlands Verbond van Vakverenigingen; ÖGB= Österreichischer Gewerkschaftsbund; SAK= Suomen Ammattijärjestöjen Keskusjärjestö; SGB= Schweizerischer Gewerkschaftsbund; TUC= Trades Union Congress.
Sources: Labour force and electoral data drawn from Flora et al, 1983 and 1987; union membership

data from Visser, 1987 (supplemented by national sources for Belgium, Finland and Ireland and in order to take account of non-confederated unions in France and Scandinavia). Other sources include: Austria: Lang, 1978, ch. 9; Traxler, 1982, ch. 4; Belgium: Desolre, 1981; Molitor, 1978; Denmark: Hansen & Henriksen, 1980b, esp. pp.162-4, 316-24; Rasmussen, 1986; Finland: Koskimies, 1981; Lilja, 1983, esp. ch 3; France: Dubois et al, 1978; Reynaud, 1975, ch. V; West Germany: Armingeon, 1987; Bergmann et al, 1975; Bergmann, 1985; Brandt et al, 1982; Müller-Jentsch and Sperling, 1978; Müller-Jentsch, 1985; Streeck, 1982; Ireland: Hardiman, 1986; Hillery, 1981; Italy: Regalia, 1986; Regalia et al, 1978; Turone, 1981, ch. IV; Netherlands: Akkermans & Grootings, 1978; Visser, 1987; Norway; Kvavik, 1976; Olsen, 1983; Sweden: Korpi, 1978; Stephens, 1979; Switzerland: Höpflinger, 1976; Parri; 1987; UK: Clegg, 1979, ch. 5; Crouch, 1978.

Table Vc: **Employers' Organisations, c. 1975, 13 European Countries**

Group	Country	1	2	3	4
Aa	Austria	H	1	1	Z
	Finland	H	1	1	Z
Ab	Denmark	H	1	1	(Z)
	Netherlands	H	1	1	(Z)
	Norway	H	1	1	(Z)
	Sweden	H	1	1	(Z)
B	West Germany	H	-	1	W
	Switzerland	H	-	1	W
Ca	Belgium	H	-	1	W/Z
Cb	UK	M	-	0.5	W/(Z)
	Ireland	M	-	0.5	W/(Z)
	Italy (north)	H	1	0.5	W/Z
D	France	M	-	0.5	X/W
	Italy (south)	L	-	0.5	X/W

Notes:

(Country boundaries as in Table IVa)
1. High (H), moderate (M) or low (L) level of organisation.
2. Strongly developed peak organisation (1) or not (-). 0.5 indicates strongly developed and centralised branch-level organisations.
3. Regularly involved as organisations with government in economic policy-making (1) or not (-). 0.5 indicates more intermittent involvement.
4. Dominant strategy in relations with unions: W=accepts collective bargaining at various levels; X=rejects dealings with organised labour; Y= required by government to come to terms with organised labour; Z= insists on centralised pattern; W/X, X/W, W/Y= mixed patterns.

Sources: Austria: Lang, 1978; Traxler, 1982, ch.4; 1986; Belgium: Desolre, 1981; Molitor, 1978;
     Denmark: Hansen & Henriksen, 1980b; Rasmussen, 1985; Finland: Koskimies, 1981; Lilja, 1983,
     esp. ch. 3; France: Bunel & Saglio, 1984; Lefranc, 1976, esp. pp. 159ff and 191ff; Reynaud, 1975,
     ch. III; West Germany: Armingeon, 1987; Bergmann, 1985; Bunn, 1984; Müller-Jentsch, 1985;
     Ireland, Hardiman, 1986; Hillery, 1981; Italy: Treu & Martinelli, 1984; Turone, 1981, ch. IV;
     Netherlands: van Noorden, 1984; Norway; Kvavik, 1976; Olsen, 1983; Sweden: Skogh, 1984;
     Switzerland: Katzenstein, 1984, ch. 3; Parri, 1987; UK: Armstrong, 1984; Clegg, 1979, ch. 3;
     Grant & Marsh, 1977

of their industrial relations systems. In group A (Austria, Sweden, Norway, Denmark) unions had been deeply engaged throughout the post-war period in a wide range of national-level institutions that enabled/required them to participate in economy-wide and more detailed decision-making on wage movements, labour market policy and other matters. These are the cases where the GPE model can finally be seen in practice. It is notable that Denmark remains clearly a member of this group even though it has lost some of the centralisation that our thesis requires for GPE. This draws our attention to the fact that disengagement from GPE once it exists requires dislodging organised labour from the place it has secured. In the mid-1970s, with the Social Democrats in government, there was unlikely to be any push in such a direction. By the early 1980s, with increased unemployment and a bourgeois government, some decline in GPE in the Danish system can be detected, but that lies beyond the scope of this article. With the exception of Denmark, the countries found in this group are those predictable by our thesis on the basis of the independent variables obtaining in the mid 1970s.

The remaining groups also continue as we would expect. Similar institutions for national participation by union leaderships existed in Belgium and the Netherlands (Group B) as in Group A, though limited to a generally narrower range of issues. Similar again are Group C, Germany and Switzerland, except that there remains in these countries something of a split between national-level participation by confederal and union leaders and more localised collective bargaining.

In Finland, Britain and Ireland (Group D) we also find in the mid-1970s steps towards greatly increased national involvement by central union leaderships, probably more intensively in Finland but prominent in all three cases. This group is distinguished from all the foregoing by the recency of these moves. They date back to the late 1960s, though in the UK there had been an earlier 'false start' in the 1940-50 period. The institutions do not yet have the intricate complexity of constantly growing scope for exchanges typical of GPE as such, so we should speak (as we did of Scandinavia in the 1930s and Austria in the 1950s) of incipient GPE. It is relevant for our thesis that, while these countries (except perhaps Ireland) were notable for union strength in the mid-1970s, they all ranked low on centralisation. This must cast some doubt on the viability of the GPE model. Looking forward a few years, by the early 1980s a decline in union power had taken place in the UK and perhaps also Ireland, but not in Finland where unemployment has remained low and labour participation central to political stability. An account of the 1980s might therefore see Denmark and Finland changing places between Groups A and D, with the latter group

**Table Vd: Institutional Development in Industrial Relations, c.1975,
                    13 European Countries**

Group	Description	Country
A	Unions deeply involved in very wide range of bi- and tripartite administrative organs	Austria Denmark Norway Sweden
B	Similar to A but less extensive	Belgium Netherlands
C	Similar to B, but split between national-level administrative participation and more local but controlled collective bargaining	West Germany Switzerland
D	Incipient patterns of union involvement as in A and B	Finland Ireland UK
E	Incipient political exchange	Italy
F	Little development	France

Notes:

(Country borders as in Table IVa)
Sources: Austria: Lang, 1978, ch. 7; Marin, 1982; Traxler, 1982, ch. 4; Belgium: Desolre, 1981; Molitor, 1978; Denmark: Hansen & Henrikson, 1980b, p. 345ff; Rasmussen, 1986; Finland: Helander, 1984; Helander & Anckar, 1983; France: Dubois et al, 1978; Reynaud, 1975, chs. V, IX; Sellier, 1978; West Germany: Brandt et al, 1982; Müller-Jentsch & Sperling, 1978; Ireland: Hardiman, 1986; Italy: Regalia et al, 1978; Regini, 1981; Treu, 1983; Turone, 1981, 140-68; Netherlands: Akkermans & Grootings, 1978; Visser, 1987; Norway, Kvavik, 1976; Olsen, 1983; Sweden: Korpi, 1978; Switzerland: Höpflinger, 1976; Katzenstein, 1984; Parri, 1987; UK: Crouch, 1978; 1982; Middlemas, 1983.

no longer characterised as incipient GPE.

Italy shares several of the characteristics of Group D: scope for overcoming the alienation of the labour movement being pursued by a variety of political and industrial forces. But the degree of institutional development for such integration remains much weaker: the concept of political exchange remains more suitable for describing the situation. But Italy should no longer be grouped with France, where very little activity of even this kind took place outside moments of crisis, though were we giving a full account of industrial relations systems we would comment on the growth of collective bargaining in that country. That these countries should rank last is again predicted by our thesis.

3. Conclusions

The above discussion has demonstrated the usefulness of the idea of GPE as a means of describing a form of industrial relations that differs from collective bargaining or crisis political exchange, and the dependence of the existence of that model on certain properties of union power and union and employer organisation. It has also shown how extensive GPE has been as a tendency towards which many systems move, but at the same time it has both shown the absence of either inevitability or irreversibility in that process.

The general assertion of established theories of industrial relations, that labour's growing strength, if not suppressed, will lead to increased contract relations with employers, is confirmed. We have also seen that continued growth in labour's power will lead to a capacity to act at state level, but this is not a simple function of union power, as the cases of the British TUC (high power but for long poor state capacity) and the Finnish SAK, the Belgian FGTB, the Dutch NVV, and the Swiss SGB (the other way round) show.

A centralised labour movement will begin to engage in GPE rather than persist with pure bargaining alone, but the process has often been very slow and should not be seen as irreversible. Change will remain unilinear except in the case of (a) a decline in labour's power or (b) a change in its level of decision-making capacity, with examples of (a) having been Austria and Germany in the 1920s, and of (b) being Denmark and the Netherlands, losing capacity now, and Finland currently gaining it.

There is a paradox in that a mix of centralised political action and localised bargaining seems associated with an instability of GPE structures in Denmark, Finland, Italy and the UK, but with extreme stability in Germany and Switzerland. The answer lies in the different forms of articulation between the levels. In the former list of countries autonomous and often oppositional shop-steward or similar rank-and-file movements led decentralised action. In Germany and Switzerland the lower levels were anticipated, even shaped by union leaderships, employers and/or the law. Indeed, rather than representing oppositional forces they have often been focusses for identity-inducing structures at company level.

We may also venture an answer to a final question. In the 1930s in Scandinavia, and elsewhere after World War II, desperate, crisis political exchange was able to generate what eventually became stable GPE models. Why did the spate of similar, slightly less panic-ridden, activity in the 1970s not have a similar outcome? In those earlier years the labour market was, except in Finland and Ireland, dominated by manual work in manufacturing industry. *Ceteris paribus*, this was fertile soil for the erection of country-wide organisations of capital and labour with certain strategic goals. What was often lacking was mutual acceptance by the social partners and the state of each other's long-term survival. In particular, the option of excluding organised labour altogether was always present for the other two actors.

As the century has progressed there has been, more or less, an increasing willingness of the two sides to come to terms with each other, but a decline in both the willingness of workers to be co-ordinated by a solidaristic organisation, and, perhaps more important, a collapse of the manual manufacturing model of employment.

'Solidaristic organisation' presents us with an interesting irony. In the first instance such solidarities focus and concentrate identities at levels other than the nation state and therefore work directly against the generation of national-level identity. These may be class solidarities (as in Scandinavia at one time), religio-cultural ones (as in Belgium, the Netherlands, Switzerland) or a combination of the two (as in Austria, France, Italy). GPE systems eventually became established where such solidarities helped construct centralised organisations able to participate in strategic bargaining — though this was by no means a sufficient condition for effective centralisation as the French and Italian cases show. Where it did work, solidarities that had initially undermined national identity subsequently helped construct institutions that became, as hypothesised at the outset of this article, a base for forging national co-operation. Precisely because leaders, especially of labour, were co-ordinating combative organisations, they were able to mobilise loyalty and obedience; which they then used to enter relationships with their 'enemies', the employers, in order to secure co-operation.

To complete the irony, in recent decades the sub-national solidarities have atrophied, partly because of the very success of the national institutions. But since the latter have been erected on the base of the former, they are in turn threatened. We see the symptoms of this in such phenomena as the secularisation of the Netherlands and the eruption in the late 1960s of decentralised industrial militancy impatient with centralised union forces that had come to represent 'bureaucracy' rather than an increasingly unrealistic class solidarity (Streeck, 1982).

Either the mid-1930s or the immediate post-war years were moments, in various countries, when class solidarities, national co-operativeness and the dominance of the manufacturing economy peaked. Neo-corporatism may have been 'discovered' in the 1970s, but the heyday of it and its modus operandi (generalised political exchange) was from around 1935 or 1945 to around 1965. The 1970s seem in terms of our model of institutional development (Table Vd) the peak of elaboration of GPE, but by then the supports were crumbling.

Since then countries have moved in contrary directions. Where GPE models already existed in the mid 1970s, there was often commitment to keep them working, if often with reduced ambitions. Elsewhere, the failure of new 1970s experiments has led to a search for very different solutions — including both mild returns to the repression of organised labour and a new search for means of securing the identity of workers to their companies, or to the capitalist system, that do not require the intermediary of unions performing within GPE.

Note

This is the revised draft of the paper for the workshop: 'Political Exchange: Between Governance and Ideology', Badia Fiesolana, Florence, December 15-18 1986, organised by Bernd Marin. I am grateful to participants in the original seminar and at a seminar in the department of sociology, University of Leeds, for valuable critical comments.

The Political Calculus of Inflation and Unemployment in Western Europe
A Game-Theoretical Interpretation[1]

Fritz W. Scharpf

1. Introduction

Political scientists and economists with a comparative bent have for some time been fascinated by the opportunities for theory testing and theory building provided by the large-scale "natural experiment" of the worldwide economic crisis that began in the early 1970s. Compared to the preceding decade, the middle and late 1970s and the early 1980s were a very difficult period for the highly industrialized Western countries. Economic growth and employment growth were reduced by half, while rates of unemployment and inflation levels were on the average twice as high (Table 1).

But even as the average economic and employment performance of all OECD countries declined after 1973, the relative distance between the more successful and the less successful countries increased for most indicators of economic performance. Equally interesting is the fact that cross-national differences do not seem to correspond to conventional economic hypotheses (Therborn, 1986). Even the almost tautological link between economic growth and employment is weak ($R^2 = 0.32$)[2], and the relationships between economic and employment growth on the one hand and inflation on the other hand are neither strongly positive (as the once-popular "Phillips curve" had suggested) nor negative (as was often claimed in the late 1970s) but simply nonexistent (with R-squares of 0.02 and 0.06, respectively).

A glance at a scatterplot of part of the same data (Figure 1) reveals even more clearly that at every level of employment change (negative, zero and positive), there have been countries with low and others with high rates of inflation, and the same is true for the other indicators as well. Confronted with the worldwide crisis, different countries apparently have achieved differing profiles of economic performance — some reaching a compromise among several goals, some doing poorly in most respects, and some doing extremely well in one dimension and extremely poorly in another.

Political scientists have attempted to explain this variance in a series of cross-national quantitative studies. In pursuit of the elusive question "Does Politics Matter?" they focused

**Table 1:   Changes in Gross Domestic Product, Employment, and Consumer
Prices, Average Rates of Unemployment 1963 (1968)-73 and 1973-83**

	GDP GROWTH		EMPLOYM GROWTH		UNEMPLOYMENT		INFLATION	
	63:73	73:83	63:73	73:83	68:73	73:83	63:73	73:83
CAN	5.7	2.8	3.6	2.3	5.4	7.8	3.7	9.3
USA	4.1	2.2	2.6	1.9	4.6	7.1	3.6	8.3
JAP	9.8	4.2	1.5	0.9	1.2	2.0	6.2	8.2
AUS	5.6	2.5	3.3	0.9	2.0	5.5	4.0	11.2
NZ	4.0	2.0	2.4	1.1	0.3	1.9	5.4	13.4
A	5.1	2.6	-0.1	0.0	1.5	2.2	4.2	6.1
B	4.9	2.1	0.8	-0.7	2.5	7.9	4.1	8.0
CH	4.1	0.6	0.8	-0.7	-	0.4	4.5	4.7
D	4.4	1.9	0.0	-0.7	1.0	3.8	3.6	5.0
DK	4.0	1.7	1.4	0.0	1.0	6.9	6.3	10.4
F	5.5	2.6	0.9	0.1	2.5	5.4	4.7	10.9
SF	4.9	3.2	0.2	1.1	2.6	4.6	6.2	11.8
GB	3.3	1.6	0.2	-0.5	3.3	6.7	5.3	13.3
I	5.0	2.4	-0.5	0.7	5.7	7.3	4.9	16.2
N	4.3	3.9	1.7	1.8	1.7	2.0	5.3	9.4
NL	5.1	1.9	0.7	0.6	1.5	6.5	5.5	6.7
S	4.0	1.8	0.6	0.9	2.2	2.3	4.9	9.9
AVERAGE	4.9	2.4	1.2	0.6	2.4	4.7	4.8	9.6
RANGE*	1.4	0.9	1.2	0.9	2.2	1.6	0.9	3.1
COEFF. VAR.**	0.3	0.4	1.0	1.6	0.7	0.5	0.2	0.3

* Relative Range = (Maximum - Minimum) / Average
** Coefficient of Variability = Standard Deviation / Average

GDP 73-83:	EMP	73-83: R^2 = 0.32
GDP 73-83:	INFLA	73-83: R^2 = 0.02
EMP 73-83:	INFLA	73-83: R^2 = 0.06
EMP 73-83:	UNEMP	73-83: R^2 = 0.01

Source: OECD Historical Statistics 1960-1984.

first on the party-political orientation of national governments, finding that left-of-center governments were indeed associated with lower rates of unemployment and higher rates of inflation than conservative governments (Hibbs, 1977). When that relationship, which had been established for the 1960s, did not hold up in the 1970s, the focus shifted to "tripartite" institutional arrangements linking the state with peak associations of capital and labor, whose relevance for the general "governability" of countries had been postulated by Philippe Schmitter's (1974; 1981) theory of "neo-corporatism." In particular, it could be shown in a considerable number of studies using a variety of indicators that, by and large, countries with powerful, organizationally concentrated and centralized labor movements and left-of-center governments had done relatively well in economic terms during the 1970s (Cameron, 1978; 1984; Schmidt, 1982; 1983; Paloheimo, 1984; Lange and Garrett, 1985).

But, once again, the explanations that were successful in one decade did not survive far into the next. Some of the former model countries got into trouble in the 1980s, and other countries that were clearly not dominated by parties of the Left, and in which organized labor was weak and fragmented, were doing relatively well. In response, the "corporatist" model was revised to emphasize the functional equivalence of labor-dominated concerta-tions between organized economic interests and the state and of Japanese or Swiss-style "corporatism without labor" (Schmidt, 1986; Garrett and Lange, 1986; Wilensky and Turner, 1987).

Although I have no quarrel with the quest for radically simplified explanatory theories that are testable with available data in quantitative cross-national studies, I think that most studies of the world economic crisis have underestimated the need for, and the difficulties of, developing "grounded theory" (Glaser and Strauss, 1967; Glaser, 1978) in political

Figure 1:   Inflation and Employment Changes 1973-1983

Inflation 73: 83

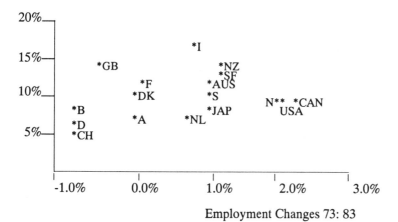

Employment Changes 73: 83

economy. In particular, it seems that political science studies have suffered as much from ignoring the underlying (and changing) economic problems as economic studies are usually (but not invariably: see Flanagan, Soskice and Ulman, 1983) suffering from a neglect of institutional differences among countries. Comparative studies based on the neo-corporatist paradigm have been criticized for the imprecision of the institutional variables employed (Therborn, 1986: 98-101). More damaging, however, is the theoretical weakness of the linkages postulated between these institutional arrangements on the one hand, and the economic outcomes to be explained on the other. However difficult, we must try to disentangle the interaction between changes in the economic environment, the economic strategy choices available to national policy makers, and the institutional conditions facilitating and constraining such choices, if we hope to develop explanations of economic performance that are not so easily upset by the mere passage of time (Scharpf, 1984; Hall, 1986; Martin, 1986a).

In my own understanding (Scharpf, 1981), institutional conditions do not determine public policy, and they can never fully explain policy outcomes. But they do define the identity, and hence the institutional self-interest, of "corporate actors" (Coleman, 1974) as well as the "repertoire" of legitimate and routinized policy responses.[3] Countries will be economically successful if their institutionally defined repertoire contains responses that permit the fashioning of coordinated "strategies" which, under given conditions, are able to achieve politically preferred goals.

One implication of this view is immediately obvious: Institutional repertoires affect economic outcomes by constraining strategy choices, facilitating some and excluding others. Thus their effect can only be defined in relation to particular strategies that are actively or hypothetically considered — just as the effect of particular strategies is always relative to a given economic environment and to a set of political goals which are actively or hypothetically considered. Hence it is *a priori* implausible to assume that a particular set of institutions would be *generally* favorable to economic performance, regardless of the economic environment and the goals actively pursued by political actors.

Furthermore, and unfortunately for theory-oriented research, all three sets of variables — institutionally defined repertoires, economic conditions, and political goals — interact strongly with one another, and they also change over time. Under stable economic conditions, policy repertoires will usually be adjusted to permit the attainment of political priorities — or else political goals will be redefined to eliminate any persistent "dissonance" with what is economically or institutionally feasible. Thus in the stable and economically benign 1960s, practically all countries were institutionally able to formulate and implement reasonably successful full-employment strategies — and in the more hostile international environment of the mid-1980s almost all countries had struck full employment from their list of attainable and actively pursued political goals.

Only when there is a significant and relatively sudden change of the external economic environment, while political goals are still unchanged, and while the adaptation of policy repertoires is impeded by institutional inertia (Hannan and Freeman, 1977; 1984) might one

be able to isolate the influence of institutional conditions on economic performance —
because it would then be possible that the strategies required to cope with the new problems
might be beyond the institutionally defined capabilities of some, but not all, countries. Thus
the worldwide economic crisis after 1973, confronting all industrialized countries with the
same external shock, did indeed provide a unique opportunity for theory-oriented research.
But that opportunity can be exploited only if the real complexity of the economic,
institutional, and political issues involved is reflected in the theoretical model used.

2. The Puzzle

In the spirit of the "most similar case" strategy (Przeworski and Teune, 1970) the following
analysis is based on a study of the economic and employment policies pursued by four
Western European countries, Austria, Great Britain, Sweden, and West Germany (Scharpf,
1981, 1984, 1987b). All of them were governed, in the first critical years after 1973, by Socialist, Social Democratic or Labour parties that had a clear political commitment to
maintaining full employment. Furthermore, on the eve of the crisis all four countries found
themselves in rather similar, and on the whole quite comfortable, economic circumstances
(Table 2).

Britain, for once, did not look at all like the "sick man of Europe" in 1973, achieving the
highest rate of economic growth and doing relatively well on inflation. By comparison,
Austria and Sweden might have had more reason to be worried about their relative performance. Yet immediately after the onset of the crisis in the fall of 1973, the four countries began
to move apart economically (Table 3).

Table 2:   Economic Performance Indicators for 1973 (in %)

1973	A	D	GB	S
GDP GROWTH	4.9	4.7	7.6	4.0
GDP INFLATION	7.6	6.4	7.1	7.0
UNEMPLOYMENT	1.1	0.8	3.0	2.5

Source: OECD Historical Statistics 1960-1984.

Table 3:   Average Performance Indicators 1974-1979 (in %)

1974-1979	A	D	GB	S
GDP GROWTH	2.9	2.3	1.5	1.8
GDP INFLATION	6.0	4.8	16.0	10.6
UNEMPLOYMENT	1.8	3.2	5.0	1.9

Source: OECD Historical Statistics 1960-1984.

Between 1974 and 1979, Britain became clearly the worst case of the four, with the lowest rate of economic growth, by far the highest rate of inflation, and the highest unemployment as well. By contrast, Austria now had the best all-round record, with the highest economic growth, the second-lowest inflation and the lowest unemployment. Even more interesting is the contrast between the two countries with intermediate performances: West Germany suffered the largest increase in unemployment compared to 1973 and achieved the greatest degree of price stability; Sweden was even able to reduce unemployment during the first five years of the crisis but suffered from two-digit inflation.

My attempt to explain this puzzle will proceed at several levels: I will begin with a brief characterization of the economic environment after 1973, and of the strategic options available to economic policy makers, followed by a brief overview of the actual policy choices in each of the four countries. I will then proceed to develop an explanatory model that relates economically feasible policy choices to the institutional self-interest of the major economic-policy actors under changing conditions of the economic environment. Within the confines of this article it is obviously impossible to give a full account of the conditions and processes of economic-policy making in the four countries. Instead, I will try to present the outline of a theoretical argument that, while still radically simplifying the "story" of real-world events, tries to capture more of its "institutional logic" than other theoretical models seem able to do.[4]

3. Economic Problems and Policy Choices After 1973

For the industrialized democracies in general, the dominant problem of the 1970s was economic "stagflation" — the simultaneous occurrence of exceptionally high rates of inflation and of levels of mass unemployment unheard of in the postwar period. In order to understand the intractability of the problem, it is useful to distinguish between causes on the demand side and on the supply side of the markets for goods and services (Malinvaud, 1977). Inflation could be either of the "demand pull" or the "cost push" variety, and unemployment could be either "Keynesian" (if firms were unable to sell as much as they would have liked to produce at current prices and costs) or "classical" (if firms did not find it profitable to produce more at current prices and costs). It was also possible that more than one type of problem was manifest at a given time (Figure 2).

In the early 1970s, the world economy had already suffered from a good deal of demand inflation, which had been initiated by the US decision to finance the Vietnam war without raising taxes. Price rises accelerated significantly, however, when the powerful cost push of a raw materials boom and of the first oil crisis was added in 1973/74. At the same time, the twelve-fold increase of the oil bill within a few months constituted a sudden transfer of purchasing power from the oil-consuming industrial countries to the oil-exporting countries. As these were not immediately able to spend their new wealth in the international markets for goods and services, OPEC surpluses jumped from 8 Billion US Dollars in 1973 to 60 Billion in 1974 (OECD Economic Outlook 28: 125). The immediate consequence was a demand gap of corresponding magnitude in the industrialized countries which, if it was not compensated, would generate "Keynesian" unemployment.

For this combination of cost-push inflation and demand-gap unemployment, national macro-economic policy makers and the prevailing practice of Keynesian demand management were ill prepared. Their major policy instruments were government fiscal policy and central bank monetary policy.[5] Both could be used to reflate aggregate demand, by increasing government expenditures or cutting taxes, and by increasing the money supply and lowering interest rates. Alternatively, both instruments could be used restrictively, by reducing the fiscal deficit and the money supply. As both sets of instruments affect the same parameters of aggregate demand, they needed to be employed in parallel in order to be effective. Under the conditions of stagflation, that meant that governments were able to fight either inflation or unemployment, but not both at the same time. Worse yet, in trying to solve one problem they would aggravate the other one (Figure 3).

The dilemma could be avoided only if economic policy makers were not limited to the

Figure 2: Typology of Economic Policy Problems in the 1970s

Source of Problem

	Demand Side	Supply Side
Inflation	Demand Pull Inflation	Cost Push Inflation
Unemployment	Demand Gap ("Keynesian") Unemployment	Profit Gap ("Classical") Unemployment

Nature of Problem

Figure 3: Effects of Fiscal and Monetary Policy Under Conditions of Stagflation

	Demand Gap Unemployment	Cost Push Inflation
expansionary	helps a lot	hurts
restrictive	hurts a lot	helps

Fiscal and Monetary Policy

use of fiscal and monetary policy, but were also able to influence wage settlements, which, although they affect aggregate demand as well, have a larger and more direct impact upon the supply side of the economy (Figure 4). Thus the inclusion of wage policy in the macro-economic tool kit greatly increased the range of problems that macro-economic policy could deal with (Weintraub, 1978).

Quite apart from the controversy about whether unions were actually responsible for the rise of inflation in the early 1970s, the direct impact of wages on the costs of production made wage restraint a highly plausible defense against the rising tide of cost-push inflation. In practical terms, that meant that the unions would need to refrain from exploiting their full bargaining power — which was considerable as long as the government was able to maintain full employment. In order to succeed, they would have to accept settlements which, when discounted by the increase of labor productivity, kept the rise of unit labor costs below the current rate of inflation.[6] In "exchange," the government was then free to use its own policy instruments to reflate aggregate demand in order to maintain full employment.

If that optimal "concertation"[7] of government and union strategies was practiced, it was possible to avoid both a steep rise of unemployment and runaway inflation, even under the crisis conditions of the mid-1970s (but not in the 1980s).[8] If, however, the unions were unwilling or unable to practice wage restraint, inflation would continue; and if the government would not reflate the economy, unemployment would increase (Figure 5).

Figure 4:   Effects of Wage Policy Under Conditions of Stagflation

	Demand Gap Unemployment	Cost Push Inflation
Wage Policy		
moderate	hurts	helps a lot
aggressive	helps	hurts a lot

Figure 5:   Levels of Inflation and Unemployment as Outcomes of Government and Union Strategies Under Conditions of Stagflation

	Wage Policy	
Fiscal and Monetary Policy	moderate	aggressive
expansionary	inflation: moderate unemployment: low	inflation: very high unemployment: low
restrictive	inflation: low unemployment: high	inflation: high unemployment: very high

If we now take a cursory look at the actual policy patterns in the four countries (Figure 6), it is clear that the economically optimal concertation between government macro-economic policy and union policy (represented by "X's" in the top left cell in each of the coordination matrices) was not consistently achieved.

(a) In *1974*, the immediate response of government policy to the beginning crisis was expansionary in all countries except West Germany — and even there the fiscal deficit increased as much as it did in the other three countries. The overall deflationary effect was due to the tight-money policy of the central bank. At the same time, the unions in all four countries continued their more or less aggressive wage strategies (Table 4, below). As a consequence, employment was stabilized in all countries except West Germany, which suffered very large job losses in 1974-76, but had the lowest rate of inflation of all OECD countries.

(b) By *1976*, however, the severity of the crisis was realized everywhere, and unions had begun to moderate their wage claims — earliest in Germany and most dramatically in Britain, where inflation had exceeded 24% in 1975. In the "Social Contract" with the Labour

Figure 6: **Coordination of Government Policy and Union Wage Policy: 1974-1982**

Union Wage Policy (m = moderate, a = aggressive)

Government Policy	1974 m	1974 a	1976 m	1976 a	1978 m	1978 a	1980 m	1980 a	1982 m	1982 a
AUSTRIA										
expansionary	0		X		X		X			
restrictive									0	
FR GERMANY										
expansionary					X		X			
restrictive	0		0						0	
GREAT BRITAIN										
expansionary	0	X								
restrictive				0		0		0		
SWEDEN										
expansionary	0		0		X		X			
restrictive									0	

government, the Trades Union Congress agreed to limit wage and salary increases to six pounds per week for everybody in 1976 and not much more in 1977. Only in Sweden did the unions still pursue an aggressive wage policy, whereas the Bourgeois coalition government, new in office after more than forty years of Social Democratic rule, was doing everything in its power to defend full employment.

(c) After another two years, in *1978*, policy coordination improved in West Germany and Sweden, and deteriorated in Great Britain. With inflation below 3%, and with the help of considerable American pressure at the Bonn Summit of 1978 (Putnam and Bayne, 1984), Chancellor Schmidt was finally able to persuade the *Bundesbank* of the wisdom and feasibility of a substantial fiscal and monetary reflation of domestic demand. As the unions continued on their course of wage moderation, employment in West Germany profited until 1980 from the country's assumption of the "locomotive" role. In Sweden, the unions now also accepted the need for wage moderation, even though unemployment was actually falling.

By contrast, the British Labour government, in an effort to defend the pound against devaluation and to push down inflation that was still above 15%, had switched to a half-hearted monetarism in spite of comparatively high levels of unemployment. Inflation declined below 9% in 1978, but now the unions were no longer able to uphold their part of the Social Contract. The crippling strikes of the "Winter of Discontent" and the high wage settlements that ended it pushed inflation up again and prepared the ground for Margaret Thatcher's election victory in the spring of 1979.

(d) By *1980*, therefore, the new British government was practicing a brand of monetarism

Table 4:   Consumer Price Inflation and Annual Increases of Unit Labor Costs in Manufacturing, 1974-1980 (in %)

	1974	1975	1976	1977	1978	1979	1980
AUSTRIA:							
Inflation	9.5	8.4	7.3	5.5	3.6	3.7	6.4
Unit L.C.	9.7	15.1	0.5	5.6	1.2	-1.8	5.9
GREAT BRITAIN:							
Inflation	16.0	24.2	16.5	15.8	8.3	13.4	18.0
Unit L.C.	24.0	32.6	12.7	11.7	14.9	17.2	21.0
SWEDEN:							
Inflation	9.9	9.8	10.3	11.4	10.0	7.2	13.7
Unit L.C.	12.9	19.3	16.7	11.1	8.3	-0.1	9.3
FR GERMANY:							
Inflation	7.0	6.0	4.5	3.7	2.7	4.1	5.5
Unit L.C.	9.1	6.8	0.6	5.3	5.0	2.4	7.3

Source: OECD Historical Statistics 1960-1984.

that was not half-hearted at all, while the unions initially continued the aggressive wage drive that had led to the defeat of the Labour government. As a consequence, inflation returned to high levels while unemployment began to rise steeply. In the other three countries Keynesian concertation continued as before, even as the international economic and monetary environment was again worsening under the double impact of the second oil crisis and of the American conversion to monetarism.

(e) But by *1982* the changes in the international environment had worked their way through the policy-making processes of all four countries. Monetary policy became restrictive everywhere, and even Austria and Sweden, which were still, or again, governed by Social Democrats, tried to reduce fiscal deficits under the compulsion of escalating interest rates. At the same time, the unions in all four countries, either out of insight or under the compulsion of rapidly rising unemployment, not only moderated their wage claims but accepted significant real-wage losses. In short, the variance among the macro-economic strategies of the four countries had all but disappeared by 1982.[9]

4. The Perspectives of Macro-Economic Actors

In the 1970s, however, countries still had a choice among macro-economic strategies with significantly different outcomes. So why were not all of them able to achieve, and maintain, the optimal concertation of fiscal and monetary reflation and union wage moderation that would have defended full employment and price stability at the same time?

The problem was not primarily a cognitive one: After some initial misjudgments of the nature of the crisis, the double threat of cost-push inflation and demand-gap unemployment, as well as the characteristics of an economically optimal policy response, were well understood in all four countries. Policy makers were also not yet inhibited by the notion that demand reflation might be entirely without effect upon the real economy, or that wages ought to be settled entirely by the laws of supply and demand in the market. Collective bargaining was effective in all four countries, and wages were understood as a "political price" whose determination could also be influenced, within limits, by considerations of macro-economic policy. But it was also understood, explicitly in Britain as part of a pre-election agreement between the TUC and the Labour Party (Crouch, 1982; Bornstein and Gourevitch, 1984), and implicitly in the other three countries, that cooperation could not be compelled. The record of statutory wage and price controls in the late 1960s and early 1970s, in Britain and in the United States, had been so negative (Frye and Gordon, 1981) that voluntary wage restraint was the only option seriously considered in the four countries (Flanagan, Soskice, and Ulman, 1983).

But if the economics of the problem were so essentially simple, and reasonably well-understood by policy makers, why wasn't the optimal strategy practiced everywhere throughout the whole period? The reason, I suggest, lies in the inevitable discrepancy between the perspective of macro-economic theory on the one hand, and the action perspectives of those "corporate actors" who are actually involved in macro-economic policy choices on the other hand. They are, each of them, pursuing their own versions of the

Figure 7:   Macro-Economic Coordination: The Union View

Wage Policy

Fiscal and Monetary Policy	moderate	aggressive
expansionary	real wages: low unemployment: low	real wages: moderate unemployment: low
restrictive	real wages: moderate unemployment: high	real wages: high unemployment: very high

collective interest — and these are influenced not only by their differing politico-economic ideologies, but also by the perceptions associated with their specific functional roles ("you stand where you sit") and by their self-interested concerns with organizational survival and growth, re-election, and career advancement. In an attempt at heroic simplification, it may suffice to distinguish only three sets of such actors — elected governments, central banks, and labor unions[10] — in an attempt to explain macro-economic outcomes in the 1970s.

Closest to the view implied by macro-economic analysis is the perspective of *elected governments* which are held politically accountable for both inflation and unemployment (as well as tax increases, unbalanced budgets, balance-of-payments crises and devaluations of the currency). Thus the government view of policy choices and outcomes is likely to correspond to the analysis presented above (Figure 5). *Labor unions*, however, upon whose cooperation the successful fight against stagflation critically depends, are likely to view the world from a different perspective (Figure 7). Although unemployment, or at least the threat of *rising* unemployment, must be of even greater importance to them than it is to governments, inflation is not one of their primary concerns. Instead, it is plausible to assume

Figure 8:   Macro-Economic Coordination: The Central Bank View

Wage Policy

Fiscal and Monetary Policy	moderate	aggressive
expansionary	inflation: moderate capital incomes: moderate	inflation: very high capital incomes low
restrictive	inflation: low capital incomes: very high	inflation: high capital incomes: moderate

that they will be preoccupied with real wage increases whenever there is no threat of rising unemployment.[11]

Finally, it may be assumed that *central banks*, if they are sufficiently independent to have an orientation differing from that of the elected government, will tend toward a professional perspective that primarily emphasizes price stability. In addition, they are likely to be concerned with the level of capital incomes[12] whose decline could trigger a sequence of capital outflows, devaluation and domestic inflation (Diagram 8).

5. Two Games of Macro-Economic Coordination

The differing world views of the actors will, of course, affect their evaluation of the outcomes of macro-economic coordination — and these may be represented in the form of a game-theoretic outcome matrix.[13] If the economic analysis summarized in the descriptive tableaus (Figures 5, 7 and 8) above is accepted, the order of preferences is relatively easy to derive for unions and central banks. By and large, the goals of central banks are fully compatible with one another, so that they will consistently prefer less inflation and higher capital incomes. By comparison, union preferences are conditional, but still unambiguous: Under conditions of full employment, they will prefer higher real wage increases — but if unemployment is rising, their foremost concern must be to save the jobs of their members. Elected governments, however, are faced with the trade-off between inflation and unemployment. They would of course prefer to avoid both problems — but if they cannot do so, they have no obvious once-and-for-all ranking of the possible mixes of outcomes.

In order to simplify, I will represent the basic ambivalence of government preferences by constructing two distinct games of macro-economic coordination, labelled "Keynesian" and "monetarist".[14] Both are played between the government and the unions;[15] the possible strategies of both sides (expansionary or restrictive fiscal and monetary policy, moderate or aggressive wage policy) are the same in both games; and so are the real-world consequences

Figure 9: **The Keynesian Game of Macro-Economic Coordination**
(Preferences of both players rank ordered 1 to 4)

	UNIONS	
GOVERNMENT	moderate	aggressive
expansionary	(1)　　　　2 1	(2)　　　　1 2
restrictive	(3)　　　　3 3	(4)　　　　4 4

associated with these strategies. The two games differ only in the assumed valuation of these consequences by the (composite) player "government."

In the *Keynesian game*, which was in fact played in almost all Western countries after 1973, the government considers unemployment as the most serious problem and treats inflation as a secondary (but still important) concern (Figure 9). Thus the government would clearly prefer to achieve the macro-economically optimal "concerted" strategy of fiscal and monetary reflation and union wage restraint in cell 1 of the diagram. The worst case for a Keynesian government is the combination of demand deflation and aggressive union wage policy (cell 4), which would lead to very high unemployment and moderate inflation. The remaining two cases are of intermediate attractiveness. Their ordering depends on the relative importance of the concern about inflation.

From a union point of view, however, the government's optimum outcome (cell 1) would be only the second best solution. As long as full employment is in fact maintained, it is in their immediate self-interest to shift to an aggressive wage policy in order to achieve the best outcome with low unemployment and higher real wages (cell 2). That this outcome is also associated with rising inflation may be an unfortunate side effect for the unions, while it may become a major political concern. Nevertheless, within the Keynesian game the government could not now switch to a deflationary strategy unless it was willing to accept its own worst-case outcome with very high rates of unemployment (cell 4).

The Keynesian game, however, was not the only one that could be played. If either the central bank was able to impose its own preferences, or if the government was politically able and willing to treat inflation as the paramount problem, and to tolerate high levels of unemployment, the character of the coordination game would change (Figure 10). Now the government would most prefer a combination of very low rates of inflation and moderately high unemployment (cell 3), while cell 2 with very high inflation and low unemployment would become its worst-case outcome.

But if the government is willing to play the monetarist game, the options of the unions deteriorate dramatically. If they continue with an aggressive wage policy (as British unions

Figure 10:   The Monetarist Game of Macro-Economic Coordination

	UNIONS	
GOVERNMENT	moderate	aggressive
expansionary	(1) 2 2	(2) 4 1
restrictive	(3) 3 1	(4) 3 4

did for a while after Margaret Thatcher's victory in 1979), they will end up in their own worst-case situation (cell 4), in which profit-gap unemployment caused by excessive wage increases is added on top of the demand-gap unemployment created by government policy. Thus it is now in their self-interest to shift to wage restraint in order to avoid, or at least reduce, further job losses and to improve their expected outcome from the worst case to second-worst (cell 3). For a monetarist government, however, this would be the best outcome from which it would have no reason to depart.

As the government has a dominant strategy in both games — expansion in the Keynesian, deflation in the monetarist case — both games have an equilibrium solution in which neither side can improve its outcome by a unilateral change of strategy (Rapoport, Guyer, and Gordon, 1976: 18). It is in both cases defined by the unions' self-interested response to the government's strategy. Yet the underlying power relations are entirely different: In the Keynesian game, the unions are powerful because of the government's commitment to full employment — and they are entirely powerless when confronted with a monetarist strategy. By exploiting the former they may achieve their best short-term outcome, while they are forced to "collaborate" with the latter in order to avoid their worst-case outcome.[16] At least in the economic environment of the 1970s, union power was very much a function of government strategy.

6. The Choice of Coordination Games

An explanation of economic outcomes in the 1970s thus needs to focus on the choice between the Keynesian and monetarist games that could have been played. In three of the four countries, that choice was formally exercised by elected governments. In West Germany, by contrast, the government's fiscal response to the onset of the crisis (which was as expansionary as that of the other countries) was largely neutralized by the tight-money policy of the central bank. Thus the explanation for the de-facto monetarism of West German economic policy in 1974/75 is primarily to be found in the exceptional degree of institutional autonomy enjoyed by the *Bundesbank* (Woolley, 1985; Kloten, Ketterer, and Vollmer, 1985) and in the tactical brilliance with which it executed its shift to monetarism without risking an open political conflict with the government and the unions (Scharpf, 1987b: 165-177).[17] When Keynesianism was practiced thereafter in West Germany, it was "on probation" and likely to be revoked at the first sign of rising inflation.

If we put the German case to one side, what factors can then explain the choice of games in the other three countries? In the literature, there are essentially two competing strands of theory dealing with the issue: From a "class-politics" perspective, what game is being played depends essentially on the class orientation of the party in power (Hibbs, 1977; 1982; Fiorina, 1978; Tufte, 1978) and on the "power resources" of the labor movement favoring the ascendancy of labor-oriented parties (Korpi, 1983; Esping-Andersen, 1985). The theory of "political business cycles" on the other hand (Nordhaus, 1975; McRae, 1977; Frey and Schneider, 1978; 1979; Peel, 1982; Lowery, 1985) emphasizes the anticipation of voter reactions by all governments, regardless of their party affiliations.[18] Assuming that voters will respond more negatively to unemployment than to inflation, the theory predicts cyclical changes between Keynesian full-employment policy before, and monetarist anti-inflation policy after, general elections.

Applied in isolation, the power of both models to explain economic policy outcomes seems less than overwhelming[19] — which is not much of a surprise, as both theories tend to focus on the motives of economic policy makers, and to ignore the conditions under which the preferences of governments can, or cannot, be translated into effective policy. But it is nevertheless promising to combine these hypotheses with the game theoretical model of macro-economic coordination developed above. The connection could be provided by the notion of a "linkage" between separate games played by one player against different opponents (Kelley, 1984; Denzau, Riker, and Shepsle, 1985; Shepsle, 1986; Putnam, 1986). In the first "coordination" game, the outcomes of macro-economic policy are jointly determined by the government and the unions, while in the second "politics" game[20] the government responds to (its anticipation of) positive or negative voter reactions to these outcomes.[21]

Furthermore, it seems reasonable to assume that different groups of voters will respond differently to macro-economic strategies. Simplifying again, I propose to lump these various groups into three socio-economic strata (Figure 10). The first stratum is without property and depends for its livelihood on relatively insecure jobs in the secondary labor market (Piore, 1979) and on government transfers. The second stratum of skilled blue and white collar workers and professionals derives its income from more secure jobs in the primary labor market, but also from substantial property holdings (Miegel, 1981). The third stratum of self-employed professionals, managers, entrepreneurs, and rentiers[22] depends primarily on profits and the returns of real and financial assets and is not directly affected by the labor market.

If these assumptions are granted, it is plausible that voters in the lower stratum have most to fear from a monetarist strategy associated with high unemployment and cutbacks in welfare spending, and that voters in the upper stratum would respond negatively to a Keynesian strategy associated with rising inflation, declining real interest rates and aggressive union wage demands. By contrast, voters in the middle stratum would have reason to be more ambivalent in their preferences. Their jobs are more secure than those in the lower stratum, but if unemployment rises and companies fail, they may feel even more threatened because they are likely to fall so much deeper. On the other hand, although these middle voters may even profit from inflation as home owners and debtors, they are likely to respond negatively to the disruption of established expectations associated with rapidly rising prices.[23]

In addition, we need to introduce a set of assumptions about how governments might differ in their dependence on the electorate. Simplifying again, the model presupposes that the choices of the "government" are exercised by one of two competing parties, or coalitions of parties, with contrasting class bases of political support.[24] "Bourgeois" parties[25] appeal

Figure 11:   Class Bases of Keynesian and Monetarist Strategies

Beneficiaries of Monetarism

```
                        ***                          Rentiers/Capitalists
                          ***                      Managers/ Entrepreneurs
     Upper Stratum          ***                    Self-Employed Professionals
                              ***
                        Employed***                          Professionals
                              ***
     Middle Stratum  Skilled White ***                       and Blue Collar
                                   ***                             Workers
                              ***
                        Unskilled        ***                       Workers
                                        ***
                        Unemployed Workers   ***
                                           ***
     Lower Stratum   Welfare Clients          ***
```

Beneficiaries of Keynesianism

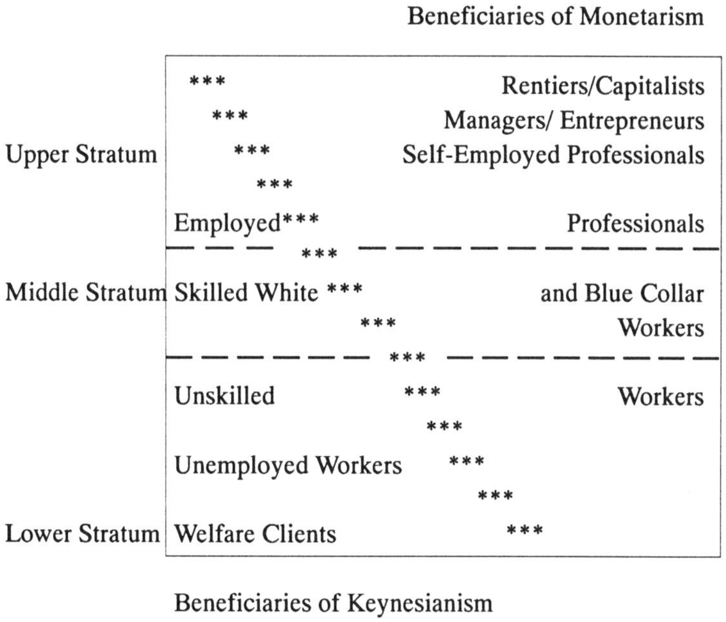

primarily to voters in the upper socio-economic stratum, while "Labor" parties have their electoral stronghold in the lower stratum. Each government identifies ideologically with the interests of its core clientele and favors macro-economic strategies that serve these interests. But it also will try to select policies that assure its reelection. If policies do not serve the interests of its core clientele, the model assumes that the government will lose some of their support,[26] but will not be able to attract votes from the core clientele of the opposition. If that were all there is to the politics game, Labor governments would (under the economic conditions of the 1970s) always have pursued Keynesian strategies, and Bourgeois governments would always have chosen to play the monetarist game.

But each government will also be defeated if it loses the volatile support of the middle stratum of voters. As they are potentially concerned with both, unemployment and inflation, their choices depend not on a general preference for either Keynesian or monetarist strategies but, rather, on specific economic circumstances and perceived consequences for their own interests.[27] In general, it is reasonable to assume that middle voters will respond positively to a situation in which both problems, inflation and unemployment, are avoided, and that they will respond negatively to a combination of high inflation plus high unemployment. When unemployment is low and inflation high, however, their response is likely to be asymmetrical: Whereas a shift from a Labor government to the Bourgeois opposition is plausible as a protest against high rates of inflation, the reverse shift is less probable if middle voters assume that under a Labor government inflation could only get worse.

Even more difficult to predict is the response of middle voters to the combination of low inflation and high unemployment. If inflation and unemployment were perceived as symmetrical, one might now expect a negative response, with perhaps a somewhat greater tolerance for Labor governments (on the hypothesis that they would be more motivated to return to full employment).[28] This response is indeed likely when unemployment is a relatively new phenomenon. But once unemployment has persisted for some time, its political implications are likely to change.

While inflation is, by and large, perceived as a collective evil that irritates even those whose incomes keep up with prices, that is not generally true of unemployment. It is only the *threat* of mass joblessness, especially when it is experienced for the first time after almost two decades of full employment, that approximates a collective evil. But once unemployment has in fact risen, voters will realize that only a minority of the labor force is in fact affected — and it is also fairly obvious who is likely to be in that minority. For those who are not (and that is the overwhelming majority of the middle voters), unemployment is at best an "altruistic problem," whose salience depends entirely on the "moral climate" of the country[29] and of the times, but it is not a problem of their economic self-interest. Thus, if we continue to assume self-interested voting among the middle layer of the electorate, we would predict support for Bourgeois as well as for Labor governments under conditions of low inflation and long-term unemployment.

With this we are now able to return to the "linkage" between the macro-economic "coordination" game and the "politics" game. One way to present it is in the form of "nested" games where the outer frame is provided by the coordination game which effectively determines the various combinations of inflation and unemployment to which the different strata of the electorate will respond in the politics game. As these will respond differently to governments of different political persuasions, each cell of the coordination game will contain two variants of the politics game, one for Labor and one for Bourgeois governments (Figure 12).

Obviously, *cell 1* of the coordination game (obtained through a combination of Keynesian reflation and union wage restraint) did provide the optimal economic environment for the politics game from the perspective of a *Labor government*. The interests of its core clientele (and its own political preferences) were satisfied, and middle voters had no reason to defect.

For a *Bourgeois government*, however, the same situation was less attractive since its own ideological preferences as well as the interests of its core clientele could not be satisfied by a Keynesian strategy. But as upper-stratum voters could not benefit from defecting to the Labor opposition, the government was still politically secure — and it could not improve its position by switching to a monetarist strategy as as long as middle voters would still respond negatively to a rise of unemployment.

But if a union wage offensive shifted the Keynesian game into *cell 2*, as was likely under the assumptions introduced above, a *Labor government* would become extremely vulnerable in the politics game. While its core clientele would be satisfied, middle voters would respond negatively to the rapid increase of inflation and the Bourgeois opposition would present a highly credible alternative. Thus, if the government could not persuade the unions to shift back to wage moderation (and thus to cell 1), it was was faced with two equally unattractive political options: It could choose to stick to its Keynesian guns, even if that meant almost certain electoral defeat, or it could gamble on a switch to monetarism (whose short-run effect would be the worst-case outcome of cell 4) in the hope that the unions might then move toward wage restraint quickly enough to permit the government to reach the relatively safe haven of cell 3 before the next election.

However, if a *Bourgeois government* found itself in the same economic situation (cell 2), its political survival would be less in danger, as middle voters could not expect a more vigorous anti-inflation strategy from the Labor opposition. Given the political risks associated with a switch to monetarism and an initial massive increase of unemployment (cell 4),[30] a Bourgeois government might well prefer to continue the Keynesian game even in the absence of union wage restraint (and in doing so, its chances of political survival might might be better than those of a Labor government).

Figure 12:   Voter Responses to Coordination Game Outcomes

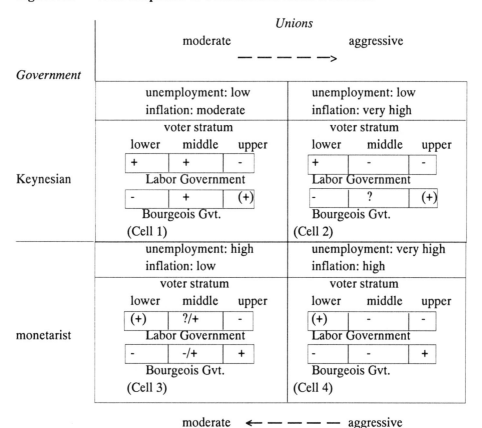

The economic environment of *cell 4*, with very high unemployment and still high rates of inflation, was politically viable for neither party. Perhaps a *Labor government* might do marginally better with the middle voters if they feared that a shift to the Bourgeois opposition could only make unemployment still worse. On the other hand, its own core clientele would suffer the most, while a *Bourgeois government* would at least begin to satisfy the interests of its upper-class clientele and would profit from their improving morale. Nevertheless, it is plausible to assume that either government would lose if elections were held during a period in which the economy found itself in cell 4. But the coordination game was unlikely to remain in cell 4 for long. If the monetarist game continued, the unions were forced by rising unemployment to moderate their wage claims. Thus, if governments managed to hang on long enough for this shift to become economically effective and politically salient, they would face more attractive prospects.

Cell 3, finally, was Janus faced. Its political implications were entirely different, depending upon whether it was entered from cell 1 or from cell 4. In the first case, the political response would have been negative, as middle voters would be confronted for the first time with a significant rise of unemployment under conditions where there was not even much concern about inflation to justify the switch to monetarism. Unlike independent central banks, therefore, rational governments, Labor or Bourgeois, would not shift to the monetarist game as long as they found themselves in cell 1.

When cell 3 was entered from cell 4, however, the politics game was of an entirely different character. Now the return to union wage restraint would help to reduce inflation visibly, and as business profits improved, unemployment would at least be stabilized and might even decline somewhat. As a consequence, joblessness would no longer appear as a personal threat to voters in the middle stratum. Under these conditions, cell 3 would become the political optimum for a *Bourgeois government.* Its own core clientele was pleased by the economic effects of the monetarist strategy, and the support of middle voters was initially assured by favorable comparisons to the preceding period. If it was plausible to blame a predecessor Labor government for its initial rise, the political salience of continuing unemployment would be greatly reduced,[31] and after a while dissonance-reducing psychological mechanisms would blunt its moral salience as well.

For a *Labor government*, by contrast, the situation was less comfortable. Although the unconcern of middle voters would assure its short-term political survival, continuing unemployment would hurt and demoralize its own core clientele. Thus the government would be under strong political pressure to move back to a Keynesian full-employment strategy (cell 1). If it did so, however, it was now uncertain of the continuing support of the middle stratum, whose sensitivity to inflation must have increased as they lost their fear of unemployment. At the least, a Labor government that returned to Keynesianism after a monetarist interlude would be vulnerable to be defeated as soon as inflation would rise again.

7. How and When Did Corporatism Matter?

The model is now sufficiently complex and realistic to be plausibly applied to the historical experience of macro-economic choices in the four countries between 1974 and 1982. What we are now able to add to the economic analysis presented in section 3 above is an explanation of government choices between Keynesian and monetarist strategies following from the logic of the "politics" games played within each of the cells of the outer "coordination" game (Figure 13).

The linkage between both games is established by the assumption that it is the prospect of winning or losing general elections which will determine a government's willingness to stay in, or enter into, a given cell of the coordination game, and thus, by implication, its choice between the Keynesian and monetarist strategies.[32]

In *1974* all four countries were governed by Labor parties, and all four governments found themselves in macro-economic positions which were vulnerable in the politics game. In Austria, Britain and Sweden the governments were able to assure full employment while the unions obtained inflationary wage settlements. In Germany, by contrast, the central bank enforced a tight money policy that limited, but could not avoid, the rise of inflation, and caused extremely high job losses. The model would predict that if these situations should continue until the next general elections,[33] all four governments would be politically vulnerable. Hence all had an interest in moving away from their uncomfortable positions. For this, however, they depended on the unions, as no government could have directly accessed a more secure political position by the exercise of its own economic-policy options.

By *1976*, nevertheless, only one country, Sweden, had not changed its position within the coordination game — and the Swedish Social Democrats were indeed defeated by a Bourgeois coalition in the fall of 1976.[34] In the other three countries the unions had helped to improve the government's political prospects by a move to wage moderation. But only in one country, Germany, can this move be explained within the present model as a self-interested response to rising unemployment. In Austria and Britain, institutional factors not yet discussed must be drawn upon to explain the unions' willingness to shift to a pattern of Keynesian concertation which, from the perspective of short-term economic payoffs, was only the second best solution which they could obtain.

By *1978*, Swedish unions had also shifted to wage moderation while the Bourgeois government remained firmly committed to full employment. Even in Germany, the federal government was now able to shift toward a full employment strategy, after inflation was more or less under control. Thus, Austria, Sweden and West Germany were now (and until 1980) following a course of Keynesian concertation which was politically optimal for Labor governments, and at least politically viable for the Swedish Bourgeois coalition, but which depended upon union wage restraint not yet explained within the model.

In Britain, by contrast, both the government and the unions had departed from Keynesian concertation by 1978 for reasons which may be plausibly interpreted within our model. The government had shifted to monetarism in the hope of reaching cell 3, and thus to break

Figure 13: Historical Sequences of Coordination and Politics Games

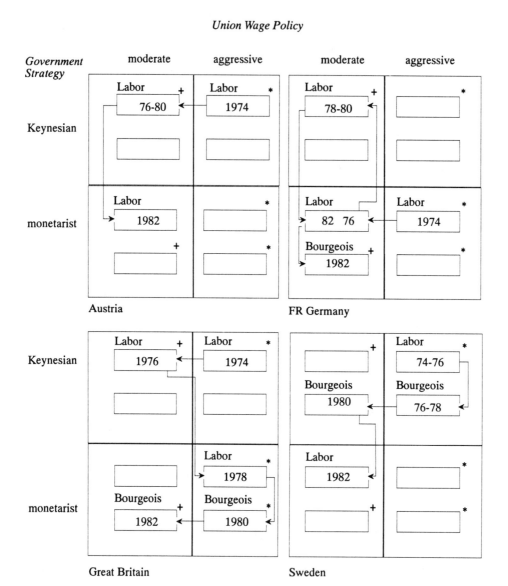

* =   politically vulnerable position
+ =   politically secure position

persistent inflationary expectations without a dramatic increase of unemployment. At the same time, the unions had resumed their wage offensive in the hope of reaching cell 2, and thus to improve the real-wage position of their members after two years of extreme wage restraint. In the end, they both found themselves in cell 4, and hence in a position which was politically non-viable for the Labor government in the 1979 general elections.

Later developments also seem to conform well to the model: After their victory in 1979, Margaret Thatcher's Conservatives had sufficient time to wait for the unions to shift back to wage moderation under the compulsion of very high unemployment. When that point had been reached by *1982*, the Bourgeois government was politically secure. In Germany, the Social Democrats were ousted when the Free Democrats switched coalitions in the fall of 1982. At that time unemployment was rapidly increasing as a result of another heavy dose of monetarism applied by the *Bundesbank* in response to the second oil-price crisis. The new Christian-Liberal government, however, could blame its predecessors for the rise of unemployment and was able to win comfortable majorities in subsequent elections.

In Sweden, the Bourgeois government did not survive the externally imposed shift to monetarism (as a consequence of which unemployment had begun to creep up by 1982), but the Social Democrats' hold on power seemed also tenuous, even though the devaluation of the *kronor* kept Swedish unemployment at comparatively very low levels. The same is by and large true of Austria, where the unions have been even more cooperative than in Sweden, but where the commitment to fixed exchange rates against the *Deutsche Mark* precluded devaluation, so that the rise of unemployment did more to undercut Labor support.

To summarize: There were in the 1970s and early 1980s two positions within the coordination game at which a government might be secure within the politics game (cell 1 for Labor and cell 3 for Bourgeois governments), and there were a number of positions at which governments were politically vulnerable. But the chances of survival were unevenly distributed: While Bourgeois governments, once they had reached their politically preferred position could count on the self-interested collaboration of the unions in the coordination game, the same was not true of the politically preferred position of Labor governments: It represented a political equilibrium but not a coordination equilibrium. If unions would follow their own short-term preferences in the coordination game, Labor governments would find themselves in a politically untenable position (cell 2). If the government then looked only to its own political survival, it would be tempted into a desperate shift to monetarism which, even if it succeeded politically, would increase unemployment dramatically. If it failed, as it did in Britain, it would help to establish a Bourgeois government that was politically secure in spite of continuing high unemployment.

Thus, if both Labor governments and unions were to follow their short-term institutional self-interests, the result would have been a sequence of unstable game-situations which could only come to an end in a Bourgeois-monetarist constellation that represented a stable equilibrium in the politics game as well as in the coordination game. From the perspective of the labor movement, however, that sequence was a disaster for Labor parties as well as for unions — and one that was easy to anticipate.[35] The question is, therefore, under which conditions the sequence could have been interrupted and reversed before the Bourgeois-monetarist equilibrium was established. What was required is clear enough: The unions would have to be willing and able to forgo short-term wage gains in order to allow the government to reach cell 1 of the coordination game, where it was in its own political self-interest to defend full employment. That was the essence of the "neo-corporatist-Keynesian concertation" achieved in Austria between 1976 and 1980, in Britain between 1976 and 1978, and in Sweden and West Germany between 1978 and 1980.[36]

What was involved was not in the strict sense a question of "political exchange" (Pizzorno, 1978, Marin, 1985). To the extent that a Labor government pursued full-employment strategies, it was acting out of self-interest — not to reward the unions. It had nothing else to offer them in return for wage moderation, and it could only warn them of its own impending political demise, not threaten it. What was in question, instead, was the unions' capacity of "self-management" (Elster, 1979; Schelling, 1984), that is their ability to avoid both the "temporal trap" of favoring short-term over longer-term definitions of self-interest and the "social trap" of favoring competitive sub-group interests over the collective interest of the union movement (Messick and McClelland, 1983). It is here that institutional explanations of economic-policy successes and failures during the 1970s finally come into their own: Solidarity, as well as the ability to anticipate the future in present choices, is undercut by competition between individual unions, and it is facilitated (though not assured) by organizational concentration in the union movement and by the effective centralization of collective bargaining decisions.

In Britain, to begin with the most obvious case, the extreme fragmentation of union organization (the TUC alone still had over one hundred member unions in the 1970s), and the decentralization of collective bargaining to the level of individual firms, plants, or even the shop floor within plants create enormous competitive pressures within the union movement (Barnes and Reid, 1980). Negotiators in each of the small bargaining units tend to exploit fully the ability to pay of profitable firms and the bargaining strength of scarce skill groups — and they would suffer in inter-union competition if their own settlements were more moderate than those achieved elsewhere. Under such conditions, voluntary wage restraint, even if its economic or political benefit to the union movement as a whole were obvious, is a collective good whose attainment is highly vulnerable to free-riding.

By contrast, the free-rider problem is significantly reduced in the other three countries whose institutions, though quite different, conformed to a greater degree to the "neo-corporatist" model. In Austria and West Germany, the national union movements consist of no more than 16 or 17 industrial unions that do not compete against each other. Collective bargaining is also quite centralized within each union, with effective decisions taken at the national level even if regional settlements may differ. Under such conditions, union negotiators must be concerned about job losses in weaker firms or regions, and they are less free to exploit pockets of local bargaining strength. They must, in other words, permanently work to achieve a collective or solidaristic definition of the self-interest of divergent groups of workers in order to assure their own organizational survival (Streeck, 1981b). An even more inclusive perspective is introduced by the formal role of the central union federation in collective bargaining in Sweden and Austria (Marin, 1982), and by the *de facto* wage leadership of the largest industrial unions in West Germany (Streeck, 1982, 1984).

Thus, in one way or another, a collective definition of the self-interest of the union movement could be worked into the normal processes of collective bargaining by large, "encompassing" (Olson, 1982) organizations on the union side. At the same time, organizational centralization assured union leaders some (limited) freedom to pursue longer-term strategies even in the face of rank-and-file discontent, and it provided them with opportunities to present and defend more "enlightened" and longer-term definitions of union self-interest in internal discussions.

Thus Austrian and German unions were able to practice wage restraint after 1975 in a spirit of "business as usual" that was hardly noticed by anybody outside of professional circles. In Britain, by contrast, the success of the Social Contract in 1976 and 1977 depended entirely on a most extraordinary exertion of political and moral pressure by government and top union leaders. Local bargaining units and shop stewards were browbeaten into compliance by a national campaign to "give a year to Britain," replete with appeals to the "spirit of Dunkirk" and to the solidarity of the labor movement with an embattled Labour government. The emphasis was on short-term sacrifices, and the six-pounds rule itself (which wrought havoc with jealously defended wage differentials) was chosen for its maximal moral appeal and for its high visibility which did discourage evasions.

The Swedish case is less clear-cut (Martin, 1984; 1986b). The number of unions is larger than in Austria or West Germany (about 25), and there is considerable wage competition between the blue-collar unions, organized by industry, and the white-collar unions, which are mainly organized by skill level. At the same time, however, the national federation of blue-collar unions and national cartels of white-collar unions, have a larger role in collective bargaining than is true in the other countries. Yet there is also a good deal of wage drift generated by local wage rounds in the more profitable (or state owned) firms — which is then generalized to the whole economy by an ever denser network of "compensation" clauses in collective agreements. Nevertheless, whenever this was considered necessary, the Swedish labor movement was able to draw upon moral resources and an unspectacular but effective commitment to solidaristic values that were able to constrain self-interested competition between individual bargaining units.[37]

Thus it seems more plausible to ascribe the aggressive and economically damaging Swedish wage rounds after 1975 not to a fundamental institutional incapacity, but perhaps to a temporary lapse of judgment and, after 1976, to the fact the unions saw little need at first to assist the new Bourgeois government in its macro-economic management. After all, if that government had failed, it was the Social Democrats, rather than a Thatcherite party, who would have returned to office. But when it became clear, after 1978, that the Swedish economy was in fact suffering, union wage moderation was again forthcoming.

In short, if and when the union movement as a whole had reason to consider wage restraint as its own best strategy, neo-corporatist institutional conditions facilitated that choice in Austria, West Germany, and Sweden. In Britain, their absence could be compensated for a time by extreme exertions of ideological pressure and moral leadership. But it was always clear that the Social Contract was not institutionally viable as a longer-term strategy, and that the inevitable return to "free collective bargaining" would again release the pent-up pressures of wage competition. The only question was whether the breakup had to occur under dramatic circumstances in 1978, or whether a more sensitive management of government-union relations and better timing could have facilitated a more orderly retreat that might have allowed Callaghan to survive another general election.

Finally, it is perhaps worth pointing out that neo-corporatist institutions are of relevance to macro-economic policy[38] only as long as the Keynesian game is being played. If the government shifts to a monetarist strategy, wage restraint (which is still required for its success) no longer depends on the organizational concentration of the union movement and on the centralization of collective-bargaining decisions.[39] The reason is analytically straightforward: Job losses, unlike inflation, are primarily experienced not as a collective evil but as an individual risk whose avoidance is in the immediate self-interest of individual workers and, hence, not vulnerable to free-riding. As soon as unemployment is allowed to rise, therefore, the overriding interest in protecting existing jobs will motivate wage concessions not only at the level of the union movement as a whole, but also at lower levels of collective bargaining.[40] Under such conditions, there is no reason to assume that decentralized and fragmented union movements (that are otherwise characterized by greater militancy — Cameron, 1984) should be any less "docile" than highly centralized and disciplined corporatist unions are said to be (Panitch, 1979). It is thus entirely plausible, within the model developed here, that neo-corporatist institutions should explain a great deal of economic variance during the Keynesian 1970s — and much less during the monetarist 1980s.

Notes

1 The paper is based on a book length study (Scharpf, 1987b) that was completed while I was working at the Labor Market Policy Research Unit of the Wissenschaftszentrum Berlin. Earlier versions have profited from seminar discussions at the Center for Advanced Study in the Behavioral Sciences, Stanford, at the Workshop in Political Theory and Policy Analysis, Indiana University, at the Center for European Studies, Harvard University, and at the School of Business and Public Administration, California State University, San Bernardino. I have also profited from the helpful comments of Jens Alber, Jürgen Feick, Bernd Marin, Renate Mayntz, Manfred Schmidt and Douglas Webber. A shorter version was published in Journal of Public Policy (1987)7, 227-257.

2 Equally interesting is the nonexistent relationship between employment growth and levels of unemployment. It demonstrates the unsuitability of using registered unemployment (which is influenced by changes on the supply side of the labor market as much as by the demand for labor) as an indicator of *economic* performance.

3 There is a direct parallel to the anthropological concept of a culturally defined (but changeable) "repertoire of action resources" (habits, skills, and styles) from which individuals and groups are able to construct "strategies of action" (Swidler, 1986). I also find Swidler's distinction between

periods of culturally "settled lives" and "unsettled" periods (in which the cultural repertoire is redefined in non-incremental fashion) highly suggestive for an analysis of policy choices.

4 Of course, no single theory which attempts even limited generality is ever able to explain complex, real-world phenomena (as distinguished from phenomena studied in the controlled environment of the laboratory) — in the natural sciences (with the exception of astronomy) no more so than in the social sciences (Schlenker, 1974; McGuire, 1983). For my own understanding, I find it useful to conceptualize real-world events as "intersections" of processes and factors whose separate "logics" may be captured by specific explanatory theories, but whose interaction may only be accessible to historical description (Scharpf, 1987a). Nevertheless, theories do differ in the scope and significance of the "cuts" that they are able to explain.

5 In this paper, I concentrate on the explanation of *macro-economic policy*, which affects unemployment through its impact on the number of jobs offered in the economy. This is, of course, not the whole "story" (which is presented more fully in my book). Governments did resort to a variety of other strategies to prevent, reduce, or conceal the rise of *unemployment* (Wilensky and Turner, 1987). Switzerland, for instance, relied almost entirely on the repatriation of foreign workers to compensate for very large job losses (Schmidt, 1985). Sweden on the other hand reduced potential unemployment by almost four percentage points between 1974 and 1978 through "active labor market" retraining and subsidized employment. West Germany combined both strategies with the early retirement of older workers to achieve a similar reduction of the labor supply (Scharpf, 1987b: 279-293).

6 In the "Monetarist" environment of the 1980s, by contrast, wage restraint came to mean falling real wages or, at the least, reductions of real unit labor costs in order to increase the profitability of capital.

7 The term, and perhaps the strategy, was first used self-consciously in the German "*Konzertierte Aktion*" which, in 1967-69, had brilliantly succeeded in overcoming a home-made recession through demand reflation and wage restraint.

8 After the onset of the second oil crisis in 1979, the United States, which before had facilitated worldwide expansionary strategies through its relatively loose fiscal and monetary policy, switched to a monetarist tight money policy which increased real long-term dollar interests from a low of -3% at the beginning of 1980 to an average of +6% in 1982 and a high of over +8% in 1983. Given the paramount role of the U.S. dollar in the international capital markets, all other industrial countries were also forced to reduce their money supply and to raise their interest rates (Funke, 1986). As a further consequence, national fiscal policy also became less effective as an instrument of expansion (and much more expensive). In effect, therefore, most Western European countries pursued restrictive fiscal and monetary policies after 1981 — and those that did not at first (Mitterand's France, for instance) were soon compelled to follow suit in order to avoid massive outflows of capital and a dramatic devaluation of their currencies.

9 When the Social Democrats returned to power in Sweden in the fall of 1982, they achieved a limited degree of demand reflation through the competitive devaluation of the *kronor* — a strategy which not all countries could have adopted.

10 In their collective bargaining role, one might include employers' associations as macro-economic actors of marginal importance. Even though one may generally presume that the degree of their resistance to wage increases is determined by economic self-interest, it is at least conceivable that the relative toughness of their position may also be influenced by considerations including the state of the macro-economy.

But it is not plausible to assume that business associations could be a player in a macro-economic "inflation game", modelled after the Prisoner's Dilemma, in which they choose between high and low price increases while the unions choose high or low wage increases (Maital and Benjamini, 1979; Neck, 1985). Price-setting decisions (and investment decisions, for that matter), although of critical importance for the performance of the economy, are not the subject of *collective* choices in capitalist economies. The recent concern of social scientists with the "organization of business interests" (Streeck and Schmitter, 1985) should not obscure this important difference.

11 Rising rates of inflation may cut into the real value of nominal wage settlements, but from a union perspective that insight is more likely to justify aggressive wage bargaining than wage moderation.

12 Capital incomes are influenced by both policy variables: Wage moderation increases profits, and high interest rates increase income from monetary assets.

13 The game-theoretical presentation is justified by the strategic interdependence among the players. Even if governments and unions are interested in different "bundles" of outcomes, the extent to which either side will be able to achieve its goals is always determined jointly by its own action and the action of the other side. Once that basic condition is granted, the presentation of coordination problems in game-theoretic form will help to simplify and clarify the analysis — provided, of course, that the search for empirically grounded payoff matrices is not short-cut by unthinking reference to one of the standard game models (usually the symmetrical Prisoner's Dilemma).

14 It should be clear that I am describing broader political-economic strategies whose content is related to, but not identical with, the use of both terms in economics.

15 Even when the central bank is an autonomous player, it is not necessary to represent the constellation as a three-cornered game. As fiscal and monetary policy operate upon the same parameters of aggregate demand, any discrepancy between the two will affect the *de facto* choice of a single "government" strategy.

16 In my view it is thus not correct to argue, as Peter Lange and Geoffrey Garrett (1985: 799-800, 817) have done, that wage restraint is rational for unions only as long as the government will guarantee economic growth and full employment. On the contrary: That is precisely the government with whom self-interested unions will find it most difficult to cooperate. Only a government that is willing to tolerate high unemployment may count upon their self-interested moderation.

17 That is perhaps not the whole story, and it underemphasizes the role of the Free Democrats and the inflation sensitivity of German public opinion (Schmidt, 1987), but it is a more important part of the story than authors emphasizing the "power resources of the labor movement" are generally willing to concede (Korpi, 1983; Esping-Andersen and Korpi, 1984; Martin, 1986). Of course, the theoretical dispute becomes moot if power resources are defined to include the political control of central bank policy.

18 Frey and Schneider (1978; 1979) combine both assumptions: In their model, governments will pursue their own ideological preferences until their popularity falls below a critical threshold at which their re-election is in danger.

19 The class orientation of political parties did indeed matter in the switch from Callaghan to Thatcher in Britain, or from Giscard to Mitterand in France, but it does not explain the relative continuity of economic policy after changes of government in Sweden and in the United States in 1976, or in West Germany in 1982. Similarly, the theory of the "political business cycle" may perhaps explain German fiscal policy in 1980, but the Austrian and Swedish governments seem to have continued their chosen course with little regard for the timing of elections, and the Carter administration did switch to a monetarist anti-inflation strategy in 1979 which predictably increased U.S. unemployment before the 1980 elections.

20 In fact, there is a third linked game, played between union leaders and the active union membership, and a fourth one, played between different unions. I will return to these in the concluding section.

21 It is perhaps necessary to emphasize that we are trying to explain not election outcomes but policy choices, and that we are dealing with perceptions. Elections are in fact won or lost over a multitude of issues, of which the course of the economy is only one, and not always the most important one. But it is nevertheless reasonable to postulate that those who are responsible for economic policy will in fact base their decisions on an anticipation of the responses of self-interested voters to those aspects of economic performance which affect their own welfare.

22 By the logic of the classification, persons in retirement would share the interests of the upper stratum if their income is derived from savings, and they would belong to the lower stratum if they depend on tax-financed transfers.

23 Here, national differences are important. Voters in Germany seem to have a lower tolerance for inflation than those in Sweden, Austria, or Great Britain.

24 The model could accommodate coalition governments with cross-cutting class orientations, but not the "new politics" of non-class issues, movements and parties (peace, ecology, gender, life

styles, ethnic, regional, etc.).

25 Conservative parties in Britain and in the Scandinavian countries, the German Free Democrats or the Republican Party of the United States would seem to fit this class-based definition better than Christian Democratic parties.

26 It is thus assumed that in the lower and upper socio-economic strata a "clientele" orientation will predominate which prevents voters, even if they are disappointed by their "own" party, from switching to an opposition that could only be worse from their point of view (Krieger, 1985). Nevertheless, the party will pay a political price for disappointing its followers: They may stay home on election day, and their lack of enthusiasm will be reflected in reduced volunteer support and lower financial contributions.

27 The electoral response of the middle stratum is thus determined by the "anti-government" logic of Downsian rational voters, rather than by a clientelist orientation.

28 It may explain the re-election of the German Social-Liberal coalition in 1976 in spite of massive job losses (Rattinger, 1979).

29 It is here that the "power resource" theory is most persuasive: A powerful labor movement of the Scandinavian or Austrian type, with a strong presence in all societal institutions, including the mass media, may indeed exercise a degree of "ideological hegemony" that may at least postpone the shift to a neo-conservative "lifeboat ethics" and the egoistic redefinition of middle-stratum interests.

30 Here, the length of the electoral cycle and the closeness of the next general election is obviously important. Quite apart from other differences, the British five-year electoral cycle enhanced, and the Swedish three-year cycle reduced, the political feasibility of a switch to monetarism.

31 The remarkable effect which a change of government has on the "framing" (Kahneman and Tversky, 1984) of the base line from which success and failure are measured might merit more attention than it has found in political theory.

32 As was discussed above, the general shift to monetarist strategies by 1982 was exogenously caused by the pervasive impact of the American shift to monetarism. Another exogenous factor, except in Britain, is the timing of general elections.

33 As the seriousness of the economic crisis did not become obvious until the winter of 1974/75, the British elections in the fall of 1974 would not count as a test.

34 It is perhaps fair to add that Swedish Social Democrats attribute the change of government more to the dispute over nuclear energy than to a deep dissatisfaction with their management of the economy.

35 It was in fact fully anticipated in Britain, where the last years of the Labour government were full of dire warnings to the unions about the catastrophic consequences of an impending Conservative victory.

36 Alternatively, if the unions were unwilling or unable to cooperate, the monetarist equilibrium might also have been avoided if the Labor government would rather risk short term political defeat than depart from full employment. That was the course taken by the Swedish Social Democrats in 1976, but it is uncertain whether it was taken as a conscious strategic choice — and it is not clear whether the strategy of self-sacrifice would have worked as well against a Thatcherite successor government.

37 One such mechanism had been the explicit agreement on the "EFO-Model" (Edgren, Faxén, and Odhner, 1973) which had regulated wage competition between the "exposed" export sectors and the "domestic" sectors of the economy in the late sixties and early seventies.

38 Of course that does not rule out a significant role for cooperative industrial relations at the level of the firm or the industry in facilitating technical modernization and productivity-enhancing changes of work organization (Streeck, 1986). It is doubtful, however, whether these arrangements are meaningfully described as "meso" or "micro corporatism" (Teubner, 1987).

39 There might actually be a reverse relationship: Under conditions of high unemployment, it would require a highly solidaristic labor movement to design and implement an aggressive wage campaign that, by further increasing unemployment in the short run, might help to defeat a Monetarist government at the next election. On that hypothesis, the union-busting thrust of recent industrial-relations legislation in Britain, while entirely counter-productive within a Keynesian frame of reference, may actually make partisan-political sense.

40 It is still true, however, that fragmented industrial relations systems tend to generate more endogenous wage pressure than neo-corporatist ones. Even under conditions of high general unemployment, there will be firms that are doing well and skill groups that are in high demand — and these pockets of labor power will be exploited in fragmented systems. Thus, even though unemployment was much higher, the real wages of those who still had jobs rose more in Britain after 1980 than they did in Austria, Sweden, and West Germany.

Political Exchange:
A Theoretical Reconsideration and Some Empirical Evidence from Taxation

Klaus Gretschmann
Patrick Kenis

> "If you want to study the naked interplay of vested interests, study taxation"
> J.A. Schumpeter

1. Introduction

Of relatively new interest in various branches of the social sciences — such as organization-sociology, political science, institutional economics and policy studies — is the analysis of specific institutional arrangements for policy-making. These come under organisational systems, policy domains, networks of policy-making, concertational systems, marketfora, etc.

Something of what is substantially meant by such systems is described in Knoke and Laumann's definition of a policy domain: "A policy domain is a subsystem identified by specifying a substantively defined criterion of mutual relevance or common orientation among a set of consequential actors concerned with formulating, advocating and selecting courses of action (that is, policy options) that are intended to resolve the delimited substantive problems in question" (Knoke and Laumann 1982: 256). Obvious examples of such domains include — among other things — education, agriculture, housing, energy, health, technology and, last but not least, *taxation*. Participants in a particular policy-making domain comprise all those private and public sector actors, whose actions affect the collective outcome of relevant policy decisions. This involves a kind of mutual relevance taken into account by those very actors in forming expectations and performing strategies. All such policy-action systems are founded upon a comprehensive set of often informal rules which regulate the allocation and distribution of resources relevant for domain-policy decisions.

At this stage the *functioning* of such systems has been primarily by means of approaches based on case studies, while their *structure* has been studied by means of network analysis (cf. Pappi's and Schneider's contribution in this volume). While case studies offer many advantages because of their empirical "groundedness", which allows for the deriving and the testing of (partial) theoretical propositions, network analysis has demonstrated its strength in exploring and eliciting characteristics of policy systems, thus rendering these systems analytically comparable.

Nonetheless, there still seems to exist a considerable lack of convincing *theoretical* approaches useful for the analysis of the *driving forces* in those systems. What we therefore need, and are trying to develop with broad brushstrokes in what follows, is a theoretical framework geared to capture the essentials of the subject of this study political exchange. The theoretical findings will be empirically illustrated using the case of tax reform.

The article is organized in the following manner: a brief reconsideration of the idea of political exchange will serve as the starting point of our considerations (2). In view of the shortcomings of previous approaches, it appears necessary to develop a theoretical framework which allows us to explore policy systems through the study of those ways and means which actors purposely use to produce an outcome which best suits both their individul and their common interests (3).[1] These theoretical considerations will enable us to extract and to model the *logic* of political exchanges (4). Our approach will be illustrated empirically with reference to the recent three-tiered German Tax Reform (1986/1988/1990) (5). Finally, and with the aim of arriving at a "generating model" (Boudon 1979), some conclusions will be drawn concerning both the basic mechanisms and the performance of GPE, as well as its consequences for system stability (6).

2. Political Exchange in a Nutshell

For those familiar with the theoretical debate on Generalized Political Exchange, it may be commonplace that Generalized Political Exchange is a concept which — though borrowing from the received views on exchange — strongly differs from both its economic and sociological heritage. On the one hand, the strand of thought represented by mainstream economics focuses primarily on either specifying and analyzing the significance of (competitive or monopolistic) market forms for market clearance, or on formulating (stability) conditions for the "general equilibrium" of exchange systems (Arrow 1986). This proves, however, too narrow to cover strategic political (inter)actions and to consider emergent structural properties resulting therefrom. On the other hand, sociological theories devoted to the analysis of the "generalized media of exchange" in the Parsonian or Luhmannian tradition are centered upon the level of collectivity and system properties, but they lack closer consideration of the underlying (choice-logic) micro-foundations.

Notwithstanding the contribution of these approaches to clarifying how both markets and societies operate, they are — because of their level of aggregation or abstraction — by no means sufficiently apt to make sense of the basic characteristics and processes of a policy domain.

Being acutely aware of this deficit, Pizzorno in his seminal article on political exchange (1978) conceptualised industrial relations systems as political markets, while at the same time assuring the reader that he would not follow a "mere exchange theory" of the political system which might have assumed "inevitable equilibrium" and situations of "free competition among well-informed individuals". Instead, he focused upon the formation process and the role of collective entities and identities in and through the exchange of political concessions for system support. In doing so, Pizzorno breaks fresh ground in that his approach covers indeed more than mere exchanges. Although remaining implicit, aspects of emergent socio-political and socio-economic action structures and action strategies are at the core of political exchanges. Nonetheless, Pizzorno's approach, like that of the school of "Scambio Politico" in general (for an overview, see Parri 1985), has up to now refrained from specifying the *set of conditions* under which particular constellations lead — through exchange, threat, or bargaining — to specific results.

This is the background against which Marin (1985) developed his idea of a 'generalized' concept of political exchange, which holds that *contextual* elements (Marin 1985: 20) must be considered in order to reach a proper understanding of political exchange. The concept of generalized political exchange (GPE) centers upon "the logic of ongoing risky transactions between organized collective actors with functionally interdependent yet competing or even antagonistic interests" (Marin 1985: 6). However, while presenting his approach in detail, Marin's use of "generalized" no longer seems to stand for a complex set of interdependent context variables; rather, it represents "an inherently power-generating, value-adding and mutually ensuring process (1985: 36) ...; accordingly it refers to nothing less than societal reproduction and development, and that is governance of the system" (1985; 39). If our reading is correct, Marin seems to propose that Generalized Political Exchange is a kind of superstructure which provides the opportunity for continuous mediation of antagonistic interests through quid pro quo exchanges. Thereby, Generalized Political Exchange serves to further the overall welfare of the polity and to safeguard its stability within boundaries.

Notwithstanding the merit of this approach — in which attention is paid to how integration occurs both at the level of policy domains and of the polity as a whole — Marin's concept of *Generalized* Political Exchange appears a little over-generalized, in that the level of policy domain is prematurely set aside in order to concentrate instead on problems of guidance, control and stability of the macro-system. It is likely due to this 'overgeneralisation' that even *Generalized* Political Exchange lacks an actor-theoretical foundation for studying the fabric of political interactions composed of collectivities and organizations. It seems as if, up to a point, the very logic of (generalized) political exchanges is still hidden behind a veil of ignorance.

3. The Theoretical Framework

In order to raise that veil of ignorance, it seems appropriate to investigate the preconditions for political exchange or, in other words, to see what its essential ingredients are.

To answer this question, we start by considering the notion of exchange. Broadly speaking, exchange is conceived as a particular form of *coordination* of divergent interests (not necessarily of cooperation), a coordination which leads to mutual gains from trade: i.e., from transactions of goods and services. What one exchange partner owns abundantly and/

or does not value highly, can be given away for something he badly wants or needs — provided that the other parties are prepared to give it away.

As Hirschman (1977) demonstrated convincingly, market exchanges are based on "interests" and interest mediation, and they are a counter model to compulsion, to robbery and violence rooted in "passions". Therefore, exchange may be viewed as an institutional arrangement guided by rule of "if you give me this, I'll give you that". In that, it is the opposite to threat, represented by the principle of "if you don't do this, I will do that to harm you".

In everyday life, nobody would characterize as exchange a situation in which a man with a gun offers his victim life for money. Political exchange theory, however, appears to comprise the renunciation of executing a threat — to act counter to an opponent's interest — in exchange for a particular behavior or decision. Whereas exchanges in general are usually characterized along the lines of the expected surplus, i.e., mutual gains from trade, political exchange, importantly enough, involves elements of threat and counter-threat.

It may be regarded as a truism that exchanges of any sorts require as prerequisite at least two actors with different preferences, tastes or interests who have different resources at their disposal. These differences in endowment and desires make for the rationale of exchange: actors can accordingly acquire things they desire, but which they do not have — and vice-versa. In other words: unless actors have different preferences — i.e., attach different salience to particular policy elements and policy results — "political trading" will not occur.

As for the relevant *actors*, political exchange theory — unlike public choice approaches, which rest on methodological individualism — deals with collective or corporate actors. These focus, homogenize and pool the diverse preferences of their members (Coleman 1974; Vanberg 1982) and, therefore, may be regarded as a means of reducing transaction costs (Williamson 1979; Gretschmann/Kenis, this volumes). In political exchanges, the actors often have to arrange for the exchange of binding agreements and contracts despite opposing interests among their members. The reliability of a corporate or collective exchange partner in such cases becomes a function of member support within organizations. This is to say that the reliability and significance of an actors in political exchanges depends upon his capacity to deal precisely , if not exclusively, with those issues for which member support is highest. Claus Offe (1984) has pointed out that this is the reason why membership organizations operate on the strategy "to exchange *for* many, but therefore not to exchange *everything*". This observation gives rise to the question about how significant and insignificant actors are differentiated in a particular domain. We propose the following: the more an actor can either affect the interest function of any other relevant actor in the policy domain, or the overall outcome of a policy process, the more significant he is — and vice-versa. The weight of an actor is determined to a large extent by the cohesiveness and the power of the group he represents, by the quantity and quality of the information made available to him, and by the variety of possible measures and moves he can take or make.

All these factors refer to the notion of "*resources*". Interestingly enough, most resources used in political exchanges involve some kind of externalities. This means that one actor's

ability to exert influence in a policy domain crucially depends on how many other participants will be affected by one move of this actor, in that they will or will not achieve their
objectives. However, unlike simple majority systems of decision making, political exchanges appear to be able to overcome problems which result from a-priori unequal
influence-potentials. While majority systems of decision-making pay little attention to the
loosing minority in the way of compensation, political exchanges by contrast include
compensation (from exchange) for the parties which accept those results from policy-
making which are not conducive or even detrimental to their interests. This may be regarded
as a sensible way of avoiding grounds for political unrest among those parties which have
repeatedly succumbed politically.

Yet, this is not to say that political exchanges completely rule out distributional conflicts.
In *economic* markets, the distribution of the gains from trade is clearly determined by the
process of price formation, sufficiently described in theoretical literature (Arrow and Hahn
1971; Debreu 1971). Equilibrium prices in an ideal Walrasian world guarantee a perfect
market clearing. The problem of *political* exchanges is that there are neither market- nor
shadow-prices available. This has to do with the lack of an equivalent for money in political
exchange. Money is not only, as described by sociologists, a generalised medium, but is,
more importantly, a yardstick which allows us to determine equilibrium prices — and
thereby, the relative gains and losses of the market participants. However, in the absence of
political money, the rates of exchange cannot be determined for a multi-lateral exchange
network. Therefore, the distribution of gains becomes the result of strategic action (manipulation of information, power-based setting of the terms of trade, influencing the risk
structure, etc.).

This makes political exchange vulnerable to "false trading", which results in differences
between expected or promised and actual outcomes. Due to the absence of a coherent
standard, false trading cannot be excluded to become a source of permanent conflict about
the fair distribution: i.e., the *relative* advantages derived from trade or relative deprivations
suffered from trade.

Though we cannot with any certainty determine beforehand whether these conflict-
generating elements in political exchange will outweigh the conflict-settling effects
mentioned above, we should not forget, however, to point out the role of trust and faithful
cooperation as salient features of political exchanges. In political exchange, *trust-based*
rights and obligations are substituted for *law-based* rights and obligations. To illustrate this
point, let us suppose that actor A signals to B his own readiness to exchange with him and
B replies by faithfully fulfilling what is requested. In the absence of well-defined formal
legal rights, this involves a risk — namely for A, the risk of being cheated — and a cost —
for B, the foregone opportunity of cheating A by giving him less than agreed upon. But they
have jointly produced a collective good—a faithful relationship—which is a valuable asset
for future transactions. Its yield is represented by a reduction in transaction costs: that is, the
cost of monitoring each other's activities or of taking measures to insure against being
defrauded. Trust is an asset the value of which can increase and decrease with the number

of successful or unsuccessful exchanges — exchanges which would not occur otherwise, because without trust trading would become too costly. But how is it that B does not grab the opportunity to cheat? Self-commitment — that is, refraining from defrauding an opponent — is a means of optimizing returns whenever future deals and transactions with one and the same partner appear probable. As Guttman has put it (1978), rational actors who know that their counterparts will reduce their offers and contributions and thereby deteriorate the terms of trade in response to negative experience and disappointed expectations, will exhibit positive, fair offers and stick to the rules in order to induce their counterparts to increase future contributions and expand exchanges. Even *present sacrifices*, or political credit, can be regarded appropriate and therefore be accepted, in order to gain *future benefits*.

But *what* exactly is traded in political exchange? The answer often given in the tradition of the school of "Scambio Politico" is this: "the according of legitimacy to the state", "political support", "consensus and compliance" offered by private actors in exchange for "policies", "decisions", "compromises" and "options" produced by the "state" for the sake of private actors. However, such a bi-polar framing, concentrating on the public-private relationship, does not appear to us to adequately describe the nature of political exchanges. Thinking in terms of political exchange involves the notion that a public authority or a state agency has become one actor among many in a political domain (Gretschmann 1986). In this setting, the actors try to influence others' choices and actions; and at the same time, they are exposing themselves to various influences exerted by others. In the literature dealing with the political exchange approach, one finds that the modern state is no longer regarded as the "dominant player" endowed with unilateral authority over polity and economy, but rather as just another part of a "horizontal" policy network.

This is not to say, however, that the state or a public authority involved in a particular policy-making domain necessarily holds exactly the same position as the other actors involved. It may well be the "agenda-setter making the initial move" in a policy-game. The actual role it plays as well as the (as)symmetric constellation under which it acts must be specified distinctly for each empirical case dealt with. Here, it may suffice to say that, what constitutes political exchange is the fact that a public actor is interested in incorporating the other actors by letting them co-shape and co- determine policy outcomes through political exchanges. The purpose of such a procedure is to make the other actors co-responsible for any — in most cases, rather uncalculable — outcome and to ensure sufficient support for policy measures. This implies — since several actors can provide for several shares of support — that the "state" has to exchange with a sufficient number of them at the same time. In most cases, the necessary support level is a function of the number of the participants involved, as well as a function of the number of issues (Gopoian 1984) posed: Take a situation in which the "state" offers tax preferences to special interest groups in order to achieve their compliance. Changing their relative welfare position might prompt other groups, which had been content with the distribution beforehand, to react by withdrawing their former support. Eventually, this may lead to an overall increase in the number of support providing and stabilizing measures.

Since all actors in political exchange are basically interested in achieving as much support as possible for their own objectives, every actor is faced with the necessity of (a) determining the amount of support necessary for this purpose, (b) estimating and influencing the capacities of relevant exchange partners, (c) limiting exchange assets and resources of opponents, (d) controlling the access to political markets. It can be (1) that support involves a variety of forms of compliance; and (2) that the relevant actors resolve problems (a) through (d) differently.

Finally, a short remark seems to be in order as to what is meant specifically by the term "*generalized* political exchange". One might assume that "generalized" refers to the large number of actors involved in, and affected by, political exchange. On the other hand, "*generalized*" might refer to the difference between parametric and strategic activities, that is between a situation with exogenous constraints as opposed to a constellation of endogenous constraints, dependent upon the choices and rewards of others. Since we have already ascribed both characteristics — number of actors and reflexitivity — to *political* exchanges, something else seems to be implied by "generalized". We believe that the "differentia specifica" of *Generalized* Political Exchange is a "relational repeatability", which ensures the option of future exchanges. Despite changing actor constellations in a policy domain — i.e., despite the "exit" of some actors and the "entry" of new ones, the established mode of "political exchange" continues to exist. In this context it can be argued that "generalized" refers to the differentiation between "process utility" and "goal utility": While the latter deals with the actual outcome of an exchange, the former is concerned with the process which leads to an outcome, a process which is *in itself* regarded as valuable. The same goes for GPE: regardless of how often and in what configurations it actually works, the existence of this institutional device benefits the polity as a whole — regardless of whether or not individual actors in a policy field derive gains from concrete transactions.[2]

4. The Logic of Political Exchange

In order to fully grasp political exchange and generalized political exchange and reveal their characteristic features, we must first understand the dynamics arising from the interactions and moves differently endowed and interested actors make within a specific action space. The logic of the dynamics of political exchanges, based on strategic action resulting from the actors' experiences of the past and expectations about the future, is covered in the model presented below.

In order to demonstrate how political exchange works, we have depicted in Figure 1 the interests of actors A and B for alternatives X and Y in a simple (two actors, two interests)[3] model of a policy domain. This implies that we measure both the interest of A and the benefits which accrue to him along the axis OX; and those of B, along OY. Let us assume that, as a consequence of their different endowments, A and B have at their disposal two different but restricted action spaces: the dotted line delineates A's leeway; the dashed line, B's. Let us now assume a starting point S for any policy process; let us further assume that the actions of A and B are exclusively guided by short-run and self-interested motives; and let us finally consider a situation in which both actors act alternately with A having the initial move. Then we can expect the following process: A will move from S to T, the latter representing the maximum he can gain in view of his restricted action space. Thereby, A will win benefits T'T''. This development, however, is detrimental for B, since A's gains are achieved only at the expense of a loss S'S'' in B's interest function. Consequently, B will answer by moving from V to U where he maximizes his interest given the relevant constraint. Now B has realized some gains by diminishing A's interest which, in turn, results in A moving next to V, and so on and so forth.[4]

Interestingly enough, this process shows evidence of inherently perverse dynamics (moving towards origin), since in the end both will be worse off — considering the outcome of each actor's moves countered by the other. The basic element of this process is the short-sightedness of the parties involved. If either were able to consider the long-term consequences of his moves — i.e., the countermoves of the opponent — he might be able to influence the overall outcome in the direction of a jointly favorable result.

As can easily be seen from Figure 2 — where we have dropped the assumption of restricted spaces — the logic of jointly favorable results consists of moving towards point M, which represents a maximum of the interest realization of both parties. Unfortunately,

Figure 1   The Logic of Political Exchange I

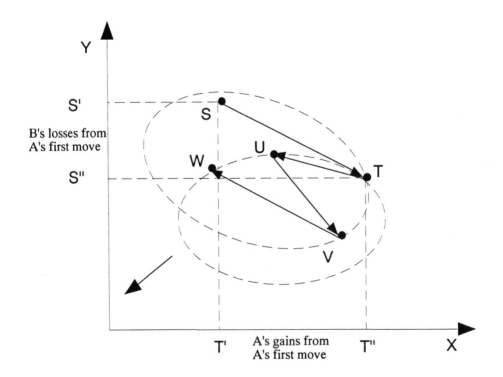

from there a gain can be derived only from conflict moves: that is, M —> Y' in favor of B
at the expense of A, or M —> X', the reverse. Once having reached M, the only possibility
for further "jointly favorable" action is to create additional leeway by shifting Y'X' to
Y"X", thus making M' a possibility. We shall demonstrate below that this possibility has
played an important role in the course of the German tax reform debate.

At this point the reader may wonder were "exchange" comes into play. The answer is
twofold. Firstly, and referring to Figure 1, welfare economics has proven conclusively that
A's move from S to T might be tolerable for B and 'benign' for the system: i.e., an improvement of the overall portion of gains and loss, if and only if A is willing to (over)compensate
B's losses S'S" from his gains T'T" and if B in exchange renounces his TV move. Such a
compensation is worthwhile as long as T'T" > S'S"; in other words, *net* gains can be
achieved. Exchange here implies a positive sum game — which is, however, not necessarily
free of conflict. As pointed out in section 3, the main conflict in political exchange, where
not primarily physical resources but rather activities, obligations, promises or information
are traded, lies in determining the "terms of trade" or "relative prices": what is a move, or
the willingness not to move by one party, worth to the other?

The second point where exchange plays a decisive role in our model, is in triggering the
move and in stabilizing the path to M in Figure 2. In order to avoid the pursuit of their myopic
self-interests, the actors have to offer each other advantageous items through exchange. In

Figure 2   The Logic of Political Exchange II

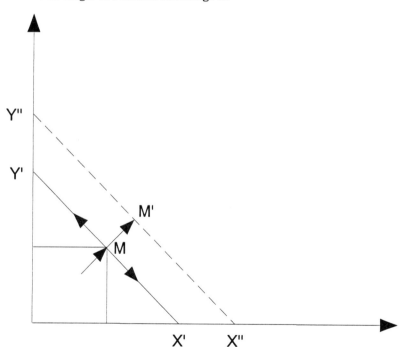

this way, exchange prevents the system from moving towards the 'origin' and enables it to turn towards M.

These considerations clearly demonstrate that political exchange is not simply an institutional device for recurrent transactions, but that it is also a means to discover opposing interests and divergent intentions *as mutually compatible*. In so doing, political exchange contributes to improving the steering capacity and steering results (pay-offs) of policy-making. This will be demonstrated below using the example of the three-tiered German Tax Reform (1986/1988/1990).

5. The German Tax Reform Package as Political Exchange

While economic tax analyses rest on the assumption that individual or corporate taxpayers are passive adjusters to tax legislation who react through adjustments in savings, spendings, work effort, investment behaviour, etc., political studies of taxation have primarily conceived taxpayers as actively influencing both tax legislation (for example, by means of lobbying) and tax implementation (by influencing bureaucratic interpretation of tax laws or by going to the courts) (Breton 1974, Finer 1975). The process of how organisational actors in the area of taxation (inter)act with each other in order to avoid losses or even gain advantages (Aumann and Kurz 1977), has so far been a widely neglected field (Folkers 1983). Presumably, this has to do with the fact that the fiscal game is vastly more complex than e.g. the more coherent field of "wages, prices and employment" regulated through a corporatist set-up.

Various and numerous tax interests are pitted against one another. As Forte and Peacock have observed, "conservationists will support pollution taxes, whereas car-owners, will oppose petrol tax increases; retired persons will support preferential tax treatment of pensions, whereas workers with families will look for improved tax exemptions for children ... Capital and labor will have a combined interest in the car industry in opposing automobile and petrol taxes, whereas both restaurant owners and employees will oppose tightening-up of record keeping for tax purposes, as recent Italian experience has shown" (1981: 9) . Therefore, research in taxation not surprisingly reveals some strange bedfellows. Complex tax structures, for which Richard Bird once coined the term "Tax Kaleidoscope", are a natural result of this heterogeneity among taxpayers' interests.

In what follows, we will analyze the multiplicity of interests and their interplay — through political exchanges of any sort — triggered by the recent German "three-step" Tax Reform Package (1986-1988-1990).

5.1 Causes and Concepts

Generally speaking, the starting point for most tax reforms or tax amendments are economic malfunctions, political dissatisfaction or unintended side-effects on other policy domains arising form the existing tax system. Political objectives (above all to win elections), economic necessities (e.g., to boost a sluggish economy), fiscal requirements (for example,

Table 1   Factors Determing the Process of Interest Mediation and Exchange in the Tax Reform Debate

1 ACTORS	2 HOW AFFECTED BY TAX REFORM	3 OBJECTIVES	4 RESOURCES/ THREAT POTENTIAL	5 ATTITUDE TOWARDS REFORM	6 CONCESSIONS AND EXCHANGES
GOVERNMENT	Loss of fiscal revenue because a net tax relief is intended.	To optimize fiscal revenues while minimizing political costs. To win votes and elections. To justify proclaimed economic policies.	Legal enactment and enforcement of tax measures.	Initiator and principal proponent.	1. Offers selected tax preferences and/or specific public goods in exchange for support of the reform as a whole. 2. Resources for revenues to produce net benefits from reform for the ___ policy in exchange for political support of a "less-state ideology" and for private business' promises to boost the economy.
BUSINESS a) Big Business (BDI) tax liabilities by	Reduction of corporate tax rate at the top — from 56% to 50% will reduce Tax provisions to in- 3 billion DM. Some depreciation allowances will be cut down.	Favourable tax treatment of investment. employment via crese rates of return.	(a and b) Business determines level and structure of (in-)activities.	(a and b) Complaints that private households taxrelief will be considerably higher' than business'.	1. Government promises to keep up or even enlarge subsidies to industry. 2. Assures that no increase in VAT is planned. 3. Offers subsidized credits to small- and medium-sized firms (6 billion DM). 4. Guarantees "grandfather clauses" and other "phasing-in" provisions. 5. Business assures "grudging consent", since business expects increase in domestic demand through tax relief for households.
b) Small Business (ASU, ZDH)	Relief of tax burden through a lowered top rate of income tax (56% to 53%) and a new tax scale with lower marginal rates.	Suitable transition period to adjust corporate planning. "Calculability" and continuity of tax policies.	The latter also affect economic growth and thereby, the tax base.	Complaints unequal treatment of corporate and uncorporated firms through different top rates.	

Table 1   Cont.

1 ACTORS	2 HOW AFFECTED BY TAX REFORM	3 OBJECTIVES	4 RESOURCES/ THREAT POTENTIAL	5 ATTITUDE TOWARDS REFORM	6 CONCESSIONS AND EXCHANGES
UNIONS	Considerable tax relief for employees increases take-home pay of clientele.

Cancellation of some selective tax exemptions and allowances for particular groups of employees. | Fair after-tax distribution of income.

Job creation to re-establish a high level of employment. | Strike.

Political pressure.

Withdrawal of system support. | Refuse to accept tax reform because high incomes would profit overproportionately. Could well live with a higher level of tax burden if the money raised would be spent to finance a public job creation programme. | 1. Government offers a moderate extension of public deficit spending via cheaper credits as a means to stimulate growth and employment.
2. Government adds a "social component" to the tax reform by "raising the floor"; the base amount of tax-free income will be raised. This will remove half a million low-wage earners from the tax-rolls.
3. Politicians encourage the unions to move for higher wages in the next bargaining round. |

Table 1   Cont.

1 ACTORS	2 HOW AFFECTED BY TAX REFORM	3 OBJECTIVES TAX REFORM	4 RESOURCES/ THREAT POTENTIAL	5 ATTITUDE TOWARDS REFORM	6 CONCESSIONS AND EXCHANGES
JURISDICTIONS a) States (*Länder*)	Will lose revenues according to their share (of 42,5%) of the income tax total.	(a and b) Safeguard their fiscal autonomy and jurisdiction to tax.	(a) Possibility to refuse or deny consent to tax reform in the second house of the bicameral German parliament which represents the "*Länder*". Possibility to appeal to the Constitutional Court.	(a and b) No tax reform without an adequate compensation for the fiscal losses through a reorganization of the revenue-sharing and fiscal equalization system.	1. Federal government offers municipalities special and badly needed cheap credits (21 billion DM). 2. Federal government makes concessions in intergovernmental fiscal relations. 3. Despite fierce opposition by those states which are governed by Social Democrats, the Fed. succeeds to gain support of the majority of Christian Democratic States.
b) Municipalities	Suffer losses up to 15% of income tax total.	To keep their revenues from taxation constant.	Reduction of public investment on the level of the municipality, where 3/4 of all public investments are made. Threat to raise the trade tax levied by local authorities, which would run counter the tax reform intentions.		

Table 1   Cont.

1 ACTORS	2 HOW AFFECTED BY TAX REFORM	3 OBJECTIVES	4 RESOURCES/ THREAT POTENTIAL	5 ATTITUDE TOWARDS REFORM	6 CONCESSIONS AND EXCHANGES
SPECIAL INTEREST GROUPS					
a) Fiscal Administration (German Tax Union)	Has to carry out the changed tax laws, and this means additional work effort.	"Administrative ease".	Specific information and know-how; fiscal administration determines the degree.	No reform without additional personnel posts in tax offices. Instead of scale corrections and top rate variations tax administration plead for tax simplification.	No promises, offers or results up to this point. Therefore, partial collaboration with unions and Taxpayers Associations.
b) Taxpayers' Association (Bund der Steuerzahler)	Through all those measures which affect private households.	Tax simplification. Lower tax burden.	Possibility to activate taxpayer-voter protest. Pressure through the press. Can further non-compliance of the individual tax-payer through special recommendations and legal support.	Basic direction of reform is agreed. However, it is not radical enough. Simplicity and fairness are sufficiently considered. Negative vertical equity is criticized.	Grudging consent but tries to fathom future joint efforts (with unions, fiscal authorities, etc.) to correct the reform.
(c) Association of Professional Tax Consultants	Change of Tax Code provides new demanding for their services (raises profits). Additional training is required to adapt to alterations in the tax code.	High incomes from consulting. Keep up barriers to new competitors.	Determine degree and quality of tax-compliance. Dispose of significant information. Have an influential lobby.	Vested interest in conserving the complications and loopholes of tax system. Tax policy is called upon to guarantee steadiness (to avoid adjustment costs).	Claims for further relief of business taxation and more tax preferences for self-employed. No negotiation with government so far.

to lower high deficits), or social and distributional considerations (horizontal and vertical inequities,[5] bracket creep,[6] etc.), are often the sources of tax reform efforts.

As can be shown, these factors have also played a crucial role in the German case: (1) In 1985, one year before the elections, the conservative-liberal government promised a "grand" tax reform in three steps for the years 1986, 1988 and 1990, a reform involving massive income tax reductions — 20 billion DM for 1986 and 1988, and 44 billion for 1990 — for business and households, in order to win votes. (2) In the face of a 9% unemployment rate, the tax reform idea had been designed as a means to stimulate economic growth, to promote capital formation and investment, to improve the incentives to work, and, thereby, to stabilize employment. Against this background, the tax reform may be regarded as a substitute for a public employment program which the social-democratic opposition demanded. (3) The tax reform was intended to mitigate the effects of bracket-creep by introducing a linear-progressive tax scale, and to undo horizontal inequities by broadening the tax base. A couple of tax preferences were to be curtailed if not eliminated; loopholes were to be closed; and marginal tax rates, particularly at the top, were to be lowered. (4) Needless to say, the fiscal reduction aspect was also considered: of the 44 billion DM tax relief (for the 1990 part of the package), the "net" reduction should amount to only 25 billion while 19 billion relief were to be compensated by cutting subsidies and tax preferences or by a rise in *indirect* taxes.

5.2 Actors, Interests, Resources and Exchange Strategies

After the first proposal became public, various organized interests suggested alternative interpretations of the problems to be tackled and the adequate measures to be taken:1 i.e., to be incorporated in the tax reform concept. Coalitions of actors (Sabatier 1986) — opponents and proponents — attempted to influence the shape of the reform model.

Table 1 offers an overview of the factors determining the process of interest mediation and exchange during the course of the tax reform debate. Column (1) identifies the relevant actors; column (2) specifies how actors are affected by the intended changes; column (3) denotes the main objectives the actors pursue; column (4) lists the relevant resources each actors has at his disposal, which can be used in "political exchange" activities; column (5) classifies the position and attitude of each actor towards tax reform; column (6) shows exchange offers and concessions made.

We now consider the matrix in more detail. We have identified a set of seven organisational actors most relevant for the working of the tax reform. These are: (1) government; (2) business such as the BDI (Federation of German Industry) for big business and ZDH (Central Association of German Handicrafts) or ASU (Association of Independent Businessmen) for small and medium sized industries; (3) the unions, represented by the DGB (German Trade Union Federation); (4) the territorial authorities (*Länder*) represented by the "Bundesrat" (Federal Council) and the municipalities organized in the DST (Federation of German Towns); (5) the DSG (German Tax Union) which represents the fiscal administration and their members; (6) the Taxpayers' Association (Bund der Steuerzahler); and finally

(7) the Association of Tax Consultants (Steuerberater Deutschland).

The notion of the importance of these actors has been gained from the frequency and the size of their public statements in newspapers, political magazines, television, etc. Non-organised actors — e.g., the ordinary citizen taxpayer — has been excluded from our analysis. Although taxpayers have the possibility of non-compliance, their bargaining power is very low and they are consequently considered to be of only very limited relevance for political exchanges.

According to the basic formulas of combinatorics, these seven core actors can theoretically combine pairwise in 21 different ways. 56 possibilities result if multiple combinations are taken into account. Surprisingly enough, however, the number of (partial) collaboration, coalition and exchange relations — which we found empirically — is far lower.

The government needs to be viewed as the prominent actor and the dominant player in this policy domain, since it holds a central position through dealing — bilaterally or multilaterally — with *all* the other actors. With reference to the basic features which characterize the 1986-1990 reform-package (see section 5.1 above), our first observation is that federal government will definitely suffer financial losses from the core elements of the reform, that is, from the tax relief granted to taxpayers. In fact, the taxshare in GNP has dropped from 24.2% (1985) to 22.5% (1990). In turn, government reckons on winning votes and "political support" by lowering the tax burden. In this regard, the reform serves two purposes: The tax reform proposal has been to demonstrate that (1) an important step towards the objective of "less state" has been taken, and that (2) government offers a better-suited instrument to tackle unemployment than the opposition does. The reform is held to be an effective means of fostering growth and employment by giving more leeway to private initiative (cf. Government Information Office 15/87).

Since government is the principal proponent of the reform-undertaking, it tries to win support (a) by offering selective tax preferences or public expenditures and regulations to particular interest groups and associations, and (b) by pointing out that the tax reduction will benefit the polity as a whole and all its members. The former we call a *particularistic strategy*, the latter a *populistic strategy* of political exchange.

As far as business is concerned, big business will profit considerably from the reduction of the corporate income tax which will be put into effect in 1990. Maximum rates will be lowered from 56% to 50% involving a net relief of 2.5 billion DM. For small and medium sized business — which accounts for 90% of all firms — the "normal" income tax is the main "business tax". This means that small business will benefit particularly (by five billion DM) from the revision of the previous income tax rate structure into a less steeply progressive scale with lower marginal rates across the whole range. Moreover, top rates will be lowered to 53%. However, business will also suffer some losses (about 2 billion DM) since some special depreciation allowances and tax preferences will be abolished along with other measures to (re)finance the reform.

Both attitudes and objectives of business are at hand: In order to secure a sufficiently high "rate of return", business wants to maintain special tax provisions, and to keep tax shelters and loopholes, and argues that a smooth transition from the old to the new tax code should be guaranteed in order to facilitate corporate planning adjustments. Otherwise — and this seems to involve an overt threat — firms' decisions in favour of more investment would be "jeopardized". Whilst the state influences the firms' after-tax profile through imposing a particular tax rate, the firms in turn are free to determine the size of the total tax receipts through decisions on employment and production.

With specific reference to this mutual dependency, the Federation of German Industry has repeatedly criticized the reform as not far reaching enough to stimulate investment. The Federation therefore called for larger tax reliefs in order to compensate for increasing risks in volatile markets (HB 90). Moreover, business associations complain that the pressing burden from trading-taxes and from the net worth tax for companies will not be altered by the reform. However, business representatives have welcomed the unburdening of private households from the tax pressure as a means to further domestic demand and savings. While increases in demand means an increase in the sales volumes, savings — i.e., capital formation — leads to lower interest rates for loans. Business would profit from both.

In order to win the support of business for the reform plan, government has offered a major business tax reform for 1991 involving a thorough revision of the corporate income tax code, of the local trade taxes and of the business wealth tax. In monetary terms, these measures promise to ease company tax burden by 25 billion DM. Moreover, publicly-provided credit funds (6 billion DM) shall be made available to small and medium-sized firms at very low interest costs, in order to improve their economic situation. In exchange for these "measures", business has recently signaled preliminary "grudging consent" to the reform plans.

Whereas business has turned out to be a proponent, however half-hearted, of the reform concept, unions regard themselves as strict opponents. The unions' interest in matters of taxation is twofold. They strive for a "just" after-tax distribution of income: in other words, for vertical equity and, with high unemployment, they call for public job creation programs. The tax reform as designed is seen as fulfilling neither.

Unions maintain that through the tax reform the conservative-liberal government is redistributing after-tax income from labour to capital. The purported reform purpose, namely to stimulate economic growth and employment, is seen merely as window-dressing. The gain received by employees in the form of tax reliefs, meaning higher take-home pay, would be (more than) offset by measures to (re)finance the reform. Indeed, in 1988 the government decided to increase from 1989 on the tax on petrol and tobacco , the burden of which is borne primarily by low- and medium-income earners. In the view of the unions, the net winners will be business and high-income-earners, whereas the ordinary citizen will lose because of several tax revisions: formerly tax-free, employer-provided fringe benefits will become imputed taxable income; additional earnings from Sunday and overtime work shall no longer be object to a favorable tax treatment; the so-called tax-free Christmas and Employees' allowances will be eliminated — allowances which once had been introduced into the tax code as a means of compensating for the advantage given to entrepreneurs and self-employed to shape transactions, so as to receive the most favorable tax treatment Therefore, the unions were very disinclined to accept the tax reform proposals.

However, although the unions have powerful resources at their disposal such as strikes, political pressure, and wage bargaining instruments, their actual reactions have materialized to be remarkably moderate. Presumably, this has to do with three facts: firstly, for the distributional objective, the tax reform plan involves a so-called "social component". The amount of basic tax-free income will be raised so that about half a million low-wage earners will be removed from the tax rolls. Secondly, average middle class "skilled workers", who constitute a powerful clientele of unions, are likely to be among those taxpayers who benefit most in relative terms. After the reform, they will have a disposable income 12% higher than previously. Thirdly, the unions were publicly encouraged by some politicians to enforce high wage claims in the next bargaining rounds. This is by no means a selfless "appeal", because income increments stand for additional tax receipts. In that, this indicates a sort of quid pro quo deal between government and unions.

Even more resourceful are the jurisdictions: i.e., the *Länder* (state) and the municipalities. Since the *Länder* are lawfully entitled through the revenue sharing system of fiscal federalism to 42.5% of income tax total and the municipalities to 15%, their fiscal situation will be impaired by the reform. The *Länder* will have to bear revenue losses up to 11 billion DM (for 1986-88) and another 12 billion (for 1990) and the municipalities up to 3.5 billion.

Fiscal autonomy being one of their prominent interests, both the Bundesrat, a kind of second chamber representing the *Länder's* interests, and the Federation of German Towns have called for a reorganisation of the fiscal equalization system (cf. FAZ 101: HB 85; HB 106).

Since the consent of the Bundesrat is a necessary precondition for changing the tax code through parliament, the government was forced to offer concessions. It did so by increasing the federal block grants to the *Länder* by 5% per year from 1986 on, and by supporting the *Länder* to keep wage increases in the public sector at a very low rate (86/87: 3.5%; 1988: 2.4%; 1989: 1.4% in nominal terms) (DBB 1990). In order to prevent the municipalities from engaging in 'counter productive reactions' — e.g., increasing local trade taxes or decreasing local public investment — the federal government made extensive loan commitments for local projects.

Last but not least, special interest groups play a decisive role in the making of tax policies.

The financial administration, organized as the "German Tax Union", has to carry out and implement tax revisions. This involves additional work efforts, lowering the "administrative ease". No tax reform can be made without a close collaboration between government and fiscal authorities. The latter are endowed exclusively with the information and know-how necessary to achieve taxpayers' compliance (Kinsey 1987). This fact, which finds its expression in the level of revenue collected, highlights the important role played by tax authorities in tax reform. Accordingly, the German Tax Union has claimed that it would be impossible to carry out the reform plans without additional manpower: i.e., 2000 new job openings (HB 67). This argument is strongly supported by the following figures. Whereas during the last decade the number of "tax cases" has increased by about 200%, only 40% additional manpower was employed. This development will worsen if the reform plans materialize. Negotiations between government and tax authorities on this matter are still going on.

However, the tax reform promises tax simplification and therefore is responsive to another argument made by tax officials: namely, that justice and equity can only be guaranteed if the tax code were cleared of overcomplexities. 120 tax statutes, 220 ordinances regulating tax treatment, and about 1000 administrative tax regulations are testimony to the fact that simplification of the tax system is badly needed. The complexity and ambivalence of tax laws allow the clever and wealthy to exploit loopholes and use tax shelters. The ordinary citizen has neither the information for loophole-finding nor the means to consulting professional tax advisers. As this has also been argued by the Taxpayers' Association (*Bund der Steuerzahler*), mutual support and a joint appeal to Parliament in favour of a more simple and just tax system has been stipulated (FAZ 171).

The German Taxpayers' Association is a pressure group representing taxpayers' interests. Being an Olson-type (Junkerheinrich 1986), latent interest association, its main political resource is the mobilization of public opinion. Main objectives are bringing about a lower tax burden for households, a simplification of the tax system (HB 227), a general roll-back of "Leviathan", a cutback of waste and red tape in the public sector. The basic elements of the tax reform such as lower rates, a broader base, the revision of the schedule are accepted and the reform plan is even defended against, for example, state and local sector interests (Karl-Bauer-Institut 1987). The Taxpayers' Association is in accord with the Unions in complaining about possibly regressive effects of the reform plan; it agrees with business and unions that government should not increase indirect taxes to collect the revenues necessary for refunding the reform. It is generally argued that a larger share of state expenditure (subsidies) should be cut in order to finance this reform.

Finally, the Association of Tax Consultants has repeatedly addressed both government and the public on matters related to tax reform. Tax revisions usually provide consultants and specialists with additional demand for their services, thereby raising their profit. At the same time, however, they have to develop new strategies for the sake of their clients, which introduces costs for gathering information, acquiring new know-how, etc. Therefore, the political aim they pursue can be derived from self-interest: tax advisers have a vested interest in maintaining as complex a tax system as possible in order to secure their position as experts, and they plead for steadiness in tax policies in order to avoid "adjustment costs". This was, in fact, the core of a resolution proposed to government during the course of the tax reform process (HB 219). In this way, they may be regarded as the adversaries of unions and the Taxpayer's Association. Ultimately, the Tax Consultants' Association made its support for the reform dependent upon the government's concession not to extend the liabilities of tax advisers for the compliance of their clients. As tax consultants play a major role in taxpayers' compliance, their support of the reform plans is badly needed.

From what has been said above, it is clear that government and its "political trading partners" have made some exchanges in order to win and not to lose from the tax reform plans. Moreover, three sets of coalitions can be identified:

a) An *"equity coalition"*, calling for lower tax burden and more distributional justice and "social elements" to be incorporated into the reform model. The Trade Unions and the German Taxpayers' Association have joined forces here.

b) An *"efficiency coalition"*, composed of government, business and partially — the Fiscal Administration and Tax Consultants. Their aim is to successfully design the tax system so as to arrive at a growing and more efficient economy.

c) A *"revenue coalition"*, which primarily aims at an efficient system of tax collection to guarantee sufficient resources to finance public activities. The proponents here are government, *Länder* and municipalities.

Although these three coalitions differ distinctly as to how to allocate the gains from the tax reform to different uses, all actors seem to share a covert common belief: namely, that tax rates determine the tax base — i.e., income. A rate-variation automatically expands or narrows the GDP (Auerbach 1986, Adams 1981).[7] This means that, in the face of the tax reductions envisaged, *every* actor can hope for some gains from the reform as a whole. This, the reader may remember, closely resembles the exchange logic involving a shift of the ultimate constraint as outlined in Figure 2. Government, as well as state and local authorities, expect to suffer short term revenue losses; in the long run, however, the economy will, it is held, be stimulated by lowering the tax burden — which will in turn lead to increased economic growth and, consequently, rising revenues. Unions can hope that unemployment will be curtailed if lower tax rates do indeed contribute to a more rapidly growing economy. Business can hope to increase after-tax profits. Taxpayers hope to enjoy increased take-home pay. Tax authorities can hope for a better remuneration and more manpower if revenues really rise in the post-reform tax system.

In sum, all actors have formed at least partly positive expectations about the advantages of the reform as such, independent of any "positional gains" they can derive by means of political exchanges. These expectations are based on a view of the situation common to all of the actors involved in the domain of tax policy-making.

6. By Way of Conclusion: Stabilizing or Destabilizing Effects of Political Exchange

Dependent on whether and how the expectations mentioned above materialize, tax reforms will be in the future subject to periodic overhaul as indeed they have been in the past. Schmoelders (1971) has coined the term "Permanent Tax Reform" as a way of indicating that one reform will be subject to the next. Empirical evidence confirms this proposition: in the last ten years we have witnessed as many as 46 revisions of the income tax code in Germany. Such frequent revisions have become part of the actors' expectations.

This "permanency" of tax changes is due to the fact that — despite the reality that political exchange helps to make others' choices of action calculable and, up to a point, predictable — an actor ascribes probabilities to the various strategies of other actors, probabilities which are continuously adjusted in the light of others' actual behavior. At the same time, the actor has to consider in his own choice of strategy that the opponents will likewise take into account the actor's own activities. This is a prediction problem analogous to the problem of regression analysis, in which varying degrees of confidence exist about parameter estimates — depending on the number of observations, relationships among variables and other factors. As long as it is difficult to predict others' behavior and the resulting development with satisfactory accuracy, there is very little likelihood of a continuous system stability (Mutti 1984:17).

As far as the tax reform is concerned, benefits and costs of tax changes are uncertain because there exist variations in, and thus uncertainty about, the actors' reactions and behavior in response to the occurred changes. Since all actors involved are acutely aware of these dynamics, our proposition is that political exchanges increase the probability that any compromise will be found, but that political exchange at the same time generates uncertainty about how long the compromise will endure (under changing conditions). In other words, political exchanges make for a solution, but this very solution creates its own problem of adjustment.

If the organisational actors in the domain of tax policy making strive for relative positional gains and neglect the absolute benefits which accrue to all of them to different degrees, why then should they not "defect" from the (previous) compromise when they see a chance to improve their relative position in a new constellation?

Recall Fig. 1 depicting the logic of political exchange. The conducive moves explained there are adequate only as long as the framework — i.e., the axes of coordinates — remain fixed. We must be aware, however, that the moves made can well shift the whole system of coordinates (imagine a rotation in the origin). This would induce actors to start moving again so as to achieve a new mutually acceptable solution — a new "equilibrium", as it were (see Appendix).

Put succinctly, our hunch is that the political exchanges — through which a particular outcome of tax-policy making is achieved — alter the data constellation of the reference system which is relevant to the actors' behavior. In technical terms, political exchanges do not simply change the parameter values within an existing structural model of reality but rather the structural relations of which the model is composed: that is, the structure of the policy domain. This is an effect akin to Heisenberg's "indeterminacy principle".

This leads us to the conclusion that political exchange is a device for coordinating divergent interests and intentions and, thereby, creates a certain form of stability — namely, reliability and calculability. It is the same time, a source of ever newly-evolving uncertainty which springs from the necessity to continuously adjust expectations. In our view, this ambivalence is the very essence of political and generalized political exchange.

Appendix

As an example of what is said above, consider the following simply model:

(1) $T_t = a + bz_t + cT_{t-1} + u_t$

where T is a political target variable (e.g., tax revenue), z is a policy variable (e.g., tax rate, or tax base) and u is a stochastic disturbance term with the usual properties; t-subscript indicates time.

Now assume a linear feed-back control given by:

(2) $z_t = d + kT_{t-1}$

with d and k being parameters which describe political behavior of the participants in domain policy-making, behavior which affects the outcome. Political Exchange can be viewed as a steering and coordinating mechanism with the tendency to set the parameters d and k so as to minimize deviations from the political target T:

(3) $E(V) = E(T_t - T')^2$

with T' the desired level of T and E denoting expected value. Given the assumption that the parameters in equation (1) are independent from d and k, the optimal setting of d and k are

(4) $k = -c/b$ (5) $d = (T' - a)/b$.

Proof:

Substituting (3) through (1) and (2) yields

$E(V) = E(a + bz_t + cT_{t-1} + u_t T')^2$

$= E(a + bd + bkT_{t-1} + cTt-a + u_t -T')^2$

$= E(a + bd + T_{t-1}(bk + c) + u_t - T')^2$

For k = -c/b we have: Tt-1 (bk + c) = Tt-1 (c-c) = 0

for d = (T' - a)/b respectively:

a + b (T' - a)/b - T' = a + T' - a - T' = 0.

This leads to

$E(V) = E(u_t)^2 = 0$.

Political exchange processes thus do influence the target variable T_k, and the effects on T_t through changes in the parameters d and k can be clearly predicted.

Now suppose that the parameters *a and b are themselves a function of the policy parameters d and k*:

(6) $T_t = a(d,k) + b(d,k) z_t + cT_{t-1} + u_t$.

The optimal settings are then

(9) $k = -c/b(d,k)$ and

(10) $d = (y - a(d,k))/b(d,k)$ (the derivation is analogous to the one above).

It is clear that in such cases, although political exchange has effects on the target variable T_t these effects are indeterminable. The degree of control necessary for determining the policy performance requires complete knowledge about the functions (a (d,k) and b (d,k), but these — like moving targets — vary with the choice of d and k itself.

Quod erat demonstrandum!

Notes

1 Coleman (1986) has argued in a more elaborate way for a research program akin to this one.
2 Notable here is the similarity in meaning between this concept of "generalized" and the one used by Parsons concerning his generalized media of exchange. What led Parsons to the introduction of his concept was the fact that in social life many relations are established between and among diverse phenomena, tendencies and so on. The capacity to transcend and thereby relate diverse things makes up the generality of a medium of exchange. This capacity of bridging the diversity of diversities without therefore having to rely on mechanisms such as amalgamation or identification of individual identity with collective identity, makes up the crux of generalized political exchange as noted above. But whereas Parsons and his followers locate the solution to this bridging problem at the level of the collectivity, we do so from the actual situation of purposive actors. Whereas the concept of generalized media of exchange — evolutionarily developed as a materialized answer to the problem of double contingency — may hold for many highly differentiated social systems, most policy domains cannot rely on to such systemic integrative mechanisms but depend rather on a continuous process of reproducing their generality through ongoing actions.
3 This simple case can be generalized without any problem for a n-person m-interest constellation. However, since this no longer leads to a diagrammatic exposition but rather demands advanced mathematical tools, we have for purposes of clarity chosen the simple version.
4 One point might be important to mention here: The reason why A will not return from B's U to T again, but try another a bit less favorable point V, is due to learning. A recognizes that his first move was overly demanding, once he has been confronted with B's U-move. So, he will be a bit more modest by going to V instead of back to T. The same goes for B not moving from V back to his max. position U but rather to W.
5 Public economists usually differentiate between the concepts of horizontal and vertical equity. Horizontal equity involves the rule that taxpayers in the same circumstances should pay an equal amount of taxes: i.e., they are to be treated alike. In order to ensure vertical equity, it is necessary to determine the amount to be taken from the "more able": i.e., the richer taxpayers. Taxpayers who dispose of different levels of resources — e.g., income or wealth — obviously have different abilities to contribute.
6 "Bracket creep" means that as nominal incomes rise due to inflation, more and more taxpayers fall into tax brackets originally put in place to apply only to the very wealthy.
7 The RWI has calculated that the growth effect of the 1986-1988 tax reduction would amount up to 0.5% of GNP growth, accompanied by a drop in unemployment by 115,000 employees.

Control as a Generalized Exchange Medium within the Policy Process?
A Theoretical Interpretation of a Policy Analysis on Chemicals Control

Volker Schneider

1. Introduction

One of the key concepts in the political and social sciences of today is the concept of exchange. Its theoretical currency seems ubiquitous and its empirical applications range from the explanation of micro-phenomena as single acts to the emergent properties of global social systems. The best-known and most numerous applications of this program are undoubtedly located at the individual and group level (cf. Homans, Blau, Thibeau/Kelley etc.). Less well-known, but much more interesting are applications of this conceptual framework to political macro-phenomena such as political culture, legitimacy, structures of politics, interest groups, modernization processes and specific political configurations such as 'clientelism' or 'neo-corporatism' (Waldmann 1972, 1973 Salisbury 1970, Schmidt et al. 1977, Eisenstadt/Roninger 1980).

An important aspect of the exchange concept points to some far ranging metatheoretical implications. Especially in the American social and political sciences, the exchange concept emerged within a behaviouristic and individualistic stream of theory development which conceived itself as an alternative to the functionalistic models of political and social reasoning. Although there have been some attempts to reconcile the two hostile conceptions (cf. Clark 1972) or to develop the idea of exchange between social subsystems or 'systemic interchanges' (see Parsons, Eisenstadt, Luhmann), the main stream of exchange theory always had been embedded less in system-functionalism than in structuralist or actor centered approaches, where actors, their voluntary strategies and the relations and interdependencies between actors (e. g. networks) had been the main focus of analysis.

Interestingly, during the late seventies a stream of "empirical theory" developed which used the exchange concept in a way which differed sharply from individualistic conceptions but rejected at the same time the traditional functionalist explanation for political institutions. The new basic feature of this conceptual development was undoubtedly the discovery of the importance of the empirically identifiable actors, their interests, their resources and their strategies for explaining institutional arrangements and political processes in contemporary politics and society. One of the first milestones in this track of theory building was

Pizzorno's explanation of cooperative industrial relations as deliberate strategies of labour, industry and government and not as the effect of some kind of ideological domination. In this respect he did not conceive cooperative arrangements between capital and labour as an effect of a pre-existing cooperative political culture (national mentality!!) or institutional structure, but as the outcome of a process of political exchange between the three main societal actors in contemporary society, between state, capital and labour (Pizzorno 1978). Another example more closely related to policy analysis was given by Scharpf (1985) who relates stable and durable relationships between actors in policy formulation processes (bargaining, cooperation, coordination) to exchange networks. Later Lehmbruch was one of the first authors within the debate on neo-corporatism to conceive intermediary relationships in corporatist arrangements as "political exchange" (Lehmbruch 1983; see also Lehmbruch 1985). Although in Streeck/Schmitter (1985) the concept of political exchange is not explicitly used, their attempt to show that the structure of organized interests and their relations with the government, where the government licenses, recognizes, gives access to policy making, and even supports interest organizations financially in exchange for information, control of its members and political support implicitly uses the "exchange idea" (Streeck/Schmitter 1985). Within the corporatist discussion, however, exchange relations usually meant those between the state and leading business organizations. Thus Bernd Marin's approach can be seen as going beyond these conceptual limits and systematizing and generalizing the basic idea that some specific political configurations and policy-making processes could be analyzed as dynamic exchange processes (Marin 1985).

Another field of discussion very much related to this approach is the German concept of "informal administrative action" (Bohne 1981) or "administrative self-binding" (Hoffmann-Riem 1982), which especially tries to explain exchange going on at the implementation level. Such exchange arrangements take place in stalemate situations between implementing agencies and regulated groups in which the government does not have sufficient resources to control and effectively police norm deviations. At the same time, however, the implementation target groups are unable to fend off regulative interventions perfectly. Both sides are therefore interested in a cooperative compromise whereby the state lowers the regulative burden and the regulated commit themselves to a cooperative stance regarding the application of regulations. Results of such a compromise are very often arrangements at the operative implementations level that save the administration economic resources. Such implementation arrangements can, according to Thrasher (1983:376), be generalized as resource exchange: "...behaviour within implementation structures can be discussed in terms of individuals engaged in a process of interpersonal exchange. These exchanges are necessary because individuals do not possess the resources needed to implement policies and are forced to seek the help of others both inside and more importantly outside their own organization."

Even if all these theoretical efforts vary sometimes significantly in their operational concepts, one important common denominator of all these new facets of exchange theory seems to be the focus of a strategic actor-orientation in explaining today's more and more complex political and social arrangements and processes. Although all of these new concepts hardly ever relate their metatheoretical foundations explicitly to methodological individualism, in practice they owe a great deal to these methodological principles. In these concepts political explanations focus on concrete actors and the relations between actors, be it an individual, an organization or a group, and not to "systems" or systemic properties. Another important aspect of the exchange theory is that exchange relations emerge out of "voluntary social action" and not through coercion (Blau 1983:208). Exchange relations also imply a utilitarian rationality of action: An exchange relation can neither be established nor maintained unless both parties involved stand to gain some kind of benefit from it (Scharpf 1978: 354).

The idea of the exchange relations existing not only between two or three actors but within a whole web of exchange flows, i.e. exchange within a whole system of actors who are tied together by a network of reciprocal resource flows, leads almost necessarily to a conception of a spatial generalization of exchange links, thus: generalized exchange. This idea of generalization through extension seems to be an important aspect of Marin's concept of generalized political exchange (Marin 1985).

From this perspective 'generalized exchange' should be understood as an antonym for restricted exchange, which is exchange restricted to dyadic relations such as barter and exchange which is limited to sporadic and isolated exchange acts. In contrast to this, generalized exchange relates to a highly functionally differentiated system, in which a multiplicity of interdependent actors is tied together through extended and recurrent exchange relations.

The concept of generalized exchange with respect to its spatial extension was originally introduced by Lévi-Strauss (1949) in a study of marriage systems. According to this concept, specific marriage rules and strategies logically lead to a long chain of families linked by kinship relations. This makes the constitution of long-distance alliances between culturally rather divergent groups possible. An analogous approach to the question of exchange in political life, therefore, would be that modern societal or policy sectors are also tied together on the basis of complex and integrating exchange relations.

The intention of this paper is the application of this concept of generalized political exchange to an empirical policy process. In order to clarify some conceptual problems within the ongoing debate, I will first discuss the specificity of interactions which exist on the basis of exchange relations. Secondly, I will try to elaborate the specificity of the political in political exchange. Finally, I will discuss the problem of the generalization of exchange relationships which then will be related to the problem of exchange media. The treatment of the last question will lead me to the introduction of the Marxian concept of money as "general equivalent" or generalized media. This will then be linked to the question of whether there is any political "general equivalent" similar to money in economic exchange. The answer will be found in the concept of "control over events/outcomes" as a kind of exchange currency or accounting unit (Coleman). After a short outline of this concept in general it will be specified and linked to the question of control in policy-making processes (actors, interests, resources, power positions and strategies of control) and will be applied to the issue of chemicals control.

2. The Specificity of the 'Political' in Political Exchange and the Question of Generalized Media

The concept of exchange implies a basic assumption about man and society. If exchange is conceived as the act of giving one thing for another, it is basically an individualistic concept: it is inseparably related to the autonomy of the individual actor, which has the ability and power to decide and to make choices, it presupposes therefore a modern conception of society, which is less governed by holistic norms (ideologies, religions etc.) than by "interests" (for this interpretation see the Dumont 1977, Rosanvallon 1977, Hirschman 1978). Exchange should be conceived as an autonomous and voluntary action which happens only when both parties decide to engage themselves in that kind of relation. In this sense exchange it is clearly an antonym to robbery. The proverb "fair exchange is no robbery" suggests such a meaning. As such it implies also the recognition of the autonomy and the property rights of each exchange partner.

In order to see the specificity of exchange relations between actors it is useful to look at the whole array of possible relationships between actors. If an actor wants to get some "thing" or resource from another actor, he has several means. If he is able to coerce or threaten others, he can simply force the other side to give him something for nothing. If he is less powerful or if he has no power at all, he can only appeal to the other actor's charity. In other words, exchange can be conceived as a specific organizing principle for a resource flow, where actors are dependent on each other and transfer things, goods or other values on a voluntary basis.

This conception of exchange is very clearly stated in Adam Smith's "Wealth of Nations":

"Nobody ever saw a dog make a fair and deliberate exchange of one bone for another with another dog. Nobody ever saw one animal by its gestures and natural cries signify to another, this is mine, that yours; I am willing to give this for that. When an animal wants to obtain something either of a man or of another animal, it has no other means of persuasion but to gain the favour of those whose service it requires. A puppy fawns upon its dam, and a spaniel endeavors by thousands attractions to engage the attention of its master who is at dinner, when it wants to be fed by him. Man sometimes uses the same art with his brethren, and when he has no other means of engaging them to act according to his inclinations, endeavors by every servile and fawning attention to obtain their good will. He has no time, however, to do this upon every occasion. (...) and it is in vain for him to expect it from their benevolence only. He will be more likely to prevail if he can interest their self-love in his favour, and shew them that it is for their own advantage to do for him what he requires of them. Whoever offers to another a bargain of any kind, proposes to do this. Give me that which I want, and you shall have this which you want, is the meaning of every such offer; and it is in this manner that we obtain from one another the far greater part of those good offices which we stand in need of." (1979: 26)

The extensive presentation of this well-known classical quotation is intended to support the argument that exchange — be it social, economic or political — is always governed by the same logic: It involves a voluntary transfer of resources between actors on the basis of at least some kind of reciprocity. Exchange thus can be understood as one form of solving the basic problem that one actor needs the other actors' cooperation if he is to realize his goals and interest. Political exchange thus does not mean a different logic of exchange but the intrusion of the exchange logic into politics and policy formulation. This means that the decision-making procedure of an authoritative allocation of values and resources could be also governed by exchange relations. With these kinds of relations the rules of the game in politics are transformed in such a way that "struggle", pressure, the use of force, or Carl Schmitt's "adversarial" relations are no longer the prevailing logic in the authoritative allocation of resources and values, but rather cooperation and bargaining, thus: exchange. Politics based on exchange would mean that generally binding decisions are not "imposed" by a winning coalition. They are the result of an exchange process, which, however, does not necessarily have to be an equilibrium. Exchange does not imply that each party would benefit from transactional relationships to the same degree. Asymmetrical or unequal exchange is a ubiquitous feature of political life; the fact that exchange systems are not open for everyone is also well known. In exchange networks power appears as unequal structural locations. This is an important subject for structural analysis based on the "network approach" (Knoke/Kuklinsky 1982, Burt 1982, Marsden 1983). Cooperation through exchange — and this is important to note — does not mean that the interests between the involved actors suddenly converge to a single point. As Professor Baldwin pointed out during the GPE conference, the strength of the exchange concept is that it allows the simultaneous conception of conflict and cooperation. Marin's concept of "antagonistic cooperation" also fits well into this context: because these very conflicts of interest exist, the actors are forced to cooperate and to choose the exchange strategy as a mode of conflict regulation (1985:154). Thus exchange does not mean neutralization of conflicting interests; within the institutional arrangements, which only facilitate and generalize long-term cooperation, the struggle of interests will go on, the actors being only more limited in the choice of their strategies and means.

"Exchange" is based on two preconditions: the first is that the actors have to be dependent on each other. If actors were totally self-sufficient there would be no need for exchange. The actors thus have to perceive each other's respective resources as valuable. The value of resources may depend on the one hand upon an actor's need for a resource and on the other hand upon the general availability (substitutability) of that resource. Dependency could also exist indirectly, if the actors jointly control a given event or action which affects them. Therefore, an actor who controls this given outcome or event only to a small degree needs the cooperation of other actors in co-determining the outcome. The second precondition is a more strategic one: the actors must have learned or must be convinced that the problem of interdependence must be solved by cooperation rather than by threat or coercion.

This model of dependency and exchange strategic behaviour on the basis of a jointly controlled outcome has been very clearly formulated by J. S. Coleman (1971, 1973). His — admittedly rather simple — model starts with a situation of interdependence in which the actions of certain actors have consequences for others. If actor B is affected by A's action, and if B is self-interested, then B is interested having some effect on this action, so that its consequences will be at least not wholly harmful. If force or coercion is excluded from the arsenal of means B has at his disposal for convincing A to act in an expected way, B could "buy" a given behaviour or the commitment to behave in a certain way from A.

If one considers the existence of not only a two-actor set but a system of actors who are interested in a whole array of issues and action outcomes, a complex network of exchange relations is involved. In order to conceptualize this some assumptions have to be made: First, every actor is driven by the desire to realize as much interests it can in each of these outcomes. Secondly the intensity of the actors interests varies among the different issues as well as its capacities to control the different action outcomes. It is very plausible to assume that the actors will attempt to gain more power over those action outcomes which interest them most and that they will shift their control capacities from action outcomes in which they are only slightly interested to outcomes in which they are very much interested. In U.S. Congress this kind of exchange is known as logrolling.

Within Coleman's model the actors are essentially exchanging "proportions of control" which they have at their disposal over different issues in the decision-making process. Actors thus trade control over events in which they have little interest for control over ones in which they are very much interested. The "terms of trade" in exchange relations are determined by dependency ratios, which again determine the supply and demand of control for each issue. Thus, the "price of control" depends on the one hand on the structure of interest dependencies (i.e. on the degree to which the different actors control events in which other actors have interests) and, on the other hand, on the control structure. The structure of control is to be understood as a matrix of power relations which expresses the degree to which actors are able to control their interest on their own and the degree to which the actors' interests are controlled by other actors. In such action systems control capacities are generally unequally distributed among actors.

In legislative "games" where control capacities are homogeneous (votes), "control" can be operationalized without greater difficulties as a quota of votes. If a perfect market as well as certain other model assumptions are supposed (e.g. the allocation principle, see for details Kappelhoff 1977), the prices or value of a "unit of control" can be determined with matrix algebra. This price for the control capacities over one event then could be interpreted as the value which the event has for the whole actor system (Kappelhoff 1977:10).

At the model level there are a series of assumptions which make it difficult to use this concept for the analysis of real word phenomena. Applications of this exchange logic to empirical situations are complicated especially where different types of control resources are involved. Aside from the "perfect market assumption" (which in economics also exists only in text books), especially the multiplicity of resources within the actor system makes the "homogeneity" of control means problematic. This creates the problem of how to find one common denominator for all resources to which the homogeneity assumption can be applied. Such an application of Coleman's model to empirical exchange situations within community politics was realized by Marsden/Laumann (1977) as well as by Pappi/ Kappelhoff (1984). In these situations there was at the empirical level obviously no such single and unified "control capacity" as the votes in legislative decision making. Empirically more realistic, these authors conceptualized a set of public decision-making processes which assumed that the total control over the given set of public decisions would be exerted with the aid of 10 different resources such as authority, money, land, expert knowledge etc. The implicit idea in this approach was that all different resources finally function as "capacities to control" some part of the decision-making outcome. The different influence resources thus had been essentially discounted to a common denominator: "control". This unit then expressed the effectiveness of each resource in controlling events or outcomes. Although very different in substance and shape, expert knowledge and authority, for example, were treated as "commensurable" with regard to the proportion of control they have over events or action outcomes. As all different resources are only means to control events, the proportion of control they command thus could be understood as a unit of account or currency in exchange processes in political life (Pappi/Kappelhoff 1984:102).

This basic idea could be generalized, and "control over outcomes" could be seen as the "general equivalent" for political transactions, comparable to money in economic transactions. It is clear that such an equivalent would not cover all the functions and attributes money has in economic processes (fungibility, means of payment, means of storage of values etc.), and that it would not even have any material existence, but, however, as money it would function as a 'yardstick' for resource valuation. It is clear, too, that many resources are not fungible or transferable. Positional resources, such as, for instance, the power to legislate, are legally not transferable. Exchange processes therefore work on the basis of commitments to carry out certain actions or to decide in a given way, which could be called "political credit" (Pappi/ Kappelhoff 1984:101).

If the capacity to control events could be conceptualized as a currency within a given action system, the question of whether control could be seen as a "political money" (Coleman 1970) arises. Would it be possible to see control as a generalized medium in political life? This question leads to much more fundamental problems. If the problem of generalized exchange media is considered, the question arises of why and how media are involved in exchange relations and which specific properties characterize generalized media? Rather simply put, media are means which facilitate exchanges. In this respect money was a social invention which enabled actors to assign degrees of economic value to extremely diverse and, in the first place, incomparable objects. By this they became exchangeable. Money translated the "terms of trade" between exchangeable goods into one generalized 'yardstick'. If we proceed with the same example, a further question is: What makes money a "generalized medium"? It seems that its most important property in this respect is its universality. Its currency is not restricted to a singular or particular exchange act, but is able to intermediate almost every exchange situation. This facilitative function of exchange is due to the fact that money by convention is accepted to value almost all commodities and services. Whereas classical theories of money related this general acceptance to the intrinsic value of money (ultimately based on gold or silver), recent theories of money treat it like a sole numeraire, that is, a mere scale on which the relative prices (and therefore scarcities) of the various goods being produced are expressed. In order to be such a unit of account money does not need a physical or material existence. If in the political sphere actors also trade with resources, and even if it is extremely difficult to value political resources with respect to their effects on preferred outcomes, there must be some general numeraire in political exchange, some sort of "political money" (Coleman 1970). Although much woollier than the control concept, such generalized accounting could also be conceived as a criteria of "relevance": In processes of policy making different actors have different preferences for policy outcomes, and they mobilize resources in order to influence these outcomes. Most outcomes are jointly determined and controlled by a plurality of actors. A single actor who intends to realize his interests consequently has to convince others to act in a way that is compatible with his policy preferences. This given actor will then be dependent on other actors to the degree to which these actors control the policy outcome. Within the whole policy system a kind of 'structure of mutual relevance' emerges, which expresses the ensemble of interdependencies within the actor set. Exchange relations will be related to this relevance structure. If, for example, a private organization does not affect or control governmental performance in the treatment of a policy problem in a significant way, it will be excluded from participation. If governmental activities do not affect an organization, it will not be interested in participation (Olsen 1981:495). And if private organizations are allowed to participate, essential control capacities are exchanged. These capacities could be based on very different resources: money, decision making authority, mobilizing capacities, control over members etc. The common denominator, however, is control of the policy outcome.

3. Policy-Making as an Exchange Process: The Case of Chemicals Control in the Federal Republic of Germany

The following part of the paper will illustrate the application of the exchange concept to an empirical policy process, the formulation and implementation of a chemicals control policy in the German Federal Republic, which I have analyzed on other occasions (Schneider 1985, 1986, 1988). The basic idea of this application could be outlined in the following way: in controlling toxic chemicals, government and administration are heavily dependent on scientific expertise and "political information" about likely reactions and strategies of those to be "regulated". Only to a small degree can these resources be provided by the regulators (government and administration). The regulators are therefore dependent on other "policy actors" (industry, unions, scientists, consumers and environmentalists etc.). However, by means of the monopoly on legislative competencies, the governmental sector controls the setting up of legal norms and rules which affect some of the policy actors. The close cooperation between the government and industrial associations, trade unions and scientific institutions thus can be interpreted as basically conditioned by interest interdependencies and the dynamics of exchange relations: The government allows these groups to participate in some of its own originally exclusive rights to legislation in exchange for the provision of information and self-binding behavior which in turn facilitates a more effective and efficient control of chemicals by the government.

3.1 The Problem of Chemicals Control

Chemicals control will be one of the major socio-technical problems of the next decades. Man-made chemicals are the cause of an increasing number of (fatal) diseases. Large-scale disasters and accidents such as those in Seveso in Italy, Bhopal in India, Kepone in the United States and, very recently, at Sandoz in Switzerland are only a few of the most prominent examples which have served to raise peoples' consciousness regarding open or latent chemical poisoning of man and environment. Whereas chemicals have been produced since the last century, their harmful effects have only become visible in the last twenty years. Only since the 1950s has the exposure to chemicals been controlled at the workplace and only since the mid-70s have industrial chemicals in particular been subject to pre-marketing control with regard to their harmful effects on health and the environment. Whereas political intervention in the past was often triggered only when a chemical substance in use proved to be dangerous, a new policy approach has developed since the mid-70s which essentially entails preventive measures for controlling dangerous chemicals. Some countries passed legislation prescribing the attesting and examination of new chemicals before allowing their use. Since Switzerland (1969) and Japan (1973) passed the first laws requiring pre-marketing notification regarding new chemicals, many other industrial countries have followed.

In West Germany, a Chemicals Act (Chemikaliengesetz) was passed by the Bundestag in 1980 and went into effect in 1982. This new law has given the government authority to restrict the marketing of new chemicals which, having been tested, prove to be dangerous to human health and the environment. In addition the government also has the power to place some restrictions on existing chemicals if they are considered hazardous. Any factory intending to market a new chemical substance — except for laboratory or testing purposes — has to give notice to a governmental agency (the Bundesanstalt für Arbeitsschutz und Unfallforschung) 45 days before starting to market it. The notification has to state the chemical composition of the substance, its intended use, the amount of annual production, a description of the possible environmental and health effects as evidenced by any tests done by the factory and a description of the chemicals expected by-products. This regulatory intervention which involves financial, technical and temporal burdens on chemical innovation and production has been considered to be the major governmental intervention into the German chemical industry.

The issue of chemicals control in Germany was not initiated by national policy actors but by foreign countries, especially by France and the United States. The first official consideration of this issue was triggered when the French began to formulate a national chemicals control policy. This advance in its turn initiated the legislation of an EEC chemicals control directive, which was intended to avoid technical and administrative barriers to chemicals trade within the Common Market (cf. Kenis/Schneider 1986). Another factor paralleling the emergence of this issue was the American initiative for international policy harmonization in chemicals control within the Organization for Economic Cooperation and Development (OECD). This was an attempt to internationalize the regulatory burden which had been put on the American chemicals industry by the U.S. Toxic Substance Act (TSCA) in 1976.

An essential feature of the policy formulation process of the German Chemicals Act was the close connection to policy formulation at the European Community and the OECD level. Another main feature was that the decisions about the fundamental structure and scope of the Chemicals Act had been made at an early and relatively secret stage prior to the bill being presented to the Bundestag. During this period there was an intensive process of information exchange for review and consultation between the Chemicals Producers Association (Verband der chemischen Industrie e. V. = VCI) and different executive branches of the federal government. The VCI, which has the de facto monopoly on representation within the chemical sector and speaks with one voice for the whole German chemical industry, was consulted from the very moment that the legislative initiative came from within the German Ministry of the Interior. This association had representatives and experts in all national and international commissions, committees and working groups which were involved in this legislative project.

Only in a very late policy phase, in 1979, was the issue drawn into the visible arena of public discussion. It was only after this point that there was a more open structure of access to the policy process. The bargaining compromise between the government and industry was presented to a wide range of interest groups and independent experts in the fields of industry, environmental protection, consumerism, trade unions and science. Almost at the same time the European Community legislated a directive prescribing chemicals control measures in its member states and provided a rather detailed orientation for the national regulative frameworks. In autumn 1979, the bill was submitted to the Bundesrat, the upper house of representatives of the 11 state governments of the Federal Republic, which accepted the bill and proposed amendments only in very minor details. In November 1979, the bill was introduced into the lower house of the German government, the Bundestag. Since all major issues and potential conflicts of interests had been resolved and intermediated by proceeding consultation the bill passed the Bundestag in 1980; only one independent deputy voted against the proposal. Two years later, in 1982, the Chemicals Act went into effect and was implemented by a network of different governmental agencies. Its regulatory provisions call for a close cooperation with industry in the application of the act. In the German chemicals control system the role of industry is so important that it has been described as a "legally controlled self-regulation of the chemicals industry". In comparison to the American TSCA, the provisions of the German Chemicals Act are much "softer", although it has been acknowledged that the US law, depending on its implementation structure, is not applied as 'toughly' as it could be (for a TSCA comparison see Schneider 1985).

3.2 An Interpretation of the Chemicals Control Policy Based on Political Exchange Theory

How could this complex process of policy making be explained within the model outlined above, in which actors try to control outcomes and exchange influence resources? A first step is certainly the identification of the policy actor system within which the chemicals law was formulated. Using the positional, decision-making and reputational approach, I was able to identify a policy actor set of 47 organizations which were strongly engaged in the policy process and a core actor set of 26 very influential organizations (Schneider 1986b). For the sake of the application of the outlined concept it is essential to reduce some complexity by condensing the whole actor-set of 47 organizational actors in into the following "groups" or sectors:

- governmental sector: government, the administration, parliament, parties and international intergovernmental organizations;
- industrial sector: national and European associations representing industrial interests;
- labour sector: affected labour unions;
- public interests sector: environmentalists and consumers;
- science sector: different scientific institutions involved in policy-making.

There were converging as well as diverging interests among these actors and "sectors" with respect to the formulation of this policy. The governmental sector basically was interested in treating the chemicals problem in such a way that it would vanish from the public eye and from the national and especially from the international agenda. But at the same time the government was interested in keeping its financial obligation as low as possible. The chemical industry was very interested in lightening the unavoidable regulatory burden which it would soon be forced to bear. In addition, because of its strong export orientation, it was relatively open-minded regarding the issue of international policy harmonization. At this time, the party machinery was not at all interested in this issue because it did not attract much public attention. Environmentalists, consumers and scientific institutions were proponents of tough regulation but entered into the policy arena only at the last minute. The mobilization of the environmentalists reached its peak only when the law had passed the parliament.

The different resource positions and interdependencies of these actors become apparent if we consider the specific task structure related to chemicals control. In order to set up a preventive chemicals control system, it is necessary: to insure that physical and toxicological information about new and existing chemicals is gathered; to establish standards and limits for toxicological properties in chemical substances; to develop a decision-making structure to evaluate this information on the basis of the developed standards; to establish an administrative control structure which guarantees that no chemicals will be produced or put on the market without a prior evaluation of their potentially harmful effects on health and environment.

At all four levels, the government is heavily dependent on the cooperation of industry. The government has very limited access to the specialized expert knowledge and research as well as laboratory facilities required to gather information and to set standards. More than 95% of all R&D expenditures in the German chemicals sector stem from the chemicals industry (Häusler 1989:25). The state only has a handful research institutes in the area of ecological chemistry and toxicology.

The effective implementation of a chemicals control system also requires very detailed and specialized information about the behaviour and the likely reactions of the regulated firms (this is one of the basic insights of the German implementation research; cf. Mayntz 1983). At this level, the resources of government are limited, too. Usually ministerial officials and bureaucrats come in contact only with larger firms. Relevant information about the conditions, interests and strategies of the 4.000 small and medium-sized chemical enterprises is only accessible through the channels of the single industrial association of the German chemicals industry, the VCI. The industry in contrast is indirectly dependent on the government because its finances and its innovation facilities will be affected by the way it will be regulated.

In a parliamentary democracy the parliament and the parties constituting it have the formal powers to control the output of a regulatory policy. A well-known feature of policy making within the Federal Republic of Germany, however, is the predominance of the executive branch. In Germany policy programs are heavily predetermined during the pre-parliamentary phase of legislation. In the German governmental system the ministerial sections are the strategic policy formulators. The sections are the loci where the majority of policy programs are initiated, designed and formulated (Mayntz/Scharpf 1975:67ff). In the process of the German Chemicals Act the same phenomenon could be observed: It was in fact the executive and not the parliament that controlled the policy design.The decisions regarding the Chemicals Act had essentially been prepared and made within expert committees and ad-hoc-groups, to which only a limited number of organizations received access.

Although government and industry were the major actors within the policy formulation, the policy process was not totally restricted to these two key actors. If government and industry are inclined to agree to a compromise in the sense that the state would lower the regulative burden and the industry would commit itself to a cooperative stance in the application of the law, there is still a risk that the public might veto such an arrangement. As the results of such a compromise generally lead to a rather low regulation level, such an arrangement also depends on the behaviour of groups which are able to mobilize the public opinion against such a compromise or "cooperative policy solution". Such a potential mobilizer was the trade union, which had been integrated in the decision making process only at a later stage. Government and industry thus needed at least some support from the powerful "IG Chemie" and coopted it into the decision making bodies as well.

Other possible mobilizers were the environmentalists and consumers. In the formulation of the law, however, these groups played their mobilizing role to a much lower degree. The consumers, potentially very much concerned about this kind of issue and equipped with professional staff, did not even attempt to play this role: they are organized in what is almost a prototype of a corporatist interest organization, which has the representation monopoly and is financed to 90% by the German government.

The complex dependencies and the multiplex flows of resources between the different sectors could be seen as an integrated exchange network. In order to determine structural actor positions (or "sector positions") it would be necessary to measure all these flows. Although such an undertaking is virtually impossible, some methods have been developed within the "network approach" which provide instruments for a rough approximation.

For an estimation of the relative position of each sector* with regard to different types of resources, I applied an approach which Laumann and Pappi (1976:193ff) used in a study of community politics. Interviewing the actor set specified above, I asked every informant to make a judgement regarding each organization they knew well enough as to which one of 9 specified resources in the policy process it controlled. Each respondent also indicated what he believed to be the resource base of his organization. The resource indexes were then computed as ratios between attributed resources and numbers of judgments. For each of 23 policy organizations this resulted in a profile of resource "equipment". From the point of view of the resource profiles the matrix also indicates the unequal distribution of a given resource among the actor set. From these profiles I computed two kinds of indices of profile similarity that were then subjected to a multidimensional scaling with the program

* The following sector abbreviations were used: GOV for the governmental sector, IND for industry, LAB for labour, ENV for environmentalists and consumers and SCI for science.

Figure 1   The Structural Similarity of Actors' Resource Equipment

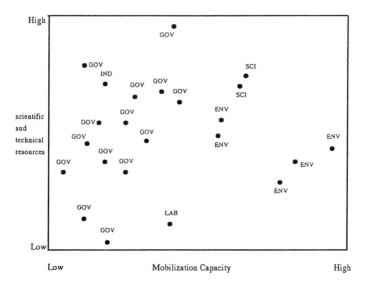

MINISSA (N). The results were two-dimensional solutions with stress values of 0.09 and 0.14. The scalings are represented in Figures 1 and 2. In Figure 1 the geometrical distances represent the similarity of actors represent with respect to the resources they possess.

In Figure 2 the geometrical distances between the points represent the structural similarity of resources with respect to the actors who possess them. The filled-in circles in Figure 2 indicate clusters of resources on the basis of a hierarchical cluster analysis.The relative distribution of a selection of 3 resources with respect to the 5 actor categories is presented in Table 1. In correspondence with the 3 clusters I condensed the resources "expert knowledge" and "personal and technical equipment" to the resource "expertise" , and "good image" and "mobilizing capacity" as general capacity to "support" a policy within its own

Table 1   Distribution of Selected Influence Resources Among the 5 Policy Actor Categories (Sectors)

Sector	NOrg	NJudg.	Expertise	Decision	Support
GOV	14	91	0.21	0.44	0.11
IND	1	19	0.34	0.13	0.05
LAB	1	7	0.21	0.25	0.32
ENV	5	22	0.07	0.04	0.32
SCI	2	9	0.17	0.14	0.20
Sum	23	148	1.00	1.00	1.00

NJudg = Number of judgments;
NOrg = Number of organizations judged.

Figure 2   The Structural Similarity of Influence Resources

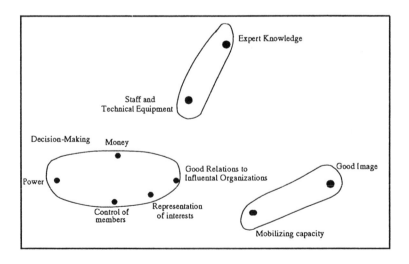

organization and within the public arena.

Table 1 shows that industry was thought to have the most expert knowledge, while the governmental sector was considered to have the highest decision-making power. With respect to "support" or "mobilizing capacity", environmentalists and labour were thought to take the lead. It is interesting that labour was also considered to be very influential within the decision-making process, although as a non-governmental sector it has no formal rights in decision-making at all. The fact that labour had been perceived as an actor who was de facto influential in decision-making could therefore be interpreted as the result of an exchange process in which government incorporated labour into policy-making in exchange for cooperative behavior in the sense that it would not mobilize its members.

Using network analytical methods (cf. Knoke/Kuklinsky 1982) I have also tried to measure and represent some positions within the resources network directly. The data for this analysis were collected by informant interviews among the above specified policy actor set. In order to measure relations of information exchange, for instance, the informants were asked to name all organizations with which they had a regular information exchange on matters of chemicals control. These responses were represented in an asymmetrical square binary matrix with 1's in the matrix cell wherever an organization reported such an information exchange. From this matrix an index of centrality was computed (centrality based on closeness).

Another influence resource within the policy system is "access to the decision-making fora" in the policy formulation process. Within a total set of 20 decision making committees at the national and international level I identified a subset of policy formulation committees as strategic loci within the process of policy formulation. The membership in these committees may be considered as a rough indicator for "access to the whole decision-making machinery" (for a compilation of the total set of committees see Schneider 1988:145). The "access positions" of different actor categories were then measured as the number of one actor block's committee memberships related to the maximal possible memberships which a block could have. This corresponds to Freeman's "centrality based on degree" (Freeman 1977).

A third index tries to capture the influence or power positions of the different "sectors" in the policy making process. This index was measured as the mean power reputation of each of the 5 actor categories. The more an actor block was mentioned as influential in the policy process, the better its "power position" is. The results of this procedure are presented in Table 4, where each entry represents the mean position of each actor block. For the sake of better comparability, the mean values were rescaled in such a way that the maximum value of each column was transformed to the maximum 1.

According to this table, industry not only occupies the most central position within the information exchange network, but it also has the best access position within the set of policy formulation committees. Within the network of power reputation, however, the government is at the top. Interestingly, with respect to all three resources, the core actor groups have been government, industry and labour. The least influential groups have obviously been the environmentalists. Government's dependence on industry at the level of expert knowledge, scientific information and support within the implementation phase seems to be the central factor, which could explain its network position. As rough as these network analytical estimations tend to be, nevertheless they seem to draw a picture which is also compatible with common-sense observations. In this respect it is interesting to see how the German government felt about the interdependency between industry and government. Two former officials from the German Federal Ministry of Interior point out:

"Chemicals control policy, because of the particular problem situation, depends to a large degree on the cooperation between government, industry, trade unions and science. This environmental assessment of chemicals requires a good deal of scientific, technological and economic information, which the administration does not have and can only get from those concerned. Since the provision of appropriate, reliable information from industry and science can be secured only to a limited extent through compulsion, cooperative relations between government, industry and science are necessary conditions for the guarantee of a sufficient supply of information. (Hartkopf/Bohne 1983: 304 ff. My own translation; see Schneider 1985:180).

On the background of the outlined interdependencies, the German Chemicals Act seems to be a textbook example of a cooperative solution to a policy problem. The specificity of this solution is very striking when compared to the American approach. In the U.S. the formulation as well as the implementation were characterized by adversarial relations and hard conflicts between industry and government. Government and parliament imposed the regulatory measures on industry, the latter fought against regulation at every opportunity and with all the resources it could muster (Brickman et al. 1985). Consequently, although the U.S. TSCA prescribed tighter controls, the administration did not have the resources to break industry's resistance at the implementation stage. In Germany, in contrast, industry, labour and government have been involved in bargaining in order to find a solution which will lighten the regulative burden placed upon industry and save scarce resources for the administration. As a rule the major organized interests in Germany seem to get access to decision making in exchange not only for important information but also for responsible and cooperative behaviour during the enforcement stage of an act. In the German chemicals control policy political and technical issues concerning the application of the law have been resolved as much as possible early in the phase of policy design. Policy formulation has been

Table 2   **The Positions of the Actor Categories within Chemicals Control Policy Networks**

Sector	N.Org.	Information	Access	Power
GOV	21	0.916	0.955	1.000
IND	3	1.000	1.000	0.935
LAB	4	0.841	0.805	0.341
ENV	8	0.760	0.410	0.080
SCI	11	0.858	0.596	0.131

based on consultation and bargaining between the regulators and the regulated. Public officials and representatives of the industry have cooperated since the initial stage of the policy process. This provided government with indispensable information and political support for effective implementation. Industry, in exchange, had the opportunity to co-determine the way in which it will be regulated. The dynamic force which seems to explain the German policy outcome in chemicals control is, therefore, exchange.

Note

This paper was presented at the meeting "Political Exchange: Between Governance and Ideology" at the European University Institute in Florence, 15-18 December 1986. I would like to thank Helena Flam, Bernd Marin, Fritz Scharpf and Uwe Schimank for their critiques of earlier versions of this paper. I am also grateful for the suggestions Erhard Friedberg, Franz U. Pappi and James S. Coleman gave me during the workshop.

Political Exchange on a Perfect Market?
An Alternative Model and an Empirical Test

Peter Kappelhoff
Franz Urban Pappi

Social science exchange theory can be built on individualistic premises and contrasted to the collectivistic version from Durkheim to Lévi-Strauss (cf. Ekeh 1974). The individual-istic theory on which we will focus our discussion has two theoretical ancestors, the perfect market model of neoclassical economics and the sociological exchange theory of Homans (1958), Blau (1964) and Thibaut and Kelley (1959). The main difference between economic and social exchange can be summarized as follows: social exchange can not be understood without taking into account its embeddedness in a social structure (cf. Granovetter 1985). This has the consequence that the terms of a single transaction are normally left unspecified. Somebody is doing somebody else a favor who then has an unspecified duty to pay back a "fair" amount of resources at a later time (cf. Voss 1986: 56). In this situation a price system which can clear the market is extremely unlikely to develop, especially when one takes into account in addition that an equivalent of money as a medium of exchange is missing. But what is unlikely is not impossible and there may be social and political situations to which perfect market models can be applied.

One case in point is the practice of log-rolling in parliaments where votes for different collective decisions are traded according to demand and supply factors (but see arguments to the contrary by Shubik 1984). Coleman has developed a legislative game which he generalized to an action theory for well-defined social systems. This model can be seen as a special application of a perfect market model for social and political situations (cf. Cole-man 1973; 1986: 85-136). We shall present the main ideas of this model together with a modification developed by Marsden (1983). In Marsden's model, exchange between actors no longer follows the logic of a perfect market but is restricted to exchanges according to an access network. In addition, actors favorably situated in the access network are permitted to "buy" resources according to exchange ratios with other actors which are skewed in their favor.

After the presentation of the original model and its modification we shall first use simulated data to show some of the consequences of the modified model. Then we shall apply the modified model to a community elite system and we shall investigate the consequences different model assumptions have for the derived power structure of this empirical system.

1. The Perfect Market Model and its Modification

According to Coleman's model actors exchange their influence resources to gain access to those resources which are best suited to their interest profile. In the basic model, actors are interested in events (issues) which are controlled, partially, by other actors. In this way, actors become interdependent.

In the legislative game each member of parliament has one vote for each decision. Thus the control matrix C is quite straightforward to measure, with one special, very important feature. The system is treated as a closed system with respect to i (i = 1,2...n) members of parliament. Thus the control over event k (k = 1,2...m) by the set of actors can be expressed as a fraction of the overall control in the system for this event, that is the total of n votes. The fractions, of course, sum up to 1 for each event.

$$\sum_{i=1}^{n} c_{ki} = 1.0 \tag{1}$$

In the same way, we can express the interests of each actor in the events as a fraction of his total interest in the system, if we are able to close the system with respect to events, too, and if we assume that each actor does not save part of his control for purposes not covered by the fixed set of events. With these assumptions, the interest matrix X can be standardized in an analogous way as the control matrix:

$$\sum_{k=1}^{m} x_{ik} = 1.0 \tag{2}$$

What we call interest here, are empirical measures of the amount of interest each actor has in the events. In an economic model, the events would be divisible goods for which the actors have preferences in varying amounts, that is on an interval scale. For collective decisions, Coleman assumes that the actors exchange control without paying attention whether the control given away will finally be used for or against a certain proposal, that is for or against the actor's directed interest y_{ik}. This Y-matrix is the X-matrix with plus and minus signs added to each entry according to the 'yes' or 'no' preference of the actor for each proposal.

The most serious problem of the perfect market analogy for collective goods instead of divisible, private goods is strategic behavior or free riding. Why should actor i buy more control over event k when he already knows that 51% of the votes are in favor of his preference? This question would not be meaningful if it would make sense to trade in more votes than are necessary for a simple majority. With a probabilistic decision rule Coleman avoids the problem of majority votes for his model (1973:88-89). According to this rarely applied rule a motion is passed if a randomly picked committee member is in favor of it.

With the perfect market assumption prices or values of control over the different events will clear the market for which demand equals supply. Let v_k denote the value or price of event k. Then the supply S_k of control over this event is given as

$$S_k = \sum_{i=1}^{n} v_k c_{ki} = v_k \text{ , because } \sum_{i=1}^{n} c_{ki} = 1 \qquad (3)$$

The demand for control D_k is derived from the central behavioral assumption of the model, the rule of proportional resource allocation: actors allocate their power, that is their resources weighted by equilibrium prices, proportionally to their interest to gain their optimal share of final control C_{ki}^* over each event. This means

$$C_{ki}^* = \frac{x_{ik} p_i}{v_k} \qquad \text{or} \qquad v_k C_{ki}^* = x_{ik} p_i \qquad (4)$$

where p_i denotes the power of actor i. Equation (4) can also be seen as an implicit definition of the fundamental notion of interest in the Coleman-model: "...according to the definition of interests as the fraction of his resources that he will allocate to an event at equilibrium it is also true that the amount of value he devotes towards controlling event [k] is also given by $[x_{ik} p_i]$" (Coleman 1986: 89). From the definition of power as the holding of valued resources, we have

$$p_i = \sum_{l=1}^{m} v_l c_{li} \qquad (5)$$

and therefore

$$D_k = \sum_{i=1}^{n} v_k C_{ki}^* = \sum_{i=1}^{n} x_{ik} p_i = \sum_{i=1}^{n} x_{ik} \left[\sum_{l=1}^{m} v_l c_{li} \right] \qquad (6)$$

Equating $S_k = D_k$ gives a set of equations which are solvable for the v_k's. Since the equilibrium prices are only defined relative to one another one has to introduce

$$\sum_{k=1}^{m} v_k = 1 \qquad (7)$$

as an additional restriction.

The dynamic aspects of this equilibrium theory can either be analysed as a process in which the actors adjust their control "from its present state to equilibrium" according to (4) (Coleman 1986: 93) or as a process where "the power of an actor is determined by weighting the supply of generalized resources held by that actor against other actors' demands for those resources" (Marsden 1983: 694). The adjustment process through time is driven by discrepancies between resource outflows and inflows of the actors in the latter case. Inflows of resources will increase the power of i and outflows will decrease it. In equilibrium, of course, the inflows and outflows of generalized resources or power balance.

The important information for this process are the interest interdependencies z_{ij} between actors:

$$z_{ij} = \sum_{k=1}^{m} x_{ik} \, c_{kj} \qquad (8)$$

As X and C are row stochastic, the entries of Z sum to 1 rowwise, too. Thus the row vector $\{z_{2j} | j = 1,...n\}$ e.g. denotes the dependence of actor 2 from the j other actors and the column vector $\{z_{i2} | i = 1,...n\}$ are the latters' dependencies from 2. When we weight these dependencies with the power of the respective row-actors, we grasp the dynamic aspect of the system with the following equation (for its derivation cf. Marsden 1983: 694-695):

$$\frac{d_{pi}(t)}{dt} = \left[\sum_{j=1}^{n} p_j(t) z_{ji} - \sum_{j=1}^{n} p_i(t) z_{ij} \right] \qquad (9)$$

The first term within the brackets corresponds to the effective demand for i's resources and the second term is i's supply to the other actors or his demand for their resources. The (t) term denotes the time reference of power.

This system of inflows and outflows of resources through time towards an equilibrium point is equivalent to a continuous Markov process. The table of transition rates G is directly derived from the Z-matrix:

$$G = XC - I = Z - I \qquad (10)$$

Thus equation (9) can be written in matrix terms:

$$\dot{P}(t) = P(t)G \qquad (11)$$

Equating this derivative with zero, gives the equilibrium vector for power.

We are now ready to introduce Marsden's alternative to the perfect market assumption of Coleman. Under this assumption there do not exist any restrictions for the resource flows according to the transition rates derived from the dependencies among actors. But assume that we have asked the actors with whom they exchange resources and whom they avoid. Because for an exchange to take place we need two persons we may symmetrize the empirical exchange network. Then we block the resource flows within G whenever we have a report that a pair of actors are not exchange partners even if they depend on each other and renormalize the diagonal elements accordingly. Given that this system has an unique solution - and it will have one if the remaining G is still one connected component - we can reach a modified equilibrium of system power even without the assumption that everybody can exchange with everybody else (cf. Marsden 1983: 693-698).

Marsden's second modification which makes the model even more realistic pertains to the behavior of actors centrally located in the exchange network. In Coleman's original model the actors behave as price takers. On a dyadic basis the rates of exchange between i and j (R_{ij}) are derived from the matrix of interdependencies:

$$R_{ij} = \frac{z_{ji}}{z_{ij}} \qquad (12)$$

When i and j exchange resources the terms of trade are the more in favor of i the more j depends on i and the less i depends on j. Exchange ratios greater than 1.0 denote favorable terms for the row actor and unfavorable ones for the column actor. Note that the terms of trade according to the model of restricted access are the same for actors who are directly connected as in the perfect market model. Only the indirect resource flows between not directly connected actors are different from the ones of the perfect market model.

According to the power-dependence theory of Emerson (1962), Marsden now allows price-making behavior in dyadic exchange if an actor is better connected than his partner so that he has more alternative sources of supply and more people interested in the control he offers. Thus he will be able to exploit his "monopoly power" vis-à-vis his partner to a certain extent. The resources of well connected actors will be more expensive than on a perfect market or on a market with restricted access in which all the actors are price takers (see Marsden 1983: 704-705 for the mathematical formulation of the price-making mechanism).

2. A First Application of the Restricted Access Model to Hypothetical Data

We start our analysis with a hypothetical action system of five actors. This is very similar to the hypothetical action system 2 introduced by Marsden (1983: 700-702). Our system has the same patterns of dependencies and, as well, of exchange ratios ("terms of trade") between actors; but the actual figures are changed to obtain more skewed exchange ratios so that the effects of access restrictions are stronger. The interest dependency matrix is given in Table 1 together with the exchange ratios between actors.

Also shown are the analyzed exchange systems together with the terms of trade between actors. The direction of favorable exchange is indicated by an arrow.

System I is the original Coleman-version of the model, where we have a perfect market with no exchange restrictions whatsoever. All actors can exchange with one another according to the terms of trade. This formulation would correspond to the continuous time Markov-model reformulation given by Marsden (1983: 695). More in the spirit of the original idea of Coleman one would argue that the actors don't exchange among themselves according to the terms of trade, but with a central bank which buys and sells control over events for a fixed market price.

Systems II to IV give exchange restrictions which all form a chain pattern with different positions of the actors within a chain. System V shows a cyclic pattern. The arrows indicate to what degree the exchange balance is biased in favor of the actor to whom the arrow points. Of course, the exchange ratios are taken from Table 1b for the respective pair of actors.

Table 1

a) Interest dependency of the hypothetical action system (Z-matrix)

	1	2	3	4	5
1	0	.455	.273	.182	.091
2	.273	0	.182	.455	.091
3	.091	.273	0	.182	.455
4	.455	.182	.273	0	.091
5	.182	.273	.455	.091	0

b) Exchange ratios in the hypothetical action system

	1	2	3	4	5
1	/	0.6	0.33	2.5	2.0
2	1.66	/	1.5	0.4	3.0
3	3.0	0.66	/	1.5	1.0
4	0.4	2.5	0.66	/	1.0
5	0.5	0.33	1.0	1.0	/

c) Analyzed exchange systems

I) no exchange   restrictions (perfect market)

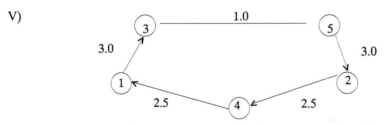

The arrows indicate the resource flows in the chain. As we shall see, they can be used to find out which actors gain or loose power compared to the power distribution for the perfect market. We want to demonstrate that only the pattern of the exchange ratios in the restricted exchange network, that is the direction of flows in the network, and not the formal position in the restricted exchange network per se determine these power shifts. Each actor, whether peripheral or central in the exchange network, will gain power, if his more favorable exchange relations in the restricted access network are saved, whereas his less advantageous relations are cut. Compared to the perfect market, an actor gains power by avoiding exchanges with actors on whom he depends most and by establishing relations with actors who depend on him. The rationale for this kind of strategic action to reduce power dependencies is somewhat double-edged, since it boils down to avoiding dependencies by ignoring them. In his seminal book about exchange and power in social life Blau (1964) discusses four conditions of independence (p. 125): strategic resources, available alternatives, coercive force, and ideals lessening needs. If one excludes the third strategy in the context of our discussion, the first refers to an improvement of the resource endowment, the second to alternative exchange relations, and the fourth to a change of interests. Thus, cutting off exchange relations with actors, on whom one heavily depends, that is the opposite of the second strategy proposed by Blau, can result in a real reduction of these dependencies only if it is accompanied by an improvement of the actors' own resource endowment or a change in value patterns, which lessens his interest dependencies.

System II is the exchange system studied by Marsden for his hypothetical action system 2. Since all resource flows are directed towards actor 2, he will gain power. To make the picture more clear, the following systems III and IV show a one direction resource flow. In both cases actor 3 is at an extreme pole of the resource flow. In system III he will loose virtually all his power, whereas in system IV which is constructed to include the most unbalanced resource flows of the system, he will gain as much power as possible, though his formal position in the network is identical to his position in system III.

In system V all formal positions are equivalent. The resource flow in the system forms a cyclic pattern. Sources and sinks of resource flows cannot easily be identified. We conclude that exchange structures containing loops are more difficult to handle than simple tree structures, which besides chain structures and hierarchies also encompass star structures similar to the hypothetical action system 1 studied by Marsden. Intuitively we expect the changes in the power structure to be smaller for the cyclic system V. Actor 3 seems to be in the best position since, with the terms of trade of 3, his "resource inflows" from actor 1 are favorable compared to his "resource outflows" to actor 5 with the terms of trade of 1.

To confirm our intuitive deductions arrived at so far, we give the resulting power distribution for systems I to V in Table 2.

Table 2   **Power Distribution in the Hypothetical Action System for Exchange Systems I to V**

Exchange system	Power of actors				
	1	2	3	4	5
I	.199	.229	.220	.195	.157
II	.190	.317	.211	.141	.141
III	.600	.096	.032	.240	.032
IV	.217	.035	.650	.087	.012
V	.225	.150	.267	.172	.186

Input data see Table 1.

To illustrate the functioning of the system, we solve the power distribution for system II analytically. In equilibrium the flows towards and from each actor will balance. Therefore, we have five equilibrium conditions which can formally be derived from the equilibrium equation

$$P_e \cdot G = 0, \tag{13}$$

which directly follows from (11). G contains those elements of the Z-matrix for which an exchange relationship is existing. The main diagonal of G is then the sum of the row values, with a negative sign. To make the figures easier to handle we multiply the elements of G by 11 and arrive at:

$$(p_1, p_2, p_3, p_4, p_5) \cdot \begin{pmatrix} -2 & 0 & 0 & 2 & 0 \\ 0 & -6 & 0 & 5 & 1 \\ 0 & 0 & -5 & 0 & 5 \\ 5 & 2 & 0 & -7 & 0 \\ 0 & 3 & 5 & 0 & -8 \end{pmatrix} = 0 \tag{14}$$

We therefore have the following equilibrium conditions:

$$5p_4 = 2p_1 \tag{15}$$

$$2p_4 + 3p_5 = 6p_2 \tag{16}$$

$$5p_5 = 5p_3 \tag{17}$$

$$2p_1 + 5p_2 = 7p_4 \tag{18}$$

$$p_2 + 5p_3 = 8p_5 \tag{19}$$

It follows

$$p_5 = p_3, \ p_2 = 3p_3, \ p_4 = \frac{15}{2}p_3 \text{ and } p_1 = \frac{75}{4}p_3$$

Together with the norming condition

$$p_1 + p_2 + p_3 + p_4 + p_5 = 1,$$

we get $p_5 = p_3 = \dfrac{4}{125}, \ p_2 = \dfrac{12}{125}, \ p_4 = \dfrac{6}{25}$ and $p_1 = \dfrac{3}{5}$

These are the results shown in Table 2. The other results are computed with our general computer routine and may contain rounding errors.

Our predictions for changes in the power distribution are confirmed in all instances, but we are very careful to comment only on such simple cases where all factors producing changes point in the same direction, and so our predictions were quite foolproof. In general, the situation is more complicated. Actor 1 in system IV, for instance, is in a quite favorable position, since all the resource flows from actors 5, 2 and 4 point in his direction and the terms of trade are substantially skewed in his favor. On the other hand, most of the power resources only "pass through" and finally reach actor 3, who clearly gains most power. Therefore, the actual balance of flows for actor 1, taking into account all direct and indirect flows in the system, cannot be evaluated merely by inspection. As the results in Table 2 indicate, actor 1 finally comes out with a small increase of power of .217, compared with .199 in the perfect market structure. We conclude that predictions with regard to changes in the power structure in the restricted access model can be made only in very special cases, i.e. where changes for direct and indirect exchange relations all point in the same direction. In these cases the impact of access restrictions can be very substantial. This is best shown by actor 3, who holds 65 per cent of the power in system IV but only 3.2 per cent of the power in system III, compared with 22 per cent for the model without access restrictions.

The cyclic system V is more complicated than the simple chain systems II to IV. Chain systems can be solved from their ends and in general this applies to all tree structures. It means that the equilibrium condition of equal inflows and outflows for actors can easily be carried over to the exchange relations themselves. For each exchange relation resource flows have to be equal in both directions, that is, exchange is really balanced between actors. This is not generally the case for systems containing loops as indicated by system V. Here we have a power resource differential of about 0.036 ($p_i\, g_{ij} - p_j\, g_{ji}$), which permanently flows through the system, even at equilibrium. Each actor gains from one exchange partner what he loses to the other. This unbalance of resource flows has to be conceptually separated from unequal exchange ratios which lead to power differentials between actors. The resource flows in the restricted access network are unbalanced even if one takes these power differentials into account. Since the model rests on the assumption of dyadic social exchange relationships based on mutual trust and equilibrated advantages for both actors, this unbalance of resource flows could impair the stability of the system, unless all actors are aware of the overall dependencies generated by the cyclic flow of power resources, a situation similar to the Kula exchange described by Malinowski.

3. A Second Application of Models to the Empirical System of a Community Elite

A community elite can be interpreted as a system of influence wielding aiming at the resolution of community conflicts. The conflicts or issues will be finally settled by collective decisions. This process of influence wielding is supposed to be similar to log-rolling in the better delineated system of a parliament. In contrast to this latter situation, we conceive of a community elite not only as the members of the city council but as a broader system of the incumbents of the top leadership positions within the different institutional sectors of a community. As far as these leaders take each other into account as consequential

actors for collective decisions on behalf of the community, they form the social system of
the elite.

Elsewhere, we have described the community of Altneustadt and its elite (Laumann and
Pappi 1976). After this first study, we have investigated the elite of this German city a second
time in 1978, to gather all the data which are necessary for an application of Coleman's
original model of collective action (1973; 1986). Since we have already analysed the power
structure of this community elite in terms of the original Coleman model (Pappi and
Kappelhoff 1984), we are now in a position to evaluate the changes in the power structure
by taking restricted access and price making behavior into account.

Altneustadt is a middle-sized, self-contained city whose elite was dominated at that time
by a broad coalition of the Christian Democrats (CDU) with businessmen and prominent
leaders of the religious and educational sector. The Social Democrats (SPD) as the major
opposition party was less well integrated within the elite system. To give a short description
of the major institutional affiliations of the elite personnel we present the distribution of the
primary leadership positions of the 71 elite members with whom we are concerned here: 16
have primary affiliations in the economic sector; 6 are from the public administration; 12
are CDU politicians; 8 are SPD politicians; 14 represent voluntary associations and 15 the
cultural sector with religion and education.

Instead of presenting the major results of the exchange processes or the power distribution for the 71 individuals we shall aggregate our major results for these institutional sectors.
Because one has an intuitive notion of the normal power bases of these sectors, the consequences of the different models for the power distribution can be better evaluated for these
groupings.

A second device to group the individual elite members is to identify structurally
equivalent actors within the multiple network of general power and influence relations.
Using a blockmodelling technique we identified six general positions for the multiple
network of power reputation, discussion of community affairs and exchange processes
(Kappelhoff and Pappi, 1987). The first group in this case is a power elite at the top of the
structure, then a CDU and a SPD block of city council members, a group of small
businessmen as the hangers on of the power elite and two peripheral groups, the culture
block and the residual category of other notables. With the exception of the SPD-councillors
all other groups belong to the dominant CDU-coalition.

In addition to the institutional sectors, we shall present our results for this grouping, too.
But we should emphasize that all results derived from the application of the models of
resource exchanges were computed for individual elite members as units of analysis. We use
the two types of groupings only as a convenient device to present our results.

In the case of a community elite, there are, of course, reasons to replace the assumption
of a perfect market by the more realistic one of a socially structured exchange process. First
of all we do not have a generally accepted medium of exchange like money in this case.
Official decision making authority as an elected public official or authority stemming from
a leading position in the public service are the final implementative resources in the

influence process, but, of course, other resources are also important in shaping the influence processes. A list of these resources would include among others economic resources, special expert knowledge, influence in subgroups, and reputation as an honourable broker (for a more detailed discussion of the resources included in our application of the Coleman-model see Pappi and Kappelhoff, 1984). These resources, with the partial exception of economic resources, are neither alienable, nor can they be converted easily into each other. Instead, relations of mutual trust are a precondition for agreements between actors to apply their resources in each other's interest (see Marsden 1983: 691). Since there has to be a certain amount of social trust in advance to get the exchange relation started, one could imagine that ideological similarity functions as a base for building up mutual exchange relationships. This would result in a cleavage structure with good opportunities for resource mobilization and interest regulation within ideological homogeneous political coalitions but with few opportunities for conflict settlement in the system as a whole. As we know, this is, in a broad sense, exactly what we would expect from the political system of Altneustadt, where we have the dominant CDU coalition and the quite isolated SPD opposition. But if the system is to function as a whole, there have to be institutionalized exchange relations to bridge the gap between ideological opposite groups which can operate as a functional equivalent for mutual trust, stemming from ideological and social similarity. Otherwise the system would depend on accidental and casual bargainings to use one's resources on behalf of the interest of another actor in exchange for a promised reciprocal at a later point of time. Such risk taking behavior of political entrepreneurs can, of course, be a first step to build up mutual trust and durable exchange relationships. But this kind of relationship is more of special importance in crisis situations which cannot replace institutionalized exchange relationships between opposing political groups in the everyday business of politics. In the case of Altneustadt we expect that the political work in the city council and its subcommittees will offer the opportunities for the CDU and SPD city council fractions to build up this kind of institutionalized exchange relationship. If these kinds of relationships predominate, they can change the character of the political system from an antagonistic to a cooperative party competition and finally to a grand coalition of political parties centred around the city administration, as it was found for some small German communities (cf. Zoll 1974 e.g.). The structure of such a kind of exchange system should give a close approximation to the perfect market model (maybe with expert knowledge as the most important resource). But for Altneustadt with its deep cleavage between the dominant CDU coalition and the SPD opposition, we expect deviations from a perfect market structure in the above described direction which should lead to a gain in power for the CDU coalition, especially for the most central groups of the coalition, and a loss of power for the peripheral SPD opposition.

a. The Operationalization of the Exchange Network

Now we will introduce our operational measure of the access network for the modified Coleman-model, called the exchange network in our study. We could have used a proxy measure, as for instance the discussion of community affairs network, which was also used by Marsden and Laumann (1977) in their study of the Towertown community elite in order to estimate the interest dependency among actors. But to come as close as possible to the main idea of the Coleman-model of purposive actors exchanging control to realize their interest, we asked more directly for the exchange partners in community affairs. We give the exact wording of the exchange network question, which immediately followed the question with regard to the discussion partners in community affairs:

"Community politics consist not only of discussions but also of negotiations and concrete preparation of specific decisions. Thus, one sometimes participates in decisions in which one has little interest oneself in order to do someone a favor. The other person is thereby obligated to the first and one can, perhaps, get something back on this obligation. Thus, relations of mutual support form themselves. Which persons on this list are for you possible partners in such cases?"

The logic of the model and, as well, the theoretical meaning of the relation lead us to expect the exchange relationship to be symmetric. This does not mean that the exchange relationship is balanced but only that resource flows occur in both directions. As a matter of fact it is exactly the degree of unevenness of the exchange relationships, which lead to the power differentials between actors. Because we cannot expect the nominations in response to the exchange question to form a perfect symmetric pattern, we have to symmetrize the relation. We decided to code an exchange relation as existent, if at least one of the exchange partners gave a nomination.

We have two reasons to prefer this less restrictive procedure. The main point is the so-called sociodynamic law, which states that relations between two persons are more likely to be reported by the person with the lower status than the other way round. In the case of friendship choices this means that sociometric stars get a lot of nominations from the middle and lower status people which they do not return; in some cases they may not even be aware of the existence of such relations at all. Translated to the case of power hierarchies and exchange relations, we expect less powerful people to report exchange relationships with more powerful people on whom they are objectively more dependent but which are not reciprocated in general, because they are of minor importance to the more powerful. To strengthen this argument we give power differentials for all four possible choice patterns in a dyad. From the Z-matrix[1] of objective interest dependencies we compute the difference $|z_{ij} - z_{ji}|$ as an indicator of the dependency of actor i on actor j. When the difference has a positive sign i is more dependent on j than the other way round.

As we see from Table 3, we get the expected result. The value for the mean dependency differential of 13.5 for unreciprocated choices is quite high compared with the mean overall dependency value of 14.1 (1/71). Also of interest is the column which gives the absolute power differentials $|z_{ij} - z_{ji}|$. Here the value of the mean dependency differential for unreciprocated choices goes up to 18.3, but for reciprocated choices the value is only 8.9, which shows reciprocated exchange relations to be much more balanced than unreciprocated ones. At a first glance the result for the sum of the dependencies $z_{ij} + z_{ji}$ is surprising. Originally we had thought of this sum as an indicator of the overall strength of the relationship and had

Table 3   **Dependency [a] and Exchange Relations in Dyads**

Type of dyad	Dependencies between actors [b]			
	$z_{ij} - z_{ji}$	$z_{ij} + z_{ji}$	$\lvert z_{ij} - z_{ji} \rvert$	N
i <—> j	0	33.3	8.2	50
i —> j	13.5	38.8	18.3	256
i <— j	-13.5	38.8	18.3	256
i - - - j	0	26.8	11.9	4408
all dyads	0	28.2	12.5	4970

a) The dependencies z_{ij} between actors are from the interest-interdependence matrix $(Z = X\,F\,R)$ of the extended Coleman-model (see Footnote 1).
b) Entries are multiplied by 1000.

expected it to be largest for reciprocated choices. But it turned out that the value for the unreciprocated choices is, with 38.8, higher than for the reciprocated ones with 33.3 (the expected value is 28.2). This means that unreciprocated choices in general involve at least one powerful actor whereas the reciprocated choices are, to a considerable degree, between the powerless actors.

Altogether, these data support a ranked clusters model of the exchange relationship with reciprocated choices inside a group of peripheral actors and inside a smaller group of powerful actors, and with unreciprocated choices directed to the power center. This interpretation is supported by a triad census analysis of the exchange network. The only substantial structural effects here are a modest reciprocity and hierarchy effect (see Kappelhoff 1987).

All these empirical results for the unsymmetrized exchange relation support our decisions to symmetrize the network by completing unreciprocated choices the other way round. Another formal reason for this less restrictive procedure is the connectivity of the network. To take only the reciprocated choices would have resulted in 46 isolates and four components of $n_1 = 2$, $n_2 = 2$, $n_3 = 3$, and $n_4 = 19$. Since connectivity of the access network is a necessary precondition for the application of Marsden's modification of the Coleman-model in which restricted access and price making behavior are taken into account (see Marsden 1983: 697), only one actor of our elite system (N = 72, see Pappi and Kappelhoff 1984) is lost by our less restrictive procedure. This is a self-employed artisan from the economic sector, who is quite powerless holding only 0.6 per cent of the total power of the system. The other 71 actors form a connected component in the symmetrized exchange network and are the basis of our further analysis.

b. The Structure of the Exchange Network

Before we give the results of our analysis of the changes in our power structure due to restricted access and price making behavior, we take a look at the structure of the exchange network between the six sectors of the community elite defined by institutional affiliation

Table 4   Structural Characteristics of the Exchange Network

a) Institutional sectors

	N	average number of exchange relations	row-resp. [a] column effects [b]	Network densities [c] and interaction effects [b] between blocks [d]					
				1	2	3	4	5	6
1 economy	16	6.5	-.54	18 / 1.81	9 / -.13	16 / .44	1 / -1.85	4 / .13	4 / -.40
2 city administration	6	11.7	.62	9 / -.13	27 / -.04	22 / -.32	13 / -.12	15 / .32	20 / .30
3 CDU	12	12.8	.66	16 / .44	22 / -.32	38 / .39	13 / -.16	9 / -.34	16 / -.01
4 SPD	8	7.8	-.23	1 / -1.85	13 / -.12	13 / -.16	57 / 2.96	3 / -.72	7 / -.10
5 voluntary associations	14	5.0	-.13	4 / .13	15 / .32	9 / -.34	3 / -.72	11 / .98	4 / -.37
6 culture	15	6.7	-.08	4 / -.40	20 / .30	16 / -.01	7 / -.10	4 / -.37	14 / .60
	71	7.9							

b) Power structure groups

	N	average number of exchange relations	row-resp. column effects	1	2	3	4	5	6
1 Power elite	15	10.3	.56	27 / .32	15 / .94	8 / -.23	8 / -.15	23 / -.25	7 / -.63
2 Small business	9	4.1	-.79	15 / .94	11 / 1.97	3 / -.03	1 / -.91	2 / -1.45	2 / -.52
3 Other notables	16	5.1	-.27	8 / -.23	3 / -.03	3 / -.36	6 / .34	21 / .47	5 / -.20
4 Culture	11	5.1	-.41	8 / -.15	1 / -.91	6 / .34	7 / .74	22 / .68	3 / -.69
5 CDU city council	10	15.3	.92	23 / -.25	2 / -1.45	21 / .47	22 / .68	44 / .40	20 / .16
6 SPD city council	10	7.6	-.00	7 / -.63	2 / -.52	5 / -.20	3 / -.69	20 / .16	36 / 1.88
	71	7.9							

a) Row- and column effects are identical, since the network is symmetrized.
b) Effects of the log-linear model discussed by Marsden (1981a).
c) Actual, out of possible relations, in per cent.
d) The upper row gives densities and the lower row interaction effects.

and also between the six empirical blocks resulting from a blockmodel analysis of the power structure. In Table 4 we present the matrix of block densities, together with the interaction effects (inbreeding and distances between blocks) of a log linear analysis (see Marsden 1981a) and also the average number of exchange relations for the blocks and the corresponding row and column effects of the log linear analysis. Since the exchange network is symmetrized, the density and interaction effects matrices are symmetric by definition and row and column effects (for indegrees and outdegrees) are identical.

What effects for the power distribution between blocks can we expect from the structure of the exchange network? The most central sectors are the CDU and the city administration for the theoretical blocking, and the CDU city council and the power elite for the empirical blocking. In both cases, these blocks are clearly outstanding with respect to average choice frequency, which is especially true for the CDU city council with an average of 15.3. This is clearly higher than the average of 10.3 for the power elite and reflects the role of the CDU city council as the bargaining center of the political system in routine affairs (see Kappelhoff and Pappi 1987). The other blocks have quite similar choice frequencies, which are somewhat lower than the overall average of 7.9. Especially peripheral is the small business block with an average of 4.1. This is partially compensated by its exceptionally close relation to the power elite.

Because of space limitations we cannot comment on the density and interaction effect matrices in detail. For the institutional sectors we want to stress the fact, that the most central sectors, the CDU and the city administration, have the lowest inbreeding and show a very balanced pattern of distances to all other sectors. That, once again, highlights the role of these sectors as bargaining centers. The largest distances are between the economy and the SPD, which perfectly fits in with the ideological distances between these groups. This is also evident for the small business and the SPD city council with regard to the power structure groups. Here the distances between groups show more structure. Here small business is close to the power elite and distant from other groups with the exception of the CDU city council, which is at the center of the structure.

From our analysis of the exchange structure between blocks we expect an increase in power derived from Marsden's model, for the most central blocks, the CDU and the city administration among the institutional sectors, and the CDU city council and the power elite among the power structure groups. The CDU city council should gain more than the power elite. The other groups should loose, especially the small business block which is only connected to the power elite. These expectations rest on the assumption that central groups gain power, taking restricted access and price making behavior into account, whereas peripheral groups should loose. This is obviously the case for the price making behavior model, since the terms of trade between actors are modified according to their number of exchange relations, which is a measure of centrality. But as we have shown already with hypothetical data, this is not generally true for the restricted access model. It will be contingent on the nature of the Z-matrix and the access network.

c. Changes in the Power Structure due to Restricted Access and Price Making Behavior

In section 2 we learnt that it is not always easy to predict changes in the power distribution due to restricted access. To get some indications, we present the aggregated terms of trade between blocks in Table 5. Because we deal with exchange ratios we use the geometric mean as an aggregation device. We present the average terms of trade first for the perfect market and then for the restricted access model, where we consider only those interest interdependencies, which are activated by an exchange relation. We cannot comment in detail on the overall structure of the terms of trade. We just mention the outstanding role of the power elite and, after it, of the CDU city council among the power structure groups, and of the CDU and, after it, the city administration among the institutional sectors. In both blockings the SPD ranks third in the exchange hierarchy, with the economy respectively the small business block on the fourth place, and culture at the bottom. These two exchange hierarchies for the institutional sectors and the power structure groups are perfect in the sense that each group has favorable average exchange ratios with all groups lower in the exchange hierarchy.

There are no dramatic changes in average exchange ratios between blocks for the restricted exchange network. But for the groups at the top of the exchange hierarchy there is an unimportant tendency towards more favorable terms of trade. Therefore, one would expect these groups to gain power in the restricted access model. Altogether the changes are often difficult to interpret in detail. As an instance, the economy has a worse exchange ratio with the SPD in the restricted model. But this result for the institutional sectors is not in accord with parallel shifts in exchange ratios for the power structure groups. Here the SPD city council looses against the small business as well as against the power elite which contains the top positions of the economic sector. The only systematic tendency we see in the data is the small shift of average exchange ratios in the restricted access network in favor of the more powerful.

There are two explanations for this finding. The first is that people, especially those at the bottom of the power hierarchy, tend to name more easily those exchange partners who have more power than those on an equal level. In this context we refer to the results of our investigation in the asymmetric structure of the exchange network in section 3a. But we are reluctant to decide whether this is really an artefact of our research instrument or whether it reflects a pattern of the real exchange structure. There are also good reasons for this second interpretation, because exchange relations with the powerful may be most vital in the case of highest dependency to secure badly needed resources. This would also result in a bias of exchange relations in favor of the more powerful in the restricted access network. In Table 6 we give the results of the power distribution between blocks for the different models.

Here again we want to stress the fact that the models operate on the individual level of the 71 actors and that the results are aggregated afterwards for convenience of better presentation and interpretation. We did not standardize for block size since we consider block size a determinant of the overall power of a block. But we give the expected power for the equal power distribution as a control device. The results for the perfect market model

Table 5   **Average Exchange Ratios [a] Between Blocks for the Perfect Market and the Restricted Exchange Model [b]**

a) Institutional sectors

	1	2	3	4	5	6
1 Economy	1.00	0.73	0.54	0.88	1.33	1.94
	1.00	0.68	0.43	0.31	1.85	2.68
2 City administration	1.37	1.00	0.78	1.24	1.82	2.89
	1.47	1.00	0.89	1.47	2.83	2.70
3 CDU	1.84	1.29	1.00	1.55	2.41	3.90
	2.34	1.12	1.00	1.84	4.24	5.17
4 SPD	1.14	0.81	0.64	1.00	1.58	2.54
	3.26	0.68	0.54	1.00	1.20	2.67
5 Voluntary associations	0.75	0.55	0.41	0.63	1.00	1.61
	1.85	0.35	0.24	0.83	1.00	1.09
6 Culture	0.52	0.35	0.26	0.39	0.62	1.00
	0.37	0.37	0.19	0.37	0.92	1.00

b) Power structure groups

	1	2	3	4	5	6
1 Power elite	1.00	3.55	3.65	4.52	1.37	2.28
	1.00	4.00	4.21	5.77	1.38	2.71
2 Small business	0.28	1.00	1.02	1.24	0.40	0.66
	0.25	1.00	0.69	0.93	0.23	1.39
3 Other notables	0.27	0.98	1.00	1.26	0.36	0.59
	0.24	1.46	1.00	1.06	0.35	0.60
4 Culture	0.22	0.80	0.79	1.00	0.28	0.46
	0.17	1.07	0.94	1.00	0.26	0.56
5 CDU city council	0.73	2.52	2.79	3.58	1.00	1.68
	0.72	4.32	2.82	3.84	1.00	1.27
6 SPD city council	0.44	1.52	1.68	2.16	0.60	1.00
	0.37	0.72	1.67	1.77	0.78	1.00

a) Geometric means.
b) Upper rows give the exchange ratios for the perfect market and lower rows for the restricted exchange model.

confirm our expectations and will not be discussed further. The average power of group members reflects the exchange hierarchy found for the average terms of trade between groups. Quite surprising are the results of the restricted access model. There are no changes

Table 6   Changes in the Power Structure[a] for Models Including Restricted Access and Price Making Behavior[b]

a) Institutional sectors

	N	equal power	perfect market	restricted access	price making behavior
1 Economy	16	22.6	22.5	22.7	19.6
2 City administration	6	8.4	13.1	12.9	16.1
3 CDU	12	16.9	30.7	30.4	38.9
4 SPD	8	11.3	10.3	10.5	9.7
5 Voluntary associations	14	19.7	14.6	14.6	8.5
6 Culture	15	21.2	8.8	8.9	7.4

b) Power structure groups

	N	equal power	perfect market	restricted access	price making behavior
1 Power elite	15	21.2	43.6	43.1	47.2
2 Small business	9	12.7	6.9	6.7	4.4
3 Other notables	16	22.6	12.0	12.4	7.8
4 Culture	11	15.5	6.1	6.3	4.1
5 CDU city council	10	14.1	20.0	19.9	25.8
6 SPD city council	10	14.1	11.4	11.6	10.7

a) Power is shown in per cent of total system power.
b)(bèta) = 2 and (gamma) = 1/8 for equation (24) in Marsden 1983: 704.

at all which are worth mentioning. The exchange structure of the Altneustadt community elite simply reproduces the power structure resulting from the perfect market model.

There are two reasons why we are reluctant to stress the substantive interpretation of this result. First of all, we know of no other application of the restricted access model to real exchange systems of our size, so we must be very careful with the assessments of the results in general. And secondly, from our discussion of the functioning of the model in section 2, we would expect the power elite to gain power, because all exchange ratios to other groups are more favorable than for the perfect market (see Table 5), but the power elite looses 0.5 per cent of its power which is the largest deviation from the perfect market for all groups, but in the wrong direction. The other groups at the top of the exchange hierarchy, the CDU city council, and the CDU and city administration for the institutional sectors, also loose power.

We can offer only a very tentative explanation for these results, which rests on analogies drawn from our analysis of resource flow in the cyclic system V. The average density of 7.5 for the exchange network is quite high, so that we can expect a very well connected structure with many cycles of different lengths. This could lead to a certain resource flow to the bottom of the exchange hierarchy, as indicated by the positive power differential for actor 5 between system V and the perfect market model, though the average terms of trade between actor 5 and the "block" of actors 1, 2, 3 and 4 are worse than in the perfect market model. The change of the power distribution between system IV and V depends on one link (between actor 3 and 5). The influence of such strategic "cyclic links" cannot be detected from the analysis of aggregated terms of trade between blocks.

More encouraging are the results from the model including price making behavior. Deviating from Marsden (1983) we choose (bèta) = 2 and (gamma) = 1/8 as parameters for the function F(i,j) (equation (24), Marsden 1983: 704), which transforms exchange ratios in favor of the actor with more exchange relations. The smaller value of (gamma) gives a greater latitude for modification of the exchange ratio. The question whether the disadvantaged actors will accept the resulting deterioration of exchange ratios remains open to empirical investigation. As expected, the groups in the center of the exchange network gain power. These are the CDU city council (+ 5,9%) and the power elite (+ 8,1%) and the city administration (+ 3%) for the institutional sectors. There is a linear relationship between frequency of exchange relations (cf. Table 4) and change in power due to price making behavior. Thus, centrality in the exchange structure can be seen as a secondary resource (cf. Boissevain 1974), which in the case of the community elite in Altneustadt gives additional power to the already powerful groups and, therefore, leads to a further concentration in the power structure.

What consequences have these results for the functioning of the political system of the community elite? We want to discuss this point from the position of the SPD opposition, which confronts the overwhelming majority of the dominant CDU coalition formed by the other five groups for both types of blocking. At the beginning of this section, we asked whether there would be sufficient institutionalized exchange relations to overcome ideological cleavage between the two coalitions to foster the minimal conditions for conflict settlement and functioning of the system as an entity. Our results suggest that the CDU and the city administration serve not only as integrators for the CDU coalition, but for the community elite altogether since the SPD, while quite isolated as shown by the highest inbreeding in the exchange structure, has good connections to these two groups and is isolated only from the rest of the CDU coalition. The SPD ranks third in the exchange hierarchy, while the economy which also shows substantial inbreeding in the exchange network, ranks fourth. Whereas the SPD approximately holds its position in the power structure, both for restricted access and price making behavior, the economy, especially the small business group, looses substantially. This is also true for the other groups on the periphery of the CDU coalition. The centralization of the power structure favoring the center of the CDU coalition, therefore, is not to the detriment of the SPD coalition but to the periphery of the CDU coalition. Of special interest here is the position of the power elite

Table 7   **Changes in Power [a] for the Two Most Powerful Members of the Community Elite**

	equal power	perfect market	restricted access	price making behavior
City mayor	1.4	7.5	7.4	11.6
City manager	1.4	5.6	5.5	7.8

a) Power is given in per cent of total system power.

which contains the city mayor (CDU) and the head of the city administration besides the leaders of the economic sector. We give the power for these two actors separately, to show that, due to a central position in the exchange network, secondary resources are concentrated in the CDU and the city administration and not in the power elite per se.

Compared to perfect market power, the city mayor gains 4.1 per cent and the city manager 2.2 per cent of the total system power. They are clearly in the center of the bargaining system of the community, as one would expect from their institutional positions. Their combined gain of 6.3 per cent, more than explains the overall gain of 3.6 per cent for the power elite altogether. As a more detailed analysis shows, the loss of power for the rest of the power elite block is mainly at the expense of the economic leaders. Thus, we conclude, that the exchange system of the Altneustadt community elite is not integrated by the power elite but by the CDU as a political party and as a fraction of the city council together with the city administration.

4. Further Considerations

Power in the Coleman-model is conceptualized as control over valued resources, which have impact on the outcomes of events and are of interest for the actors of the system. In the case of a community power structure this can be seen as a formalization of Dahl's concept of decision making power with regard to issues over which there is observable conflict of (subjective) interests (Dahl 1961, Lukes 1977: 11-16). The control over the agenda of politics and the ways in which potential issues are kept out of the political process, that is the second face of power (Bachrach and Baratz 1970, Lukes 1974: 16-21) cannot easily be incorporated into the Coleman model. Even the inclusion of influence processes into the model (cf. Marsden 1981b) captures only the shaping of interests in issues which are already on the political agenda and, therefore, can be conceptualized as events in the exchange system. Completely out of the realm of the model is the third, structural dimension of power (Lukes 1974: 21-25), the mobilization of bias due to organizational and systemic effects, which cannot be reduced to the behavior of individual actors.

These limitations of our analysis are obvious in the case of the economic sector. Quite characteristically we found the economy only poorly integrated into the exchange network and only fourth in its position within the exchange hierarchy. The system is dominated by the CDU and the city administration, a finding which perfectly fits in with the results of most German community studies, where the political parties and the administration form the center of the decision making structure. If we would take into account structural aspects of power a possible result might be that the position of the economy gets strengthened. This, at least, is indicated by several studies, which stress limitations in the autonomy of community elites. For instance, communities depend heavily on taxes based on the profits of local enterprises, so that all actors of the community elite have to take the interests of these enterprises into account. This kind of quasi automatic influence (Zoll, 1974) is prior to the influence in the decision making process of the community elite we studied here, since it determines the rules of the game for all groups in the system, whatever their ideological position and interests.

Notes

1) $Z = XC$ (see equation (8)). We operationalized the control matrix as the product of an impact matrix F (how efficacious are the influence resources for a decision on each event?) and a resource possession matrix R (which percentage of a resource is owned by each actor?). Then we get a derived control matrix as $C = F R$. We asked respondents for estimates of the entries of F and we gathered information on R from local experts (see Pappi and Kappelhoff, 1984).

Territorial Politics and Political Exchange:
American Federalism and French Unitarianism Reconsidered

Leonardo Parri

1. Introduction: A Theoretical Framework

Exchange Processes in Contemporary Politics

In the present post-liberal era (Lowi, 1969) the governance (Marin, 1987) of the social system can no longer be assured through sovereignty, that is through the authoritative imposition of the "will of the state" upon social interests and dynamics. Nowadays, in fact, functional interest organizations[1] can virtually insure the governance of entire social sub-systems (Willke, 1990). Rebus sic stantibus, governance ceases to be the exclusive concern of the state and becomes a common matter of concern with the functional interest organizations. Public policy-making and implementation are no longer decree-based reflections of state intentions but are the result of a process of interaction (Friedberg, 1990) where the state, no longer powerful enough to compel the private actors to comply with its will, must negotiate over the content of the policy output and outcomes. Public policies become the arena where a constellation of interdependent public and private actors, possessing mutually relevant resources for the issue at stake, negotiate and relate to each other in patterns which can vary from simple dyadic links to complex networks (Marin, 1985). Within these dyads or networks, actors influence each other so that they behave in a way congruent with their goals: this is done by offering one's own behavior modification in exchange for that of the other(s). "Possibilities for action" (Crozier and Friedberg, 1978) linked to the possession of mutually valued resources are exchanged. Politics is no longer an authority relation between a powerful public governor and a weak private governed and become similar to an exchange relation between public and private equals: unilateral dominion is replaced by contracted agreement (Bobbio, 1984). The state becomes semi-sovereign, no longer the center of the social system but a decentrated (Marin, 1987) body among other powerful private organizations. The purpose of this essay is to show that the developments depicted above concern not only the relations between the state and the functional segments of the society, as shown by the current literature, but also regard the relations between the (central) state and the territorial segments of society, that is the subnational governments.[2] In contemporary territorial politics the relations between the national and subnational governments can no longer be seen in terms of hierarchical subordination — in unitary settings — or indifference — in federal settings; rather, they must be understood as a reciprocal exchange of "possibilities for action", just as in present functional politics.

The first section will give the theoretical grounds which form the basis of the above presented hypothesis, in sections 2 and 3 this territorial exchange assumption will be proved on the basis of American and French territorial politics. Section 4 includes both comparative notes and concluding considerations.

The Development of the Relations between the Central and the Peripheral Politico-Administrative Structures

An adequate understanding of the relations between the different units of territorial representation, the levels of government, requires a brief summary of the historical development of the vertical articulation of the politico-administrative structures. The classical liberal state was committed to a minimal set of policy functions which were "such that they have to be administered at the center" (Rose, 1985: 15). They were matters of "high politics": foreign affairs, war, justice, finance and money. The peripheral governments were concerned with "low politics": urban welfare, public order and infrastructures, rural problems etc. In American "dual federalism" and in British "self-government" the central and peripheral governments possessed different policy functions and were separate from each other. In unitary systems the center's agencies, especially the prefectures, exerted legal and financial control over the peripheral units of government. The traditional dialectic "central authority/local freedom" (Dente, 1985: 393) assured a substantial vertical division of the attributions and ensured more or less wide spaces of autonomy for the peripheral governments. In both systems the "dual polity" model (Rose, 1985) modulated the country's politics.

The emergence of the welfare interventionist state beginning from the thirties brings about the multiplication of the state policy functions, the administration of which needs a nationwide deliverance apparatus composed of a capillary network of decision-making and implementation structures. Both the old and the new central ministries create a nationwide *déconcentré* apparatus of field offices. A decisional and/or implementation role concerning the new policy functions is often assigned to historically pre-existent *décentralisé* subnational governments or to centrally appointed or locally elected special single-purpose jurisdictions (Smith, 1985). A multilevel structure of decision-making and implementation consequently emerges, determined not only by historical-administrative legacies but also by the territorial multidimensionality of the new policy problems (Scharpf, Reissert and Schnabel, 1976). The decisional and implementation prerogatives concerning a policy function are therefore no longer divided between the levels of government, but rather are shared, every level being responsible for a specific policy segment and all the levels cooperating with each other. "Dual federalism" gives way to "cooperative federalism", while in unitary settings the integrational model of central-local relations (Kjellberg, 1985) and the integrated administration pattern supplant the old dichotomy tutelage/autonomy. Traditional legal-constitutional separations in federal and prefectoral control in unitary systems lose their importance in intergovernmental relations as the consequence of the emergence of nationwide integrated public policies implying functional control and cooperation (Dente, 1983). Central and peripheral governments become closer, united as they are in welfare-interventionist policies they manage jointly. The picture of the peripheral governments' separation from or subordination to the center, in federal and unitary settings respectively, no longer holds true. There is no more intergovermental indifference or dependence, but both in federal and unitary countries intergovernmental mutual involvement and interdependence (Scharpf, Reissert and Schnabel, 1976; Grémion, 1976; Tarrow, 1978; Donolo and Fichera, 1981; Graziano, 1982; Wright, 1982; Rhodes, 1983, 1985; Sharpe,1985; Dente, 1985). Given this interdependence, the goals of the different levels of government are partially common and partially different. A mixed-motive game based on both conflict and cooperation develops within intergovernmental interactions (Mény and Wright, 1985: 5; Smith, 1985: 94). In such a situation, the central government has no possibility of unilaterally imposing its will on the peripheral governments, which in turn are neither defenseless nor passive: negotiating and compromising therefore becomes the only possible modus vivendi in intergovernmental interactions.

Intergovernmental Relations and Political Sociology: The Concept of Territorial Politics

The politico-administrative structure of the present welfare-interventionist state is differentiated following two main lines of logic: the functional and the territorial one (Hanf,1 981; Muller, 1985).[3] This implies the presence of different territorial levels of government, as mentioned in the previous section, which are internally differentiated among functional administrative sectors according to the various different policy functions. Each territorial level of government is therefore a complex organization, the internal cohesion of which is indeed continually threatened by centrifugal tendencies developed by its different functional sectors. Leaving the consideration of these fragmenting tendencies to the empirical part, one can conceive intergovernmental relations as relations between complex organizations in the course of the formulation and implementation of nationwide integrated public policies. Following interorganizational theory (Benson, 1975; Scharpf, 1978; Galaskiewicz, 1982) and the "policy approach" method,[4] the common formulation and implementation of a nationwide integrated public policy by the different government levels can be conceptualized as the emergence of a more or less complex network of interorganizational exchange relations (Cook, 1977; Aldrich and Whetten, 1981). Within this network, the different intergovernmental units are interdependent: given their diverse territorial location and structural features, they do not possess all the valued resources for the achievement of their goals, and consequently exchange them among each other and negotiate about their reciprocal behavior.

Going a step forward, one can transform this pattern of intergovernmental relations occurring in the vacuum of the administrative world, where "pettifogging bureaucrats" fight "abstract battles over local autonomy" (Tarrow, 1978: 2), into a model of territorial politics. Within this model, every level of government as an organization is in close contact with its socio-cultural, economic and political relevant environment and, as suggested by the "policy approach", deals with the organizations existing in this environment both during the formulation and implementation of the public policies. In such a situation, every level of government is not just a complex organization with administrative, financial and juridical character, but a complex organization also with a politico-representative character due to its close interaction with the social, economic and political organizations of the relevant environment within its jurisdiction. On the basis of this "openness", the organization called "government at the level X" can be considered a conceptual unit of political sociology (Sartori, 1968) and as such can be defined as a complex organization formed by the executive cabinet (the chief executive and his ministers); the different administrative departments and the connected advisory commissions collecting the "interested" and "relevant" representatives of the social, economic and cultural forces of the corresponding territorial level; the representative assembly composed by the elected deputies, most of the time members of political parties, and its legislative commissions. Synthesizing the main findings from the relevant literature (Tarkowsky, 1982: 219; Rhodes, 1985: 42; Smith, 1985: 92-95), four basic resource domains controlled by the governmental organization can be identified: resources connected to the control a) of an administrative apparatus, b) of financial means, c) of juridical-institutional prerogatives, d) of politico-representative capabilities.

a) The control of an administrative apparatus implies the possession of skill and knowledge resources, human and material and also authority resources (regulations rights etc.).

b) The control over a governmental budget implies the possession of monetary resources.

c) Juridical-institutional prerogatives imply first of all the possession of public authority resources[5] (laws, decrees etc.) and of symbolic resources deriving from the constitutional status of the government.

d) The existence of a representative assembly elected in the correspondent territorial jurisdiction and of an executive responsible to it, makes — through the mediation of the political parties which have participated in the voting — the government level into question the representative of its "territory", meant as "the collectivity dwelling on the territory, its interests, its cultural world" (Giannini, 1986: 76).[6] This representative character of the organization "government at the level X" is strengthened by the presence of formal (administrative advisory commissions) and informal (clientele relations with the local interests, connivances with the local policy-targets) connections with the functional and non-functional interest organizations existing in the correspondent territorial jurisdiction.

This openness toward its relevant environment gives a "political potential" (Donolo and Fichera, 1981: 53) to the government level into question, that is it gives the possession, with

respect to the assigned territory, of alliance-representational,[7] symbolic and information resources. Within the dynamics of territorial politics, meant as negotiated interaction between
governments with a "political potential", every level of government conceives a strategy of
action involving certain organizational goals and the kind of actions needed for their
"satisficing" achievement. During the formulation and implementation of nationwide intergovernmental public policies, these strategies of mutual influence become operative. The
result of these processes of intergovernmental negotiation is dependent on the power
(im)balances which emerge between the different government levels. In this theoretical
framework, power is meant as a relational concept (Emerson, 1962; Cook, 1977; Baldwin,
1978; Crozier and Friedberg, 1978), that is, power is "the unbalanced exchange of
possibilities for action between a set of interdependent ... actors" (Friedberg, 1990). To put
it more clearly and limiting oneself to a dyadic relation, the power of A with respect to B
is the ability that A shows entering in relation with B — to influence B's behavior in a way
congruent with his goals, allowing for the fact that B would have not changed his behavior
in the way desired by A if the latter had not entered in relation with him. With B's behavior
is meant the "possibilities for action", with respect to A, that B has on the basis of the
resources at his disposal. In order to convince B to behave in a way congruent with A's own
goals, A enters into negotiation with him and, during this negotiation, in exchange for the
desired behavior modification of B, A offers a modification of his own behavior according
to B's supposed or requested needs and goals. In such a context, the power (im)balance
between A and B — that is, the terms of trade of the mutual exchange of "possibilities for
action" — will be in A's favor:
1) the more B values A's behavior modification for the obtaining of his own goals and the
   less B is able to satisfy his own goals entering in relation with some other actor (C,D etc.);
2) the more A is able, relative to B's ability, to develop a negotiation strategy which converts
   possessed resources into influence.

   In every national context, the different territorial articulation of the politico-administrative structure and of the political parties and functional interest organizations which constitute the relevant environment of the various governments will bring about a different
distribution of the power resources among the levels of government and a different configuration of the intergovernmental policy problems. Consequently, different, country-specific,
action strategies and power (im)balances in territorial politics will emerge.

The Notion of Centralization: A Critique and a Reconceptualization

One of the more frequently used notions in the analysis of territorial politics is that of
centralization. The evaluation of the "centralization level" has always been an obligatory
step in every research effort and still remains a key element of research. Nevertheless, the
concept has been defined in far too many and often unsatisfactory ways. Consequently, in
this section a notion of centralization will be presented which avoids some of the shortcomings of previous attempts and which is compatible with the theoretical framework I have
expounded.

The classical concept of centralization, both in federal and unitary settings, has centered on the estimation of the vertical distribution of the juridical-institutional prerogatives between the levels of government (Fesler, 1965; Smith, 1985: 1). This traditional approach has proved inadequate because of its exclusive concentration on the top-down configuration of the politico-administrative structure, bringing about the consequent neglect of the presence of "political", informal, bargained (Palumbo, 1975; Trigilia, 1982) politico-administrative internal dynamics deriving from bottom-up thrusts. Consequently, there have been "illusions" with respect to the real centralization level (Hanf and Scharpf, 1978; Toonen, 1983). The most recent approaches in the literature have not only limited themselves to the juridical-institutional prerogatives, but have also looked at the territorial distribution of the administrative (number of employees, workload etc.) and budgetary (income, expenditures) resources.

Nevertheless, both the classical and the more recent approaches have in common a zero-sum conception of the vertical territorial distribution of the power resources within the politico-administrative system. What is gained by one level of government is lost by another (Ashford, 1979: 77). On the contrary, the amount of power resources to be distributed among the levels of government has never been fix, but has diachronically increased, owing to the development of new policy functions linked to the emergence of the welfare-interventionist state (this amount has indeed decreased in some cases, owing to recent trends of deregulation and budgetary restraint). Furthermore, the conventional approaches neglect the existence of politico-representative capabilities, the so-called "political potentials", which are at the disposal of the different levels of government and which are able to counterbalance the lack of administrative, juridical and financial resources. Another limit of the conventional approaches is their static vision of the internal vertical working of the politico-administrative structures, implicitly consistent with the "dual polity" pattern. Contemporary territorial politics shows instead a highly dynamic character, given the lasting interactions and negotiations between levels of government during the policies' formulation and implementation. A simple static measurement of the power resources at the disposal of the levels of government says too little about the real power (im)balance within the politico-administrative structure. In a dynamic and interactive framework such as that of the integrated administration policies, the intergovernmental power (im)balance can be rightly conceived only as the distribution of the mutual influence capabilities emerging from intergovernmental policy-linked negotiations. As a matter of fact, sticking to the above presented relational concept of power, the only possible notion of centralization is one which is dynamic and idiosyncratically policy-linked, where the higher the centralization level is, the bigger is the influence the central government has upon the specific intergovernmental policy outputs and outcomes. In such a framework, the level of centralization is determined by the specific power (im)balance emerging between the different levels of government in the course of the considered interorganizational policy-making and implementation process that links them together.

Functional, Territorial and Generalized Political Exchanges

Territorial politics is one of the three crucial forms of political dynamics in present polities, the other two being functional and party politics. Three different political circuits, the territorial, the functional and the party, can be considered as the foci of these forms of politics (for the concept of political circuit see Offe, 1981 and Parri, 1985, 1987b). I conclude this section by comparing the exchange activities occurring in the functional political circuit (FPC) that I have mentioned in the introduction, with those in the previous sections I have discovered occurring also in the territorial political circuit (TPC). There are two principal forms of exchange of "possibilities for action" occurring during the formulation and implementation of public policies in the FPC: the simple dyadic and the complex, transaction chain-based, one called respectively functional political exchange (FPE) (Pizzorno, 1978; Parri, 1985, 1987a) and generalized political exchange (GPE) (Marin, 1985). Simple dyadic FPEs between the state and functional interest organizations[8] have been discovered to occur during the formulation and implementation of sectoral public policies (Lehmbruch, 1984; Cawson, 1986). When transsectoral public policies, such as e.g. macro-economic management, are considered, there is the possibility of the emergence, under certain conditions, of a transaction chain-based GPE (Marin, 1985, 1987a).

Within the TPC there is only the possibility of the emergence of simple dyadic forms of exchange, which I call territorial political exchange (TPE), while transaction chains do not develop for reasons which will soon be analyzed.

On the blueprint of the definition of FPE, I define TPE as the relation between two public actors (the central government and a regional/state one or a regional/state territorial interest organization; the central government and a communal one or a communal territorial interest organization; a regional/state government and a communal one or a communal territorial interest organization) which takes place during the formulation and implementation of a public policy and within which a negotiation, on the basis of the possessed reciprocally valued power resources, occurs in order to formulate and implement the policy goals. Therefore, a TPE occurs when one of the two public actors, normally the one at the higher territorial level, allows the other to influence the content of the public decisional (within intergovernmental commissions and advisory bodies or through informal intergovernmental contacts) and implementation processes (through various forms of intergovernmental executive cooperation), so that it can profit from part of the public policy outputs and outcomes, and when, in exchange for this, the latter gives its consensus to the former, i.e. it puts at the other's disposal its power resources in order to guarantee the efficacy and the effectiveness of the public policy in question.

I now consider the reasons for the non-emergence of transaction chain-based TPE within the TPC. At the basis of GPE in the FPC there is a complex policy problem of a transsectoral character, e.g. macroeconomic management, involving many actors in a potentially endless policy game with a non-finite time horizon that brings about the production of veritable public goods such as for example macroeconomic stability. In the TPC the policy problems at stake are less complex and of sectoral character: the obtaining of a grant; the management of a specific intergovernmental policy which may concern pollution, regional employment, urban welfare etc.; the struggle surrounding the alleged misuse of control prerogatives of the central government concerning a certain act or policy of a subnational government, etc. Moreover, the number of the policy-involved actors is almost always institutionally prescribed; normally two: the central government and a subnational government, cartel of subnational governments or territorial interest organizations; or at the maximum three, when the central government is confronted at the same time with regional/state and local governments.The policy game in territorial politics is limited in time and scope, solvable through relatively clearly defined and not open-ended policy steps, and it brings about the creation of categorical goods (in the territorial sense, that is goods concerning a specific problem within a specific area).

Rebus sic stantibus, while the complex transsectoral policy problems within the FPC require for their solving a high coordination of the actors, a high internalization of the externalities of their actions, a common definition of the problem at stake and a considerable mutual trust, the simpler policy problems emerging within the TPC can also be solved "satisficingly" by means of a medium-low coordination of the actors, a low internalization of the externalities of their actions, and they tolerate for their solving a low level of mutual actors' trust and an only partially common or diverse definition of the policy issue at stake. In the first — functional — case, the policy problem can only be solved through the emergence of complex multilateral different rules of the game which put a premium on the compliance with the overall network-systemic imperatives with respect to the pursuit of the organizational self-interest of the actors. If these rules of the game are respected, the actors will benefit from the total long-term systemic payoffs produced by the working of the transaction chain and from a substantial reduction of the uncertainty level surrounding their action strategies. In the second — territorial — case, several rules of the game are already formally, normally bilaterally, prescribed by legal and administrative norms. When, beside these, informal rules of the game develop, as unavoidably happens, these rules bring about mutually rewarding two party transactions, side payments, log-rolling and other forms of barter which are so common in the intergovernmental literature. The organizational self-interest of the actors at the maximum enlightened by some medium-term calculations domi-nates the negotiations in territorial politics.

While the complex functional policy game is highly precarious and requires the fulfilment of all the above-mentioned requirements in order not to break down and be viable — that is, it needs a "problem-solving" style of negotiation (Scharpf, 1985) bringing about the transaction chain typical of GPE — the territorial policy game is simpler, more stable and can tolerate without breaking down the less demanding above-presented conditions, which are typical of a bargaining style of negotiation (Scharpf, 1985) and bring about the emergence of barter-like dyadic TPE.

Beyond these differences which put GPE at one extreme of the continuum of exchange complexity, actors' mutual involvement and fine-tuned coordination, and TPE (and FPE) at the opposite extreme, there are also striking similarities between the two. Both GPE and TPE (FPE) involve all the mutually relevant actors of a policy process, and in both cases there are no clear yardsticks to measure the valuables exchanged. Despite the different ways of dealing with them, both GPE and TPE (FPE) are mixed-motive games solved through antagonistic cooperation (Marin, 1985). The dimension of informality, crucial in GPE, also assumes an important role in TPE: without the informal practices which go beyond or emerge alongside the large body of formal regulations and norms, territorial politics would show serious rigidities and bottlenecks and would present several perverse effects. While in GPE one can speak of "bounded informality" (Marin, 1987a), in TPE, where the formal regulations are numerous and often circumvened or modified, it makes sense to speak of "bounded formality". While the core of the functioning of GPE are informal rules limited by the systemic constraints of the policy game, the core of the modus operandi of TPE consists in formal juridical, administrative and financial rules limited by the constraints linked to the particular desiderata of the intergovernmental policy actors. Part of these desiderata emerge and are taken into account through the development of informal, often also rule-breaking, conducts and negotiations between the governmental actors. Last but not least, both in the FPC and in the TPC the supposed key policy coordinator, the state or central government, is forced to negotiate with functional and territorial interests respectively. These interests, especially through the vehicle of the just mentioned informality, transform the written iron rules of sovereignty into partially empty prerogatives: Decree in functional politics and hierarchy in territorial politics are substituted by GPE (or FPE) and TPE respectively.

2. Territorial Politics in the United States

Introduction

I will now apply the above-presented theoretical framework to two aspects of territorial politics in the U.S. and in France: the decisional and implementation policy-game structured around the concession of policy-linked conditional grants/subsidies from the national to the subnational governments; and the more general argument of the centralization level, i.e. the power (im)balance between the national and subnational government levels. A previous elementary knowledge of the basic articulations of the U.S. and French politico-administrative structures is required. The first case I present is the American one.

Narrow, Fragmented TPEs and Categorical Grant-Based Territorial Politics

In the lifecycle of "dual federalism" in the U.S. there was no TPC but rather intergovernmental indifference. A veritable TPC developed only with the emergence of "cooperative federalism" after the New Deal and especially after the Second World War (for periodizations of U.S. federalism see Beer, 1973; Wright, 1981 and Walker, 1981a). In this article I concentrate almost exclusively on federal-state relations, which are the crucial nexus in

U.S. territorial politics.

The principal device through which federal-state relations were established in the U.S. has been the categorical grant. According to this, the federal government decides that the achievement of a certain policy goal must be favored nationwide: federal money is then put at the disposal of the states as a goal-reaching incentive. The states have to establish their own policy program. If this program meets the policy requirements set up by Washington (called "strings"), the state in question receives a part of the necessary financial resources from the federal government (for the several kinds of existing categorical grants see Elazar, 1984: 74-80). Every policy program is managed by a federal agency (and its field level subordinated agencies) responsible for a certain policy function in connection with a homologous state agency. The former can refuse or block the money to the latter if it does not meet the federal policy-requirements, but the federal agency has anyway no hierarchi-cal-juridical prerogatives with respect to the state agency. As a matter of fact, categorical grants, according to a Supreme Court decision of 1923, are considered to be a voluntarily accepted instrument of policy incentivation.

The number and variety of categorical grant programs has proliferated since the thirties and especially since the sixties, giving rise to new federal and state policy function-specialized agencies. The generating mechanism of the categorical grant is a federal-based policy community called the "iron triangle" (Seidman, 1975) or "issue network" (Milward and Francisco, 1983): Congressmen with "political entrepreneur" characteristics (Colella and Beam, 1981) try to satisfy their functional constituencies by making alliances with functional interest organizations in order to obtain the issuance of a functionally-targeted categorical grant. Close links with and, diachronically seen, the creation of new congres-sional committees charged with the care of the policy function in question plus their large staff and close connections with the federal policy-functional agency facilitate the success of this congressional "politics of distribution" (Kettl, 1984: 77) aimed at obtaining the consensus of a myriad of functional and subfunctional Washington-based interest organi-zations, following a typical pluralist pattern centered around "pressures" and dyadic barter transactions (Wilson, 1982). The result of these categorical FPEs are federal categorical grant programs which can be utilized, because of the institutional constraints of federalism, by the functional interest organizations only if they are transformed in state categorical grant programs co-managed with Washington. So, in American politics, the development of FPEs within the FPC gives rise to the development of federal-state relations and to the associated emergence of a TPC.

How was the development of a categorical grant-based "cooperative federalism" judged in the U.S.? The dramatic increase of the percentage of state plus local revenue (16,8% in 1960, 31,7% in 1980) and spending (10% in 1960, 25% in 1980) covered by all kinds of federal categorical grants; the growth of the attached federal regulations; the states' impossibility, given the pressures of their constituencies, to refuse Washington's string-attached money; all this would have brought about a de facto centralized federalism (Beer, 1973; Kempf and Toinet, 1980), the "Europeanization of America" (Lowi, 1978), a "prefectorial federalism" (Elazar, 1981) where field level federal agencies, charged with tasks of supervision of grant-aided state policies, would have imposed the nationalization of U.S. subnational politics (Hoffenbert, 1971; Hanus, 1981). After the intergovernmental indifference of "dual federalism" the de facto hierarchical device of the categorical grant would have brought about a top-down centralized TPC. A less superficial analysis of U.S. territorial politics presents instead another picture, much different from that of a hierarchical relation and closer to that of a bargained relation. As shown by several authors (Levine, 1969; Ingram, 1977; Sharansky, 1978; Elazar, 1984), during the formulation and implementation of the grant policy programs the officers of the state agencies are able to influence the federal agencies officers' conduct and are thus not merely passive recipients or sheer executors of the federal will. At the formulation level in Washington, the national associations of the state administrative officers are able, on the basis of their administrative skill, to influence the content of the categorical grant programs and often these programs are inspired by already existing state policy programs. The phase of the grant management at the state level, when the state agency sets up and implements, under the supervision of the federal agency and its field offices, the subnational grant policy program is not a phase of simple inducement-compliance to the federal financial, functional and legal "strings", but rather a process of federal-state bargaining, a mixed-motive game between actors who reciprocally need the others' resources in order to achieve their goals. This policy-linked bargaining process between levels of government on the basis of the possessed valued resources corresponds to the definition of TPE cited earlier. In this TPE the resources in the hands of the federal agency are financial (the grant); administrative (the policy program skill); juridico-institutional (supervisory prerogatives of reviewing state regulations, laws, budgets and performance levels concerning the grant program management). The resources in possession of the state agency are financial (the rest of the program's funds, allotted by the state legislature); administrative (the offices in the field, their skill, the information deriving from the contacts with the policy-targets); and politico-representative (the support of the program's clientele within the state, the possibility of contacting the congressman of the coterminous electoral college in order that he performs "pressures" in Washington, via the congress committee which control the federal agency in question, with the aim of softening the zeal of the federal field officers involved).

On the basis of the available resources, the federal and state agencies negotiate the TPE: the former looking for the maximum of compliance to the national "strings", the latter trying to adapt the state grant programs to the specific subnational conditions. The result of this power relation is a compromise that materializes in a "slippage" of the federal control (the same has proved to be true for the management of the federal block grants, van Horn, 1979) that leaves spaces for the subnational desiderata. As a matter of fact, the "feds" never fully exploit their supervisory prerogatives, preferring informal mechanisms of consultation, persuasion and cooperation. The device of the withdrawal of federal funds is only rarely used and a general state consensus with the goals of the federal program supported by minimally adequate staff and funding endowments is judged as satisfactory. The fact that

the categorical grant management occurs through TPE and not through hierarchical compliance to federal requirements is confirmed by the circumstance that, despite the large
diffusion of federal grant-aided state policies, the policy variations between the state have
not declined (Kemp, 1978; Dye, 1984) even in the most federally-intruded policy sectors
(Sharansky, 1978: 107-119).

The Reaction of the Chief Executives; Block and General Grants as an Instrument of
Widening the Scope of and the Control upon TPEs

The escalation of the categorical grant policies as the dominant modus operandi within the
TPC brought about what was called "picket fence federalism" (Sanford, 1967: 80). The
"vertical functional autocracies" (Beer, 1976: 158) constituted by the professionalized
staffs of the federal and state policy-functional agencies, pass through, like a series of
vertical stakes, the levels of government. The so-called chief executives or generalists, the
governors, mayors etc. were unable to control and coordinate the large amount of narrow,
categorical based TPEs managed by the federal agencies and their homologous state
agencies. These were in fact only nominally under the authority of their chief executives,
but in reality they enjoyed considerable autonomy, supported by their links with the federal
officers, above, and the functional policy-targets, below. When in the sixties the categorical
grant programs boomed, the subnational chief executives began an action oriented towards
the reduction of the functional fragmentation of U.S. territorial politics and at the enhancement of their control over the TPEs. The already existing but indeed dormant and
underorganized territorial interest organizations comprising the representatives of the
various subnational government executives were revitalized and strengthened (Haider,
1974) as the principal instrument of influence in Washington. At the end of the sixties, the
so-called "intergovernmental lobby" formed by the territorial interest organizations[9]
became one of the major political forces in Washington (Beer, 1977). In their battle for the
creation of new rules of the game governing the TPEs, which aimed at obtaining less
functionally fragmented and more territorially integrated grants, more monitorable by the
subnational chief executives, the territorial interest organizations had (and still have) to face
the opposition of a large part of the congress, of the federal policy-functional agencies and
of the Washington-based functional interest organizations. "Political entrepreneurs" in the
congress are committed to the strong categorical grant-oriented pattern of "congressional
federalism" (Walker, 1981a: 107), which allows them to boast about the sponsorship of the
different grant programs with respect to their functional constituencies. The federal
"functional autocrats" and their clients, the functional interest organizations, are afraid of
losing control over the management of the federal manna in favor of the alleged minority-
unresponsive and patronage-oriented governors and mayors. By contrast, federal coordinating bodies like the OMB (Office of Management and Budget, up to 1970 BOB, Bureau
of the Budget), the ACIR (Advisory Commission for Intergovernmental Relations) and the
federal chief executive, especially when the president is a Republican, supported the efforts
of the territorial interest organizations. The endeavours of the territorial interest organiza-

tions in Washington in fact brought about some success starting from the late sixties:

a) A series of measures increased the subnational chief executives' possibilities of control and of territorial coordination with respect to the categorical grant applications and management within their jurisdiction (the Intergovernmental Cooperation Act in 1968, the Joint Funding Simplification Act in 1974, the BOB's circulars A-80 and A-85 in 1967 and A-95 in 1968);

b) the widening of the scope of the TPEs through the creation of block grants (BG; starting from the Partnership for Health Act in 1966) and general grants (General Revenue Sharing, GRS, introduced with the State and Local Fiscal Assistance Act in 1972). BGs contain few federal "strings", are targeted for broad policy sectors and allow subnational chief executives to decide on the specific utilization of federal money, and thus to gain a position of control over the state functional and subfunctional agencies and more independence vis-à-vis their federal homologous. The general grants connected with the GRS are virtually without any federal "string" and give almost total freedom of choice to the subnational chief executives.

The mobilization of the "political potential" of the subnational governments through the rebirth of the territorial interest organizations has brought about several changes in the U.S. territorial politics. In 1970, the categorical grant quota of the federal transfers was 96,6%, while in 1982 it decreased to 79% leaving more space to BGs and GRS; the subnational governments, thanks to the new enhanced juridico-institutional prerogatives in the management of BGs and GRS with respect to the categorical grant regulations, have strengthened their bargaining position in the negotiation of TPEs. The Reagan administration, despite reductions which it imposed on the financial resources given to the subnational governments, has continued the efforts to consolidate into BGs categorical grants (see the Omnibus Budget Reconciliation Act of 1981) and to suppress federal regulations which limit the freedom of action of the subnational governments (see the OMB's executive orders 12291 and 12372) (Williamson, 1986; Cole and Taebel, 1986).

The Federal State Power Balance in U.S. "Cooperative Federalism"

What about the centralization level, i.e. the federal-state power balance after fifty years of "cooperative federalism"? I have already shown that, if one looks at the concrete functioning of the intergovernmental public policies, the thesis of an increased level of centralization supposedly beginning in the thirties has proved false: the increased "intergovernmentalization of everything and everyone" (Kettl, 1984: 74) did not bring about hierarchical top-down federal-state relations but TPEs where "the flow of power was not unidirectional but complex and interactive" (Beer, 1976: 163-4). Nevertheless, centralist interpretations of the U.S. territorial politics stress that the federal government has enormously increased its administrative, financial, juridico-institutional and politico-representative power resources, especially after the "Great Society" period of the early sixties. This would have brought about a restriction of the "possibilities for action" of the states and drastic changes in the federal-state power balance. These interpretations neglect, as was already argued by president Lyndon B. Johnson in the sixties, that the power resources at the disposal of the different levels of government in the federal system are not a finite quantity, so that what is gained by Washington is lost by the states (Fried, 1981: 27). The distribution of the power resources between government levels has no zero-sum characteristics: The emergence of the welfare interventionist state has brought about the increase of the total amount of administrative, financial, juridico-institutional and politico-representative resources of all levels of government in the U.S. and has also brought about a multiplication of the policy arenas where these resources are mobilized during the negotiation of TPEs (Beer, 1978). Something one may refer to as "polarity principle" (Eulau, 1973) has guided the development of U.S. federalism: an increase in the power resources of Washington has stimulated the increase, as a power balancing strategy, in the state power resources (Tarrow, 1978). This process can be observed in all the four resource domains I have conceptualized:

a) The state administrative apparatus has become considerably more professionalized and rationalized, following and sometimes anticipating the developments at the federal level (McKay, 1982): more and more a three-tiered cabinet structure is substituting the old uncoordinated state administrative organization (Bodman and Garry, 1983). From the quantitative point of view, since the Second World War the employees of state and localities have shown a higher rate of increase than the federal ones (military employees excluded). Governors are no more "reactionary bosses in smoke-filled rooms" who have virtually no control of the administrative apparatus, but have developed managerial attitudes (Sabato, 1978). Nowadays, a state planning department office under the governor's control has become more and more widespread (Elazar, 1984).

b) Since the sixties the state tax efforts have strongly developed in order to increase their policy capabilities (Wright, 1981). Recently, many states have introduced a personal income tax and reformed their fiscal system in order to make it more elastic (Walker, 1981b). Reagan's federal financial restraint has further stimulated the state fiscal efforts.

c) Looking at the juridico-institutional domain, one can see that not only the state legislative activity has greatly evolved and has been strongly enhanced, but sometimes the state have been pacesetters in new issue areas and have anticipated with their policies the federal initiatives (Elazar, 1984). State constitutional reforms have been undertaken in order to reshape the politico-administrative apparatus in a way more congruent with the new policy exigencies (Walker, 1981b).

d) The state relations with their functional policy-targets and their territorial constituencies have increased with the development of new state and intergovernmental policies that have witnessed the position of the state political and administrative institutions as the most accessible point of the national polity.

Because they have been able to enhance the power resources at their disposal, the states have not only avoided becoming hierarchical subordinates of Washington, but have defended their power position in the negotiation of TPEs with the federal government.

3. Territorial Politics in France

Introduction

Classical views of politics in France see the French unitary "state-nation" (Hayward, 1973: 13) as the guardian of the undividable common interest of the country (Gourevitch, 1980). Strongly autonomous from the French society, thanks to its high level of structural differentiation, institutionalization and centralism (Birnbaum, 1982), the French state is alleged to be able to protect "the national interest" both from particular functional and territorial interests. Decree-based policies are regarded as preventing the emergence of both pluralism and corporatism and of the connected FPEs or GPE (Birnbaum, 1982; Wilson, 1983), while hierarchy- and tutelage-based central-local relations are seen as preventing any subnational autonomy and the connected TPEs (Hoffmann et Al., 1966; Berger, 1974). This picture has been proved to be inaccurate with respect to the reality of French functional politics: while stronger than other European states, the French state, even during the fifth Republic, has developed more or less pluralist or corporatist FPEs, and has not been able to govern the society *par décret* (Suleiman, 1974; Wright, 1983; Keeler, 1985; Mény, 1985). Is the same true also for French territorial politics?

The Jacobin Leviathan and Territorial Representation

While leaving aside the powerful big cities, capable of strong influence on Paris, and concentrating on medium-small cities, villages and the department, I examine first of all the power resource balance between the national and subnational governments in France as depicted by the classical studies carried out during the sixties ands the seventies.[10]

a) Communes and departments do not possess or control de facto an administrative apparatus of their own and must therefore resort to the strongly *déconcentré* (1,600,000 officers, of whom only 32,000 working in Paris) and highly skilled state administrative machine.

b) Only about 40% of the subnational revenue is raised through local taxes. State transfers are therefore of crucial importance to the communes and departments.

c) Subnational governments possess only limited juridico-institutional prerogatives, mainly in the domain of infrastructure, welfare and planning. Moreover, these prerogatives are not exclusive but shared with the state. Communes and departments are autonomously administrated *collectivités territoriales* but at the same time also administrative *déconcentrés* units of the central state coming under its authority.

d) The politico-representative capabilities of the central state are very high in France due both to the ideological *jacobin* tradition and to the direct election of the chief of the national executive. Nevertheless, the *girondin* political potential of the subnational governments has always remained high: *la France périphérique* possesses a veritable army of elected officers (36,000 mayors plus 500,000 communal councillors, 96 presidents of the general council of the department, PGCD, plus 3000 general councillors of the department, GCD), whose local rooting, support and legitimacy are considerable, also thanks to elements like the strong *esprit de clocher*, the depoliticization of local politics (Kesselmann, 1967; Tarrow, 1979) and the extreme fragmentation and smallness of the subnational units of governments.

How is this extreme imbalance in power resources concretized in territorial politics? The answer seems obvious: it is concretized in a top-down hierarchical relation between the national and the subnational governments (see, e.g., the dominating role of the prefect in departmental politics). It is the prefect, not the PGCD, who directs the departmental administration, convenes the general council of the department, decides its agenda, prepares the dossiers to be examined in the sessions and proposes the budget. He is also the president of the numerous advisory commissions which bring together the representatives of the departmental functional interest organizations. Through the *tutelle administrative sur les actes*, the prefect conditions the mayors and places limits on their space of manoeuvre. While the administrative tutelle has softened from the sixties on, new forms of *tutelle*, such as the technical and the financial one, have flanked it adding to the old legality control forms of functional and financial control of merit. The combined modus operandi of these two kinds of *tutelle* is particularly evident if one looks at the ways subnational government obtains state grants and subsidies for local capital investments. The French system of subsidization of subnational governments closely resembles the U.S. system of categorical grant allotment (Ashford, 1982: 253): both offer an incredible variety of opportunities, constituting a highly fragmented system of transmission of national policy objectives to the subnational governments (in France the system privileges the subsidization of subnational capital spending, while in the U.S. specific subnational policy programs are also subsidized). Take e.g. the case of a French commune that wants to build a public construction and take advantage of the subsidies made available by the ministry X and of the loans made available by one of the several agencies of the CDC, *Caisse des Dépôts et Consignations* (Ashford, 1980, 1982; Branciard, 1984). The subsidy is allotted if the *dossier technique* concerning the construction respects the various requirements desired by the ministry (in the U.S. called "strings"). As said earlier, the commune does not possess the administrative skill to prepare an acceptable dossier and is therefore obliged to resort to the subdepartmental state officers of the ministry X, who receive extra remuneration for this A.T.G.C. (*Aide Technique à la Gestion Communale*). The recourse to a less expensive private project-agency instead brings about the non-acceptance of the dossier, so that de facto the subdepartmental state officers are monopolists on the technical market and can, according to some mayor, "dictatorially" (Becquart-Leclercq, 1976: 27) influence the content of the communal project. After the subsidy is allotted, the mayor can ask an agency of the CDC for an integrative state loan. The loan is conceded only if the subnational officer of the ministry of finances, the powerful TPG (*Trésorier Payeur Général*), evaluates the budgetary situation of the commune as sound and if the CDC present financing lines are not in conflict with the communal project. In 1977 the mayors, in the *Rapport Aubert —Questionnaire des Maires de France* attacked the *aspects de mendicité* existent in the subsidy/loan system and asked for less dependence through the creation of *dotations générales* (i.e., block grants). In such a situation, where the joint action of the state administrative, technical and financial *tutelles* appear to almost totally limit the "possibilities for action" of the subnational governments, territorial politics seem to exclude the presence of TPEs and to be managed through the hierarchical subordination of the province to Paris.

TPEs and the "Locus minoris resistentiae" of the Jacobin Leviathan

If one goes beyond the mayors' instinctive protests against the *État* and beyond the formalism of the juridico-institutional analyses, an alternative picture of French territorial politics emerges (Worms, 1966; Crozier and Thoenig, 1975; Thoenig, 1975, 1978; Dupuy, 1985; Rondin, 1985). Faced with the apparition of a *pouvoir périphérique* (Grémion, 1976), the above depicted top-down hierarchy becomes a "negotiated hierarchy" where the subnational governments still preserve "possibilities for action".

Let me first of all reconsider the mayor-subdepartmental state officer relation. While it is true that the the the latter possesses administrative and juridico-institutional resources of which the former is devoid, the mayor, for his part, has behind him the whole of the "political potential" of the commune in the form of politico-representative capabilities. If the state officer is inflexible and formalist in dealing with him in matters concerning the communal investment project presentation and/or implementation (in fact, the subdepartmental state officers also have a crucial role in the concrete realization of the capital investment), the mayor can — being the "voice" of "his" commune — make complaints to the subprefect or the GCD of his *canton*, who are both in a position of formal or informal supremacy with respect to the state subdepartmental agent. One has, moreover, to consider that for the state subdepartmental officer the mayor is not only a policy-demander but also a policy-target and policy-client. As policy-target a non-cooperative mayor means that the state officer will be not able to achieve the policy goals, as they are desired by Paris, which are linked to the subsidy allotment and investment realization. This lack of efficacity and effectiveness will bring about various criticisms on the part of his superiors in the ministry. As policy-client a non-cooperative mayor means a loss of the personal fees attached to the A.T.G.C.[11] for the state officer. The mayor and the subdepartmental state officer are therefore interdependent: the former cooperates with the latter if this informally softens the Parisian technical requirements, and takes into consideration the peripheral desiderata in the project presentation and implementation.

Similar dynamics of interdependence also emerge between the prefect and the PGCD. The latter has behind him the "political potential" of, on average, 30 GCD and 90 mayors. For the ministry of the interior in Paris a good prefect is not a Jacobin hard-liner imposing the letter of the formal regulations, but a *pater familias* who prevents the emergence of *histoires* within the department and the *remontée vers Paris* of unsolved peripheral problems. As the *institution pivot* (Rondin, 1985: 85) of the department, the prefect must be able to mediate and integrate all the different interests within the area and secure good development of the relations between the state field officers and the various subnational governments. In order to do so, the prefect needs a *relais* with the so-called *pays réel*. The PGCD with all the sub-departmental personal connections linked to his considerable political potential can give to the prefect the necessary information about the claims and exigence of the *cantons* and communes. This information is particularly precious for the presentation of the departmental budget, which is the main stake in departmental politics. While it is the prefect who, thanks also to the cooperation of the PGCD, de facto establishes the budget, the visible initiative on this matter is left to the PGCD who must appear to be the real boss of the department and a skilful "political entrepreneur" vis-à-vis the GCD and the mayors. The prefect and the PGCD should therefore be considered as interdependent (for a specification of the various interdependence areas see Worms, 1966).

Moreover the prefect, far from being the mere representative of Paris in the department, is also the *porte-parole* of the departmental desiderata in Paris. As a matter of fact, the easier it will be to rule the department and to compose its internal conflicts, the more the communes and their department obtain state subsidies and loans, the higher they are ranked in the national *plan* priorities, and the larger are the tolerated local exceptions to central rules.

The lower levels of the state administrative apparatus can therefore be seen as the locus minoris resistentiae of the Jacobin Leviathan. Prefects and subdepartmental state officers are not in fact able to unilaterally impose the central rules on the subnational governments. They run the risk of giving rise to a wave of local malcontent and the blockage of the whole mechanism of territorial politics. The peripheral "political potentials" can not be neglected, every central norm has a local "accommodation". Even the administrative tops in Paris know about the necessity for negotiation and thus leave a certain freedom to their field subordinates. The *tutelle* relations are indeed not top-down one-way but two-ways and also bottom-up. They are to a certain extent reversed and also deserve the interest of the province in Paris (Grémion, 1976: 321). The center has only a "negotiated power" (Rondin, 1985: 80) based on a "tempered centralization" (Wright, 1983: 291) and characterized "more by interdependence than by hierarchy" (Crozier and Thoenig, 1975: 14). The mixed-motive game of TPE emerges also in France as the crucial modus operandi of territorial politics.

In France three further mechanisms facilitate the transmission of the subnational desiderata to the center and the connected realization of TPEs. The first mechanism, also found in the U.S., is the presence of territorial interest organizations, the most powerful of which are the AMF, *Association des Maires de France* and the AMGVF, *Association des Maires des Grandes Villes de France*. The influence of the mayors is particularly strong in the senate, not to mention the hundreds of administrative advisory commissions where the mayoral associations are present. The other two mechanisms are specifically French and are based on an individualistic and quasi clientelistic (Médard, 1981) mobilization of the subnational "political potentials". The first mechanism is the *réseau relationnel* analyzed by Becquart-Leclercq (1979), where the mayors, acting as "administrative activists" (Tarrow, 1979) look for the maximum number of appropriate personal relations within the administrative apparatus and with the national deputies or senators in order to obtain favors, exceptions and other forms of tolerated *illégalisme du droit* (Becquart-Leclercq, 1979: 11) from the central government. The third mechanism is the *cumul des mandats* (Reydellet, 1979), thanks to which the subnational elected representatives who cumulate a national mandate of deputy or senator can easily defend and support the interests of their commune or department in the Parisian assemblies and ministries.

Changing the Central-Local Power Balance: The Impact of the Defferre Reforms

The different laws and decrees which have followed the basic initial act presented by Gaston Defferre (*Loi du 2 mars 1982 relative aux droits et libertés des communes, des départements et des régions*) in order to complete the decentralization reform, have brought about a clear mutation in the central-local power resource (im)balance in France (for the literature on the topic see, among others: Ashford, 1983; Dupuy and Thoenig, 1983; Chevallier et al., 1984; Rondin, 1984; Sadran, 1985; Kesselmann, 1985; Thoenig, 1985).

a) Juridico-institutional prerogatives. The basic principle of the reform was to transfer to the communes, departments and regions coherent blocks of prerogatives previously possessed by the state. This goal, difficult to arrive at in a system of integrated administration (see the interesting comments of the transfer-bill rapporteur J.P. Worms in Branciard, 1984: 80) was partially achieved. The three levels of subnational government (the region abandoned its inferior status of *établissement public* and became a *collectivité territoriale*, like the communes and departments) subtracted from the state part of its juridico-institutional prerogatives: the commune mainly urban planning ones, the department mainly infrastructure and social welfare ones, the region mainly economic ones (some of the prerogatives of the region were indeed totally new). The prefect was renamed *Commissaire de la République*, CDR, and his a priori *tutelle administrative sur les actes* of the subnational governments abolished. The subnational acts now become directly executive and the CDR has only the right of an a posteriori denouncement of a "suspect" act to an administrative tribunal. A similar procedure abolished the a priori controls of the subnational expenditures made by the finance state officers.

b) Administrative apparatus. The whole of the state *déconcentré* offices which performed the transferred policy functions were consigned to the respective subnational government. Following the already existent communal model, the PGCD and the president of the regional council substituted the departmental and regional prefect at the head of the departmental and regional administration. The department in particular benefited from the reform: part of the prefectoral administration was transferred to it; a new role, that of the director of the departmental administration, was created. Consequently the department, breaking the monopoly of the state field officers, can now give technical assistance to the communes. For the new instituted economic tasks it has to perform, the region has the right of ex novo creating the administrative staff it needs.

c) Financial means. State perceived taxes were transferred to departments and regions in order to finance their new policy functions. A *Dotation Générale de Décentralisation*, DGD, initially compensated the costs not covered by the tax transfer. In response to an old demand coming from the subnational governments, two kinds of block grants were instituted: the *Dotation Générale de Fonctionnement*, DGF, and the *Dotation Générale d'Equipement*, DGE. The latter substituted part of the state transfers previously received through subsidies and loans for capital investments.[12]

d) Politico-representative capabilities. The transformation of the region in a *collectivité territoriale* and the introduction of the direct election of the regional council have almost ex novo created a new "political potential" representing around 1/20 of the nation's territory. More generally, the new policy functions at the disposal of the subnational governments have enhanced the amount of subnationally controlled and distributed policy resources and therefore have increased the likelihood of having policy-clients whose interests are linked to those of the subnational governments. The suppression of the *tutelles* has, moreover, increased the direct responsibility of the subnational elected toward their respective constituencies. They can no more "evade accountability using the state as a scapegoat" (Kesselmann, 1985: 167), or point to the "bureaucratic blindness" of the prefect or of the state officers as being responsible for their own policy failures. The abolition of the *tutelles* puts an end to the era of centralization as a "general system of unresponsability" (Dupuy and Thoenig, 1983: 964) and brings the subnational elected closer to their constituencies.

Drawing a first conclusion, one can say that the Defferre-reforms, by contrast with the U.S. case, have brought about a zero-sum redistribution of the power resources within the TPC. What was lost by the French central state was transferred to, and therefore gained, by the subnational governments (with the exception of the totally new resources obtained by the regions for their ex novo created tasks). The prefect, the subprefects, the departmental directions of several ministries, the TPG, lost part of their power resources in favor of the subnational elected and their subordinated administrative officers. All these changes will modify the nature and the internal power (im)balance of the TPEs in France in ways which further research will investigate. As foreseen e.g. by Croisat and Tournon (1984), one may think that the old Worm's (1966) interdependent couple formed by "*le préfet et ses notables*" (i.e. the PGCD, the GCD and the mayors) will be transformed, owing to the power changes described above, in a new couple of interdependants formed by "le Président du Conseil Général du Département et son CDR".

A first conclusion which can be presented concerns the development of the federal-state power balance in the U.S. with respect to the central-local one in France. In the American case, the power balancing mechanism of Eulau's (1973) "polarity principle", according to which the subnational governments react with an increase in their own power resources as a response to a strengthening of the national government, has freely developed thanks to the institutional opportunities of federalism. In the French case, this "polarity principle" has been obstructed by the institutional constraints of the unitary state. The reinforcement of the subnational governments has therefore followed extra-institutional, informal and semi-legal ways, sometimes tolerated, sometimes repressed by Paris. Starting from the sixties, especially at the communal and regional levels, skilled and progressive elected have, together with the so-called provincial *forces vives*, tried to strengthen the role of their subnational governments with several initiatives which were beyond or close to the edge of legality. In order to meet the new exigence of the changing environment during and after the crisis of the seventies, the *"notables rouges"* (Lacorne, 1980) of the municipalities controlled by the left, departments and regions developed several subnational policy initiatives. When the left came to power in 1981, on the basis also of the subnational experiences of the *notables rouges*, it used the strong machinery of the Jacobin state to change the central local power (im)balance along *girondin* lines, legalizing and formally institutionalizing what were formerly semilegal and informal subnational policies. What in federalist settings takes place to incrementalism, in unitary settings is a lasting casus belli requiring struggle and tensions and which ends in deep reforms.

4. Comparative Conclusions

At the end of this essay some comparative conclusions are required. I have tried to reach the initial aim, that is to demonstrate that exchange processes in contemporary complex polities do not only concern functional but also territorial politics. The two cases presented, namely the paradigm of decentralized federalism and that of centralized unitarianism, were chosen for their highly representative character. In this respect the concept of TPE, as exchange of "possibilities for action" between levels of government, has in my opinion proved to be flexible and heuristic enough to cover and explain the internal dynamics of territorial politics in two very different institutional systems, and it has, I think, once more proved the limits of a merely juridical approach to the examined topic.

The role of the subnational governments in contemporary territorial politics emerges from the developed analysis as living, dynamic and viable. In both countries I have examined the modus operandi of what has been considered the crucial instrument of the centralizing attack on the subnational governments: the policy-linked conditional grant/subsidy allotted by the central government. Beyond every superficial impression, the grant/subsidy policy has proved to be only to a certain extent the locus of the transmission of the national goals to the subnational units, but has also proved to be the locus of consideration of the subnational desiderata and of their partial acceptance by the center. The mechanism which permits this flexible compromisory mutual adjustment is the TPE with its hierarchy-breaking dynamics of negotiation. Consequently, the French subsidy system, and the same is true for the U.S. categorical grant system, cannot be considered "the oppressive instrument of an overcentralized government", but rather "the cement which holds the system together" (Ashford, 1982: 314), permitting, through the connected TPEs, the partial satisfaction of both the national and subnational policy desiderata.

In both countries examined the subnational governments have to be considered living, dynamic and viable also because of their ability to impose the partial substitution-consolidation of the policy-linked categorical grants/subsidies with a less conditional and wider scope grant/subsidy system (the BGs and GRS in the U.S. and the DGF and DGE in France). This allows for the increase of the subnational "possibilities for action" and reinforces the subnational power position in the connected TPEs.

Another element of vitality of the politico-administrative periphery has been the ability of U.S. and — even if this was for a long time obstructed by institutional constraints — French subnational governments of facing the increase of the amount of the power resources possessed by the national government. Only if the "polarity principle" is working, the subnational governments can cross the threshold below which the power resource imbalance is too high and hierarchy relations are not yet broken by the emergence of TPEs. Whenever and wherever TPEs are found in territorial politics, one can judge this finding as an indicator of the vitality of the subnational governments, like FPEs and GPE are an indicator of the vitality of the functional interest organizations.

Notes

1 Functional interest organizations are articulated on the basis of "functional representation" (Tarrow, 1978: 4), following the divisions given by the social organization of production, that is along class, sectoral and professional lines in a non-territorial way.
2 The subnational governments are the units of "territorial representation", the basis of which is the "choice of officials through geographic areas" (Tarrow, 1978: 4), independently of functional criteria.
3 The functional logic is non-territorial and organizes public administration and the "corporatist" representative institutions linked to it according to the articulation of the social producton and service sectors and to the welfare policy-functions. Cutting across these functional articulations, the territorial logic leads to an areal-vertical articulation of the public administration and the elective representatives assemblies that follows the geographic structuration of the policy-problems and of the legitimation needs of the state.
4 According to the "policy approach" (Hjern and Hull, 1981: Ham and Hill, 1986: 39-46), public policy formulation and implementation has to be seen as the emergence of, almost always informal, networks linking the public administration with the private actors concerned by the policy, called "policy-targets". The decisional and implementing public actors do not in fact possess the whole of the resources needed for an efficacious and effective policy management and must therefore negotiate with the private policy targets (Hanf, 1982; Mayntz, 1983). In this way, private cooperation to policy in policy formulation and implementation is exchanged for private influence on the output and outcomes of the public policy. Several contributions (Hanf and Scharpf, 1978; Mayntz, 1980; Hjern and Porter, 1981; Barret and Hill, 1984) have shown that the subnational governments, when charged with tasks of integration and implementation of central decisions, modify and adapt the central policy directives, which are indeed often "open" and ambiguous, in a way that follows the subnational desiderata. All this with the complicity and under the pressure of the private policy-targets of the field.
5 Given the importance of the formal juridical regulations in the study of territorial politics, I reject any "alegalism" (Rose, 1985: 24) that neglects the fact that "government is not just another organization" (Sharpe, 1985: 381). Public authority resources, despite their efficacy and effectiveness limits, are a kind of resource that matters particularly in the study of territorial politics, forming a big part of the structural framework of intergovernmental action.

6 Through territorial representation, materialized in national and subnational elective assemblies, every individual member of the nation-state acquires a "territorial citizenship" (Rokkan, 1975: 171) that, independently of his functional (productive or welfare) position, guarantees him the right of being assisted and protected by the national community. Moreover, subnational territorial representation and citizenship is the basis of what B. Constant called "pouvoir municipal", that is the right of a certain level of independence and diversity of the subnational units with respect to the national one.

7 Alliance-representational resources derive from the formation of a relatively stable relation between an organization, in our case a level of government, and other organizations or groups of its relevant environment. As a consequence, a more or less formal relation of alliance or delegation between two organizations can develop, so that one of them represents the interests of the other within decisional and implementation arenas where the latter has no access. In this way, the representing or delegated organization has at its disposal part of the resources of the other, external, one (Benson, 1975: 233-234).

8 I define simple dyadic functional political exchange (FPE) as the relation between a public actor (the national or a subnational government) and a private actor (a national or subnational functional interest organization), which takes place in the course of the formulation and implementation of a public policy, and within which a negotiation, on the basis of the reciprocally valued possessed resources, occurs in order to formulate and implement the policy goals. Therefore, an FPE occurs when the public actor allows the functional interest organization to influence the content of the public decisional (within advisory commissions, through informal pressures, in concertative bodies, etc.) and implementation processes (through the formal acceptance of the functional interest organization's participation in the implementation process or through informal "implementation structures"), so that it can profit from part of the public policy outputs and outcomes, and when, in exchange for this, the latter gives its consensus to the former, that is it acts utilizing, or putting at the other's disposal, its power resources in order to guarantee the efficacy and the effectiveness of the public policy into question. For the definition of GPE see Marin (1985).

9 These are: the NGC, National Governors Conference (1908); the ICMA, International City Management Association (1915); the NLC, National League of Cities, former AMA, American Municipal Association (1924); the USCM, United States Conference of Mayors (1933); the COSGO, Council of State Governments (1933); the NACO, National Association of Counties (1937); the NLC, National Legislative Conference (1948) (Beer, 1976).

10 I now consider the pre-1982 situation. The effects of the Defferre-Reforms will be taken into account in section 3.

11 A reform of the A.T.G.C.-system occurred in 1979-80 creating a central fund and introducing standard fees for the payment of the state field officers (Ashford, 1982: 314-5).

12 A first consolidation of subsidies and the creation of small DGF and DGE occurred already in the late seventies under the center-right government.

List of Abbreviations Used in the Text

A.T.G.C.	Aide Technique à la Gestion Communale
BG	Block Grant
BOB	Bureau of the Budget
CDC	Caisse des Dépôts et Consignations
CDR	Commissaire de la République
DGE	Dotation Générale d'Equipement
DGF	Dotation Générale de Fonctionnement
FPC	Functional Political Circuit
FPE	Functional Political Exchange
GCD	General Councillor of the Department
GPE	Generalized Political Exchange
GRS	General Revenue Sharing
OMB	Office of Management and Budget
PGCD	President of the General Council of the Department
TPC	Territorial Political Circuit
TPE	Territorial Political Exchange
TPG	Trésorier Payeur Général

Political Intervention —
Operational Preconditions for Generalized Political Exchange

Helmut Willke

1. Defining the Problem

Generalized political exchange (GPE) is a category of an external observer whose frame of reference is the idea of interchange between interdependent, functionally differentiated societal subsystems. This is a valid view if one looks at systemic (i.e. interorganizational or intersectoral) interplay from the vantage point of individual or collective actors trying to coordinate their divergent intentions or strategies.

The concept of GPE captures a configuration of recent developments in advanced western societies, which gradually superimposes itself on liberalistic and pluralistic structures of interest mediation and political influence. The newly emerging structures of corporated political exchange, that is the emergence of a set of powerful, centralized, functionally differentiated interest organizations, are not exactly new to the student of politics in modern societies. Quite new, however, is an awareness, that these emerging structures have far-reaching consequences for the political system and the political processes of modern democracies (Marin 1985, 20ff).

In contrast to the liberal format of influence and pressure politics of a plurality of interest groups these countries are moving towards an officially organized collaboration between the state and large interest organizations in public policy making. In order to assess this new situation it is crucial to realize that this is a two-way traffic: on the one hand the corporated interests aggregate and mediate their constituencies' demands and feed them into the political system; they provide first-hand experience, detailed information and know-how and work out propositions, models and alternatives for the policy making process. On the other hand the state regards interest organizations as administrative and implementing instruments, as means for the achievement of public purposes — actually for doing part of the state's very own job, that is the implementation of its policies.

This is indeed a puzzling situation. It is true that political exchange and mediation work both ways: interest organizations feed information into the political system and the political system feeds implementation programs back into the interest organizations. The point, however, is that in *both* ways the interest organizations provide services for the state or the administration — and this of course raises the question what they get in return.

In order to answer this question we must differentiate. The specific returns of this form of collaboration are different for each particular interest organization. For instance, in the West German *Concerted Action* the unions expected as an exchange for their collaboration an increasing influence on economic policy in general — instead of being restricted to wage bargaining. The employers expected a pacifying and stabilizing effect of the Concerted Action, because the unions would have to postpone any form of class struggle if they agreed to become involved in a concerted action. These specific returns are essential to explain the exchange logic of societal discourse systems. There is a more general and maybe more important aspect of exchange relations between the state and societal subsystems, however; it comes into focus when we consider the premisses of this form of collaboration. These premisses are:

1. Because of the exceeding complexity, specialization and efficiency of societal subsystems the state becomes *dependent* on at least three capacities of these corporated subsystems: their capacity for detailed and specialized information and know-how; their capacity for decentralized implementation; and their capacity to withhold compliance and social consensus. The prerogative of the state for societal guidance and policy making is not unchallenged any more. The state meets serious competition from resourceful and self-determining societal subsystems, e.g. the economy, science and technology, education, the health system or multi-national corporations. And its cunning, so to speak, is to convert this competition into collaboration and to pay for it.

2. The currency in which the state is able to pay is *power*. Power is the political system's medium of exchange or medium of communication, and it is coded in the form of *law*. In order to gain the compliance of the relevant corporated subsystem the state risks parts of its competence for policy formulation, that is, part of its sovereign power. This risk is the stake in a gamble in which common gain is possible but not certain. The state trivializes elements of its autonomy in policy making into bargaining currency and trades it in for guidance opportunities in traditionally autonomous societal areas. The net effect of this process is an increasingly intricate interplay between state and societal subsystems whereby all participants *lose parts of their specific autonomy* and gain access into other, previously autonomous domains. In this sense it is correct to speak of the semi-sovereign functions of corporated interest organizations and complementarily of the *semi-sovereign State* (Willke 1986a).

3. The fact that the state gives up elements of its power and autonomy of policy making in return for access into societal areas of autonomy — e.g. autonomy of collective bargaining, autonomy of science, autonomy of forming voluntary associations, autonomy of decentralized territorial units, etc. — is indicative of the inescapable interdependencies of the functionally differentiated parts of complex societies. These interdependencies are recursive, multiple and complex and therefore defy simple mechanisms of decomposition. Most important, they defy hierarchic organization. Hierarchy is an adequate form for the bureaucratic administration or guidance of relatively simple and moderately complex problems or processes. For highly complex problems and processes, however, a need arises

to go *beyond bureaucracy*, beyond hierarchy.

The pressing contemporary problems of advanced societies like economic policy, technology and science planning, infra-structures, health policy or reform of educational systems are too complex for bureaucratic procedures. The adequate management of these problems calls for forms of information processing and problem solving which are able to cope with high complexity, variation and uncertainty. The development of societal dis-course systems shows that advanced societies have already adapted to this need. Societal discourse systems are prototypes of non-hierarchical, *circular or reticular* structures without center or top. They are assemblies of basically equal and interdependent actors, representing parts of the whole of society. Both sides, the state as well as the societal actors have to adjust to these new roles; but it is the state's role which changes most drastically from authoritative hierarchic top to primus inter pares (Willke 1983; 1986).

4. The rationale of this change is its necessity for administration and policy making in complex, turbulent environments. And the problem of *political design* then is, as Anderson puts it, "to create institutions for the effective coordination of organizations which have a vital role to play in the execution of public policy or it is to design forums in which putatively hostile or competitive interests will be caused to deliberate and arrive at a common policy." (Anderson 1976, 144).

It seems that the emergence of GPE-structures in advanced societies reflects the need for structural, institutional, and procedural changes in policies and politics in order to increase the guidance capacities of these societies. Administrative and bureaucratic (hierarchic) forms of societal guidance of course remain operative, mostly in certain basic public functions of order and due process; however, more elaborate forms of policy formation, implementation and impact monitoring develop in critically important problem areas, mainly social welfare arenas and fields of technological, macro-economic, and infra-structural design. These areas defy simple rules and regulations. They imply professional know-how, innovative and responsive organizations, knowledge-based operational proce-dures, and problem-prone technologies: multi-national corporations, huge medical centers, agro-business-conglomerations, new strategic weapon systems, international financial and foreign currency transactions, international debts and securities markets, large energy production systems, major informational and media networks, specialized research and analysis facilities, etc. Most or all of these systems are far too complicated to understand (Churchman 1968, XI). As a rule there is no chance of effective political control or guidance of these problem areas but, instead, there are quite sophisticated ways in which these corporated systems take advantage of the growth of "uncontrollables" and "blind spots" of the traditional political process.

It is, therefore, safe to conclude that democratic governments of the West "lack the intellectual capacities to master the complexities which have emerged as a result of heedless economic growth and chaotic political development... Everywhere powerful sectional economic and political interests subvert any coherent view of the public interest." (Sinai 1978, 211). On the other hand, there are undoubtedly efforts to build up new forms to control and guide these developments, sometimes even explicitly aimed at restoring a democratic political process and reducing the immense risks involved. "Looking-out institutions", offices of technology and risk assessment, offices of management and budget, concerted actions, conferences on nuclear plant security, guidelines for experimental work with retroviruses and recombinant DNA, trilateral commissions, international debt management conferences, world trade and GATT discussions — and so on. Nobody even seems to ask the question how this turmoil of activities might be coordinated, linked to the democratic political process, and be combined to some sort of rational process of selecting bearable technical, economical, and environmental risks, of selecting fundamental technological alternatives, of selecting alternative futures and possible societies.

In a very profound and disquieting way, modern technological and industrial societies have reached a level of *organized social complexity* which by far surpasses the intellectual capacities of individual actors and goes beyond the limits of small segments and limited aspects. But we have lost control, it seems, over the interrelation of these aspects and segments, over the combined effects of the many elements. Let us briefly retrace what has happened. For sociological purposes it is convenient to distinguish three stages in the evolution of modern societies: a primitive level characterized by segmental differentiation (aggregation of same parts), a mezo level characterized mainly by class differentiation, and a modern level characterized by functional differentiation. Functional differentiation in its developed form is a product of the process of occidental rationalization, as analyzed by Max Weber. It means that certain aspects of communal life — aspects like economical, political, scientific, technological, religious, educational or any other activities — are increasingly separated from each other, become more and more specialized, produce separated occupational roles, professions and specialists and finally become incorporated in a relatively autonomous, functionally differentiated and specialized subsystem of society — subsystem like economy, political system, science system, educational or health system, technology, religion, mass communication, and many more. All these subsystems develop their specific rationalities, their specific options and demands, goals and means, functions and products. All this together makes for a very strong centrifugal dynamic of modern societies. The parts drift apart and the question is what remains to preserve and integrate the whole of society. Indeed, this is, in my opinion, the central question and the central problem of modern western societies.

The traditional answer, of course, is that it is the *state* which unites and integrates the whole of society. We have to realize, however, that the state and the traditional political systems (parties, parliaments and administration) seem to have reached the limits of their guidance capacity. The main subsystems like economy, science, technology, health and educational system are far too complex to be guided by the simple means of law and money. The internal complexity of these subsystems, their capacity for self-determination and the production of specialized options, their time perspectives and planning horizons are beyond the limited rationality of the political subsystem. We appear, therefore, to confront a seemingly inescapable paradox: "in the complex modern societies, the less foreseeable the future, the more is foresight required; the less we understand, the more is insight needed; the fewer the conditions which permit planning, the greater is the necessity to plan." (Ruggie 1975, 136). Yet, a comprehensive model of systems steering or societal guidance is too complex for our simple minds and policies: and the incremental model is too simple for our complex societies. There seems to be no way out of this trap.

Indeed, the impression of staggering complexities, of necessary and risky transactions between interdependent and competing collective actors (Marin 1985, 6), and of unsolvable guidance problems (e.g.: ungovernability) of modern societies seems to have been a strong motive to look for practical solutions in empirical politics and "find" structures of neo-corporatist interest intermediation or of generalized political exchange.

However, it seems advisable to be cautious about focussing on exchange relations without first trying to specify the characteristics, capacities, and limitations of the actors involved. The GPE-view might profit from a complementary but incongruent perspective which focusses on the conditions for the possibility of exchange between autonomous systems. At first sight this undoubtedly demands a somewhat forced alienation: to take into consideration, and account for the *uncertainty and riskiness of exchange relations* in spite of their ubiquitiousness. This riskiness results from one aspect of functional differentiation which still seems quite neglected in theories of societal guidance, namely the joint growth of interdependencies *and* independencies between autonomous subsystems of society. Whereas GPE stresses interdependencies, the more serious *problems* of interchange and coordination derive from the independencies and finally the autonomy of societal subsystems. Contemporary subsystems like economy, political system, science, education, health, religion, law, art, etc. can be understood as strictly autonomous, that is operationally closed, self-referential systems. They operate according to own standards, specific rules of self-organization, own selective criteria, and primarily in order to continue their own operations (autopoiesis). All this makes them independent in fundamental aspects of their functioning, it makes them "inner-directed", and predominantly sensitive to the conditions and contingencies of their autopoietic reproduction (for general outlines see Maturana 1982; Zeleny 1981; Luhmann 1984; for specific studies Luhmann 1983 and 1984a (economy); Luhmann 1983a and 1985 (law); Luhmann 1985a (religion); Luhmann 1986 (education); Luhmann 1984c (art).

Still, of course, there are inter-system-relations. These, however, need to be understood as more precarious and more complicated than exchange theory or interorganization theory would have it. During the course of "occidental rationalization" (in Max Weber's sense) various areas of general social communication have developed specific media of internal communication, specialized semantics, codes and programmes for operations of a certain kind: be this economic transactions mediated by money, or political processes according to specific rules for the transformation of power, or scientific research coded in terms of truth/falsification, or religious practice mediated by belief. This process of differential specialization of various areas within society accelerated the evolution of society by triggering internal evolutionary processes of the differentiated domains. This in turn increased the overall complexity of society as well as the complexities of its subsystems. Above all, it means that the parts as well as society in general, have to cope with their internal complexity which, on the one hand, produces myriads of options and contingencies and, on the other hand, needs to be contained and controlled by standard operation procedures of creating internal order and identity. There is an impressive amount of interdisciplinary evidence (e.g. from the theory of autopoiesis, from second order cybernetics, from black-box theory, or from cognitive sciences) for the assumption that *self-referentiality* is necessary and functional for a system to cope with its own complexity (in addition to Maturana 1982, Zeleny 1981 and Luhmann 1984 cited above see: v. Foerster 1981; Glanville 1982; Hofstadter 1984). Of course, any system first of all is a problem for itself, and this problem spells out: continuation and self-production in space and time by the highly improbable ordering of contingencies in the face of chance perturbations. This is the somewhat paradoxical foundation of complex systems: that they can become operative as systems only in the form of complex systems (that is: as systems with a high internal complexity) and that on the other hand, this very complexity continually threatens to overwhelm and disorganize the system.

In order to cope with its own complexity, a system uses a simplified model of itself to organize its own operations. It uses a self-description, a sort of internal blue-print, to inform itself and thus control the validity of possible operations. Without this self-description a social system simply would not be able to decide which of the myriads of contingent operations fit into its own self-reproducing procedures and which would go awry.

If, then, all these characteristics of complex societal subsystems are taken together (functional differentiation, self-referentiality, internal ordering of operations via self-description, and hence operational closure and autopoiesis) it appears that modern societies have two distinct problem areas. One which is widely recognized and also at the base of GPE: this is the complex interdependencies between specialized subsystems following from the primacy of functional differentiation. And one which seems to be quite neglected, that is the high degree of *autonomy* of these subsystems which makes them unsusceptible and indifferent to their environments. Both problems together seem to lead to an evolutionary trajectory of the whole of society which ranges — depending on observer — from suboptimality to irrationality. Societal guidance or evolutionary strategies therefore imply work at both ends of the problem range. To rely on traditional concepts in trying to "solve" this problematic situation — be this a neo-conservative primacy of the state or a neo-liberal primacy of free markets — means to propagate "fatal strategies" (Baudrillard 1983). The structuring of modern societies follows an architecture of complexity which demands major revisions in describing the logic of societal control, coordination, guidance — and exchange.

In order to approach this problem it seems necessary to look very closely at the problem of political intervention into autonomous systems as an operational precondition for exchange relations. *Any exchange involves mutual or circuitous interventions into self-organizing, autonomous systems.* Only if these interventions can be set up as strategies of effective modification of systems' behavior is there a chance to establish exchange relations which alleviate and not aggravate the problem of societal guidance.

In the following section an attempt is made to illustrate this phrasing of the problem by analyzing one type of political-economic exchange. This exchange is characterized by a complicated and mostly intransparent concatenation of systemic interventions. The general directions of these interventions derive from national perceptions of international competition, and they result in the formation of a new gravity center for macro-economic guidance. The objective of this section is to reflect on the idea that an emerging neo-mercantilism of the most advanced and innovative societies provides a new frame of reference for core aspects of GPE. The final section of this paper restates this theme by investigating some of the intricacies of successful intervention.

2. A Mixed-Motive Game and Some Detours to Exchange

Three of the most advanced and massive contemporary examples of political strategies towards macroeconomic management are surprisingly bashful about their economic intentions. In all three cases a naive observer, reading the relevant documents, definitely would get the impression that he is informed about policies of promoting science and fundamental research; that the objective is to increase R&D budgets; and that the realization of the technotronic society was the dominant policy objective.

This particular policy game started with the Japanese — more precisely: MITI's-decision to start the *Fifth Generation Computer Project* (FGCP). It aims at
* freeing computer technology from the reigns of IMB compatibility;
* advancing from data processing to knowledge processing and artificial intelligence;
* and, most remarkable, thereby promoting and implementing the transformation of Japanese society.

The main legitimization of that Titanic effort was "social ends": "The Japanese would say that they are going down this route for social ends. The Japanese elite has a view of a near future in which Japan has a rapidly ageing population, faces a skills shortage, and continues to have an almost total dependence on imported natural resources. What Japan seeks is to reduce that import dependence as much as possible. This is not a new policy; Japanese have for some years been saying that their future is intimately tied to the knowledge-intensive and knowledge-driven industries." (Malik 1983, 207).

Obviously, the message of this project was well understood — whatever the message was. Two years after the inauguration of the project at the Fifth Generation Tokyo Conference of October 1981, President Reagan launched the American response to the challenge: SDI. I imagine that this reasoning is puzzling to some degree. So let me explain. SDI is all kinds of things. But Star War imagery put aside, it is first of all and explicitly a science promotion program. It's predominant implicit goals are advances in communication technologies (C-3: communication, command, control), in software engineering, and programming. It so happens that the most realistic and down to earth parts of SDI perfectly match the Japanese Fifth Generation Computer project. Quite sayingly, *David Parnas* speaks of "software wars" (Parnas 1986, 49ff).

In direct response to the Japanese challenge the American agency DARPA (Defence Advanced Research Projects Agency) started SCI (Strategic Computing Initiative). Since there is no way in the United States to organize such an effort through the collaboration of private industries, only the State was left to do this. The Department of Defence took over the role of the Japanese MITI, and to some degree even necessarily so, because there is no MITI in the United States. So, for example, the Pentagon provided a budget of about 50 million Dollars for SCI in 1984, almost exactly the amount of the budget of the Japanese project in that year. Leading American scientists quite clearly stated the challenge-response character of the two projects (Feigenbaum/Mc Corduck 1984, 40). In January 1984 the first five-year-phase of SDI started, explicitly declared as a "research programme" (Presidential Directive No.119), and provided with prospective funds of about 26 billion dollars.

With due delay even the Europeans joined this game. On November 6th 1985 the European Commission and 18 European governments started EUREKA (European Research Coordination Agency). EUREKA promotes the cooperation of firms and research institutes in high-tech areas, e.g. laser-technology, bio-technology, robotics, or communication technology. It provides variable funding, according to need and significance of the projects. Quite openly EUREKA was considered and declared to be the European "civil response to SDI" (Keller 1986, 11ff) and a start to participate in the technology race with Japan (Hahn 1986, 48). The EUREKA-declaration of Hannover states: "EUREKA's goal is to improve the productivity and competivity of European industries and national economies in the world market through increasing cooperation between corporations and research institutes ..." (Europa-Archiv 2/86 of 25.01.1986, pp. D-39 ff.).

EUREKA comes on top of two more specific European science programmes. Initiated in 1980 and established in 1983 the European Commission's ESPRIT (European Strategic Programme for Research and Development in Informational Technologies) focusses on micro-electronics, software technology, advanced information processing, computer-aided production, and office-technology. Its budget is about one billion dollar and it funds adequate research projects with 50% of their R&D costs (Hüncke 1986, 11; Schütze 1985; 35ff). An even more specific programme is RACE (Research and Development in Advanced Communication Technologies for Europe) which can be seen as a direct response to the American and Japanese 'threat' of worldwide technological dominance.

In combination with quite a number of more specialized programmes — including e.g. BRITE (Basic Research in Information Technologies for Europe), COST (Coopération européenne dans le domaine de la recherche scientifique et technique), JET (Joint European Torus), and ESA (European Space Agency) — EUREKA is becoming a crystallization point for a "European Technology Community", that is a concerted political action to meet the conjoint Japanese-American science and technology challenge.

What does all this mean? In my opinion, the most important point is, that the traditional forms of GPE — mainly neo-corporatist arrangements at national or regional levels, concerted actions, "scambio politico", income-policy, social-economic councils, etc. — rapidly are getting transformed into secondary objectives by a super-structure of world-wide competition for scientific-technological-economic predominance. Quite contrary to neo-classical economic doctrine this meta-game about breakthroughs in fundamental research, core technologies, and advanced socio-technical production-system-management propels the world economy rights back to (neo-) mercantilism. And quite paradoxically it seems to push the state into a position of encompassing societal guidance in spite of massive evidence of ungovernability and complexity overload.

2.1 A Mercantilist Resuscitation?

A mercantilist resuscitation becomes less improbable as the goals of national macro-economic management shift from the production of internal consensus and compliance to external excellence or even superiority in world-wide socio-economic competition. The chain reaction of national high-tech programmes triggered by Japan's Fifth Generation project brought into the open a new pattern of state involvement in societal management: the transition from macro-economic management to encompassing societal guidance.

The dominant principle of evolutionary change from feudal to modern society is the functional differentiation of society into subsystems. The process of functional differentiation is quite well understood and analysed as an historical process. Much less understood seem to be the consequences of this fundamental change in societal structure. Even today, we tend to think of modern societies as hierarchically structured systems, with State and politics as the top of the hierarchy, providing for binding decisions for the whole of society. However, in a strict sense, functionally differentiated systems are characterized by interdependence, not by hierarchy: functionally differentiated societies have no established rank order between functions, subsystems or rationalities. "They have to rely on changing priorities and can institutionalize functional primacies only on the level of subsystems. They cannot describe themselves as 'hierarchies' ... they have no top and no center" (Luhmann 1984c, 65).

However, practical politics and policies still build on the misconception of the State as a general societal problem solver. In this role, the modern State necessarily must become overburdened; it must assume responsibilities it cannot bear; it must elicit hopes it cannot fulfil. In highly developed, functionally differentiated societies, there is no single hierarchical top instance or central institution which can adequately represent the complexity of the whole of society, or which would be able to build up the requisite variety (internal complexity) for overall societal problem solving. The analogous lesson for example has been learned in organization theory and organizational practice. This has lead to remarkable efforts in organization development to overcome hierarchical structures and centralized problem solving. In the case of the theory and practice of the State, progress has not been so overwhelming. However, one major step in untangling the paradox of the State and its implications for GPE and — more generally — for societal guidance appears to lie in realizing three points:

1) The image of the State as an entity in juxtaposition to society in general, confounds logical and also empirical levels. The political system of a society is one of the many subsystems following the functional differentiation of society. Its rationality is a partial one, just like that of all other societal subsystems and it has an "inclusive" dynamic just like all other subsystems. And this is the reason why, on the one hand, as a subsystem it cannot transcend its particularity and its partial rationality; and why, on the other hand, the State has to fill in the gap and satisfy the quest for societal unity. Untangling this tangled hierarchy means to realize, that the State cannot fulfil the function of the superstructure of society, but instead operates as the infrastructure of the political system. This is what is meant by conceptualizing the State as the self-description of the political system. Mixing up the levels of society and the level of societal subsystems means to overburden the State with the sum of societal problems, whereas as an institution it is built to handle the problems of the political system alone.

2) Of course, this leaves the question what, if not the State, is there to represent and organize the unity of society. As long as there is no answer to this question the State necessarily fails to fulfil a commitment which it cannot avoid to assume within the present context of conceptualizing and describing the Welfare State.

3) So I think that one way to proceed from here is to accept the partiality of the State as the institutional core of the political system and prepare for the necessity of a much more complex construction for those exchange processes between autonomous societal subsystems and their acting major organizations which now become necessary in order to produce the integration and manageability of a modern non-hierarchical or "heterarchical" society.

A central part of this more complex construction seems to be the idea to take into account the consequences of the formative principle of modern "western" societies. This type of societal formation is characterized by the primacy of functional differentiation, ensuing complex interdependencies between the specialized subsystems, over-production of specialized options (including externalities) within the subsystems, a high degree of autonomy of the internal operation procedures, and, following from all this, an evolutionary trajectory of the whole of society which definitely is centrifugal and possibly suicidal.

This, then, is the baffling situation: in the wake of neo-corporatist thinking, implying powerful, organized, highly complex and competent societal actors, we detect a profound weakness of unrestrained strength. Only if these collective actors can be aligned in an interactive concatenation of mutual self-restraint and self-control, is there a chance to reduce the excessive amount of negative externalities, and to increase combinatorial gains. In the case of a company, this appears to be quite obvious: only if management succeeds in making "organizational intelligence" out of the inner-directed, centrifugal activities of the differentiated departments (product design, purchasing, manufacturing, finance, R&D, personnel, marketing, etc.) can it hope to beat the competition. Of course, a nation is not a company. Is it?

But there seem to exist functionally equivalent problems, since modern societies, too, are complex, functionally differentiated systems. If the impression is not entirely aberrant that there is developing a new quality of international competition, and if a society (or a community of societies) wants to take part in this game, then there is a definite need to produce an adequate level of "societal intelligence" in order to be able to compete.

To be sure, this is not meant to amount to a resurrection of *Hilferding's Organisierter Kapitalismus*. Capitalism is much too narrow a definition for modern society's purposes. Rather, the argument aims at organized complexity in the sense of developing forms of organizing the complexity of contemporary societies. More specifically, it aims at *organized political exchange*, meaning that the national political systems (and their states) are pushed into a new role of organizing the complexities of society, or a new role of societal guidance.

A most intricate and probably paradoxical reason for this conspicuous role of the political system is the fact of its anachronistic national format. Whereas most — if not all — other subsystems of modern societies, mainly science, technology, economy, art, sport, even to some degree religion, education or popular culture, have transcended national boundaries and developed into *lateral world systems*, the political subsystems of modern societies remain the guardians of territorial division and separation. Whether the evolution of lateral world systems has been encouraged and promoted by the background security of territorially defined national sovereignty; whether in the contrary the narrow-minded fixation of "small units" hampers the coming into being of a world society; or whether the symbolics of national identification simply visualize the demarcation of centers and peripheries, and thus provide the stratification of a world system, accentuating the architecture of its complexity — all these are unanswered questions. The fact remains, that the current and foreseeable future world dynamics result — to a degree which probably still is underestimated — from an opaque mixture of evolutionary strategies of spatially defined areas — USA, Japan, Europe, South-East-Asia, Soviet Bloc — on the one hand, and a pervasive, worldwide competition between these strategies on the other hand.

The disquieting part of this observation is the self-fulfilling circularity of the process. The actors involved in this meta-game assume, and maybe expect, adverse strategies and therefore 'observe' strategic moves. Whether these observations are realistic or not is of secondary importance. The entire process is self-sustaining insofar as the mere anticipation of adverse strategies forces actors to react. Those reactions, of course, confirm the assumptions of competing actors — and the rat race is on. The official documents of FGCP, SDI, and EUREKA are abundant with incidents of this type of reaction circles. All three parties solemnly declare to react to perceived challenges, to secure attained positions, to defend their share of world market transactions, to improve their competitive edge, etc. As far as reactive cycles and self-reproducing processes are concerned, all this is not exactly new. The arms race is a prominent further example. However, at least two aspects seem to be quite new and worthwhile to ponder: the inclusiveness of the new game and its political consequences.

Inclusiveness means that this game of global competition is not restricted any more to separated and specialized domains of societal activities, say military confrontation, economic competition or technological excellence. A really disturbing feature of the new political game is its conjunctive quality: a concentration and concoction of all aspects of societal efficiency in an overall competition for generalized reputation and excellency. Until now, it seemed feasible that the Russians and Americans are superior in military strength, the Japanese in technological production, the Germans in economic export, the French in savoir vivre, or the Italians in muddling through. But the rules of the game appear to change. A core "iron triangle" of tight scientific-technological-economic interdependencies (with massive consequences for military technology and strength, an aspect which will be neglected here) evolves as a new gravity center of generalized societal capacities. It doesn't suffice any more for a nation to excel in one of these domains. For the triggering effects, spin off, and trickle down effects of innovations in one of these areas multiply the overall effects. So, it becomes risky and potentially dangerous to neglect one of these fields, to neglect their interdependencies, or to neglect cumulating effects. Various drives to enforce the development of assumed or real trigger-technologies (e.g. 4 or 16 mega-bit chip, operational laser, AI-driven robots) attest to a spreading fear to loose ground if certain strategically placed technologies are occupied or dominated by the competition.

A few numbers may indicate that this is not just fear and fantasy: The USA and Japan together control 90% of the world market in semi-conductors. Europe doesn't count. Between 1963 and 1983 the share of high technology products of all exports decreased for OECD-countries from 58% to 43%, for the USA from 27% to 21%, and increased for Japan from 5% to 23% according to one source (Narjes 1986, 1). According to another source (Rinsche 1986, 5) during the same time period the share of high-tech products of all exports moved from 23% to 25% for the European Community, from 29% to 38% for the USA, and from 16% to 42% for Japan. Whatever the calculating base, it is obvious that major changes have occurred during the past twenty years, and it is not unreasonable to assume that more is to come. One indicator are the estimated overall expenditures for R&D during the five year period from 1986 to 1991: they are about 1.000 Billion ECU (European Currency Units, right now approximately one ECU = one US dollar) for the USA, the twelve EC-countries together and Japan each about half this amount. Relative to its GNP Japan spends about 30% more for R&D than the European Community (Narjes 1986, 1).

It is not too farfetched, then, to conclude that the over-riding goal of somehow "successfully" participating in the emerging world-wide socio-economic competition leads to a tightening of interdependencies, particularly between science, technology, and economy. This creates an "iron triangle" or a new *dominant coalition* which threatens to align other facets of social life (e.g. education, university curricula, public communication, cultural reproduction) according to the gravity lines of high-tech productivity concerns. This sort of inclusiveness constitutes a counter-movement to functional differentiation, comparable to the emergence of a military-industrial or a welfare-industrial complex. But whereas these examples of a lumping together of different societal functions in retrospect appear short lived and contingent upon special circumstances, the new constellation of a scientific-technological-economic syndrome might prove more stubborn. It is a concatenation of crucial sectors of modern societies under the auspices of prosperity and (hopefully) peaceful reputation. Possibly this is one of the reasons why everybody seems to like the idea of strengthening that syndrome, without inquiring much into the consequences.

However, one impact definitely will be a transformation of the role of national political systems and their states. To some degree the participating states will become the management departments of huge corporations, putting "Japan Inc." versus "American Society, Inc." (Zeitlin 1973), and the "European Technology Community" somewhere in between. Although this image certainly is exaggerated and onesided, it highlights a creeping resuscitation of mercantilism. Again it is the role of the state to organize and coordinate a societal effort of protecting and promoting national economies. Again it is the political system which subsidizes long-range research projects, provides starting aids, fosters initiative, buffers risks, and in general facilitates contextual conditions of a great variety in order to create a "climate" of technological and productive innovation (for comparison see v. Justi 1761 on "Kameralistik").

Of course, you might argue that this is nothing new and that the modern political systems have done this all along. I think that this standard argument is misleading, although there is no doubt that the political subsystems never really have stopped to somehow interfere with economic processes. It is misleading because it disregards threshold phenomena. The degree, quality, directedness, and legitimizing rhetoric of the *emerging neo-mercantilism* set it apart from Keynesian or Neo-Keynesian approaches. The focal point of political activities is not any more to prevent something "bad", e.g. economic depression, unemployment, civil unrest, or political delegitimization. The point now is to actively pursue the "goodies" the world market offers to competent competitors. The difference is obvious even on a small scale: for example the case of "Späth-Kapitalismus" of Suebia (one of the States of the Federal Republic, headed by a Prime Minister with the name of 'Späth'). For some years now, this example of practical neo-mercantilism has drawn some attention because instead of hiding economic intervention behind a veil of defensive excuses the administration of that country aggressively *wanted* to promote and mediate technological innovation, and explicitly so in order to increase exports. One of the effects of this policy was the creation — mediated by political maeutics — of a huge technological corporation by merging Daimler-Benz, MBB, Dornier and AEG.

If it makes at least some sense to describe world market dynamics, international competition, the emerging dominance of a scientific-technological-economic iron triangle, and of neo-mercantilism within the presented frame of reference, then one should expect some consequences in particular for the involved political subsystems and the mechanisms of generalized political exchange. For example, it is hard to see "exchange relations" between science and politics. There are definitely political interventions into science, then "some" spin-off effects on technology, then "some" causal (instrumental) effects on the economy, and finally "some" secondary effects of economic performance on the political system. But the entire arrangement resembles a black box in which causal relations, intention-impact concatenation, or feed-back and feed-forward circles are quite opaque.

A striking difference between mercantilism and neo-mercantilism is the fact that the state today has to deal with a variety of powerful, autonomous societal actors (subsystems, organisations, collective actors), and that the state definitely is not in a position any more to arrange things by decree. Therefore, in order to come to grips with GPE it seems necessary to look very closely into the problems of political intervention into autonomous systems as an operational precondition for exchange relations.

3. Political Intervention, Transaction Chains, and Exchange

The basic function of the state ('state' again being an abbreviation for 'political-administrative system') has been to avoid anarchy by protecting its subjects, maintaining territorial integrity, enforcing law, and levying taxes. Control was operative at the level of individuals, either as non-members or as members of a "dominant protective agency" (Nozick 1974, 15ff and 101ff; see also Rose 1976). There have been, however, important changes *within* societies that challenge the control capacity and thus the internal sovereignty of the state.

First of all, there is the fact, that — contrary to an individualistic conception of society — "organized groups, and not individuals are the protagonists of political life in a democratic society" (Bobbio 1984, 6). The rise of the great associations, organizations, trade unions, professions and corporations indicate the powerful thrust of functional differentiation of modern societies, and it indicates a profound change in the level and scope of possible and possibly necessary control in society. Initially crystallizing around focal organizations like factories, banks, hospitals, schools, universities, voluntary associations, political parties, etc. the present fully-fledged societal subsystems (e.g. economy, health system, education, science, technology, culture, etc.) demand an altogether different relation with the state for power and control and they continuously increase their internal differentiation, complexity and autonomy in a self-reinforcing way.

On the one hand, this means, that indeed "society consists of a constellation of governments, rather than an association of individuals held together by a single government" (Unger 1976, 193). These 'private governments' have their own interests and goals, their own rationalities and resources. And within their niches these subsystems follow their specific evolutionary trajectories which, taken together, give modern societies a definite centrifugal drift. There is no way for the state (and with it for the political system) to penetrate the eigen-complexities of developed subsystems. Which courses science and technology should take, which new medical methods and treatments should be pursued, which measures taken against dying forests, which new academic courses to be offered, which bio-genetic experiments forbidden, etc., all this is beyond the control and guidance capacity of the political-administrative system. Even if it wanted to guide, it would necessarily rely heavily on the professional judgement of the very subsystems that supposedly were to be guided. This amounts to the very consequential argument that under present conditions the traditionally basic guidance function of the state is severely limited because any type of societal guidance predominantly means *self-guidance* of resourceful organized actors.

As outlined in Section 1, the problem of "political design" or of purposeful and organized political exchange derive from a simultaneous increase of the interdependencies and independencies of societal actors. The autonomy of societal subsystems is well entrenched not only legally through basic rights and constitutional demarcation lines (Luhmann 1965). Practically more important seem to be the functional provisions for inner-directedness, operational closure, and self-referentiality in guaranteeing a considerable degree of *indifference* of these systems to external perturbations.

The problem of political design then is to establish the *exchange logic of a network of autonomous actors*. This logic implies multiple interventions and "fitting" transaction-chains between operationally closed systems. It implies the accordation of adverse interests as well as surmounting a basic indifference of self-containing and self-referential systems. Why should economic actors react to political measures? They usually don't. Why should firms, associations or interest organizations comply to laws, political persuasion programmes or appeals. They usually don't. Instead, they calculate in cost-benefit-terms and disregard morals (pecunia non olet). Even in using money as a means of intervention there is a perennial unlimited-dollar-misunderstanding between politics and economy: the intentions of a specific policy all too often are transformed, mitigated or even reversed by economic actors because they operate according to their own standards and rationale, e.g. not thinking in terms of implementation but in terms of opportunity realization (see for the relevant phenomena of "moral hazard" and "adverse selection" Baecker 1988, 33ff). Working basically self-referentially, the economy or any other subsystem will be impressed by events in its environment only very selectively and according to its own selective criteria. The political use of money still is different from the economic use of money (Lindblom 1982). And this difference needs to be reflected if one aims at effective macro-economic interventions.

One way of organizing the interrelation of different autonomous actors, is to let things happen through gradual, mutual, incremental adjustment, to go with the fluctuations wherever they develop. The consequence is incrementalism, or more general, *evolution*. Evolution means "muddling through" the chance variations of contingencies by solving present problems in a decentralized way, in a short range time perspective, locally, and within the circumstances at hand. The intelligence — and the costs — of evolution lie in restricting the possibilities of change to adapting to stochastic changes of possibilities. Muddling through solves the dilemma of functional differentiation by asymmetrically stressing local autonomy and *"order through fluctuations"* (Prigogine 1976). For example, the gradual fluctuations of world-economic gravity centers from Europe to America to the Pacific area shows this pattern of incremental change and adaptation. It is probably safe to say that no actor or group of actors has consciously designed this to happen. Instead, a multitude of different factors were woven together in an undirected evolutionary process.

A second way to organize systemic interrelations is *planning*. Central planning presupposes a centre or a hierarchical top in societies, be this the state, the economy or any other subsystem or organization. Planning under the primacy of the state means general, obligatory laws. These laws describe and prescribe future preferred states of affairs and they direct administrative action through purposive programs and goal-directed forms of intervention (Willke 1983a). Societal planning by the state or by public administration must assume, that it is possible and rational to intervene directly into whichever societal subsystem by means of law. Planning under the primacy of the economy means, on the other hand, the preponderance of long-range economic calculations and of considerations of rentability over all other criteria of decision making. Both forms of planning postulate clear priorities and posteriorities and so solve the dilemma of functional differentiation by asymmetrically stressing central decision making and *order through hierarchy*.

There is ample evidence however, that planning has failed as a methodology of organized societal change. Among other reasons this is due to a fundamental mismatch between the hierarchical structure of planning and a non-hierarchical or "heterarchical" (McCulloch) organization of complex systems.

Guidance is a third way of organizing societal change. Guidance consists of two complementary parts: a reflexive, decentralized framing of contexts which may serve as common "world views" or common orientations for all organized societal actors; and self-guidance of all subsystems within the limits of their autonomy. A decentral framing of contexts is supposed to mean, that a minimum of common orientation of "world view" among societal actors seems indispensable for constituting and maintaining a complex differentiated society. However, these common contexts cannot be generated any more by a central unit or an hierarchical top decision maker. No single actor or organization or subsystem can generalize its own specific rationality or world view and declare it binding for all others. For no single subsystem is in a position to transcend the internal complexity and impenetrability of all other highly developed subsystems. No single individual or corporate mind can construct an adequate internal map of the overall complexity of society; nor can it "understand" all parts and the intricacies of their operations. So centralized directives necessarily are suboptimal (for a good presentation of suboptimality see Zeleny 1982: 47ff).

Whereas it seems common sense that under conditions of high complexity central planning and direct intervention must remain suboptimal, it is far less evidence to many social scientists that evolution is suboptimal, too. The logic of evolution, however, is not positive selection and thus, optimization of a certain ecological domain; rather it is negative selection (Campbell, 1969: 73ff) or the exclusion of lethal variants. So, evolution does not allow for adequate reactions to perceived long-range risks or deviation amplifying trends. For example, these trends might be caused by negative externalities or unintended consequences of purposive action. This means that something more than muddling through is necessary to cope with the current, seemingly 'natural' dramaturgies of global problems, ranging from overpopulation, resource exhaustion, environmental pollution, or arms race, to the risks of a forced high-technology race. This 'something more' could be societal guidance, perceived as a strategy which respects the integrity of autonomous subsystems and still promotes organized structural change by shaping specific contextual patterns (see Willke 1984).

More precisely: societal guidance as a political strategy seems to be possible if it works with contextual interventions instead of direct, decree-type regulations. "Contextual interventions" refer to the fact that complex self-referential systems operate according to the specific logic of their "distinctions directrices" (Luhmann 1985a), deriving operationally relevant information *only* from differences which make a difference within their specialized media of communication (for the underlying concept of information see Bateson 1972, 315ff, 381, 453ff; for the concept of media of communication see Luhmann 1984, 205ff). Interventions in this sense aim at changing environmental conditions of system-environment relations (which in condensed, domesticated societal arenas usually are inter-system-relations). Interventions necessarily work indirectly because all they can do is conditionalize contextual conditions. The autonomous operational procedures define a system's discriminating criteria and thus its sensitive spots. Only the system itself can implement changes in its standard operating procedures. If they are implanted from outside, they provoke immune reactions or even the collapse of the autonomy of the system. This means that changes can only be realized as self-implemented changes and that interventions, therefore, are effective if they facilitate, initiate or promote processes of self-transformation of the target system (Willke 1984a).

Although this sounds very theoretical, there is no denying the fact that societal guidance actually operates in this way, for example, in the form of concerted actions or various forms of neo-corporatist practice (Schmitter 1983; Willke 1983).There are considerable guidance activities going on within and between all parts of society. The political systems of modern welfare societies cannot escape the pressure to intervene in practically all societal problem arenas, be this family, schooling, science, traffic, home building, energy consumption or whatever. But also, the economy, or religion, military, culture, technology or other sectors try hard to guide societal processes in an effort to intentionally change their respective societal environment in a preferred direction.

It is not at all surprising that these diverse efforts at societal guidance actually happen. What may come as a surprise, however, is the fact to what degree these efforts fail. Often they produce detrimental effects and even more often they are but a waste of time and resources. Arguing from the vantage point of the theory of self-referential systems, these failures should be expected. For highly developed societal subsystems are intransparent even to self-observation. Their specialization, operational closure, and their self-referential way of structuring events make them opaque and resistant to unrefined external intervention. Although autopoietic systems are by no means completely independent from their environment, it is apparent that direct intervention works as little as cannon boat diplomacy or big stick policy. Therefore, it becomes exceedingly important to specify in which respects a certain autopoietic system is independent and cannot be directed through external intervention, and in which respects it is open to external stimuli. For example, economic communications come into being by referring to payments oriented by prices, within a frame of cost-benefit-calculations. These communications become specialized and self-referential as a special medium of communication — money — evolves and as these communications get organized by a dualistic code which only distinguishes between property and non-property (Luhmann 1983; Baecker 1986). Modern economies have refined this operationally closed game to an amazing degree, including banks, stock markets, or future markets. Still, of course, there are relations between the economy and external systems, for example, technology, politics, nature, labor or other segments of its environment. Relations are realized through *transactions*, "the transfer of something valued between systems" (Kuhn 1974, 9). Transactions follow from a very artful combination of price-oriented (self-referential) and opportunity-oriented (other-referential) considerations. They are prototypes of "transferential operations" (Braten 1984, 161) which establish a selective and loose coupling of autonomous systems.

Rethinking GPE in terms of societal guidance capacities first of all means to examine feasible policies for the improvement of "social technologies" for the structuring of complex dynamic systems. This can be done by looking at empirical evidence for innovative concertation networks or discourse systems or social rule systems (Burns/Flam, 1986). A lot can be gained from international comparison e.g. of conflict and interest mediation systems, of policy concertation, etc., (and the vast literature on neo-corporatism has done exactly that. For the particularly interesting case of Japan see Marin 1987, 20ff for a general description, and Weber 1987 for details). And, of course, this can be done by looking for new ideas concerning the architecture of complexity.

It is not without irony that we do know, or pretend to know, the exact ratings of main competitors (Japan, USA, Europe, USSR) as regards innovative capacities in advanced technologies, be this computers, factory automation, life sciences, advanced materials, optoelectronics or whatever (see Special Report, Fortune Oct.13, 1986). But what makes the differences? It is definitely not intelligence, nor size, nor natural resources. It seems to be a productive hypothesis to postulate that the decisive differences are those of social and guidance "technologies", that is to say, differences in the rules and metarules of establishing order and direction between autonomous, loosely coupled social systems.

Looking for new ideas in this domain definitely demands to move beyond the traditional dichotomies of State and market, of supply-side and demand-side policies, centralization vs. decentralization, regulation vs. deregulation, etc. The idea of *heterarchical contextual guidance* basically means:

- There are non-hierarchic relations between societal subsystems and actors involved in a problem-oriented policy, be this drug abuse, epidemic risks, a shift in industrial structure, or a viable energy production systems mix.
- The type of "possible" intervention is highly specific: purposive action is restricted to managing contextual parameters through joint interventions that may mature into transaction chains. The goal is to create mutually compatible and "resonant" (s. Luhmann 1986a) contextual conditions which instigate processes of self-directed change of the relevant autonomous systems.
- The autonomy of the relevant systems needs to be respected not for altruistic reasons but for reasons of 'enlightened' self-interest. Autonomy of a highly developed system

includes: its specific rationality, information-producing and processing capacities, its built-in problem solving routines and operational know-how, its capacity for decentralized implementation and impact monitoring, its special competence and contribution to a differentiated overall system. From the point of view of contextual guidance all this should be used as assets for coordinated self-guidance, and not treated as obstacles to outer-directed change.

• Coordination and guidance activities aiming at viable forms of 'compatible heterogeneity' necessitate a shift of focus from unity to diversity. A suitable measure for judging the "quality" of societal systems, therefore, cannot be unity anymore, or consensus or even lack of conflict; instead it should be the capacity of a differentiated system for tolerating ambiguity, for coping with differences and divergent rationalities, and for processing contradictions.

All this appears to be quite clear and easily understandable as long as we look not at ourselves but at our neighbors, for example at the present drama of "glasnost" and "perestroika" in the Soviet Union and the break-down of State-socialist systems. However, the point is that modern Western societies need even more transparency of societal discourses in order to come to grips with the centrifugal tendencies, disruptive option overload, and damaging externalities of their powerful subsystems. Contextual guidance means to influence contextual parameters of the standard operating procedures of societal actors in such a way that the "prisoners dilemma" can be overcome, i.e. that co-evolution or even cooperation is possible in spite of remaining conflicts of interests.

In the special case of self-referential social systems, guidance then is a process which succeeds in establishing patterned connections between a system and external interventions in spite of the 'inner-directedness' of systemic processes. In most general terms, this type of connection between system and intervention demands a *grammar of transformational rules* which allow for the transfer of external conditions into the internally determined operational cycles of an acting unit. This kind of interrelation between two or more structurally determined systems obviously happens in each instance of co-evolution of distinct systems when there is some interactive behavioral coupling — be this on the basis of general structural coupling, of the co-evolution merely of transferential mechanisms, or of even more selective gate-keeper devices which permit the controlled infiltration of external stimuli into the system. For example, it seems possible to circumvent the "immune reaction" of an autopoietic system against external interventions by coupling in a sluice-like manner dispositions (in the system) and events (in its environment) or by coupling systemic operational rules and external messages which pertain to these rules. The latter example illustrates the possibility to eventually change the rules through messages which contain information about rules. Taking into account that in social interaction all structures of events "have a self-closing or cyclical character", as Allport (1954: 288) has put it long ago, the problem is to couple different sequences of events in order to arrive at concerted action and instructive interaction.

In other words, the point is to find those "transferential operations" (Braten) or "interface devices" (Waller 1983: 1) which make it possible for the intervening as well as for the guided system to shift between self-referencing and other-referencing. The difference between the two perspectives could be used to extend self-observation to the faculty of *reflexion*. At the level of modern societies political intervention can operate as a medium of guidance — and thus policy programmes be a mediator of political intervention into societal subsystems — only if these interventions succeed in facilitating transferential operations between partially autonomous actors and so promote reflexion as a modus of controlled co-evolution.

All this amounts to a logic of exchange which hinges upon sequences of conditioning environmental parameters of inter-acting social systems. Definitely, exchange is not the transportation of fixed entities (e.g. actions or meaning) between social systems. Rather, it means the concertation of internal orientations through transactions which respond to external opportunity structures for internal operations.

Apparently, the new types of political exchange programs that have been mentioned in this paper — FCGP, SDI, EUREKA — have learned this lesson. All of them have overriding economic intentions. But they work indirectly. They invest into science, create new opportunity structures, and facilitate transactions between science, technology, and economy — and then wait and see what happens.

Games within Games:
On the Politics of Association and Dissociation in European Industrial Policy-Making

Arthur F. P. Wassenberg

"On ne sort de l'ambiguité qu'à son détriment",
Cardinal de Retz.

1. Introduction

There is more than one reason to expect that between now and 1992 the issue of industrial cooperation will continue to figure prominently on the policy-agenda of the European Economic Community (EEC). Around that time, according to official narrative, the internal barriers will have been removed and the economic integration will be a fait accompli. The auxiliary narrative centers around two perceptions: the threat posed by the Japanese American hegemony in the field of advanced technologies — the challenge — and the conviction that individual European companies and individual member states are incapable of finding a suitable answer to that threat if they do not coordinate their strategies in one way or another — apparently the response.

Academic treatises and press releases talk about Europe, Japan and the United States as if the latter represent concrete entities. Yet, according to a recently published Gallup poll, performed for the European Commission in Brussels, more than two thirds of the U.S. population have never heard of the EEC. Only 1% knows that the EEC has twelve members. Since the second last poll in 1973, American familiarity with the EEC has gone down considerably. EEC Commissioner Willy De Clerq, who is responsible for EEC-U.S. relations, feels that the EEC should try to attract more American attention. "Whereas 86% of Americans consider the ties with Europe important", says De Clerq, "only 29% of them know about the EEC". In his opinion, the results of the poll prove that Americans still see Europe as a region that mainly excels in the production of art, music, drama and fashion. Americans do not have a high opinion of European high tech knowledge. Half of the interviewees (interviewed in November 1987) thought the U.S. leads the way in high tech knowledge, 42% thought Japan does. Only 4% thought of Europe in this connection. Maybe this assessment of European capabilities helps to explain why Americans say to expect to profit rather than to lose by the EEC market.

Conversely, what do Europeans know about their opposites on the other side of the Atlantic? And about the *Dritte im Bunde*, Japan, itself surrounded by a ring of rapidly developing competitors in the Pacific? Apparently, mutual ignorance does not prevent the international imitation of methods and mores. American strategies and tactics of intercorporate conflict and cooperation — assisted by official and semi-official allies from the political and the legal establishment — find their way into Europe. This happens at an astonishing pace.

Europe gets acquainted with a relatively new phenomenon: intercorporate raids. The primary reaction, from private as well as public players, appears to be somewhat frail or maladroite. However, one may expect that a modus vivendi will be found. Organizations seem to learn the rules of a new game. That game can be called 'antagonistic cooperation'. The aim of this chapter is to explore the principles of antagonistic cooperation, not only among firms but also between firms, governments and administrative agencies.

In order to get a first-hand impression of the typical stratagems and spoils associated with this type of game (among firms and part of a social and political establishment) we start with an enlightening short story. Next the implications of this specific, but less and less exceptional form of cooperation will be traced for the stability of interorganizational relations. As will be demonstrated below, understanding the rules of a game does not necessarily imply that one controls the logic of such a game: neither in terms of the stability of resulting coalitions (and oppositions) nor in terms of their creativity. The essentials of antagonistic cooperation will be illustrated by a case-study of interorganizational cooperation in one field of European industrial policy-making (information technology).

Case-studies do not produce conclusive knowledge. In this chapter, an elaborate case-study serves to demonstrate the merits of a specific perspective: a perspective that chooses *triadic* relationships as the basic unit of analysis for the explanation of the dynamics of inter-organizational cooperation, rather than the more usual *dyadic* (exchange-theoretical and conflict-sociological) approaches to strategy formulation and policy-making.

2. Phantom Capitalism

How consensually does 'Europe' define the Japanese/American challenge, and how far does its willingness and capacity reach to answer the challenge in a concerted fashion? Because of Europe's lack of experience with the 'American' mix of intercorporate conflict and cooperation, it seems as if a new phantom is haunting the old continent. Not long ago the phantom was spotted in Brussels, the capital of a kingdom and the nerve centre of the EEC. The plot could have been borrowed from a (neo-)gothic novel.

The opening move was for a Mr. Carlo de Benedetti, in Italy acclaimed as the representative of a new industrial elite and in the rest of Europe admired for the flair with which he had succeeded — like a *conquistador* — in weaving a web of financial and industrial companies within a short space of time. Early in the year 1988, he announced that he had acquired a considerable interest in one of Belgium's eldest financial and economic sanctuaries: the *Société Générale*. He announced that he had chosen the Société Générale as a stepping stone in the formation of a "truly European" network of companies (under his indisputable supervision, of course). This network would make it possible to face the completion of the EEC in 1992 without fear. According to De Benedetti's formula, Europe would, from that moment on, be ready for the confrontation with other economic power blocks.

The reaction of the Société Générale's board of directors was not enthusiastic. During a quickly organized press conference, the assembled journalists inquired into all the details. Why, for instance, did the Société Générale not welcome the Italian tycoon, who was reported to be a very rich, extremely competent and quite suitable partner for the formation of a European holding? Société Générale's managing director René Lamy grew angry and roared:

"We do not want Belgium to be financially and economically controlled by Turin. We will never agree with De Benedetti's imperialist proceedings. We do not wish to be colonized. He claims that he wants to modernize us, he accuses us of being a feudal organization. Nonsense! Furthermore, Italy is also familiar with feudal conditions and maybe De Benedetti himself forms part of them.

He is bent on absolute control. He says he is not, but I dare him to prove that. He cannot, because I have a letter, in which he states that he wants to be the key shareholder. We will not submit to this kind of stratagem. We will not submit to this act of aggression."

The battle for Belgium Incorporated was attended by a battle in the media.[1] The Société Générale was forced into an uncomfortable position, especially in the international financial media. "De Benedetti's attitude forms a refreshing contrast to the secretiveness and arrogance of the complex that dominates Belgium", said *The Wall Street Journal*, clearly hoping for De Benedetti's victory. "This victory is in the interest of the Belgian citizens who pay far too many taxes, while the government and Société Générale have allowed large parts of industry to come to a halt", wrote the Bible of the financial world. Belgium did sorely need a "mover and shaker like De Benedetti".

Shortly afterwards it was De Benedetti's turn to demonstrate his local knowledges. In a Belgian broadcast he said: "Société Générale and its supporters disregard Belgian, or rather Flemish, demands. I am a true capitalist. I believe that a company is owned by its shareholders. The board of directors does not work for its own sake, but for the shareholders. The board of directors is obliged to present the shareholders with good results; if it doesn't, it has failed. Looking at Société Générale, I see that results have dropped back. Economic growth is insignificant, the board of directors adopts a feudal attitude toward the shareholders. The board disregards the shareholders' and the country's demands, for it has not solved the unemployment problem and the demands of Flemish employers are disregarded."

On the French-speaking channel he added that the *credibility* of the board of directors was very low and that profits were only modest. In short, the Société's board of directors and all its supporters had failed, as witnessed by the unemployment figures, the company's figures and the price of shares.

Moreover, as may happen with sophisticated raiders or *black knights*, De Benedetti appeared to be well-informed about typically Belgian political sensibilities. Belgium's Société Générale has always represented and still represents a Walloon/Brussels stronghold to Flanders. The board was always recruited from the conservative, French-speaking catholic atmosphere, the nobility and the surroundings of the Royal Court. There were close ties between the Court and Société Générale: until Boudewijn ascended the throne, the king had always been represented in the board of the holding. Flemish interests have always been and still are great, whereas Flemish influence on the top of the organization has always been restricted. On the one hand, the Société Générale is not in the least popular, the economic mastodon is a symbol of the old Belgium, dominated by Walloons. On the other hand, the Société is considered a safe investment by many Flemings. More than two thirds of the army of small shareholders can be found in prosperous Flanders. Consequently, two reactions, mirroring Société Générale's internal tensions, did become visible after De Benedetti made his offer. The financial and political establishment, silently backed by the Royal Court and some 10 families of the nobility, had not yet recovered from the shock. They were doing everything to ward off "this *conquistador*" (it was Secretary of State Eyskens who coined the term). The Public Prosecutor was even contemplating an investigation. Small share-holders in the Walloon provinces launched an initiative to keep the "Société Générale in Belgian hands". On the other hand, a group of Flemish shareholders was preparing legal steps in support of De Benedetti. The Flemish financial press had all the time emphatically chosen De Benedetti's side. The editor in chief of *Trends* weekly: "We have always thought of Société Générale as a junta that feeds itself. It is an unsympathetic organization. It was high time something happened."

In the meantime, both Belgium and the rest of Europe are greatly interested as to the outcome of this spectacular stock exchange fight. Not only Belgian interests are at stake, on the whole De Benedetti's plan for building a large European holding is seen as a forerunner of a Europe without internal frontiers, that is a forerunner of the internal market. Clearly, the overtone of international press comments on the collision just described was: "It already seems clear now who is going to take important economic decisions in future. Certainly not governments and parliaments."

This appeared to be a realistic estimation in view of the following rounds in the game. Shortly after the events described above, the French financial group Compagnie Financière de Suez made itself known as the third party in the hunt for the Société Générale. The French, taking the role of the *white knight*, came to the rescue of the board of the Belgian holding. They bought 10% of the Société's stocks in a large and controversial transaction. In its defence of the Belgian conglomerate against De Benedetti, ally Suez was backed by three other French companies: the investment bank Lazard Frères, the industrial giant CGE and the waterworks Lyonnaise des Eaux. Together they possessed around 20% of the Société's shares. That was almost enough to block the board's decisions.

This new round in the battle for the Société complicated the takeover fight considerably. A large part of the groups involved was connected by mutual participations. De Benedetti's next move was to speak with top man Michel François-Ponchet of the French bank *Paribas*. An Italian-French alliance would have far-reaching consequences, since Paribas indirectly had a great interest in the *Gevaert* holding of André Leysen who had presented himself, in an earlier round, as another white knight.

Leysen wanted to buy 10 million out of the 12 million new shares, issued by the Société. Both De Benedetti and Leysen wanted to restructure the somewhat dusty Société Générale into an enterprise of European size, that was ready to do battle. As could be expected, the black and the white knights soon decided to have a number of talks, but De Benedetti's demand for a decisive vote formed a stumbling block. Through Paribas De Benedetti was said to want to bring more pressure to bear on Leysen, in order to persuade him to cooperate against the French Suez group.

With the latter manoeuvre, the takeover fight would now spread to France. Suez and Paribas, both only recently privatized, were long-standing rivals. Furthermore, the French interference also involved the second largest Belgian holding Groupe Bruxelles Lambert, because that holding had a large interest in Paribas. Should De Benedetti and Leysen have formed an alliance, this would have meant a complete turnabout. In that event it would have been in the Italian interest that Leysen appeared to have bought 10 million shares. On the other hand, the Société's defense, which existed in the issue of 12 million new shares, would prove a suicide attempt.

The exceptionally complicated nature of the takeover fight underlines once more the mutual interests of the parties involved: the actors get increasingly entangled in their self-woven webs. Suez, for instance, holds 10% of the shares in Cerus, the French holding of De Benedetti. Cerus and Société Générale hold, in their turn, 1.5% of the Suez shares. Both groups also hold a seat on the board of directors of the French group.

For a while Gevaert's top man Leysen, seconded by a range of sympathizing institutional investors, seemed to be a reliable ally of the Société. He stated: "We want to anchor the Société in Belgium. We want the centre of decision making to remain in Belgium and we do not want one shareholder to claim a decisive role, as my friend De Benedetti does." Shortly afterwards, the *white knight* of the first hour proved to be a brittle fiancé of the Old Lady, as the Générale is called in Belgium. Soon the group around Leysen fell apart. Because of an attractive offer by De Benedetti, they let themselves be parted, even though shortly before that they had sworn each other allegiance forever. Davignon, the second man of the Société and generally viewed as the successor of present managing director Lamy, touched upon part of the hidden logic of the game: in the *Financial Times* he stated that although the Société's friends still had 50% of the shares, *"the only factor that still unites the group is their shared distrust of De Benedetti"*. The next logical step followed swiftly. Near the end of February, 1988, Carlo De Benedetti, André Leysen and the Belgian holding Cobepa decided to join forces in the battle for the control of Société Générale. And of course: in close harmony *black* and *white* declared that the fresh coalition's aim was to contribute to a "solid Belgian anchoring" of the largest Belgian holding.

Financial analysts concluded: *De Benedetti has decidedly reinforced his position by winning over Leysen, dividing the Belgians and on top of that bringing in Suez's deadly rival Paribas (through Cobepa), respectively.*

How will *industrial* analysts interpret the viability of this type of networks? And how will *political* analysts interpret the quality of a European integration that is founded on such a substructure of impromptu and self-entangling industrial coalitions? Different paradigms lead to different answers.

3. Dyad Versus Triad Power

From an *institutionalist* perspective, the performance of Europe's communitarian institutions is measured in terms of legitimate decision making and rational problem solving. From that frame of reference — essentially a view 'from the top' looking for things as normative integration, authoritative decision-making and rational solutions — the answer is bound to be rather disconsolate. The *counter*-institutionalist perspective implies an entirely different conceptual framework, and entirely different places for assembling evidence on Europe's performance in terms of political-economic integration. Starting from a pragmatic/minimalist concept of integration — i.e. integration defined as the interorganizational coordination of expectations and factual behaviour, without a priori assumptions on the moral or material ground of that coordination — the counter-perspective tends to come up with a less idealistic, though not necessarily more optimistic, assessment. The counter-institutionalists, operating with a view 'from the bottom' and looking for more informal forms of collusive and divisive behaviour in the twilight-zones between public institutions and private organizations, will show a keener sense for the peculiar aspects of what might be called "the evolution of *antagonistic* cooperation". From this view, the quality of European integration will be related to, first, the predicted stability of resulting coalitions, and, secondly, to the creativity of such coalitions in an industrial and political sense.

The effective results of the intercorporate contest described above, such as the composition of the winning coalition and the price to be paid for the control of the Société, cannot be accurately predicted. A degree of unpredictability or indeterminateness is added to the coalitional and counter-coalitional dynamics by the presence of a quickly expanding circle of indirectly interested 'allies'. *Philips*, for instance, declared to be interested to join De Benedetti's *Europe '92* (a holding company established to fight the supporters of the Société Générale again from another angle) because that manoeuvre opens an opportunity for Philips to acquire influence in the management of the Société. Philips' interest in the Société has to be understood, apart from other motives, by the fact that the latter owns a minority share in Alcatel. *Alcatel* (a telecommunications joint venture between the French CGE and the European subsidiary of the American ITT) happens to be Philips' main rival in Belgium since Alcatel's daughter Bell Antwerp (combining with Asea-Siemens) managed to score off Philips' offer for the complete renewal of the Belgian telephone network. Besides, Europe '92 offers ample opportunities to meet De Benedetti's youngest ally, André Leysen of Gevaert, who is also vice-president of the supervisory board of Philips. In addition, Philips and De Benedetti use to meet at other places: *AT & T*, Philips partner in APT, owns a 25% share in Olivetti, De Benedetti's home-base. Finally, De Benedetti and Philips' former president Dekker may exchange views and coordinate ambitions directly with Davignon, vice-president of the Société, by another *mutualité*, the 'Roundtable of European Industrialists'. The evolution of 'cooperation° passes through a mosaic of ad hoc entries and emergency exits.

In spite of the virtual disorientation stemming from this labyrinth of drifting and switching loyalties, it is not impossible to discover a modicum of *order* in the evolution of the game. Order is produced by two, at first sight, opposing forces: at one side one must admit that the game is governed by a definite 'logic-of-indeterminateness' — an expression (Schelling, 1969) suggesting ample room for strategic choice but at the same time implying a large measure of unpredictability. However, once strategic choices are made, forms of cooperation and commitments develop that, *because of* continuing rivalries and sentiments of distrust, can not be revoked with impunity — suggesting, as in a captive alliance, decreasing room for strategic choice but increasing degrees of predictability of the emerging order. Order is a bastard.

As exemplified in the introductory short story, three elements play a pre-eminent role in the evolution of that order:

1) the degree of *cohesion* of the (groups of) organizations that can be regarded as the relevant players (e.g., the foreseeable erosion of the common Flemish/Walloon defence because of internal contradictions)
2) the degree of uncertainty with regard to the actual bargaining *power* of the various players (a function of the intensity and the asymmetry of their interdependence) and, as a resultant of the interaction between cohesion and bargaining power,
3) the degree of *credibility* of the players in this kind of mixed motive/multiple level game.

Unlike what is suggested by our conquistador, "credibility" is not an actor attribute. Credibility is a reflexive attribute that conditions the evolution of the game. When the *conditioning* of the game escapes from the protagonists' control, a growing, potentially persistent discrepancy between the players' intentions (logic of action) and the game's rationality (logic of interaction) occurs. This observation has far-reaching implications for the explanatory power of the paradigm that prevails in the analysis of strategy formulation and policy making: the dyadic or exchange-theoretical approach. A trilateral or triadic approach deviates radically from a dyadic approach, both in its assumptions and its implications. In a triad power approach, actors are not involved in *exchange* transactions, but in decisions whether or not to *invest* in the (re)production of mutual power relationships. Power, in this context, means: the capacity to enlarge or restrict the room for strategic choice, for one-self or for others, as a function of the availability of a third party that may serve as a substitute for existing coalitions. In one sentence: power refers to the presence of entry barriers for others and the absence of entry and *exit barriers for oneself*. Decisions to invest in power-*sharing* are based on profit and loss expectations. In situations of inter-organizational interdependence, profit and loss expectations are of a circular or reflexive nature: they are a function of what one party expects that other parties expect to gain or to loose from cooperation or conflict.

In the following paragraphs, we will elaborate the trilateral or triad power perspective. We will show how this perspective explains the stability and creativity of networks (coalitions generating coalitions) by (1) tracing the changing structures of dependence, (2) describing the associated activities of the actors, (3) analyzing the interplay of intra- and interorganizational dynamics, and (4) explaining the intended and unintended consequences of actors' activities as a result of the interplay of intra- and interorganizational dynamics. The following considerations underlie this sequence. Industrial change tends to redefine the distribution of power and authority — between as well as within organizations. Essentially, the social scientific analysis of industrial change is the analysis of a political-economic game: new technologies redefine stakes, positions and the structure of existing networks. Only part of the resulting redefinition can be seen as purposeful or 'controlled'. Therefore, the 'limits to intentionality' deserve a central place in the analysis of associative versus dissociative behaviour. Deviations from intentionality arise from differences between the logic of the individual actors (micro) and the logic of the game (meso). Perhaps the origin of the 'cycle' leading to ever growing discrepancies between the intentions of the actors and the outcomes of the game can be found in the following 'principle': under conditions of (1) strategic interdependence and (2) uncertainty about the symbiotic or competitive nature of that interdependence (the 'nature' of interdependence is not given but open to manipulation or negotiation) *tactical moves tend to take the place of strategic intentions.*

When uncertainty exists about the significance of the long term commitments that interdependent actors are willing to enter, tactics are preferred over strategies. Willingness to enter long term commitments in the area of new technologies — e.g, micro electronics, biotechnology and telecommunication — is tempered by uncertainties associated with the shift from the classical economies-of-scale to the new economies-of-scope. *Scope* here refers to the organizational requirements c.q. capacity to cope with several ambiguities at the same time: new technologies cut across traditional sectors (e.g. agricultural, service and industrial sectors); new technologies cut across traditional functional management areas (i.e. they tend to obscure the demarcations and to upset the managerial hierarchy between R&D, production, marketing and finance); new technologies disturb the internal and external politics of accommodation between labour, capital and management (while redefining the principles of mobility, substitutability, scarcity, centrality and associational capability); new technologies tend to blur the borderlines between internal and external organizational relations (entrepreneurship comes to be defined as an unstable mix of intrapreneurship, subcontracting, management buy outs and inter-firm strategic partnerships). Together these developments will alter existing patterns of checks and balances — not only on the outside but also inside organizations: *internal checks will determine external balances while external checks will determine internal balances of power and authority.* Organizations able to handle these contingencies probably understand what is meant by the exploitation of economies-of-scope. Do such organizations exist? One of the more recent developments in the science of organization-and-environment, the so-called "Market versus Hierarchy"-paradigm, suggests a possible answer. The M & H-approach is based on two hypotheses: under conditions of rapidly changing technology, economic organizations are confronted with problems of sectional self interest, opportunism of contracting partners, information impactedness and so on; the inability to anticipate (and penalize) this type of 'environmental surprises' in a conventional system of market exchange will stimulate organizations — according to the M & H-paradigm — to integrate resource and product market requirements and reduce costs associated with bounded rationality ("endemic to turbulent environments and innovative, non-routine conditions"). This happens by internalizing product and resource markets within as few system boundaries as possible; such internalization would substitute *exchange* relations for *authority* relations.

In the light of the ambiguities listed above, the M & H-thesis sounds plausible. Coping capacity associated with the type of arena and the type of "environmental surprises" described above, means coping with several dilemmas. In the next section some of them are mentioned. They provide a first impression of the kind of 'judo' politics that one may expect when private, public and mixed organizations are confronted with the need of "domestication" of new conditions of interdependence.

4. Antagonistic Cooperation: The Anatomy

Given conditions of (1) strategic interdependence and (2) uncertainty about the symbiotic or competitive nature of that interdependence, organizations face several dilemmas. Dilemmas generate ambiguity, especially with regard to the question how organization's rivals or potential strategic alliances will respond to this common set of ambiguities. The management of ambiguity is the management of choice: the choice of partners, issues and timing — in such a way that one's own flexibility is maintained (A's 'deniability') while the behaviour of opponent(s) is made or kept as predictable as possible (B's 'reliability'). As argued before, credibility in this type of encounters depends on the internal cohesion of the actors — a set of internal *faculties* representing decision making power — and on their external leverage — a set of external *facilities* representing bargaining power. Differences in faculties and facilities among the actors will determine the degree of asymmetry in the trade-off between A's deniability and B's reliability.

Several dilemmas complicate the trade-off. For instance economies-of-scale are attractive as barriers against new entrants but reduce flexibility (scale creates exit barriers). Market concentration implies power but creates oligopolistic vulnerability. Reducing the costs associated with inventories enhances flexibility but heightens sensitivity to adversary tactics (strikes). New technologies create cross-sector flexibility but jeopardize internal cohesion and identity (especially in situations of shortening product life cycles). Most of these dilemmas can be expressed in terms of a strategic partnerships-paradox, in which the solution of the paradox has to be found in some optimal mix — however intuitively defined — of partners, issues and timing. Forces that tend to stabilize partnerships are: advantages of scale, financial motives, market considerations, R&D and production agreements, and risk-sharing. Forces that tend to destabilize partnerships are: increasing R&D- and decision making costs, reduced flexibility, involuntary technology and market transfers, loss of autonomy and identity, loss of jobs and career perspectives, and conflicts of fair return-on-investment-sharing. The paradox encourages opportunistic behaviour (the trade-off of between 'deniability' and 'reliability'). Winning, loosing or any other form of (temporary) compromise will depend on the distribution of internal decision making power and external bargaining power of the protagonists. Given the mutually destructive potential of such a setting, the resulting regime may be called a game of antagonistic cooperation.

The De Benedetti's case can be seen as the prototype of the evolution of a game of antagonistic cooperation, whereby organizations (negotiators) have to face the following facts (Wassenberg 1985: 167-8):

1) The negotiation *agenda* is not planned in detail. As a consequence of the fact that both the roles and rules of the game, and norms and values are ill-defined, the evaluation of gains and losses as well as opinions about the actual content of the issues at stake, may shift significantly during the negotiation process.

2) The negotiation *arena* is imperfectly defined — a condition apt to generate obscurity in various respects. It is, for instance, not to be expected that the respective actors can be considered as plenipotentiaries operating on behalf of internally homogeneous constituencies or in name of cohesive bureaucratic/corporate elites. In other words, variables such as (inter)organizational discipline, predictability or compliance can be very problematic. In addition, some vital questions, concerning the scope and the limits of the arena, arise: on what level, apart from formal assignments, are the negotiators operating *de facto*: the organizational, the interorganizational or the conglomerate level of (inter)organizational networks? As a result of vagueness about the horizontal and vertical structure of the arena, the credibility of threats and commitments may shift significantly (as the agenda does) during the negotiation process.

3) Finally, the *time* dimension is hardly ever sufficiently defined. Duration, recurrence and pace of the negotiation are in themselves subject to bargaining tactics. The negotiability of agenda and/or arena depends on the negotiability of time. It is precisely the time-bound nature of issues and types of dependence that questions the assumption that the attributes of issues, or the attributes of interdependence might in some way be treated as "objective" attributes (that is, as properties autonomously defined or exogenously predetermined). The effective control of time, on the contrary, allows for the strategic and tactical manipulation of the attributes of issues and/or types of dependence. The consequence is again that threats and commitments may shift significantly during the negotiation process.

It seems questionable whether encounters in this type of world can be described adequately in exchange-theoretical terms, like market-transactions in the usual or in the metaphorical sense. What rather seems to be at stake, is negotiating about the (re)production of a negotiated order, that is: negotiating, among actual or prospective stakeholders, about *(dis)investments* in mutual power arrangements on the basis of (interactive) expectations about the social, political and economic returns on (dis)investments and their relative distribution.

In view of the uncertain control of the spatial/temporal setting, negotiating about partners, issues and timing — and about a common, that is: reliable definition of the *outsiders* — has to be interpreted as search-behaviour. For the actors this means that they have to discover the decomposability of the negotiated order — in terms of issues (agenda), entry & exit options (arena) and time (timing). Reasoning from the distinction introduced before, one may imagine that the management of ambiguity and choice in this type of game, that is: *the quest for controlling the negotiated order*, can be expressed in terms of two generic types:

1) organizations trying to manipulate the decision making power of their opponents/ partners, and/or

2) organizations trying to manipulate the bargaining power of their opponents/partners.

The way in which organizations react to external threats and opportunities depends, primarily, on the composition of their internally dominant coalitions. The composition of internally dominant coalitions, however, depends, in the long run, on the correct assessment of the credibility of the threats and promises -the mix of commitments — expressed by the organization's rivals/ partners.

Misalliances are born out of incorrect assessments. In general, misalliances arise from situations in which defensive tactics have to conceal a lack or impossibility of offensive strategies. Those situations may be expected in the area of new technologies, that is: in areas where the conditions of strategic interdependence and uncertainty about the symbiotic or competitive nature of interdependence prevail. Looking at some recent illustrations, misalliances with concomitant supplanting of strategy by tactics can be expected when the following, more specific conditions hold: uneven levels of commitments, changing strategic objectives, the world moves faster than your partner does, big firm-small firm mismatch, inadequate internal structures and incentives for cooperation, insufficient executive attention, misjudging distribution capabilities, overestimating technology and underestimating competition, power struggles & power vacuum and, finally, lack of an internal sense of direction and consensus. Listen to a De Benedetti's latest proselyte and *connoisseur*, Gevaert's president André Leysen:

"The last months I have made (two) mistakes. the first was to think that the Société Générale had friends. I knew that the Générale did not have a sublime reputation in Flanders. Wallonia had the feeling to be abandoned by the Générale. And in the Brussels establishment nobody rose to defend the Générale. (..) I underestimated that.

"Secondly, I did not sufficiently take into account the totally different worlds of thought separating the industrial and the financial world. I am myself an industrialist. When an industrialist reaches an agreement, say on investments, it is valid for ten *years*. Everything in the financial world appears to be much more mobile; more often than not the long term covers not many more than ten *minutes*. It is all very labile" (*NRC-Handelsblad*, 13-4-1988).

In order to see to what extent the framework developed above enhances our understanding of the realities of association and dissociation in European industrial policy-making — *la donna è mobile* — let us first present a short overview of the context in which those realities are embedded.

5. The Context

The urgencies alias unruliness of existing modes of industrial cooperation in Europe appear regularly on the EEC's agenda. The attention is justified by two observations: the threat posed by the Japanese/American hegemony in the field of advanced technologies and the perception that individual companies and individual member states are incapable of finding a suitable answer to that threat if they do not cooperate in one way or another.

A first warning signal was given as early as 1967. In that year a best-seller named *Le Défi Américain* was published (Servan Schreiber, 1967). Since not every European — the warning was addressed to him — accepts a warning cast in French sentences, an English translation (which could also make the Americans, and maybe even the Japanese understand) appeared in the same year. As the title indicates, the message only dealt with the American contribution to the "invasion" of European markets. The American penetration was ascribed to the possession of superior technology and management skills. Now, more than 20 years later, it seems as if especially Japan has taken the American challenge to heart. The Europeans, whom the author started out to save, have preferred an increase in their investments in the United States to an adjustment of their management style or an intensification of intra-community cooperation.

Servan-Schreiber foresaw two ill chances: industrial "annexation" if the erosion of financial resistance within European companies would continue, or industrial "satellitization" when European companies opted for a "complementary" role, and for exploitation of "foreign licenses" vis-à-vis American industry. Having remarked that the Japanese manoeuvre to overtake the U.S. in the field of electronics would only take a "few years", the author stated that there was only one real solution: recovery of Europe's competitive position. This recovery would require:
1) *"taille et gestion"*: formation of large industrial entities that can compete with the American giants, not only in size but also in management;
2) *"grandes opérations"*: selection of a number of big operations in the field of advanced technologies in order to protect or restore Europe's autonomy in essential places;
3) *"pouvoir fédéral"*: a minimum of federal power serving as promoter of and security for communitarian enterprises;
4) *"méthodes d'association"*: transformation of the mutual relations between industrial entities, universities and politics;
5) *"éducation"*: deepening and broadening the education of young people, permanent vocational retraining and in-service training for adults;
6) *"énergies captives"*: release of energy out of outdated structures, by means of a revolution in organization methods: a revolution accompanied by a renewal of elites and social relations.

All this sounds familiar. In retrospect, two things are conspicuous. In the first place: an enormous confidence — then, and now — in large-scale financial, physical and organizational initiatives as a defence against the obtrusive technological and organizational superiority of the two other power blocks. From our present point of view, this can be called a generic plea. What strikes is the absence of a specific plea for intelligent combinations of industrial, political and human capital — in which not primarily scale (quantity), but rather the combination of separate technologies (quality) is chosen as the starting point of a European counter-offensive.

A second conspicuous characteristic — in this case not a continuity, but a sign of reorientation — is a complaint, ignored in the late 1960s, but central to the late 1980s: the wretched business of procedural and tariff barriers between the member states. Were these barriers of a less frustrating nature in 1967? It sounds improbable, since the conventional wisdom did not change since that time: economies-of-scale — the 'quantitative' constant in the argumentation for harmonization of the internal market — cannot be realized in combination with an abundance of bureaucratic and other obstacles. Is there perhaps another reason for the omission of this point in earlier days?

The question gains in importance because the Japanese/American invasion appears not to be hindered, let alone to be prevented, by the European bureaucratic obstacles. Given Europe's reported backwardness, it could even be argued that (earlier) uniformization of the European market would only have increased the invasion risk. Do the complaints about fragmentation and bureaucracy not serve as a kind of collective *alibi*, which blames the own lagging behind almost exclusively on the opponent's size and not on his dexterity in taking all kinds of European obstacles? Could that rationalization be the explanation for the unanimity with which Europe's recovery of its competitive powers is in the first place associated with homogenization of the market and own increase in scale? Is there, moreover, no inconsistency in the argumentation that the reigning "champions" of Europe are too big for the home markets of the individual member states, if one does not at the same time admit that the *sum total* of those individual capacities will, by definition, be too big for the EEC as a whole? Viewed in this way, homogenization of the European market can only lead to intensified *intra-communitarian* competition; a competitive struggle that European concerns will probably prefer to enter assisted by.... their American and Japanese partners (the paradoxical outcome of all this will be an increase of the invasion risk mentioned earlier). The quantitative bias, lending priority to arguments of scale over arguments of scope, leads to logical and practical absurdities. An alternative interpretation of the causes for Europe's inferiority complex which does not merely point to the size and streamlining of the internal market, may bring other remedies to light.

6. Mixed Motives

At first sight, there appears to be no lack of competition within the EEC. The scene is characterized by rivalry between companies (on the market and in their race for government support), rivalry between member states (although their race is impeded by the uncoordinated rivalry between different Ministries and Departments on a national level) and, on top of this, rivalry between the General Directorates on the level of the European Commission.

This complicated pattern of rivalries coexists with different forms of cooperation, or something that looks like it.

Cooperation means coordination of decisions by companies, pressure groups and states. Basically, there are two forms of coordination: *ex post* via the price mechanism (market transactions) or *ex ante* via organization (integration of decisions within an organized context). Integration of decision making — 'organizing the market' — is preferred to coordination through the market — 'the price mechanism' — when the coordination does not yield reliable information about the predispositions, expectations, real intentions and expected consequences of companies', pressure groups' and governments' behaviour. Uncertainty about these matters occurs especially in the case of the production of complex capital goods and of complicated forms of (after sales) service. Under these circumstances, contracting parties are confronted by two characteristic complications: a perspective of long-term planning combined with uncertainty about the life span of products and production processes, and uncertainty about the price, quality and availability of resources and buyers.

This uncertainty is even more apparent in periods of rapid and far-reaching technological change: price indications are even less reliable as a context for information and interpretation, and the market mechanism fails as a basis for coordination. Technological change unsettles the familiar ideas about (inter)national markets and destabilizes the markets for capital, knowledge, labour, management and political-organizational or 'institutional' capital. To sum up: the company's environment becomes less predictable and negotiable. The only way in which the environment can be made somewhat more manageable is by a search for shared risks. Risk sharing demands cooperation. Growing uncertainty on the side of both demand and supply, however, leads to mutual distrust. Mutual distrust leads to opportunistic behaviour — varying from not sticking to an agreement to giving a flattered picture of one's own capacity or concealing strategic and tactical intentions (see Jacquemin 1985: 91-154 for a survey of strategic and tactical variants).

Opportunism does not stem from either bad character or evil intent. It rather derives from uncertainty about the chances of success for organizational plans and uncertainty about the setup the opponent(s) has chosen. At the same time, interdependence does force each party to take the other's manoeuvres seriously. Take the example of companies entering into a cooperative agreement in the field of research and development (that is to say, companies that still have a long way to go before they enter the market as potential competitors). Contracting parties should be on the alert for the chance that at least one party only entered the agreement to gain the largest possible amount of information and knowledge, while minimizing its own contribution, so that at the most suitable moment it can switch, not seldom by means of an alternative coalition, to an aggressive competition strategy.

According to the literature, this pattern occurs most often in *international* agreements that enable a not so well equipped partner to use his participation as a means of taking advantage of an "apprentisage accéléré" (Jacquemin 1986: 3). Jacquemin also points to conflicts of interest with companies that, voluntarily or involuntarily, are not involved in cooperation agreements. The presence of a third party creates the permanent risk of a withdrawal in favour of alternative coalitions, the undermining of the cooperation formula (e.g., eroding the existing coalition through the acquisition of a license with a third party) or strategies aimed at the recovery of independence. One of the complications is that (potential) partners differ as to intentions, needs, strategies, time scope and the degree in which they are averse to risks. Next to this complication, another major obstacle feeding mutual distrust and inciting an opportunistic answer to the underlying uncertainties, is the difficulty of finding a fair formula for the division of both the results and the costs of the joint (research and development) efforts.

As referred to earlier, some are of the opinion that opportunism's contagion can only be averted by replacing separate market transactions with organized decision making. Williamson (1975) distinguishes two stadia or gradations: cooperation between companies while their independence is maintained (teams), or complete fusion into a new entity (hierarchy). Decision making should be coordinated when opportunistic behaviour is feared for. According to Williamson (1975: 2040) this fear is well-founded under the following circumstances:

1) the *actual* or *financial* impossibility of acquiring and incorporating all information necessary to completely reliable decision making;
2) *small numbers*: when a great number of players is involved, disappointed or duped parties can always (threaten to) move on to other partners, under better competitive conditions; in the case of small numbers the escapist solution is lacking;
3) *range of information*: because information is connected with a certain context, its value decreases when it is offered in bits and pieces; persons that have an overall picture of information, or can assemble the bits and pieces, are a jump ahead of those who lack such a picture or the 'assemblage key';
4) *atmosphere*: exchange relations and transactions do not take place in a neutral atmosphere; the relation itself can be a source of satisfaction or dissatisfaction for the partners.

Williamson thinks that under these conditions[2] parties will decide to replace separate contract relations by decision making in teams; or, when this formula is not an adequate defence against opportunistic impulses, by hierarchical decision making. Two questions arise: how is such a substitution of "hierarchy" for "market" done? and perhaps more seriously: is hierarchy really an effective remedy for opportunism?

Concerning the first question: so far the literature based on Williamson's ideas consists in theoretical improvements rather than in empirical research which helps to establish where this substitution of market transactions by the formation of teams and hierarchical coordination occurs in practice, and how this transition is made. After all, the decision to replace market transactions by coordinated decision making — e.g., the formation of cartels, joint ventures, combined research efforts, sharing of distribution facilities — is *in itself* a transaction that may contain opportunistic elements. What defence can be put up against this? The answer to that is not likely to be found in the laboratory. Only field work in concrete industrial arenas where structures of dependence are assessed, opponents' intentions are explored and alliances are entered into, will yield the required answers.

Concerning the second question: even in "perfect" hierarchies opportunistic logic takes its toll. The manipulation of information — by management with regard to the production line, by lower echelons with regard to higher echelons, by contractors or divisions with regard to the coordinating management — appears to be a well-tried method for acquiring or keeping the desired freedom of action for the own group, division, department or echelon. Empirical literature shows that this holds true both for companies (recorded for those that are prospering, but recorded even more convincingly for companies that are caught up in a struggle for survival: Nelson, 1981; Wassenberg, 1983; Leibenstein, 1987) and for government institutions.

7. Inside Hierarchies

Recent literature suggests that public and private bureaucracies have something in common: they share a built-in interest in the reduction of uncertainty. Their aims and modes of operating, however, are different. On the one hand, government bureaucracy ideal-typically aims at the 'repeatability' of behaviour (both in society and between and within the departments of the state apparatus); repeatability is supposed to be promoted by *standardization* and the *enhancement* of competition between client-systems and, to a lesser degree, between the interdepartmental domains. On the other hand, market-dominating firms, or firms aspiring to that position, search for the 'predictability' of behaviour (not just of competitors, but also of input-suppliers, customers and governmental actors); predictability, in this stylized representation, is supposed to be promoted by *differentiation* and the *suppression* of competition (these terms refer to efforts at establishing hierarchical relationships in industry or in the market-sector as a whole and to establish exclusive connections in specialized niches in the governmental bureaucracy). In one word, still ideal-typically speaking: public bureaucracies look for 'Weberian' equalities whereas private bureaucracies look for 'Schumpeterian' inequalities. However, a shared search for limited liability seems to keep the two cultures on speaking terms. How do actors reconcile their own search for limited liability with the search for predictability of their counterparts? Supposedly by sharing, that is: by *obscuring* liabilities.

For a couple of years now, convincing arguments have been put forward for paying more attention to the dynamics of internal bureaucratic competition — as opposed to Weberian notions of unquestioned hierarchy or, the other extreme, the notion of atomistic competition between monolithic bureaus and agencies — as exemplified by the conceptual, rather than empirical tradition of Niskanen. A useful survey of these arguments may be found in the *Logic of Bureaucratic Conduct* (Breton & Wintrobe 1982). As Breton & Wintrobe argue (1982: 89-90) the mainstream literature on public bureaucracy departs from the "monopoly assumption" embodied in the supposition "that bureaucracy may be modelled as a single bureau, and that decision makers within that bureau have a single objective or set of objectives, so that the bureau itself behaves as a monolithic unit". The authors propose that "competition is the most general assumption to make about bureaucracy — no less in government bureaus than in private corporations. Impediments to competition do arise in bureaucracies. But we believe that these impediments are best understood as restrictions imposed within a general framework of competition."

In our opinion the most promising extension of the paradigm proposed by the authors is their proposal to interpret intra-bureaucratic competition not as a struggle by individual bureaus for jobs or budgets as such but rather as competition for "positions" or "membership" in "bureaucratic networks" and as "the competition for resources between networks and bureaus" (1982: especially chapter 6). Again, in our terms this has to be seen as a non-trivial shift from a (short term oriented) exchange theoretical to a (medium term oriented) investment perspective. Breton & Wintrobe believe that inter-bureau competition does not eliminate but on the contrary, enhances the capacity for managerial or bureaucratic discretion (in their terminology: "the capacity for selective behavior"). This perspective is a useful expedient for understanding not just "the capacity for selective behaviour" but, more enlightening, the capacity to consolidate selective behaviour by the institutionalization of limited liability — a capacity that will help to explain an intriguing phenomenon in European strategy-formulation and policy-making: the *survival of the fittest deficiencies*.

Before clarifying this phenomenon, however, we have to correct for a missing link in the above-presented outlook on bureaucratic life. While stressing the prevalence and the importance of intra-bureaucratic competition for the explanation of middle and lower level bureaucratic conduct, most students of public bureaucracy — Breton & Wintrobe among them — fail to specify where they suppose top level bureaucrats and/or their "sponsors" — ministers and politicians in the legislature — get their inspiration from when selecting and embarking on policy objectives and priorities. Put more succinctly: what the Logic of Bureaucratic Conduct lacks in the reconstruction above, is an intimate analysis of the essence of interaction — ranging from competition to collusion — between private and public organizations.

It is not possible, however, to give an adequate description of that interaction, without mentioning some peculiarities of the other side of the fence: strategy formulation, policy-making and the selection of tactics in the market. In spite of a number of structural and behavioural *analogies* between public and private organizations, it will become clear that it is not wise to conclude that the *interaction* between the two might be adequately described as simply competition (or impediments to competition) multiplied by two. After all the differences in faculties and facilities between public and private hierarchies (see above and in less ideal-typical terms, the case-study below) are as important as the analogies and interdependencies between them. The repeated encounters between, what one may call a surrogate-market (government bureaucracy) and a surrogate-hierarchy (firms on the market, alone or *en comité*) suggest a type of outcome different from a mere convergence-by-repetition predicted by a virtually 'uniform' logic of bureaucratic conduct. Without denying or underestimating the consequences of public-private commonalities in the urge for uncertainty reduction and the mutuality of aspirations for limited liability, limiting oneself to a description of public-private similarities and affinities — a primitive version of the thesis of the bureaucratic symbiosis à la Galbraith put forward in this *New Industrial*

State — would come close to an inadvertent restoration of the questionable belief about the monolithic behaviour of bureaus (even a more unrealistic proposition when applied to a culturally more heterogeneous and structurally more complex level of interest aggregation, with longer time spans of feedback, as in the European case).

8. Inside Markets

In addition to a revised theory of the logic of "bureaucratic action", a revised theory on the Olsonian logic of "collective action" is needed to grasp the subtleties of oligopolistic and other varieties of concerted behaviour in the market. The real puzzle is to find out how the two logics become intertwined, that is: how the dynamics of the negotiated order emerging from incomplete or postponed rivalries *within* bureaucratic organizations, feed on the dynamics of the negotiated order emerging from incomplete or postponed antagonism *among* bureaucratic organizations.[3)]

As in the analysis of the logic of bureaucratic conduct, it proves to be fruitful to analyze market conduct and structure in terms of *transactions* and transactional *networks*, rather than in terms of the firm or the market as the basic unit of analysis. As briefly mentioned above, the "transactional" approach, though not new in the (interrupted) tradition of institutional economics, experienced recently a new take-off.

Given the conceptualization of industrial and technological change that we proposed earlier — especially the part referring to deliberate or spontaneous changes in the dependency structure of industries, vertically as well as horizontally — the policy making context resembles the situation in which Daems, on empirical grounds (Daems 1983: 35-54) and Williamson, on deductive and programmatic grounds (Williamson, 1975; Williamson & Ouchi, 1983) expect a gradual transition from market-type contracting (between autonomous organizations) to hierarchical formations (in which the initially autonomous partners are incorporated). The *hierarchical* formula for coordinating inter-organizational behaviour is expected to prevail when (existing or emerging) inter-firm relationships are characterized by: (1) uncertainty, (2) a high frequency with which the transactions recur and (3) the degree to which durable transaction-specific investments are required to realize least-cost supply.

The discriminatory power of these variables — Williamson & Ouchi (1983: 14) speak of "critical dimensions" differentiating transactions — is based on the behavioural assumptions of "bounded rationality" and "opportunism". As they explain:

"Whereas bounded rationality suggests decision-making less complex than the usual assumption of hyper-rationality, opportunism suggests calculating behaviour more sophisticated than the usual assumption of simple self-interest. Opportunism refers to "making false or empty, that is, self-disbelieved threats or promises", cutting corners for undisclosed personal advantage, covering up tracks, and the like (...). (I)t is not essential that all economic agents behave this way. What is crucial is that *some* agents behave in this fashion and that it is costly to sort out those who are opportunistic from those who are not" (Williamson

& Ouchi, 1983: 16-7; italics in the original).

It is not clear why the pejorative connotation of "opportunism" is needed in a theory of opportunism-controlling behaviour as long as explanations in terms of threats-and-opportunities, or of threats-and-promises as normally used in the theories of international relations, seem to suffice. In the latter branch of theory formation, the management of opportunism is considered to be nothing more than the result of *power*-wielding. As proposed earlier, power can be defined as: the capacity of an actor to manipulate the room for strategic choice of his opponent(s). In order to stress the relational character of power, especially in our context of inter-firm strategy formulation and industrial policy-making, *bargaining* power should be seen, then, as a function of the cost to oneself of imposing a loss of strategic and tactical choice upon one's bargaining-partner(s). As Leysen, the former *white knight* who turned into a secondant of the *black knight* in our ghost-story, declared, on the eve of the decisive shareholders meeting of the Société Générale:

"If we (parties from both sides, *AW*) do not reach an agreement, the Générale becomes absolutely ungovernable. Neither the one nor the other party can move. (..) Therefore a deal has to be made. Otherwise we wreck the property we all paid a high price for" (*NRC-Handelsblad*, 13-4-1988).

One source of opportunism, identified by Williamson as information impactedness, seems especially informative for our understanding of (the transactional varieties of) the coordination and monitoring of interorganizational conduct. Williamson (1975: 31) circumscribes *information impactedness* as:

"a derivative condition that arises mainly because of uncertainty and opportunism, though bounded rationality is involved as well. It exists when true underlying circumstances relevant to the transaction, or related sets of transactions, are known to one or more parties but cannot be discerned by or displayed for others."

These contingencies make the transactionalist approach a powerful candidate for explaining the propensity for hierarchization of initially market-like relationships:

"Faced with bounded rationality on the one hand and the proclivity for some human agents to behave opportunistically on the other, the basic organizational design issue essentially reduces to this: organize transactions in such a way as to economize on bounded rationality while simultaneously safe-guarding those transactions against the hazards of opportunism" (Williamson & Ouchi, 1983: 17).

In the case of recurring, uncertain and idiosyncratic exchange-relationships ("idiosyncratic" means: durable transaction-specific *investments*) hierarchy is supposed to be a superior formula for economizing on transaction costs — as opposed to market-contracting between non-integrated, autonomous actors — because incorporation is thought to represent more "sensitive governance characteristics and stronger joint profit-maximizing features".

Daems, working within the confines of the same transactional approach, adds a third organizational formula that — in terms of (1) the structuring of the conditions of *ownership*, (2) the distribution of joint *returns* and (3) the enforcement of interorganizational *compli-*

ance — represents another arrangement, somewhere between the Williamsonian extremes of market & hierarchy: the federative form. The concept of a "federation" — we would say: an inter-organizational network *without* clear-cut and undisputed hierarchical prerogatives but ruled by the more or less compelling, sometimes even coercive rules of a negotiated order, however 'spontaneously' established — comes closer to the real-life phenomena of interfirm strategies and industrial policy-making than the M & H-extremes.

Starting from the dimensions just mentioned, Daems (1983: 39 ff) defines a "market" as a structure of interaction in which there is (1) no shared ownership, (2) separateness in the distribution of returns, while (3) prices play the role of compliance-mechanism. At the other end of this three-dimensional space we find a "hierarchy" in which there exists (1) consolidated ownership, (2) a pooling of returns for the corporate partners and (3) formal (legal) rules for the supervision over joint production and distribution by the respective establishments etc. The intermediate form, a "federation", is defined as a construct in which the respective organizational participants remain (1) statutarily independent but engage in (2) pooling returns (pooling may take several forms: sharing profits, dividing market, joint acquisition and allocation of orders and so on). Concerning (3) the principle of compliance in the federative case, firms rely on "joint decision-making" for coordination, allocation and monitoring of participants' conduct.

"Cartels are federations", states Daems, "but not all federations are cartels". Another example, in Europe and Japan, may be firms linked through extensive interlocking stockholdings ("financial groups"). Another federative variety can be mentioned: network-coordination etc. by interlocking directorates. In short, all these varieties of inter-firm coordination can be called "federations" as long as the network does not rely on a central administration office to supervise the group members.

Daems supposes or postulates the existence of "institutional competition", apparently not as a nominalist metaphor but as a realistic fact of economic life:

"Institutional arrangements (markets, hierarchies, federations), very much like technologies, compete with one another. In a competitive world with free institutional choices these institutions will survive that promise the highest net return to the co-operating units in the long run" (Daems, 1983: 44).

The supporting, axiomatic reasoning seems simple. In the first place,

"If no benefits can be obtained from concerted actions there is no point to use scarce resources to organize an institutional arrangement be it a market, a federation or a hierarchy for the exchange of information and the enforcement of contract" (Daems, 1983: 41).

Why then is it that under certain conditions concerted action is organized by means of hierarchies and under other conditions federations and markets are used? In order to "organize" his case Daems points to the same determinants that Williamson used for explaining the emergence of other coordination and compliance mechanisms taking precedence over market-contracting as a means of coordination, namely: (1) the degree of uncertainty involved in fully completing the transaction (2) the size of transaction-specific investments, and (3) the frequency of recurrence of the transaction.

The higher the values of these variables, the more pressing the need for reliable information exchange and inter-firm compliance in that industry. Hierarchy may be expected when uncertainty, frequency and size reach their highest values, markets at the lowest opposite and federations in between. Since Daems assumes that the three institutional alternatives differ in their effect on the "joint return to concerted action" (1983: 41), he can formulate his law-like principle of "institutional competition": assuming for a moment equal installing and operating costs, "hierarchy" will be preferred to "federation" to "market" only if the first communicates information better and/or enforces compliance more effectively. Illustration:

"The greater the amount of resources that is irreversibly committed for specific or transacting-specific purposes the more the need exists for tight compliance. Since hierarchies, for a variety of reasons, have superior enforcement mechanisms and information networks, it seems plausible to postulate that consolidated ownership and supervision will be more used in industries where the co-ordination, allocation and monitoring processes of concerted actions are subject to the considerable uncertainty or require resources for highly specialised and unique uses" (Daems, 1983: 43).

The reader may feel doubts about the declared superiority of hierarchies as an enforcement mechanism, for several reasons. First, we can refer to the growing, rather skeptical literature on the "bureaucratic phenomenon" (see the section above about the emergence of "surrogate markets" within hierarchies). Next, interorganizational stability tends to reinforce intra-bureaucratic competition: the external stability reached by oligopolization or cartellization breeds internal rivalries between factions — cliques of functional, professional or sector-specific chiefs with their immediate subordinates — competing for a position in the "dominant coalition" at the top of the hierarchy. Phrased in terms of a paradox: the more effective hierarchy appears in controlling *inter*organizational opportunism, the higher the probability — other things equal — that *intra*organizational opportunism becomes substituted for external opportunism. Internal opportunism, however, tends to destabilize external relationships and commitments, in the sense of reducing their credibility. Linking the dynamics of external and internal competition in this way comprises, as we will see below, the thrust of a triadic power theory.

Perhaps more important, serious doubts should surround Daems' assumption that there exists such a thing as *free* competition among "institutional alternatives". It seems rather rash to assume that there is a free floating demand and supply for institutional substitutes, that is: complete transparency of the (dis)advantages associated with each alternative; no "hidden defects" or externalities or at least no information-costs for acquiring insight in those defects c.q. effects; perfect "mobility" and prompt "delivery" of the substitutes once decided upon (perfect substitutability); no vested interests in, or oppositions against proposed reorganization of existing institutional arrangements; and so on. It is not without irony that Williamson, Daems and other transactionalists consider the market-based form of contracting too rudimentary for understanding and monitoring the subtleties of vertical contracting or idiosyncratic exchanges in general (i.e. exchanges in the case of high levels

of uncertainty, information impactedness and irreversible, transaction-specific investments). Given that outlook on the organization of economic life, it does not seem valid to
assert or assume at the same time that the market should be deemed to be capable to handle
such a *hyper*-idiosyncratic transaction as the decision to switch from one institutional
arrangement to another. Trust in the Invisible Hand governing the enlightened competition
among institutional substitutes does not seem justified.

Let's return to practice to see the implications of this approach — the interplay between
internal cohesion and external interdependence cast in a triad setting — for the politics of
association and dissociation in European industrial strategy formulation and policy-
making.

9. European Deficiencies

It does not sound illogical: "organize transactions in such a way as to economize on bounded
rationality while simultaneously safe-guarding those transactions against the hazards of
opportunism". How faithful does industrial practice follow academic logic? The same
conditions that (neo-)transactionalists want to consider as a stimulus to hierarchy or to
federalisation, seem to frustrate the rise of efficient institutional arrangements from the
"competition among institutions". What separates propensity from potential are bounded
rationality and.... the hazards of opportunism. That is the reason why the large-scale
"concerted action", pleaded for by advocates of the European case, remains so unsuccessful. If a form of communitarian cooperation is decided upon at all (*Esprit, Eureka*), it is never
certain whether what is involved here is a European industrial *renaissance* or a *pre-emptive
strike*, aimed at the prevention of a threatening transatlantic or even, as in De Benedetti's
case, an intra-European combination. This ambiguity pursues both public and private
players on the European stage. Overshadowed by the logic of opportunism, "voluntary"
cooperation only seems feasible when there is a tight concentration of profits and a
dispersion of costs as wide as possible.

In the Japanese or the American context, this can be more easily arranged than in the
European context. The often mentioned size of the Japanese and American markets gives
them more possibilities, not only because of a more favourable relation between costs and
profits (the conventional argument of scale), but especially because of the less prominent
presence of the "small numbers" risk (see page 15 above), ad 2)). Furthermore, the
symbiotic relation between government and national companies gives a greater hold on the
asymmetric distribution of costs and benefits. In Japan, this hold is given by the Department
of International Trade & Industry (until the end of the sixties by establishing industrial-
political priorities, but recently rather with the motive of commercial-political self-control
in view of imminent protectionist retaliations). In the United States, an analogous role is
played by the driving force of military and space travel orders. Under those circumstances,
it is worthwhile to suppress opportunistic inclinations and to search for the protection or
discipline of more hierarchical forms of decision making. In the EEC, this kind of 'rewards'
is for the most part lacking (even the military cooperation that is starting up may not prove

to be an exception).

In comparison with national companies, labour unions and governments, multinationals have more possibilities to use opportunistic methods and at the same time keep ahead of the opportunism of others, or — literally — to keep it at a distance. They can do this because of their territorial flexibility. Political and social fragmentation and cultural diversity in Europe offer alert multinationals the opportunity to transform a relatively moderate lead (based on their own hierarchy *across* frontiers) into a considerable lead in decision making (vis-à-vis governments and unions based on hierarchy *within* frontiers). Multinationals produce Schumpeterian inequalities that nation-states (and other nationalistic institutions) reproduce in Weberian style. Profiting by this anti-thesis, European companies enter into all kinds of alliances generating a less and less transparent web of non-European joint ventures. All this is done according to individual definitions of urgency and profit. These definitions do not necessarily run parallel to the EEC's interests.

The ill-coordinated web of alliances with Japanese and American companies may thwart the development of an autonomous European answer to the American/Japanese challenge. In order to restore the balance in the European arena, different strategies can be proposed. Those strategies should offer an alternative to the irrational (in the sense of too costly, started too late and because of that illusory) character of a European imitation race, in which each member state for itself, and the EEC against Japan and the U.S., *ex post* appear to have chosen the same "spearheads" and "champions".[4]

Given a situation of interdependence, there are, in principle, two ways of pushing back the role of opportunism: in the first place, fighting opportunism through delegation of authority and internalization of market transactions (the transactionalists' variant). This option loses its significance when parties lack the capability of, or interest in changing the conditions that serve as a seed-bed for the logic of opportunism. The second option is to confront opportunists on the supply side with a non-trivial risk of opportunism on the demand side, that is to say: discouraging the logic of opportunism by creating an element of *reciprocity* between suppliers and buyers. The latter requires some coordination or organization of the demand side: *demand pull* is a necessary corrective of the danger of a blind imitation race triggered by the technological "imperative" or *technology push.*

In order to judge the reality value of these options, insight is needed in dependence structures, bargaining power and decision making processes, primarily on a micro- and meso-level: companies, departments and European directorates, their meeting places included. One of the possibilities to test the qualities of the framework developed above, is to take an example, rich enough to demonstrate the hazards of opportunism in a triad power setting and the evolution of antagonistic cooperation at work. The selected case is called *Esprit*.

10. Esprit: A Multi-Level Game

Europe is experimenting with new forms of industrial cohabitation. One of them is the European Strategic Programme for Research in Information Technology (ESPRIT). The internal dynamics of *Esprit* can only be understood if we take two external realities into account.

In the first place, the reality that justifies the basic philosophy of Esprit: the international conditions of competition between Japan, the United States and Western-Europe. This is the global setting or "Triad Power" in the usual sense (Ohmae 1985). The global setting sets the pace; it is the *drive* behind Esprit. Secondly, there is the reality that will determine the operational outcomes of Esprit: a loose-knit assembly of intra-European but non-Community framed agreements and programmes like Eureka. *Geo*-politically, Eureka (European Research Coordination Agency) is the European reaction to the U.S. Strategic Defense Initiative programme. *Regio*-politically, Eureka is the nationalist and national champions' device for escaping from the supranational discipline associated with programmes emanating from the Community's headquarters. *Industry*-politically, Eureka seems to be inspired by a "market pull" orientation competing with the "technology push" orientation of the Community programmes. This loose-knit assembly of initiatives and activities is based on a bilateral philosophy: negotiations are primarily governed by the partially cooperative, partially competitive dyad Paris-Bonn with other nationalities — shifting from case to case — as the third party, tipping the balance and completing the "Triad Power" on the regional level. It is this regio-political setting that sets the effective limits of or the *scope* for Esprit. While strategically escorted by these two realities, Esprit itself can be seen as the product of yet another kind of "Triad Power", i.e. as the outcome of ongoing negotiations between multinational companies, national politicians and supranational officials. Split by the bipolarity (and the contradictions) of the global and the regional setting, the communitarian setting is bound to define the *spirit* of Esprit.

Though differing sharply in terms of stakes and resources as well as in the kind of strategic choices available in each setting, the *formal* logic-of-shifting alliances within the communitarian setting is analogous to coalitional logics within the regional or the global setting. The coexistence of the global, the regional and the communitarian setting — in fact a *mosaic* of triad powers — determines the room for strategic choice of the participants in Esprit. The actors differ in their relative capabilities to influence the returns from investment in the respective power-settings. As argued before, investments will be based — apart from sheer necessity — on profit and loss expectations. Circularities arise as far as definitions or perceptions of necessity appear to be based on what the actors expect about the investment behaviour of the relevant 'others'. How *rational* (purposeful, calculated, controlled) are the decisions of the respective actors — multinational companies, national governments, supranational institutions — to participate or not to participate in the different settings? And what about the coordination of strategic choices *across* the different settings? And maybe even more pertinently: what about the *freedom* to choose?

11. The Uses of Power

The Esprit experience demonstrates how the effectiveness of power — in itself not more than a potential — depends on a balanced use of that potential, that is: on negotiating and lobbying skills. For our purposes the difference between the art of negotiation and the craft of lobbying is largely a matter of degree: lobbying is negotiating in disguise — i.e. the preparatory act of exploring the aspiration level and influencing the *expectations* of one's opponent(s) — while negotiating is transforming the results of lobbying into effective *commitments*. Negotiating and lobbying, though differing in terms of explicitness and resolution, should be seen as complementary activities. As argued before, the specific mix will vary according to: (1) the *degree of uncertainty* created by the ambiguity of choice (the selection of partners, issues & timing as a function of the diversity of interests at stake); (2) the *internal cohesion* of the various stakeholders; (3) the *degree of interdependence* between the stakeholders, and (4) the *degree of mobility* of the stakeholders, i.e. their relative access to the global, the regional and the communitarian reaches of the mosaic of power mentioned above.

Uncertainty, cohesion, interdependence and mobility are interrelated. For instance: mobility — i.e. the relative ease of substituting the regional for the communitarian setting, or substituting the global for the regional setting and vice versa — qualifies the impact of interdependence and uncertainty. Entry and exit options constitute the hard core of bargaining power. Bargaining power, in principle, means influence.

Translated into the politics of industrial policy-making this means that effective strategy-formulation may be defined as the art of exploiting the opportunities and minimizing the constraints of uncertainty and interdependence by manipulating — as far as feasible — the conditions of mobility. (One of the most crucial aspects of these conditions appears to be the *timing* of mobility from one level of the mosaic of power to another.) Effective industrial policy-making can be defined as the art of coordinating one's strategic choices across different levels of the power mosaic. Practically, effectiveness is a matter of choosing the right (mix of) level(s) and choosing the right timing. Analytically, speaking about the consequences of entry and exit options is senseless without a specification of the dimensions of time and space as these apply to the different parts of the mosaic.

Making strategic choices is not enough. Choices have to be implemented. Under conditions of interdependence, implementation means lobbying and negotiating. Effective lobbying and negotiating can be defined as: the art and science of securing agreement between two or more interdependent parties that are trying to maximize their outcomes by finding an acceptable balance of commitments. Assuming a modicum of shared interests among firms, governments and public officials in reducing uncertainty, the need to find an acceptable balance is strengthened by a sense of strategic interdependence[5] but relaxed for differences in opportunities of mobility (the differential accessibility of the power mosaic). Power differentials, due to mobility differentials, can be recognized by the criteria of acceptability in defining a balance of commitments. It is here that the game of antagonistic cooperation begins: one party offers another party compensation for the latter's lack of mobility opportunities (entry and/or exit barriers) in exchange for his support in reducing the risks of uncertainty of the former party (e.g., with regard to his long term investments) and/or interdependence (e.g., the risk of captive alliances). Most of the time, as exemplified by the story of Esprit, the "balance of commitments" is not a dyadic, but a triadic affair introducing *series* of shifting coalitions. The serial character of the game offers chances for correcting imbalances but does not foster the stability of the newly found equilibria.

Where the conditions of mobility and the resulting commitments inform us about the logic of the game, the term politics refers to the logic of the actors: their attempts to structure a situation of interdependence in such a way that their individual goals are promoted. As explained earlier, the expression 'individual' goals is somewhat misleading. When talking about the goals and the logic of actors we should not forget that we are dealing with phenomena of a high internal complexity: actors' are no monoliths. Internal complexity explains why bargaining power is not a sufficient condition for wielding influence. In order to produce reliable/credible commitments, actors have to be internally cohesive. Cohesion — an internal asset — supplements external negotiation power. In that sense effective lobbying and negotiating can be said to be dependent on the skilful management of the *interplay* between faculties (the stability or reliability of intra-organizational coalitions) and facilities (the stability or predictability of inter-organizational alliances or partnerships). Intra-organizational and inter-organizational bargaining are of equal importance. The interplay of both determines the ultimate credibility of resulting commitments. Quite often, as we happened to see in the Générale's case and as we will see again below, the instability of the policy arena(s) and, consequently, doubts about the credibility of concluded commitments, are due to the intra-actor ambiguity of so-called 'individual' goals — rather than to *inter*-actor controversies or conflicts of interest. Strategic uncertainty and coalitional dilemmas originate primarily from these sources: *intra*-actor fragmentation or rivalry, generating unreliable responses to critical *inter*-actor resource interdependences, rather than the other way around.

To summarize: it is wise to keep in mind that not only a governmental organization, but also a business firm is a political coalition and the executive in the firm is a political broker. In the words of James March: "The composition of the firm is not given; it is negotiated. The goals of the firm are no given; they are bargained". This assessment reminds us of the possibility that effective lobbying and negotiating may sometimes mean: finding a balance of commitments by accommodating to or manipulating the internal cohesion and resolution *of one's opponent(s)*. Let us see what insight these notes offer for our understanding of the negotiated order around Europe's information technology.

12. The Uses of Esprit

Driving force behind the EEC's answer, around 1977, to the dramatic deterioration of its international position in information technology (IT) was Viscount Davignon, former commissioner for Industry in the European Commission. Around that time Davignon invited the twelve leading IT-companies in Europe (3 from Germany, 3 from Great Britain, 3 from France, 2 from Italy and 1 from the Netherlands) to discuss possible remedies for Europe's position. Against the background of earlier failures of communitarian inter-firm cooperation (*Unidata*: Philips/Siemens/CII, started in 1972, dissolved in 1975 when CII opted for a merger with the US-firm Honeywell Bull), the participants of the 1977 Round Table decided to restrict discussions to cooperation in the area of "pre-competitive" research. After roughly 4 years the European Commission formulated the Esprit-programme. After a 1-year pilot stage, the European Council of Ministers gave its official fiat: the 28th of February 1984 Esprit started with a threefold official mission: (1) promotion of intra-European cooperation in pre-competitive R&D in the area of IT, (2) procurement of basic technologies to improve Europe's mid term and long term competitive capacity on the world market, (3) promotion of European standardization.

The restriction to *pre*-competitive cooperative efforts has to do, apart from some negative private reminiscences, with the public strictness of the Treaty of Rome-regulations on cartels and other collusive practices. (In practice, the label appears to be rather elastic because as long as the interested firms will argue that they need additional or continued "research", the cooperation is supposed to be of a "pre-competitive" nature.) The Esprit-programme is divided into two stages (ESPRIT I: 1984-1988, ESPRIT II: 1989-1993) to accommodate goals and means to changing conditions in the (global) IT-sector. Half the funding (750 mln ECU for the first 5-year term) is provided by the Community. The rules for selecting proposals are competitive on terms of merit and stringent about both commercial exploitation and the dissemination of results.

The public/private structure of the management of Esprit has to be subdivided into three circuits, roughly corresponding with the earlier mentioned 'Triad Power' on the community level (see Figure 1).

As asked before: how *rational* are the decisions to participate or not to participate in the communitarian 'part' of the mosaic of power? How to find an acceptable balance of commitments *across* the different settings of the mosaic of power? And what about the actors' differential *freedom* to choose at all? To answer those questions, one should at least know more about the logic of the respective actors.

13. The Logic of the Actors

In case of strategic interdependence, rational organizations — private and public alike — may be expected to follow a simple behavioural axiom: increase one's own limited liability or 'deniability° while promoting or maintaining one's opponents' reliability. In terms introduced before[6]: actors will try to maximize their chances of free entry and free exit in any decision-making setting — i.e. keeping their position as flexible as possible by avoiding long term commitments — while hoping or stimulating that the opposite will hold for their bargaining partners. Asymmetries in commitments make life much easier, but not necessarily more stable. There is a clear trade-off between the desire for flexibility and the quest for stability. Much of the actual and the future behaviour of the partners in Esprit, depends essentially on the question how the actors will cope with the following dilemma: how much *loss of strategic choice* in exchange for how much *gain in stability* in the communitarian setting in exchange for how much *improvement in competitive capability* in the global and

**Figure 1   'Triad Power' on the Community Level: The Architecture of
                ESPRIT**

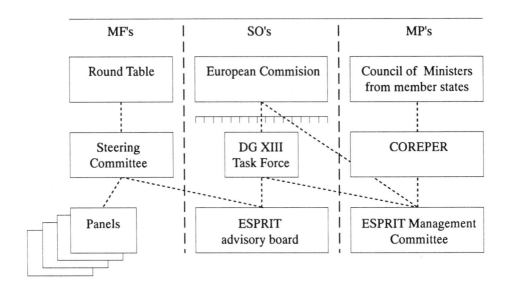

the regional reaches of the mosaic of power?

MF's, SO's and MP's probably differ in their preferred solution of the dilemma, for the
following reasons. The three participants differ in terms of their internal cohesion as well
as in terms of manoeuvrability — i.e. in their relative freedom to enter or to withdraw from
the respective parts of the power mosaic. As a consequence, the actors differ in terms of
accountability. Inequalities between MF's, SO's and MP's in 'individual' accountability are
reinforced by typical inter-actor differences, not only in terms of their subjective time
horizon (to some extent a 'voluntaristic' element) but also in terms of the objective time span
of feedback (the non-voluntaristic 'measurability' of each others actions). The 'strategic
triangle' of manoeuvrability, accountability and timing — representing a power continuum,
decreasing from MF's to MP's with SO's presumably occupying a position in the middle
— will determine the differential response to the dilemma formulated above: the trade-off
between strategic choice, stability and competitive potential. The *scope* of investments in
public/private partnerships and programmes like Esprit depends on one's position on the
continuum.

The empirical literature on interorganizational bargaining and decision-making suggests
that integrated public/private participation is most likely in issue-areas with "small
organization sets where interdependence is shared by small numbers of governmental
agencies and organized interests". Thus, integrated participation prevails where societies
segment into functionally autonomous sectors, especially sectors characterized by small

numbers of well-defined, stable interests, so that for each policy topic it is easy to specify stable rules about which organizations can participate, which problems and solutions are relevant, and which rules of the game are legitimate. Specialized systems prevent policies from becoming garbage cans, from becoming fortuitous results of the intermingling of loosely coupled processes. Olsen (1981) concludes from a review of research findings "that integrated participation occurs where predictability, certainty, compromises, recognition, role differentiation, and effective representation outwards offer high benefits, and where the costs are low of commitment and rigidity (..)". His words echo the implicit assumptions on which exchange-theory bases the birth of social order but contradict the explicit assumptions on which, not without irony, transactionalists predict the birth of hierarchy and federation, ousting exchange relations from the market:

"(I)ntegrated participation is more prevalent where there is little ambiguity concerning the extent and character of interdependence and power. For instance, integrated participation is most likely in policy topics which interest only a few organizations, or which are controlled by a few organizations that have stable divisions of intra-organizational labor and power. Secondly, integrated participation concentrated on policy topics where organizations' interests and preference orderings are reasonably well specified, where the magnitude and character of value disagreements are clear, and where organizations know how much of the attainment of one goal they are prepared to sacrifice in order to attain other goals somewhat more fully. Finally, integrated participation focuses upon policy topics where the causal world is well understood, where decisions have predictable consequences, and where it is easy to know who has competence and expertise" (Olsen 1981: 510-1).

In the case of Esprit none of these conditions appear to hold. The number of participants in Esprit does not suggest the presence of a "small organization set of governmental agencies and well-organized interests" with stable rules about insiders and outsiders, stable and unambiguously defined interests, consensual rules of the "European game" and a clear conception of the scope of interdependence. This reality refers not only to (inter-)governmental relationships, nor exclusively to public/private asymmetries in manoeuvrability and bargaining power, but also to inherent ambiguities, not to say contradictions, between European firms that are supposed to cooperate within the communitarian setting. Perhaps illustrative for the quality of intra-European interfirm relationships is the fact that from the sharp increase of concentration of operations in high-technology sectors like electricals, electronic engineering, chemicals and mechanical engineering, the share of *Community* joint ventures is still distinctly in the minority (European Commission 1985: 196-8). Statistics suggest that this type of cooperative agreements is more frequently used to catch up in areas where European technology has fallen behind that of U.S. and Japanese competitors than as a means of expanding business within the European Community. The majority of R&D cooperation is between partners of different nationalities, but most of these involve firms from non-EEC countries, with U.S. firms occupying a predominant role.

The available literature suggests that cooperative agreements, for instance in R&D as in the case of Esprit in its "pre-competitive" make-up, are fragile and unstable constructions confronted with various difficulties, leading generally to early breaking ups, buy-outs or mergers. In the words of an expert and adviser of the European Commission, justifying a more lengthy quote:

"This situation is aggravated within Europe where the majority of R&D arrangements are multicountry and where divergent objectives, strategies, domestic regulations, and institutions often combine with sociopsychological factors such as nationalistic feelings and attachment to familiar working methods.

These arrangements have a number of important handicaps. A cooperative agreement is a compromise between a desire for collaboration and an intention of maintaining independence, so that the organizational structure reflecting such an ambiguity is usually complex. Various clauses of the legal structure express this concern and imply heavy transaction costs of negotiation, especially for transnational ventures. Partner selection and the possibility of defining well-balanced contributions is the first barrier. An especially important fear is that one partner will be strengthened by the cooperation in such a way that it will become a dangerous competitor. This situation is of course more probable for horizontal agreements than for vertical ones. In the latter case, complementarities allow the benefits to be distributed according to the respective activities and products. In the case of cooperation between competitors, a geographical partition is the most obvious system of trying to solve the problem but has a side effect on existing competition.

At a second stage, the management of existing cooperative agreements is also costly, especially in R&D where technological conditions are changing rapidly and unpredictably. As it is not possible to maintain complete control over the functioning of the cooperation, it is necessary to construct complex contracts containing explicit clauses concerning confidentiality and transmission of information; and patent, trademark and copyright licenses. In fact, in joint R&D, there are fundamental limits on the ability to protect intellectual property, especially when technology advances at a rapid pace and competitors can invent around existing patents.

Finally, it is not easy to divide the benefits of a cooperative agreement in R&D, given that scientific knowledge has many aspects of a public good and that its results are not often easily incorporated. Disputes about joint appropriation, exclusivity and sharing (*ratione loci* or *ratione materiae*) of the results are often the source of disagreements.

All of these elements suggest that even in the context of a very tolerant antitrust policy, without positive public actions, European cooperation in R&D will remain a limited and unstable phenomenon" (Jacquemin & Spinoit 1986: 492-4).

Yet Esprit exists. How to explain the miracle? Neither exchange nor transaction theory seem to offer an answer. Let us have a closer look at the logic of the various actors. Part of the *Eurocracy*'s passion for the take-off of new policy programmes can be found in old frustrations: the credibility, and hence the prestige, of the Community were eroded by such diversities as the economic crisis, uncontrollability of the agricultural budget, disappointing results of the reorganization of ailing sectors like steel, demonstrations of persistent protectionism of the member states, and so on. In that institutional and psychological state of readiness a reprise of the American/Japanese *Défi* had to be welcomed as an inspiring common cause. Seen from the perspective of the credibility and the prestige of the European top of *private industry*, part of the passion for Esprit can be found in the intended/expected 'side payment' of a European Commission's preparedness to adopt a more friendly attitude vis-à-vis cartel-like behaviour of European firms. But the most important part of the paradox of the 'impossible' flair of Esprit lies in our opinion in the condition that multinational firms tend to *win as much*, or more, *as they say to loose* from the contradictions of European "intergovernmentalism". On the one hand, one may say that organizations are less likely to participate in issue-areas which are undergoing major changes, the more so during periods when the organizations themselves are undergoing changes in values, perspectives, priorities or resources: "organizations remain reluctant to participate until priorities and resources, and thus their interdependencies, become clearer" (Olsen, 1981: 511). On the other hand, the stakes of the game do not allow for waiting. And more importantly: the only effective way to test priorities, resources and the structures of interdependence, is participating in Esprit *as long as* multinational firms do not give up their freedom to move, simultaneously or sequentially, from the communitarian setting to other parts of the power mosaic. As we have seen, this is exactly what the MF's practice. That practice has far-reaching consequences for the logic of the game, i.e. for the balance of commitments originating from the distribution and the uses of bargaining and decision-making power. Compared to MF's, MP's and to a lesser degree SO's do not have comparable external facilities and internal faculties.

14. The Logic of the Game

The preceding sections try to show that the politics of association and dissociation in European industrial policy-making can be usefully conceived as *four*-level game: on the one hand the *national* game where domestic groups (national champions with affiliated interests) seek to maximize their interests by pressuring their own governments to adopt favourable policies, and politicians in search of power and prestige by constructing or following coalitions among those groups; on the other hand the *international* game, to be subdivided into three, more or less substitutable but separate games: the global, the regional and the communitarian sub-game.

A most vital characteristic of this multi-level game is that moves that are rational for a player at one board (e.g. supporting a national champion or subsidizing a bi-national technology project) may be quite irrational for that same player at another board (e.g. promoting a multi-lateral programme or welcoming joint ventures between more than two European firms). Nevertheless, there are powerful incentives for attending at each of the games and monitoring their outputs. Players have to tolerate some differences in rhetoric between the games (which is why, as one observer says, each summiteer gives his own news conference after a summit). Moreover, rhetoric intended for one set of players may upset bargains struck at the other table and so on (Putnam, 1984).

The political complexities for the players in this multi-level game are staggering, quite apart from the bounds of rationality due to technical-economic complexities. Any key player at the international table who is dissatisfied with the outcome may upset the game board, and conversely, any national leader who fails to satisfy an adequate number of his fellow players at the domestic table risks being evicted from his seat. Moreover, each national leader already has made a substantial investment in building a particular coalition at the domestic board, and he will be loathe to try to construct a different coalition simply to sustain an alternative policy mix that might be more acceptable internationally. Conversely, each multi-national firm having invested in international joint ventures (whether European or not) will refuse to dissolve his coalition simply to accommodate domestic or communitarian critics.

Economic adversity further complicates the game, by making it more nearly zero-sum and by reducing the policy "gains from trade" that might allow side-payments to disaffected participants. Even in theory there is no guarantee that any solution exists that will simultaneously satisfy the needs of the key players, and if such a solution exists in principle, the uncertainties of practical politics — the counterparts of Clausewitz's "fog of battle" — may prevent the players from reaching it (Putnam 1984: 48-50).

The outcome of the complexities of the four-level game comes close, at first sight, to what Scharpf describes as "frustration without disintegration and resilience without progress" — thus characterizing the real existence of European policy-making since the mid-1960s:

"In ongoing joint-decision systems, from which *exit is excluded or very costly*, non-agreement would imply the self-defeating continuation of past policies in the face of a changing policy environment. Thus, pressures to reach agreement will be great. The substance of agreement will be affected, however, by the prevailing style of decision-making. In its ability to achieve effective responses to a changing policy environment, the "bargaining" style is clearly inferior to the "problem solving" style. But the preconditions of "problem solving" — the orientation towards common goals, values and norms — are difficult to create, and they are easily eroded in cases of ideological conflict, mutual distrust or disagreement over the fairness of distribution rules. Thus, reversion to a "bargaining" style of decision-making (..) seems to have been characteristic of the European Community ever since the great confrontations of the mid-1960's. The price to be paid for that is not simply a prevalence of distributive conflicts complicating all substantive decisions, but a systematic tendency toward sub-optimal substantive solutions (..)" (Scharpf 1985: 40; *italics added*).

Perhaps this assessment should be called an understatement in the case of industrial policy problems confronting Europe, if for multinational firms and, to a lesser degree, for national politicians exit from the communitarian framework appears *not* to be excluded or if the costs of exit are compensated by the benefits of participation in other (global or regional) industrial policy games. The substantive results will be less than sub-optimal if the rationality of the corporate strategy of multinational firms, incidentally supported by national politicians interested in protecting their national champions, drives out the rationality of industrial policies on a Community level. The disappointing results of that substitution process, while not providing an adequate answer to the problem of excess capacity and other problems may inspire to a second substitution effect: the substitution of an endless series of short term trade guerilla tactics for long term, structural industrial policies and corporate strategies. The result, then, may be frustration *and* disintegration.

The coincidence of (1) the complexities of the four-level game -with an unequal distribution of bargaining power among the participants due to unequal barriers to entry and/ or exit for each of them — and (2) a horizontal orientation in the prevailing policy programmes — intending or pretending cooperation among the main competitors in the European arena — is apt to produce misalliances and trained incapacities.

15. Conclusion

Something strange seems to happen with policy programmes like Esprit. As argued in an earlier section, the *spirit* of Esprit is contingent on the strategies and tactics pursued in two other settings: the global and the regional setting of industrial policy-making. There is no formal device or institutionalized platform to coordinate the decisions and commitments made across the three settings. The only principle of integration is a complex web of interlocking directorates and joint ventures of multinational firms which manage to participate simultaneously in the global, the regional and the communitarian networks. They form the core of the overall mosaic of power. Their bargaining power, not only vis-à-vis their public partners but also vis-à-vis their private partners, rests on their superiority in terms of mobility: to a certain extent they may move from one setting to another (and back) following the principle that they participate only in some form of concerted action if the inducements they receive in one setting are better than what they would get elsewhere. That is the driving force underlying the evolution of antagonistic cooperation.

Yet, preceding paragraphs suggest that there are limits to mobility. Politicians have their prisoners' dilemmas. Entrepreneurs have their deal busters. *Both* may have their doubts about the long term stability of firm-to-firm and firm-to-government — let alone government-to-government — commitments. Under those conditions it becomes understandable that short term tactical considerations (even in order to consolidate internal coalitions!) drive out long term strategic aims. That may be lucrative for *conquistadores*, but it is not very promising for the stability and creativity of the resulting networks that should form the infra-structure of European integration.

In that respect, *vertical* alliances (see, for instance, the complementary cooperation between the partners in the aircraft construction consortium *Airbus*-industries) prove to be a safer investment in mutual power relations. Vertical combinations have a built-in check against opportunism: because of entry and exit barriers on the network level, it is profitable to trust each other's interests and intentions. On the other hand, because of an open structure on the level of the individual organizations — the participants agree, on a rotating basis, to station top quality staff and line in an independent Airbus-organization — there is a built-in incentive to creativity. To *Esprit*'s architecture — a web of exclusively horizontal alliances — the opposite formula applies: open networks and closed organizations. The latter is not an excellent recipe for the reduction of opportunism and the increase of creativity.

Notes

1 Our summary of the affair is based on a series of articles and press releases that accompanied De Benedetti's manoeuvres vis-à-vis the Société Générale in the international financial press and in the main Dutch newspapers *NRC-Handelsblad* and *De Volkskrant* (January-April, 1988).

2 Closer reading reveals that the third characteristic ("information impactedness") is the key variable in Williamson's explanation of the "internalization" of operations that are originally market transactions.

3 For the formulation of a political contingency-theory linking the rise and decline of intra-organizational *oligarchies* to the rise and decline of interorganizational policy *cartels*, see Wassenberg (1982). The analysis of the workings of the suggested contingency-principle and evidence of its predicted outcome — "the survival of the fittest deficiencies" in policy-making — can be found in an elaborate reconstruction of 20 years of industrial policy-making in the shipbuilding & offshore industry in the Netherlands (Wassenberg, 1983).

4 The risk of an imitation race is not at all imaginary, or even already a reality, if the popularity of publications like Kenichi Ohmae's *Triad Power: the Coming Shape of Global Competition*, may be taken as a measure. In it a world is announced (and advocated) that is divided into three geo-political spheres of influence under hegemonic supervision of Japan, the U.S. and Europe — essentially, it amounts to shared superiority based on *identical* technologies attached to product-market combinations.

5 See the section *Inside markets*.

6 See above *Esprit: a multilevel game*.

Productivity Coalitions and the Future of Unionism
Disintegration of Generalized Political Exchange?

Paul Windolf

1. The Devolution of Collective Bargaining[1]

a) Productivity coalitions have become a new focus of research in industrial relations to analyse recent changes in managerial strategies and in collective bargaining (Negrelli 1982, Streeck 1984). Though there is no precise definition of the concept, it usually refers to structural transformations in the industrial relations system: Firstly, the centre of collective bargaining shifts from the branch or national level towards the level of the enterprise. The firm becomes more and more important for productivity agreements and for new forms of participation. Examples for the devolution of collective bargaining are found in France, where the socialist government introduced a new labour law obliging the firm's management to negotiate with union representatives at least once a year about wages and hours of work.[2] In West Germany, the collective agreement on the shortening of working time was opened to a second-round negotiation between the works council and management on the enterprise level. For Britain, Brown (1986) has shown that management was able to overcome sectional interest bargaining by concentrating the negotiations on the enterprise level.

Secondly, the antagonistic relationship between management and the unions is replaced by a more co-operative style of bargaining. This development is seen by some writers as a temporary armistice due to the economic crisis, others interpret it as a permanent change in the "cultura conflittuale" (Accornero 1983, Rieser 1985). An adverse relationship of power is gradually transformed into a symbiotic relationship in which co-operation is exchanged for participation in decision making. Instead of imposing new forms of work organization management seeks the co-operation of the workforce when decisions on new investments are taken. This kind of bargaining also implies a shift from quantitative to more qualitative demands (Streeck 1981).

Thirdly, the concept of productivity coalitions points to a tendency to replace contract relationships by an internal agreement between individual workers (or groups of workers) and management. This is the most problematic consequence of productivity coalitions because it signals a permanent weakening of the union movement. Management deliberately bypasses unions and collective bargaining and addresses the workforce directly to negotiate productivity agreements. In this case the collective contract is replaced by an intraorganizational agreement. Or, to put it in another language, the representative institutions of industrial democracy (e.g. works council, union sections) are replaced by a "direct" democracy. Examples of this tendency are found in the French steel industry where employers — after the defeat of the unions — tried to directly co-operate with the workforce through quality circles and team work (Groux/Levy 1985, Eisenhammer 1987).

The concept of "productivity coalitions" revives the ideology of community (Gemeinschaft) propagated by employers in many European countries during the interwar period in reaction to the radical Marxist ideology and the rise of communist parties. Class society and antagonistic interest groups were to be replaced by "a community of production in which all members are organically interwoven" (Maier 1970: 47). Productivity coalitions also strongly rely on decentralization and on competitive strength. The concept amalgamates the ideology of "Gemeinschaft" with recent neoliberal ideas of deregulation, market competition, and the dismantling of large interest organizations. The firm becomes a "community of fate" which demands an unconditional commitment of its workforce. In Germany, for instance, the Works Council Act of 1920 established a bargaining unit on the enterprise level elected by all employees regardless of their union membership or ideological complexion. The works council movement became a centre for co-operative bargaining between management and the work force and for the conflict-free implementation of technical change (Winkler 1984: 283). The German unions accepted Fordism and Taylorism as a means to increase productivity and to regain shares in the world market which Germany had lost after the war. But the German unions also insisted on co-determination to influence the implementation and the speed of the assembly line (Stollberg 1981: 82, 98).

b) Productivity coalitions have ambiguous meanings and functions. They are used by management to regain control over the labour process but, nevertheless, are supported by the workforce. It would be misleading to conclude that these coalitions will soon fall apart as happened with the human relations school and company unionism during the interwar period (Durand 1986, Nelson 1982). They reflect the active support of workers for the restructuring plans of management and, what is more important, they foreshadow a loss of loyalty and legitimacy of the unions. Productivity coalitions are no "liaison d'amour" but, as in politics, an exchange alliance to protect the workers' jobs. The following examples which became prominent for industrial relations in Britain and Italy illustrate the ambiguity of their functions.

In September 1980 Fiat informed the unions that about 24.000 employees were to be laid off. The motor company was on the brink of bankruptcy and had to reduce its output by about 450.000 cars per year to become profitable. The unions called the workers immediately out for a strike blocking the company for more than six weeks. Until mid October negotiations between management, unions, and the government dragged on without tangible results. On October 14 about 40.000 FIAT employees demonstrated in Turin demanding the end of the strike and a "right to work". Not only foremen, white collar workers and technicians but also skilled workers and assembly line operators participated in the famous "march of 40.000" through Turin which marked a turning point in the Italian industrial relations.[3] With hindsight an article of a prominent member of the Italian communist party, published in November 1979, became a prophecy. Amendola reproached the unions for their losing contact with the rank and file. Faced with the challenge of new technology and the inevitable reduction of the workforce they proved unable to formulate a coherent strategy and to prevent outbreaks of violence in the plants. Unless the unions would go through a process of "drastical changes and self-critique" he prophesied a decisive defeat of the union movement (Amendola 1979: 13).

A similar turning point was observed in industrial relations in the British motor car industry. Since 1975 the government had to lend each year more money to British Leyland to prevent the largest, state owned motor car company from going bankrupt. In October 1979 the incoming new managing director M. Edwardes addressed the workforce directly by a referendum asking for the approval of a recovery plan. The plan included the lay off of about 25,000 workers, the abolishment of restrictive practices, and the introduction of a new flexible work organization. The workforce approved the plan by a majority of 87% of those voting. When management tried to put the plan into action the union of the transport workers (TGWU) called their members out for a strike. About 22,000 workers walked out but returned to work after a week because the largest metal workers union (AUEW) refused to support the strike. The terms of the recovery plan approved by the referendum were then implemented by management (Willman et al. 1985: 82, 185). Each time when negotiations with unions reached a deadlock management used the referendum as a kind of "direct democracy" to legitimize new restructuring and redundancy plans.

Both examples have been taken from the motor car industry which in recent years not only suffered from a deep recession but also introduced new technology and a new work organization.[4] The economic crisis and the introduction of new technology are both conditions favourable, if not for the stability, at least for the set up of productivity coalitions.[5] The examples illustrate, in a nutshell, the issues which will be discussed below: the weakening of central union control, the participation of workers in managerial decisions without participation of unions, the cooperative alliance between groups of workers and management, the use of the referendum as a kind of "direct" democracy.

In many firms the economic crisis has not strengthened management but has weakened both the firm and the unions. Driven to the brink of bankruptcy management tried to get the cooperation of the workers even if it was previously opposed to any kind of participation (Ramsay 1977). As there are not gains but losses to distribute management is more prepared to share responsibility even if such participation violates the basic principle of management's right to manage. Examples for this a kind of cooperation are Chrysler, British Leyland, Pirelli, General Motors, the French steel industry.

The shift from branch to enterprise bargaining and the growing importance of qualitative demands reflect the weakening of centralized corporatist arrangements which flourished in many European countries during the sixties and early seventies. The "decline of unionism" which became a common place in the industrial relations literature in the United States is now complemented by the "decline of corporatism" in Western European countries (Lash 1985). Even though some scholars used the term "micro-corporatism" for these new forms of enterprise bargaining (Teubner 1987: 21) it must not be forgotten that "micro"-corporatism differs in many respects from "macro"-corporatism, i.e. the generalized political exchange between unions, employers's associations, and the state.

Micro-corporatism tends to destroy the solidarity between workers employed in lame-duck enterprises and those working in prospering firms — a solidarity upon which the strength and efficiency of unions is based. They also further the flourishing of sectional interests and particularistic groups which exploit their individual market strength. "The decomposition of comprehensive bargaining aggregates by .... decentralization is nothing else but the very 'return to the market' that is at the core of the neo-liberal offensive against corporatist rigidities" (Streeck 1984: 295). Last but not least the term "micro-corporatism" neglects the tri-partite character of collective bargaining under corporatist regimes. For instance, on some occasions an income policy has been "sold" for an active labour market policy. The unions did not fully exploit their market strength expecting a government programme to support full employment. Unions and employers associations are bound to take the macro-economic consequences of their claims and concessions into account. This kind of political exchange cannot be implemented on the enterprise level.

The following sections will further develop the concept of productivity coalitions and the devolution of collective bargaining. In Section 2 it will be shown to what extent the changing technical and economic environment has supported the emergence of productivity coalitions. In Section 3 the concept of participation is discussed. In Section 4 recent experiments with participation and flexibility in Italy, Great Britain, France, and the Federal Republic of Germany will be analysed.

2. From Mass Unionism to Productivity Coalitions

Are productivity coalitions a transitory phenomenon due to the economic depression and the crisis of the welfare state or do they indicate a structural change in industrial relations? Since the 19th century the union movement suffered from cyclical down swings in membership and power. Membership in German unions went down from a peak of 7.3 Mill in 1919 to 3.9 Mill in 1926 (Stollberg 1981: 75). The American unions recovered from the depression of the thirties and gained more than 4 Mill. members within a few years. The question whether centralized mass unionism suffers from a cyclical downswing or whether it is an outdated form of interest representation has to be discussed within a wider historical perspective.[6]

In table 1 an evolutionary model of different subsystems of society is shown. It represents a heuristic concept which clarifies the relationship between different subsystems and their mutual impact. The table may be interpreted in two directions: Firstly, we may look at each subsystem separately and examine the evolutionary development of, for instance, the work organization, the union organization or the function of law. Secondly, the table may also be interpreted in a horizontal way. This implies two kinds of arguments: The first is a causal argument. We may ask in which way technology and new forms of work organization influence the structure of unions and the relationship between unions and the government. We may also analyse the impact of leads and lags in the different subsystems. Are there structural incompatibilities between the different subsystems? If, for instance, the labour process changes towards a re-professionalization ("end of Taylorism") whereas the structure of unionism remains unchanged (mass unions), could this lag in the development of the union organization explain the "decline of unionism"?

a) In a study on the French automobile industry Touraine (1955) developed already in the early fifties an evolution model to describe the transformation of the work process and the skills of workers. He argues that during the interwar period the traditional craft organization of the production process (stage A) was transformed by the introduction of scientific management (Taylorism, Fordism). Centralization and bureaucratization of the work organization and a deskilling of the workforce are well known consequences of this kind of "scientific" management (stage B). Touraine also foresaw a stage C during which full automation would be introduced replacing direct labour and leading to a reskilling of jobs. At the beginning of the eighties the discussion on the consequences of technical change on the skills of workers gains momentum again. Some writers believe the "end of Taylorism" and the end of mass production to be imminent. Piore/Sabel (1984) use the term "industrial divide" to characterize the historical transitions from craft to mass production (interwar period) and from mass production to flexible specialization which they believe will become the dominant production paradigm for the foreseeable future. The essence of the many empirical studies is that new technology offers opportunities for a re-professionalization of industrial work. The large groups of unskilled assembly workers are disappearing and replaced by highly qualified maintenance workers and quality controllers (Kern/Schumann 1985, Baethge/Overbeck 1986, Littek/Heisig 1986).

Table 1:   Evolution of Work Organization and Interest Representation

evolutionary stage	work organization	structure of union organization	relationship betw. state and unions	role of law
A	crafts (skilled)	craft unionism	voluntarism (pluralism)	contract law
B	assembly line (unskilled)	mass unionism	corporatism	substantive law
C	flexible work organization (reskilling)	productivity coalitions	decentralization (controlled autonomy)	procedural (reflexive) law

b) Do we observe a similar "second divide" in the structure of unionism which would open new perspectives for interest representation? Changes in the structure of unionism are also described in table 1 in a three-step model. Craft unions were replaced by mass unions which organized large numbers of unskilled assembly workers. In many countries this transformation was accompanied by serious conflicts. In the US the structural incompatibilities between craft unionism on the one hand and the emerging new forms of work organization (Fordism) on the other caused a split in the union movement. The traditional craft unions proved unwilling and unable to organize the interests of the assembly line workers who were more aggressive in their industrial actions and more radical in their political ideology (Tomlins 1985). For Britain, Hobsbawm (1984) analysed the transition from craft to mass unionism at the turn of the century with the emergence of the "New Unionism". Since then a complicated process of mergers between different unions took place transforming many craft unions into "general" mass unions (Undy et al. 1981).

The bureaucratized and centralized unions which developed under the regime of the assembly line become more and more inadequate to meet the demands of a highly differentiated working class. The argument is more clearly understood if one looks at the consequences of Taylorism for the skills and differentiation of the workforce. Traditional theories of professionalism assume that the more the division of labour advances the more the structure of professions and the characteristics of individual workers become differentiated. The paradoxical outcome of Taylorism, however, was not professional differentiation but de-differentiation of skills and professionalism. The most extreme forms of Taylorism and Fordism were extinguishing individual differences. Variations in work tasks and skills required at the assembly line became so tiny that it was correct to assume that all workers did, more or less, the same job. The similarity of working conditions and skills, and the homogeneity of values, political orientations, and life style were essential for an efficient interest representation within mass unions.

If we put it in terms of the Durkheimian sociology the "organic solidarity" of the craft unionism was replaced by the "mechanical solidarity" of mass unionism. The "mechanical" solidarity develops in societies or groups with a low degree of differentiation where all members share the same values and have similar life styles (Durkheim 1973: 70, 98).[7] The community of steel and automobile workers represented an ideal group for mass unionism. The irony of Taylorism was that it furthered (mass) unionism even though Taylor's outspoken intention was to curb the spread of union organizations (Jacoby 1983). The unintended consequences of "scientific management" were to extinguish individual differences and to make workers more inclined to defend their interests collectively.

Since the early eighties, unskilled workers at the assembly line are gradually substituted by advanced technology. They are replaced by a heterogeneous workforce differing in skill, responsibility, working time and ranging from rather unqualified computer-dependent workers to highly qualified professionals. Additionally and independent from changes in the labour process the expansion of the educational system provided a growing proportion of the population with higher education. About 40% of a cohort pass through some kind of college education in the US and Japan; the enrollment rates in Western European Universities reach in some countries 30-35%. The unskilled, once the dominant majority in the labour force, became a minority. The growing differentiation and heterogeneity of education, working conditions, skills, political orientations, and lifestyle (Goldthorpe 1984: 318) threaten the internal integration of unions. The devolution of collective bargaining and the emergence of productivity coalitions are not only due to the economic crisis but are also a response to the growing differentiation of the workforce.

So far, the contours of a "new" unionism are only vaguely perceived. Management rediscovers the human relations school of the interwar-period arguing that personnel management may take over those functions previously fulfilled by unions (Strauss 1984). Firms set up team work and quality circles giving many responsibilities back to the worker. The question upon which I shall come back is how unions might be able to adjust their organizational structure to this development.

c) The fourth column tries to squeeze the many steps, through which the relationship between the government and interest organizations was transformed, into a three-stage model. Voluntarism denotes a system of industrial relations which was built upon the collective strength of union organizations and did not rely on government support. The early history of unionism shows that the liberal state and the ideology of "contract law" was hostile to the existence of large interest organizations. Union organizations were seen as paralysing labour markets in the same way as trusts perverted the functioning of product markets (Wedderburn 1971).

The advent of corporatism was closely related to the growth of mass unions and the welfare state. Business corporations, unions, employers' associations, and the state coalesced into a large, encompassing regulatory complex. The bargaining system was centralized and the state played an important role providing, for instance, a representation monopoly (as in Italy for the public service) or legal rights to co-determination (as in Germany). "Corporatism can be defined as a system of interest representation in which the constituent units are organized into a limited number of singular, compulsory, noncompetitive, hierarchically ordered and functionally differentiated categories, recognized or licensed (if not created) by the state and granted a deliberate representational monopoly within their respective categories ..." (Schmitter 1974: 93). The central features of this system are centralized bargaining and generalized exchange between employers, the state, and unions. Sectional interests are cleared within the organizations, generalized exchange is based on the mutual trust that today's advance concessions will not be left unrequited. An important option for corporatist strategies is that political and economic commodities may be exchanged in different markets which allow for leads and lags (Marin 1985).

With the economic downswing and the financial crisis of the welfare state this kind of interest representation lost much of its attraction. Many Western European governments switched from a macro-economic, Keynesian regulation to a neo-liberal deregulation of the economy. If, for instance, the government refuses to implement an active labour market policy, because she does not feel responsible for the level of unemployment the tri-partite, centralized concertation becomes an empty box. There are not many economic programmes left which the unions might wish to influence. The centre of economic regulation moved down from the government to the enterprise level which is more difficult to control.

Lash (1985: 217) maintains "that there is a long-term trend towards decentralisation of Swedish industrial relations". The Metal Employers Association demands a shift of centralized bargaining (one of the cornerstones of Swedish corporatism) down to the enterprise level. Management is interested in "productivity deals for which local unions would be held responsible" (Lash 1985: 221). The fragmentation of collective bargaining undermines the solidarity pact which was so important for Swedish labour market policy. A second threat to Swedish corporatism is the growing competition between white and blue collar unions. In many industries the blue collar workers losing their jobs are replaced by professional workers. The competition reflects the increasing power of the white collar/ professional workers' unions which do not accept the trend-setting pretensions of the traditional blue collar unions any longer.

However, corporatism is more than a mere solidarity pact. Its supporters claim that centralized concertation and the search for compromise would make it more easy to modernize the economy or, at least, to reduce the social costs of modernization. Corporatism is also threatened when the system becomes so entrenched and rigid that firms sacrifice modernization for the sake of stability and consensus in their bargaining with unions and the state. In a comparative study Czada (1984) claims that "corporatist" countries (e.g. Austria) do not lack behind "pluralist" countries (e.g. USA) in their endeavour to modernize the economy. However, given the serious difficulties of the state-owned industries in Austria this seems to be too optimistic a view. Traxler (1987b: 75) admits that their are two dangers for Austria — the most "corporatist" country in Western Europe: First, the corpo-ratist system may lose its capacity for problem solving (e.g. for modernization). Secondly, even if it is successful in adjusting the Austrian economy to new conditions in the world market (which remains to be seen) the concertation machinery might be unable to control centrifugal tendencies. The problem of who bears the brunt of modernization (e.g. steel workers) undermines the centralized bargaining system and strengthens the attitude to "beggar-my-neighbour". Employers are asking for the "deregulation" of rigid working times and for "flexibility" in dealing with security of employment contracts (Traxler 1987b: 72). In a summary on recent research on Austrian corporatism Grande/Müller (1985: 20) conclude that corporatism was successful in stabilizing the economy but might be too rigid to further innovation.

d) Some authors maintain that decentralization is the only way to stabilize the system of industrial relations. The interests and motives of union members became too heterogeneous to be represented by a centralized agency. Teubner (1983: 272) argues that "functional differentiation requires a displacement of integrative mechanisms from the level of the society to the level of the subsystems. Centralized social integration is effectively ruled out today and cannot be achieved by legal, economic, moral, or scientific mechanisms." He in-troduces the concept of "controlled autonomy" to show how society may overcome the disintegrating consequences of a growing differentiation of its subsystems.

Advocates of controlled autonomy do not preach deregulation. On the contrary, the concept is compatible with a further "juridification" of industrial relations (Simitis 1984, Clarke 1985). Yet, the kind of law has to be changed. It is no longer substantive law which is to be implemented by centralized bureaucracies but procedural law which provides institutions and procedures for self-regulation.

The concept of controlled autonomy is closely related to the changing function of law. With the growth of the welfare state substantive law became a dominant type of social regulation.[8] For many social and economic activities the state imposed standards and substantive norms to correct the outcome of market competition (e.g. redistribution of income, working time, social security, etc.). Substantive law, corporatism, and the welfare state are complementary institutions.

Procedural law (reflexive law in Teubner's terminology) does not set standards or substantive norms. Instead, it provides institutions and procedures for self-regulation, for an autonomous bargaining and for reaching consent between conflicts of interest. "Instead of the comprehensive regulation of substantive legal rationality, reflexive law restricts legal performance to more indirect, more abstract forms of social control ..... Reflexive law will neither authoritatively determine the social functions of other subsystems nor regulate their input and output performances, but will foster mechanisms that systematically further the development of reflexion structures within other social subsystems" (Teubner 1983: 275).

Devolution and autonomy must not necessarily destroy centralized control. The institutions of "controlled autonomy" are built upon the pre-existing corporatist organizations. The autonomy of subsystems has to be "controlled" in order to prevent their disintegration. The central authority has to set general norms — though on an abstract and generalized broad level — which guide the subsystems. The simultaneous existence of a generalized control and decentralized autonomy is reflected in the contradictory terminology which Teubner (1983) uses (e.g. "decentralized integration" or "regulated autonomy").

e) However, on closer inspection the concept of "controlled autonomy" does not seem to be a step ahead in the evolution of law or of industrial relations. The concept revives ideas of voluntarism and liberal pluralism. In many countries, industrial relations and education systems have since long been governed by "controlled autonomy". In a historical analysis of the roots of American pluralism Stone (1981: 1509) argues that the leading ideologists of industrial relations in the US have seen the industrial relations system as a "mini-democracy with self-government and autonomous regulation". Stone shows that "industrial pluralism is the view that collective bargaining is self-government by management and labor: management and labor are considered to be equal parties who jointly determine the conditions of the sale of labor power."

Industrial pluralists started from the assumption of parity between management and workers and of a balance of power between the different interest groups within a social subsystem. However, there is no reason to believe that this balance of power exists. Governments were well aware of the imbalance of power between unions and management and have taken different actions depending on their political complexion: If unions were believed to be too strong, strike laws were enacted. If capitalists were believed to be too strong, the right to lock out was limited and union rights were enlarged. Without this correcting mechanism of an outside third party the imbalance of power causes disintegration and the system of bargaining falls apart. The imbalance of power was one reason for the vanishing of voluntarism. Antagonistic interest groups endowed with different amounts of power push industrial pluralism towards an outside arbitrator. The inbuilt instability was one reason for the transformation of voluntarism to corporatism and towards the interference of the state in favor of one party of the game. The imbalance of power and with it the instability of the system reappears in Teubner's model of "controlled autonomy".

A second criticism is that Teubner neglects the "logic of collective action" and the perverse effects of sectional interests. Olson (1982: 31) has shown that small decentralized interest organizations tend to follow sectional interests incompatible with the "general interest" of society or with the efficiency of the economy. For instance, a disproportional increase in wages or the benefit of a restrictive practice completely accrues to the small group whereas the losses due to these practices are equally distributed among all members of society (inflation, low productivity). The larger and the more comprehensive the interest organization the higher the share of the losses the group has to bear as a consequence of its sectional interest representation. This is a strong argument for encompassing and highly centralized interest organizations (Traxler/Vobruba 1987).

Within the liberal system of voluntarism perverse effects of sectional interests were controlled by market competition. Groups that acted outside or against the economic logic were eliminated from the market. Under corporatist regimes highly centralized organizations — supported by union securities or a state-granted monopoly position — control the perverse effects. It is hard to see how sectional interests are controlled by "controlled autonomy".

3. The Concept of Participation

Autonomy, "autogestion", and decentralization being keywords of the French union movement during the sixties (Mallet 1969, Sellier 1984) have been taken over by neo-liberal thinkers to propel their ideas of a new responsibility and of a decentralized market society. Unions demanded "autogestion" to achieve participation and self-determination for workers in the enterprise. In the neo-liberal terminology the concept refers to deregulation and market competition between "autonomous" groups.

Where "flexible specialization" becomes the dominant production design management demands to be exempted from rigid regulations of the corporatist regime. "Flexibility" is the catch word which covers any change management intends to introduce (see section 4.2). Working time, wages, internal mobility, and security of employment have to be adjusted to the particular circumstances of the enterprise. On the workers' side qualitative demands become important. They centre around claims for information, consultation, and participation if management intends to change the product or to introduce new technology. On many occasions, management is willing to negotiate these claims because participation in decision making is expected to change the "cultura conflittuale" towards a more co-operative style of bargaining.

It is precisely for this reason that parts of the union movement have opposed participation and co-determination schemes. They argue that the participation of workers in managerial decision making would constantly expose the worker to a managerial counter-socialization. Participation is collaboration which destroys solidarity and with it the union movement as an independent power in society.

Regardless of the validity of this argument participation models flourish in many European firms.[9] Some of them on a stable, institutionalized basis, others as a temporary experiment. An analysis of selected models of participation may show how unions and management perceive and deal with the dilemma of decentralized interest representation. The different models are analysed here from two points of view: Firstly, may participation replace centralized negotiations within corporatist institutions? Do participation models integrate the various demands of a differentiated workforce? Secondly, to what extent are unions able to control participation? Is it introduced with or without unions or even against the unions?

The term "participation" covers rudimentary forms of consultation as well as highly institutionalized forms of co-determination with veto rights. A few characteristics of the concept are briefly mentioned in order to clarify the following discussion.

One important dimension is the level of participation: Whether workers may influence only marginal managerial decisions (e.g. some aspects of the work organization) or whether they are able to influence the strategic enterpreneurial decisions of the firm. A second dimension concerns the level of formality: Whether they have grown out of custom and practice or whether they are institutionalized either by law (e.g. German co-determination) or by collective agreement (i.e. comitati paritetici in Italy). A third dimension refers to the "cultura conflittuale" of the union: whether participation models have to grow within a system of antagonistic interest representation (e.g. some unions in France and Italy) or whether a more co-operative culture of joint management exists (Rieser 1985). This dimension which represents in a shorthand formula the traditions, basic values and the history of the unions has a decisive influence on the success or failure of participation.

A forth dimension refers to the power of unions to punish an assumed misconduct of management. What are the legitimate sanctions against breach of contract? May unions call upon third party arbitration, or are they able to take legal action when rights to participation are violated, or are they allowed to use the strike weapon? (As will be seen there is no participation model that allows the strike as a legitimate weapon for settling disputes.) A final dimension is the institutional implementation of participation: whether new committees are created which are separated from the formal decision making channels of the firm or whether participation is integrated into already existing bodies of the organization (e.g. board of directors).

These dimensions are used as analytical tools to describe the variety of participation models recently implemented in some European countries. They are interpreted as continuous scales which give an idea of the distance a union has to overcome if it takes part in a participation experiment that radically differs from its traditional culture of bargaining. To illustrate the point the following example is helpful. Before 1978 participation at British Leyland was based upon the "principle of mutuality". Management was not allowed to change the work organization without collective bargaining and, the essence of the principle was that management had to pay for every change (Willman et al. 1985: 68). This kind of participation grew out of an antagonistic relationship (violations were sanctioned by strike), it was informal (custom and practice), and of a low level (only some aspects of the work organization). If this system is replaced by co-determination on the Board of Directors, the participation model becomes highly formalized, requires a co-operative style of bargaining (strike weapon is not allowed), and even strategic decision making is covered by the model. The experiment of the British Post Office which is analysed below will show to what extent such a shift requires a change in basic values and ideologies of the unions.

4. Flexibility and Participation: Four Case Studies

4.1 Experiments with Participation in Italy and Britain

a) In 1984, after two years of negotiation, an agreement was signed between the three representative Italian unions and the IRI-management.[10] The agreement contains detailed regulations for a one-year experiment in participation. IRI is an Italian holding company which manages all nationalized enterprises in the different industries (e.g. ship building, steel, electronics, building material). As many IRI-firms were in economic trouble the agreement also obliges management and the unions to co- operate in the restructuring of the firms and in an active labour market policy. The introduction of new technology, an efficient work organization, and the requalification of the workforce were the most important objectives management and the unions wanted to achieve (Treu 1986, Pedrazzoli 1985).

The agreement illustrates the hypothesis that productivity coalitions are more likely to be introduced in times of economic depression. Management accepts more easily a participation machinery if the firm is in trouble. Ramsay (1977) has put forward a cyclical theory of participation: In times of depression management is willing to co-operate in a participation experiment to share the losses with the workforce. If the performance of the firm improves participation is dismantled. The evidence for this hypothesis is, however, not convincing. Most participation schemes introduced in hard times fail already at the beginning. Unions are usually reluctant to collaborate in restructuring plans and to legitimize the lay off of a substantial part of the workforce if they do not get anything in exchange. If experiments survive the economic trouble they are likely to last for a longer period.

The IRI-agreement is an experiment limited to a few industries (electronics, shipbuilding) and to a period of one year. Given the important position of the nationalized firms within the Italian economy an experiment which proved successful here might well be extended to other sectors and to the private industry.[11] This illustrates a second hypothesis: Models of participation are more easily implemented in nationalized industries or in the public sector provided that a social-democratic government or a centre-left coalition is in power. To put it differently: If participation models are introduced in the public sector as an experiment to prepare the ground for a change in the "cultura conflittuale" of a country, the experiment is contingent upon the outcome of the political process. (The participation experiment in the British Post Office was finished when the conservative government came into office, see below.)

The IRI-agreement created permanent institutions (Comitati Consultivi Paritetici) for a stable and continuous process of consultation and participation. Committees were set up on different hierarchical levels: plant, enterprise, industry, and finally, on the level of the IRI-Holding-Company. Additionally, regional committees were established cutting across the different nationalized industries. The committees consist of an equal number of members of management and of representatives of the three largest unions (9 members from each side on the industry level, 6 from each side on the enterprise level). The Committees meet every four months, but may also be convened by any of the parties concerned.

The creation of a network of committees with a co-ordinating institution at the top comes very close to what has been termed "meso-corporatism", i.e. institutionalized participation encompassing a large economic unit. Participation limited to the enterprise or even plant is likely to follow sectional interests; the network of IRI-committees created by the agreement may provide an opportunity to enlarge the horizon of sectional interest representation. Apart from many declarations of good will the agreement assigns three important tasks to the committees:

- Management has to inform union representatives about the strategic decisions of the enterprise, particularly about new investments, the introduction of new technology, and the selling or buying of plants. It also has to give detailed information about its future personnel policy, the level of employment, and the conditions of work. The unions have to be informed about the early stages of project design and have to be integrated into the implementation of the economic, industrial, and personnel policies. Consultation should go beyond a pure negotiation of the consequences of managerial decision making. The information is to be given so early that the unions can propose their own suggestions and counter-projects. The unions did not want to assume the role of a fire-guard but to influence the strategic decision making of management.[12]
- A second objective of the Committees is to negotiate and to submit a joint report to top management which gives the different views and recommendations of the members about investment plans, introduction of new technology, and industrial policy. However, the proposals of the report are not binding, neither for management nor for the unions.
- Thirdly, the unions had to accept a dispute procedure which is expected to reduce the widespread use of mini-strikes (micro-conflittualità). Management and unions agreed

on joint consultation procedures and a cooling-out period during which industrial action is not allowed. As the procedure is quite complicated it is unlikely to be very successful.

The agreement also defines the legal status of the Committees. It says that "the tasks and the activities of the Committees must not affect the autonomy of the parties and their responsibility in collective bargaining" (IRI 1986: 71). Institutions responsible for participation on the one hand and for collective bargaining on the other are carefully separated from each other. The "Comitati Consultivi Paritetici" do not have the right to negotiate and its proposals do not bind any of the parties. (In the British Post Office agreement, analysed below, more or less identical formulations will be found.)

The "separation of power" between participation and collective bargaining reveals a complicated relationship between the two institutions. How can unions bring their influence to bear if they participate in joint consultation but do not have veto rights to prevent management from enforcing its decisions? And what happens if one party fails to adhere to its contractual obligations? The strike is a legitimate weapon for collective bargaining, it is a problematic weapon to enforce the unions' point of view within institutions for participation. The empirical evidence shows that strikes usually undermine participation experiments. Participation introduces a different "exchange logic" in the relationship between management and unions. Participation has to rely on a 'deferred gratification' pattern and on the mutual trust that the parties will honour the spirit of an agreement which cannot specify the details of the day-to-day business.

In 1985 a local union (Milano) took legal action against IRI charging the holding company of breach of contract. It argued that the union was not informed in due time of the decision to sell a subsidiary which belonged to the IRI-Holding. When the court's decision was still pending the unions and management negotiated an amendment to the IRI-agreement. An arbitration procedure was negotiated stipulating that this agreement and the consultation procedure should not give rise to legal action by any of the parties involved (Treu 1986: 406). The amendment illustrates that both management and unions tried to control disputes arising from the contract and to avoid third-party interference, let alone strikes or other industrial actions. The parties also agreed on the prolongation of the experiment for another year and the extension to other industries including a time table which shows that within a few years more or less all industrial companies belonging to IRI will be covered by the contract.

The agreement does not give veto-rights to the unions. Unions may submit their proposals but these are not binding. The agreement is an exchange contract: Strategic information is exchanged for co-operation. Management is obliged to inform unions about future investments and restructuring plans. The information may give unions a lever to put pressure upon management and to demand true veto-rights. Management expects the unions to co-operate in the restructuring of plants, in the introduction of efficient work practices and, particularly, in controlling the many mini-strikes. Whether management and unions receive what they expect remains to be seen. So far, the IRI-agreement is an experiment. The fact that the agreement was renewed and enlarged after one year seems to indicate that expectations were not completely frustrated.

b) In January 1978 the British Post Office started a two-year experiment with participation of union members on the Board of Directors. The conceptualization and negotiations about the scheme went back to the early seventies when the Labour Party and the TUC made various proposals to enlarge industrial democracy. In 1977 the Bullock Report (1977) was published recommending industrial democracy on the Board of Directors on the basis of the famous 2X + Y formula: En equal number of managers and union representatives (X-members) was to be complemented by a limited number of outside, independent nominees (Y-members).

Throughout the seventies management as well as parts of the union movement were hostile to participation and co-determination. The Post Office management objected that on lower levels of the hierarchy many opportunities for consultation and information of the firm's workforce already existed. Participation of union members on the Board would weaken economic considerations in managerial decision making. The unions, too, raised many objections. They argued that the participation scheme "constitutes a form of incorporation through which capitalist control of industry would be further legitimated and sustained". A second objection came from collective bargaining practitioners. They argued that "within the existing structure of society the role of the trade union is to act as an independent opposition to management in the pursuit of members' interest" (Batstone et al. 1983: 3, 4).

However, enthusiasm for industrial democracy was still strong enough in the late seventies to overcome the resistance. In July 1977 legislation was passed by Parliament to enable the national experiment to take place. The British government then appointed seven managers, seven union members and five outside members for the Post Office Board. A point of disagreement concerned the selection of union officials. The unions did not accept any interference of the government or of the Post Office in the selection of their members who were to sit on the Board. A compromise was found when the unions promised to select only senior members of "national standing" who did not have voting rights or executive functions on union committees responsible for collective bargaining. Neither management nor the unions wished to mix up enterpreneurial decision making with wage bargaining even though many issues were expected to come up in both institutions. Similar to the IRI-agreement both functions were carefully kept apart.

Union officials were integrated into the existing Post Office Board; new committees for participation were not created. This arrangement was supposed to raise serious conflicts of interest for the union officials (which were less acute for union members in the Comitati Consultivi Paritetici). Management insisted upon the joint responsibility of the Board members for all decisions. One of their arguments to oppose the participatory scheme was, in fact, that "the inevitable conflict of interest between collective responsibility for Board decisions and continued accountability to union members would be inimical to efficient management" (Batstone et al. 1983: 21). How would union officials deal with confidential information and how would they decide? After the tow-years experiment it turned out that the handling of confidential information did not raise serious problems. Union officials sitting on the Board only communicated with the top-secretaries of their union. On many occasions union officials also voted with management but, nevertheless, tried to bring the special interests of unions to bear.

Union officials wanted to get involved in the strategic decision making from the early stages of project planning; they wanted to consider the different options and to take part in the implementation of new investments and restructuring operations of the business. As one union member put it: "The present position is one in which the unions are virtually confined to sand-papering off the rough edges of decisions which they have had no hand in shaping. .... To be meaningful a system of participation must involve unions in both policy formulation and implementation ..." (Batstone et al. 1983: 22).

The experiment lasted only two years. It began in January 1978 and was not renewed after the conservative party had won the elections in 1979. Management became very hostile to the participation model for several reasons: First, between 1977 and 1979 "industrial relations had grown worse, disputes had increased, and performance declined" (p. 154). Management's expectation of joining a productivity coalition with the workforce was frustrated. Unions did not support some restructuring plans implemented during the period but opposed them by strike actions. Second, management became disillusioned about the behavior of the union officials on the Board. "The union nominees, for all their good intentions, lacked the necessary calibre to contribute to Bord debate and had focussed upon often detailed personnel and industrial relations issues, strengthening the inward-looking features of the Board at a time when it was necessary to adopt a more outward approach" (p. 154).

But also union officials became disenchanted. They fell victim of strategies which members of large bureaucracies work out to bypass and paralyse the decision centres of the organization. Projects when they finally arrived at the Board level had been filtered out. Options were deliberately omitted and the proposals made by the think-tank of the bureaucracy appeared as being inevitable. On many occasions important decisions did not reach the Post Office Board but were taken at the Management Board which was formally subordinated to the Post Office Board. Senior management sitting on the Management Board controlled and filtered information to prevent union officials from getting involved in important projects. Union officials were too isolated in a managerial environment to get the information elsewhere. "The Board consisted of 19 individuals who met for the equivalent of six or seven working days a year" (p. 67). They had to face a professional staff of about 1,300 members at Headquarters.

There are many similarities between the IRI-agreement and the Post Office experiment. In both cases, union officials were hoping to obtain strategic information to influence managerial decision making. Management expected unions to co-operate in the restructuring of the business. In the Post Office, these expectations were frustrated and both parties lost interest in the experiment. Nevertheless, one of the main reasons to explain the failure is the changing political environment. When the conservative government came into office the experiment was running out. It made it clear from the beginning that it had no interest in renewing the agreement. This shows that such experiments are contingent upon the outcome of the political process. If they are successful at all, they can only work in the long run. Union members have to acquire the necessary expertise to bring their counter-projects to bear. Lower managers, for instance, objected to "having to educate our Board members and it was claimed that they could no longer respect a Board that had to be spoonfed on first principles" (p. 69). Mutual trust which is important for a deferred exchange pattern also requires perseverance.

Hugh Scanlon argues that "the best form of industrial democracy is the extension of collective bargaining to which we know no limit" (Terry 1986: 163). But this optimistic view neglects the complicated relationship between collective bargaining and participation/ co-determination. For collective bargaining the strike is a legitimate weapon whereas industrial action tends to undermine participation experiments.

The Post Office experiment was wrecked on the ambiguous relation ship between strike and veto-rights. If unions are incorporated into participation schemes they have to have a chance to bring their counter-projects to bear without resorting to industrial action. If they have to rubberstamp and legitimize managerial decisions without being able to influence them union officials will soon lose interest. It also appears difficult for them to convince the rank and file and to prevent union members from taking industrial action. If unions have no veto-rights the costs of abandoning the participation scheme are low. Striking a balance between the hostile reactions of their members (whose expectations were frustrated) and the benefits of the experiment the unions came to the conclusion that the balance was negative.

Willman et al. (1985) have shown that the participation experiment at British Leyland was discontinued for similar reasons. In the late seventies management of British Leyland was experimenting with different forms of participation. When it became obvious that union officials were used to legitimize the lay-off of about twenty thousand workers without being able to influence the restructuring plans they left the joint committees.

4.2 Collective Agreements on Flexibility in France and West Germany

Flexibility became a catch-all concept to describe the transformation of the labour process and, what is more important, to legitimize whatever changes management has made in recent years. Changes which promised more flexibility were justified per se. It is almost impossible to give the term "flexibility" a precise meaning. It is directed not against a particular form of work organization but against barriers to change. In fact, there is no "flexible" work organization since all kinds of organization tend to become institutionalized and resistant to change. Flexibility means: anything goes. Taken as a political programme flexibility is directed against the very process of institutionalization. What management demands is to reduce the costs of change (Calvet 1986).

Flexibility cannot be achieved if management has to pay for every change in work practices it wishes to make. The productivity agreements which were concluded in many British firms in the sixties (Flanders 1970: 51) or the principle of "mutuality" which governed industrial relations at British Leyland differ radically from the present demands for flexibility. Flexibility means permanent change as part of the working conditions. When change becomes permanent the costs for change have to be reduced to a minimum.

Unions whose power is based on the control of the labour process were particularly weakened during the present crisis. "The more the interests to be represented are linked to specific working conditions ... the more the structure of interest representation is transformed in response to technical change" (Pizzorno 1977: 172). Whenever seniority rights, restrictive practices, and demarcation lines are an important condition for the stability of union power, the demand for flexibility must have disastrous consequences. If details of the work organization cannot be laid down in written agreements, if change becomes permanent and institutionalized, if change as such is no longer a lever for obtaining a higher remuneration package — how can unions exercise control over the work process?

One way in which unions reacted to this dilemma was a division of labour between the central union organization and workers' representatives on the plant level. Broad guidelines were negotiated in national agreements, detailed application and monitoring of general rules were left to local representatives. This institutional arrangement must give much autonomy to the local representatives. They have to organize a side management on the plant level to check the implementation of "flexibility". Local units must control transfers within the internal labour market, monitor the work organization, and the implementation of flexible time regimes. They need professional knowledge and have to be representative, i.e. accepted and legitimized by all workers (and not only union members).

Two collective agreements, recently negotiated in France and in Germany, illustrate the division of labour between a central bargaining unit and a local institution which checks the implementation on the plant level. Though both agreements have been negotiated in a different institutional environment they have many formal and substantive characteristics in common.

a) In May 1984 the French National Confederation of Employers (CNPF) and the three representative unions started negotiations on "flexibility". This time the employers (and not the unions) asked for collective bargaining demanding a flexible working time and a modification of the lay-off procedure. The central demand behind the employers' initiative was the abrogation of parts of the labour law.

The French labour law, a Bill of Rights for the working class, is in many firms more important than collective agreements. Given the relative weakness of the French union movement, the unions preferred to get from the state what they could not get from the employers. The demand of employers to abrogate parts of the labour law put the unions in a particularly difficult situation (Soubie 1986).

The sequence of negotiations before 1984 differs considerably from what happened after 1984. Before 1984 the unions usually too weak to obtain concessions from the employers addressed the state for labour legislation. Depending on the government in office and on the pressure the unions were able to mobilize more or less favorable labour laws passed the Parliament. Subsequently, the laws — though modified and adjusted to the particular circumstances in the different industries and firms — were taken over by collective agreements.

In May 1984 this sequence was reversed. The socialist government which by that time had already lost much of its popularity asked the unions to go ahead and to negotiate an abrogation of the labour law. The legal regulation of working time, of lay offs, and of time limited contracts was to be made "flexible", i.e. a central piece of social security was to be repealed. The government intended to wait for the outcome of collective bargaining and to revise the labour law according to the compromise reached between unions and employers.

The Employers' Association asked first for a modification of the law on the standard working time. As this demand has been put on the bargaining table in many European countries a few remarks on flexible time schedules are helpful for an understanding of the strategies of unions and employers (Schlecht 1987). Flexibility of working time has become a very powerful instrument for rationalization and higher productivity in recent years. Three parameters have to be negotiated to determine a flexible time schedule. First, the standard working time has to be fixed (e.g. 38 hours per week). Second, a range has to be defined within which the actual working time is allowed to fluctuate. The employers wanted this range to be as wide as possible (e.g. actual working time may fluctuate between sixty and twenty hours per week), the unions wanted to reduce it as much as possible (only half an hour per week). In figure 1 the actual working time fluctuates between 40 and 36 hours per week. Third, the period has to be defined during which the standard working time has to be reached on average. The employers wanted this period to be as long as possible (e.g. one year); the unions wanted to shorten this period. The German metal unions fixed it at two months. In Figure 1 the period for which the average is computed stretches over six months.

It is obvious that the wider the range within which the actual working time is allowed to fluctuate and the longer the period during which the standard working time has to be obtained on average, the more advantages a flexible arrangement has for the employer and the more meaningless the "standard" working time becomes. Employers may reduce overtime payment to a minimum because overtime is paid back in the second half of the period by leisure time. A further advantage is that the firm's labour force may be adjusted to seasonal changes in output without hiring or firing workers. The working time of a core workforce may, for instance, be adjusted to the seasonal cycles by working fifty hours during peak times and and only thirty hours when production has to be reduced. This "just-in-time" system for the workforce economizes on recruitment, training, and lay off costs. When the actual working time is allowed to fluctuate within a very wide range (e.g. between sixty and twenty hours) even the difference between full-time and part-time workers and between full-time and short-time working diminishes.[13] Deregulation and flexibility of working time means that "anything goes".

Of crucial importance are two questions: Firstly, how are the parameters of the flexible time system determined, i.e. how long is the standard working time, how wide is the range, and how long is the period for which the average is computed. Secondly, which parameters are negotiated on what level. The French employers wanted to negotiate broad guidelines

Figure 1:   Flexible Time Schedule

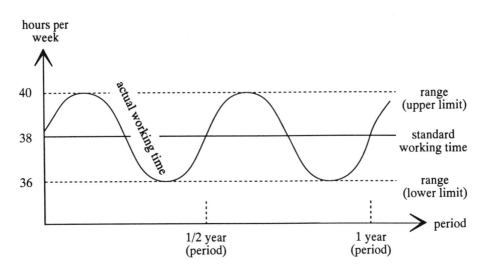

with t e unions at the national level but to leave the precise definition of the three parameters open) a second-round negotiation at the branch and the firm level. It is obvious that the emplc yment effects of a 35-hour week — negotiated at the branch level — may be offset by a] articularly "flexible" arrangement for the other two parameters — negotiated by produ :tivity coalitions on the shop floor.

As :cond demand which the French employers put on the bargaining table concerned the abrog tion of state control over lay offs. French firms have to ask the Labour Administration for au horization when they want to lay off workers. The procedure is quite complicated: Mana ;ement has to inform the works council (comité d'entreprise) which is allowed to discu ; the issue up to ninety days. Only after the written opinion of the "comité d'entreprise" is available may the employer submit a demand for lay-offs to the Labour Administration. Before management is finally allowed to lay off up to six months may pass during which the worker receives full pay. The bureaucratic control of lay-offs is the French equivalent for laws protecting employment in other countries (e.g. "cassa integrazione" in Italy). The Employers' Association demanded to cancel the state control and to shortcircuit the process by only informing the "comité d'entreprise" (Loubéjac 1986).

Thirdly, the employers asked to relax legal restrictions on part time, time limited contracts, and temporary work with the effect that the firm can more easily recruit temporary workers. This demand is closely related to the abrogation of the lay-off procedures. Social security and protection of employment is only granted for standard working contracts but not for temporary work. The proposal of employers was, in fact, a demand for a reduction in social security costs. Since the mid-seventies the French labour law allows time-limited contracts. Recent research has shown that about 30%-40% of the new unemployed had previously a time-limited contract. These kinds of contracts enforce the segmentation of labour markets and the marginalization of particular groups of workers (Salzberg 1985).

When the employers presented their demands the CGT rejected them straight away; FO and CFDT were arguing that abrogation of the labour law was inevitable.[14] Accepting some of these demands today had the advantage of getting something in exchange instead of being forced to accept all of them tomorrow when a new conservative government was expected to change the labour law.

In December 1984 a contract was worked out (but not yet signed) in which the employers obtained some concessions.[15] For instance, the period for which the standard working time was to be computed was fixed at one year, but the other two parameters — the standard time itself and the range — were left open to a second-round bargaining, particularly to negotiations at the branch level. Enterprise bargaining was restricted: If no branch agreement existed firms were not allowed to negotiate an abrogation of the labour law. Unions also obtained rights to information when new technology was to be introduced.

However, the concessions employers made were too little to convince the rank and file. FO and CFDT rallied behind the CGT and refused to sign the contract. The irony of the agreement of 1984 is that the incoming conservative government abrogated in 1985 the state control of lay-offs without giving the unions anything in exchange.

The agreement of 1984 is an example of a division of labour in collective bargaining between different levels. Broad guidelines, this time for the abrogation of labour law and for give-back contracts, are negotiated on higher levels, details of the regulation are open to a second-round bargaining lower down in the hierarchy. However, it has been shown that guidelines negotiated centrally may be offset by flexible regulations on the firm level. Unless the organizational and ideological links between productivity coalitions and the national unions are strong enough to prevent such outcomes the delegation of bargaining competence may end up in a fragmentation of the union movement (see various agreements mentioned in Sellier 1986).

b) In 1978/79 the German steel workers struck six weeks for the 35-hour week and lost the strike. Since then the German unions tried again and again to break the employers' resistance to accept a reduction of working time. In 1984, after a long a embittered strike which paralysed the automobile industry for six weeks a reduction of 1 1/2 hour was achieved. Why so much effort for so little a result?

The union's policy is more easily understood if one looks at the relationship between low economic growth, unemployment, and the decline of unionism. Since the depression of the mid-seventies the unions can no longer attract new members by high wage increases and a redistribution of income. In many years the inflation rate was well above the wage increase. During the same period the unemployment rate increased from 3% to about 10%. In the strongholds of unionism — steel, automobile, chemical industry — many jobs were lost and with them the union members. The demand for a lower working time replaced the demand for higher wages. The reduction of the working time was a union goal behind which all workers could rally, not only those with work but also the unemployed. It was a means and a hope to regain ideological strength and lost terrain. Because of their rights to co-determination on working time German unions are able to put pressure upon management. The standard working time is fixed in collective agreements which are legally binding. The works councils have a veto right when management wants to work overtime.

The research institute of the unions carried out many studies to demonstrate that up to 60% of a working time reduction could be used for the creation of new jobs. The reduction of working time was a policy for a global regulation of the economy to reduce unemployment and to protect the remaining jobs. Since the late seventies the German government had increasingly abandoned a global Keynesian economic policy and had favored neo-classical laissez-faire. The unions tried to step in and fought for a central regulation of working time because it promised at least a moderate reduction of unemployment.

When the employers presented their counter-strategy — flexibility of working time — the unions offered embittered resistance. From the beginning of the strike it was clear that the employers' demand for flexibility would offset the positive employment effects and, thus, wreck the union's strategy to regain strength and credibility.

As employers and the union were unable to find a compromise, an agreement was, finally, found through arbitration.[16] Unions obtained a reduction of the standard working time to 38.5 hours, but the agreement was opened up to second-round bargaining with the works councils for a flexible use of working time. The range was fixed at 3 hours (between 37 and 40 hours per week); the period during which the standard working time (38.5 hours) had to be obtained on average was fixed at two months. The firms were also allowed to negotiate different regulations for different groups of workers. The firms were particularly interested in obtaining a more flexible regulation for qualified workers and employees. The unions were not able to prevent the "flexibilization" of working time, but they enforced a precise definition of the three parameters of flexibility (standard time, range, period).

Three years later, in May 1987, the metal unions concluded a new agreement, this time without industrial action. The standard working time was further reduced to 37.5 weeks, but the period during which the standard time had to be obtained was extended to six months. The range for fluctuations was not precisely defined but left open to shop floor bargaining. Thus, the unions paid for a further reduction of the standard time with more flexibility.

The crucial question for the unions remains to what extent the works councils are willing and are able to respect the "spirit" of the collective agreement. As has been shown above the employment effects of a working time reduction may be more or less offset depending on the degree of flexibility which is negotiated on the level of the enterprise. Different studies which have looked at the implementation of the collective agreement on the enterprise level confirmed the union's expectation that the works councils did not accept an excessive use of flexibility.[17] This may be explained by the high proportion of members of the works council belonging to an industrial union (about 80%). There is usually no competition between rival organizations which may prevent the works councils from falling in line with the union policy.

5. Conclusions

a) Is the devolution of bargaining only a cyclical tendency which will be reversed with the next swing in the economic wave or does it represent a stable structural shift in the system of industrial relations? Any cyclical shift observed at its beginning may be wrongly taken for a long lasting trend. In a comparative study on recent trends in industrial relations in Western Europe Treu (1985: 41) argues that "among the most prominent aspects of convergence is the trend towards centralization of the collective bargaining structure". Sellier puts forward a different hypothesis. Analysing recent developments in French industrial relations he points to the remarkable change of attitudes of the French Employers' Association. Before the economic crisis the employers refused to negotiate locally because they regarded enterprise bargaining as being little short of "anarchy" (Sellier 1986: 773). After 1975 French employers were in favour of enterprise agreements. Whenever possible they try to reach an agreement on the firm level. Sellier explains the change in attitudes by the changing labour market conditions which affected employers and unions in opposite directions (see also Streeck 1984: 296).

Before 1975 a second-round enterprise bargaining was very tempting for workers to exploit their strong position in the labour market. Employers tried to avoid the inflationary affects of enterprise bargaining by concentrating negotiations on the branch or even national level. After 1975 when the unions were too weak to put pressure upon management they were less at a disadvantage when negotiating centrally. Sellier interprets the shift of collective bargaining towards the enterprise level as a cyclical movement contingent upon the relative power of unions and employers.

In section two I have argued that the shift towards enterprise bargaining and the formation of productivity coalitions is strongly influenced by technical change, new forms of the work organization, and the structural transformation of world markets. The trend towards decentralized bargaining is likely to survive the present economic crisis.

b) One institutional option to control centrifugal tendencies is the implementation of a Works Council system. Though this might sound paradoxically, the analysis of the flexible working time system in section 4.2 has shown that the German Works Council may buffer the negative consequences of decentralization. Provided, however, that the unions do not lose their hold on the Works Councils. If the unions are successful (as they were in West-Germany) in integrating the Works Councils by "interlocking directorates" into the union movement the Works Councils may check and control the firm's personnel and economic policy. If the unions lose this control the Works Councils will, in fact, strengthen the centrifugal tendencies.

Another obstacle has to be taken into account which may make it difficult to implement a Works Council system. Decentralization has a different impact on the central union organization depending on the relative strength, ideological complexion, and autonomy of the local units. In Italy and Britain, for instance, tendencies towards decentralization to the firm level usually strengthen the more radical wings of the union movement.[18] A revalorization of the position of the German Works Council, however, strengthens the more moderate wings of the union movement. The works council elected by all employees of the company is usually more prepared to accept a managerial point of view than the union officials of the central headquarters. Decentralization has different effects on the union movement in different European countries. It strengthens different political trends depending on the internal organization of the unions. This makes it difficult to put forward a general hypothesis about the outcome of decentralization.

d) Marin (1982, 1986) has shown that the strength of corporatist arrangements is based upon a "generalized political exchange". Concessions being made in one subsystem at a particular point in time are rewarded later on in another subsystem. For instance, the acquiescence of the unions to accept lay-offs in the steel and automobile industry may be rewarded by a generous law to use the unemployment insurance for reskilling programmes. This kind of "generalized political exchange" is more difficult to accept if productivity coalitions are cut off from more encompassing organizational networks. They are forced to restrict the exchange to the firm level. This is one reason to explain why the participation model at British Leyland failed. The workers expected immediate rewards for their acceptance to lay off 25.000 workers which management was not able to give at that time.

Notes

1   The present article has been written when I was a Jean Monnet Fellow at the European University Institute, Florence. I am very grateful for helpful comments to B. Bercusson, M. Lazarson, B. Marin, and P. Schmitter.
2   One of the most important reasons for this regulation was to force the employers to recognize unions as a legitimate bargaining agent (Soubie 1983, Amadieu 1986).
3   For details see L'Espresso 21 Sept. 1980, pp. 188-195 ("Torino ha la febbre, l'Italia si ammala"); L'Espresso 19 Oct. 1980, pp. 260-274 ("Guai ai vinti!"); Comito (1982).
4   In France, management and unions were unable to reach an agreement on a recovery plan for the Peugeot plant at Poissy. The dispute led to the bankruptcy of the former Chrysler/Simca plant (Windolf 1985). In Germany, the introduction of new technology in the motor car industry was negotiated on the shop floor between management and the works council without industrial dispute (Windolf 1985a).
5   A tendency towards decentralization and the emergence of productivity coalitions has been observed in many European countries although the different authors use different terms: "micro-corporatism" (Teubner 1987:21); "co-operative alliances" (Streeck 1984:297); "syndicalisme d'entreprise" (Amadieu 1986:pp. 495-500); "accordo di produttività, rapporti di coalizione, coinvolgimento del sindacato" (Negrelli 1982: 508); etc. etc.
6   Galbraith (1972) prophesied in the late sixties the "decline" of unionism: "The union belongs to a particular stage in the development of the industrial system. When that stage passes so does the union in anything like its original position of power (p. 275)." "The loss of union membership is not a temporary setback pending the organization of white-collar employees and engineers but the earlier stages of a permanent decline (p. 264)."
7   The evolutionary development shown in Table 1 is circular rather than linear. It starts with a qualified workforce (A), passes through a stage of dequalification (B), and returns to a stage of reskilling (C).
8   Formal/substantive law are concepts developed by M. Weber (1978). Formal law ("formales Recht") only regulates the "formal" procedures of a market economy; substantive law (materielles Recht) sets standards and goals which have to be attained. See also Nonet/Selznick (1978).

9 Research reports on the introduction of new technology and participation of workers in several Italian firms are given in "Quaderni di Formazione ISFOL" (Istituto per lo Sviluppo della Formazione Professionale dei Lavoratori), No. 3, 1985. A report about French firms introducing participation models is given in: Le Monde Affaires 23 May 1987: "L'entreprise, la coqueluche des politiques".

10 The agreements are published in: Rivista Italiana di Diritto del Lavoro 4 (1985), pp. 10-19, part III and 5 (1986), pp. 70-76, part III. Detailed information is given in a special issue of "Industria e Sindacato", No. 21, 31 May 1985: "Il futuro delle relazioni industriali — modelli a confronto". (Translations from the agreements by the author.)

11 In July 1984 the Italian Metal Employers' Association published a pamphlet which clearly shows that private employers do not accept the participation model negotiated for IRI. On the contrary, they recommend to reduce the influence of the unions (see "Imprese e lavoro" in: Rivista Italiana di Diritto del Lavoro 4 (1985), pp. 36-52). The hard line was confirmed when in early 1987 Alfa Romeo was taken over by FIAT. The prestigious motor car firm Alfa Romeo was in public ownership and belonged to the IRI-Holding-Company. FIAT refused to take over the IRI-contract. The "Comitati Consultivi Paritetici" were disbanded.

12 Information on investment and new technology is the most important benefit unions receive from participation agreements. They regard it as a first step to obtain rights to co-determination on the introduction of new technology (Windolf 1985a). In Italy some collective agreements on information rights were concluded in the mid-seventies, but only on the level of the industry, i.e. employers had to inform the unions about the future development of the industry, but not about individual firms (Della Rocca/Negrelli 1983). Even this information was given reluctantly (Romagnoli 1985: 160).

13 The demands of the employers and the reactions of the unions are reported in: Handelsblatt 3 Febr. 1987; 24 Febr. 1987; 25 March 1987.

14 CGT = Conféderation Générale du Travail" (largest French union, strong communist influence); CFDT = Confédération française démocratique du travail (affiliated to the French Socialist Party); FO = Force Ouvrière (founded in 1946 after the split of the CGT, "independent" union).

15 The agreement is published in: Droit Social 1985, no.2, pp. 99-103 (Protocole du 16 décembre 1984 sur l'adaptation des conditions d'emploi).

16 The agreement is published in: Recht der Arbeit 1984, no. 6, p. 362-63.

17 Results of a survey on the implementation of flexible working time are reported in: Handelsblatt 24 Febr. 1987; see also Seifert (1986).

18 The Alfa-Romeo/FIAT agreement of 1987 provides an interesting illustration for this hypothesis. When FIAT took over Alfa Romeo a new collective agreement had to be negotiated. Productivity at Alfa Romeo was 35-40% lower compared to FIAT. For several years Alfa Romeo was a big loss maker. FIAT insisted on new work practices and on the disbanding of group work introduced by a collective agreement in 1981. Negotiations between the unions and FIAT took place at Rome, at the headquarters of the three representative Italian unions (CGIL, CISL, UIL). Since February 1986 the works council (consiglio di fabbrica) at the Alfa Romeo plants had not convened. It was not involved in the negotiations. The unions tried to negotiate a restructuring plan centrally and to keep the more radical local union sections out. When the unions organized a referendum to get the results of the agreement confirmed by the workforce, 9760 workers voted yes, 9688 voted no. The tiny majority in favor of the referendum illustrates the weakness of the strategy and the vulnerability of the headquarters to local pressures. (La Stampa 4 April and 27 May 1987).

Joint Regulation, Meso-Games and Political Exchange in Swedish Industrial Relations

Victor A. Pestoff

1. Introduction

1.1 Socio-Economic Bargaining

Socio-economic bargaining or negotiations between divergent interests permeate Swedish society and have long served as a symbol for the politics of compromise. Major areas of social, economic and political relations fall outside the competitive sphere and are governed by social barter or political exchange rather than impersonal market forces and party competition.

However, socio-economic bargaining in Sweden differs in a number of respects — including the degree of governmental intervention and formal institutionalization — from socio-economic planning procedure in several continental European countries. The Swedish government has never found it necessary to establish a Social and Economic Council, which constitutes the focal point of studies of concertation on liberal corporatism (see Lehmbruch, 1977 & 1984). Instead, informal negotiations concerning macro-socio-economic goals between the leaders of labor-market organizations, the government, the Central Bank and, at times, the opposition parties have shifted in form and venue in the period since World War II. Negotiations at Harpsund, Haga and Rosenbad represent this phenomenon at different times and in different settings (see Nedelmann & Meier, 1979 and Pestoff, 1984a). Nor was it necessary, as it was with the Austrian Chamber of Commerce (see Marin, 1982), to stipulate mandatory membership in a single national peak organization in order to bring the various organized interests together at the negotiating table. Rather, negotiations and bargaining between the various concerned organized interests started in a number of diverse arenas as early as the late 1930s and early 1940s. These arenas included not only wages and working conditions, agricultural and food prices and housing rents but also raw-material prices for the wood and paper industries, taxi fares and, more recently, crisis industries and/or economically depressed areas, to name but a few. Thus, the Swedish system of socio-economic bargaining is comprehensive, encompassing the most important arenas of society.

Socio-economic bargaining may be tripartite, but in Sweden it often takes a bipartite form. Collective bargaining and industrial relations are a special case of joint regulation which will be explored in greater detail below. Centralized organizations represent the interests of capital and labor, and they are sometimes constrained by minimal state intervention in certain areas, but the state is usually a junior partner. Mostly, however, collective agreements between them are, at best, exposed to *post hoc* comments by the Secretary of Finance. A different situation faces the authorities in the area of consumer policy. In lieu of a "spontaneous and independent" consumer movement, the government encouraged various women's organizations to collaborate in forming an interlocutor for well-organized producers during the 1940s and 1950s (Pestoff, 1988a and 1989). When this failed, it turned to the trade unions instead, coopting them alongside the consumer cooperatives into functioning as a countervailing power (*ibid.*). In the area of agricultural and food policy, a similar development resulted in the creation of the Consumer Delegation of the Swedish Agricultural Marketing Board in 1963, at the initiative of the government. Ever since then, the semi-annual agricultural compensation and food-price negotiations supervised by the Board have normally been left up to the Consumer and Producer Delegations or the "partners" themselves. However, here the government and the *Riksdag* set their seal of approval on food-price agreements. Annual rent negotiations between well-organized tenants and landlords provide yet another example of negotiation without governmental interference.

1.2 Meso-Games

Common to many of these examples of a "negotiated economy" (Hernes, 1978) is a temporal proximity which permits informal coordination between various arenas, rather than a dependence on grandiose, formal package deals between all economic interests. However, certain of these arenas are more directly interrelated by virtue of the participation of the same organized actors and the similarity of the issue content. Thus, collective bargaining and various aspects of industrial relations share many common denominators. By industrial relations, I mean in particular work-environment regulation, co-determination, labor-market insurance and economic democracy. Each of these areas is a separate sector within the trans-sectoral arena of industrial relations. Additional examples, such as the Labor Court, arbitration and mediation will not be examined herein.

All these are highly interrelated, but not to the extent of being mirror images. Each has its own rules of the game and balance of power, and therefore its own distinct institutional structure and dynamics. Each area of industrial relations may be envisioned as a separate, but nevertheless kindred meso-game (Marin, 1985), following its own logic and finding its own solution at the meso level. However, developments in one area of industrial relations may affect those in other areas. Thus, prolonged intransigence and irreconcilable differences in one area may eventually rule out continued compromise in another. The interrelation of these meso-games is one of the topics explored in this chapter.

However, even individual areas of industrial relations can often be divided into a number of sub-areas, as the work environment readily illustrates. It is first at this lower level of abstraction that it becomes possible to describe the bi- and tripartite cooperative institutions of joint regulation and to see the corporative network established to facilitate cooperation and conflict resolution in Swedish industrial relations.

Finally, developments at the meso level are not only interrelated, but also exert influence on the macro level. The total lack of compromise in any one meso-game may not only negatively affect developments in other areas of industrial relations: it may also result in a crisis for the political system itself. The very rules of the game for public socio-economic bargaining or tripartism may be questioned. Corporative institutions which ensure integrated but balanced participation by organized capital and labor in public policy-making may be challenged by one or the other. A threat to boycott these corporative institutions, combined with the development of informal techniques for obtaining influence, may seriously jeopardize such institutions.

1.3 Joint Regulation

However, before the interrelation of various meso-games in Swedish collective bargaining and industrial relations is examined, a number of comments are warranted by Traxler's contribution to this volume. In it, he attempts to combine various perspectives on industrial relations found in Marxism, systems theory and actor-centered theory (this volume). In doing so, he focuses on the material and institutional conditions as well as the intentional actions of organized capital and labor and the state. In discussing the problems of organizing and institutionalizing collective action by the interdependent but antagonistic interests of capital and labor, he calls attention to the class-specific nature of the problems facing each one of these groups (*ibid.*). In particular, he notes that their organizational dilemmas are complementary, rather than identical. The problem of labor is to recruit members, i.e. one of associability, while that of capital is to obtain members' loyalty, i.e. one of governability (*ibid.*). Neither capital nor labor is able to solve its organizational problems unaided. Once they recognize each other as interlocutors and approve the rules regulating their relationship (*ibid.*) in collective bargaining, they therefore revert to reciprocal assistance.

From a Swedish perspective, it should be noted that mutual recognition occurred more than 80 years ago, while the principles governing collective-bargaining procedures were agreed on nearly 50 years ago. Several of the examples Traxler employs to illustrate reciprocal assistance, including the deduction of trade-union dues by employers and higher wage rates for employees who refuse to be part of the centralized wage agreements, are easily observed in Sweden.

Swedish experience — the highest union density in the world (80-90 per cent of employees are unionized) and one of the most centralized employers' organizations anywhere — thus does more than merely corroborate the effectiveness of the long-standing reciprocal assistance between organized capital and labor. However, once firmly established, both organized capital and labor have continued to develop their own organizational properties and capacities. They have not only surmounted the organizational dilemmas they faced; they have even successfully surpassed them, and perhaps also transposed them. Thus, organized labor no longer has to struggle to obtain members among blue- and white-collar workers, since it already has their near-total adhesion. Rather, the growing divisions between civil-servant and private-employee unions are rapidly turning cohesion into the principal dilemma facing the Swedish trade unions.

The organizational innovations of Swedish employers have greatly augmented their capacity for governance, and also help to explain their unusual degree of centralization. The economic and legal obligations placed on SAF's members can result in severe penalties for non-complying members. Members can be and have been fined up to 3 per cent of their total annual wage bill for permitting excessive wage drift or for breaking ranks during collective-bargaining rounds. Fines imposed directly on Volvo or Saab-Scania by SAF in the late 1970s illustrate efforts to curb wage drift. The fate of a member company during the 1986 round of collective bargaining for salaried employees underlines SAF's options in terms of members who break ranks, or who even suggest doing so. One member firm, in an interview on local radio, stated that it had no desire to lock out its employees as SAF had ordered. The labor dispute was subsequently resolved without an open conflict. Nevertheless, this firm was expelled from SAF and its relevant branch EO. It also forfeited its 3 per cent guarantee commitment. SAF has therefore successfully resolved the problem of governance or cohesion. Evidence presented below suggests that its efforts are now aimed at obtaining the adhesion of all private firms. Thus, both organized capital and labor have resolved the basic organizational dilemmas traditionally facing them. It may therefore be stated that their organizational development justifies reference to "Swedish exceptionalism".

According to Traxler, whereas the antagonistic and asymmetrical relationship may result in reciprocal assistance in the area of collective bargaining, owing to a mutual interest in cooperating to overcome their organizational dilemma, this is not the case when it comes to corporative-interest intermediation. Capitalists' role in accumulating and reinvesting capital results in the social primacy of capital accumulation and the economic domination of labor by capital (*ibid.*). This leads to an asymmetry in strategic options facing capital and labor. Besides the conflictive nature of the pursuit of their interests, there is an inequality. Labor must take the offensive and initiative in promoting its interests, while capital can limit its activities to defending and upholding its privileges (*ibid.*, see also Streeck, 1988).

Once again, Swedish experience bears witness to this asymmetrical relationship in collective bargaining and industrial relations. However, since the social primacy of capital itself was called in question by the wage-earner funds, an era of overt conflict has replaced the politics of compromise. Collective bargaining and industrial relations are institutionally separated from politics, and the most visible signs of the political crisis resulting from the wage-earner funds may, for the time being, be the institution of lay representation in public policy-making. However, even Swedish industrial relations shows clear indications of negative developments, owing to the struggle over the wage-earner funds. Employers now seem intent on deinstitutionalizing industrial relations and decentralizing collective bargaining.

1.4 Institutional Class Conflict

The role of organized labor and capital in modern capitalist societies is contingent upon a number of factors. Historical traditions, the strength of organized labor and the domination of social democratic parties are among the factors traditionally cited to explain variations in the institutionalization of class conflict in advanced industrialized nations. Two recent studies examine these variations broadly and in depth, and need not be recapitulated here (Crouch & Pizzorno, eds., 1978 and Goldthorpe, ed., 1984).

The role of organized labor and capital should be envisaged not only in terms of institutionalized class conflict, but as part of a general pattern of social and political bargaining — one which also reflects historical traditions, the strength of organized capital and labor, etc. More specifically, collective bargaining, work environment regulation, industrial and/or economic democracy are independent but integral components of an overall system of social and political bargaining. However, this larger context is all too often ignored, overlooked or merely written off as the "environment" when various aspects of industrial relations are analysed. Certain isolated elements are examined out of context. Generalizations concerning the institutionalization of class conflict or social and political bargaining are made with little or no reference to the numerous other relevant aspects, or to the institutional setting.

One intention of this paper is to focus on the interrelationship between institutionalized class conflict and social and political bargaining in Sweden. Collective bargaining, work-environment regulation, co-determination, joint labor-market insurance and economic democracy are all interrelated at the macro and micro levels, as well as at the meso-level. This paper aims to clarify the nature of this interrelationship at the meso-level.

The role of organized capital and labor varies from one area to another in Sweden. There is a greater or lesser degree of joint regulation by capital and labor in the different sectors mentioned above. In those characterized by extensive joint regulation, the very reliance on solutions which are mutually acceptable to organized capital and labor precludes the need for the state to assume major responsibility. However, the state is seldom entirely absent from any of these arenas. Its role as an employer grew dramatically in the 1970s, but it usually plays a subordinate role to organized capital and labor, by legitimizing their joint-regulation efforts and/or providing the legal support and institutional framework enabling joint regulation to continue functioning successfully. But Traxler's distinction between state regulation and direct intervention in joint-regulation systems of capital and labor seems to miss this point. The theoretical argument concerning "state-free regulation of industrial relations" ignores the practical consequences. The more successfully capital and labor resolve the problems of industrial relations through joint regulation, the smaller the burden on the state and the less the need for it to intervene directly. Consequently, the greater the resources available to it for establishing overall socio-economic goals, governing, etc. Thus, in comparative terms, whether the state is burdened with repeated crises of industrial conflict or not is of no small importance, as the increasing level of strikes among civil servants in the 1980s illustrates.

The literature on private-interest government argues that the state devolves power from the public sector to private organizations which then, embellished with quasi-public status, are able to govern their own members. But both historically and in terms of the options facing policy-makers, this appears oversimplified. To the extent that organized capital and labor had already successfully resolved their open clashes, it was not necessary for the state to assume responsibility for bringing order to this sector of society. Admittedly, the threat of state intervention could, and in Sweden in the 1930s did, spur these antagonistic organizations to seek compromise rather than conflict, thus changing it from one of the countries with the highest figures for strikes to one of those with the lowest after the 1938 Saltsjöbaden Agreement.

Furthermore, the very establishment of mutual cooperation between the antagonistic interests of organized capital and labor yields alternatives that would simply not exist without joint regulation. Organized capital and labor do not necessarily seek or promote political solutions to economic and social problems. Rather, they reach agreements which resolve the problems before the state is obliged to intervene. Such agreements often result in bipartite structures, which serve as forums for their mutual cooperation. Thus, we find that the organized interests of capital and labor actively extend their sphere of control rather than merely receiving powers devolved from the state.

1.5 Organizational Participation in Public Policy-Making

Sweden was described as an "organizationally saturated" society by G. Heckscher more than 40 years ago (1946), when he also distinguished between totalitarian corporatism in Italy and "free" or democratic corporatism in Sweden (*ibid.*). Already at that time, he noted that organizational participation in Swedish public policy-making was very extensive, permeating the whole of society (*ibid.*). He analyzed the growth and development of this participation in terms of the unique needs of the state during periods of general mobilization of economic, social and military resources precipitated by the two World Wars and the Great Depression (*ibid.*).

The roots of this participation can be traced back more than a century (see Back, 1967 on the period 1870-1910). In Scandinavia, the right of association and the feudal privileges enjoyed by guilds survived longer than in the rest of Europe (Bendix, 1964). The interval between the dissolution of Swedish guilds (1846) and the removal of restrictions on economic interest organizations (1864) was exceptionally short (Pestoff, 1977). Business interest associations and trade unions began to appear shortly afterwards (Pestoff, 1977 and 1988b). Crouch argues that the shorter the interval between the destruction of ancient guilds and the construction of typically modern interest organizations, the more highly motivated both the state and these organizations are to cooperate in establishing neo-corporatist institutions (this volume).

Organizational participation in public policy-making takes place through formal as well as informal channels. Figure 1 below outlines and numbers the various steps of the Swedish legislative process, from the formal initiative of a motion to the *Riksdag* until its final implementation. Interest organizations feature as legitimate participants in some of these steps. This represents points where they are formally integrated into public policy-making. Interest organizations have also developed informal channels of influence. Thus, integrated organizational participation in public policy-making is highly visible, formal and permanent owing to the institutions of *ad hoc* parliamentary commissions (No. 5), the *remiss* system (No. 6) and lay representation on the governing boards of central administrative agencies (No. 14). Less visible — and perhaps less formal and legitimate, but not necessarily less permanent — participation in the legislative process takes place in at least three additional ways.

First, the *Haga*-like consultations (No. 0) prior to the initiation of a Bill in the *Riksdag* provides one alternative. Secondly, the practice of circulating draft proposals (*delning av koncept till regeringsbeslut*) to private bodies (between Nos. 4 & 5 and Nos. 7 & 8), before their approval by the Government-in-Council, is now well established. It is similar to the *remiss* system in some respects, but confined to a few powerful interest organizations. Thirdly, several business organizations acknowledge contacts with individual MPs on an *ad hoc* basis (No. 1), as well as systematic contacts with standing committees of the *Riksdag* (No. 10) and with the political parties or the whole *Riksdag* (No. 11). This phenomenon is similar to the American practice of lobbying. Finally, business organizations also maintain informal but direct contacts with the directors of central administrative agencies (No. 14). Both the second and third informal channels of influence have been developed by sectoral or branch associations rather than peak organizations, but with the tacit consent of the latter.

Each of these phases in turn will be discussed briefly in order to provide a clearer conception of the full range of organizational participation in public policy-making. Consult Figure 1 for details.

In terms of organizational participation in public policy-making, we observe that in the sphere of consultation on general economic policy (step No. 0) both organizations and the state have retained their freedom of participation. Thus consultations on income policy have taken neither a formal nor a binding form in Sweden. Nor is there a Social and Economic Council. Note the similarity between Sweden and Austria in this respect (see Marin, 1987a). Moreover, in terms of agenda setting, organizations can themselves engage in activities designed to obtain a place on the current political agenda for an issue they feel strongly enough about, if they support it energetically.

Unlike their counterparts in most other Western democracies, government departments in Sweden do not play a prominent role in the early phases of law-making, nor later in their implementation. This may primarily be explained in terms of the very limited staff resources at their command. Thus Royal Commissions or *ad hoc* committees (No. 5) appointed by the responsible minister normally constitute a preliminary stage in the formulation of government legislative proposals. A variety of interest organizations are traditionally represented on such committees.

We find, however, that the participation of both organizations and politicians in *ad hoc* parliamentary committees is declining rapidly in favor of that of civil servants. The latter

Figure 1   The Legislative Process — 14 Steps From Initiation to Implementation in Brief

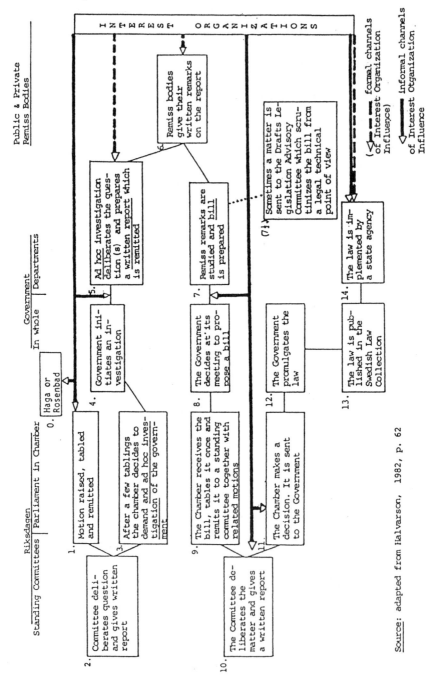

Source: adapted from Halvarson, 1982, p. 62

now contribute nearly two-thirds of the members of such committees, while MPs and organizational representatives constitute the remaining third, on an equal basis. Organizational participation has, however, expanded systematically in the *remiss* system (No. 6). Professional and general interest organizations have, ever since the 1920s, remitted a written reply to almost all of the proposals made by *ad hoc* parliamentary committees. Employee and employer organizations have increased their participation over the decade, remitting their reactions to nine-tenths and two-thirds respectively of all *ad hoc* parliamentary committees (see Pestoff, 1984a, for further details).

The above-mentioned, little-known process called the "circulating of draft proposals for decisions by the Government-in-Council" (*delning av koncept till regeringsbeslut*) demonstrates certain similarities to the *remiss* system, but serves quite different functions. Drafts of the government's proposals usually concern one of two matters, either the instructions for a given *ad hoc* parliamentary committee (between Nos. 4 & 5) or a draft Bill before it is sent to the *Riksdag* (between Nos. 7 & 8). This informal process is limited exclusively to a few business interest associations and perhaps to a limited number of additional interest organizations. The handful of selected participants in this process are the best staffed and financed organizations in Sweden. It is considered the most important channel of influence by initiated organization spokesmen (see Pestoff, 1983a, 1983b and 1984b for further details).

Finally, before turning to policy implementation, it may be noted that yet another informal practice has taken root, one which shows certain similarities to the American phenomenon of "lobbying". It has nevertheless adapted itself to Swedish conditions and, thus far, proved less corrupt. Numerous business interest organizations maintain regular and systematic contacts with one or more standing committees of the *Riksdag* (No. 10) or with individual members (No. 1) or other groups of members (No. 11). They have developed this practice into an art and such contacts are deemed very important and influential by many of them (see Pestoff, 1984b for further details). Even the central administrative agencies are increasingly subject to these informal pressure-group tactics.

Once a Bill has been passed by the *Riksdag* and promulgated as a law, it must be implemented. But, as noted earlier, in Sweden government departments are relatively small organizations with limited staff resources. Instead, the central administrative agencies and boards are responsible for executing policy decisions. Thus, the central task for government departments is to plan for policies or changes in existing programs, while policy implementation clearly belongs to the domain of the central administrative agencies. Major legislative reforms often take the form of "frame laws" (*ramlagar*), which provide the impetus and direction of the desired changes and set certain constraints, but otherwise give central administrative agencies (No. 14) a free hand to work out the detailed implementation of the reform.

Lay boards were first introduced into modern Swedish public administration in 1908 with the establishment of the National Power Administration (*Vattenfall*). By the late 1970s, approximately four out of five central administrative agencies were governed by lay boards.

Hadenius groups the 481 lay representatives found on these 62 boards into three categories: civil servants, who occupy 41 per cent of the seats; politicians, who have 23 per cent, and interest group representatives, who occupy 36 per cent (1978: 26).

There is a clear tendency towards an overall balance in lay representation between trade unions on the one hand and business and employers' interests on the other. This results in a corporate tripartite constellation in which the politicians and civil servants represent the "neutral" interests of the state.

Parity or a balance of forces in interest-group representation is found both in traditional sectors, where opposing interests are articulated through clearly demarcated organizations, and in less clearly delimited sectors. Agencies responsible for implementing labor-market policy or work-environment regulation belong to the classic areas in which the opposing interests of workers and employers are organized into trade unions and employers' organizations. But even in areas such as agricultural (food) policy or consumer policy, where one of the opposing parties (the consumers) notoriously faces difficulties in formally organizing itself, the evidence suggests a policy of promoting numerical parity or a balance of forces in the composition of the governing bodies of central administrative agencies. In the case of consumer policy, a corporate pattern of coopting the trade unions and consumer cooperatives into filling the gap is pursued. Parity is thus achieved by indirectly matching the organizational representation of producer and consumer interests (Pestoff, 1988a).

This evidence suggests that achieving parity or a balance of forces in interest-group representation is a norm behind the tripartite or corporate constellation of Swedish lay boards. Taken as a whole, Swedish public policy-making provides ample evidence of parity or balanced representation of interest groups in most phases discussed above. Lobbying provides the most striking exception. This distinct tripartite pattern cannot therefore be attributed to the motives of a single sector or policy area. Thus it does not seem realistic to assume that the purpose of parity is to produce a "hostage" effect in one area (such as work-environment regulation), thereby accommodating and attenuating conflicting interests, while producing a "balancing" effect for the purpose of accentuating or exacerbating a conflict of interest in another sector or area (such as consumer policy).

1.6 Corporatism and Political Exchange

Political scientists and sociologists in a number of countries note that Sweden has well-articulated neo-corporatist institutions. Some maintain that these institutions place Sweden among the leading corporatist democracies. Schmitter's distinction between "societal corporatism" and "state corporatism" (1974) is similar to Heckscher's. Sweden ranks high among the countries characterized by societal corporatism, according to Schmitter (1981). Lehmbruch places Sweden among the leading Western nations in terms of strength of corporatism (1982). Crouch distinguishes between neo-corporatist and liberal polities, and places Sweden among the former (1985). Paloheimo draws similar conclusions (1984). Finally, Wilensky uses three categories for the 18 OECD countries included in his study, i.e. "corporatist democracies", "corporatism without full-scale labor participation" and "fragmented and decentralized political economies" (1983).

Neo-corporatism focuses on institutionalized cooperation of the organized, antagonistic interests of labor and capital and the performance of various political economies according to Marin (1983, p. 199) or the cooperative regulation of class conflict (*ibid.*, p. 209). Bargaining channels develop, according to Wilensky, for the interaction of well-organized, highly centralized blocs, especially labor, employer and professional associations in countries with relatively centralized governments which routinely seek the advice of such organized interests. Furthermore, the peak bargains reached by federations of labor, employers and other professional interests not only help to blur previous distinctions between public and private; they are normally very broad in scope, rather than merely focusing on limited labor-market issues (1983, p. 71). Such bargains normally cover the major issues of modern political economy, such as inflation and economic growth, prices and wages, investments and taxes, unemployment, the balance of payments and exchange rates, as well as social policy. Marin also discusses comprehensive systems of interest inter-mediation, '... which extend the negotiation space and thereby bind opponents to each other. Although this increases the conflict potentials through enlarged competences, it simultane-ously disperses them over a large number of cooperative bodies and raises the costs of these interdependent conflicts, allowing for a piecemeal processing of demands'. (1983, p. 215)

Thus, he concludes, cooperative intermediation works either comprehensively or not at all.

In this volume, Marin discusses the permanent yet tenuous transactions between func-tionally interdependent organizations with competing or even antagonistic interests, such as organized labor and capital, which are not regulated by law. He refers to such ongoing bargaining as generalized political exchange (1985 and above), which he defines as: 'mutually contingent, macropolitical and economic transactions between autonomous, organized collective actors with divergent/competitive/antagonistic but functionally inter-dependent interests, the binding character of which cannot be based on law and contract.' (*ibid.*, p. 8)

A central feature of the processes he describes is an ordered interdependence of multidimensional transactions. This ordered interdependence may be either hierarchic, horizontal or sequential. Thus, a comprehensive set of interrelated meso-games helps to ensure the governance of the whole system. This is not achieved by a single historical compromise, although this might well facilitate it, but should rather be conceived of as a cor-poratist mode of interest intermediation which develops over long periods of time. We are thus clearly not dealing with fragmented and decentralized political economies with disconnected, encapsulated, isolated collective actors or parts, but rather with an extended network of interdependent actors and parts (*ibid.*).

The unique combination of conflict and cooperation accounting for the concept of generalized political exchange suggests the transformation of class struggle into a perma-nent series of skirmishes of position between collective actors with mutually contingent interests. The rules of the game define the opportunity structure for political transactions as

well as the constraints on the possible strategies. Associational politics may also concern
the rules of the game itself, their scope, what game to play, who may play and in which meso-
game, etc. The current Swedish debate about lay representatives on the governing boards
of public administrative agencies is one such struggle over the rules of the game.

Marin concludes that the very process of political exchange transforms opposed or
antagonistic, yet interdependent, interests into mutually contingent and compatible ones.
But such transformation takes time and evolves through enduring long-term relations
(*ibid.*).

It may be argued that public policy-making in Sweden, as presented above, provides a
set of arenas for autonomously organized but interdependent interests for mutually
contingent transactions. Furthermore, it may be maintained that interdependence is characteristic not only of the relations between interests, but also of relations between the
various micropolitical and microeconomic arenas and their roles in any given macropolitical and economic transactions.

The distinction between the state and non-governmental organizations (NGOs) is
blurred in corporate democracies. Organizations representing private interests are accorded
a formal role in the formation of public policy in areas of major concern to themselves; in
return, they assume both responsibility for and a formal role in the effective implementation
of such policy (Goldthorpe, 1984). Since this implementation normally includes the
representatives of organized capital and labor, it undermines the institutional separation of
the industrial and political spheres (Fulcher, 1976). But it also means that trade unions are
obliged to refrain from exploiting their economic power in collective bargaining to the full,
in exchange for the opportunity to exercise political power or political influence in social
bargaining in the political sphere (Pizzorno, 1978 and Goldthorpe, 1984).

Joint regulation in industrial relations and encompassing socioeconomic bargaining in
Sweden provide a unique setting for examining the interrelatedness of meso-games. The
tendency for unions to convert their market strength into political measures designed to
promote the interest of the working class — in a broader and more permanent fashion than
they can achieve by industrial action alone is reinforced by the existence of institutions for
integrated organizational participation in public policy-making. The centralization of trade-
union movements and the strength of the Social Democratic Party will greatly enhance
organized labor's opportunities for participating in political exchange (Wilensky, 1983,
Pizzorno, 1978 and Korpi, 1983). However, when the Social Democrats are in opposition
capital may become the power broker if its political allies form a weak coalition government, as developments in Swedish industrial relations in the last 10 years demonstrate.

2. Meso-games in Swedish Industrial Relations

2.1 Collective Bargaining

Industrial conflict is institutionalized, to a greater or lesser extent, in all capitalist societies.

But in Sweden it is unique in traditionally taking the form of joint regulation by organized labor and capital. According to the institutional theory of industrial conflict, conflict on the nature of society was eventually replaced by conflict on unequal distribution within the existing social order (Fulcher, 1976). The owners of capital accepted unions as legitimate bargaining partners, and labor reconciled itself to the persistence of capitalism and concentrated its energies on improving its position in society (*ibid.*). In Sweden, this was formalized in the December Compromise of 1906. The Swedish Trade Union Confederation (LO) accepted the rights of employers at plant level to hire and fire employees freely and to manage production relations without restriction, in exchange for union recognition (Hadenius, 1983).

In 1938 the Swedish Employers' Confederation (SAF) and LO signed the Saltsjöbaden Basic Agreement. This laid down the procedures for collective agreements and was designed to limit industrial conflicts. An additional result was to stave off previous conservative and a subsequent Social Democratic proposal for legislation to protect "third parties" from strikes and lockouts (*ibid.* and Fulcher, *op. cit.*).

By the 1950s, Sweden had rapidly been transformed from a country with one of the highest levels of strike activity and working days lost per 1000 employees to that with the lowest absolute levels. During the early 1950s, a centralized collective-bargaining model was established. Then, from 1957 to 1983, workers and private employers bargained in three stages. First, a central agreement was reached between SAF and LO, which set the economic limits for subsequent negotiations and also included a clause concerning peace during the course of negotiations. Branch-wide agreements were negotiated between SAF and LO's respective affiliates. Finally, negotiations at the plant or firm level filled out the details of the central and branch agreements.

This system worked smoothly and averted open conflicts until 1977 when, under the non-socialist government, 220,000 salaried employees were locked out for two weeks. Then in 1980 the country's largest labor-market conflict ever broke out. Nearly three million workers were locked out by their employers or on strike for a few weeks in April and May of that year. The Chairman of SAF reassured his member firms that their lockout decision was "an investment for the future". Labor-market conflicts have recurred periodically since then, often in the public sector, although on a smaller scale. In 1983, SAF announced its refusal to negotiate centrally any more, and its intention to limit collective bargaining to branch-wide agreements in the future, with the ultimate aim of merely reaching company-wide agreements. The varying length (11-23 months) of the branch agreements negotiated in 1983 confirmed this policy. However, the Social Democratic government intervened and coordinated the length of all the branch-wide agreements, through the national mediation facilities. Without this intervention, it seems unlikely that the system of centralized collective bargaining would have survived. Since then, SAF has repeatedly expressed its preference for branch-wide and company-wide agreements.

The "rights" laid down in the December Compromise remained unchallenged for more than 60 years of industrial relations in Sweden. However, both Marin and Fulcher argue that the persistence of gross inequalities and the domination of capital at plant level imply an unequal balance of power which cannot prove stable in the long run (1987 and *op. cit.*, p. 51). Marin also calls attention to tensions between an unstable local inequality and parity at the macro level, which can lead to conflicts over the rules of the game (*op. cit.*). The political reforms of the 1970s which come under the heading of working-life reforms or industrial democracy may be seen as an effort to redress this unequal local balance. Although initially shrouded in near-consensus between the political parties, they nevertheless represent a clear break with the earlier pattern of joint regulation by organized capital and labor. Social Democratic governments had no reason to interfere as long as both parties to the 1938 Basic Agreement guaranteed its smooth implementation. This did not absolve the state from all responsibility for collective bargaining and industrial relations, but it did remove the necessity for emergency intervention to deal with labor market catastrophes. Instead, the state could concentrate on overall macroeconomic planning and labor market policy and thus leave the details of collective bargaining to organized capital and labor. Nor did this preclude legislation dealing with particular problems such as occupational accidents and workers' protection. But joint regulation could provide a basis for such regulation, in the form of agreements between organized capital and labor. These often required only a few modifications and legal terminology to be applicable to all employers and employees, rather than just the original parties to the agreement.

However, a new pattern became apparent in the late 1960s and early 1970s. Organized labor turned to the Social Democratic Government to seek retribution when its efforts to redress the unequal balance of power between capital and labor at plant level by means of joint regulation proved futile. Thus, at the macro level legislation backed by broad majorities tipped the scales in favor of organized labor in the early 1970s, while they remained in favor of capital at the local plant level. Tensions growing out of these differential balances of power at the macro and micro levels were not experienced identically by organized labor and capital. The message was dramatically carried home to organized labor when the wildcat strikes broke out in the late 1960s. It sought to alleviate these tensions by attempting to redress the balance of power at the micro level by the legislative process. But these very changes caused new tensions, now among employers. They could tolerate a relatively equitable balance at the macro level as long as the balance at the micro level remained in their favor. But when the local balance was threatened by legislation designed to democratize work life they could no longer tolerate it. The closer the local balance came to approximate equity, the more necessary it became for them to challenge and redress the balance at the macro level. This could best be achieved by attempting to alter the meso-level balances and thereby destabilizing the macro balance. Thus, after the nonsocialist election victory SAF initiated an offensive to revise "the extremes" of recent work-life legislation.

Pizzorno notes that unions under-exploit their power in the labor market in order to achieve political influence (1978). The discrepancy between collective bargaining and political influence may, however, have a destabilizing effect. Equilibrium in the political market is achieved by virtue of the fact that union leaders are capable of autonomously defining the ends toward which collective action should be directed (*ibid.*). By sacrificing shortterm benefits in favor of power, leaders obtain a near-monopoly in the interpretation of the movement's long-term interest. There is a constant risk of an interpretation gap between union leaders and rank-and-file members. If the gap becomes too wide, it jeopardizes the equilibrium in political exchange. This is normally expressed through new or oppositional groups who claim to represent the interests of members better than current leaders, or through wildcat (unauthorized) strikes (*ibid.*).

Wildcat strikes of the late 1960s and early '70s in Sweden brought the problems of poor work environment and inadequate worker influence at plant level to the forefront. These strikes spurred the trade unions to propose solutions to problems and also raised public awareness. This awareness, in turn, paved the way for the political consensus surrounding the legal reforms which culminated in work-environment and co-determination laws in the mid-1970s.

2.2 Work-Environment Regulation

Co-determination and the amelioration of the work environment help to illustrate the above point. Both areas became subject to legislation designed to increase the power of labor at plant level. They were, of course, closely interrelated in the drafting of the reforms and the final legal texts. However, there was more extensive joint regulation of the work environment than of co-determination. In 1942, SAF and LO reached an agreement to establish the bipartite Joint Industrial Safety Council (ASN) and to lay down guidelines for local work-environment promotion efforts, including the appointment of safety delegates for all workplaces with more than five employees, and of bipartite safety committees for all workplaces with more than 50. A revision of industrial safety legislation in 1949 placed these rules for local safety cooperation on a statutory basis. Technical developments and rationalization in the 1950s and 1960s necessitated the revision of work safety standards, and in the 1960s the largest private companies began to provide occupational health services. A new compromise between SAF and LO in 1967 laid down the rules for local occupational safety and set the guidelines for occupational health services in the private sector. The following year, a number of branch-specific agreements were reached by the respective branch unions and employer organizations.

However, in its negotiations with SAF, LO was unable to secure an agreement on all its demands for improved work-environment regulation. These demands mainly concerned the right to decide on work environment matters at the plant level. LO therefore began to seek political support for a revision of the 1949 Workers' Protection Act which would meet some or most of its unfulfilled expectations (Nordfors, 1985). A partial revision of this law in 1973 expanded the employees' powers in such matters. Interestingly enough, the bipartite compromise of 1967 was now (1974) renegotiated, and the subsequent Work Environment Agreement between SAF and LO included several new provisions not found in the 1973 law. A further revision of the law frames many of these joint-regulation provisions in statutory terms (ibid.).

In 1972, the National Board of Occupational Safety and Health was reorganized to include a governing council consisting of lay representatives nominated by labor-market organizations thereby increasing the corporatist representation of labor.

2.3 Co-Determination

In 1946, SAF, LO and TCO had reached an agreement on joint company councils, and minor revisions were made in 1958, one year after the centralized agreement between SAF and LO became the established pattern of collective bargaining. In the second half of the 1960s, both LO and SAF consistently rejected the idea of legislation concerning the representation of employees on their companies' boards when it was repeatedly proposed by both the non-socialist parties and the Communists (Hadenius, 1983). The Work Environment Act (AML) of 1974 makes numerous references to the proposed Codetermination Act (MBL) of 1976. This is necessary, since reforming the work environment proved impossible as long as SAF and its members maintained their unlimited "rights" at plant level. But all such issues could not be dealt with by AML, so many of them were left to MBL, which became a necessary condition for reforming the work environment.

Both AML and MBL are paving or framework enactments. The *Riksdag* merely sets general guidelines, leaving the details to other bodies. In the case of the former, the tripartite National Board of Occupational Safety and Health is responsible for filling out the details. Where the latter was concerned, a collective agreement was intended to define the details of the law. However, it has proved much more difficult to reach an agreement to specify MBL than to continue and expand joint regulation of the work environment. The 1974 Work Environment Agreement (AMA) between LO and SAF went one step farther than the Act (AML) of a few months earlier. In 1978, the Federation of Salaried Employees in Industry and Services (PTK) became one of the principal parties to AMA, which was then revised again in 1983. However, the unions met stiff opposition from private employers in negotiating a collective agreement on MBL. The consumer-cooperative employers reached a collective agreement with their employees in 1977, followed by nationalized industries in 1978 and private employers in 1982. A branch agreement was reached between SAF and the National Union of Insurance Company Employees in 1979. The 1982 agreement, known as the Development Agreement, is a national "framework agreement", but to date very few local agreements have been reached in the private sector. The unions complain that this reform is mainly a "paper tiger" in the private sector. Thus, with minor exceptions, the Co-determination Act preceded genuine collective bargaining, while the work-environment field has always been subject to joint regulation.

2.4 Labor-Market Insurance

Certain types of labor-market insurance were subject to negotiations between organized labor and capital as early as the 1960s. Such joint regulation gained momentum in the early 1970s. The first negotiated agreement between SAF and LO, concerning occupational group life insurance (TGL), was reached in 1963. Severance pay supplements were the subject of the next agreement (AGB) which came in 1965. Sick pay and disability pensions were covered by a joint SAF-LO agreement (AGS) in 1972. The following year, special supplementary pension insurance (STP) was established, and in 1974 Labor Market No-fault Liability Insurance (TFA) was agreed upon. Together these five insurance agreements are known as labor-market insurance.

Today, two and a half million wage-earners are covered by sick pay and disability pension insurance, and nearly as many applicants have been recompensed since the outset. The assets of this particular insurance scheme now total nearly 15 B SEK, while those of the sup-plementary pension scheme hold over 25 B SEK. Altogether, the assets of these labor-market insurance schemes amounted to 18.6 B SEK in 1980 and 46.4 B SEK in 1985. A similar growth rate over the next five-year period would result in well over 100 B SEK by 1990.

Labor-market insurance schemes are based on agreements between SAF and LO, and the premiums are paid by the employers. In 1986 these premiums amounted to 5.75 per cent of wages before taxes. The boards of the first four of these insurance schemes are identical in composition, i.e. with the same persons as representatives, including three each from LO and SAF, plus a chairman. The board of the fifth is similarly composed, but also includes a representative from PTK, as well as the managing directors of a cooperative and a private insurance company.

Labor-market insurance was only once subject to legislation. The Occupational Injury Insurance Act of 1977 resulted in higher compensation for injury insurance than for ordinary sick pay. It covered workers outside the SAF/LO sphere, such as civil servants, and also broadened the definition of occupational injury to cover any factor in the work environment with a (proven) unfavorable effect on employees' physical or mental health.

2.5 Wage-Earner Funds

As we have seen above, joint regulation as a whole has changed since the era of the Saltsjöbaden Basic Agreement. In the ensuing decades, it remained largely problem-free and straightforward. Then, in the 1970s, a decade of legal reforms was ushered in. Initially, these commanded broad political support, and improved the trade unions' position vis-à-vis employers. But by the end of the decade, the spirit of compromise had been replaced by one of animosity and confrontation over the wage-earner funds (Åsard, 1986). Initial support for LO's proposed reforms had given way to adamant opposition. On December 21 1983, the Social Democrats' bill on the wage-earner funds was passed by 164 votes to 158, with the Communists abstaining (*ibid.*). Shortly before, on October 4, nearly 80,000 managers and business owners had marched through the streets of Stockholm in protest against the bill. Continued rabid opposition on the part of private businessmen has made it difficult for the government to use the funds as intended. Recently, critical voices from leading trade unionists have been heard concerning the impact and future of the Funds.

The author of the initial proposal for economic democracy in 1976, R. Meidner, maintains today that the wage-earner funds have failed to achieve a single one of their objectives. This is largely due to the fact that they are so circumscribed by restrictions stemming from attempts to make them more palatable to the employers (DN, 7.1.87). Former LO Chairman, G. Nilsson, concurred when he stated that the funds are a "harmless marginal joke" rather than a reform designed to usher in economic democracy (*Pockettidning* R, No. 3-4, 1986). However, S. Malm, LO's present chairman, argues that the wage-earner funds were and are a political burden on the Social Democratic Party (*ibid.*). The chairman of the Metal Workers' Union, L. Blomberg, goes further, stating that the funds are set up in an unfortunate fashion since they provoked such a strong reaction from employers (*DN*, 26.2.87).

The wage-earner funds amassed 3.4 B SEK in the 27 months between their inception in January 1984 and April 1986. At the limit of their period of accumulation of new capital through payroll and corporate profit taxes, the National Audit Bureau (RRV) calculates that they will have 16.5 B SEK at their disposal for investments.

However, unlike labor-market insurance, which merely loans its assets to public and private investors, the wage-earner funds buy stocks on the stock market and make direct investments in private companies. They thereby gain a say in the management of individual companies. This impinges on the ultimate prerogative of individual capitalists and undermines their privileges as a class. Traxler notes that labor's class interests are ambiguous, while those of capital are unequivocal, since they coincide with society's interests in capital accumulation (*op. cit.*, p. 30).

Numerous trade unionists have, in fact, questioned the wisdom of diluting the position of labor as wage-earners by aspiring to obtain a role normally reserved for the owners of capital. They have queried how the roles as employers and employees can be simultaneously combined. The response of representatives of Swedish capital to the challenge has been both clear and concise: they have flatly rejected all proposals for wage-earner funds, no matter how watered-down, and rallied to defend their class privileges and social position in terms of capital accumulation. The Swedish business interest associations have played an active role in the struggle against the wage-earner funds, and they are still doing so. They established a special *ad hoc* front organization to lead this struggle, under the name of the 4th October Committee (Hansson, 1984 and Pestoff, 1988b). Thus, when forced on the offensive by proposals they considered odious, organized capital demonstrated flexibility in adapting tactics normally associated with trade unions, such as mass demonstrations etc.

If the wage-earner funds proved divisive for the labor movement and helped to bring differences between LO and the Social Democrats to the fore, it can be argued that they resulted in the opposite effect among employers. Twenty-five years of centralized collective bargaining almost eliminated competition between employers on the labor market, since wage rates and employment conditions were negotiated in three stages — centrally, branchwise and at company level. Only at the last stage did individual firms enter the picture. But decentralizing collective bargaining implies a reintroduction of competition among SAF's member firms, in particular for the youngest and best skilled workers. This could accentuate differences between diverse employer groups. Large multinationals producing for the export market, such as Volvo, Electrolux, Ericsson, Asea, Saab-Scania, etc., would be pitted against small employers serving the domestic market in competition for the best workers. Small firms are bound to lose in such competition. But this could strain the class solidarity of employers and pose problems for SAF's internal governance.

At the same time, decentralization of collective bargaining should imply a corresponding decentralization of resources for collective action by employers — unless, of course, other functions could justify the lion's share of membership dues, conflict funds and staff remaining in the hands of the central organization after it has outlived its function in centralized collective bargaining. The issue of wage-earner funds served to galvanize opinion among diverse groups of employers and provided SAF with the breathing space as well as the room to manoeuver in finding and adjusting to a new role. A recent survey among SAF's members shows that a majority feel that a strong central organization is necessary in future in order to promote the political interests of free enterprise. The wage-earner funds undoubtedly made a significant contribution to the existence of an awareness among businessmen of the need for, and the importance of, their active participation in politics.

2.6 Lay Representation on the Governing Bodies of Central Administrative Agencies

Lay representation on the governing bodies of central administrative agencies was discussed previously in section A.5. It can be seen as an official institutionalization of the rules of the game of cooperative interest intermediation, in addition to providing for integrated organizational participation in public policy-making. Balanced representation based on numerical parity embodies the very principles of joint regulation. A challenge it can be conceived as challenging the rules of the game of cooperative interest intermediation and joint regulation.

Following reform proposals made by a parliamentary *ad hoc* committee known as *Verksledningskommittén* (VLK), the two most important business interest associations, SAF and the Federation of Swedish Industry, have openly challenged this public institution of lay representation (*DN*, 12.10.85). They have suggested that private enterprise should no longer nominate representatives to such governing councils, and no longer formally partici- pate in implementing public policy (*SvD* 26.03.87, 10.04.87 and *DN* 5.04.87). However, their well-developed lobby activities and public-opinion campaigns ensure them continued access through informal channels of influence (Pestoff, 1988a and 1988b).

But labor appears completely unprepared for this development, and trade unions have not yet begun to explore these alternative channels of influence. They have therefore rejected any curtailment of lay representation in their *remiss* answers to VLK's proposals. Moreover, TCO argued that such a proposal would, if carried through, disband a crucial mechanism for reaching consensus in important social and economic questions and lead to growing social tensions and open confrontations between different groups (*DN*, 6.85). Nevertheless, it seems likely that the Conservative Party may join the Liberal Party in condemning the institution of lay representation as "corporativism", thereby placing the issue squarely on the national political agenda and helping to create an "overload pluralist" situation. The

Social Democrats would be forced to defend the "undemocratic" practice of maintaining extensive interest-group participation in public policy-making, in a neo-liberal age of growing individualism.

If private enterprise should go so far as to boycott this official channel of influence, then it would prove difficult to maintain integrated organizational participation in the implementation phase of public policy-making in Sweden. Labor would also have to relinquish its own formal representation, but without having informal techniques to fall back on. This would seriously undermine labor's accessibility to the public domain.

2.7 Style and Institutions of Conflict Resolution

In spite of the increasing reliance of organized labor on cooperation with the Social Democratic Party when efforts to modify joint regulation agreements were unsuccessful in the early 1970s, the institutions of joint regulation were not dismantled. Instead, they were developed and extended, often by means of legislation. They were never entirely replaced by public assumption of responsibility for industrial relations. However, the degree of public or political involvement varies from one area to another. Once joint regulation becomes established, public responsibility becomes less necessary. Conversely, the weaker the grounds for negotiations and mutual compromise between the interdependent but antagonistic interests of organized labor and capital, the greater the importance of finding political solutions. This relationship can briefly be summarized in the following figure on the style and institutions of conflict resolution in Swedish industrial relations.

The style of conflict resolution at the meso level can be divided into two categories, either conflict and confrontation or consensus and compromise. Societal institutions for conflict resolution are either interest intermediation or party politics. At the meso level, interest intermediation is undertaken though negotiated joint resolution. The failure of this institution can result in an issue becoming politicized and being taken up by the political parties in the parliament. Joint regulation is based on negotiated agreements, which can only be reached if both parties accept the outcome; i.e. they must reach a unanimous decision. Thus, in effect any single party has a veto. Parliamentary politics is competitive by nature and democratic decision-making procedures simply require majority support. Parties in the minority cannot therefore normally veto the proposals of the majority.

The axes in the figure represent alternative combinations of style and institutions of conflict resolution. The main axis combines compromise and interest mediation, in cell "c", and conflict with party competition, in cell "b". Both these combinations have a separate logic of their own and demonstrate considerable stability and legitimacy, in terms of the solutions they produce. The opposite is true of the remaining two cells, i.e. "a" and "d". They lack a logic of their own and do not normally result in stable or accepted solutions to conflicts.

The changes ushered in following the Social Democratic election defeat in 1976 had a clear impact on joint regulation in Swedish industrial relations. The natural political ally of the trade unions turned the reins of government over to the employers' two political allies

Figure 2 **Style and Institutions of Conflict Resolution in Swedish Industrial Relations**

Institutions for   Conflict Resolution
interest inter-   party politics
mediation

Style of conflict
resolution:

a	b
	WEF
	LR-? ↗ ↑
conflict & (CCB - ?)	
confrontation ↑	
LR '	
CCB ? ◄-- CD (WEF?)	
consensus & WER ⎱ ◄----►	
compromise LMI ⎰	
c	d

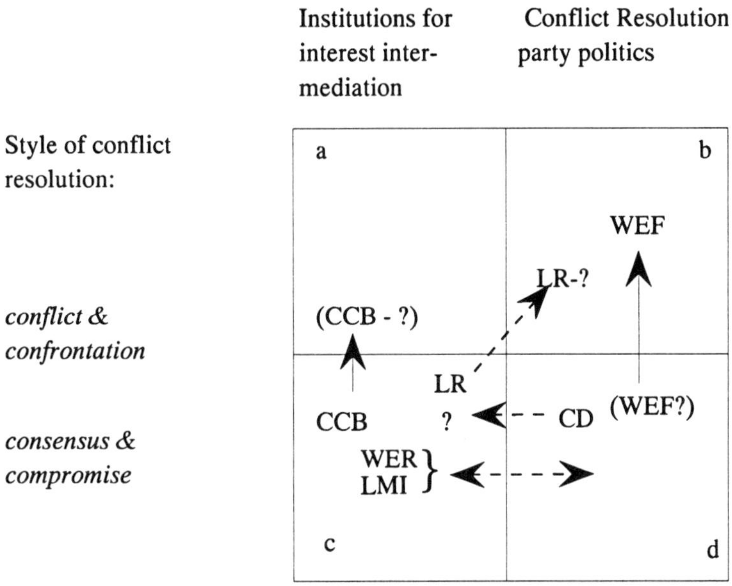

CCB = centralize*d collective bargaining (1957-81)*
CD = co-determination
LMI = labor-market insurance
LR = lay representation
WEF = wage-earner funds
WER = work-environment regulation

plus the political ally of the producer cooperatives. These three parties' lack of cohesion placed SAF in the privileged position of being a power broker among warring coalition partners.

In summarizing the various meso-games of Swedish industrial relations, we note that centralized collective bargaining was solidly located in cell "c" during the period 1938-1977. However, starting with the lockout of 1977 and the general labor conflict of 1980, wage negotiations have tended to move towards cell "a", since SAF has aspired to dismantle the centralized system it once forced upon the trade unions in the 1950s. Their only major hurdle is not the trade unions, but the opposition of the Social Democratic Government. But if collective bargaining becomes located here and labor market conflicts increase dramatically, nothing can prevent the *Riksdag* from regularly interfering in labor negotiations and even legislating collective agreements, as sometimes happens in Denmark, thus moving them into cell "b".

Work-environment regulation is clearly lodged in cell "c"; so, too, is labor-market insurance. Both have occasionally been broadened and strengthened through the legislative process and abetted by a large consensus in the *Riksdag*. However, they depend primarily on the logic of compromise through joint regulation.

Co-determination was promoted chiefly by political initiatives, which were initially rejected by both organized labor and capital but later accepted by the former, though not the latter. The prime mode of implementation was supposed to be through collective bargaining or joint regulation. Since unanimous decisions are required, the employers could use the lack of agreement to delay implementing such legislation. Finally, the longer the lapse between the initial proposal (in 1976) and the final *Riksdag* decision (1983), the more divisive the wage-earner fund proposals proved to be. They clearly belong to the upper right-hand area of political confrontation. Lay representation has now been openly challenged by organized capital and one of the political parties. It seems likely that it too may prove decisive in political terms and thus move from cell "c" to cell "b".

Thus, we find that each meso-game has its own rules and develops according to its own logic. They are nevertheless interrelated, both at the meso and at the macro levels. However, before we explore the exact nature of this relationship, closer attention will be given to one particular meso-game where joint regulation has proved very successful, namely work-environment regulation.

3. Joint Regulation and the Institutional Network(s) of Work Environment Policy in Sweden

We have seen above how joint regulation was the primary motive and method for developing work-environment policy. Organized labor and capital played a leading role in these developments. It was not until the early 1970s, once negotiations had failed to satisfy the demands of organized labor, that labor's growing concern over the work environment pursued alternative channels. Political conditions were ripe for a wave of reforms in working life and near-consensus facilitated such legislation. Turning from negotiations and legislation, however, we find that joint regulation is also the primary motive and method behind the institutional network(s) of Swedish work-environment policy.

Work-environment policy found its first official expression with the establishment of the Labor Inspectorate (*Yrkesinspektionen*, YI/LI), which started operations with three labor inspectors in 1889. In 1905, the Association for Occupational Safety (FFA/AOS) was established as a non-governmental body to promote occupational safety. One-third of its income came from public funds as early in 1912. In 1987 it had 18 employees and a budget of 16 M SEK. Its board comprises representatives of organized labor and capital plus public agencies in the field.

The Swedish Joint Industrial Safety Council (*Arbetarskyddsnämnden*, ASN/JISC) was the bipartite body set up according to the occupational safety agreement between SAF and LO in 1942. In 1987 it employed 26 persons and has a budget of 20 M SEK. It has served as a model for similar bipartite bodies for civil servants and employees of the consumer cooperatives (SAN & KAN). In 1978 JISC was expanded to include the representatives of salaried employees in private enterprise (PTK).

The Workers' Protection Act of 1949 set up *Arbetarskyddsstyrelsen* (the National Board of Occupational Safety and Health, NBOSH), which was amalgamated with the Labor Inspectorate in the 1974 legislation on work environment. The board of the new agency includes four lay representatives of organized labor (2-LO, 1-TCO & 1-SACO), two of organized capital (SAF), two members of the *Riksdag*, one representative of public employers (SAV) plus two from the agency itself. In addition, a regional tripartite council was set up in 1973 for each of the 19 Regional Labor Inspectorates. In 1983 NBOSH had 755 employees and LI had 700. Their joint budget was 324 M SEK. The Work Environment Fund (AMS/WEF), which was set up in 1972, in 1987 employed 51 persons and has a budget of 530 M SEK. It finances research into work-environment and co-determination issues on the basis of a wage levy. It has a tripartite governing body, with six representatives from organized labor, the same number of employer representatives and a similar number of public representatives.

Thus, for the first sixty years of Swedish work environment policy, LI was the sole public authority dealing with worker safety, and it lacked any form of lay representation. Today, NBOSH and WEF are clear examples of tripartism. There are an additional 30 central administrative agencies with some form of responsibility for work-environment matters. Most of them have lay representatives on their boards, but these are not normally nominated by organized labor and capital. More important, however, are all the other numerous bipartite institutions dealing with work-environment policy which are bodies for joint regulation between organized labor and capital. But the state normally provides some economic support for these efforts in accordance with the pattern established with AOS at the turn of the century. The non-governmental work-environment bodies add up to well over 100, most with their own specialization. A brief survey of these includes the following features (Pestoff, 1985).

1. Occupational health services in private industry and for civil servants, with approximately 600 local occupational health centers. OHCs were set up according to the 1967 SAF/LO/PTK agreement on work environment, and now cover 80% of all private employees in Sweden. In addition, there are ten branch-specific health service organizations, of which the best developed is the Construction Industry Foundation for Industrial Safety and Health (*Bygghälsan*, BH). BH was set up in 1968; by 1982, it employed 282 persons and had a budget of 100 M SEK. It operates 12 regional and 20 local offices, plus 17 mobile health service units. It has numerous bipartite committees.

2. There are 50 bipartite work-environment committees, of which 34 are branch-specific, eight deal with specific problems in certain industries and two deal with labor-market insurance. In addition, there are three central bipartite bodies for work-environment issues, JISC (mentioned above) for SAF, LO and PTK, another for civil servants (SAN) and a third for employees of the consumer cooperatives (KAN). The branch-specific and special work

environment committees are run and serviced by SAF's affiliates. These consist of an equal number of employer and employee representatives and promote safety projects related to the work environment, e.g. improvements in safety gloves and safety-technique materials, safety-delegate training courses, etc. These projects are financed by grants from the Work Environment Fund.

3. At all workplaces with five or more employees, trade unions appoint one or more safety delegates, and at all workplaces with 50 or more employees the Work Environment Act calls for the establishment of a bipartite safety committee, in which the employees have a majority. There are nearly 110,000 safety delegates, whose activities are partially financed by public funds, which amounted to 50 M SEK in 1984.

4. Bipartite labor-market insurance schemes established in the 1960s and '70s provide insurance covering occupational group life insurance, severance pay, sick pay and disability pensions, supplementary pensions and liabilities for occupational injury for all employees. Together, their assets exceeded 46 B SEK in 1985.

This brief survey of non-governmental bodies established via joint regulation shows that bipartism, based on organized capital and labor, is just as extensive in Swedish work-environment regulation as tripartism, if not more so. This important point has gone unnoticed by earlier writers, who have focused on a single agency, such as the Labor Inspectorate (Kelman, 1981 and Lundberg, 1982). In fact, joint regulation is the rule in Swedish work-environment regulation, and strictly technocratic public regulation by experts is the exception. And when the state is present in tripartite bodies, it appears to play the role of junior partner to organized capital and labor. Developments in this area have been almost entirely dependent upon consensus between them and the result of negotiations between them. Labor has been forced to take the initiative in these developments, while capital could content itself with a defensive strategy, as Traxler postulates (*op. cit.*).

The state supports, helps to finance and in other ways encourages joint regulation of the work environment, but does not try to initiate it, nor to direct it. It steps in only when a stalemate occurs between organized capital and labor, and only then to reinstate the normal order of joint regulation. This was evident in the period of broad political consensus favoring the improvement of the work environment.

It is also important to note that the consensus which underpins the development of work-environment regulation is not merely based on bilateral barter but should, rather, be conceived of as political exchange. There are clear rules of the game, formalized in the agreements between organized capital and labor. Permanent bipartite and tripartite institutions are established to implement these agreements. This is an ongoing development rather than an *ad hoc* or once-and-for-all reform strategy. Furthermore, both parties to these developments recognize the close interrelationship between the work environment and collective bargaining. Swedish industry has come to realize that wage increases make little difference today, because it cannot attract young workers unless the work environment is improved, according to business spokesmen.

The Work Environment Act of 1977, together with the Codetermination Act, greatly augmented the powers of safety delegates and safety committees at individual workplaces, and of regional safety delegates in different branches. This was an important change in an expanding network of institutions which are together responsible for regulating the work environment. We are thus faced not by a single agency or two, but rather by a complex institutional network for work-environment regulation. Although there is some variation from branch to branch, this complexity is exemplified by the network found in the building and construction industry, as shown in Figure 3 below.

This institutional network consists of no fewer than five levels, from workplaces through local trade union branches up to the national level for each branch, in addition to the peak or central level which brings together all the divergent branches. The main actors are employers and employees, organized through their respective associations; local and regional safety delegates; the National Board of Occupational Safety and Health, with 12 regions; the Labor Inspectorate, divided into 19 regions, each with a Regional Labor Inspectorate Council; branch-specific work-environment committees, and a national occupational safety council. Thus we find a very complex network in which the national peak organizations, their national branch associations, the regional and local bodies of the national branch associations and local bodies of the national branch associations at the worksites, and a variety of public authorities at corresponding levels interact to regulate the work environment in Sweden (Pestoff, 1985).

An important feature of this institutional network is its corporative nature, one which mixes bipartite and tripartite bodies, as well as public and private. This complex network illustrates the interrelation and interdependency of the antagonistic interests of organized capital and labor in work-environment regulation. The wide variety of institutions found here and their complex relation to one another also demonstrates the overall nature of the setting in which organized capital and labor promote their interests. It goes far beyond simple bilateral barter, although this may well take place in any isolated component of this complex network. The very complexity of this institutional network bears witness to the overt political nature of the pursuit of antagonistic interests in work environment regulation. It also provides a good example of the complexity of the interrelation and interdependency of these interests in political exchange.

4. Conclusions

Crouch's contribution to the workshop on political exchange focuses on the organizational dimensions of labor, its capacity to make political exchanges and its participation in macro-level socioeconomic bargaining, as seen from an historical and comparative perspective (this volume). Labor's organizational capacity is related to the degree of centralization and strength of its organization. Its capacity to make political exchanges is related to the accessibility of the public domain and the development of industrial relations. Labor's position on these dimensions is neither given nor static, but varies both temporally and spatially (*ibid.*). When these variables are combined, Crouch derives a potential range of the

Figure 3   The Institutional Network of the Construction Industry's Work Environment Programme

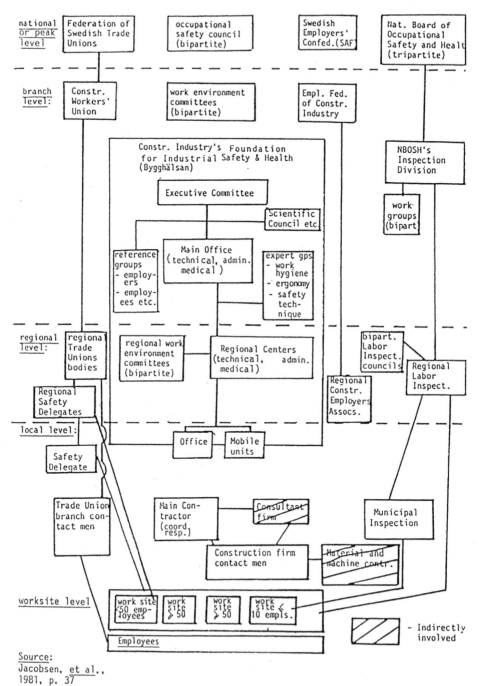

Source:
Jacobsen, et al.,
1981, p. 37

types of labor-movement participation in industrial relations, spanning from a "union-free" environment or economy to their full participation in generalized political exchange, with intermediate categories such as "paper tigers" and "pure" collective bargaining (*ibid.*). He proceeds to analyze changes in the positions of various Western European labor movements during the 20th century (*ibid.*). The Scandinavian countries demonstrate maximum capacity for generalized political exchange as early as the 1930s and 1940s (*ibid.*). In the 1960s, however, the power of labor began to disaggregate in Western Europe, and 1968 was a turning point in many countries, ushering in an upsurge of industrial conflict which made collective-bargaining systems unmanageable or threatened the centralized coordination of corporatist systems (*ibid.*) Although this temporarily gave labor the initiative in industrial relations, by 1980, Crouch argues, a new era of deinstitutionalization undermined labor's position. This resulted in "overload pluralism" that was incompatible with generalized political exchange and restored the initiative in industrial relations to management, who (re)asserted the importance of the company level, where they dominate the balance of power, as opposed to the national or industrial level, where large unions operate in their preferred milieu (*ibid.*).

In Sweden, this deinstitutionalization coincided with the nonsocialist governments of the 1976-82 period, and the resurgence of perennial industrial conflicts, starting with the major labor-market conflict of 1980. In 1983, the Social Democrats attempted to shore up centralized collective bargaining, which organized capital intends to scuttle.

The Brookings Institute's analysis of the Swedish economy (1986) recommended a new historic compromise between organized capital and labor, similar to that of nearly 50 years ago in Saltsjöbaden, in order to ensure continued smooth economic growth. This appeal fell on deaf ears. The famous EFO model between SAF, LO and TCO for technical calculation of the overall leeway for pay increases was often used in the early 1970s, but then fell into disuse some years later. It was constructed by the main economic experts of these same three organizations, and bore their initials — Edgren, Faxen and Odhner. In early 1987, a follow-up report, "Pay Formation in the Economy of the 1990s" was prepared by Faxen, Odhner and Spånt, the latter having now succeeded Edgren as chief economic adviser at TCO (1987). The FSO report proposes the further development of the EFO model, something that corresponds well with the recommendation of the Brookings Institute. SAF's weekly journal was quick to criticize the FOS report, pointing out that Faxen was now retired and his proposals no longer carried any authority among organized employers.

It appears that SAF's adamant opposition to the wage-earner funds is now equaled by intransigence toward compromise in collective bargaining. Whether this implies a systematic strategy for preventing socio-economic bargaining in other fields, or merely a desire to limit labor's influence to wages and working conditions, restricted to the company level, remains to be seen. Note that the "bread-and-butter unionism" which satisfies itself with company-level collective bargaining might also be conceived of as the first step in an effort to roll back generalized political exchange, with the ultimate aim of a "union-free" economy. But Crouch's analysis of political exchange makes it clear that this would be an arduous task involving an extensive overt social struggle, including greatly increased labor-market conflicts. Moreover, certain aspects of generalized political exchange are beyond the immediate influence of organized capital, since they involve the organizational features of labor itself. These include its degree of centralization and the organizational strength of Swedish trade unions. However, other aspects are more readily subject to the direct and indirect influence of organized capital, including the development of industrial-relations institutions and accessibility to the public domain. The attitudes of the leaders of organized employers that large-scale labor conflicts are "an investment for the future" or that "the Swedish rate of unemployment is ridiculously low and must come up to the European level", when combined with a thrust for company-level wage agreements, clearly expresses an intention to deinstitutionalize industrial relations as far as possible.

Furthermore, growing employer criticism of "corporativism" focuses on certain formal and institutional features of access to public policy-making. This criticism also illustrates the growing political crisis over the rules of the game of social and economic bargaining and the politics of compromise. At present, one pivot of this bargaining is the public institution of interest organizations nominating representatives to the governing councils of central administrative agencies, discussed above in sections A.5 and B.6.

Deinstitutionalization of industrial relations and reduced accessibility to the public domain will not result in an immediate and total termination of all social and economic bargaining and cooperative interest intermediation in Sweden. It will, however, significantly change the nature and scope of such bargaining. Organized capital and labor may sit down to negotiate over limited technical issues, and the state may even be present or a party to such negotiations. But Marin argues that simple political barter and generalized political exchange are different phenomena. The *quid pro quo* of political barter, whereby under-exploitation of wage demands results in undeniable immediate benefits, such as lower taxes, increased social transfers or a decisive voice in a current legislative reform, is a necessary but insufficient condition of generalized political exchange. Political barter in numerous interdependent markets must be hierarchically ordered before generalized political exchange can replace simple political barter (1985).

Generalized political exchange is therefore:
'... multi-dimensional transactions... involving the exchange of a variety of variables, including consensus, support, concessions, guarantees, mutual respect of political status, rights and duties... access to authoritative decision-making, effective membership control, commitment to compromised rules, renunciation of strategic exit and voice options, power of withholding, etc. — all this reduces to the single dimension of compliance with quite specific and highly differential rules of the game' (*ibid.*).

'Political exchange implies the transformation of class struggle into a permanent war of position between collective actors with mutually conflicting interests... But opposed or antagonistic interests are interdependent to the point of mutual contingency and it is the very process of political exchange which transforms these antagonistic interdependencies into compatible interests.'

Such transformation, however, takes time and is the product of enduring long-term relationships rather than a single agreement (*ibid.*).

Marin states that political exchange does not develop by itself through certain regularities in political confrontation and compromise, or from unintended outcomes, but rather represents collective efforts to regulate politics. The rules of the game define the opportunity structure for political transactions and set the constraints for political strategies. Political exchange takes place within these constraints, but there is also a power struggle over the rules themselves, their scope, the game to be played, etc. (*ibid.*).

The wage-earner funds ushered in a new era in Swedish politics, one in which conflict is replacing compromise as the kingpin of the political system. Unlike the working-life reform program of the 1970s, which commanded a broad political consensus, the Wage Earner Fund Act of 1983 was passed by only a very small margin in the *Riksdag*.

Organized capital and the three non-socialist parties have been uncompromisingly opposed to the wage-earner funds. Recently, they threatened to boycott a leading commercial private bank (Handelsbanken), which intended to commence lucrative commercial transactions with one of the funds. The board directors and their families were also physically threatened (*SvD*, 16.2.87). The chairman of the bank accused the funds' opponents of employing McCarthyist and fascist tactics, and questioned the legitimacy of such methods in democratic societies (*SvD*, 16.2 & 3.3.87). The chairman of LO, Stig Malm, castigated the opposition to the funds with these and similar accusations (*SvD*, 19.2.87), while most businessmen defended their "right to protest" and/or "to do business with whoever they choose" (*SvD*, 12, 17, 19, 20, 21, 22 and 27.2.87).

This debate, and the methods employed by the opponents to wage-earner funds, led the Chairman of the Metal Workers' Union, Leif Blomberg, to the conclusion that the funds functioned in an unfortunate fashion (*DN*, 26.2.87). He argues:

'We also have to take seriously — extremely seriously the militant right-wing attitude among opponents which takes the form, for example, of blind resistance to wage-earner funds, indifference to workers' demands for substantial training for new tasks and occupations in an age of high technology, and a cold disregard of monotony, stress and jobs which physically wear out (burn out) teenage working women' (*ibid.*).

He condemns the "ideology of hate" which, in his view, dominates right-wing thinking. But this hate must nevertheless be taken seriously. He continues:

'The funds are a minor issue, but opposition to them is symbolic and demonstrates an opposition to sickness insurance etc. which is much clearer now than ten years ago. We see in our contacts with...(our employers) that they have become increasingly right-wing and militant, and that is the most serious development for the political and trade union labor movement' (*ibid.*).

Capital clearly has the initiative in Swedish industrial relations and socio-economic bargaining. The future of generalized political exchange will depend on the intentional actions of capitalists: not only existing material and institutional conditions, but their intentional actions will also affect these conditions.

A second important conclusion is that politics does matter. Neither political parties nor organized labor and capital are solely motivated by economic realities, to which they must slavishly conform or perish. Such simple economic determinism ignores the intentional aspects of contemporary developments in Swedish joint regulation. It is currently in a deep crisis, but not because of economic developments. Rather, it is in the midst of a political crisis and as yet still uncertain whether it will be able to survive intact. The changes ushered in by the Social Democratic election defeat in 1976 have proved a challenge to the very essence of cooperative interest intermediation. The politics of consensus and compromise is rapidly being replaced by the politics of conflict and confrontation, as joint regulation begins to lose its role as the kingpin of Swedish industrial relations.

Thus, attempts to rectify the imbalance in local power relations between organized capital and labor at the plant level, through the work-life legislation of the early 1970s, led to steps aimed at altering the balance between them at the national level, once political changes provided the opportunity. This opportunity was found in the aftermath of the 1976 election. Numerous steps were taken in a number of independent but interrelated areas of industrial relations, ultimately changing their nature from compromise and cooperation to conflict and confrontation.

List 1   Laws and Agreements on Labor-Market Issues in Sweden

1889	YI: Labor Inspectorate
1901	Compensation for accidents at work
1905	FFA: Association for Occupational Safety
1906	SAF-LO mutual recognition agreement
1938	Saltsjöbaden Basic Agreement on labor peace
1942	ASN: Swedish Joint Industrial Safety Council
1946	SAF/LO and SAF/TCO agreements on company councils
1949	ASL: Workers' Protection Act
	ASS: National Board of Occupational Safety and Health
1957	Centralized SAF/LO collective bargaining
	Referendum on supplementary pensions (ATP)
1958	Minor revisions of SAF/LO/TCO agreement on joint company councils
1963	TGL: occupational group life insurance — SAF & LO
1965	AGB: supplementary severance pay insurance — SAF & LO
1967	SAF/LO work safety compromise and occupational health services
1968	Bygghälsan (the Construction Industry's occupational health service)
1969-71	Wildcat strikes about working conditions

1972	AGS: sick pay & disability pension insurance — SAF & LO
	AMS/WEF: Work Environment Fund
1973	STP: Special supplementary pension insurance — SAF & LO
	Work Environment Act (AML) (prop. 1973: 130)
	YI & NBOSH = SBOSH & bipartite regional bodies for YI
1974	Work Environment Agreement (AMA) — SAF & LO
	TFA: No-fault liability insurance for occupational injuries SAF & LO
	SAF, LO & TCO Agreements regarding works councils
1976	Non-socialist government
	LO/SAF/PTK agreement on training of local safety delegates
	Trade-union representation on company boards; Codetermination Act (MBL)
1977	Occupational Injury Insurance Act
	New Work Environment Act (AML)
1978	PTK joins the AMA between SAF and LO
1980	General labor-market conflict
1982	Social Democratic election victory
1983	Revision of 1974 AMA
	Wage-earner funds

List 2 Abbreviations Used in the Text

AGB	Supplementary severance pay insurance (1965)
AGS	Negotiated Group Sickness Insurance (1972)
AMA	Work Environment Agreement (1974)
AML	Work Environment Act (1973 & 1977)
AMS/WEF	Work Environment Fund (1972)
ASL	Workers' Protection Act (1949)
ASN/JISC	Swedish Joint Industrial Safety Council (1942)
BH	Construction Industry Foundation for Industrial Safety and Health (1968)
DN	Dagens Nyheter
FFA/AOS	Association for Occupational Safety (1905)
KAN	Cooperative Work Environment Council
KF	Swedish Cooperative Union and Wholesale Society (1899)
LO	Swedish Trade Union Confederation
LR	lay representatives
PTK	Federation of Salaried Employees in Industry and Services
MBL	Co-determination Act (1976)
NBOSH	National Board of Occupational Safety and Health (1949)
NGO	Non-governmental organization
OHC	Occupational health center

RRV	National Audit Board
SAF	Swedish Employers' Confederation (1902)
SAN	Work Environment Council for Public Employees
SAV	National Agency for Government Employers
STP	Special supplementary pension insurance (1973)
SvD	Svenska Dagbladet
TCO	Central Organization of Salaried Employees
TFA	Labor-market No-Fault Liability Insurance Scheme (1974)
TGL	Occupational group life insurance (1963)
YI/LI	Labor Inspectorate (1889)
B SEK	billion Swedish kronor
M SEK	million Swedish kronor

References

Accornero, A. (1983) 'La cultura conflittuale del sindacato', *Giornale di Diritto del Lavoro e di Relazioni Industriali* 5: 263-85.

Adams, R.D. (1981) 'Tax Rates and Tax Collection', *Public Finance Quarterly* 9: 415-30.

Adorno, T.W. (1972) 'Zum Verhältnis von Soziologie und Psychologie', pp. 42-85 in T.W. Adorno *Gesammelte Schriften*. Vol. 8. Frankfurt: Suhrkamp.

Akkermans, T. and Grootings, P. (1978) 'From Corporatism to Polarisation: Elements of the Development of Dutch Industrial Relations', in C.J. Crouch and A. Pizzorno (eds) *The Resurgence of Class Conflict in Western Europe since 1968.* Vol I. *National Studies.* London: Macmillan.

Aldrich, H. and Whetten, D.A. (1981) 'Organization-Sets, Action-Sets, and Networks: Making the Most of Simplicity', in P.C. Nystrom and W.H. Starbuck (eds) *Handbook of Organizational Design.* Vol. 1. London: Oxford University Press.

Allport, F. (1954) 'The Structuring of Events: Outline of a General Theory with Applications to Psychology', *Psychological Review* 61: 281-303.

Amadieu, J.F. (1986) 'Les tendances au syndicalisme d'entreprise en France — quelques hypothèses', *Droit Social* 6: 495-500.

Amendola, G. (1979) 'Interrogativi sul 'caso' Fiat', *Rinascita* 43: 13-5.

Andersen, T.P. (1976) *Staten og Storkonflikten i 1925.* Copenhagen: Selskabet til forskning i urbejderbevægelsens historie.

Anderson, C.W. (1976) 'Public Policy and the Complex Organization: The Problem of Governance and the Future Evolution of Advanced Industrial Society', in L. Lindberg (ed.) *Politics and the Future of Industrial Society.* New York: McKay.

Anderson, C.W. (1979) 'Political Design and the Representation of Interests', pp. 271-97 in P.C. Schmitter and G. Lehmbruch (eds) *Trends Toward Corporatist Intermediation.* Beverly Hills/London: SAGE Publications.

Armingeon, K. (1987) 'Gewerkschaften in der Bundesrepublik Deutschland 1950-1985: Mitglieder, Organisation und Aussenbeziehungen', *Politische Vierteljahresschrift* 28(1): 7-34.

Armstrong, E.G.A. (1984) 'Employers' Associations in Great Britain', in J.P. Windmuller and A. Gladstone (eds) *Employers Associations and Industrial Relations. A Comparative Study.* Oxford: Clarendon Press.

Arrow, K.J. (1986) 'Rationality of Self and Others', *Journal of Business* 59: 385-400.

Arrow, K.J. and Hahn, F. (1971) *General Competitive Analysis.* San Francisco: Holden.

Åsard, E. (1986) 'Industrial and Economic Democracy in Sweden — From Consensus to Confrontation', *European Journal of Political Research.*

Ashford, D.E. (1979) 'Territorial Politics and Equality: Decentralization in the Modern State', *Political Studies* 27: 71-83.

Ashford, D.E. (1980) 'La Tutelle Financière: New Wine in Old Bottles', in D.E. Ashford (ed.) *National Resources and Urban Policy.* New York: Methuen.

Ashford, D.E. (1982) *British Dogmatism and French Pragmatism. Central-Local Policy-Making in the Welfare State.* London: Allen and Unwin.

Ashford, D.E. (1983) 'Reconstructing the French 'Etat': the Progress of the Loi Defferre', *West European Politics* 6: 262-70.

Auerbach, A. (1985) 'The Theory of Excess Burden and Optimal Taxation', pp. 61-127 in A. Auerbach and M. Feldstein (eds) *Handbook of Public Economics*. Vol. 1. Amsterdam: North Holland Publ. Comp.

Aumann, R.J. and Kurz, M. (1977) 'Power and Taxes', *Econometrica* 45: 1137-1161.

Bachrach, P. and Baratz, M.S. (1970) *Power and Poverty*. New York: Oxford University Press.

Back, P.-E. (1967) *Sammanslutningarnas roll i politiken 1870-1910*. Skellefteå: Västerbottens tryckeri.

Baecker, D. (1988) *Information und Risiko in der Marktwirtschaft*. Frankfurt: Suhrkamp.

Baethge, M. and Oberbeck, H. (1986) *Zukunft der Angestellten —Neue Technologien und berufliche Perspektiven in Büro und Verwaltung*. Frankfurt: Campus.

Baldamus, W. (1961) *Efficiency and Effort*. London: Tavistock Publications.

Baldwin, D.A. (1978) 'Power and Social Exchange', *American Political Science Review* 72: 1229-42.

Baldwin, D.A. (1990) 'Politics, Exchange, and Cooperation' in B. Marin (ed.) *Generalized Political Exchange. Antagonistic Cooperation and Integrated Policy Circuits*. Frankfurt/Boulder, Colorado: Campus Verlag/Westview Press.

Banting, K. (ed.) (1986) *The State and Economic Interests*. Toronto: University of Toronto Press.

Barbadoro, I. (1973a) *Storia del sindicalismo italiano dalla nascita al fascismo*. Vol. I. *La Federterra*. Florence: La Nuova Italia.

Barbadoro, I. (1973b) *Storia del sindicalismo italiano dalla nascita al fascismo*. Vol. II. *La CGIL*. Florence: La Nuova Italia.

Barnes, D. and Reid, E. (1980) *Governments and Trade Unions. The British Experience 1964-1979*. London: Heinemann.

Barrett, S. and Hill, M. (1984) 'Policy, Bargaining and Structure in Implementation Theory: Towards an Integrated Perspective', *Policy and Politics* 12: 219-40.

Bateson, G. (1972) *Steps to an Ecology of Mind*. New York: Jason Aronson; German translation (1983) *Ökologie des Geistes*. Frankfurt: Suhrkamp.

Batstone, E. et al. (1983) *Unions on the Board*. Oxford: Basil Blackwell.

Baudrillard, J. (1983) *Les stratégies fatales*. Paris: Grasset.

Becquart-Leclercq, J. (1976) 'Relational Power and Center-Periphery Linkages in French Local Polity', *Sociology and Social Research* 62: 21-42.

Becquart-Leclercq, J. (1979) 'Réseau relationnel, pouvoir relationnel', *Revue française de science politique* 29: 102-28.

Beer, S. (1973) 'The Modernization of American Federalism,' *Publius* 3: 50-95.

Beer, S. (1976) 'The Adoption of General Revenue Sharing: A Case Study in Public Sector Politics', *Public Policy* 24: 127-95.

Beer, S. (1977) 'Political Overload and Federalism', *Polity* 10: 5-17.

Beer, S. (1978) ' Federalism, Nationalism, and Democracy in America', *American Political Science Review* 72: 9-21.

Bendix, R. (1964) *Nation Building and Citizenship*. New York: Random House.

Bendix, R. (1974) *Work and Authority in Industry*. Berkeley: University of California Press (first published 1956).

Benson, K.J. (1975) 'The Interorganizational Network as a Political Economy', *Administrative Science Quarterly* 20: 229-49.

Berger, J. (1978) 'Intersubjektive Sinnkonstitution und Sozialstruktur. Zur Kritik handlungstheoretischer Ansätze der Soziologie', *Zeitschrift für Soziologie* 7: 327-34.

Berger, J. and Offe, C. (1982) 'Functionalism versus Rational Choice. Some Questions Concerning the Rationality of Choosing One or the Other', *Theory and Society* 11: 521-26.

Berger, S. (1974) *The French Political System*. New York: Random House.

Berger, S. (ed.) (1981) *Organizing Interests in Western Europe: Pluralism, Corporatism and Transformation Politics*. Cambridge, MA: Harvard University Press.

Bergmann, J. (1985) 'Gewerkschaften — Organisationsstruktur und Mitgliederinteressen', in G. Endruweit et al. (eds) *Handbuch der Arbeitsbeziehungen: Deutschland, Österreich, Schweiz*. Berlin: de Gruyter.

Bergmann, J. et al. (1975) *Gewerkschaften in der Bundesrepublik Deutschland.* Frankfurt: Campus.

Birnbaum, P. (1982) 'The State versus Corporatism', *Politics and Society* 4: 477-501.

Blalock, H.M. Jr. (1961) *Causal Inferences in Nonexperimental Research.* Chapel Hill: University of North Carolina Press.

Blau, P.M. (1964) *Exchange and Power in Social Life.* New York: Wiley and Sons.

Blau, P.M. (1983) 'Social Exchange', pp. 204-14 in P.M. Blau *On the Nature of Organizations.* Malabar, Florida: Krieger.

Blum, A.A. (ed.) (1981) *International Handbook of Industrial Relations.* London/Westport, CT: Greenwood Publishing Group.

Bobbio, N. (1984a) 'Contratto e contrattualismo nel dibattito attuale', in N. Bobbio (ed.) *Il futuro della democrazia.* Torino: Einaudi.

Bobbio, N. (1984b) 'The Future of Democracy', *Telos* 61: 3.

Bodman, L. and Garry, D.B. (1983) 'Innovations in State Cabinet Systems', in D.A. Zimmerman and J.F. Zimmermann (eds) *The Politics of Subnational Governance.* Lanham: University Press of America.

Bohne, E. (1981) *Der informelle Rechtsstaat.* Berlin: Duncker und Humblot.

Boissevain, J. (1974) *Friends of Friends: Networks, Manipulators and Coalitions.* Oxford: Basil Blackwell.

Bornstein, S. and Gourevitch, P. (1984) 'Unions in a Declining Economy: The Case of the British TUC', pp. 13-88 in P. Gourevitch et al. *Unions and Economic Crisis: Britain, West Germany and Sweden.* London: George Allen and Unwin.

Boudon, R. (1979) 'Generating Models as a Research Strategy', pp. 151-63 in R.K. Merton, J.S. Coleman and P.H. Rossi (eds) *Qualitative and Quantitative Social Research. Papers in Honour of Paul F. Lazarsfeld.* New York: Free Press.

Bowman, J.R. (1982) 'The Logic of Capitalist Collective Action', *Social Science Information* 21: 571-604.

Branciard, M. (1984) *La décentralisation dans un pays centralisé.* Lyons: Chronique Sociale.

Brandt, G. et al. (1982) *Anpassung an der Krise: Gewerkschaften in den siebziger Jahren.* Frankfurt: Campus.

Braten, S. (1984) 'The Third Position — Beyond Artificial and Autopoietic Reduction', *Kybernetes* 13: 157-63.

Breton, A. (1974) *The Economic Theory of Representative Government.* London: Macmillan.

Breton, A. and Wintrobe, R. (1982) *An Economic Analysis of Competition, Exchange, and Efficiency in Private and Public Organizations.* Cambridge: Cambridge University Press.

Brickman, R., Jasanoff, S. and Ilgen, T. (1982) 'Chemical Regulation and Cancer: A Cross-National Study of Policy and Politics'. Report prepared for the National Science Foundation.

Brizay, B. (1975) *Le patronat: histoire, structure, stratégie.* Paris: Editions Seuil.

Brookings Institute (1986) *The Swedish Economy.* Washington, D.C.: Brookings Institute.

Brown, W. (1986) 'The Changing Role of Trade Unions in the Management of Labour', *British Journal of Industrial Relations* 24: 161-68.

Bullock, Lord (1977) *Report of the Committee of Inquiry on Industrial Democracy.* London: HMSO.

Bundesminister für Forschung und Technologie (ed.) (1984) *Bundesbericht Forschung* 1984. Bonn.

Bunel, J. and Saglio, J. (1984) 'Employers' Associations in France', in J.P. Windmuller and A. Gladstone (eds) *Employers Associations and Industrial Relations. A Comparative Study.* Oxford: Clarendon Press.

Bunn, R.F. (1984) 'Employers' Associations in the Federal Republic of Germany', in J.P. Windmuller and A. Gladstone (eds) *Employers Associations and Industrial Relations. A Comparative Study.* Oxford: Clarendon Press.

Burt, R.S. (1982) *Toward a Structural Theory of Action.* New York: Academic Press.

Calvet, J. (1986) 'La nécessité d'une flexibilité et d'une mobilité dans l'industrie automobile contemporaine et les difficultés pour y parvenir', *Droit Social* 11: 735-40.

Cameron, D.R. (1978) 'The Expansion of the Public Economy: A Comparative Analysis', *American Political Science Review* 72: 1243-61.

Cameron, D.R. (1984) 'Social Democracy, Corporatism, Labour Quiescence, and the Representation of Economic Interest in Advanced Capitalist Society', pp. 143-78 in J.H. Goldthorpe (ed.) *Order and Conflict in Contemporary Capitalism. Studies in the Political Economy of Western European Nations*. Oxford: Oxford University Press.

Campbell, D. (1969) 'Variation and Selective Retention in Socio-Cultural Evolution', *General Systems* 14: 69-85.

Cawson, A. (ed.) (1985) *Organized Interests and the State. Studies in Meso-Corporatism*. London: SAGE Publications.

Cawson, A. (1985a) 'Varieties of Corporatism: the Importance of the Meso-Level of Interest Intermediation', in A. Cawson *Organized Interests and the State. Studies in Meso-Corporatism*. London: SAGE Publications.

Ceri, P. (1990) 'Social Exchange and Political Exchange: Towards a Typology' in B. Marin (ed.) *Generalized Political Exchange. Antagonistic Cooperation and Integrated Policy Circuits*. Frankfurt/Boulder, Colorado: Campus Verlag/Westview Press.

Chevallier, J. et al. (1984) *L'institution régionale*. Paris: Presses Universitaires de France.

Chlepner, B.S. (1956) *Cent ans d'histoire sociale en Belgique*. Brussels: Institut de Sociologie Solvay.

Churchman, W. (1979) *The Systems Approach*. New York: Delta.

Clark, T.N. (1972) 'Structural-Functionalism, Exchange Theory, and the New Political Economy: Institutionalization As a Theoretical Linkage', *Sociological Inquiry* 42(3-4): 275-98.

Clarke, J. (1985) 'The Juridification of Industrial Relations — A Review Article', *Industrial Law Journal* 15: 69-90.

Clegg, H.A. (1972) *The System of Industrial Relations in Great Britain*. Oxford: Basil Blackwell.

Clegg, H.A. (1979) *The Changing System of Industrial Relations in Great Britain*. Oxford: Basil Blackwell.

Cole, R. and Taebel, D.A. (1986) 'The New Federalism: Promises, Programs, and Performance', *Publius* 16: 3-10.

Colella, C.C. and Beam, D.R. (1981) 'The Political Dynamics of Intergovernmental Policy-Making', in J.J. Hanus (ed.) *The Nationalization State Government*. Lexington, MA: Lexington Books.

Coleman, J.S. (1964) *Introduction to Mathematical Sociology*. New York: Free Press.

Coleman, J.S. (1970) 'Political Money', *Political Science Review* 64(4): 1074-87.

Coleman, J.S. (1971) 'Collective decisions', in H. Turk and R.L. Simpson *Institutions and Social Exchange — The Sociologies of Talcott Parsons and George C. Homans*. Indianapolis: Bobbs-Merrill.

Coleman, J.S. (1973) *The Mathematics of Collective Action*. London: Heinemann Educational Books.

Coleman, J.S. (1974) *Power and the Structure of Society*. New York: Norton.

Coleman, J.S. (1986a) 'Social action systems' in J.S. Coleman *Individual Interests and Collective Action. Selected Essays*. Cambridge: Cambridge University Press.

Coleman, J.S. (1986) *Individual Interests and Collective Action. Selected Essays*. Cambridge: Cambridge University Press.

Coleman, J.S. (1990a) 'Forms of Rights and Forms of Power' in B. Marin (ed.) *Generalized Political Exchange. Antagonistic Cooperation and Integrated Policy Circuits*. Frankfurt/Boulder, Colorado: Campus Verlag/Westview Press.

Coleman, J.S. (1990b) *Foundations of Social Theory*. Cambridge, MA: Harvard University Press.

Comito, V. (1982) *La Fiat tra crisi e restrutturazione*. Roma: Riuniti.

Contini, G. (1985) 'Politics, Law and Shop-Floor Bargaining in Post-War Italy', in S. Tolliday and J. Zeitlin (eds) *Shop-Floor Bargaining and the State*. Cambridge: Cambridge University Press.

Cook, K.S. (1977) 'Exchange and Power in Networks of Interorganizational Relations', *Sociological Quarterly* 18: 62-82.

Cook, K.S. (1990) 'Exchange Networks and Generalized Exchange. Linking Structure and Action' in B. Marin (ed.) *Generalized Political Exchange. Antagonistic Cooperation and Integrated Policy Circuits*. Frankfurt/Boulder, Colorado: Campus Verlag/Westview Press.

Cook, K.S. and Emerson, R.M. (1978) 'Power, Equity, and Commitment in Exchange Networks', *American Sociological Review* 43: 721-39.

Cook, K.S., Emerson, R.M., Gillmore, M.R. and Yamagishi, T. (1983) 'The Distribution of Power in Exchange Networks: Theory and Experimental Results', *American Journal of Sociology* 89: 275-305.

Croisat, M. and Tournon, J. (1984) 'Centralisation et Pluralisme. Le paradoxe français', *International Political Science Review* 5: 415-28.

Crouch, C.J. (1978) 'The Intensification of Industrial Conflict in the United Kingdom', in C.J. Crouch and A. Pizzorno (eds) *The Resurgence of Class Conflict in Western Europe since 1968.* Vol. I. *National Studies.* London: Macmillan.

Crouch, C.J. (1979, 1982) *The Politics of Industrial Relations.* London/Glasgow: Fontana.

Crouch, C.J. (1985) 'Conditions for Trade Union Wage Restraint', pp.105-139 in L.N. Lindberg and C.S. Maier (eds) (1985)

Crouch, C.J. (1986) 'Sharing Public Spaces: States and Organized Interests in W. Europe', in J.A. Hall (ed.) *States in History.* Oxford: Blackwell.

Crouch, C.J. and Pizzorno, A. (eds) (1978a) *The Resurgence of Class Conflict in Western Europe since 1968.* Vol. I. *National Studies.* London: Macmillan.

Crouch, C.J. and Pizzorno, A. (eds) (1978b)*The Resurgence of Class Conflict in Western Europe since 1968.* Vol. II. *Comparative Analyses.* London: Macmillan.

Crozier, M. and Friedberg, E. (1978) *Attore sociale e sistema.* Milano: Etas libri.

Crozier, M. and Thoenig, J.-C. (1975) 'La régulation des systèmes organisés complexes. Le cas du système de décision politico-administratif local en France', *Revue française de sociologie* 16: 3-32.

Czada, R. (1984) 'Zwischen Arbeitsplatzinteresse und Modernisierungszwang', pp. 135-183 in H. Wimmer (ed.) *Wirtschafts- und Sozialpartnerschaft in Österreich.* Wien: Verlag des Verbandes der wissenschaftlichen Gesellschaften Österreichs (VWGÖ).

Daems H. (1983) 'The Determinants of the Hierarchical Organization of Industry', in A. Francis et al. (eds) *Power, Efficiency and Institutions.* London: Heinemann.

Dahl, R.A. (1961) *Who governs? Democracy and Power in an American City.* New Haven/ London: Yale University Press.

Dahrendorf, R. (1959) *Class and Class Conflict in Industrial Society.* London: Routledge and Kegan Paul.

Debreu, G. (1971) *Theory of Value.* New Haven: Yale University Press.

Della Rocca, G. and Negrelli, S. (1983) 'Diritti di informazione ed evoluzione della contrattazione aziendale (1969-1981)', *Giornale di Diritto del Lavoro e di Relazioni Industriali* 5: 549-79.

Delsinne, L. (1936) *Le mouvement syndicale en Belgique.* Brussels: Castaigne.

Dente, B. (1983) 'Gli obiettivi del controllo centrale. Per un'analisi comparata delle relazioni tra centro e periferia', *Rivista italiana di scienza politica* 12: 379-412.

Dente, B. (1985) *Governare la frammentazione.* Bologna: Il Mulino.

Denzau, A., Riker, W. and Shepsle, K. (1985) 'Farquharson and Fenno: Sophisticated Voting and the Home Style', *American Political Science Review* 79: 1117-34.

Deppe, F. (1979) *Autonomie und Integration: Materialien zur Gewerkschaftsanalyse.* Marburg: Arbeiterbewegung und Gesellschaftswissenschaft.

Desolre, G.G. (1981) 'Belgium', in A.A. Blum (ed.) *International Handbook of Industrial Relations.* London/Westport, CT: Greenwood Publishing Group.

Donolo, C. and Fichera, F. (1981) *Il governo debole.* Bari: De Donato.

Drewes, G. (1958) *Die Gewerkschaften in der Verwaltungsordnung.* Heidelberg: Verlagsgesellschaft 'Recht und Wirtschaft'.

Dubois, P. et al. (1978) 'The Contradictions of French Trade Unionism', in C.J. Crouch and A. Pizzorno (eds) *The Resurgence of Class Conflict in Western Europe since 1968.* Vol. I. *National Studies.* London: Macmillan.

Dumont, L. (1977) *Homo aequalis. Genèse et épanouissement de l'idéologie économique.* Paris: Gallimard.

Dunlop, J.T. (1958) *Industrial Relations Systems.* New York: Holt, Rinehart and Winston.

Dupuy, F. (1985) 'The Politico-Administrative System of the Departement in France', in Y. Mény and V. Wright (eds) *Centre-Periphery Relations in Western Europe.* London: Allen and Unwin.

Dupuy, F. and Thoenig, J.-C. (1983) 'La loi du 2 mars 1982 sur la décentralisation. De l'analyse des textes à l'observation des premiers pas', *Revue française de science politique* 33: 962-85.

Durand, C. (1986) 'Les syndicats et la politique industrielle', *Sociologie du Travail* : 304-22.

Durkheim, E. (1973) *De la division du travail social*. Paris: PUF (first published 1893).

Dybdahl, V. (1982) *Det nye samfund pa vej, 1871-1913*. Copenhagen: Gyldendal.

Dye, T. (1984) 'Party and Policy in the States', *Journal of Politics* 46: 1097-1116.

Ebertzheim, R. (1959) *Les syndicats ouvriers en Belgique*. Liège.

Edgren, G., Faxen, K.-O. and Odhner, C.-E. (1973) *Wage Formation and the Economy*. London: Allen and Unwin.

Ehrmann, H.W. (1957) *Organized Business in France*. Princeton, NJ: Princeton University Press.

Eisenhammer, J. (1987) 'Longwy and Bagnoli — A Comparative Study of Trade Union Response to the Steel Crisis in France and Italy', in Y. Mény and V. Wright (eds) *The Politics of Steel — Western Europe and the Steel Industry in the Crisis Years (1974-1984)*. Berlin: de Gruyter.

Eisenstadt, S.N. and Roniger, L. (1975) 'Patron-Client Relations as a Model of Structuring Social Exchange', *Comparative Studies in Society and History* 1: 42-77.

Ekeh, P. (1974) *Social Exchange Theory*. London: Heinemann Educational Books.

Elazar, D.J. (1981) 'Is Federalism Compatible with Prefectoral Administration?' *Publius* 11: 3-22.

Elazar, D.J. (1984) *American Federalism. A View from the States*. New York: Harper and Row.

Elchardus, M. (1988) 'Austauschtemporalitäten. Selbstorganisation zum Zweck gesellschaftlicher Steuerung', *Journal für Sozialforschung* 28(4): 391-416.

Elchardus, M. (1990) 'The Temporalities of Exchange. The Case of Self-Organization for Societal Governance' in B. Marin (ed.) *Generalized Political Exchange. Antagonistic Cooperation and Integrated Policy Circuits*. Frankfurt/Boulder, Colorado: Campus Verlag/Westview Press.

Elster, J. (1979) *Ulysses and the Sirens. Studies in Rationality and Irrationality*. Cambridge: Cambridge University Press.

Elster, J. (1982) 'Marxism, Functionalism, and Game Theory. The Case for Methodological Individualism', *Theory and Society* 11: 453-82.

Elster, J. (1989) 'Wage Bargaining and Social Norms', *Acta Sociologica* 32(2): 113-136.

Emerson, R.M. (1962) 'Power-Dependence Relations', *American Sociological Review* 27: 31-41.

Endruweit, G. et al. (eds) (1985) *Handbuch der Arbeitsbeziehungen: Deutschland, Österreich, Schweiz*. Berlin: de Gruyter.

Erd, R. and Müller-Jentsch, W. (1978) 'Ende der Arbeiteraristokratie? Technologische Veränderungen, Qualifikationsstruktur und Tarifbeziehungen in der Druckindustrie', *Prokla* 35: 17-47.

Esping-Andersen, G. (1985) *Politics against Markets. The Social-Democratic Road to Power*. Princeton: Princeton University Press.

Esping-Andersen, G. and Korpi, W. (1984) 'Social Policy as Class Politics in Post-War Capitalism: Scandinavia, Austria, and Germany', pp. 179-208 in J.H. Goldthorpe (ed.) *Order and Conflict in Contemporary Capitalism. Studies in the Political Economy of Western European Nations*. Oxford: Oxford University Press.

Eulau, H. (1973) 'Polarity in Representational Federalism: A Neglected Theme in Political Theory', *Publius* 3: 153-71.

European Commission (1985) 'Fourteenth Report on Competition Policy'.

Fafchamps, J. (1961) *Les conventions collectives en Belgique*. Brussels: La Pensée Catholique.

Faxen, K.-O. et al. (1987) *Lönebildning i 90-talets samhällsekonomi*. Stockholm: LO, SAF and TCO.

Feigenbaum, E. and McCorduck, P. (1984) *The Fifth Generation*. Reading, MA: Addison-Wesley.

Fesler, J.W. (1965) 'Approaches to the Understanding of Decentralization', *Journal of Politics* 27: 536-66.

Finer, S.E. (ed.) (1975) *Adversary Politics and Electoral Reform*. London: A. Wigram.

Fiorina, M.P. (1978) 'Economic Retrospective Voting in American National Elections: A Microanalysis', *American Journal of Political Science* 11: 426-73.

Flanagan, R.J., Soskice, D.W. and Ulman, L. (1983) *Unionism, Economic Stabilization and Incomes Policies: The European Experience*. Washington, DC: Brookings.

Flanders, A. (1970) *Management and Unions — The Theory and Reform of Industrial Relations*.

London: Faber.

Flora, P. et al. (1983) *State, Economy and Society in Western Europe 1815-1975*. Vol. I *The Growth of Mass Democracies and Welfare States*. London: Macmillan.

Flora, P. et al. (1987) *State, Economy and Society in Western Europe 1815-1975*. Vol. II *The Growth of Industrial Societies and Capitalist Economies*. London: Macmillan.

Foerster, H. v. (1981) *Observing Systems*. Seaside, Cal.: Intersystems Publications.

Folkers, C.G. (1983) 'Zu einer positiven Theorie der Steuerreform', pp. 189-211 in K.H. Hansmeyer (ed.) *Staatsfinanzierung im Wandel*. Berlin: Duncker und Humblot.

Forte, F. and Peacock, A. (1981) 'Tax Planning, Tax Analysis and Tax Policy', pp. 3-28 in A. Peacock and F. Forte (eds) *The Political Economy of Taxation*. Oxford: Basil Blackwell.

Fox, A. (1966) *Industrial Sociology and Industrial Relations*. London: HMSO.

Fox, A. (1974) *Beyond Contract: Work, Power and Trust Relations*. London: Faber and Faber.

Fox, A. (1985) *History and Heritage*. London: Allen and Unwin.

Freeman, L.C. (1979) 'Centrality in Social Networks: Conceptual Clarification', *Social Networks* 1: 215-39.

Frey, B.S. and Schneider, F. (1978) 'An Empirical Study of Politico-Economic Interaction in the United States', *Review of Economics and Statistics* 60: 174-83.

Frey, B.S. and Schneider, F. (1979) 'An Econometric Model with an Endogenous Government Sector', *Public Choice* 34: 29-43.

Fried, R. (1981) 'Prefectorialism in America?' *Publius* 11: 23-9.

Friedberg, E. (1990) 'Generalized Political Exchange, Organizational Analysis, and Public Policy' in B. Marin (ed.) *Generalized Political Exchange. Antagonistic Cooperation and Integrated Policy Circuits*. Frankfurt/Boulder, Colorado: Campus Verlag/Westview Press.

Frye, J. and Gordon, R.J. (1981) 'Government Intervention in the Inflation Process: The Econometrics of 'Self-Inflicted Wounds'', *American Economic Review* 71: 288-94.

Fulcher, J. (1976) 'Class Conflict: Joint Regulation and its Decline', in R. Scace (ed.) *Readings in the Swedish Class Structure*. Oxford: Pergamon Press.

Funke, M. (1986) 'Nominalzinsen, Realzinsen und internationale Kapitalbewegungen.' WZB Discussion Paper IIM/LMP 86-11. Berlin: Wissenschaftszentrum Berlin.

Galaskiewicz, J. (1982) 'Interorganizational Relations', *Annual Review of Sociology* 11: 281-304.

Galbraith, J.K. (1972) *The New Industrial State*. London: Deutsch.

Galenson, W. (1949) *Labor in Norway*. Cambridge, MA: Harvard University Press.

Galenson, W. (1952a) *The Danish System of Labor Relations*. Cambridge, MA: Harvard University Press.

Galenson, W. (1952b) 'Scandinavia' in W. Galenson (ed.) *Comparative Labor Movements*. New York: Prentice Hall.

Garrett, G. and Lange, P. (1976) 'Performance in a Hostile World: Economic Growth in Capitalist Democracies, 1974-80', *World Politics* 38: 517-45.

Giannini, M.S. (1986) *Il potere pubblico. Stati e amministrazioni pubbliche*. Bologna: Il Mulino.

Giddens, A. (1982) 'Commentary on the Debate', *Theory and Society* 11: 527-39.

Glanville, R. (1982) 'Inside Every White Box There Are Two Black Boxes Trying To Get Out', *Behavioral Science* 27: 1-11.

Glaser, B.G. (1978) *Theoretical Sensitivity. Advances in the Methodology of Grounded Theory*. Mill Valley, CA: Sociology Press.

Glaser, B.G. and Strauss, A.L. (1967) *The Discovery of Grounded Theory. Strategies for Qualitative Research*. Chicago: Aldine Atherton.

Goldthorpe, J.H. (1984a) 'The End of Convergence — Corporatist and Dualist Tendencies in Modern Western Societies', pp. 315-43 in J.H. Goldthorpe (ed.) *Order and Conflict in Contemporary Capitalism. Studies in the Political Economy of Western European Nations*. Oxford: Oxford University Press.

Goldthorpe, J.H. (ed.) (1984) *Order and Conflict in Contemporary Capitalism. Studies in the Political Economy of Western European Nations*. Oxford: Oxford University Press.

Gopoian, D. (1984) 'What Makes PAC's Tick? An Analysis of the Allocative Patterns of Economic

Interest Groups', *American Journal of Political Science* 28: 259-81.

Gourevitch, P., Martin, A., Ross, G., Allen, C., Bornstein, S. and Markovits, A. (1984) *Unions and Economic Crisis: Britain, West Germany and Sweden.* London: George Allen and Unwin.

Gourevitch, P.A. (1980) *Paris and the Provinces. The Politics of Local Government Reform in France.* London: Allen and Unwin.

Government Information Office (15/87) *Aktuelle Beiträge zur Wirtschafts- und Finanzpolitik: Steuerreform 1986/88 und 1990.* 14. April 1987.

Grande, E. and Müller, W.C. (1985) 'Sozialpartnerschaftliche Krisensteuerung oder Krise der Sozialpartnerschaft?' in P. Gerlich et al. (eds) *Sozialpartnerschaft in der Krise —Leistungen und Grenzen des Neokorporatismus in Österreich.* Wien: Böhlau.

Granovetter, M. (1985) 'Economic Action and Social Structure: The Problem of Embeddedness', *American Journal of Sociology* 91: 481-510.

Grant, W. and Marsh, P. (1977) *The CBI.* London: Hodder and Sloughton.

Graziano, L. (1982) 'Introduzione all'edizione italiana', in L. Graziano, P.J. Katzenstein and S. Tarrow (eds) *Centro e periferia nelle nazioni industriali.* Roma: Officina.

Greenwald, A., Pratkanis, A.A., Leippe, M.R. and Baumgardner, M.H. (1986) 'Under What Conditions Does Theory Obstruct Research Progress?' *Psychological Review* 93: 216-29.

Grémion, P. (1976) *Le pouvoir périphérique. Bureaucrats et notables dans le système politique français.* Paris: Editions Seuil.

Gretschmann, K. (1986) 'Measuring the Public Sector: A Contestable Issue', pp. 139-58 in F.X. Kaufmann, G. Majone and V. Ostrom (eds) *Guidance, Control and Evaluation in the Public Sector.* Berlin/New York: de Gruyter.

Groux, G. and Lévy, C. (1985) 'Mobilisation collective et productivité économique — Le cas des 'cercles de qualité' dans la sidérurgie', *Revue française de sociologie* 26: 70-95.

Gruner, E. (1963) 'Koalitionsrecht und gewerkschaftliches Wachstum im schweizerischen Hochkapitalismus', *Mélanges d'histoire économique et sociale* 2: 319-41.

Gusman, S. et al. (1980) *Public Policy for Chemicals: National and International Issues.* Washington, DC: The Conservation Foundation.

Guttman, J. (1978) 'Understanding Collective Action', *American Economic Review* 68: 251-55.

Habermas, J. (1970) *Zur Logik der Sozialwissenschaften.* Frankfurt: Suhrkamp.

Hadenius, A. (1976) *Facklig organisationsutveckling.* Uppsala: Statsvetenskapliga föreningen i Uppsala.

Hadenius, A. (1978) 'Ämbetsverkens styrelser', *Statsvetenskaplig tidskrift.*

Hadenius, A. (1983) *Medbestämmande reformen.* Stockholm: Almqvist and Wiksell.

Hahn, W. (1986) 'EUREKA. Ein neuer Weg für mehr Zusammenarbeit in Europa', *Mitteilungen des Hochschulverbandes* 1: 47-51.

Haider, D. (1974) *When Governments Come to Washington. Governors, Mayors and Intergovernmental Lobbying.* New York: The Free Press.

Hall, P. (1986) *Governing the Economy. The Politics of State Intervention in Britain and France.* Cambridge, MA: Polity Press.

Halvarson, A. (1982) *Sveriges statsskick.* Stockholm: Liber.

Ham, C. and Hill, M. (1986) *Introduzione all'analisi delle politiche pubbliche.* Bologna: Il Mulino.

Hanf, K. (1978) 'Introduction', in K. Hanf and F.W. Scharpf (eds) *Interorganizational Policy Making. Limits to Coordination and Central Control.* London: SAGE Publications.

Hanf, K. (1982) 'Regulatory Structures: Enforcement as Bargaining', *European Journal of Political Research* 10: 159-72.

Hanf, K. and Scharpf, F.W. (eds) (1978) *Interorganizational Policy Making. Limits to Coordination and Central Control.* London: SAGE Publications.

Hannan, M.T. and Freeman, J. (1977) 'The Population Ecology of Organizations', *American Journal of Sociology* 82: 929-64.

Hannan, M.T. and Freeman, J. (1984) 'Structural Inertia and Organizational Change', *American Sociological Review* 49: 149-64.

Hansen, S.A. and Henriksen, I. (1980a) *Sociale bydninger, 1914-1939.* Copenhagen: Gyldendal.

Hansen, S.A. and Henriksen, I. (1980b) *Velfaerdsstaten, 1940-1978*. Copenhagen: Gyldendal.

Hansson, S.O. (1984) *SAF i politiken*. Stockholm: Tiden.

Hanus, J.J. (ed.) (1981) *The Nationalization of State Government*. Lexington, MA: Lexington Books.

Hardiman, N. (1986) 'Centralised Collective Bargaining: Trade Unions, Employers and Government in the Republic of Ireland'. Unpublished doctoral thesis. Oxford: University of Oxford.

Hardin, R. (1982) 'Collective Action as an Agreeable n-Prisoners' Dilemma', pp. 123-35 in B. Barry and R. Hardin (eds) *Rational Man and Irrational Society?* London/Beverly Hills/New Delhi: SAGE Publications.

Hartkopf, G. and Bohne, E. (1983) *Umweltpolitik 1 —Grundlagen, Analysen, Perspektiven*. Opladen: Westdeutscher Verlag.

Hayward, J. (1973) *The One and Indivisible French Republic*. London: Weisenfeld and Nicholson.

Heckscher, G. (1946, 1951) *Staten och organisationer*. Stockholm: KF tryckeri.

Heidenheimer, A.J. (1980) *Unions and Welfare State Development in Britain and Germany: an Interpretation of Metamorphoses in the Period 1910-1950*. Berlin: Internationales Institut für Vergleichende Gesellschaftsforschung.

Helander, V. (1984) 'Corporatism or Quasi-Corporatism: The Development of Prices Policy Mechanisms in Finland 1968-1978', in H. Paloheimo (ed.) *Politics in the Era of Corporatism and Planning*. Tampere: The Finnish Political Science Association.

Helander, V. and Anckar, D. (1983) *Consultation and Political Culture: Essays on the Case of Finland*. Helsinki: Societas Scientiarum Fennica.

Hempel, C.G. (1965) *Aspects of Scientific Explanation*. New York: Free Press.

Hernes, G. (1978) *Förhandlingsøkonomi og blandningsadministrasjon*. Oslo: Universitetsforlaget Oslo.

Hibbs, D.A. (1977) 'Political Parties and Macroeconomic Policy', *American Political Science Review* 71: 1467-87.

Hibbs, D.A. (1982) 'On the Demand for Economic Outcomes: Macroeconomic Performance and Mass Political Support in the United States, Great Britain, and Germany', *Journal of Politics* 44: 426-62.

Hillery, B.J. (1981) 'Ireland', in A.A. Blum (ed.) *International Handbook of Industrial Relations*. London/Westport, CT: Greenwood Publishing Group.

Hinrichs, K. (1988) *Motive und Interessen im Arbeitszeitkonflikt*. Frankfurt/New York: Campus.

Hirsch, F. (1977) *Social Limits to Growth*. London: Routledge and Kegan Paul.

Hirschman, A.O. (1977) *The Passions and the Interests. Political Arguments for Capitalism before Its Triumph*. Princeton, NJ: Princeton University Press.

Hjern, B. and Hull, C. (1981) 'Implementation Research and Empirical Constitutionalism', *European Journal of Political Research* 10: 105-16.

Hjern, B. and Porter, D.O. (1981) 'Implementation Structures. A New Unit of Administrative Analysis', *Organization Studies* 2: 211-27.

Hobsbawm, E.J. (1984) 'Der 'New Unionism'. Eine komparative Betrachtung', in W.J. Mommsen and H.G. Husung (eds) *Auf dem Wege zur Massengewerkschaft*. Stuttgart: Klett-Cotta.

Hoffenbert, R.I. (1971) 'The Nationalization of State Politics', in R.I. Hoffenbert and I. Sharansky (eds) *State and Urban Politics. Readings in Comparative Public Policy*. Boston: Little Brown.

Hoffmann, S. et al. (1963) *In Search of France*. Cambridge, MA: Cambridge University Press.

Hoffmann-Riem, W. (1982) 'Selbstbindung der Verwaltung', pp. 190-234 in D.H. Scheuning, W. Hoffman-Riem and B. Raschauer (eds) *Selbstbindungen der Verwaltung*. Berlin/New York: de Gruyter.

Hofstadter, D. (1984) *Gödel, Escher, Bach: An Eternal Golden Braid*. Harmondsworth: Penguin.

Höpflinger, F. (1976) *Industriegewerkschaften in der Schweiz*. Zürich: Limmat Verlag.

Horn, C.E. v. (1979) *Policy Implementation in the Federal System: National Goals and Local Implementors*. Lexington, MA: Lexington Books.

Hünke, H. (1986) 'Schlüsselstellung der Informationstechnik', *Das Parlament* 33-34 (16.8.86): 11-12.

Hyman, R. and Brough, I. (1975) *Social Values and Industrial Relations. A Study of Fairness and

Inequality. Oxford: Basil Blackwell.

Ingram, H. (1977) 'Policy Implementation through Bargaining. The Case of Federal Grants-in-Aid', *Public Policy* 25: 449-526.

Jackson, P. and Sisson, K. (1976) 'Employers' Confederations in Sweden and the United Kingdom and the Significance of Industrial Infrastructure', *British Journal of Industrial Relations* 14(3): 306-23.

Jacobsen, A. et al. (1981) *Förbättring av arbetsmiljö genom regionella skyddsombuden.* Stockholm: Sv. Byggarbetarför., R117.

Jacoby, S.M. (1983) 'Union-Management Cooperation in the United States — Lessons from the 1920s', *Industrial and Labor Relations Review* 37: 18-23.

Jacquemin, A. (1985) *Sélection et pouvoir dans la nouveau économie industrielle.* Paris/Louvain-la-Neuve: Economica-Cabay.

Jacquemin, A. (1986) *Compétition européenne et coopération entre entreprises en matière de recherche développement.* Luxembourg: European Commission.

Jacquemin, A. and Spinoit, B. (1986) 'Economic and Legal Aspects of Cooperative Research: A European View', reprinted from The Annual Proceedings of Fordham Corporate Law Institute. New York: Matthew Bender and Company.

Junkerheinrich, M. (1986) 'Organisations- und Konfliktfähigkeit von Steuerinteressen', *Die Verwaltung* 19: 213-29.

Justi, J. v. (1761) *Politische und Finanzschriften über wichtige Gegenstände der Staatskunst, der Kriegswissenschaften und des Cameral- und Finanzwesens.* Kopenhagen und Leipzig (Fotoreproduction Darmstadt 1970).

Jørgensen, P.F. (1975) *Den samvirkende Fakforbund: Kompetencespørgmål i mellemkrigstiden.* Copenhagen.

Kahneman, D. and Tversky, A. (1984) 'Choice, Values, Frames', *American Psychologist* 39: 341-50.

Kappelhoff, P. (1977) 'Markt- und Netzwerkansatz bei der Analyse von Machtbeziehungen: Kollektive Entscheidungen als Tausch von Kontrolle'. Arbeitsbericht. Wien: Soziale Netzwerke.

Kappelhoff, P. (1987) 'Die Triade als System dichotomer Variablen', pp. 162-76 in F. U. Pappi (ed.) *Methoden der Netzwerkanalyse.* München: Oldenbourg.

Kappelhoff, P. and Pappi, F.U. (1982) 'Restricted Exchange in Altneustadt. Analyse sozialer Netzwerke'. Working Paper. Kiel: Institut für Soziologie der Christian-Albrecht Universität.

Kappelhoff, P. and Pappi, F.U. (1987) 'The Political Subsystem of a Community Elite: Blockmodelling the Power Structure'. Universitetet i Oslo: Institutet for Sosiologi. *Sociologisk Årbok*: 231-64.

Karl-Bräuer-Institut (1987) *Keine Abstriche an Steuersenkung 1990.* Wiesbaden: Bund der Steuerzahler.

Kastendiek, H. (1981) 'Die Selbstblockierung der Korporatismus-Diskussion. Teilproblematisierungen der gesellschaftlichen Politikorganisation und gesellschaftspolitische Entproblematisierungen korporativer Strukturen und Strategien', pp. 92-116 in U. v. Alemann (ed.) *Neokorporatismus.* Frankfurt/New York: Campus.

Katzenstein, P.J. (1984) *Corporatism and Change. Austria, Switzerland and the Politics of Industry.* Ithaca: Cornell University Press.

Keeler, J.T.S. (1985) 'Situating France on the Pluralism-Corporatism Continuum. A Critique and an Alternative to the Wilson Perspective', *Comparative Politics* 17: 229-49.

Keller, H. (1986) 'EUREKA — eine Idee mit Zukunft', *Das Parlament* 33-34 (16.8.86): 11 ff.

Kelley, H.H. (1984) 'The Theoretical Description of Interdependence by Means of Transition Lists', *Journal of Personality and Social Psychology* 47: 956-82.

Kelman, S. (1981) *Regulating America, Regulating Sweden: a Comparative Study of Occupational Safety and Health.* Cambridge, MA: MIT Press.

Kemp, K.A. (1978) 'Nationalization of the American States. A Test of the Thesis', *American Politics Quarterly* 6: 237-47.

Kempf, H. and Toinet, M.-F. (1980) 'La fin du fédéralisme aux Etats-Unis?' *Revue française de science politique* 30: 735-75.

Kenis, P. and Schneider, V. (1987) 'The EC as an International Corporate Actor: Two Case Studies in Economic Diplomacy', *European Journal of Political Research* 15: 437-57.

Kern, H. and Schumann, M. (1985) *Das Ende der Arbeitsteilung — Rationalisierung in der industriellen Produktion.* München: Beck.

Kesselman, M. (1967) *The Ambiguous Consensus.* New York: Knopf.

Kesselman, M. (1985) 'The Tranquil Revolution at Clochemerle: Socialist Decentralization in France', in P.G. Cerny and M.A. Schain (eds) *Socialism, the State and Public Policies in France.* London: Francis Pinter.

Kettl, D. (1984) 'The Maturing of American Federalism', in R.T. Golembiewsky and A. Wildavsky (eds) *The Costs of Federalism.* New Brunswick and London: Transaction Book.

Kinsev, K.A. (1987) 'The Social Dynamics of Tax Encounters'. Conference paper. American Bar Foundation.

Kjellberg, F. (1985) 'Local Government Reorganization and the Development of the Welfare State', *Journal of Public Policy* 5: 215-39.

Kloten, N., Ketterer, K.-H. and Vollmer, R. (1985) 'West Germany's Stabilization Performance', pp. 353-402 in L.N. Lindberg and C.S. Maier (eds) *The Politics of Inflation and Economic Stagnation. Theoretical Approaches and International Case Studies.* Washington, DC: Brookings.

Knoellinger, C.E. (1960) *Labor in Finland.* Cambridge, MA: Harvard University Press.

Knoke, D. and Kuklinski, J.H. (1982) *Network Analysis.* Beverly Hills: SAGE Publications.

Knoke, D. and Laumann, E.O. (1982) 'The Social Organization of National Policy Domains', in N. Lin and P.V. Marsden (eds) *Social Structure and Networks.* Beverly Hills: SAGE Publications.

Korpi, W. (1978) *The Working Class in Welfare Capitalism.* London: Routledge.

Korpi, W. (1983) *The Democratic Class Struggle.* London: Routledge.

Koskimies, J. (1981) 'Finland', in A.A. Blum (ed.) *International Handbook of Industrial Relations.* London/Westport, CT: Greenwood Publishing Group.

Krieger, H. (1985) "Anti-Regierungs-' oder 'Klientelthese'? Wirkungen persönlicher Betroffenheit von Arbeitslosigkeit im Rahmen des etablierten Parteienspektrums (1980-85)', *Politische Vierteljahresschrift* 26: 357-80.

Kuhn, A. (1974) *The Logic of Social Systems: A Unified, Deductive, System-Based Approach to Social Science.* San Francisco: Jossey Bass.

Kvavik, R.B. (1976) *Interest Groups in Norway.* Oslo: Universitetsforlaget Oslo.

Lacorne, D. (1980) *Les notables rouges.* Paris: Presses de la FNSP.

Lafferty, W.M. (1971) *Economic Development and the Response of Labor in Scandinavia.* Oslo: Universitetsforlaget Oslo.

Lang, W. (1978) *Kooperative Gewerkschaften und Einkommenspolitik: das Beispiel Österreichs.* Frankfurt: Peter Lang Verlag.

Lange, P. (1984) 'Unions, Workers and Wage Regulation: the Rational Bases of Consent', pp. 98-123 in J.H. Goldthorpe (ed.) *Order and Conflict in Contemporary Capitalism. Studies in the Political Economy of Western European Nations.* Oxford: Oxford University Press.

Lange, P. and Garrett, G. (1985) 'The Politics of Growth: Strategic Interaction and Economic Performance in the Advanced Industrial Democracies, 1974-1980', *Journal of Politics* 47: 792-827.

Lash, S. (1985) 'The End of Neo-Corporatism? — The Breakdown of Centralised Bargaining in Sweden', *British Journal of Industrial Relations* 23: 215-39.

Laumann, E.O. and Pappi, F.U. (1976) *Networks of Collective Action.* New York: Academic Press.

Leckebusch, R. (1966) *Entstehung und Wandlungen der Zielsetzungen, der Struktur und der Wirkungen von Arbeitgeberverbänden.* Berlin: Duncker und Humblot.

Lefranc, G. (1967) *Le mouvement syndical sous la troisième république.* Paris: Payot.

Lefranc, G. (1976) *Les organisations patronales en France.* Paris: Payot.

Lehmbruch, G. (1977) 'Liberal Corporatism and Party Government', *Comparative Political Studies* 10: 91-126.

Lehmbruch, G. (1982) 'Neo-Corporatism in a Comparative Perspective', pp. 1-28 in G. Lehmbruch and P.C. Schmitter (eds) *Patterns of Corporatist Policy-Making.* London/Beverly Hills: SAGE Publications.

Lehmbruch, G. (1983) 'Neokorporatismus in Westeuropa: Hauptprobleme im internationalen

Vergleich', *Journal für Sozialforschung* 23(4): 407-20.

Lehmbruch, G. (1984) 'Concertation and the Structure of Corporatist Networks', pp. 60-80 in J.H. Goldthorpe (ed.) *Order and Conflict in Contemporary Capitalism. Studies in the Political Economy of Western European Nations*. Oxford: Oxford University Press.

Lehmbruch, G. (1985) 'Sozialpartnerschaft in der vergleichenden Politikforschung', *Journal für Sozialforschung* 25(3): 285-303.

Lehmbruch, G. and Schmitter, P.C. (eds) (1982) *Patterns of Corporatist Policy-Making*. London: SAGE Publications.

Leibenstein, H. (1987) *Inside the Firm: The Inefficiencies of Hierarchy*. Cambridge, MA: Harvard University Press.

Lévi-Strauss, C. (1967) *Les structures élémentaires de la parenté*. 2 ed. Paris: Mouton and Maison des Sciences de l'Homme (first published 1947).

Levine, L. (1969) 'Federal Grants-in-Aid: Administration and Politics', in D.J. Elazar et al. (eds) *Cooperation and Conflict: Readings in American Federalism*. Ithaca, Ill.: F.F. Peacock Publishers.

Lewin, L. (1980) *Governing Trade Unions in Sweden*. Cambridge, MA: Harvard University Press.

Lilja, K. (1983) *Workers' Workplace Organisations*. Helsinki: School of Economics.

Lindberg, L.N. and Maier, C.S. (eds) (1985) *The Politics of Inflation and Economic Stagnation. Theoretical Approaches and International Case Studies*. Washington, DC: Brookings.

Lindblom, C. (1982) 'The Market as Prison', *Journal of Politics* 44: 324-36.

Littek, W. and Heisig, U. (1986) 'Rationalisierung von Arbeit als Aushandlungsprozeß', *Soziale Welt* 37: 237-62.

Lockwood, D. (1981) 'The Weakest Link in the Chain? Some Comments on the Marxist Theory of Action', *Research in the Sociology of Work* 1: 435-81.

Loubéjac, F. (1986) 'Sur la suppression de l'autorisation de licenciement', *Droit Social* 3: 213-19.

Lowery, D. (1985) 'The Keynesian and Political Determinants of Unbalanced Budgets: U.S. Fiscal Policy from Eisenhower to Reagan', *American Journal of Political Science* 29: 428-60.

Lowi, T.J. (1969) *The End of Liberalism*. New York: Norton.

Lowi, T.J. (1978) 'Europeanization of America? From United States to United State', in T.J. Lowi and A. Stone (eds) *Nationalizing Government. Public Policies in America*. London: SAGE Publications.

Lübbe, H. (1975) 'Was heißt 'Das kann man nur historisch erklären'? Zur Analyse der Struktur historischer Prozesse', pp. 154-68 in H. Lübbe *Fortschritt als Orientierungsproblem*. Freiburg: Rombach.

Luhmann, N. (1965) *Grundrechte als Institution*. Berlin: Duncker und Humblot.

Luhmann, N. (1975) 'Einführende Bemerkungen zu einer Theorie symbolisch generalisierter Kommunikationsmedien', in N. Luhmann *Soziologische Aufklärung 2*. Opladen: Westdeutscher Verlag.

Luhmann, N. (1983) 'Die Einheit des Rechtssystems', *Rechtstheorie* 14: 129-54.

Luhmann, N. (1983a) 'Das sind Preise', *Soziale Welt* 34: 153-70.

Luhmann, N. (1984) *Soziale Systeme. Grundriß einer allgemeinen Theorie*. Frankfurt: Suhrkamp.

Luhmann, N. (1984a) 'Die Wirtschaft der Gesellschaft als autopoietisches System', *Zeitschrift für Soziologie* 13(4): 308-27.

Luhmann, N. (1984b) 'Das Kunstwerk und die Selbstreproduktion der Kunst', *Delfin* 3: 51-69.

Luhmann, N. (1984c) 'The Self-Description of Society: Crisis Fashion and Sociological Theory', *International Journal of Comparative Sociology* 25(1-2): 59-72.

Luhmann, N. (1985) 'Society, Meaning, Religion Based on Self-Reference', *Sociological Analysis* 46(1): 5.

Luhmann, N. (1985a) 'Einige Probleme mit reflexivem Recht', *Zeitschrift für Rechtssoziologie* 6; English translation (1984) 'Some Problems with 'Reflexive Law". Paper given at the Conference 'Autopoiesis in Law and Society'. Florence: European University Institute. Oct. 1984.

Luhmann, N. (1985b) "Distinctions directrices' — über Codierung von Semantiken und Systemen'. Manuscript. Bielefeld.

Luhmann, N. (1986) 'Systeme verstehen Systeme', in N. Luhmann and K. Schorr (eds) *Zwischen Intransparenz und Verstehen*. Frankfurt: Suhrkamp.

Luhmann, N. (1986a) *Ökologische Kommunikation*. Opladen: Westdeutscher Verlag.

MacRae, C.D. (1977) 'A Political Model of the Business Cycle', *Journal of Political Economy* 85: 239-63.

Macneil, I.R. (1974a) 'The Many Futures of Contracts', *Southern California Law Review* 47: 691-816.

Macneil, I.R. (1980) *The New Social Contract. An Inquiry into Modern Contractual Relations*. New Haven: Yale University Press.

Macneil, I.R. (1981) 'Economic Analysis of Contractual Relations: Its Shortfalls and the Need for a 'Rich Classificatory Apparatus'', *Northwestern University Law Review* 75: 1018-63.

Macneil, I.R. (1985) 'Relational Contract: What We Do and Do Not Know', *Wisconsin Law Review* 3: 483-525.

Macneil, I.R. (1990) 'Political Exchange as Relational Contract' in B. Marin (ed.) *Generalized Political Exchange. Antagonistic Cooperation and Integrated Policy Circuits*. Frankfurt/Boulder, Colorado: Campus Verlag/Westview Press.

Maier, C.S. (1970) 'Between Taylorism and Technocracy — European Ideologies and the Vision of Industrial Productivity in the 1920s', *Journal of Contemporary History* 5: 27-61.

Maier, C.S. (1975) *Recasting Bourgeois Europe*. Princeton, NJ: Princeton University Press.

Maital, S. and Benjamini, Y. (1979) 'Inflation as a Prisoner's Dilemma', *Journal of Post Keynesian Economics* 2: 459-81.

Malik, R. (1983) 'Japan's Fifth Generation Computer Project', *Futures* 15: 205-10.

Malinvaud, E. (1977) *The Theory of Unemployment Reconsidered*. Oxford: Basil Blackwell.

Mallet, S. (1969) *La nouvelle classe ouvrière*. Paris: Editions Seuil.

March, J. and Simon, H.A. (1967) *Organizations*. New York/London/Sidney: Wiley.

Marin, B. (1982) *Die Paritätische Kommission. Aufgeklärter Technokorporatismus in Österreich*. Vienna: Internationale Publikationen.

Marin, B. (1983) 'Organizing Interests by Interest Organizations: Associational Prerequisites of Corporatism in Austria', *International Political Science Review* 4(2): 197-216.

Marin, B. (1985) 'Generalized Political Exchange. Preliminary Considerations'. EUI Working Paper 85/190. Florence: European University Institute, reprinted in B. Marin (ed.) (1990).

Marin, B. (1985a) 'Austria — The Paradigm Case of Liberal Corporatism?', pp. 89-125 in W. Grant (ed.) *The Political Economy of Corporatism*. London: Macmillan.

Marin, B. (1986) *Unternehmerorganisationen im Verbändestaat. Politik der Bauwirtschaft in Österreich*. Wien: Internationale Publikationen.

Marin, B. (1987) 'Contracting without Contracts. Economic Policy Concertation by Autopoietic Regimes beyond Law?' EUI Working Paper 87/278. Florence: European University Institute; reprinted in G. Teubner (ed.) (1990) *State, Law, Economy as Autopoietic Systems*. Milano: Guiffré.

Marin, B. (1987a) 'From Consociationalism to Technocorporatism: The Austrian Case as a Model-Generator', pp. 39-69 in I. Scholten (ed.) *Political Stability and Neo-Corporatism. Corporatist Integration and Societal Cleavages in Western Europe*. London: SAGE Publications.

Marin, B. (ed.) (1990) *Generalized Political Exchange. Antagonistic Cooperation and Integrated Policy Circuits*. Frankfurt/Boulder, Colorado: Campus Verlag/Westview Press.

Marin, B. and Mayntz, R. (eds) (1991)*Policy Networks. Empirical Evidence and Theoretical Considerations*. Frankfurt/New York: Campus Verlag (forthcoming).

Marsden, P.V. (1981a) 'Models and Methods for Characterizing the Structural Parameters of Groups', *Social Networks* 3: 1-27.

Marsden, P.V. (1981b) 'Introducing Influence Processes into a System of Collective Decisions', *American Journal of Sociology* 86: 1203-35.

Marsden, P.V. (1983) 'Restricted Access in Networks and Models of Power', *American Journal of Sociology* 88(4): 686-717.

Marsden, P.V. and Laumann, E.O. (1977) 'Collective Action in a Community Elite: Exchange, Influence Resources, and Issue Resolution', pp. 199-250 in R.J. Liebert and A.W. Imersheim (eds) *Power, Paradigms and Community Research*. London/Beverly Hills: SAGE Publications.

Martin, A. (1984) 'Trade Unions in Sweden: Strategic Responses to Change and Crisis', pp. 189-359 in P. Gourevitch et al. *Unions and Economic Crisis: Britain, West Germany and Sweden.* London: George Allen and Unwin.

Martin, A. (1986a) 'The Politics of Employment and Welfare: National Policies and International Interdependence', pp. 157-240 in K. Banting (ed.) *The State and Economic Interests.* Toronto: University of Toronto Press.

Martin, A. (1986b) 'The End of the 'Swedish Model?' Recent Developments in Swedish Industrial Relations'. Manuscript. Cambridge, MA: Harvard University Center For European Studies.

Marx, K. (1969) *Das Kapital. Kritik der politischen Ökonomie.* Vol. 1, MEW 23. Berlin: Dietz (first published 1890).

Maturana, H. (1982) *Erkennen: Die Organisation und Verkörperung von Wirklichkeit.* Braunschweig/ Wiesbaden: Vieweg.

Matzner, E., Kregel, J. and Roncaglia, A. (eds) (1987) *Arbeit für alle ist möglich. Über ökonomische und institutionelle Bedingungen erfolgreicher Beschäftigungs- und Arbeitsmarktpolitik.* Berlin: Sigma.

Mayntz, R. (1983) 'The Conditions of Effective Public Policy: a New Challenge For Policy Analysis', *Policy and Politics* 11(2): 123-43.

Mayntz, R. (1986) 'Generalized Political Exchange — Searching for the *contrat social* in a center-less society'. Paper presented at the workshop 'Political Exchange: Between Governance and Ideology', organized by B. Marin and A. Pizzorno, European University Institute. Florence. December 14-18.

Mayntz, R. (1986a) 'Corporate Actors in Public Policy: Changing Perspectives in Political Analysis', *Norsk Statsviten Skapelig Tidskrift* 3: 7-25.

Mayntz, R. (ed.) (1980) *Implementation politischer Programme.* Königstein: Hein.

Mayntz, R. and Nedelmann, B. (1987) 'Eigendynamische soziale Prozesse: Anmerkungen zu einem analytischen Paradigma.' in *Kölner Zeitschrift für Soziologie und Sozialpsychologie* 39(4): 648-668.

Mayntz, R. and Scharpf, F.W. (1975) *Policy-Making in the German Federal Bureaucracy.* Amsterdam: Elsevier.

McCarthy, C. (1977) *Trade Unions in Ireland, 1894-1960.* Dublin: Institute of Public Administration.

McGuire, W.J. (1983) 'A Contextualist Theory of Knowledge: Its Implications for Innovation and Reform in Psychological Research', pp. 1-47 in L. Berkowitz (ed.) *Advances in Experimental Social Psychology.* Vol. 16. Orlando, Florida: Academic Press.

McKay, D. (1982) 'Fiscal Federalism, Professionalism and the Transformation of American State Government', *Public Administration* 60: 10-22.

Médard, J.-F. (1981) 'Political Clientelism in France: The Center-Periphery Nexus Reexamined', in S.N. Eisenstadt and R. Lemarchand (eds) *Political Clientelism Patronage and Development.* London: SAGE Publications.

Mény, Y. (1984) 'Decentralisation in Socialist France: The Politics of Pragmatism', *West European Politics* 7: 65-79.

Mény, Y. (1985) 'La légitimation des groupes d'intérêt par l'administration française'. Paper presented at the IPSA Congress. Paris.

Mény, Y. and Wright, V. (eds) (1985) *Centre-Periphery Relations in Western Europe.* London: Allen and Unwin.

Merlini, C. (ed.) (1984) *Economic Summits and Western Decision-Making.* London/Sidney: Croom Helm.

Messick, D.M. and McClelland, C.L. (1983) 'Social Traps and Temporal Traps', *Personality and Social Psychology Bulletin* 9: 105-10.

Middlemas, K. (1978) *Politics in Industrial Society.* London: André Deutsch.

Middlemas, K. (1983) *Industry, Unions and Government: 30 Years of the NEDC.* London: Macmillan.

Miegel, M. (1981) *Sicherheit im Alter. Plädoyer für die Weiterentwicklung des Rentensystems.* Stuttgart: Bonn Aktuell.

Milward, B.H. and Francisco, R.A. (1983) 'Subsystems Politics and Corporatism in the United States', *Policy and Politics* 11: 273-93.

Molitor, M. (1978) 'Social Conflicts in Belgium', in C.J. Crouch and A. Pizzorno (eds) *The Resurgence of Class Conflict in Western Europe since 1968*. Vol. I. *National Studies*. London: Macmillan.

Muller, P. (1985) 'Un schéma d'analyse des politiques sectorielles', *Revue française de science politique* 35: 165-188.

Müller-Jentsch, W. (1983) 'Versuch über die Tarifautonomie', *Leviathan* 11: 118-50.

Müller-Jentsch, W. (1985) 'Berufs-, Betriebs-, oder Industriegewerkschaften', in G. Endruweit et al. (eds) *Handbuch der Arbeitsbeziehungen: Deutschland, Österreich, Schweiz*. Berlin: de Gruyter.

Müller-Jentsch, W. and Sperling, H.-J. (1978) 'Economic Development, Labour Conflicts and the Industrial Relations System in West Germany', in C.J. Crouch and A. Pizzorno (eds) *The Resurgence of Class Conflict in Western Europe since 1968*. Vol. I. *National Studies*. London: Macmillan.

Mutti, A. (1984) *Scambio Politico e Incertezza*. Mimeo. Università di Pavia.

Mutti, A. (1990) 'The Role of Trust in Political Exchange' in B. Marin (ed.) *Generalized Political Exchange. Antagonistic Cooperation and Integrated Policy Circuits*. Frankfurt/Boulder, Colorado: Campus Verlag/Westview Press.

Narjes, K.-H. (1986) 'Europas Chancen stehen auf dem Spiel', *Das Parlament* 36, 33-34 (16.8.1986): 1-2.

Neck, R. (1985) 'Das österreichische System der Sozial- und Wirtschaftspartnerschaft aus politisch-ökonomischer Sicht', *Journal für Sozialforschung* 25(4): 375-403.

Nedelmann, B. and Meier, K.G. (1979) 'Theories of Contemporary Corporatism: Static or Dynamic?' pp. 95-118 in P.C. Schmitter and G. Lehmbruch (eds) *Trends Toward Corporatist Intermediation*. Beverly Hills/London: SAGE Publications.

Negrelli, S. (1982) 'La Pirelli dopo l'autunno caldo — Studio di un caso', *Giornale di Diritto del Lavoro e di Relazioni Industriali* 4: 485-516.

Nelson, D. (1982) 'The Company Union Movement 1900-1937 — A Reexamination', *Business History Review* 56: 335-58.

Nelson, P.B. (1981) *Corporations in Crisis: Behavioral Observations for Bankruptcy Policy*. Praeger: New York.

Nonet, P. and Selznick, P. (1978) *Law and Society in Transition —Toward Responsive Law*. New York: Harper.

Noorden, W. v. (1984) 'Employers Associations in the Netherlands', in J.P. Windmuller and A. Gladstone (eds) *Employers Associations and Industrial Relations. A Comparative Study*. Oxford: Clarendon Press.

Nordfors, L. (1985) *Makten, hälsan och vinsten*. Lund: Studentlitteratur.

Nordhaus, W. (1975) 'The Political Business Cycle', *Review of Economic Studies* 42: 169-90.

Nozick, R. (1974) *Anarchy, State, and Utopia*. New York: Basic Books.

Offe, C. (1970) *Leistungsprinzip und industrielle Arbeit*. Frankfurt: Europäische Verlagsanstalt.

Offe, C. (1975) *Berufsbildungsreform. Eine Fallstudie über Reformpolitik*. Frankfurt: Suhrkamp.

Offe, C. (1981) 'The Attribution of Political Status to Interest Groups: Observations to the Western German Case', pp. 123-28 in S. Berger (ed.) *Organizing Interests in Western Europe: Pluralism, Capitalism and the Transformation of Politics*. New York: Cambridge University Press.

Offe, C. (1984) 'Korporatismus als System nichtstaatlicher Makrosteuerung', *Geschichte und Gesellschaft* 10: 234-56.

Offe, C. and Ronge, V. (1976) 'Thesen zur Begründung des Konzepts des 'kapitalistischen Staates' und zur materialistischen Politikforschung', pp. 54-70 in C. Pozzoli (ed.) *Rahmenbedingungen und Schranken staatlichen Handelns*. Frankfurt: Suhrkamp.

Offe, C. and Wiesenthal, H. (1980) 'Two Logics of Collective Action. Theoretical Notes on Social Class and Organizational Form', *Political Power and Social Theory* 1: 67-115.

Ohmae K. (1985) *Triad Power: The Coming Shape of Global Competition*. New York/London: Free Press.

Olsen, J.P. (1981) 'Integrated Organizational Participation in Government', pp. 492-515 in P.C. Nystrom and W.H. Starbuck (eds) *Handbook of Organizational Design*. Vol. 2. *Remodelling*

Organizations and their Environments. Oxford: Oxford University Press.

Olsen, J.P. (1983) *Organized Democracy*. Bergen: Universitetsforlaget.

Olson, M. (1965) *The Logic of Collective Action. Public Goods and the Theory of Groups*. Cambridge/London: Harvard University Press.

Olson, M. (1982) *The Rise and Decline of Nations. Economic Growth, Stagflation, and Social Rigidities*. New Haven/London: Yale University Press.

Paloheimo, H. (1984a) 'Distributive Struggle, Corporatist Power Structures and Economic Policy of the 1970s in Developed Capitalist Countries', pp. 1-46 in H. Paloheimo (ed.) *Politics in the Era of Corporatism and Planning*. Tampere: The Finnish Political Science Association.

Paloheimo, H. (1984b) 'Pluralism, Corporatism and the Distributive Conflict', *Scandinavian Political Studies* 1: 17-38.

Paloheimo, H. (ed.) (1984) *Politics in the Era of Corporatism and Planning*. Tampere: The Finnish Political Science Association.

Palumbo, D.J. (1975) 'Organization Theory and Political Science', in F.I. Greenstein and N.W. Polsby (eds) *Handbook of Political Science*. Vol. 2. Menlo Park, California: Addison-Wesley.

Panitch, L. (1979) 'The Development of Corporatism in Liberal Democracies', pp. 119-46 in P.C. Schmitter and G. Lehmbruch (eds) *Trends Toward Corporatist Intermediation*. Beverly Hills/London: SAGE Publications.

Pappi, F.U. and Kappelhoff, P. (1984) 'Abhängigkeit, Tausch und kollektive Entscheidung in einer Gemeindeelite', *Zeitschrift für Soziologie* 13(2): 87-117.

Parnas, D. (1986) 'Software Wars', *Kursbuch* 83: 49-69.

Parri, L. (1985) 'Political Exchange in the Italian Debate'. European University Institute. Working Paper 85/174.

Parri, L. (1987) 'Neo-Corporatist Arrangements, 'Konkordanz' and Direct Democracy: The Swiss Experience', in I. Scholten (ed.) *Political Stability and Neo-Corporatism*. London: SAGE Publications.

Parri, L. (1987a) 'Staat und Gewerkschaften in der Schweiz (1873-1981)', *Politische Vierteljahresschrift* 28(1): 35-58.

Parsons, T. (1959) 'General Theory in Sociology', pp. 3-38 in R.K. Merton, L. Broom and L.S. Cottrell (eds) *Sociology Today*. New York: Basic Books.

Parsons, T. (1966) 'Suggestions for a Sociological Approach to the Theory of Organizations', pp. 32-47 in A. Etzioni (ed.) *Complex Organizations*. New York: Holt, Rinehart and Winston.

Parsons, T. (1971) 'On the Concept of Political Power', in S.N. Eisenstadt *Political Sociology*. London/New York: Basic Books.

Pedrazzoli, M. (1985) 'Sull'introduzione per via contrattuale di comitati consultivi paritetici nel gruppo IRI', *Rivista Italiana di Diritto del Lavoro* 4: 217-39.

Peel, D.A. (1982) 'The Political Business Cycle — Have We Seen the End of it?', *Long Range Planning* 15: 30-33.

Pestoff, V.A. (1977) *Voluntary Associations and Nordic Party Systems*. Stockholm: Department of Political Science.

Pestoff, V.A. (1983a) 'The Organization of Business Interests in the Swedish Chemical and Drug Industries', Stockholm: AASBI RR No. 9.

Pestoff, V.A. (1983b) 'The Organization of Business Interests in the Swedish Food Processing Industry', Stockholm: AASBI RR No. 8.

Pestoff, V.A. (1983c) 'The Organization of Business Interests in the Swedish Building and Construction Industry', Stockholm: AASBI RR No. 12.

Pestoff, V.A. (1984a) 'Konsumentinflytande och konsumentorganisering den svenska modellen' (Consumer Influence and Consumer Organization — the Swedish Model) Stockholm: Finansdept., DsFi 1984: 15.

Pestoff, V.A. (1984b) 'The Swedish Organizational Community and its Participation in Public Policy-Making', Stockholm: AASBI RR No. 6.

Pestoff, V.A. (1985) 'Corporatist Patterns in Swedish Work Environment Regulation', Barcelona: ECPR paper.

Pestoff, V.A. (1988a) 'Exit, Voice and Collective Action in Swedish Consumer Policy', *Journal of Consumer Policy*: 1-27.

Pestoff, V.A. (1988b) 'The Politics of Private Business, Cooperatives and Public Enterprise in a Corporatist Democracy—the Case of Sweden', Stockholm: stencil and Naringslivsorganisationerna och politiken i Sverige.TCO.

Pestoff, V.A. (1989) 'Organisationernas medverken och förhandlinger i svensk konsumentpolitik' (Organizational Participation and Negotiations in Swedish Consumer Policy) in K. Nielsen and O.K. Pedersen (eds) *Forhandlingsøkonomi i Norden* (A Nordic Negotiated Economy) Copenhagen and Oslo: DJØF and Tano. Reprinted in *Socialrätts vetenskaplige Tidskrift*.

Pettigrew, T.E. (1967) 'Social Evaluation Theory: Convergences and Applications', pp. 241-315 in D. Levine (ed.) *Nebraska Symposium on Motivation*. Lincoln: University of Nebraska Press.

Piore, M.J. (ed.) (1979) *Unemployment and Inflation. Institutionalist and Structuralist Views*. White Plains, NY: M.E. Sharpe.

Piore, M.J. and Sabel, C.F. (1984) *The Second Industrial Divide*. New York: Basic Books.

Pizzorno, A. (1977) 'Fra azione di classe e sistemi corporativi — Osservazioni comparate sulle rappresentanze del lavoro dei paesi capitalistici avanzati', in A. Accornero et al. (eds) *Movimento sindacale e società italiana*. Milano: Feltrinelli.

Pizzorno, A. (1978) 'Political Exchange and Collective Identity in Industrial Conflict', pp. 277-98 in C.J. Crouch and A. Pizzorno (eds) *The Resurgence of Class Conflict in Western Europe since 1968*. Vol. II. Comparative Analyses. London: Macmillan.

Pockettidning, R. (1986) 'Maktjakten — i storfinansens spår'.

Prigge, W.-U. (1985) 'Arbeitgeber- und Unternehmensverbände', in G. Endruweit et al. (eds) *Handbuch der Arbeitsbeziehungen: Deutschland, Österreich, Schweiz*. Berlin: de Gruyter.

Prigogine, I. (1976) 'Order Through Fluctuation: Self-Organization and Social System', pp. 93-133 in E. Jantsch and C. Waddington (eds) *Evolution and Consciousness. Human Systems in Transition*. London: Addison-Wesley.

Prost, A. (1964) *La CGT à l'époque du Front Populaire 1934-1939*. Paris: Colin.

Przeworski, A. and Teune, H. (1970) *The Logic of Comparative Social Inquiry*. New York: Wiley-Interscience.

Przeworski, A. and Wallerstein, M. (1982) 'The Structure of Class Conflict in Democratic Capitalist Societies', *American Political Science Review* 76: 215-38.

Putnam, R.D. (1984) 'The Western Economic Summits: A Political Interpretation', in C. Merlini (ed.) *Economic Summits and Western Decision-Making*. London/Sidney: Croom Helm.

Putnam, R.D. (1986) 'The Logic of Two-Level Games: International Cooperation, and Western Summitry, 1975-1986'. Manuscript. Cambridge, MA: Harvard University Department of Government.

Putnam, R.D. and Bayne, N. (1984) *Hanging Together. The Seven-Power Summits*. London: Heinemann.

Ramsay, H. (1977) 'Cycles of Control — Worker Participation in Sociological and Historical Perspective', *Sociology* 11: 481-506.

Rapoport, A., Guyer, M.J. and Gordon, D.G. (1976) *The 2 x 2 Game*. Ann Arbor: University of Michigan Press.

Rasmussen, E.J. (1985) '25 Years of Labour Government and Incomes Policy'. Unpublished doctoral thesis. Florence: European University Institute.

Rattinger, H. (1979) 'Auswirkungen der Arbeitsmarktlage auf das Ergebnis der Bundestagswahl 1976', *Politische Vierteljahresschrift* 20: 51-70.

Rauscher, A. (1985) 'Richtungs- oder Einheitsgewerkschaft', in G. Endruweit et al. (eds) *Handbuch der Arbeitsbeziehungen: Deutschland, Österreich, Schweiz*. Berlin: de Gruyter.

Redaktionskollektiv Gewerkschaften (1972): 'Thesen zur Gewerkschaftsanalyse', *Prokla* 2: 87-108.

Regalia, I. (1986) 'Centralisation or Decentralisation? An Analysis of Organisational Changes in the Italian Trade Union Movement at the Time of Crisis', in O. Jacobi et al. (eds) *Technological Change, Rationalisation and Industrial Relations*. London: Croom Helm.

Regalia, I. et al. (1978) 'Labour Conflicts and Industrial Relations in Italy', in C.J. Crouch and A.

Pizzorno (eds) *The Resurgence of Class Conflict in Western Europe since 1968.* Vol. I. *National Studies.* London: Macmillan.

Regini, M. (1981) *I dilemmi del sindacato.* Bologna: Il Mulino.

Rehbinder, E., Kayser, D. and Klein, H. (1985) *Chemikaliengesetz: Kommentar und Rechtsvorschriften zum Chemikaliengesetz.* Heidelberg: C.F. Müller.

Reydellet, M. (1979) 'Le cumul des mandats', *Revue de droit et de la science politique en France et à l'étranger* 95: 693-768.

Reynaud, J.-D. (1975) *Les syndicats en France.* Tome I. Paris: Editions Seuil.

Rhodes, R.A.W. (1983) *Control and Power in Central-Local Government Relations.* Hands: Gover.

Rhodes, R.A.W. (1985) 'Intergovernmental Relations in the United Kingdom', in Y. Mény and V. Wright (eds) *Centre-Periphery Relations in Western Europe.* London: Allen and Unwin.

Rieser, V. (1985) 'Cultura della razionalizzazione e relazioni industriali in Italia e in Germania', *Inchiesta* (Oct.- Dic.): 28-35.

Rinsche, G. (1986) 'Konkurrenz und Kooperation. Schlüsselworte der europäischen Zukunftssicherung', *Das Parlament* 36, 33-34 (16.8.86): 5-6.

Rokkan, S. (1975) 'I voti contano, le risorse decidono,' *Rivista italiana di scienza politica* 5: 167-76.

Romagnoli, U. (1985) 'L'anno-zero della democrazia industriale', *Politica del Diritto* 16: 157-63.

Rondin, J. (1985) *Le sacre des notables.* Paris: Fayard.

Rosanvallon, P. (1979) *Le capitalisme utopique. Critique de l'idéologie économique.* Paris: Editions Seuil.

Rose, R. (1976) 'On the Priorities of Government: A Developmental Analysis of Public Policies', *European Journal of Political Research* 4: 247-89.

Rose, R. (1985) 'From Government at the Center to Nationwide Government', in Y. Mény and V. Wright (eds) *Centre-Periphery Relations in Western Europe.* London: Allen and Unwin.

Ross, A.M. and Hartmann, P.T. (1960) *Changing Patterns of Industrial Conflict.* New York: Wiley.

Ruggie, J. (1975) 'Approaches in Policy Analysis and Design', in T. La Porte (ed.) *Organized Social Complexity.* Princeton, N.J.: Princeton University Press.

Sabatier, P. (1986) 'Policy Analysis, Policy Oriented Learning and Policy Change: An Advocacy Coalition Framework'. Mimeo. University of California: Davis.

Sabato, L. (1978) *Goodbye to Good-Time Charlie.* Lexington, MA: D.C. Heath.

Sadran, P. (1985) 'L'évolution des relations centre-périphérie en France'. Paper presented at the IPSA Congress, Paris.

Salisbury, R.H. (1970) 'An Exchange Theory of Interest Groups' pp. 32-67 in R.H. Salisbury *Interest Group Politics in America.* New York: Harper and Row.

Salzberg, L. (1985) 'Les contrats à durée determinée en 1984', *Document l'INSEE* 24. Paris: INSEE.

Samuelsson, K. (1968) *From Great Power to Welfare State.* London: Allen and Unwin.

Sanford, T. (1967) *Storm over the States.* New York: McGraw Hill Book.

Sartori, G. (1968) 'Alla ricerca della sociologia politica', *Rassegna italiana di sociologia* 9: 597-639.

Scharpf, F.W. (1978) 'Interorganizational Policy Studies: Issues, Concepts and Perspectives', pp. 345-70 in K. Hanf and F.W. Scharpf *Interorganizational Policy Making.* London/Beverly Hills: SAGE Publications.

Scharpf, F.W. (1981) 'The Political Economy of Inflation and Unemployment in Western Europe: An Outline', WZB Dicussion Paper IIM/LMP 81-21. Berlin: Wissenschaftszentrum Berlin.

Scharpf, F.W. (1982) 'Der Erklärungswert 'binnenstruktureller' Faktoren in der Politik- und Verwaltungsforschung', pp. 90-104 in J.J. Hesse (ed.) *Politikwissenschaft und Verwaltungswissenschaft.* PVS Sonderheft 13. Opladen: Westdeutscher Verlag.

Scharpf, F.W. (1984) 'Economic and Institutional Constraints of Full-Employment Strategies: Sweden, Austria, and West Germany (1973-1982)', pp. 257-90 in J.H. Goldthorpe (ed.) *Order and Conflict in Contemporary Capitalism. Studies in the Political Economy of Western European Nations.* Oxford: Oxford University Press.

Scharpf, F.W. (1985) 'The Joint-Decision Traps: Lessons from German Federalism and European Integration'. WZB Discussion Paper IIM/LMP 85-1. Berlin: Wissenschaftszentrum Berlin.

Scharpf, F.W. (1987a) 'Anmerkungen aus der Sicht der Institutionenforschung', pp. 341-50 in E.

Matzner, J. Kregel and A. Roncaglia (eds) (1987) *Arbeit für alle ist möglich. Über ökonomische und institutionelle Bedingungen erfolgreicher Beschäftigungs- und Arbeitsmarktpolitik.* Berlin: Sigma.

Scharpf, F.W. (1987b) *Sozialdemokratische Krisenpolitik in Europa. Das 'Modell Deutschland' im Vergleich.* Frankfurt: Campus Verlag.

Scharpf, F.W., Reissert, B. and Schnabel, F. (1976) *Politikverflechtung. Theorie und Empirie des kooperativen Föderalismus in der Bundesrepublik.* Kronberg: Skriptor.

Schelling, T.C. (1969) *The Strategy of Conflict.* Oxford: Oxford University Press.

Schelling, T.C. (1984) *Choice and Consequence.* Cambridge, MA: Harvard University Press.

Schelling, T.C. (1984a) 'What is Game Theory?' pp. 213-42 in T.C. Schelling *Choice and Consequence.* Cambridge, MA: Harvard University Press.

Schienstock, G. (1981) 'Towards a Theory of Industrial Relations', *British Journal of Industrial Relations* 19: 170-89.

Schlecht, M. (1987) 'Ausweitung der Betriebszeiten?', *WSI-Mitteilungen* 40: 27-35.

Schlenker, B.R. (1974) 'Social Psychology and Science', *Journal of Personality and Social Psychology* 29: 1-15.

Schmidt, M.G. (1982) 'Does Corporatism Matter? Economic Crisis, Politics and Rates of Unemployment in Capitalist Democracies in the 1970s', pp. 237-58 in G. Lehmbruch and P.C. Schmitter (eds) *Patterns of Corporatist Policy-Making.* London/Beverly Hills: SAGE Publications.

Schmidt, M.G. (1983) 'The Welfare Sate and the Economy in Periods of Economic Crisis: A Comparative Study of Twenty-Three OECD Nations', *European Journal of Political Research* 11: 1-26.

Schmidt, M.G. (1985a) 'The Politics of Labour Market Policy. Structural and Political Determinants of Full Employment and Mass Employment in Mixed Economies'. Paper presented at the XIII World Congress of the International Political Science Association. Paris: IPSA.

Schmidt, M.G. (1985b) *Der Schweizerische Weg zur Vollbeschäftigung. Eine Bilanz der Beschäftigung, der Arbeitslosigkeit und der Arbeitsmarktpolitik.* Frankfurt: Campus.

Schmidt, M.G. (1986) 'Politische Bedingungen erfolgreicher Wirtschaftspolitik. Eine vergleichende Analyse westlicher Industrieländer (1960-1985)', *Journal für Sozialforschung* 26(3): 251-73.

Schmidt, M.G. (1987) 'West Germany: The Policy of the Middle Way'. Manuscript. Berlin/ Heidelberg: The Comparative History of Public Policy Project.

Schmidt, S.W., Guasti, L., Landé, C.H., Scott, J.C. (1977) *Friends, Followers and Factions.* Berkeley: University of California Press.

Schmitter, P.C. (1974) 'Still the Century of Corporatism?', *Review of Politics* 36(1): 85-131.

Schmitter, P.C. (1981) 'Interest Intermediation and Regime Governability in Contemporary Western Europe and North America', p. 285-330 in S. Berger (ed.) *Organizing Interests in Western Europe.* Cambridge: Cambridge University Press.

Schmitter, P.C. (1982) 'Reflections on Where the Theory of Neo-Corporatism Has Gone and Where the Praxis of Neo-Corporatism May Be Going', pp. 259-79 in G. Lehmbruch and P.C. Schmitter (eds) *Patterns of Corporatist Policy-Making.* London/Beverly Hills: SAGE Publications.

Schmitter, P.C. (1983) 'Democratic Theory and Neocorporatist Practice', *Social Research* 50(4): 885-928.

Schmitter, P.C. (1985) 'Neo-Corporatism and the State', pp. 32-62 in W. Grant (ed.) *The Political Economy of Corporatism.* London: Macmillan.

Schmitter, P.C. and Brand, D. (1979) 'Organizing Capitalists in the United States: The Advantages and Disadvantages of Exceptionalism'. Paper presented at the American Political Science Association Meeting.

Schmitter, P.C. and Lehmbruch, G. (eds) (1979) *Trends Toward Corporatist Intermediation.* London/ Beverly Hills: SAGE Publications.

Schmitter, P.C. and Streeck, W. (1981) 'The Organization of Business Interests. A Research Design to Study the Associative Action of Business in the Advanced Industrial Societies of Western Europe'. WZB Discussion Paper IIM/LPM 81-13. Berlin: Wissenschaftszentrum Berlin.

Schmoelders, G. (1971) 'Permanente Steuerreform', *Steuer und Wirtschaft* 48: 37-45.

Schneider, V. (1985) 'Corporatist and Pluralist Patterns of Policy-Making for Chemicals Control: A Comparison between West Germany and the USA, pp.174-92 in A. Cawson (ed.) *Organized Interests and the State. Studies in Meso-Corporatism.* Beverly Hills: SAGE Publications.

Schneider, V. (1986) 'Tauschnetzwerke in der Politikentwicklung: Chemikalienkontrolle in der OECD, EG und der Bundesrepublik Deutschland', *Journal für Sozialforschung* 26(4): 383-416.

Schneider, V. (1988) *Politiknetzwerke der Chemikalienkontrolle. Eine Analyse einer transnationalen Politikentwicklung.* Berlin/New York: de Gruyter.

Schott, K. (1984) 'Investment, Order and Conflict in a Simple Dynamic Model of Capitalism', pp. 81-97 in J.H. Goldthorpe (ed.) *Order and Conflict in Contemporary Capitalism. Studies in the Political Economy of Western European Nations.* Oxford: Oxford University Press.

Schütze, W. (1985) 'SDI oder EUREKA? Aus Politik und Zeitgeschichte', Beilage *Das Parlament* B 44/85 (2.11.1985): 30-39.

Seidman, H. (1975) *Politics, Position and Power. The Dynamics of Federal Organization.* New York: Oxford University Press.

Seifert, H. (1986) 'Durchsetzungsprobleme zukünftiger Arbeitszeitgestaltung', *WSI-Mitteilungen* 39: 216-27.

Sellier, F. (1984) *La confrontation sociale en France, 1936-1981.* Paris: PUF.

Sellier, F. (1986) 'Aménagement du temps de travail, articulation entre niveaux de négociation et conflits entre syndicats', *Droit Social* 11: 773-78.

Sellier, P. (1978) 'France', in J.T. Dunlop and W. Galenson (eds) *Western Labor in the Twentieth Century.* New York: Academic Press.

Servan-Schreiber, J.-J. (1967) *Le défi américain.* Paris: Denoël.

Sharansky, I. (1978) *The Maligned States. Accomplishments, Problems, and Opportunities.* New York: McGraw Hill.

Sharpe, L.J. (1985) 'Central Coordination and the Policy Network', *Political Studies* 33: 361-81.

Shepsle, K.A. (1986) 'Cooperation and Institutional Arrangements'. Paper prepared for the Harvard Conference on International Regimes and Cooperation, February 13-15, 1986.

Shorter, E. and Tilly, C. (1974) *Strikes in France.* Cambridge: Cambridge University Press.

Shubik, M. (1984) *Game Theory in the Social Sciences. Vol. 2. A Game-Theoretic Approach to Political Economy.* Cambridge, MA: MIT Press.

Simitis, S. (1984) 'Zur Verrechtlichung der Arbeitsbeziehungen', in F. Kübler (ed.) *Verrechtlichung von Wirtschaft, Arbeit und sozialer Solidarität.* Baden-Baden: Nomos.

Sinai I, R. 1978: *The Decadence of the Modern World.* Cambridge, MA: Schenkmann.

Sisson, K. (1979) 'The Organisation of Employers' Associations in Five Countries: Some Comments on their Origins and Development'. Paper prepared for the International Institute of Management Workshop on 'Employers' Associations as Organisation', November 14-16, Berlin.

Skogh, G. (1984) 'Employers' Associations in Sweden', in J.P. Windmuller and A. Gladstone (eds) *Employers Associations and Industrial Relations. A Comparative Study.* Oxford: Clarendon Press.

Smith, A. (1976) *An Inquiry into the Nature and Causes of the Wealth of Nations.* Vol. 1. Oxford: Clarendon Press (first published 1776).

Smith, B.C. (1985) *Decentralization. The Territorial Dimension of the State.* London: Allen and Unwin.

Soubie, R. (1983) 'L'obligation de négocier et sa sanction', *Droit Social* 1: 55-62.

Soubie, R. (1986) 'Après les négociations sur la flexibilité', *Droit Social* no. 2: 95-9, 3: 221-24, 4: 290-93.

Spitaels, G. (1967) *Le mouvement syndicale en Belgique.* Brussels: Institut de Sociologie de l'Université libre de Bruxelles.

Stegmann, D. (1980) 'Unternehmerverbände (Geschichte)', in W. and A. Albers, W. & A. (eds) *Handwörterbuch der Wirtschaftswissenschaft.* Bd 8. Stuttgart: Vandenhoeck und Ruprecht.

Stephens, J.D. (1979) *The Transition from Capitalism to Socialism.* London: Macmillan.

Stollberg, G. (1981) *Die Rationalisierungsdebatte 1908-1933.* Frankfurt: Campus.

Stone, K. v. Wezel (1981) 'The Post-War Paradigm in American Labor Law', *Yale Law Journal* 90: 1509-80.

Strauss, G. (1984) 'Industrial Relations — Time of Change', *Industrial Relations* 23: 1-15.

Streeck, W. (1981a) 'Qualitative Demands and the Neo-Corporatist Manageability of Industrial Relations', *British Journal of Industrial Relations* 19: 149-69.

Streeck, W. (1981b) *Gewerkschaftliche Organisationsprobleme in der sozialstaatlichen Demokratie.* Königstein: Athenäum.

Streeck, W. (1982) 'Organizational Consequences of Neo-Corporatist Cooperation in West German Labor Unions', pp. 29-81 in G. Lehmbruch and P.C. Schmitter (eds) *Patterns of Corporatist Policy-Making.* London/Beverly Hills: SAGE Publications.

Streeck, W. (1984) 'Neo-Corporatist Industrial Relations and the Economic Crisis in West Germany', pp. 291-314 in J.H. Goldthorpe (ed.) *Order and Conflict in Contemporary Capitalism. Studies in the Political Economy of Western European Nations.* Oxford: Oxford University Press.

Streeck, W. (1986) 'Kollektive Arbeitsbeziehungen und Industrieller Wandel: Das Beispiel der Automobilindustrie'. WZB Discussion Paper IIM/LMP 86-2. Berlin: Wissenschaftszentrum Berlin.

Streeck, W. (1988) 'Interest Variety and Organization Capacity: Two Logics of Collective Action?' Seminar paper. Konstanz.

Streeck, W. and Schmitter, P.C. (1985) *Private Interest Government. Beyond Market and State.* London: SAGE Publications.

Streeck, W. and Schmitter, P.C. (1985a) 'Community, Market, State — and Associations? The Prospective Contribution of Interest Governance to Social Order', pp. 1-29 in W. Streeck and P.C. Schmitter (eds).

Streeck, W. and Schmitter, P.C. (1985b) 'Gemeinschaft, Markt und Staat — und die Verbände? Der mögliche Beitrag von Interessenregierungen zur sozialen Ordnung.' *Journal für Sozialforschung* 25(2): 133-57.

Suleiman, E. (1974) *Politics, Power, and Bureaucracy in France. The Administrative Elite.* Princeton, NJ: Princeton University Press.

Swidler, A. (1986) 'Culture in Action: Symbols and Strategies', *American Sociological Review* 51: 273-86.

Talos, E. (1981) *Staatliche Sozialpolitik in Österreich.* Vienna: Verlag für Gesellschaftskritik.

Tarkowsky, J. (1982) 'L'influenza della periferia in un sistema centralizzato: risorse, leadership locale e integrazione orizzontale in Polonia', in L. Graziano, P.J. Katzenstein and S. Tarrow (eds) *Centro e periferia nelle nazioni industriali.* Roma: Officina.

Tarrow, S. (1978) 'Introduction', in S. Tarrow, P.J. Katzenstein and L. Graziano (eds) *Territorial Politics in Industrial Nations.* New York: Praeger.

Tarrow, S. (1979) *Tra centro e periferia.* Bologna: Il Mulino.

Terry, M. (1986) 'Shop Stewards and Management — Collective Bargaining as Co-operation', in O. Jacobi et al. (eds) *Technological Change, Rationalisation and Industrial Relations.* London: Croom Helm.

Teubner, G. (1983) 'Substantive and Reflexive Elements in Modern Law', *Law and Society Review* 17: 239-85.

Teubner, G. (1987a) 'Unitas Multiplex — Problems of Governance in Group Enterprises from a Systems Theory Viewpoint'. EUI Colloquium Paper 115/87. Florence: European University Institute.

Teubner, G. (1987b) 'Unternehmenskorporatismus. New Industrial Policy und das 'Wesen' der Juristischen Person', *Kritische Vierteljahresschrift für Gesetzgebung und Rechtswissenschaft*: 61-85.

Teubner, G. (ed) (1990) *State, Law, Economy as Autopoietic Systems.* Milano: Guiffré.

Teubner, G. and Willke, H. (1984) 'Kontext und Autonomie. Gesellschaftliche Selbststeuerung durch reflexives Recht', *Zeitschrift für Rechtssoziologie* 6(4): 4-35.

Therborn, G. (1986) *Why Some Peoples Are More Unemployed Than Others. The Strange Paradox of Growth and Unemployment.* London: Verso.

Thibaut, J.W. and Kelley, H.H. (1959) *The Social Psychology of Groups.* New York: John Wiley.

Thoenig, J.-C. (1975) 'La relation entre le centre et la périphérie en France. Une analyse systémique',

Bulletin de l'institut international d'administration publique 36: 77-123.

Thoenig, J.-C. (1978) 'State Bureaucracies and Local Government in France', in K. Hanf and F.W. Scharpf (eds) *Interorganizational Policy Making. Limits to Coordination and Central Control.* London: SAGE Publications.

Thoenig, J.-C. (1985) 'Le grand horloger et les effets de système: de la décentralisation en France', *Politiques et management public* 3: 135-55.

Thrasher, M. (1983) 'Exchange Networks and Implementation', *Policy and Politics* 11(4): 375-91.

Tomlins, C.L. (1985) *The State and the Unions —Labor Relations, Law, and the Organized Labor.* Cambridge: Cambridge University Press.

Toonen, T. (1983) 'Administrative Plurality in an Unitary State: The Analysis of Public Organisational Pluralism', *Policy and Politics* 11: 247-71.

Touraine, A. (1955) *L'évolution du travail aux Usines Renault.* Paris: CNRS.

Traxler, F. (1982) *Evolution gewerkschaftlicher Interessenvertretung. Entwicklungslogik und Organisationsdynamik gewerkschaftlichen Handelns am Beispiel Österreich.* Wien/Frankfurt: Braumüller/Campus Verlag.

Traxler, F. (1982a) 'Zur Entwicklung kooperativer Arbeitsbeziehungen. Versuch einer Prozeßanalyse', *Zeitschrift für Soziologie* 11(4): 335-52.

Traxler, F. (1985) 'Arbeitgeberverbände', pp. 51-64 in G. Endruweit, E. Gaugler, H. Staehle and B. Wilpert (eds) *Handbuch der Arbeitsbeziehungen: Deutschland, Österreich, Schweiz.* Berlin: de Gruyter.

Traxler, F. (1986) *Interessenverbände der Unternehmer. Konstitutionsbedingungen und Steuerungskapazitäten, analysiert am Beispiel Österreichs.* Frankfurt/New York: Campus Verlag.

Traxler, F. (1987a) "Entente coopérative'. Arbeitsbeziehungen in der Bauwirtschaft', pp. 231-49 in B. Marin (ed.) *Verfall und Erneuerung im Bauwesen.* Wien: Internationale Publikationen.

Traxler, F. (1987b) 'Klassenstruktur, Korporatismus und Krise. Zur Machtverteilung in Österreichs 'Sozialpartnerschaft' im Umbruch des Weltmarkts', *Politische Vierteljahresschrift* 28(1): 59-79.

Traxler, F. (1989) 'Comparing Business Interest Associations and Labor Unions: Theoretical Perspectives and Empirical Findings on Social Class, Collective Action and the Organizability of Interests.' Unpublished paper.

Traxler, F. and Vobruba, G. (1987) 'Selbststeuerung als funktionales Äquivalent zum Recht? Zur Steuerungskapazität von neokorporatistischen Arrangements und reflexivem Recht', *Zeitschrift für Soziologie* 16(1): 3-15.

Treu, T. (1983) 'Collective Bargaining and Participation in Economic Policy: the Case of Italy', in C.J. Crouch and F. Heller (eds) *International Yearbook of Organizational Democracy.* Vol. I *Organizational Democracy and Political Processes.* Chichester/New York: John Wiley and Sons.

Treu, T. (1985) 'Centralisation-Decentralisation in Collective Bargaining', *International Journal of Comparative Law and Industrial Relations* 1: 41-65.

Treu, T. (1986) 'Le relazioni industriali nell'impresa — Il Protocollo IRI', *Rivista Italiana di Diritto del Lavoro* 5: 395-425.

Treu, T. and Martinelli, A. (1984) 'Employers' Associations in Italy', in J.P. Windmuller and A. Gladstone (eds) *Employers Associations and Industrial Relations. A Comparative Study.* Oxford: Clarendon Press.

Trigilia, C. (1982) 'Modernizzazione, accentramento e decentramento politico', *Stato e mercato* 1: 45-92.

Tufte, E.R. (1978) *The Political Control of the Economy.* Princeton, NJ: Princeton University Press.

Turone, S. (1981) *Storia del sindacato in Italia 1943-1980.* Bari: Laterza.

Ullmann, P. (1977) *Tarifverträge und Tarifpolitik in Deutschland bis 1914.* Frankfurt/Bern/Las Vegas: Peter Lang.

Undy, R. et al. (1981) *Change in Trade Unions.* London: Hutchinson.

Unger, R. (1976) *Law in Modern Society. Towards a Criticism of Social Theory.* New York/London: Free Press.

Vanberg, V. (1972) *Markt und Organisation.* Tübingen: Mohr.

Vigen, A. (1950) *Rigsdagen og erhvervsorganisationern. Den danske Rigsdag 1848-1949.* Bd III.

Copenhagen.

Visser, J. (1986) 'Die Mitgliederentwicklung der westeuropäischen Gewerkschaften. Trends und Konjunkturen 1920-1983', *Journal für Sozialforschung* 26(1): 3-33.

Visser, J. (1987) *In Search of Inclusive Unionism*. Unpublished doctoral thesis. Amsterdam: University of Amsterdam.

Volkmann, H. (1979) 'Organisation und Konflikt. Gewerkschaft, Arbeitgeberverbände und die Entwicklung des Arbeitskonflikts im späten Kaiserreich', pp. 422-38 in W. Conze and V. Engelhard (eds) *Arbeiter im Industrialisierungsprozeß*. Stuttgart: Klett-Cotta.

Vorschläge des *Bundes der Steuerzahler*, p. 3.

Voss, T. (1985) *Rationale Akteure und soziale Institutionen. Beitrag zu einer endogenen Theorie des sozialen Tausches*. München: Oldenbourg.

Wagner, M. (1990) 'Fragile Hierarchies. Macroeconomic Management as an Exchange Problem' in B. Marin (ed.) *Generalized Political Exchange. Antagonistic Cooperation and Integrated Policy Circuits*. Frankfurt/Boulder, Colorado: Campus Verlag/Westview Press.

Waldman, S.R. (1972) *The Formation of Political Action: An Exchange Theory of Politics*. Boston: Little, Brown.

Waldman, S.R. (1973) 'Exchange Theory and Political Analysis', pp.101-27 in A. Effrot (ed.) *Perspectives In Political Sociology*. New York: Irvington.

Walker, D.B. (1981a) *Toward a Functioning Federalism*. Cambridge, MA: Winthrop Publishers.

Walker, D.B. (1981b) 'A Perspective on Intergovernmental Relations', in L. Richard H. (ed.) *Intergovernmental Relations in the 1980s*. New York and Basel: Marcel Dekker.

Waller, R. (1983) 'Complexity and the Boundaries of Human Policy Making', *International Journal of General Systems* 9 (1982/83): 1-11.

Wassenberg, A.F.P. (1982) 'Industrial Policy: On Prisoners, Chickens and other Animal Spirits in the Low Countries'. Paper prepared for the 12th World Congress IPSA, Rio de Janeiro, August 4-9.

Wassenberg, A.F.P. (1983) *Dossier RSV: Schijnbewegingen van de Industriepolitiek* (Dossier Rijn Schelde Verolme United Shipyards: Stratagems of Industrial Policies and Strategies). Leiden: Stenfert Kroese.

Wassenberg, A.F.P. (1985) 'Organizational Instinct: On the Political Economy of Bargaining', in A.H.G. Rinnooy Kan (ed.) *New Challenges for Management Research*. Amsterdam: North Holland Publ. Comp.

Webb, S. and Webb, B. (1965) *Industrial Democracy*. New York: Kelley (first published 1887).

Webb, S. and Webb, B. (1973) *The History of Trade Unionism*. Clifton: Kelley (first published 1884).

Weber, H. (1987) 'Wettbewerb in der dritten Dimension. Konzertiertes Marketing in Japan', in M. Glagow, D. Rumianek-Beier and H. Willke (eds) *Materialien zur sozialwissenschaftlichen Planungs- und Entscheidungstheorie*. H. 10. Bielefeld.

Weber, M. (1968) *Gesammelte Aufsätze zur Wissenschaftslehre*. Tübingen: J.C.B. Mohr (first published 1922).

Weber, M. (1978) *Economy and Society*. Edited by Günther Roth and Claus Wittich. Berkeley: University of California Press.

Wedderburn, K.W. (1971) *The Worker and the Law*. London: Penguin.

Weintraub, S. (1978) *Capitalism's Inflation and Unemployment Crisis*. Reading, MA: Addison-Wesley.

Weitbrecht, H. and Berger, G. (1985) 'Zur Geschichte der Arbeiterbewegung', in G. Endruweit et al. (eds) *Handbuch der Arbeitsbeziehungen: Deutschland, Österreich, Schweiz*. Berlin: de Gruyter.

Wilensky, H.L. (1983) 'Political Legitimacy and Consensus' in S.E. Spiro and E. Yuchtman-Yaar (eds) *Evaluating the Welfare State: Social and Political Perspectives*. New York: Academic Press.

Wilensky, H.L. and Turner, L. (1987) *Democratic Corporatism and Policy Linkages. The Interdependence of Industrial, Labor-Market, Incomes, and Social Policies in Eight Countries*. Berkeley: Institute of International Studies.

Williamson, O.E. (1975) *Markets and Hierarchies: Analysis and Antitrust Implications. A Study in the Economics of Internal Organization*. New York: The Free Press.

Williamson, O.E. (1979) 'Transaction Cost Economics: The Governance of Contractual Relations',

Journal of Law and Economics 22: 233-61.

Williamson, O.E. and Ouchi, W.G. (1983) 'The Markets and Hierarchies Programme of Research: Origins, Implications, Prospects', in A. Francis et al. (eds) *Power, Efficiency and Institutions*. London: Heinemann.

Williamson, R.S. (1986) 'A New Federalism: Proposals and Achievements of President Reagan's First Three Years', *Publius* 16: 11-28.

Willke, H. (1983) *Entzauberung des Staates. Überlegungen zu einer gesellschaftlichen Steuerungstheorie*. Königstein: Athenäum.

Willke, H. (1983a) 'Planungstheorie'. Universität Bielefeld. PET-Schriftenreihe Heft 2.

Willke, H. (1984) 'Gesellschaftssteuerung', pp. 29-53 in M. Glagow (ed.) *Gesellschaftssteuerung zwischen Korporatismus und Subsidiarität*. Bielefeld: AJZ.

Willke, H. (1984a) 'Zum Problem der Intervention in selbstreferentielle Systeme', *Zeitschrift für systemische Therapie* 2(7).

Willke, H. (1986) 'Entzauberung des Staates. Grundlinien einer systemtheoretischen Argumentation', *Jahrbuch für Verwaltungswissenschaft* 1.

Willke, H. (1986a) 'The Tragedy of the State', *Archiv für Rechts- und Sozialphilosophie* 72(4): 455-67.

Willman, P. et al. (1985) *Innovation and Management Control — Labour Relations at BL Cars*. Cambridge: Cambridge University Press.

Wilson, F. (1983) 'French Interest Group Politics: Pluralist or Neocorporatist?' *American Political Science Review* 77: 895-910.

Wilson, G.K. (1982) 'Why There Is No Corporatism in the United States?' in G. Lehmbruch and P.C. Schmitter (eds) *Patterns of Corporatist Policy-Making*. London: SAGE Publications.

Windmuller, J.P. (1969) *Labor Relations in the Netherlands*. Ithaca: Cornell University Press.

Windmuller, J.P. and Gladstone, A. (eds) (1984) *Employers Associations and Industrial Relations. A Comparative Study*. Oxford: Clarendon Press.

Windolf, P. (1985) 'Streik und Betriebsbesetzung bei Peugeot — Die französische Industriepolitik in der Krise', *Leviathan* 13: 38-69.

Windolf, P. (1985a) 'Industrial Robots in the West German Automobile Industry', *Politics and Society* 14: 459-95.

Winkler, H.A. (1984) *Von der Revolution zur Stabilisierung —Arbeiter und Arbeiterbewegung in der Weimarer Republik*. Berlin: Dietz.

Woolley, J.T. (1985) 'Central Banks and Inflation', pp. 318-51 in L.N. Lindberg and C.S. Maier (eds) *The Politics of Inflation and Economic Stagnation. Theoretical Approaches and International Case Studies*. Washington, DC: Brookings.

Worms, J.-P. (1966) 'Le préfet et ses notables', *Sociologie du Travail* 8: 249-75.

Wright, D.S. (1981) 'Intergovernmental Relations in the 1980s: A New Phase of IGR', in R.H. Leach (ed.) *Intergovernmental Relations in the 1980s*. New York/Basel: Marcel Dekker.

Wright, D.S. (1982) *Understanding Intergovernmental Relations*. Monterey, California: Brooks/Cole.

Wright, V. (1983) *The Government and Politics in France*. London: Hutchinson.

Zeitlin, M. (ed.) (1973) *American Society, Inc. Studies of the Social Structure and Political Economy of the United States*. Chicago: Rand McNally.

Zeleny, M. (1982) *Multiple Criteria Decision Making*. New York: Mc Graw Hill.

Zeleny, M. (ed.) (1981) *Autopoiesis. A Theory of Living Organizations*. New York/Oxford: North Holland.

Zoll, R. (1974) *Wertheim III: Kommunalpolitik und Machtstruktur*. München: Juventa Verlag.

Notes on the Authors

Colin Crouch

Fellow in Politics, Trinity College, Oxford, and Faculty Lecturer in Sociology at the University of Oxford.

Main research interest: the comparative study of industrial relations systems in Western Europe, with reference to both their historical development and contemporary problems.

Major book publications: *The Student Revolt* (1970); *Class Conflict and the Industrial Relations Crisis* (1977); *The Politics of Industrial Relations* (1979; 2nd edition, 1982); *Invaders of Political Spaces: Workers, Employers and the European State Traditions*, forthcoming.

Klaus Gretschmann

Associate Professor and coordinator of the EC Policy Unit at the European Institute of Public Administration, Maastricht (NL).

Graduated in economics and sociology and gained a PhD (summa cum laude) from the University of Cologne, where he held several positions in the Department of Public Economics for almost a decade. He was Jean Monnet Fellow at the European University Institute, Florence, Research Associate at Stanford, Research Fellow at the Centre for Interdisciplinary Research, University of Bielefeld, and John McCloy Distinguished Fellow at Johns Hopkins University, Washington, DC.

His fields of specialization are public economics, government expenditure, taxation, national debt, tax reform, social and environmental policies and EC policies in several areas.

Major publications: *Steuerungsprobleme der Staatswirtschaft* (1981); *Wirtschaft im Schatten von Staat und Markt* (1983); *Neue Technologie und soziale Sicherung* (with R.G. Heinze) (1989); *Präferenzen für Staatsausgaben* (with W. Becker and K. Mackscheidt) (1990); 'Measuring the Public Sector: A Contestable Issue', in Kaufman, Majone, Ostrom (eds) *Guidance Control and Evaluation in the Public Sector* (1986); 'Social Security in Transition. Some Reflections from a Fiscal Sociology Perspective', *International Sociology* 1 (1986); 'Welfare Spending Preferences: Empirical Evidence from a Logit Analysis' (1989).

058

Peter Kappelhoff

Dr. habil., Privatdozent at the Institute for Sociology, University of Kiel.

Work on social theory, especially on social exchange theory, and social networks.
Further fields of interest include mathematical sociology, social mobility, and life course studies.

Latest publication on *Soziale Tauschsysteme*.

Patrick Kenis

Research Fellow at the European Centre in Vienna, since 1988. Assistant Editor of the *Journal für Sozialforschung* since 1988. Previously Researcher and Research Assistant at the European University Institute, Florence.

Main research interests: comparative research in the fields of economic sociology, political sociology, organizational studies, "third sector" studies. At the moment engaged in a comparative study on AIDS-service organizations.

Recently finished a book titled *The Social Construction of an Industry. A World of Chemical Fibres* (1990), Campus Verlag/Westview Press.

Bernd Marin

Director of the European Centre for Social Welfare Policy and Research, Vienna, since 1988.

1984 Professor of Comparative Political and Social Research at the European University Institute, Florence, Head of the Department of Political and Social Sciences (1986-1987).

Studies of social sciences at the University of Vienna, post-graduate training at the Institute for Advanced Studies in Vienna, post-doctoral Research Fellowship at Harvard University. Since 1972 he taught sociology, political science and government in various Austrian universities. Research Fellow, later Deputy-Director of the Institute for Conflict Research in Vienna, 1975-1984.

Guest lecturer and Visiting Professor at the universities of Harvard, Columbia, Cornell, Warsaw, Zurich, Roskilde, Barcelona, Amsterdam, Tokyo, Budapest and Jerusalem, at the Institute for Advanced Studies in Vienna, at the International Institute for Management, Science Center, Berlin and at the Centre de Sociologie des Organisations (C.S.O./CNRS.), Paris.

Since 1979 Editor of the *Journal für Sozialforschung*.

Book publications: *Policy Networks* (ed. with Renate Mayntz, 1991 in preparation); *Generalized Political Exchange* (ed.) and *Governance and Generalized Political Exchange* (ed.), both 1990; *Verfall und Erneuerung im Bauwesen* (ed.), 1987; *Unternehmerorganisationen im Verbändestaat*, Bd. I, 1986; *Antisemitismus in Österreich. Sozialhistorische und soziologische Studien* (with John Bunzl), 1983; *Die Paritätische Kommission. Aufgeklärter Technokorporatismus in Österreich*, 1982; *Wachstumskrisen in Österreich?* Bd. I: *Grund-*

lagen (with M. Wagner), 1979, Bd. II: *Szenarios* (ed.), 1979; *Politische Organisation sozialwissenschaftlicher Forschungsarbeit,* 1978.

Franz Urban Pappi

Professor of Political Science, Universität Mannheim; formerly Full Professor at the Universität Kiel and Assistant Professor at the Universität Köln.

Doctoral degree from the Universität München.

Recent publications: *Methoden der Netzwerkanalyse* (1987); articles on voting behavior (chapter 9 on Germany in M. Franklin et al. *Electoral Change: Responses to Evolving Social and Attitudional Structures in Western Countries,* forthcoming); on new social movements in K. Rohe (ed.) *Elections, Parties and Political Traditions. Social Foundations of German Parties and Party Systems* (1990); on political exchange in *Jahrbuch zur Staats- und Verwaltungswissenschaft* (1990).

Leonardo Parri

Researcher at the European University Institute, Florence, where he is completing his PhD on subnational policies for small firms' technological innovation in the cases of an Italian and a French region.

Research interests: Swiss politics in comparative perspective, the theory of political exchange and of territorial politics, comparative intergovernmental relations and comparative policy analysis.

Publications on 'Political Exchange in the Italian Debate' (1985); 'Neo-Corporatist Arrangements, Konkordanz and Direct Democracy: The Swiss Experience' (1987); 'Staat und Gewerkschaften in der Schweiz (1873-1981)' (1987); 'Dimension territoriale de la politique et dynamiques d'échange' (1988), 'Territorial Political Exchange in Federal and Unitary Countries' (1989) 'Le politiche subnazionali per l'innovazione tecnologica nelle piccole imprese: le regioni Rhône-Alpes ed Emilia-Romagna a confronto' (1990).

Victor Alexis Pestoff

Research Associate at the Department of Business Administration, University of Stockholm, Adjunct Professor at the Department of Political Science, University of Helsinki, and Consultant of the European Centre Vienna.

Research interests: his dissertation *Voluntary Associations and the Nordic Party Systems* (1977) studied overlapping memberships and cross pressures in Finland, Norway and Sweden. His work since then focuses on three main areas of socio-economics, cooperatives, consumer policy and business and politics in Sweden. He is currently commencing a project on the role of co-operatives in the provision of social welfare services in Eastern and Western Europe for the European Centre for Social Welfare Policy and Research, Vienna.

Recent publications: *Between Markets and Politics —Co-operations in Sweden* (1990); *Business and Politics in Sweden* (forthcoming, 1991)

Fritz W. Scharpf

Director, Max-Planck-Institut für Gesellschaftsforschung, Cologne since 1986.

Studied law and political science at the Universität Tübingen, Universität Freiburg and Yale University (LL.M.).

Assistant Professor of Law, Yale Law School (1964-66).

Professor of Political Science, Universität Konstanz (1968).

Director of the International Institute of Management, Wissenschaftszentrum Berlin (1973-84).

Senior Research Fellow, Wissenschaftszentrum Berlin (1984-86).

Fellow, Center for Advanced Study in Behavioral Sciences, Stanford University (January-June 1987).

Research interests: organisation and decision processes in the ministerial bureaucracy; joint federal-state decision-making; implementation research; comparative political economy; federalism and European integration; game-theoretical application in empirical research.

Major book publications: *Grenzen der richterlichen Verantwortung* (1965); *Die politischen Kosten des Rechtsstaats* (1970); *Demokratietheorie zwischen Utopie und Anpassung,* 2nd ed. (1972); *Planung als politischer Prozeß* (1973); *Organisation der Planung* (with Renate Mayntz; eds.) (1973); *Politische Durchsetzbarkeit innerer Reformen* (1974); *Policy-Making in the German Federal Bureaucracy* (with Renate Mayntz) (1975); *Modernisierung der Volkswirtschaft. Technologiepolitik als Strukturpolitik* (with V. Hauff) (1975); *Politikverflechtung* (with B. Reissert/F. Schnabel) (1976); *Politischer Immobilismus und ökonomische Krise* (1977); *Politikverflechtung II* (with B. Reissert/F. Schnabel; eds.) (1977); *Interorganizational Policy Making. Limits to Coordination and Central Control* (with Kenneth Hanf; eds.) (1978); *Arbeitsmarktpolitik für Akademiker?* (with S. Gensior/J. Fiedler; eds.) (1979); *Implementationsprobleme offensiver Arbeitsmarktpolitik* (with D. Garlichs et al.) (1982); *Aktive Arbeitsmarktpolitik* (with M. Brockmann et al.; eds.) (1982); *Institutionelle Bedingungen der Arbeitsmarkt- und Beschäftigungspolitik* (with M. Brockmann; eds.) (1983); *Sozialdemokratische Krisenpolitik in Europa* (1987).

Volker Schneider

Research Fellow at the Max-Planck-Institut für Gesellschaftsforschung, Cologne.

He studied economics and political science in Berlin, Paris and Florence. PhD in Political and Social Sciences from the European University Institute, Florence.

Currently working on communications and information technology, policy networks and governance structures.

Book publications: *Politiknetzwerke der Chemikalienkontrolle* (1988) and *Technikentwicklung zwischen Politik und Markt: Der Fall Bildschirmtext* (1989).

Franz Traxler

Associate Professor of Sociology. He teaches at the University of Economics, Vienna and at the University of Vienna. Member of the Federal Academy of Public Administration, Vienna.

Research interests: industrial relations, organizational sociology and political sociology.

Book publications: *Evolution gewerkschaftlicher Interessenvertretung* (1982); *Interessenverbände der Unternehmer* (1986).

Arthur F.P. Wassenberg

Associate Professor of Strategic Network Management and Negotiation at the Rotterdam School of Management (postgraduate studies) and Erasmus University Rotterdam (graduate studies).

Graduated in economic and political sociology, cum laude, University of Amsterdam. Research fellowship International Institute of Management, Berlin (1976); Research fellowship Netherlands Institute of Advanced Studies (NIAS) (1979-80)

Research areas: political analysis of organizational behavior; organizational strategies and tactics; inter-organizational or network analysis and bargaining games; neo-corporatism and the changing balance of public and private power; European integration as a function of corporate politics and industrial strategies.

Major publications: 'Neo-corporatism and the Quest for Control: The Cuckoo Game', in G. Lehmbruch and Ph.C. Schmitter (eds) *Patterns of Corporatist Policy-making* (1982); 'Organizational Instincts: On the Political Economy of Bargaining', in A. Rinnooy Kan (ed.) *New Challenges for Management Research* (1985); 'Strategic Partnerships: Mixed Motives, Mixed Blessings', in *International Marketing Magazine* (1990); *Strategic Choice: The Unfolding of Power in Industrial Networks* (1990).

Helmut Willke

Professor of Sociology at the University of Bielefeld.

Dr.jur. Tübingen, 1974; Habilitation Sociology, Cologne 1982; Professor of Planning- and Decision-Theory, University of Bielefeld; Visiting Professor at the Universities of Johns Hopkins, Baltimore, Geneva, Institute for Advanced Studies, Vienna.

Major book publications: *Entzauberung des Staates* (1983); *Systemtheorie* (2nd edition, 1987); *Systemtheorie entwickelter Gesellschaften* (1990).

Publications in legal theory, state theory, systems theory and interventions theory.

Paul Windolf

Professor for Sociology at the University of Heidelberg.

Studied sociology, history and economics at the Universities of Freiburg, Sorbonne and Berlin (Freie Universität). Research Fellow at the Wissenschaftszentrum Berlin, London School of Economics and Stanford University; Jean Monnet Fellow at the European University Institute.

Current research projects: expansion of higher education since 1870; cross-national comparison of orientation and motivation of students; integration of the European Community and its consequences for industrial relations.

Major publications: *Berufliche Sozialisation* (1981); 'L'expansion de l'enseignement et la surqualification sur le marché du travail', *Archives Européennes de Sociologie* 25 (1984); 'Industrial Robots in the Automobile Industry — New Technology in the Context of German Industrial Relations', *Politics and Society* 14 (1984); 'Streik und Betriebsbesetzung in der Krise', *Leviathan* 13 (1985); *Recruitment and Selection in the Labour Market —A Comparative Study of Britain and West Germany* (1988) (with S. Wood); 'Who Joins the Union? — Determinants of Trade Union Membership in the Federal Republic of Germany', *European Sociological Review* 5 (1989) (with J. Haas); 'Vom Korporatismus zur Deregulierung — Thesen zum Strukturwandel der Gewerkschaften', *Journal für Sozialforschung* 29 (1989); *Die Expansion der Universitäten (1870-1985) —Ein internationaler Vergleich* (1990).

Author Index

A

B

Contents Complementary Volume
GENERALIZED POLITICAL EXCHANGE

V Towards Integrative Policy Circuits

VI Generalized Exchange Networks